Forensic Mental Health Assessments in Death Penalty Cases

Forensic Mental Health Assessments in Death Penalty Cases

David DeMatteo
Daniel C. Murrie
Natalie M. Anumba
Michael E. Keesler

OXFORD
UNIVERSITY PRESS

Oxford University Press, Inc., publishes works that further
Oxford University's objective of excellence
in research, scholarship, and education.

Oxford   New York
Auckland   Cape Town   Dar es Salaam   Hong Kong   Karachi
Kuala Lumpur   Madrid   Melbourne   Mexico City   Nairobi
New Delhi   Shanghai   Taipei   Toronto

With offices in
Argentina   Austria   Brazil   Chile   Czech Republic   France   Greece
Guatemala   Hungary   Italy   Japan   Poland   Portugal   Singapore
South Korea   Switzerland   Thailand   Turkey   Ukraine   Vietnam

Copyright © 2011 by Oxford University Press, Inc.

Published by Oxford University Press, Inc.
198 Madison Avenue, New York, New York 10016
www.oup.com

Oxford is a registered trademark of Oxford University Press
All rights reserved. No part of this publication may be reproduced,
stored in a retrieval system, or transmitted, in any form or by any means,
electronic, mechanical, photocopying, recording, or otherwise,
without the prior permission of Oxford University Press.

Library of Congress Cataloging-in-Publication Data

Forensic mental health assessments in death penalty cases / David DeMatteo ... [et al.].
p. cm.
Includes bibliographical references.
ISBN 978-0-19-538580-9
1. Forensic psychiatry. 2. Capital punishment. 3. Mental status examination. I. DeMatteo, David, 1972-
[DNLM: 1. Forensic Psychiatry—methods—United States. 2. Capital Punishment—United States. 3. Mental
Competency—United States. 4. Personality Assessment—United States. W 740]
RA1151.F653 2011
614'.1—dc22   2010045923

---

9 8 7 6 5 4 3 2 1
Printed in the United States of America
on acid-free paper

To Christina, Emma, and Jake   **(DD)**

To my family   **(NMA)**

To Drs. Friedenberg, Keesler, and Laughon   **(MEK)**

Contents

Acknowledgments	ix
Preface	xi
1 Overview of Forensic Mental Health Assessments in Death Penalty Cases	3
2 Death Penalty Litigation	25
3 Death Penalty Jurisprudence	123
4 Ethical Considerations in Death Penalty Assessments	145
5 Eligibility for the Death Penalty—Part 1: *Atkins*-Type Evaluations	164
6 Eligibility for the Death Penalty—Part 2: Competence for Execution Evaluations	200
7 Evaluations Addressing Mitigation in Capital Sentencing	223
8 Evaluations of Violence Risk in Capital Sentencing	260

9	Principles of Forensic Mental Health Assessment Applied to Death Penalty Cases	285
10	Sample Reports	317
	References	413
	Index	435

Acknowledgments

We owe thanks to many people who contributed in various ways to this book. The contributors of the sample reports deserve special thanks: Mary Alice Conroy, Kirk Heilbrun, Eileen Ryan, Karen Salekin, and Patty Zapf. Including reports from colleagues with national reputations and well-defined areas of specialization has greatly improved the value of this book. We thank Kirk Heilbrun and Don Bersoff for helping us flesh out many of the concepts discussed throughout the book, and we thank Geff Marczyk for convincing us that the field would benefit from a book like this. Additional thanks go to Anne Poulin and Steve Chanenson for their input on various aspects of criminal procedure and death penalty litigation. We also thank Ashley Batastini for reviewing the literature and Lucy Guarnera and Sarah Filone for helpful editing on several chapters. Finally, we are grateful for the support we received from Oxford University Press. We thank Regan Hoffman, our initial editor, for her patience, support, and always-pleasant demeanor. We also thank Sarah Harrington, Jodi Narde, and Anisha Shankar for seeing us through to the final product.

Preface

Forensic mental health professionals are conducting assessments in death penalty cases with increasing frequency. The continuing development of forensic psychology and psychiatry, combined with several recent decisions from the U.S. Supreme Court that have strong clinical implications, have likely contributed to this increase in forensic mental health assessments. Thus, forensic mental health professionals are now conducting assessments at every stage of death penalty proceedings, ranging from pretrial evaluations to determine eligibility for the death penalty to postsentencing evaluations conducted closer to the date of the execution.

Despite the increase in assessments in death penalty cases, and some professional literature addressing these assessments, there have been surprisingly few books that serve as comprehensive resources. Our primary goal in writing this book was to provide a resource for forensic mental health professionals who conduct assessments in death penalty cases. To that end, we provide relevant background on death penalty litigation and influential court cases, discussion of key ethical considerations, guidance on conducting various types of forensic mental health assessments in death penalty proceedings, and sample forensic reports illustrating best practices. We certainly do not consider this book to be the "final word" on conducting assessments in death penalty cases. As case law and the field of forensic mental health assessment continue to evolve, current thinking about death penalty assessments will likely change. Moreover, for some types of assessments, the field has not yet reached consensus regarding what constitutes best practices. Nevertheless, we believe this book captures the most current thinking and best practices relating to forensic mental health assessments in death penalty cases.

We hope this book will be useful for several groups. First, students in the fields of mental health, criminal justice, and law will gain a solid foundation of information related to capital punishment and the role of forensic mental health professionals in death penalty cases. Second, we hope those clinicians who conduct forensic mental health assessments in death penalty cases will benefit from the background and guidance this book provides. Of course, this (or any) book alone is not sufficient to prepare a clinician to conduct evaluations in death penalty cases; supervised training and practice are necessary to enter any new clinical role. But we do anticipate that this book will be a comprehensive reference, summarizing both the legal background and the clinical science relevant to death penalty evaluations. Finally, we aimed for the book to serve as a resource to attorneys who work with forensic mental health professionals. By reviewing the relevant science and practice guidelines, attorneys will be in the best position to understand forensic mental health assessments, work constructively with mental health experts, and challenge poor forensic work. This book, like forensic mental health assessment, lies at the intersection of law and the mental health fields. We hope it will prove helpful to students, practitioners, and scholars in each field, who often struggle with the complex and weighty work of capital litigation.

Forensic Mental Health Assessments in Death Penalty Cases

1

Overview of Forensic Mental Health Assessments in Death Penalty Cases

Historical Context

Mental health professionals have a long history of contributing their knowledge and skills to the legal system. Medical expert testimony on mental health issues dates back at least to the mid-1800s in England. Key events in establishing the relationship between psychology and law occurred as early as Wilhelm Wundt's psychology-law research laboratory in the late 1800s and the publication of Hugo Munsterberg's well-known treatise *On the Witness Stand* in 1908.[1] In the United States, mental health professionals became more integrated into the legal system in the early 1900s when they began providing clinical services to adult and juvenile offenders (Bartol & Bartol, 2006; Otto & Heilbrun, 2002). Other forensic activities of psychologists around this time included psychological fitness testing of law enforcement personnel and the

---

1. The publication of Munsterberg's *On the Witness Stand* in 1908 is often cited as an influential event in establishing a relationship between law and psychology. Although Munsterberg's book received some attention at the time it was published, his book is apparently viewed much more favorably today than it was when initially published, at least in terms of its historical value.

pretrial evaluation of criminal offenders (Bartol & Bartol, 2006). These early activities provided the foundation for a long-standing relationship between mental health professionals and the legal system. Relying on mental health professionals to evaluate adult and juvenile offenders, civil litigants, and law enforcement personnel has now become commonplace in the United States and elsewhere (Melton, Petrila, Poythress, & Slobogin, 2007).

Although medical experts have a long history of providing mental health expertise to courts, the use of psychologists as mental health experts in court is a much more recent phenomenon. Initially, courts only recognized physicians, typically psychiatrists, as being qualified to opine on psychiatric disorders (Bartol & Bartol, 2006). Psychologists were occasionally asked to testify about eyewitness testimony and other topics, but their testimony typically did not relate to mental health disorders, which was seen as exclusively in the domain of psychiatrists and other medical experts. However, nearly 50 years ago, the *Jenkins v. United States* (1962) decision from the U.S. Court of Appeals for the District of Columbia Circuit opened the doors for psychologists to be integrally involved in judicial proceedings. In *Jenkins*, a federal appellate court held that properly trained and qualified psychologists could testify as expert witnesses on mental health disorders. Following *Jenkins*, the use of psychologists as expert witnesses increased dramatically, with many thousands of forensic metal health assessments conducted each year on a variety of psycholegal issues (Melton et al., 2007; Otto & Heilbrun, 2002).

There are several more recent indicia of the growth and development of the forensic mental health disciplines. For example, there are several professional organizations devoted to law and psychology (or the related discipline of law and psychiatry), and a number of specialty journals that publish empirical, theoretical, and practice material relevant to forensic psychology and forensic psychiatry. There are also several "hybrid" law-psychology journals, typically sponsored by law schools, that publish articles on a variety of law-psychology topics. Recent years have also seen numerous books address forensic practice, some published as part of a book series dedicated to forensic psychology. The development of increasingly specialized forensic assessment instruments has also increased in recent years. The number and diversity of forensic education and training opportunities available to students and practitioners at the undergraduate, graduate, and postgraduate levels have increased considerably (see DeMatteo, Marczyk, Krauss, & Burl, 2009; Hall, Cook, & Berman, 2010; Krauss & Sales, 2006), and postdoctoral fellowships in forensic psychology can now be accredited by the American Psychological Association. Finally, the American Psychological Association's recognition of forensic psychology as a discrete specialization area in 2001 attests to the well-defined and growing subdiscipline of forensic psychology within the broader field of professional psychology.

Forensic Mental Health Assessment

Although mental health professionals in the legal system can function in a variety of roles, ranging from consultants to researchers to program evaluators, this book addresses only forensic mental health assessments conducted in the context of death penalty litigation. Therefore, defining forensic mental health assessment (FMHA) is an important task. Authorities differ when describing the scope and content of FMHA, and evolving conceptualizations of FMHA occasionally seem at odds with earlier conceptualizations. But the most recent and comprehensive conceptualizations of FMHA likely provide the greatest clarity and breadth.

Heilbrun, Grisso, and Goldstein (2009) provide a comprehensive definition of FMHA, conceptualizing it in several distinct but related ways. First, they define FMHA as a domain of assessments performed within the criminal, civil, juvenile justice, and family law systems. In this capacity, forensic mental health professionals conduct evaluations of criminal offenders, juvenile offenders, and civil litigants to assist a legal decision maker, typically a judge, in making a range of legal decisions. For example, evaluations conducted in a criminal context may focus on a variety of competencies (e.g., to waive *Miranda* rights, stand trial, plead guilty, represent one's self, or be sentenced), mental state at the time of the offense (e.g., insanity, diminished capacity), or factors related to sentencing (e.g., amenability to treatment, risk of future offending). Some evaluations in civil law contexts address mental health disability, psychological damages in personal injury (torts) cases, guardianship and conservatorship, and civil commitment. Evaluations with juveniles occur in both criminal and civil contexts, and they may include questions relating to venue (i.e., whether the juvenile's case will be adjudicated in juvenile/family court or criminal court), disposition, and abuse or neglect. Finally, evaluations conducted in family law contexts address questions related to parental fitness and child custody, among other topics.

Second, Heilbrun et al. (2009) define FMHA using a task-based classification system divided by a focus on the examinee's past, present, or future legally relevant capacities and functioning. For example, there are several types of assessments in which the evaluator is assessing an individual's mental state, motivations, attitudes, and behaviors at some point in the *past*. These retrospective evaluations include competence to waive *Miranda* rights and mental state at the time of the offense. Evaluations that describe an individual's *current* mental state and abilities include competence to stand trial, competence to plead guilty, psychological damages, mental health disability, and termination of parental rights. Finally, evaluations that attempt to address an individual's *future* behavior include sentencing, risk of future offending, and child custody evaluations.

Third, Heilbrun and colleagues (2009) define FMHA conceptually as "a domain of assessments of individuals intended to assist legal decision makers in decisions about the application of laws requiring consideration of individuals' mental conditions, abilities, and behaviors" (p. 15). FMHAs are typically performed by psychiatrists and psychologists, or occasionally social workers, specifically so that results from the evaluation can be used to help a legal decision maker to answer a specific legal question in a criminal, civil, juvenile, or family law context. The intention that the evaluation will assist a legal decision maker is one feature that distinguishes forensic assessments from more traditional clinical assessments.

Distinctions Between Forensic Mental Health Assessment and Clinical Assessment

Despite its grounding in mental health knowledge, methods, and practice, FMHA is quite distinct from traditional clinical practice. In fact, in certain situations FMHA will require procedures and routines that would be inappropriate in the context of traditional therapeutic relationships. The primary differences between forensic assessment and clinical assessment have been thoroughly described in the literature (see, e.g., Greenberg & Shuman, 1997, 2007; Heilbrun, 2001; Melton et al., 2007), and there are various ways to categorize these differences. At base, however, most of the identified differences relate to the purpose of the evaluation, identity of the client, need for informed consent, methods of evaluation and data collection, response style of the examinee, and the expected outcome of the assessment. See Table 1.1 for a summary of the distinctions.

Purpose

Perhaps the primary distinction between clinical assessments and FMHAs relates to the respective purposes of the evaluations. In a clinical context, the goal of the assessment is typically to diagnose mental health problems and develop an appropriate treatment plan. The client's psychological well-being is of paramount importance, and the client's treatment needs are at the core of the therapeutic relationship. In this regard, mental health professionals are assuming the traditional helping role.

In a forensic context, however, the purpose of the evaluation is to assist a legal decision maker or attorney. The examinee's mental health functioning and treatment needs may be explored during the evaluation, but only insofar as they are relevant to the legal question being addressed. In FMHA, the evaluator makes no effort to treat the examinee, although the evaluator may

Table 1.1 Comparing Forensic and Therapeutic Roles for Mental Health Professionals

	Forensic Examiner	Therapeutic Clinician
Purpose of evaluation	• Assist a legal decision maker, typically a judge, to make a more informed decision • Mental health needs are explored only to extent they are relevant to the legal issue being addressed	• Assist in diagnosis and treatment planning for symptoms of mental health disorders
Nature of standard(s) considered	• Medical (psychological, psychiatric) • Legal	• Medical (psychological, psychiatric)
Identity of the client, or for whom services are rendered	• The client is the party who requested the evaluation (e.g., attorney, court, employer, insurer), as opposed to the examinee	• The client and the examinee/patient are usually one and the same, including instances in which the patient was referred to the clinician by a third party
Relationship between the professional and examinee	• Objective or quasi-objective	• Therapeutic alliance is cultivated • Clinician assumes the traditional "helping" role.
Voluntariness of the evaluation	• Evaluations may be compelled by courts, employers, insurers, or at the behest of legal counsel, with no option in the traditional sense for the examinee to decline	• Relationship is typically initiated by patient, who can terminate at will • Length, course, and goals of treatment are at least partly directed by patient
Confidentiality	• Not limited to examiner-examinee; varies as a function of the identified client and the purpose of the evaluation	• Typically limited to the clinician–patient relationship unless disclosure obligations arise (e.g., child abuse, duty to protect)
Requirement of obtaining informed consent	• Because examinee's legal and liberty interests are implicated, examinee must be informed of who requested the evaluation, the purpose of the evaluation, how the results will be used, and limits on confidentiality • Formal and explicit consent (for voluntary participation) or notification of purpose (for involuntary participation) are necessary	• Consent is implied by patient typically having sought out the clinician • Obtaining informed consent is recommended
Response style of the examinee	• Because of potential for secondary gain and the fact that the evaluation may not be voluntary, there is an expectation that the examinee may conceal or distort information	• Because the evaluation is typically voluntary, clinician generally presumes client responses are honest

(*Continued*)

Table 1.1 Comparing Forensic and Therapeutic Roles for Mental Health Professionals (Continued)

	Forensic Examiner	Therapeutic Clinician
Data collection	• No presumption of reliable and truthful responses; collateral data should be utilized to confirm/refute self-report • Emphasis is placed on the accuracy of the information obtained • Corroboration of information via collateral documents or third-party sources is expected practice	• Emphasis is placed on the patient's experiences, beliefs, feelings, and perceptions of self and environment • Third party or collateral sources of information may be helpful, but may not be necessary
Sources of information	• Self-report • Psychological testing • Behavioral assessment • Medical procedures • Observations by others • Relevant documents • Collateral interviews	• Self-report • Psychological testing • Behavioral assessment • Medical procedures
Setting	• Settings can vary widely from a private office to a correctional setting with limited privacy	• Typically a private office
Pace	• Deadlines are imposed by the legal process • Less time is available for rapport building, and single-session evaluations are common	• Therapist and patient can often work collaboratively to negotiate frequency and duration of treatment, and nature of intervention and treatment goals
Written report	• Customary for a lengthy and detailed report to be written • Focus on functional legal capacities relevant to the legal issue being addressed • Expectation that the report will be entered into evidence in the legal proceeding • Follow conventions/standards in the field of forensic psychology	• If a report is written, it is typically brief and conclusory • Focus on the mental health or clinical functioning of the examinee • No expectation that anyone other than the therapist or client will ever see the report
Expected outcome of the assessment	• Testimony should be anticipated as a possible follow-up to the evaluation and report	• Testimony is unlikely and, although it may be acceptable in some limited instances, it is discouraged by ethical and best-practice guidelines

Source: Adapted and expanded from Heilbrun (2001), with additional content from Melton et al. (2007).

describe the general parameters of a treatment plan if it is relevant to the legal question being addressed (e.g., managing risk for future offending). Rather than assuming the traditional helping role, forensic mental health professionals must assume an objective stance throughout their involvement in the case.

Consent

In a clinical context, the therapist and patient typically share an implicit understanding about the purpose and goals of the evaluation and treatment. Both the therapist and patient understand that the assessment will be used to develop a treatment plan, and they further understand that the goal of the relationship is, for example, reducing clinical symptoms and improving behavior and functioning. Obtaining informed consent is a recommended practice, but far from universal.

In a forensic context, however, it is critically important that the examinee understand who requested the evaluation, the purpose of the evaluation, how the results of the evaluation will be used, and the limits of confidentiality. The examinee's legal interests, including those relating to liberty and life, can be directly impacted by the results of the evaluation. An examinee's understanding of key aspects of the evaluation—that is, who requested the evaluation, the purpose of the evaluation, how the results of the evaluation will be used, and who will be able to see the resulting report—may affect the examinee's willingness to participate in the evaluation or influence the types information provided during the interview and psychological testing. As such, formal and explicit consent (if participation in the evaluation is voluntary) or notification of purpose (if participation in the evaluation is not voluntary) is an essential aspect of forensic mental health practice.

Voluntariness and Autonomy

Most clinical assessments originate through the examinee, who enters into the professional relationship voluntarily. Typically, a client seeks treatment due to troubling mental health symptoms, such as depression, anxiety, or sleep difficulties. Although a client may feel pressured into receiving mental health treatment, perhaps by a significant other, the decision to enter treatment is ultimately voluntary in the legal sense. The client is free to withdraw from the therapeutic relationship at any time, for any reason, and typically without any negative consequences (except, perhaps, the failure to resolve the problems for which the client sought treatment in the first place).[2] Moreover, because of

---

2. In some contexts, an individual may be mandated by an employer to participate in a mental health evaluation or treatment, and not participating could result in termination of employment. However, mandated treatment is the exception rather than the rule.

the collaborative nature of the therapeutic relationship, the client typically has greater input into the nature of the interventions, targets of treatment, treatment goals, and length of the treatment.

Such voluntariness and autonomy are not typical of FMHA. In forensic contexts, examinees may be compelled to undergo an evaluation by a court, employer, or insurer, or at the strong request of their attorney. In many instances, there may be no readily available option to decline participation. In fact, failing to participate in some FMHAs could have negative repercussions on a defendant's criminal case, including the inability to offer certain affirmative defenses.[3] This lack of voluntariness and autonomy not only raises a variety of ethical implications in FMHA, but it may influence the validity of information obtained during the evaluation. These types of ethical and validity concerns are typically not present in a traditional clinical relationship.

Client

In a clinical assessment, the client is the individual being examined. In a forensic assessment, the client is the party who requested the evaluation (i.e., retaining attorney, court, employer, or insurer), and not the individual being examined. Identifying the client is not simply an academic exercise; it has important implications for the evaluator's duty to maintain confidentiality, disclose findings, and fulfill other key tasks. For example, a client in a traditional clinical relationship can expect that the mental health professional will not disclose confidential information obtained during assessment or treatment,[4] but the examinee in a forensic assessment should not expect the information he or she provides to remain entirely confidential. In many instances, the results of an FMHA will be shared with opposing counsel and the court, and the report may even become part of the public record. Therefore, the limits on confidentiality should be communicated to the examinee prior to the evaluation.

---

3. One example is a criminal defendant who wants to proffer an insanity defense. The defendant cannot agree to be evaluated by the defense's mental health expert but refuse to participate in the evaluation by the prosecution's expert. Failing to submit to an evaluation by the prosecution's expert may lead the court to reject the defendant's insanity plea.

4. There are a few notable exceptions to confidentiality in therapy, such as the mandated reporting of child abuse and the affirmative "duty to protect" that is triggered when a client makes serious threats of imminent violence against a readily identifiable third party (see, e.g., *Tarasoff v. Regents of the University of California*, 1976). But maintaining confidentiality is the general rule in a therapeutic relationship.

Response Style and Threats to Validity

Clients entering a therapeutic relationship are typically not motivated, at least consciously, to conceal or distort the information they provide to a treating mental health professional. In fact, most clients intuitively understand the importance of providing accurate and complete information to assist the treating professional in developing an appropriate treatment plan. Clients often recognize that it is in their best clinical interests to be honest and forthcoming during the assessment and treatment. Therefore, in a clinical context, there is typically an assumption that the patient's self-report is honest and reliable, and there are relatively few threats to the validity of the patient's self-report.

In contrast, legal proceedings may provide ample motivation to conceal or distort information, whether consciously or not. For example, a criminal offender may feign or exaggerate symptoms of a serious mental health disorder in an effort to avoid trial or criminal sanction (including execution). In the civil context, a litigant may fabricate or exaggerate symptoms to obtain mental health disability benefits or a financial settlement after sustaining a personal injury. In other civil contexts, an individual may deny or minimize mental health symptoms to avoid the loss of liberty associated with involuntary civil commitment, or the loss of decision-making power over his or her assets. In the family law context, a parent involved in a child custody dispute may deny even minor psychological problems or symptoms in an effort to appear well adjusted and capable of parenting. So in a forensic context, there is no assumption that the examinee provides reliable information, and mental health professionals conducting FMHAs must be alert to various threats to validity.

Data Sources and the Importance of the Examinee's Perspective

Clinical evaluation and treatment typically emphasize the examinee's experiences, beliefs, and perceptions. Understanding how examinees think, feel, and view themselves and their environment is often necessary to develop an effective treatment plan. Common data sources in a clinical context include patient self-report, behavioral observation/assessment, psychological testing, and the results of medical testing. But obtaining information from additional sources—other than the client being treated—is rarely necessary in traditional clinical assessment. There may be some instances when obtaining information from third parties is useful (e.g., when a client with cognitive impairment cannot provide historical information, or when a client is unaware of the extent of his or her deficits), but it is certainly not necessary in every clinical relationship. Moreover, the accuracy of the information a client provides is somewhat less important than the client's perceptions, which have important clinical implications.

In a forensic context, however, the accuracy of the information on which the evaluator's conclusions are based is of fundamental importance, and corroboration of information obtained from the examinee is considered a standard part of the FMHA process (see Heilbrun, 2001). Thus, assessment procedures must consider additional sources of information, besides the examinee alone. Forensic mental health professionals routinely obtain collateral information from available records (e.g., mental health, medical, criminal, employment, school) and individuals who are well acquainted with the examinee (e.g., significant other, employer, probation officer, physician, therapist). These sources provide additional information, and serve as a validity check on the information an examinee provides.

Relationship

Therapeutic relationships between a clinician and patient are often marked by empathy, support, and emotional safety. Therapists consider rapport an essential goal in the early stages of therapy, and they cultivate the therapeutic alliance throughout the relationship. By contrast, in forensic contexts, mental health professionals typically strive to remain detached from examinees (who are not the clients), and they focus on obtaining complete and accurate information relevant to the legal question that prompted the evaluation. Although establishing and maintaining rapport is important in any evaluation context, the relationship between the forensic mental health professional and examinee is not typically marked by empathy and support, which are the hallmarks of most clinical relationships. Indeed, the forensic mental health professional should inform the examinee that he or she is not working as a helping professional, but rather as an objective expert hired by a third party or appointed by the court.

Pace and Setting

Traditional clinical practice typically entails private, relatively comfortable settings in which the relationship between the clinician and patient is permitted to develop naturally over time. The length of the treatment may be open ended, and the treatment can often proceed in a natural manner without reference to external deadlines.[5] The therapist and patient are free to negotiate the

---

5. Of course, many therapeutic relationships are, in fact, somewhat time limited due to insurance company reimbursement practices. Insurance companies may limit the number of sessions for which they will provide full financial coverage based on the nature of the disorder being treated. These policies surely affect the length and course of some treatment relationships. Nevertheless, the point that traditional therapy is not subject to deadlines holds true in many instances and still serves as a distinguishing feature of therapeutic relationships.

frequency of treatment sessions, overall length of the treatment, nature of the intervention, and treatment goals. The therapist and patient can often proceed at a pace that is mutually comfortable, with no external pressure from third parties (perhaps with the exception of insurance companies). There is often no explicit time table for the treatment, although there is likely an implicit agreement to work toward improvement as rapidly as possible.

In forensic practice, however, deadlines are the norm. Due to court dates or procedural requirements, evaluators usually have a limited time frame in which to conduct an evaluation. Moreover, criminal defendants have a constitutionally guaranteed right to a speedy trial, so delays in processing and adjudicating a defendant's case (if not attributable to the defense) can result in a dismissal of the criminal charges. The deadlines inherent in forensic practice leave less time to develop rapport during evaluations and write reports after the evaluation.

Forensic evaluations also differ in terms of their setting. Whereas clinical assessments are typically conducted in private, quiet settings, FMHAs may be conducted in crowded and noisy correctional facilities that offer little privacy and poor testing conditions. Adverse testing conditions can affect the validity of the evaluator's findings.

Report

In a traditional clinical context, a written report, if one is ever created, is typically brief and conclusory. Certainly, an evaluation conducted for a specific purpose, such as one performed as part of an Individualized Education Plan (IEP) or to document neuropsychological functioning, may require a longer and more detailed report. But therapy progress reports are often short, minimally detailed, and not intended to document all aspects of the treatment session. A therapist may write a few sentences in a patient's file after each session, but there is no expectation that the therapist would write a lengthy report after each session. Often, no one other than the therapist will ever see the progress reports.

In a forensic context, however, it is customary for the evaluator to write a lengthy and detailed report that may be entered into evidence in a court proceeding. Because forensic reports are subjected to more scrutiny than clinical reports, forensic reports often follow certain conventions and include common components (see, e.g., Heilbrun, Marczyk, & DeMatteo, 2002). For example, the report should identify the sources of information upon which the evaluation is based, document the evaluator's findings, state the evaluator's conclusions relating to the legal issue being addressed, and explain the evaluator's reasoning in support of the conclusions. Moreover, a forensic report should clarify any limits on the evaluator's findings (e.g., questionable validity of test results due to noisy testing conditions; the absence of collateral records detailing previous mental health treatment or behavior while incarcerated). Forensic reports emphasize the factual bases for clinical opinions more than clinical reports do (Heilbrun, 2001; Heilbrun, Marczyk, et al., 2002; Nicholson & Norwood, 2000; Witt, 2010). Finally, the content of forensic reports differs from the content of clinical reports. Whereas clinical reports focus on the examinee's clinical functioning, forensic reports focus almost exclusively on the individual's functional legal capacities that are relevant to the legal issue being addressed. Forensic reports are more detailed regarding the information relevant to the referral question, but they are typically less detailed regarding information that is irrelevant to the referral question.[6]

Testimony

In a traditional therapeutic relationship, there is no expectation that the mental health professional will participate in a deposition or provide courtroom testimony regarding the patient. Although treating therapists are occasionally asked to testify about their patient's mental health functioning (e.g., to support the patient's claim of psychological damages in a personal injury case, or to support a litigant's claim that he or she is a fit parent), fulfilling two roles in the same case—treating therapist and expert witness—is contrary to the ethical guidelines applicable to psychologists and psychiatrists regarding dual roles (see American Academy of Psychiatry and the Law, 2005 [Section IV: Honesty and Striving for Objectivity]; American Psychological Association, 2002 [Standard 3.05: Multiple Relationships]).[7] However, in a forensic context, the evaluator should assume that courtroom testimony may be required (although in most instances it will not), and inform the examinee of this possibility.

The Quality of Forensic Mental Health Assessments

Given the influence FMHAs can have on legal decisions, the quality of FMHAs is of paramount importance. Subpar professional work can have lasting negative effects, with particularly egregious results in cases that may result in the

---

6. For example, most clinical reports would address psychologically influential events such as a history of sexual abuse. But a forensic report addressing competence to stand trial should not detail this type of personal information that is unrelated to a defendant's capacity to understand the nature of the proceedings and assist defense counsel.

7. A treating therapist could serve as a fact witness without violating the prohibition regarding dual roles. A fact witness can testify about the length of treatment, nature of the intervention, degree of impairment, and so forth, but not provide expert testimony that directly addresses the legal issue. However, it is certainly preferable not to take on *any* role outside of the treatment context.

loss of liberty or life. However, mental health professionals, even those who routinely conduct FMHAs and serve as expert witnesses in legal proceedings, vary considerably in their training, knowledge, and experience (see, e.g., Cunningham & Reidy, 2001; Tolman & Mullendore, 2003). One result of these differences is variation in the quality of forensic mental health practice. Over the past two decades, many legal practitioners and mental health professionals have expressed concern about the quality of FMHAs and related testimony, both in capital and noncapital cases, particularly with regard to the empirical foundation, objectivity, relevance, and thoroughness (e.g., Christy, Douglas, Otto, & Petrila, 2004; Cunningham & Reidy, 2001; Grisso, 1986, 2003; Lander & Heilbrun, 2009; Nicholson & Norwood, 2000; Skeem & Golding, 1998). Because courts may give great weight to the opinions of forensic mental health professionals in some legal proceedings, perhaps most notably in proceedings relating to competence to stand trial (see Melton et al., 2007; Roesch & Golding, 1980), the quality of forensic evaluations and written reports is important.

Concern about the quality of mental health evaluations performed for legal proceedings is long standing. Nearly 25 years ago, for instance, Grisso (1986) observed that forensic practice fell far short of the standards dictated by guiding ethics and scholarly consensus. Reiterating the concerns he first expressed many years before, Grisso (2003) more recently categorized the concerns about FMHAs into what he called the five "I's": *ignorance, irrelevance, intrusion, insufficiency,* and *incredibility*. Although he acknowledged progress since the mid 1980s, he nevertheless concluded that the bases for his initial concerns remained (see Grisso, 2003; see also Grisso, 2010).

Grisso (2003) noted that forensic mental health professionals performing assessments may provide *irrelevant* testimony and demonstrate *ignorance* of the legal question. For example, forensic mental health professionals may testify only about the defendant's specific symptoms and psychiatric diagnosis. They then use this clinical information to draw conclusions about the defendant's functional legal capacities, presumably unaware that the law does not typically equate a psychiatric diagnosis with any particular legal capacity.[8] For example, although certain psychiatric diagnoses are more likely to be associated with a finding of incompetence or insanity (i.e., psychotic disorders), no psychiatric diagnosis ipso facto renders a defendant incompetent or insane. Rather, the nexus between the mental health symptoms and the required functional legal capacities determines incompetence or insanity (see Morse, 1978a).

---

8. A notable exception is the U.S. Supreme Court's decision in *Atkins v. Virginia* (2002), which excluded offenders with a diagnosis of mental retardation from the death penalty. *Atkins* appears to stand alone in terms of excluding an entire class of people from the death penalty based exclusively on a psychiatric diagnosis.

Despite improvements in forensic mental health practice over the past 20 years, Grisso (2003) noted that certain clinical information, such as the defendant's decision-making skills, is often overlooked, despite its relevance to certain psycholegal questions.

Mental health professionals' tendency toward irrelevant information and ignorance of the law, however, does not prevent inappropriate *intrusion* into the legal system. According to Grisso (2003), many mental health professional intrude upon the legal fact finder's domain by answering the ultimate legal question. For example, in a competence to stand trial context, the ultimate legal question is whether the criminal defendant is, in fact, competent to stand trial. But answering the ultimate legal question—for example, stating definitively that a defendant *is* or *is not* competent to stand trial—is a controversial topic over which authorities are split.

Some argue that answering the ultimate legal question is acceptable because many judges and attorneys anticipate that the forensic mental health professional will answer the ultimate legal question in the course of the evaluation (see, e.g., Rogers & Ewing, 1989; Rogers & Shuman, 2000). Indeed, they argue that judges can better follow the flow and central theme of mental health testimony if opinions about the ultimate legal question are offered explicitly. In contrast, others argue that forensic mental health professionals should stay focused on relevant functional legal capacities, without explicitly answering the "ultimate issue" for which the judge or jury is responsible (e.g., Grisso, 1986, 2003; Tillbrook, Mumley, & Grisso, 2003). Addressing the "penultimate" legal issue may be preferable. For example, rather than directly addressing whether a defendant is competent to stand trial, the evaluator could address whether the defendant has a sufficient factual and rational understanding of the charges, proceedings, and potential penalties, and whether the defendant can assist counsel in his or her own defense. This is, of course, the standard for competence to stand trial outlined by the U.S. Supreme Court in *Dusky v. United States* (1960).

Grisso (2003) concluded that little harm may result if mental health professionals choose to address the ultimate legal question, but he emphasized the importance of fully explaining the clinical reasoning so fact finders may make informed decisions. Although Heilbrun, Grisso, and Goldstein (2009) generally recommend against answering the ultimate legal question, they concluded that the ultimate legal question could be answered if the evaluator conducted a thorough evaluation, with data and reasoning carefully described, so the legal consumer could separate such data and reasoning from the additional political and moral values embedded in some ultimate legal questions.

Finally, Grisso (2003) asserted that a failure to explain the reasoning behind one's clinical opinion can lead to *insufficiency* and *incredibility*. Mental health professionals can err by presenting conclusions that are not supported by current empirical literature or clinical data derived from the evaluation. Although this may result from several factors, some of the more common reasons include an absence of relevant research or clinical assessment instruments, inadequate data collection by the evaluator, or speculation that extends beyond the evaluation data. Consequently, the resulting clinical testimony may lack credibility in the eyes of the legal fact finder.

The Quality of Forensic Mental Health Assessments in Capital Contexts

Because of the constitutional requirement that capital sentences be individualized to the offense and offender (see *Gregg v. Georgia*, 1976), there are ample opportunities for mental health professionals to assist decision makers in capital cases (Cunningham, 2008, 2010). Indeed, the court often explicitly considers psychological phenomena—such as mental state at the time of the offense, factors influencing the offender's judgment and behavior, and factors relating to the likelihood that the offender will be dangerous in the future—in an effort to individualize the sentence in a capital case.

At the risk of stating the obvious, the quality of FMHAs performed in death penalty contexts is of great consequence. Legal decisions regarding capital punishment necessarily involve matters of life and death, and there is often little room for error, particularly when slight differences in an IQ score can determine whether a criminal offender is eligible for a death sentence (see *Atkins v. Virginia*, 2002; DeMatteo, Marczyk, & Pich, 2007). Despite the importance of FMHAs in capital cases, there is often unease about the competence of mental health professionals in capital contexts and the quality of work they produce. Cunningham and Reidy (2001) noted that the quality of FMHAs in capital cases often suffers due to inexperienced evaluators, incomplete assessment procedures, ethically questionable behavior, and a lack of specialized forensic assessment instruments. Cunningham and Goldstein (2003, p. 416) expressed concern that relatively inexperienced forensic evaluators may approach capital sentencing examinees as "guinea pigs" in their initial foray into FMHA.

However, concerns about the quality of forensic practice in death penalty contexts do not stem solely from the mental health professionals involved in these cases. The legal system and forensic mental health literature also bear some of the blame. For example, in most forensic contexts, the legal system has not yet identified enforceable "standards of care" that define minimally acceptable professional conduct (see Heilbrun & Brooks, 2010; Heilbrun, DeMatteo, Marczyk, & Goldstein, 2008). So it is difficult to hold evaluators liable for professional negligence based on subpar work. Moreover, although the substantive legal standards for some types of FMHA are well established, such as the "understand and assist" standard articulated in *Dusky v. United States* (1960) for competence to stand trial, the U.S. Supreme Court has not sufficiently articulated the substantive legal standard for some types of FMHAs. An obvious example is competence for execution (see Zapf, 2008, 2009). This leaves forensic mental health professionals in the difficult position of conducting an evaluation without explicit legal guidance on the applicable substantive legal standard.

Finally, in the forensic mental health literature, there is limited (albeit growing) guidance for forensic mental health professionals involved in death penalty cases (see, e.g., Cunningham & Reidy, 2001). To be clear, volumes have been written about death penalty evaluations in the legal and social science literature, but there is relatively little literature relating to *practice guidelines* for forensic evaluations in death penalty litigation, with some notable exceptions being Cunningham (2008, 2010), Eisenberg (2004), and Zapf (2009). Therefore, when viewed as a whole, there are *some* capital contexts in which mental health evaluations lack substantive legal guidance and clear professional guidance; this inevitably affects the quality of forensic mental health practice.

Roles of Mental Health Professionals in Capital Cases

On a broad level, mental health professionals may function in capital cases as either nonobjective consultants or objective experts. Consultants are retained to advocate for one party's desired outcome by assisting in tasks such as selecting juries, preparing witnesses, consulting on mental health issues, and assisting with trial strategy. In contrast, impartial experts are objective and primarily function to assist the legal decision maker. Though an expert may be hired by one side in a case, the expert must remain objective, even if objectivity requires reporting factual findings that are not favorable to the attorney's perspective. Typically, experts conduct comprehensive evaluations that include interviews of the defendant. But experts may also be retained to perform narrower evaluations that include only record reviews and collateral interviews without directly interviewing the defendant. Finally, an expert can serve as a teaching witness who presents empirical research or "teaching testimony" to assist the court in understanding complex information from clinical or social sciences (Cunningham, 2008). For example, an expert witness may summarize the literature on the effects that being on death row can have on mental health functioning, but without specific reference to the defendant.

In any given case, a mental health professional should function only as a consultant *or* expert, and then maintain that role throughout the case

(Committee on Ethical Guidelines for Forensic Psychologists, 1991; Cunningham, 2008). One potential exception to this principle involves moving from the role of impartial expert to the role of consultant (see Heilbrun, Marczyk, et al., 2002). In this situation, the mental health professional is moving from a role that requires impartiality to a role that does not, which may be acceptable if it is clear from the results of the evaluation that the attorney will not be asking for a report or testimony. However, shifting roles from consultant to impartial expert is almost never appropriate.

Mental health professionals can conduct several different types of FMHAs in capital cases. Although there are various ways to categorize these FMHAs, one is by referring to them as either "front-end" or "back-end" evaluations.[9] Front-end, or pretrial, evaluations are performed prior to the guilt/innocence phase of the defendant's trial, and they typically help the court determine whether a trial is appropriate (e.g., competence to stand trial evaluations) or whether an offender is even eligible for the death penalty (e.g., an *Atkins*-type evaluation to determine whether the offender is mentally retarded). In contrast, back-end evaluations are performed to inform legal decisions that occur after the defendant has been found guilty; that is, decisions during or after the sentencing phase of the trial. Such evaluations may include mitigation evaluations to inform the jury's sentencing decision, federal habeas corpus evaluations during the appeals process, and competence for execution evaluations conducted closer to the scheduled date of execution. Despite the variety of evaluations forensic mental health professionals may conduct in these contexts, Cunningham (2008) advised against conducting more than one evaluation or considering more than one legal issue in a given capital case.

Front-End Evaluations

Several types of front-end evaluations may be conducted in capital cases, although most are not exclusively related to the capital nature of the case. For example, there are a variety of front-end evaluations related to competencies, including competence to waive *Miranda* rights, competence to stand trial, and competence to waive counsel. Competence to stand trial evaluations are frequently conducted in noncapital contexts, and the applicable legal standard (*Dusky v. United States*, 1960) is used in both capital and noncapital contexts. Although the substantive legal standard is the same regardless of context,

---

9. We recognize that our categorization of evaluations as front end or back end is somewhat arbitrary and potentially misleading. For example, although we conceptualize *Atkins*-type evaluations as being front end, these evaluations may, in fact, be conducted posttrial in a few states. Moreover, although mitigation evaluations are technically back-end evaluations because they inform sentencing, they are almost always conducted pretrial because there is insufficient time to conduct the evaluation between the finding of guilt and sentencing proceedings.

competence to stand trial is often viewed as a flexible inquiry, in which the threshold for determining competence differs somewhat based on the complexities of the case. For example, the type of capacities necessary for a defendant in brief and simple proceedings for a misdemeanor theft charge are certainly less than the capacities necessary for a defendant to participate in more lengthy, complicated, and high-stakes capital proceedings.

Another type of front-end evaluation—mental state at the time of the offense—explores the defendant's mental health functioning and the possibility that a diminished capacity, extreme emotional disturbance, or insanity defense may be successfully raised at trial. Again, evaluations regarding a defendant's mental state at the time of the offense are not exclusive to capital contexts, and Cunningham and Goldstein (2003) noted that these evaluations follow a similar structure and process in both capital and noncapital cases. Nevertheless, because all aspects of a capital case are typically viewed with a higher level of scrutiny, including the decisions made by the attorney and the evaluations conducted by forensic mental health professionals, it is imperative that evaluators follow best practices in these evaluations.

One type of front-end evaluation is exclusive to capital cases. In *Atkins v. Virginia* (2002), the U.S. Supreme Court held that the execution of criminal offenders who are mentally retarded violates the prohibition against cruel and unusual punishment in the Eighth Amendment to the U.S. Constitution. Following *Atkins*, the diagnosis of mental retardation in capital cases has taken on constitutional significance, and forensic mental health professionals are occasionally asked to evaluate whether a criminal defendant meets criteria for mental retardation. Although we refer to *Atkins*-type evaluations as front end, it is important to note that the timing of these evaluations differs by state. Many states provide that these types of evaluations should be conducted pretrial to determine whether a capital trial is even appropriate, while other states do not permit such evaluations to be conducted until the defendant's guilt has been established and the proceedings move to the sentencing phase (see Cunningham, 2008; Dowling, 2003). Moreover, for defendants sentenced to death before *Atkins* was decided in 2002, *Atkins*-type evaluations will obviously occur postsentencing. Nevertheless, we conceptualize *Atkins*-type evaluations as front end, and many states have chosen to handle these evaluations in the pretrial stage of the capital proceedings (for a variety of conceptual and logistical reasons discussed later in this book). We discuss *Atkins* and *Atkins*-type evaluations in Chapter 5.

Back-End Evaluations

After a defendant is convicted in the guilt/innocence phase of a capital case, the next step in the bifurcated trial process is sentencing. During the sentencing phase, the court evaluates the defendant's moral culpability and blameworthiness in an effort to arrive at a fair and individualized sentence (Cunningham & Goldstein, 2003). In reinstating the death penalty in the United States in 1976, the U.S. Supreme Court held that the sentencing jury must make an individualized sentencing decision that takes into account the defendant's character, the defendant's criminal record, and the circumstances surrounding the offense (*Gregg v. Georgia*, 1976). Moreover, according to the Supreme Court's decisions in *Lockett v. Ohio* (1978) and *Eddings v. Oklahoma* (1982), the sentencing jury must be permitted to consider all relevant mitigating evidence the defense offers to argue for a sentence less than death. In this regard, the law appreciates that a variety of factors, including biological, psychological, and social, influence human behavior and may reduce blameworthiness to the point where a death sentence is no longer constitutionally appropriate. During the sentencing phase of a capital case, the prosecution seeks to justify imposing a death sentence by establishing the presence of one or more statutorily identified aggravating factors, while the defense argues for a sentence other than execution (typically life in prison without parole) by arguing against aggravating factors and by establishing the presence of mitigating factors. We discuss this process more in Chapter 2.

Mental health professionals may be asked to participate in capital sentencing evaluations because they are uniquely qualified to help identify and analyze potential mitigating factors, and to explain how those factors potentially shaped the defendant's thoughts and actions leading up to the offense (Cunningham, 2008; Cunningham & Goldstein, 2003). Alternately, mental health professionals may be asked to analyze the impact of only one specific factor on the defendant's thinking and behavior (Cunningham, 2008). For example, a mental health professional may be asked to opine how severe childhood abuse and neglect influenced the defendant's later behavior, with the defense hoping that a sufficient connection between the childhood abuse and capital offense will mitigate the defendant's moral blameworthiness and call for a non–death sentence. Or an expert witness retained by the prosecution may be asked to refute mitigation evidence presented by defense experts (Cunningham & Goldstein, 2003). As detailed in Chapter 7, forensic mental health professionals may play several roles in capital sentencing.

Besides considering what factors would justify the imposition of a lesser sentence in a capital case, mental health professionals may be tasked with assessing the risk of future violence posed by a capital defendant. In many death penalty jurisdictions, risk of future violence is a statutorily identified aggravating factor that can be used to justify a death sentence, so violence risk assessments assume a prominent place in some capital proceedings (Cunningham, 2010). In these types of assessments, mental health professionals examine the factors that may affect the likelihood that the defendant will engage in future violence. Cunningham and Goldstein (2003) note that this type of evaluation is particularly helpful in making sentencing decisions given that capital jurors tend to weigh heavily estimates of future dangerousness and overestimate a capital defendant's likelihood of engaging in future violence. Chapter 8 details the role of violence risk assessments in capital proceedings.

Mental health professionals can also play a role in the appeals process. Appeals offer the opportunity for the courts to examine the conviction, the legal proceedings that preceded the conviction, and sentencing (Cunningham, 2008). In most death penalty jurisdictions, there is a mandatory appeal of the conviction and sentencing, regardless of the defendant's wishes. In some cases, a capital defendant may claim that defense counsel was ineffective, which would violate the defendant's Sixth Amendment rights to effective assistance of counsel. Mental health professionals involved with state postconviction or federal habeas corpus hearings typically evaluate the mitigation, risk assessment, or other mental health evidence collected during the sentencing phase. They may be asked to offer an opinion regarding the quality of such evidence and describe any additional evidence that could have been presented to assist the defendant's case (Cunningham & Goldstein, 2003).

Mental health professionals may also be asked to evaluate whether a defendant is competent to waive appeals. Waiving one's right to appeal a death sentence effectively hastens the execution and relinquishes any legal right to stop or delay it, so mental health professionals may be asked to scrutinize the defendant's capacity for knowing, intelligent, and voluntary waiver in light of cognitive impairments, mental illness, or the potentially destabilizing conditions of death row. Anecdotal evidence suggests that these evaluations are rarely conducted given the mandatory appeals prescribed in most states' capital sentencing schemes, but mental health professionals can play a valuable role in these evaluations when necessary.

Near the last stage of the capital punishment process, a final type of back-end evaluation seeks to assist the court to determine whether the offender is competent to be executed. These evaluations are ambiguous and controversial, and they raise a variety of ethical implications for forensic mental health professionals (see Weinstock, Leong, & Silva, 2010, and Zapf, 2008, for informative discussions). Several decisions from the U.S. Supreme Court, including *Ford v. Wainwright* (1986) and *Panetti v. Quarterman* (2007), have held that prisoners must be competent to be executed. But the Supreme Court has so far declined to define a specific substantive standard for courts to use when determining whether an offender is, in fact, competent to be executed (see Appelbaum, 2007; Blanks & Pinals, 2007). The Supreme Court's decisions in *Ford* and *Panetti*, and the resulting ambiguity surrounding the appropriate substantive legal standard for determining competence to be executed, have left forensic mental health professionals struggling to identify appropriate clinical procedures for these evaluations. Although the practice literature regarding competence for execution evaluations is growing (see, e.g., Brodsky, Zapf, & Boccaccini, 2005; Ebert, 2001; Otto, 2009; Young, Boccaccini, Lawson, & Conroy, 2008; Zapf, 2008, 2009; Zapf, Boccaccini, & Brodsky, 2003), firm guidelines for these rare evaluations remain limited compared to the guidance available for other types of FMHAs. We discuss competence for execution evaluations in Chapter 6.

Overview of the Book

This book addresses the various FMHAs that may be conducted throughout the capital litigation process. These FMHAs have been shaped by the extensive death penalty jurisprudence from the U.S. Supreme Court (and other courts), and from statutory guidance provided at the federal and state levels. Through a series of cases decided over the past few decades, the U.S. Supreme Court has addressed which categories of offenders are eligible—and not eligible—for a death sentence, and it has addressed other substantive and procedural questions. Although some of these cases focus on factors for which mental health professionals can offer no particular expertise, such as the age of the offender at the time of the offense (e.g., *Roper v. Simmons*, 2005; *Stanford v. Kentucky*, 1989) and the nature of the criminal offense (e.g., *Coker v. Georgia*, 1977; *Kennedy v. Louisiana*, 2008), other cases have focused on the mental health or intellectual functioning of the offender at the time of the offense or closer to the scheduled execution.

To provide a legal context for the involvement of mental health professionals in capital cases, we discuss the multilayered capital litigation process in Chapter 2. Among other topics, we describe the sources of law that contribute to the substantive and procedural aspects of the death penalty, the structure of the U.S. court system, key players in the death penalty process, the role of death-qualified juries, and common trial and sentencing procedures. In Chapter 3, we discuss cases important for forensic mental health professionals involved in capital cases. Although our focus in Chapter 3 is mostly on cases decided by the U.S. Supreme Court, we also discuss several influential and informative cases decided by lower federal and state courts. To provide an ethical context for mental health professionals in capital cases, we discuss the ethical codes applicable to psychologists and psychiatrists in Chapter 4 and examine several key ethical considerations specific to FMHAs in capital contexts. We view Chapter 2 (death penalty litigation), Chapter 3 (death penalty jurisprudence), and Chapter 4 (ethical considerations) as foundational chapters that prepare readers for the material presented in the later chapters.

After these foundational chapters, we take a closer look at specific types of FMHAs in death penalty cases. In Chapter 5, we discuss evaluations conducted to determine whether offenders are mentally retarded and, therefore, ineligible for the death penalty based on the U.S. Supreme Court's decision in *Atkins v. Virginia* (2002). Among other topics, we address concerns about how states are defining mental retardation in the wake of *Atkins* and the challenges evaluators face when assessing intellectual functioning and adaptive deficits among prison inmates. In Chapter 6, we focus on evaluations conducted to examine an offender's competence for execution. We discuss both ethical considerations and practice guidelines relating to these types of evaluations. There are a variety of functions forensic mental health professionals perform in the sentencing phase of capital cases, and we discuss these in Chapter 7. In Chapter 8, we focus on the role of violence risk assessments in capital sentencing proceedings. In Chapter 9, we provide concrete recommendations for conducting evaluations in capital cases, focusing primarily on a set of FMHA principles that provide guidance and structure for death penalty evaluations. Finally, in Chapter 10, we illustrate current practices in death penalty evaluations by examining sample forensic reports provided by established forensic mental health professionals with special expertise in death penalty cases.

2

Death Penalty Litigation

The moratorium on capital punishment in the United States that followed the U.S. Supreme Court's 1972 decision in *Furman v. Georgia* ended 4 years later when the Supreme Court decided *Gregg v. Georgia* (1976). In *Gregg*, the Supreme Court concluded that the death penalty could be constitutional under certain circumstances, and it provided the states with some initial clarification on the distinction between constitutional and unconstitutional death penalty statutory schemes. In the years following *Gregg*, the Supreme Court decided several cases that further clarified what constitutes constitutionally acceptable death penalty practice (see, e.g., *Lockett v. Ohio*, 1978; *Eddings v. Oklahoma*, 1982).

Since the *Gregg* decision nearly 35 years ago, the Supreme Court has continued to address the constitutionality of the death penalty, sometimes as applied to various populations, such as juveniles (*Roper v. Simmons*, 2005) or individuals who are mentally retarded (*Atkins v. Virginia*, 2002), and sometimes as a response to various criminal offenses, including the rape of an adult (*Coker v. Georgia*, 1977) and the rape of a child (*Kennedy v. Louisiana*, 2008). The Supreme Court has also clarified the respective roles of the decision makers (judge and jury) in the sentencing phase of death penalty cases (see *Ring v. Arizona*, 2002; *Spaziano v. Florida*, 1984). By these decisions, the Supreme Court sought to make the imposition of the death penalty less arbitrary and reserve it for only the most deserving offenders.

The many cases decided by the U.S. Supreme Court, combined with numerous cases decided at the lower federal and state level, have created a large body of case law to guide capital proceedings. As a result, the death penalty process is relatively well developed in the roughly three dozen jurisdictions that currently allow capital punishment. Although capital and noncapital criminal cases share many procedural similarities, capital cases differ from their noncapital counterparts in several important respects. The nature of the death penalty requires special procedures and additional protections to comport with the Supreme Court mandates issued over the past 35 years. In this chapter, we review the structure of the court system in state and federal jurisdictions in the United States, describe key players in death penalty cases, and discuss the capital punishment process.

A Primer for Mental Health Professionals[1]

Sources of Law

As a starting point, some discussion on the various types of laws is necessary. In particular, it is important to address two related questions: What exactly is a law, and where do laws come from?

One source of law is constitutions, which are formal documents that define broad powers. Federal constitutional law stems from the U.S. Constitution, whereas state constitutional law originates from state constitutions. State constitutions can differ from the U.S. Constitution, but state constitutions cannot provide *less* protection than the U.S. Constitution (although they may provide more protection). Many of the rights and prohibitions discussed throughout this book originate in the U.S. Constitution, including the prohibition against cruel and unusual punishment in the Eighth Amendment and the substantive and procedural due process rights provided by the Fifth, Sixth, and Fourteenth Amendments.

Another type of law is statute. Statutes are enacted by legislatures, either at the federal level (through Congress) or state level (through state legislatures),

---

1. For attorneys or other professionals with legal training, this section is probably an unnecessary review. However, for mental health professionals, this basic overview of the legal system may be helpful to better understand capital litigation. Even for mental health professionals who have had some experience with the legal system, capital proceedings often require greater familiarity with certain legislation and case law that carry implications for forensic mental health assessments (FMHAs).

and then compiled into federal or state codes.[2] Statutes are typically designed to be broad in scope and widely applicable. One role of legislatures is to create statutes, which are then interpreted by courts in the context of specific disputes. Courts may sometimes determine that a particular statute violates a provision of the state or federal constitution, which would invalidate the statute. This is a good example of the well-known checks and balances system of the U.S. Government. When it comes to the death penalty, statutes often define the substantive and procedural aspects of capital punishment, and then these aspects are interpreted by courts in the context of specific cases. Disagreement with a court's statutory interpretation can lead to an appeal of the court's ruling, until the highest court with jurisdiction has the final say.

Common law, or case law, is made by judges in the context of a specific dispute. The role of a judge is to interpret existing law (typically statutory or constitutional), which may be quite broad, in the context of a specific criminal or civil dispute. Over time, courts create a large body of case law, and these court decisions create precedent for future courts to follow. Sometimes, however, a court may depart from established precedent because of factual distinctions between a current case and previous cases, disagreement with the previous court's interpretation of the law, or changes in the evolving standards of decency (which are particularly relevant in the context of Eighth Amendment cases); this is how new case law develops. Hundreds of court decisions have addressed capital punishment, and by doing so they have created a rich body of jurisprudence regarding almost every aspect of the death penalty.[3]

These various sources of law illustrate the vertical and horizontal dimensions of the U.S. legal system. The vertical dimension represents the separation of powers between the federal government and the states, which is embodied in the term *federalism* and protected by the Tenth Amendment to the U.S. Constitution. The federal and state governments have separate powers, and the states are sovereign in many respects. The horizontal dimension represents the separation of powers among the three branches of the government—that is, the legislative branch creates the statutes, the judicial branch interprets the statutes (thus creating case law), and the executive branch creates administrative agencies (which create administrative regulations).

---

2. A related concept is ordinances, which are enacted by local legislatures at the city, county, municipal, or borough level.

3. Another type of law is administrative law, which is made by administrative agencies (part of the executive branch of the government) to define or clarify the intent of the legislature. For example, Congress may enact a law designed to reduce pollution emission from factories, and the Environmental Protection Agency may be asked to operationalize that law in the form of administrative regulations. Administrative agencies and regulations exist at the federal, state, and local levels. Administrative law is not relevant in death penalty contexts.

Structure of the U.S. Court System

A brief overview of the U.S. judicial system is necessary to provide some context for the various procedures and events discussed throughout this book. At the broadest level, the U.S. judicial system is divided into two major branches: state courts and federal courts. There are various specialized courts within these systems (e.g., military, tax, chancery, probate, small-claims, landlord–tenant, family), but they are not relevant to death penalty litigation.[4] Within the state and federal court systems are courts that handle criminal matters (e.g., murder, rape, robbery, aggravated assault) and courts that handle civil matters (e.g., personal injury lawsuits), although the distinction is not always clear.[5]

State courts and federal courts generally have separate jurisdictions, but issues relating to jurisdiction are complex. Generally, state courts handle cases involving state matters, whereas federal courts address federal matters. For example, the crime of murder is typically characterized as a crime against the state, adjudicated in state court, and captioned as "People v. Smith," "State v. Smith," or "Commonwealth v. Smith."[6] However, if the murder victim was a federal employee (e.g., postal employee, U.S. Marshal), the murder becomes a federal offense to be adjudicated in federal court (e.g., "United States v. Smith"). Other crimes are more straightforward, although exceptions exist. For example, treason, espionage, and terrorism are always federal offenses. Automobile theft is typically a state offense (unless the stolen vehicle was a mail truck or other federal vehicle), and robbery is typically a state offense (unless the robbery victim was a federal employee or the robbery occurred on federal property). Even more complicated rules guide the adjudication of civil matters, but these are irrelevant to death penalty litigation.

---

4. A new breed of courts are known as problem-solving courts, which are specialized criminal courts designed to deal with offenders who present with specific problems, such as substance use, mental health problems, or homelessness. The theory underlying problem-solving courts is that treating the underlying causes of criminal behavior, rather than simply punishing the offenders, will be a more effective way to reduce criminal recidivism. This is based on the idea of therapeutic jurisprudence (Wexler & Winick, 1996). Of course, problem-solving courts do not decide capital cases, although capital defendants may have had prior experience in these courts.

5. Another distinction is between courts of law and courts of equity. As originally conceptualized, courts of law applied legal principles in deciding disputes and creating remedies, while courts of equity applied equitable principles designed to fix the legal wrong. For example, the most common remedy in civil courts is monetary damages. However, courts of equity can enter injunctions or decrees forbidding someone from engaging in a particular behavior, or mandating that someone act in a specific way. In the United States, most jurisdictions no longer maintain this distinction and have merged law courts and equity courts into courts of general jurisdiction that are able to fashion legal and equitable remedies appropriate for all types of cases.

6. Most states are formally designated as "states," but four states designate themselves as "commonwealths": Kentucky, Massachusetts, Pennsylvania, and Virginia. Despite lore to the contrary, the designation "commonwealth" has no particular constitutional or legal significance.

The state and federal court systems are each divided into hierarchies or tiers of different courts, with cases typically moving up the hierarchy through a system of legal appeals. A helpful way to conceptualize the state and federal court systems is by picturing two stepladders set side by side. The parallel ladders analogy is particularly helpful for two reasons. First, these ladders are useful in explaining the distinction between binding authority and persuasive authority, which has important implications in death penalty jurisprudence. Second, the ladders allow us to illustrate the procedure by which a case can "jump" from one ladder to the other ladder.

In the state court system, the bottom rung of the ladder contains the trial courts of limited jurisdiction. These courts, whose names can differ among jurisdictions (e.g., municipal courts), handle relatively minor matters, such as parking tickets, vandalism, and accrued fines. One rung up from the trial courts of limited jurisdiction are the trial courts of general jurisdiction. The state courts on this level handle the vast majority of cases, both civil and criminal. The purpose of trial courts is to determine the facts of the case and settle the dispute. The penalties applied by criminal trial courts include fines, judicially supervised release, incarceration, and death. The penalties available to civil trial courts are usually limited to monetary damages and injunctions.

The next rung up the ladder represents state intermediate appellate courts. As the name suggests, a case gets from the trial court to the intermediate appellate court through an appeal of the lower court's ruling. Grounds for appeal vary by case and jurisdiction, but they often involve procedural error (e.g., erroneous admission of evidence, improper exclusion of witnesses, improper empanelling of jurors). In contrast to trial courts, intermediate appellate courts resolve issues of law, not facts. In most contexts, appellate courts accept as true the facts as determined by the trial courts, and the focus of the decision is whether the trial court properly applied the law. Most states have two levels of appellate courts (intermediate appellate courts and the high appellate court), although some less populous states only have trial courts and high courts. In states with only one level of appellate court, appeals from the trial court go straight to the state high court.

Each state has a high court, which in most states is called the state supreme court.[7] State high courts hear cases that have been adjudicated at the trial and

---

7. Most states have different names for the trial, appellate, and high courts in their jurisdictions. For example, in New Jersey, the trial court is the Superior Court, the intermediate appellate court is the Superior Court Appellate Division, and the high court is the New Jersey Supreme Court. In Pennsylvania, the trial court is the Court of Common Pleas, the intermediate appellate court is the Superior Court, and the high court is the Supreme Court. To further complicate matters, in New York, the trial courts are called State Supreme Courts, the intermediate appellate courts are the Appellate Courts, and the high court is the New York Court of Appeals.

appellate levels. However, in most states, the state high court is a discretionary court, meaning that it is not required to hear any cases on appeal and only decides cases it accepts. Typically, the decision of a state high court is final. However, if the high court's ruling gives rise to an issue that implicates the U.S. Constitution, the case can jump from the state ladder to the federal ladder.[8] The move from the state court system to the federal court system has been an important part of death penalty litigation, as discussed later.

The federal court system, the second ladder, also has a number of courts arranged in a hierarchy. The lowest federal courts are the district courts, which function as trial courts. There are 94 district courts spread geographically across the continental United States and outlying states and territories. All states have at least one district court, and many states have several. As with state trial courts, the federal district courts are courts of general jurisdiction that hear both civil and criminal matters; they function to determine the facts of the case and resolve the dispute. However, federal courts hear cases involving federal matters. Cases move up the federal court system through a system of appeals. The intermediate federal courts are known as the U.S. Circuit Courts of Appeal. Similar to the district courts, the 13 circuit courts are spread out across the United States. The 13 circuit courts include 12 regional courts (numbered 1 through 11, plus the Circuit Court for the District of Columbia) and the Federal Circuit Court.[9] Each Circuit Court has jurisdiction over a set number of the 94 district courts. For example, the U.S. Court of Appeals for the Third Circuit has appellate jurisdiction over all of the district courts in Delaware, New Jersey, Pennsylvania, and the U.S. Virgin Islands, whereas the Eighth Circuit has jurisdiction over the district courts in Arkansas, Iowa, Minnesota, Missouri, Nebraska, and South Dakota.

At the top of the federal court system is the U.S. Supreme Court. As the highest court in the United States, the Supreme Court is charged primarily with interpreting the U.S. Constitution, although it also addresses other matters relating to federal law. The Supreme Court is composed of nine Justices, which include eight Associate Justices and one Chief Justice.[10] Each Justice is appointed

---

8. In most contexts, cases that jump from the state high court to the federal court system begin in the federal district courts, which are the trial courts in the federal system. However, in some instances, a case can jump from the state high court directly to the U.S. Supreme Court. Getting a case from state court to federal court provides the parties with a new set of courts to hear the case.

9. All of the circuit courts, except for the Federal Circuit Court, have jurisdiction over the courts in their region. The Federal Circuit Court has nationwide jurisdiction, but it only hears certain types of cases (e.g., patent, international trade).

10. The size of the Supreme Court is not established by the U.S. Constitution. Article III of the Constitution authorizes Congress to establish the number of Supreme Court Justices. The Judiciary Act of 1789 called for the appointment of six Justices. The Supreme Court was expanded to seven members in 1807, nine members in 1837, and ten members in 1863. The Judiciary Act of 1869 set the number of Justices at nine, and it has remained at this size since that time. It is constitutionally

(*Continued*)

by the President (and confirmed by the U.S. Senate) and serves for life (until death, retirement, or impeachment). The Supreme Court has discretionary jurisdiction, which means that it is not required to hear an appeal in any case. Thousands of cases are appealed to the U.S. Supreme Court each year by petitioning for a *writ of certiorari*, yet the Supreme Court only agrees to hear a small fraction of those cases (Thompson & Wachtell, 2009). At least four of the nine Justices must agree to hear a case for a writ to be granted (the "rule of four"), and the issue must relate to the U.S. Constitution or federal law. When deciding a case, at least five of the nine Justices must agree for there to be a majority opinion, although four votes can be sufficient if at least two of the Justices abstain from voting. The Supreme Court has jurisdiction over all cases decided by the federal circuit courts and all cases from the state high courts that are based on the U.S. Constitution or federal law. All decisions of the U.S. Supreme Court are final.

To understand the reach, or influence, of a court's ruling, it is important to note the distinction between persuasive legal authority and binding legal authority. U.S. courts follow a system of *stare decisis*, short for the Latin phrase *Stare decisis et non quieta movere*, which is roughly translated to mean, "Maintain what has been decided and do not alter that which has been established." Put simply, when a judge is faced with an issue that has previously been addressed by a court, the expectation embodied in *stare decisis* is that the judge will follow the decision of the previous court. The concept of *stare decisis* is intertwined with the issue of whether a particular court's decision should be viewed as binding authority or persuasive authority. If the earlier ruling came from a higher court in the same jurisdiction, a later court faced with the same issue in the same jurisdiction is bound to apply that higher court's ruling.[11] This is the concept of binding authority, typically referred to as *precedent*. However, courts outside of the jurisdiction of the court that previously decided an issue are not required to follow the lead of the earlier court, although the earlier court's decision may be seen as persuasive in the new court's decision making.

(*Continued*)
possible, however, for the President to attempt to increase the size of the Supreme Court by convincing Congress to appoint additional Justices. A well-known example is President Franklin Roosevelt's failed attempt to increase the size of the Supreme Court to 15 members in 1937.

11. Strictly speaking, the lower court does not *have* to follow the higher court's ruling in the sense that the lower court judge will not be dismissed from the bench for failing to follow the higher court's ruling. However, a judge who fails to follow established precedent risks having his or her decisions overturned on appeal. Moreover, in jurisdictions in which judges are elected rather than appointed, a judge may lose favor (or perhaps gain favor) with his or her constituents based on how closely the judge follows precedent. This is, of course, most likely in high-profile cases, which typically constitute a very small proportion of a judge's caseload.

Consider a few examples of persuasive and binding authority: A trial court in one city is not bound to follow the decision of another trial court in a different city in the same state. In this example, the decision in one trial court is merely persuasive authority on the other trial court. However, all courts within a state are bound to follow the decisions of the state high court. Moreover, courts in one state can certainly look to other states for guidance when faced with a similar issue, but the outside case is merely persuasive authority and not binding on courts outside the state. In the federal system, all district courts in the Third Circuit, for example, are bound to follow the decisions of the Third Circuit, but district courts in other circuits are not bound by the Third Circuit's decisions. Finally, all federal courts (district courts and circuit courts) are bound to follow the decisions of the U.S. Supreme Court.[12]

Decisions by the U.S. Supreme Court are binding on all federal courts, but not *all* decisions from the U.S. Supreme Court are binding on the states. For example, if the Supreme Court determines that a particular form of execution is unconstitutional because it constitutes cruel and unusual punishment under the Eighth Amendment, then no states are permitted to use that form of execution. In this instance, the primacy of the U.S. Constitution extends the Supreme Court's ruling to *all* courts (federal and state) in the land. But in some instances, the Supreme Court's decision may only apply to federal courts. For example, the Supreme Court's well-known decision in *Daubert v. Merrell Dow Pharmaceuticals, Inc.* (1993), which held that Federal Rule of Evidence 702 superseded *Frye* in determining the admissibility of expert evidence, is only binding on federal courts. This is because only federal courts use the Federal Rules of Evidence. As such, states were not required to adopt the *Daubert* standard, although most subsequently chose to do so.

As noted, a case that has made its way through the state court system (i.e., trial court, appellate court, high court) can potentially make its way to the federal court system, which would provide a new set of courts to hear

---

12. Other analogies may be helpful to illustrate the distinction between binding and persuasive authority. Law professors sometimes use the analogy of a family tree to illustrate the relationship between courts in the same and different jurisdictions. Imagine that the state high court is the grandfather, the state appeals (intermediate) courts are the sons and daughters, and the state trial courts are the grandchildren. If the grandfather (state high court) makes a ruling, then all of the parents (appeals courts) and all of the children (trial courts) are bound to follow the high court's decision. If, however, one of the parents (appeals court A) makes a ruling, only his or her children (trial courts set A) must follow that precedent. The other parents (appeals court B and appeals court C) do not have to follow the ruling; nor do their children (trial courts set B and trial courts set C). Another popular analogy describes court structure in the United States as a pyramid. The trial courts are at the bottom of the pyramid and are the most numerous, followed by the intermediate appellate courts in the middle of the pyramid (which are fewer in number than the trial courts), and the high court at the top of the pyramid.

the dispute.[13] In criminal cases, a writ of habeas corpus (or *habeas corpus ad subjiciendum*) is one common way for case to jump from the state court system to the federal court system. *Habeas corpus*, roughly translated as "you have the body," is technically a challenge to the legitimacy of detaining a prisoner. Several grounds exist for habeas writs, including that the defendant's conviction was obtained in violation of the U.S. Constitution (e.g., denied the Sixth Amendment right to counsel, violation of the Fourth Amendment right against illegal search and seizure). Cases heard by federal district courts via a habeas writ are then appealable up the federal court system.

Another way for a case to move from the state court system to the federal court system is by a w*rit of certiorari*. Roughly translated as "to be more fully informed," a defendant in a case heard by the state high court can in some circumstances appeal the state court's decision to the U.S. Supreme Court via a w*rit of certiorari*.[14] The Supreme Court receives roughly 7,500 petitions for certiorari each year, but typically only grants 1%–2% of the petitions (see Thompson & Wachtell, 2009). Finally, the Supreme Court's decision to hear a case does not imply disagreement with the lower court's decision (just as its declining to hear a case does not imply agreement with the lower court's decision). It simply indicates that the Supreme Court would like to address the issue in a formal ruling.[15]

---

13. Notably, the reverse situation—that is, going from federal court to state court—is impossible in the U.S. legal system.

14. *Writs of certiorari* are also used to get a case from a federal appellate court to the U.S. Supreme Court.

15. One important concept relating to jurisdiction is the distinction between subject matter jurisdiction and personal jurisdiction. A court must have both types of jurisdiction to hear a case. Subject matter jurisdiction refers to the power of a court to hear the type of claim being asserted. For example, Article III of the U.S. Constitution states that federal courts have limited types of subject matter jurisdiction. For a federal court to have subject matter jurisdiction, at least one of the following must be present: federal question (relating to the federal constitution, federal statutes, or federal treaties), diversity (which requires that the specific amount in controversy exceed a certain limit and that the parties are residents of different states), or a suit against the U.S. Government. Other grounds to establish federal subject matter jurisdiction exist, but these are several common examples.

Courts must also have personal jurisdiction to hear a case. There are several types of personal jurisdiction. With *in personam* jurisdiction, a court has power over a particular person if minimum contact is established. Minimum contact is defined differently by the states, but it may be established if the person resides or works in the state, or has a Post Office box in the state. A court has *in rem* jurisdiction if a particular piece of property is at stake. A court can also have personal jurisdiction over parties if they consent to give the court power (e.g., contracts often contain provisions specifying which court has jurisdiction to hear contract disputes). Several interesting cases have tested the limits of personal jurisdiction law. In *United States v. Satan and His Staff* (1971), the plaintiff alleged that Satan caused him misery and led to his downfall in violation of his constitutional rights. The U.S. District Court for the Western District of Pennsylvania noted that it was unclear whether the court had personal jurisdiction over Satan because no precedent existed. The court ultimately refused to proceed because the plaintiff had not instructed the U.S. Marshals as to how they could serve process on Satan. In a later case, *Water Energizers, Ltd. v. Water Energizers, Inc.* (1992), the United District Court for

(*Continued*)

Key Players in Death Penalty Cases

Before discussing the procedural aspects of capital cases, a brief review of key players in the criminal process is warranted. Given the nature of this book, we do not address the investigative aspects of the criminal process; instead, we focus only on the individuals involved in the trial process.

The Defendant

Obviously, as the individual who stands accused of a crime (state or federal), the defendant is in many respects the center of the criminal trial process. Depending on the nature of the case and the particular defendant, the role of the defendant can vary widely. For example, in some cases, a criminal defendant may take a passive role and say nothing during the trial, or the defendant may even be absent from the courtroom in certain limited circumstances (e.g., trials in absentia). In other cases, the defendant may take an active role that involves providing testimony, or even serving as his or her own attorney (referred to as *pro se* representation).

Although cases and defendants may vary considerably, the U.S. Supreme Court has held that all criminal defendants are entitled to certain constitutional protections. Many of these constitutional protections are encompassed under the principle of due process. For example, the Fifth and Sixth Amendments to the U.S. Constitution provide criminal defendants with certain rights, including the right against self-incrimination, the right to confront one's accuser, and the right to a jury trial. Other relevant constitutional protections relate to various competencies defendants must exhibit at different stages in the criminal proceedings. For example, defendants must be competent to waive their *Miranda* rights during custodial interrogation (e.g., right to remain silent, right to have an attorney present) (*Miranda v. Arizona*, 1966). If prosecuted, a defendant must be competent to stand trial (*Dusky v. United States*, 1960; *Drope v. Missouri*, 1975), and a defendant who wants to waive the right to counsel must be competent to do so (*Johnson v. Zerbst*, 1938). Given that pleading guilty results in the waiver of certain rights, defendants who choose to plead guilty must be competent to do so (*Boykin v. Alabama*, 1969). Upon a finding of guilt, a defendant must be competent to be sentenced by the judge or jury (*Green v. United States*, 1961). Finally, as discussed in Chapters 3 and 6, a defendant sentenced to death must be competent to face execution (*Ford v. Wainwright*, 1986; *Panetti v. Quarterman*, 2007).

(*Continued*)
the Southern District of New York concluded that the "existence [of Satan] is surely a necessary prerequisite for this court's exercise of personal jurisdiction" (p. 211).

Defense Attorney

Defendants are entitled to an attorney who, in turn, is obligated to serve as a zealous advocate for the defendant. Defense attorneys may be publicly appointed at no cost to the defendant (e.g., public defenders), court appointed, or privately hired. In capital cases, most defendants receive appointed counsel for indigent defendants, assistance from a capital resource center, and/or pro bono legal representation from a private criminal defense law firm. Capital defendants rarely pay for private counsel.

Attorneys must hold a valid license to practice law in each jurisdiction in which they practice, although there are procedures by which an attorney can represent someone in a jurisdiction in which the attorney is not licensed (referred to as *pro hac vice* admittance). The Sixth Amendment to the U.S. Constitution guarantees that all defendants have the effective assistance of counsel, and the failure to provide such effective assistance can be grounds for reversing the court's decision on appeal (not to mention a potential malpractice action against the attorney).

Prosecutor

In the U.S. legal system, the state (or federal) government prosecutes the defendant on behalf of the people; private prosecutions by the victim or other aggrieved individuals are not permitted. At the state level, the prosecutor can be known by several different names, depending on the jurisdiction: District Attorney, District Attorney General, City Attorney, Commonwealth's Attorney, County Attorney, Prosecuting Attorney, County Prosecutor, State Attorney, State's Attorney, or State Prosecutor. The District Attorney (DA) represents the government in the prosecution of criminal offenses. The DA is the highest ranking individual in that state's legal system, and he or she is responsible for overseeing Assistant DAs who take the lead in prosecuting cases. District attorneys are either appointed by the chief executive or publicly elected. In the federal system, prosecutors are known as "United States Attorneys," and they are appointed by the President of the United States. These attorneys serve under the U.S. Attorney General, prosecute cases in federal district courts, and are authorized to hire assistant federal prosecutors to serve underneath them.

In the U.S. legal system, as in many countries that use the adversarial system, the prosecution bears the legal burden of proving each required element of the crime. The prosecution must overcome the defendant's constitutionally guaranteed presumption of innocence by proving to the fact finder (judge or jury) the defendant's guilt beyond a reasonable doubt. Beyond a reasonable doubt is the most difficult legal burden to meet. The other legal standards, which are used in civil contexts or other aspects of criminal law (but not for findings of guilt), are preponderance of the evidence (which is the lowest burden) and clear and convincing evidence (which is an intermediary standard).[16]

The Judge

Judges preside over trial proceedings and are intended to be impartial arbiters of justice who referee the adversarial process between the defense and prosecution.[17] Although typically called judges, those who occupy positions on the state high courts or the U.S. Supreme Court are referred to as justices. In a jury trial, the judge oversees the proceedings, whereas the jury renders the verdict. If the jury returns a guilty verdict, the judge is typically responsible for determining the appropriate punishment. However, in bench trials, the judge acts as the sole fact finder and is responsible for determining guilt and handing down the sentence. A variety of decisions are left to the judge's discretion during the course of pretrial proceedings and the trial. Some of these decisions may relate to appropriate trial procedure, the admissibility of evidence, the content of jury instructions, and whether a proffered expert witness should be permitted to testify. Trial procedure in state and federal courts is governed by sets of court rules. It is not uncommon for states to have widely differing procedures, and in some states with many counties (such as Pennsylvania), each county has its own set of court rules.

The Jury

Criminal defendants are constitutionally guaranteed the right to a trial by jury through the Sixth Amendment to the U.S. Constitution.[18] The defendant may,

---

16. Some commentators and researchers have attempted to quantify the three legal burdens of proof. For example, it is not uncommon to see preponderance of the evidence quantified as 51%, followed by clear and convincing evidence at 75%, and beyond a reasonable doubt at 90%. In addition to feeling somewhat artificial, research suggests that these efforts to quantify legal burdens might not square with how jurors actually quantify them. In an early study, for example, Simon (1970) found that mock jurors placed the threshold for beyond a reasonable doubt somewhere between 70% and 74%, which is considerably lower than the "accepted" threshold of 90%.

17. This neutral role for judges in the adversarial system can be contrasted with the judge's role in the inquisitorial legal system used in some European countries. In the inquisitorial legal system, the judge is not a passive recipient of information presented by opposing sides; rather, the judge assumes primary responsibility for supervising the gathering of evidence to be used in a particular case. Also, unlike in the adversarial system, judges in the inquisitorial system actively question witnesses, whereas attorneys for each side take a more passive role. See Broeders (2003) for a helpful discussion of the use of forensic mental health professionals in inquisitorial proceedings.

18. The right to a jury trial in civil cases is guaranteed by the Seventh Amendment to the U.S. Constitution, although the U.S. Supreme Court has long held that this right is only applicable in *federal* civil cases (see, e.g., *Pearson v. Yewdall*, 1877; *Walker v. Sauvinet*, 1876). In civil cases in state

(Continued)

however, decide to waive this right and instead proceed with a bench trial in which the judge makes the factual determination of guilt. Potential jurors in a jurisdiction are randomly selected from county or state directories, such as Department of Motor Vehicle records, electoral rolls, and tax records. Although there are differences by jurisdiction, some individuals who are summoned for jury service may be exempt from serving. Automatic exemptions may exist for individuals whose jobs make it difficult for them to serve on a jury, such as physicians, law enforcement personnel, and firefighters. More generally, individuals may be exempt from jury service if it would create an undue hardship for them.

From the larger pool of potential jurors, a jury is empanelled through a process known as *voir dire*. The *voir dire* process permits the prosecution and defense to screen potential jurors through general questioning of the venire or specific questioning of each juror. The questioning may be conducted by the judge or the attorneys, depending on the jurisdiction. Through the *voir dire* process, the court and attorneys seek to uncover any biases that the potential jurors may have that would preclude the defendant from receiving a fair trial (although attorneys may have other motives in mind when excluding potential jurors). Potential jurors are typically asked questions about whether they are aware of any personal biases based on race, religion, or gender; how familiar they are already with the case (particularly if it was publicized by the media); whether there are personal or professional obligations that would make serving on the jury an unreasonable hardship (e.g., related to employment, child care, medical treatment); and whether they have any specialized knowledge or experience that might disproportionately influence the deliberation process (e.g., potential jurors who are trained as lawyers may be more able to sway the discussion).

During the *voir dire* process, the prosecution and defense are permitted to exclude a certain number of jurors without stating a reason by using a limited number of peremptory challenges. Although the attorney seeking exclusion is not required to identify a reason for excluding a particular potential juror, the U.S. Supreme Court has held that peremptory challenges cannot be used solely to exclude jurors based on race (*Batson v. Kentucky*, 1986) or gender (*J.E.B. v. Alabama ex rel T.B.*, 1994) because these are violations of the Equal Protection Clause of the U.S. Constitution. However, challenging such an unconstitutional exclusion practice is difficult because so much deference is given to attorneys during *voir dire*. In addition to excluding potential jurors

(*Continued*)
courts, the right to a jury trial may be provided by the state constitution and/or statutes. However, if a state court is enforcing a federally created right, the state is not permitted to eliminate the right to a trial by jury.

through peremptory challenges, an unlimited number of potential jurors may be excluded through challenges for cause. This type of exclusion, however, requires that the attorney seeking the exclusion identify a rational reason for the exclusion (e.g., the juror is related to the defendant, the juror has a professional relationship with the defendant, the juror has an obvious bias against the defendant).

The process of jury selection is more complicated when the prosecution plans to seek the death penalty. In capital cases, all jurors must be "death qualified." To be death qualified, a potential juror must affirm that he or she *(1)* is not unequivocally opposed to the death penalty, and *(2)* could individually vote for a sentence of death if the defendant is found guilty and facts of the case suggest that death is an appropriate punishment. Both prongs must be satisfied for a juror to be death qualified.

Legal scholars and social scientists have raised concerns about the death qualification process used in capital cases. First, some researchers have argued that a death qualified jury may in fact be pro-prosecution and biased against the defendant. According to this argument, by refusing to allow jurors who are not death qualified onto the panel, a subset of the population that might have been more sympathetic to the defense has been removed from the jury. There is no analogous selective removal for jurors who might be pro-prosecution or inherently unsympathetic. In short, death qualification is sometimes criticized as a form of selection bias that "stacks the deck" toward conviction.

Whether capital juries are indeed pro-prosecution or biased against the defendant are empirical questions and open to research. In one study, death-qualified mock jurors were more likely to render a guilty verdict than jurors who would have been excluded for their inability to be death qualified (Butler & Moran, 2002). In a subsequent study, death-qualified mock jurors assigned greater weight to aggravating factors and lower weight to mitigating factors (Butler & Moran, 2007). However, in *Lockhart v. McCree* (1986), the U.S. Supreme Court held that it does not violate the U.S. Constitution to require the use of death-qualified juries, despite social science evidence suggesting that the process results in a jury more prone to convict the defendant.

A second concern with the death qualification process is that talking with jurors about sentencing the defendant to death *before the trial has begun* may prime jurors toward a death sentence. Although criminal defendants in the U.S. legal system are presumed innocent until proven guilty, raising the issue of a death sentence before the trial has begun may cause jurors to approach the trial with preconceived biases about the defendant's actual guilt. Despite these (and other) concerns, the use of death-qualified jurors remains standard practice in all jurisdictions.

Although most juries are comprised of 12 people, the U.S. Supreme Court has repeatedly held that the Sixth Amendment does not require juries in criminal cases to be that size. For example, in *Williams v. Florida* (1970), the Supreme Court noted that the Sixth Amendment does not mention the required size of the jury, and it concluded that a 6-person jury could fulfill the functions of a jury just as well as a 12-person jury. Regardless, all federal criminal cases use 12-person juries. There is, however, some variation among the states. Only a few states permit juries of less than 12 people for felony trials, but the states are roughly equally split between 6-person and 12-person juries in misdemeanor cases.

Most states require unanimous verdicts in criminal cases, although the Supreme Court has held that there is no constitutional requirement that a guilty verdict from a 12-person jury be unanimous (see *Apodaca v. Oregon*, 1972; *Johnson v. Louisiana*, 1972). A decision agreed upon by 9 of the 12 jury members is constitutionally permissible. Nevertheless, as of this writing, all federal statutes require unanimous verdicts in felony and misdemeanor cases and, among states, only Oregon and Louisiana permit nonunanimous verdicts in criminal cases. However, in *Burch v. Louisiana* (1979), the Supreme Court held that verdicts must be unanimous if a 6-person jury is used.[19]

While the judge is responsible for interpreting the appropriate law and instructing the jury accordingly, the jury is responsible for making findings of fact and rendering a verdict on the defendant's guilt (in criminal cases) or liability (in civil cases). In a bench trial there is no jury, and the judge is responsible for making rulings on both questions of law and fact. In capital and noncapital cases, juries can make factual findings related to aggravating circumstances, which if present can be used to enhance the defendant's sentence. However, the role of the jury in capital cases differs from the role of the jury in noncapital cases in one important respect. In most noncapital cases, the jury makes a factual determination of guilt, and then the judge determines the penalty. However, in *Ring v. Arizona* (2002), the Supreme Court held unconstitutional Arizona's practice of a judge deciding between a life and death sentence. The Court held that the Sixth Amendment requires juries, not the judge, to find the aggravating factors necessary to impose a death sentence. Of note, under *Ring*, the judge can overrule the jury and reduce the sentence from death to life, but the judge cannot increase the sentence from life to death.

After hearing evidence presented by the prosecution and defense, the jury is asked to deliberate behind closed doors before reaching a verdict. If a jury is

---

19. In federal civil cases, the Seventh Amendment does not require a 12-person jury or a unanimous verdict, although federal statutes require a unanimous verdict for 6-person juries in most types of civil cases. In civil cases among the states, there is considerable variability in jury size and unanimity requirements. Less than half of the states require 12-person juries, and roughly half of the states permit nonunanimous verdicts.

unable to reach the requisite level of agreement, the result is a hung jury. In these instances, the judge declares a mistrial and the prosecution can choose to retry the case with a newly constituted jury. It is obviously taxing in terms of time, money, and other resources to retry cases, so judges are typically reluctant to declare a mistrial unless they are convinced the jury has reached an impasse. Although not encouraged or made explicit, the jury may also acquit the defendant regardless of the evidence actually presented against the defendant. This is called jury nullification, because the jury is essentially nullifying the prevailing law to arrive at a decision that it deems to be morally appropriate based on specific facts of the case. Jury nullification is most likely to occur in situations in which the jury finds the law to be unfair or too harsh in that particular case.[20]

Death Penalty Proceedings in the United States

Eligible Capital Offenses

A capital offense is an offense that may be punishable by death. When the Supreme Court effectively reinstated the death penalty in 1976 with the *Gregg* decision, it made clear that it was unconstitutional to implement a *mandatory* death sentence for certain offenses. Thus, capital offenses may be better defined as offenses for which the prosecution has the *option* of seeking the death penalty but is not required to do so. Furthermore, even if the death penalty is sought and the defendant is convicted, the punishment does not necessarily need to be a death sentence.

In death penalty states, the only capital offense is murder. At various points since the *Gregg* decision in 1976, the Supreme Court has considered the constitutional appropriateness of punishing other crimes with a death sentence, but it has consistently refused to expand the list of capital offenses. For example, in *Coker v. Georgia* (1977), which was decided just 1 year after *Gregg*, the Supreme Court was asked to consider whether the rape of an adult woman could be punishable by death. The Court ultimately upheld the

---

20. Although our discussion has focused on petit juries, some discussion of grand juries may be helpful. The grand jury is responsible for deciding whether to indict (formally charge) a suspect. While a petit jury hears evidence from the prosecution and defense in a (typically) public proceeding, a grand jury typically only hears testimony from prosecution witnesses. A defendant has the right to speak at a grand jury hearing, and he or she can be cross-examined by the prosecutor; the defense attorney plays no role in grand jury proceedings. The size of petit and grand juries also differs. Whereas petit juries consist of 6 to 12 members, grand juries are composed of between 16 and 23 members. The rules of admissibility also differ between jury trials and grand jury proceedings. Finally, most petit jurors are only required to participate in one trial, whereas grand jurors serve for the entire court term, which can be up to 18 months (although they typically only need to attend proceedings 1 day per month).

bright-line distinction between murder and all other crimes, and it concluded that the unique nature of murder makes it the only crime that can be legitimately punished by death. More recently, in *Kennedy v. Louisiana* (2008), the Supreme Court reached a similar decision when it concluded that the rape of a child could not be punishable by death.

Although murder is the only crime punishable by death, courts sometimes interpret murder broadly. The *felony murder rule* essentially creates a murder-by-proxy offense for defendants who committed a felony that was causally related to a murder, even if the defendant did not physically commit the murder. For example, in *North Carolina v. Lippard* (2002), Christopher Wayne Lippard and Charles Wesley Roache broke into the home of an elderly couple and stole the couple's truck. After crashing the truck, Roache returned and shot and killed all five members of the Phillips family. Even though Lippard never pulled a trigger, he was tried for first-degree murder under the felony murder rule. For the felony murder rule to apply, the felony must present a foreseeable danger to life, and the causal link between the felony and the murder cannot be too attenuated.

Although the Supreme Court has concluded on several occasions that murder is the only crime punishable by death (most recently in *Kennedy v. Louisiana*, 2008), some states still have some nonmurder "capital" offenses on the books. Typically, these outdated statutes receive little attention because prosecutors do not seek the death penalty for the offenses they describe. State legislatures may eventually remove these offenses from the statutory codes, although states have often been slow in removing offenses from their criminal codes (e.g., sodomy) even after they stop prosecuting them. Nevertheless, if a prosecutor were to obtain a death sentence in response to a nonmurder offense, the sentence would be struck down on appeal. Given the Supreme Court's most recent relevant ruling (*Kennedy*), it is extremely unlikely that a nonmurder offense will be punishable by death. In *Kennedy*, the Court stated: "Evolving standards of decency that mark the progress of a maturing society counsel us to be most hesitant before interpreting the Eighth Amendment to allow the extension of the death penalty, a hesitation that has special force where no life was taken in the commission of the crime" (p. 2658).

In the federal system, the U.S. Government has its own lengthy list of eligible capital offenses. Most of these are variations on murder, ranging from murder for hire (18 U.S.C. § 1958) to use of a weapon of mass destruction resulting in death (18 U.S.C. § 2332(a)). There are also, however, some crimes that are capital offenses that do not necessarily have to result in death. Some of these offenses include treason (18 U.S.C. § 2381); mailing of injurious articles with intent to kill or resulting in death (18 U.S.C. § 1716); espionage (18 U.S.C. § 794); trafficking in large quantities of drugs (18 U.S.C. § 3591(b)); and attempt to or authorizing of the murder of an officer, juror, or witness in cases involving a continuing criminal enterprise, regardless of whether the murder occurs (18 U.S.C. § 3591(b)(2)). The federal designation of nonmurder offenses as death eligible seems to contradict the recent *Kennedy* (2008) decision. However, the Supreme Court in *Kennedy* made it clear that its decision addressed crimes against persons, not crimes against the state: "Our concern here is limited to crimes against individual persons. We do not address, for example, crimes defining and punishing treason, espionage, terrorism, and drug kingpin activity, which are offenses against the State" (p. 2659). For a complete list of federal capital offenses and statutes, see Appendix A. For a complete list of the capital offenses and statute by state, see Appendix B.

The Decision to Seek the Death Penalty

When an offender commits a capital offense in a death penalty jurisdiction, the prosecutor makes the decision as to whether the state will seek the death penalty. This decision is likely influenced by many factors: specific facts of the offense (i.e., whether the nature of the offense suggests the presence of aggravating factors), the strength of the evidence against the defendant (i.e., the likelihood that the jury will convict the defendant), the wishes of the victim's family, and the availability of the resources needed to mount a capital case (which tend to be more expensive and time consuming than noncapital cases). Of course, political influences may play a role in the decision to seek, or not seek, a death sentence in a particular case. This may be particularly true in those states in which the District Attorney is an elected official and, therefore, more susceptible to political pressures. If the prosecution intends to seek the death penalty in a particular case, it must formally notify the defense of this decision within a certain timeframe prior to the trial.

The decision to seek the death penalty is a little less flexible in the federal system. In 1994, the Federal Death Penalty Act (18 U.S.C.A. §§ 3591 to 3598) was created to guide capital punishment in federal courts. This federal statute enumerates the offenses for which the death penalty is appropriate, mitigating and aggravating factors that should be considered, standards for judicial review of death penalty cases, and the classes of people who are ineligible for the death penalty (e.g., mentally retarded, pregnant, incompetent to be executed). Though the Federal Death Penalty Act has been challenged on a number of constitutional grounds, ranging from arguments that innocent people are convicted and ultimately put to death to concerns that the prosecutor (rather than a grand jury) decides whether to seek the death penalty, it has thus far been upheld.

In 1995, the U.S. Department of Justice created the Death Penalty Protocol (United States Attorneys' Manual, §§ 9–10.010), which must be followed by prosecutors in all cases in which the defendant is charged with a capital offense, regardless of whether they will ultimately pursue the death penalty (§ 9–10.020. Authorization and Consultation Prior to Seeking the Death Penalty). The standards for determining whether to seek the death penalty are outlined in § 9–10.080:

> The Attorney General's Committee and the Attorney General shall consider any legitimate law enforcement or prosecutorial reason which weighs for or against seeking the death penalty. . . The United States Attorney, the Attorney General's Committee and the Attorney General must determine whether the statutory aggravating factors applicable to the offense and any non–statutory aggravating factors sufficiently outweigh the mitigating factors applicable to the offense to justify a sentence of death, or, in the absence of any mitigating factors, whether the aggravating factors themselves are sufficient to justify a sentence of death. . . . Recognizing that there may be little or no evidence of mitigating factors available for consideration at the time of this determination, any mitigating factor reasonably raised by the evidence should be considered in the light most favorable to the defendant. . . Finally, there must be sufficient admissible evidence of the aggravating factors to obtain a death sentence and to sustain it on appeal.

The Death Penalty Protocol has been challenged in a number of cases when a prosecutor allegedly failed to follow the guidelines. To date, however, courts have held that no substantive or procedural right is actually guaranteed by the protocol and, as such, the failure to follow the protocol does not give rise to a legal grievance (see, e.g., *United States v. Lee*, 2001).

The Bifurcated Trial

In *Gregg v. Georgia* (1976), when the Supreme Court provided guidelines for what constitutes constitutional death penalty procedure, one of the requirements was that capital trials be bifurcated. In a noncapital case, the jury is responsible for determining the defendant's guilt and, if the defendant is convicted, the judge sentences the defendant. By contrast, in a capital case, the trial and sentencing are divided into two phases. The first phase of the capital trial is the guilt/innocence phase, which follows standard criminal trial procedures. If the jury returns a guilty verdict at the conclusion of the guilt/innocence phase, then the capital trial proceeds into the second phase, which is sentencing. Importantly, the sentencing jury is the same jury that decided the defendant's guilt. During the sentencing phase, the prosecution and defense make their respective cases for whether the defendant should be sentenced to death or life in prison. All federal and state death penalty cases follow this bifurcated trial procedure.

Several cases have addressed the appropriateness of empanelling separate juries for the guilt/innocence phase and sentencing phase of capital cases, but no court has upheld the procedure. In *United States v. Green* (2005), the U.S. Court of Appeals for the First Circuit held that the trial court erred by empanelling separate juries for the guilt/innocence phase and sentencing phase of the case. The court concluded that the trial judge violated the provisions of the Federal Death Penalty Act by empanelling separate juries. After that decision, other circuit courts, including the Fifth Circuit and Sixth Circuit, agreed with the First Circuit's position (see *United States v. Williams*, 2005; *United States v. Young*, 2005). The U.S. Supreme Court has so far declined to hear any cases on this issue, and we are not aware of any state courts that have addressed the issue. It is likely, however, that even if the procedure were upheld in a particular jurisdiction, the financial costs of empanelling a separate jury for the sentencing phase would be prohibitively high in many jurisdictions. Moreover, there are some conceptual reasons why empanelling a new jury for the sentencing phase does not make sense. For example, the new sentencing jury would presumably not have heard any of the evidence that led the original jury to the guilty verdict, which raises concerns about whether the punishment being imposed is in proportion to the offense and individualized to the offender, as required by the Supreme Court.

The Guilt/Innocence Phase

The guilt/innocence phase of a capital trial proceeds in much the same way as any other criminal trial. The defense and prosecution make opening statements to the jury before presenting their respective cases. Typically, the prosecution presents its case first, followed by the defense. In the U.S. legal system, the prosecution bears the legal burden of proving each element of the offense, and hence the defendant's guilt, beyond a reasonable doubt. The defense is not required to prove the defendant's innocence, although it usually seeks to create reasonable doubt in the minds of jurors by presenting a contrary version of the prosecution's case. After each side has presented its case, both sides give closing statements and the judge instructs the jury regarding relevant law and how the jury should proceed in rendering its verdict. The jury can deliberate for as long as necessary, and it is not uncommon for the jury to re-examine some evidence or ask the judge some questions. If the jury finds the defendant not guilty of the charges, the defendant is typically set free (assuming, for example, the defendant is not waiting to be tried on different charges in a different jurisdiction). If the jury is hung, or unable to reach a unanimous verdict, the judge will declare a mistrial and the prosecution is given the opportunity to retry the case from the beginning. If the jury finds the defendant guilty, the bifurcated capital trial moves into the second phase.

The Sentencing Phase

During the sentencing phase, the jury is presented with evidence of a different nature than it saw during the guilt/innocence phase. Now that the defendant's guilt has been established, the issue before the jury is whether the defendant should be sentenced to death or a term of incarceration, typically life without parole. The jury hears evidence regarding both the character of the defendant and the characteristics of the offense. While the prosecution seeks to convince the jury that death is an appropriate punishment, the defense hopes to convince the jury that the defendant, although guilty of the offense, does not deserve a sentence of death.

In response to the Supreme Court decisions reinstating the death penalty in 1976, which required an individualized sentencing decision in each capital case, modern death penalty statutes typically specify aggravating and mitigating factors designed to assist juries in reaching an appropriate sentencing decision. The prosecution presents aggravating factors, or reasons why the particular defendant is deserving of the death penalty. The purpose of aggravating factors is to narrow the class of persons eligible for the death penalty and justify imposing this more severe sentence (see *Zant v. Stephens*, 1983).

There are two categories of aggravating factors in most state death penalty statutory schemes: factors relating to the offense and factors relating to the offender. Examples of aggravating factors relating to the offense include murdering certain categories of people (e.g., police officers, correctional officers, and judges); committing murder during the course of another felony; committing murder while imprisoned; committing murder for pecuniary/financial gain; committing murder to avoid being arrested; and committing murder in a heinous, cruel, or vile manner. Examples of aggravating factors relating to the offender include a history of violent felonies and a high likelihood of being dangerous in the future. Specific aggravating factors differ from state to state, but some factors are found in many states (e.g., murder in an especially heinous, atrocious, or cruel manner). Importantly, state statutes that identify aggravating factors are exhaustive. Juries are given great latitude when it comes to mitigating factors (as will be discussed shortly), but aggravating factors must be statutorily defined and juries may not consider aggravating factors that are not listed in the statutes. For a complete list of the statutorily defined aggravating factors in each state, see Appendix C.

In addition to the defense offering its own mitigating factors, the Supreme Court has held that the defense must also be permitted to refute the prosecution's evidence regarding aggravating factors. In *Skipper v. South Carolina* (1986), the Court ruled on a South Carolina statute that listed "future dangerousness" as an aggravating factor.[21] During the guilt/innocence phase in *Skipper*, the prosecution repeatedly mentioned the defendant's propensity for violence while incarcerated. When the defense tried to proffer witnesses

---

21. Although "future dangerousness" is often mentioned as an aggravating factor, there is some evidence it is becoming less common among death penalty states (see, e.g., Keesler, DeMatteo, Murrie, & Anumba, 2010). Chapter 8 addresses FMHAs of violence risk at capital sentencing.

to counter this contention, the prosecution objected and the judge upheld the objection, thereby preventing testimony from the defense intended to refute the aggravating factor. On appeal, the Supreme Court held that the defense must be afforded an opportunity to refute the suggestion of dangerousness, and the failure to provide this opportunity was a constitutional violation.

Just as the prosecution offers aggravating factors that it believes justify a death sentence, the defense counters by presenting mitigating evidence that it believes justifies a sentence less than death. In contrast with aggravating factors, the list of mitigating factors in state death penalty statutes is not exhaustive, and juries are permitted to consider all potentially mitigating circumstances, regardless of whether they are formally listed in the statute. The only restriction placed on mitigating factors is that they must be relevant, which is a low standard that is typically interpreted liberally. The Supreme Court requires the sentencing jury to consider all relevant mitigating circumstances to ensure that *(1)* the decision to impose death is particularized to the defendant and the specific offense, and *(2)* the punishment of death is not excessive or disproportionate under the specific circumstances of the case.

States differ in terms of the mitigating factors they list in their statutes, but several mitigating factors are found across states. Examples of common mitigating factors include the following: the defendant was a "minor" participant in the offense (e.g., getaway driver or lookout as opposed to the person who actually committed the murder), the murder was committed while the defendant was under extreme mental or emotional disturbance, the defendant acted under duress, the defendant's capacity to appreciate the wrongfulness of his or her conduct or conform his or her conduct to the requirements of the law was impaired due to mental disease or defect, the defendant believed the murder was morally justified, and a low likelihood that the defendant will be dangerous in the future. Other examples of mitigating factors may include the defendant's history of childhood abuse, lack of criminal history (or violent criminal history), young age at the time of the offense, cooperating with law enforcement, or military service. Because defense attorneys are not limited in terms of the mitigating factors they can present, they usually present several. The defense's goal is to convince the jury that the defendant is not among the small subset of offenders who deserves the death penalty, and that the defendant's history and/or character make the death penalty inappropriate. For a complete list of the statutorily defined mitigating factors in each state, see Appendix D.

Occasionally, the prosecution and the defense present the same evidence, with the prosecution framing it as an aggravating factor and the defense framing it as a mitigating factor. For example, in the sentencing phase of a Florida trial, both sides emphasized that the defendant suffered from schizophrenia.

The prosecution implied that the presence of schizophrenia was an aggravating factor, whereas the defense argued that it should mitigate the defendant's sentence. The judge concluded that the presence of mental illness was an aggravating factor sufficient to satisfy the requirement that one or more aggravators be present to justify the imposition of the death penalty. On appeal to the Florida Supreme Court, both the death sentence and the use of mental illness as an aggravating factor were upheld (*Miller v. State*, 1979). Of course, the jury is free to give any amount of weight to the factors presented during the sentencing phase.

At the conclusion of the sentencing phase, the jury is once again instructed by the judge and asked to deliberate. The jury weighs the aggravating and mitigating evidence, and ultimately recommends a sentence of either death or life in prison. As previously noted, in *Ring v. Arizona* (2002), the Supreme Court held that the jury, not the judge, must find at least one aggravating factor to justify imposition of the death penalty.[22]

Automatic Appeals/Review

As a procedural safeguard, the vast majority of death penalty states have a system of automatic appeal/review, typically of both the conviction and the sentence. In these states, the automatic review is conducted regardless of whether the defendant requested or even wants the review. An automatic review typically entails having the conviction and sentence reviewed by the next higher court, which is usually a state intermediate appellate court. Many cases are appealed to the U.S. Supreme Court, although the Court declines to hear most of them. The automatic review procedure ensures that more than one court has an opportunity to review the evidence supporting the conviction and death sentence. There is no automatic review in the federal system.

There are some grounds for appeal relating to the involvement, or lack of involvement, of forensic mental health professionals in a case. For example, a defendant may argue that his or her right to effective assistance of counsel (guaranteed by the Sixth Amendment) was violated because the attorney failed to present mitigating evidence (which often involves a mental health professional). A defendant may also claim that mental health testimony presented by the prosecution's expert was erroneous. If a reviewing court agrees with these claims, the defendant may be afforded a new sentencing hearing.

---

22. Our discussion of death penalty procedures is necessarily broad. For a more complete discussion of related issues, including the differences between threshold and weighing states and how special issues govern some sentencing frameworks, we encourage readers to consult materials specifically tailored to the adjudicative process of death penalty proceedings.

Clemency

Another option for those sentenced to death is seeking clemency. Clemency is either an excusal of the previously imposed punishment or, more commonly, a reduction in the punishment. In most states, the governor plays a key role in the granting of clemency, which may be granted for a variety of reasons. (See Appendix E for a listing of the different clemency procedures used in death penalty states.) In many cases involving grants of clemency, the governor has questions about the appropriateness of the death sentence after reviewing a particular case, and the death sentence is therefore commuted to life imprisonment. An interesting use of clemency occurred in 2007, when New Jersey Governor Jon Corzine granted clemency to all convicts on New Jersey's death row the day before he signed a bill into law abolishing capital punishment in New Jersey.

The Execution

As of this writing, 35 states, the military, and the federal government have death penalty statutes. All 35 death penalty states authorize execution by lethal injection, and 17 of the 35 death penalty states authorize more than one method of execution. See Table 2.1 for a listing of the methods of execution in each state. There are several reasons why states authorize more than one method of execution. First, listing multiple methods of execution may be a state's attempt to make sure that at least one method of execution is available if other methods are ruled unconstitutional by the Supreme Court. Second, some states authorize different methods of execution depending on the date of the capital offense or the date of the sentencing. For example, in Oklahoma, electrocution is authorized if lethal injection is ever held to be unconstitutional, and firing squad is authorized if lethal injection and electrocution are both held to be unconstitutional. As another example, in Arizona, inmates sentenced after November 15, 1992, are executed via lethal injection, whereas inmates sentenced before that date can choose between lethal injection or lethal gas.

Conclusion

Death penalty litigation in the United States is complex and multilayered, and it differs in several important respects from noncapital cases. Conducting FMHAs in capital cases requires an understanding of capital procedures, the roles of key players, and various points in the criminal process at which mental health professionals can be become involved. Understanding the capital litigation process is also necessary when reviewing influential cases that have implications for FMHAs, which we address in the next chapter.

Table 2.1 Methods of Execution Used By Each State and in Federal Jurisdictions (as of 2008)

	Lethal Injection	Electrocution	Lethal Gas	Hanging	Firing Squad
Alabama	X	X			
Arizona	X		X		
Arkansas	X	X			
California	X		X		
Colorado	X				
Connecticut	X				
Delaware	X				
Florida	X	X			
Georgia	X				
Idaho	X				
Illinois	X	X			
Indiana	X				
Kansas	X				
Kentucky	X	X			
Louisiana	X				
Maryland	X		X		
Mississippi	X				
Missouri	X		X		
Montana	X				
Nebraska	X				
Nevada	X				
New Hampshire	X			X	
North Carolina	X				
Ohio	X				
Oklahoma	X	X			X
Oregon	X				
Pennsylvania	X				
South Carolina	X	X			
South Dakota	X				
Tennessee	X	X			
Texas	X				
Utah	X				X
Virginia	X	X			
Washington	X			X	
Wyoming	X		X		
U.S. Government*	X				

*The standard method of execution for federal prisoners is lethal injection. However, for offenders convicted under the Violent Crime Control and Law Enforcement Act of 1994, the method of execution is determined by the state in which the conviction took place.

Source: Adapted from Snell, 2009.

Appendix A: List of Federal Capital Offenses

- Assassination or kidnapping resulting in the death of the President or Vice President. 18 U.S.C. § 1751 [by reference to 18 U.S.C. § 1111]
- Attempt to or authorizing of the murder of an officer, juror, or witness in cases involving a continuing criminal enterprise, regardless of whether the murder occurs. 18 U.S.C. § 3591(b)(2) (though unclear if it would pass Constitutional challenge under *Kennedy v. Louisiana*, 2008)
- Bank-robbery-related murder or kidnapping. 18 U.S.C. § 2113
- Civil rights offenses resulting in death. 18 U.S.C. §§ 241, 242, 245, 247
- Crimes against persons in the United States resulting in death, committed by a person engaged in conduct transcending national boundaries. 18 U.S.C. § 2332b
- Death resulting from aircraft piracy. 49 U.S.C. § 46502
- Death resulting from offenses involving transportation of explosives, destruction of government property, or destruction of property related to foreign or interstate commerce. 18 U.S.C. § 844 (d), (f), (i)
- Destruction of aircraft, motor vehicles, or related facilities resulting in death. 18 U.S.C. § 32, 33, 34
- Death resulting from aggravated sexual abuse, sexual abuse, sexual abuse of a minor or ward, or abusive sexual conduct. 18 USC §§ 2241, 2242, 2243, 2244, 2245
- Espionage. 18 U.S.C. § 794
- First-degree murder. 18 U.S.C. § 1111
- Genocide. 18 U.S.C. § 1091
- Mailing of injurious articles with intent to kill or resulting in death. 18 U.S.C. § 1716
- Murder by a Federal prisoner. 18 U.S.C. § 1118
- Murder by an escaped Federal prisoner already sentenced to life imprisonment. 18 U.S.C. § 1120
- Murder committed by the use of a firearm during a crime of violence or a drug trafficking crime. 18 U.S.C. § 924(j)
- Murder committed during a drug-related drive-by shooting. 18 U.S.C. § 36
- Murder committed at an airport serving international civil aviation. 18 U.S.C. § 37
- Murder committed during an offense against a maritime fixed platform. 18 U.S.C. § 2281
- Murder committed during an offense against maritime navigation. 18 U.S.C. § 2280
- Murder committed in a Federal Government facility. 18 U.S.C. § 930
- Murder during a hostage taking. 18 U.S.C. § 1203

- Murder during a kidnapping. 18 U.S.C. § 1201
- Murder for hire. 18 U.S.C. § 1958
- Murder involved in a racketeering offense. 18 U.S.C. § 1959
- Murder involving torture. 18 U.S.C. §§ 2340, 2340A
- Murder of a court officer or juror. 18 U.S.C. § 1503
- Murder of a Federal judge or law enforcement official. 18 U.S.C. § 1114
- Murder of a foreign official. 18 U.S.C. § 1116
- Murder of a member of Congress, an important executive official, or a Supreme Court Justice. 18 U.S.C. § 351 [by reference to 18 U.S.C. § 1111]
- Murder of a State or local law enforcement official or other person aiding in a Federal investigation; murder of a State correctional officer. 18 U.S.C. § 1121
- Murder of a U.S. national in a foreign country. 18 U.S.C. § 1119
- Murder related to a carjacking. 18 U.S.C. § 2119
- Murder related to a continuing criminal enterprise or drug trafficking offense, or drug-related murder of a Federal, State, or local law enforcement officer. 21 U.S.C. §848(e)
- Murder related to sexual exploitation of children. 18 U.S.C. § 2251
- Murder with the intent of preventing testimony by a witness, victim, or informant. 18 U.S.C. § 1512
- Retaliatory murder of a member of the immediate family of law enforcement officials. 18 U.S.C. § 115(b)(3) [by reference to 18 U.S.C. § 1111]
- Retaliatory murder of a witness, victim, or informant. 18 U.S.C. § 1513
- Terrorist murder of a U.S. national in another country. 18 U.S.C. § 2332
- Treason. 18 U.S.C. § 2381
- Trafficking in large quantities of drugs. 18 U.S.C. § 3591(b) (though unclear if it would pass Constitutional challenge under *Kennedy v. Louisiana*, 2008)
- Use of a weapon of mass destruction resulting in death. 18 U.S.C. § 2332a
- Use of chemical weapons resulting in death. 18 USC § 2332c
- Willful wrecking of a train resulting in death. 18 U.S.C. § 1992

(*Source:* Adapted from Snell, 2009)

Appendix B: Capital Offenses by State

Alabama – Intentional murder with 18 aggravating factors (Ala. Stat. Ann. § 13A-5-40(a)(1)-(18)).

Arizona – First-degree murder accompanied by at least 1 of 14 aggravating factors (A.R.S. § 13-703(F)).

Arkansas – Capital murder (Ark. Code Ann. § 5-10-101) with a finding of at least 1 of 10 aggravating circumstances; treason. ***Revision***: Amended the definition of capital murder to include murder committed in the course of robbery, aggravated robbery, residential burglary, or commercial burglary (Ark. Cod Ann. § 5-10-101 (Supp. 2007)), effective 7/31/2007.

California – First-degree murder with special circumstances (CA PENAL § 190-190.1); sabotage; train wrecking causing death; perjury causing execution of an innocent person; fatal assault by a prisoner serving a life sentence (CA PENAL § 189); treason (CA PENAL § 37).

Colorado – First-degree murder with at least 1 of 17 aggravating factors; first-degree kidnapping resulting in death (CO ST § 18-3-102); treason (CO ST § 18-11-101).

Connecticut – Capital felony with 8 forms of aggravated homicide (C.G.S. § 53a-54b).

Delaware – First-degree murder with at least 1 statutory aggravating circumstance (11 Del. C. § 4209).

Florida – First-degree murder; felony murder; capital drug trafficking; capital sexual battery (FL ST § 782.04).

Georgia – Murder (GA ST § 16-5-1); kidnapping with bodily injury or ransom when the victim dies (GA ST § 16-5-40); aircraft hijacking (GA ST § 16-5-44); treason (GA ST § 16-11-1).

Idaho – First-degree murder with aggravating factors (ID ST § 18-4004); aggravated kidnapping (ID ST § 18-4504); perjury resulting in death (ID ST § 18-5411).

Illinois – First-degree murder with 1 of 21 aggravating circumstances (720 Ill. Comp. Stat. 5/9-1).

Indiana – Murder with 16 aggravating circumstances (IC § 35-50-2-9).

Kansas – Capital murder with 8 aggravating circumstances (KSA § 21-3439, KSA § 21-4625, KSA § 21-4636).

Kentucky – Murder with aggravating factors; kidnapping with aggravating factors (KRS § 32.025).

Louisiana – First-degree murder; treason (La. R.S. §§14:30 and 14:113).[23]

Maryland – First-degree murder, either premeditated or during the commission of a felony, provided that certain death eligibility requirements are satisfied (MD CRIM LAW § 2-202).

Mississippi – Capital murder (Miss. Code Ann. § 97-3-19(2)); aircraft piracy (Miss. Code Ann. § 97-25-55(1)).

Missouri – First-degree murder (565.020 § RSMO 2000).

Montana – Capital murder with 1 of 9 aggravating circumstances (Mont. Code Ann. § 46-18-303); aggravated sexual intercourse without consent (Mont. Code Ann. § 45-5-503).

---

23. In 2008, the U.S. Supreme Court held that the part of Louisiana's capital statute allowing for the death penalty in response to the rape of a minor was unconstitutional (see *Kennedy v. Louisiana*, 2008).

Nebraska – First-degree murder with a finding of at least 1 statutorily defined aggravating circumstance (NE ST §§ 28-303, 28-105.01).

Nevada – First-degree murder with at least 1 of 15 aggravating circumstances (NRS §§ 200.030, 200.033, 200.035).

New Hampshire – Murder committed in the course of rape, kidnapping, or drug crimes; killing of a law enforcement officer; murder for hire; murder by an inmate while serving a sentence of life without parole (RSA § 630:1, RSA § 630:5).

New Mexico – First-degree murder with at least 1 of 7 statutorily defined aggravating circumstances (Section 30-2-1 A, NMSA).

New York – First-degree murder with 1 of 13 aggravating factors (NY Penal Law § 125.27).[24]

North Carolina – First-degree murder (NCGS §§ 14-17).

Ohio – Aggravated murder with at least 1 of 10 aggravating circumstances (O.R.C. §§ 2903.01, 2929.02, and 2929.04).

Oklahoma – First-degree murder in conjunction with a finding of at least 1 of 8 statutorily defined aggravating circumstances; sex crimes against a child under 14 years of age (OK ST T. 21 §§ 701.7, 701.9).

Oregon – Aggravated murder (ORS § 163.095).

Pennsylvania – First-degree murder with 18 aggravating circumstances (18 Pa.C.S.A. § 1102).

South Carolina – Murder with 1 of 12 aggravating circumstances (§ 16-3-20(C)(a)); criminal sexual conduct with a minor with 1 of 9 aggravators (§ 16-3-655).

South Dakota – First-degree murder with 1 of 10 aggravating circumstances (SD ST §§ 22-16-4, 22-16-12, 23A-27A-4).

Tennessee – First-degree murder with 1 of 15 aggravating circumstances (Tenn. Code Ann. § 39-13-204).

Texas – Criminal homicide with 1 of 9 aggravating circumstances (Tex. Penal Code § 19.03).

Utah – Aggravated murder (76-5-202, Utah Code Annotated).

Virginia – First-degree murder with 1 of 15 aggravating circumstances (VA Code § 18.2-31).

Washington – Aggravated first-degree murder (WA ST 10.95.030).

Wyoming – First-degree murder; murder during the commission of sexual assault, sexual abuse of a minor, arson, robbery, escape, resisting arrest, kidnapping, or abuse of a minor under 16 (WY ST § 6-2-101).

(*Source:* Adapted from Snell, 2009)

---

24. In 2007, the New York Court of Appeals held that part of New York's death penalty statute was unconstitutional (see *People v. Taylor*). As a result, no executions can take place until the legislative errors are corrected.

Appendix C: Statutorily Defined Aggravating Factors by State

Alabama – Ala.Code 1975 § 13A-5-49. Aggravating circumstances

(1) The capital offense was committed by a person under sentence of imprisonment;
(2) The defendant was previously convicted of another capital offense or a felony involving the use or threat of violence to the person;
(3) The defendant knowingly created a great risk of death to many persons;
(4) The capital offense was committed while the defendant was engaged or was an accomplice in the commission of, or an attempt to commit, or flight after committing, or attempting to commit, rape, robbery, burglary, or kidnapping;
(5) The capital offense was committed for the purpose of avoiding or preventing a lawful arrest or effecting an escape from custody;
(6) The capital offense was committed for pecuniary gain;
(7) The capital offense was committed to disrupt or hinder the lawful exercise of any governmental function or the enforcement of laws;
(8) The capital offense was especially heinous, atrocious, or cruel compared to other capital offenses;
(9) The defendant intentionally caused the death of two or more persons by one act or pursuant to one scheme or course of conduct; or
(10) The capital offense was one of a series of intentional killings committed by the defendant.

Arizona – A.R.S. § 13-751. Sentence of death or life imprisonment; aggravating and mitigating circumstances; definition

(1) The defendant has been convicted of another offense in the United States for which under Arizona law a sentence of life imprisonment or death was imposable.
(2) The defendant has been or was previously convicted of a serious offense, whether preparatory or completed. Convictions for serious offenses committed on the same occasion as the homicide, or not committed on the same occasion but consolidated for trial with the homicide, shall be treated as a serious offense under this paragraph.
(3) In the commission of the offense the defendant knowingly created a grave risk of death to another person or persons in addition to the person murdered during the commission of the offense.

(4) The defendant procured the commission of the offense by payment, or promise of payment, of anything of pecuniary value.
(5) The defendant committed the offense as consideration for the receipt, or in expectation of the receipt, of anything of pecuniary value.
(6) The defendant committed the offense in an especially heinous, cruel, or depraved manner.
(7) The defendant committed the offense while:
   (a) In the custody of or on authorized or unauthorized release from the state department of corrections, a law enforcement agency, or a county or city jail.
   (b) On probation for a felony offense.
(8) The defendant has been convicted of one or more other homicides, as defined in § 13-1101, that were committed during the commission of the offense.
(9) The defendant was an adult at the time the offense was committed or was tried as an adult and the murdered person was under fifteen years of age, was an unborn child in the womb at any stage of its development, or was seventy years of age or older.
(10) The murdered person was an on duty peace officer who was killed in the course of performing the officer's official duties and the defendant knew, or should have known, that the murdered person was a peace officer.
(11) The defendant committed the offense with the intent to promote, further, or assist the objectives of a criminal street gang or criminal syndicate or to join a criminal street gang or criminal syndicate.
(12) The defendant committed the offense to prevent a person's cooperation with an official law enforcement investigation, to prevent a person's testimony in a court proceeding, in retaliation for a person's cooperation with an official law enforcement investigation, or in retaliation for a person's testimony in a court proceeding.
(13) The offense was committed in a cold, calculated manner without pretense of moral or legal justification.
(14) The defendant used a remote stun gun or an authorized remote stun gun in the commission of the offense.

Arkansas –A.C.A. § 5-4-604. Aggravating circumstances

(1) The capital murder was committed by a person imprisoned as a result of a felony conviction;
(2) The capital murder was committed by a person unlawfully at liberty after being sentenced to imprisonment as a result of a felony conviction;

(3) The person previously committed another felony, an element of which was the use or threat of violence to another person or the creation of a substantial risk of death or serious physical injury to another person;

(4) The person in the commission of the capital murder knowingly created a great risk of death to a person other than the victim or caused the death of more than one (1) person in the same criminal episode;

(5) The capital murder was committed for the purpose of avoiding or preventing an arrest or effecting an escape from custody;

(6) The capital murder was committed for pecuniary gain;

(7) The capital murder was committed for the purpose of disrupting or hindering the lawful exercise of any government or political function;

(8) (A) The capital murder was committed in an especially cruel or depraved manner.

    (B) (i) For purposes of subdivision (8)(A) of this section, a capital murder is committed in an especially cruel manner when, as part of a course of conduct intended to inflict mental anguish, serious physical abuse, or torture upon the victim prior to the victim's death, mental anguish, serious physical abuse, or torture is inflicted.

        (a) "Mental anguish" means the victim's uncertainty as to his or her ultimate fate.

        (b) "Serious physical abuse" means physical abuse that creates a substantial risk of death or that causes protracted impairment of health, or loss or protracted impairment of the function of any bodily member or organ.

        (c) "Torture" means the infliction of extreme physical pain for a prolonged period of time prior to the victim's death.

    (C) For purposes of subdivision (8)(A) of this section, a capital murder is committed in an especially depraved manner when the person relishes the murder, evidencing debasement or perversion, or shows an indifference to the suffering of the victim and evidences a sense of pleasure in committing the murder;

(9) The capital murder was committed by means of a destructive device, bomb, explosive, or similar device that the person planted, hid, or concealed in any place, area, dwelling, building, or structure, or mailed or delivered, or caused to be planted, hidden, concealed, mailed, or delivered, and the person knew that his or her act would create a great risk of death to human life; or

(10) The capital murder was committed against a person whom the defendant knew or reasonably should have known was especially vulnerable to the attack because:
   (A) Of either a temporary or permanent severe physical or mental disability which would interfere with the victim's ability to flee or to defend himself or herself; or
   (B) The person was twelve (12) years of age or younger.

California – West's Ann. Cal. Penal Code § 190.2. Death penalty or life imprisonment without parole; special circumstances

(a) The penalty for a defendant who is found guilty of murder in the first degree is death or imprisonment in the state prison for life without the possibility of parole if one or more of the following special circumstances has been found under Section 190.4 to be true:
   (1) The murder was intentional and carried out for financial gain.
   (2) The defendant was convicted previously of murder in the first or second degree. For the purpose of this paragraph, an offense committed in another jurisdiction, which if committed in California would be punishable as first or second degree murder, shall be deemed murder in the first or second degree.
   (3) The defendant, in this proceeding, has been convicted of more than one offense of murder in the first or second degree.
   (4) The murder was committed by means of a destructive device, bomb, or explosive planted, hidden, or concealed in any place, area, dwelling, building, or structure, and the defendant knew, or reasonably should have known, that his or her act or acts would create a great risk of death to one or more human beings.
   (5) The murder was committed for the purpose of avoiding or preventing a lawful arrest, or perfecting or attempting to perfect, an escape from lawful custody.
   (6) The murder was committed by means of a destructive device, bomb, or explosive that the defendant mailed or delivered, attempted to mail or deliver, or caused to be mailed or delivered, and the defendant knew, or reasonably should have known, that his or her act or acts would create a great risk of death to one or more human beings.
   (7) The victim was a peace officer, . . .who, while engaged in the course of the performance of his or her duties, was intentionally killed, and the defendant knew, or reasonably should have known, that the victim was a peace officer engaged in the performance of

his or her duties; or the victim was a peace officer, as defined in the above-enumerated sections, or a former peace officer under any of those sections, and was intentionally killed in retaliation for the performance of his or her official duties.

(8) The victim was a federal law enforcement officer or agent who, while engaged in the course of the performance of his or her duties, was intentionally killed, and the defendant knew, or reasonably should have known, that the victim was a federal law enforcement officer or agent engaged in the performance of his or her duties; or the victim was a federal law enforcement officer or agent, and was intentionally killed in retaliation for the performance of his or her official duties.

(9) The victim was a firefighter, as defined in Section 245.1, who, while engaged in the course of the performance of his or her duties, was intentionally killed, and the defendant knew, or reasonably should have known, that the victim was a firefighter engaged in the performance of his or her duties.

(10) The victim was a witness to a crime who was intentionally killed for the purpose of preventing his or her testimony in any criminal or juvenile proceeding, and the killing was not committed during the commission or attempted commission, of the crime to which he or she was a witness; or the victim was a witness to a crime and was intentionally killed in retaliation for his or her testimony in any criminal or juvenile proceeding. As used in this paragraph, "juvenile proceeding" means a proceeding brought pursuant to Section 602 or 707 of the Welfare and Institutions Code.

(11) The victim was a prosecutor or assistant prosecutor or a former prosecutor or assistant prosecutor of any local or state prosecutor's office in this or any other state, or of a federal prosecutor's office, and the murder was intentionally carried out in retaliation for, or to prevent the performance of, the victim's official duties.

(12) The victim was a judge or former judge of any court of record in the local, state, or federal system in this or any other state, and the murder was intentionally carried out in retaliation for, or to prevent the performance of, the victim's official duties.

(13) The victim was an elected or appointed official or former official of the federal government, or of any local or state government of this or any other state, and the killing was intentionally carried out in retaliation for, or to prevent the performance of, the victim's official duties.

(14) The murder was especially heinous, atrocious, or cruel, manifesting exceptional depravity. As used in this section, the phrase "especially heinous, atrocious, or cruel, manifesting exceptional

depravity" means a conscienceless or pitiless crime that is unnecessarily torturous to the victim.
(15) The defendant intentionally killed the victim by means of lying in wait.
(16) The victim was intentionally killed because of his or her race, color, religion, nationality, or country of origin.
(17) The murder was committed while the defendant was engaged in, or was an accomplice in, the commission of, attempted commission of, or the immediate flight after committing, or attempting to commit, the following felonies:
(A) Robbery in violation of Section 211 or 212.5.
(B) Kidnapping in violation of Section 207, 209, or 209.5.
(C) Rape in violation of Section 261.
(D) Sodomy in violation of Section 286.
(E) The performance of a lewd or lascivious act upon the person of a child under the age of 14 years in violation of Section 288.
(F) Oral copulation in violation of Section 288a.
(G) Burglary in the first or second degree in violation of Section 460.
(H) Arson in violation of subdivision (b) of Section 451.
(I) Train wrecking in violation of Section 219.
(J) Mayhem in violation of Section 203.
(K) Rape by instrument in violation of Section 289.
(L) Carjacking, as defined in Section 215.
(M) To prove the special circumstances of kidnapping in subparagraph (B), or arson in subparagraph (H), if there is specific intent to kill, it is only required that there be proof of the elements of those felonies. If so established, those two special circumstances are proven even if the felony of kidnapping or arson is committed primarily or solely for the purpose of facilitating the murder.
(18) The murder was intentional and involved the infliction of torture.
(19) The defendant intentionally killed the victim by the administration of poison.
(20) The victim was a juror in any court of record in the local, state, or federal system in this or any other state, and the murder was intentionally carried out in retaliation for, or to prevent the performance of, the victim's official duties.
(21) The murder was intentional and perpetrated by means of discharging a firearm from a motor vehicle, intentionally at another person or persons outside the vehicle with the intent to inflict death. For purposes of this paragraph, "motor vehicle" means any vehicle as defined in Section 415 of the Vehicle Code.

(22) The defendant intentionally killed the victim while the defendant was an active participant in a criminal street gang, as defined in subdivision (f) of Section 186.22, and the murder was carried out to further the activities of the criminal street gang.

(b) Unless an intent to kill is specifically required under subdivision (a) for a special circumstance enumerated therein, an actual killer, as to whom the special circumstance has been found to be true under Section 190.4, need not have had any intent to kill at the time of the commission of the offense which is the basis of the special circumstance in order to suffer death or confinement in the state prison for life without the possibility of parole.

(c) Every person, not the actual killer, who, with the intent to kill, aids, abets, counsels, commands, induces, solicits, requests, or assists any actor in the commission of murder in the first degree shall be punished by death or imprisonment in the state prison for life without the possibility of parole if one or more of the special circumstances enumerated in subdivision (a) has been found to be true under Section 190.4.

(d) Notwithstanding subdivision (c), every person, not the actual killer, who, with reckless indifference to human life and as a major participant, aids, abets, counsels, commands, induces, solicits, requests, or assists in the commission of a felony enumerated in paragraph (17) of subdivision (a) which results in the death of some person or persons, and who is found guilty of murder in the first degree therefor, shall be punished by death or imprisonment in the state prison for life without the possibility of parole if a special circumstance enumerated in paragraph (17) of subdivision (a) has been found to be true under Section 190.4.

Colorado – C.R.S.A. § 18-1.4-102. Imposition of sentence in class 1 felonies for crimes committed on or after July 1, 1995, and prior to July 12, 2002—appellate review

(5) For purposes of this section, aggravating factors shall be the following factors:

(a) The class 1 felony was committed by a person under sentence of imprisonment for a class 1, 2, or 3 felony as defined by Colorado law or United States law, or for a crime committed against another state or the United States which would constitute a class 1, 2, or 3 felony as defined by Colorado law; or

(b) The defendant was previously convicted in this state of a class 1 or 2 felony involving violence as specified in section 16-11-309, C.R.S., as it existed prior to October 1, 2002, or section 18-1.3-406, or was previously convicted by another state or the United States of an offense which would constitute a class 1 or 2 felony involving violence as defined by Colorado law in section 16-11-309, C.R.S., as it existed prior to October 1, 2002, or section 18-1.3-406; or

(c) The defendant intentionally killed any of the following persons while such person was engaged in the course of the performance of such person's official duties, and the defendant knew or reasonably should have known that such victim was such a person engaged in the performance of such person's official duties, or the victim was intentionally killed in retaliation for the performance of the victim's official duties:

    (I) A peace officer or former peace officer as described in section 16-2.5-101, C.R.S.; or

    (II) A firefighter as defined in section 24-33.5-1202(4), C.R.S.; or

    (III) A judge, referee, or former judge or referee of any court of record in the state or federal system or in any other state court system or a judge or former judge in any municipal court in this state or in any other state. For purposes of this subparagraph (III), the term "referee" shall include a hearing officer or any other officer who exercises judicial functions.

    (IV) An elected state, county, or municipal official; or

    (V) A federal law enforcement officer or agent or former federal law enforcement officer or agent; or

(d) The defendant intentionally killed a person kidnapped or being held as a hostage by the defendant or by anyone associated with the defendant; or

(e) The defendant has been a party to an agreement to kill another person in furtherance of which a person has been intentionally killed; or

(f) The defendant committed the offense while lying in wait, from ambush, or by use of an explosive or incendiary device. As used in this paragraph (f), "explosive or incendiary device" means:

    (VI) Dynamite and all other forms of high explosives; or

    (VII) Any explosive bomb, grenade, missile, or similar device; or

    (VIII) Any incendiary bomb or grenade, fire bomb, or similar device, including any device which consists of or includes a breakable container including a flammable liquid or compound, and a wick composed of any material which, when ignited, is capable of igniting such flammable liquid or compound, and can be carried or thrown by one individual acting alone.

(g) The defendant committed a class 1, 2, or 3 felony and, in the course of or in furtherance of such or immediate flight therefrom, the defendant intentionally caused the death of a person other than one of the participants; or

(h) The class 1 felony was committed for pecuniary gain; or

(i) In the commission of the offense, the defendant knowingly created a grave risk of death to another person in addition to the victim of the offense; or

(j) The defendant committed the offense in an especially heinous, cruel, or depraved manner; or

(k) The class 1 felony was committed for the purpose of avoiding or preventing a lawful arrest or prosecution or effecting an escape from custody. This factor shall include the intentional killing of a witness to a criminal offense.

(l) The defendant unlawfully and intentionally, knowingly, or with universal malice manifesting extreme indifference to the value of human life generally, killed two or more persons during the commission of the same criminal episode; or

(m) The defendant intentionally killed a child who has not yet attained twelve years of age; or

(n) (I) The defendant committed the class 1 felony against the victim because of the victim's race, color, ancestry, religion, or national origin.

(II) The provisions of this paragraph (n) shall apply to offenses committed on or after July 1, 1998.

(o) (I) The defendant's possession of the weapon used to commit the class 1 felony constituted a felony offense under the laws of this state or the United States.

(II) The provisions of this paragraph (o) shall apply to offenses committed on or after August 2, 2000.

Connecticut – C.G.S.A. § 53a-46a. Imposition of sentence for capital felony. Hearing. Special verdict. Mitigating and aggravating factors. Factors barring death sentence

(1) The defendant committed the offense during the commission or attempted commission of, or during the immediate flight from the commission or attempted commission of, a felony and the defendant had previously been convicted of the same felony; or

(2) The defendant committed the offense after having been convicted of two or more state offenses or two or more federal offenses or of one or more state offenses and one or more federal offenses for each of which a penalty of more than 1 year imprisonment may be imposed, which offenses were committed on different occasions and which involved the infliction of serious bodily injury upon another person; or

(3) The defendant committed the offense and in such commission knowingly created a grave risk of death to another person in addition to the victim of the offense; or

(4) The defendant committed the offense in an especially heinous, cruel, or depraved manner; or

(5) The defendant procured the commission of the offense by payment, or promise of payment, of anything of pecuniary value; or

(6) The defendant committed the offense as consideration for the receipt, or in expectation of the receipt, of anything of pecuniary value; or

(7) The defendant committed the offense with an assault weapon, as defined in section 53-202a; or

(8) The defendant committed the offense set forth in subdivision (1) of section 53a-54b to avoid arrest for a criminal act or prevent detection of a criminal act or to hamper or prevent the victim from carrying out any act within the scope of the victim's official duties or to retaliate against the victim for the performance of the victim's official duties.

Delaware – 11 Del.C. § 4209. Punishment, procedure for determining punishment, review of punishment and method of punishment for first-degree murder

(e) *Aggravating circumstances.*
   (1) In order for a sentence of death to be imposed, the jury, unanimously, or the judge where applicable, must find that the evidence established beyond a reasonable doubt the existence of at least 1 of the following aggravating circumstances which shall apply with equal force to accomplices convicted of such murder:
      (a) The murder was committed by a person in, or who has escaped from, the custody of a law-enforcement officer or place of confinement.
      (b) The murder was committed for the purpose of avoiding or preventing an arrest or for the purpose of effecting an escape from custody.
      (c) The murder was committed against any law-enforcement officer, corrections employee, or firefighter, while such victim was engaged in the performance of official duties.

(d) The murder was committed against a judicial officer, a former judicial officer, Attorney General, former Attorney General, Assistant or Deputy Attorney General or former Assistant or Deputy Attorney General, State Detective or former State Detective, Special Investigator or former Special Investigator, during, or because of, the exercise of an official duty.

(e) The murder was committed against a person who was held or otherwise detained as a shield or hostage.

(f) The murder was committed against a person who was held or detained by the defendant for ransom or reward.

(g) The murder was committed against a person who was a witness to a crime and who was killed for the purpose of preventing the witness's appearance or testimony in any grand jury, criminal, or civil proceeding involving such crime, or in retaliation for the witness's appearance or testimony in any grand jury, criminal, or civil proceeding involving such crime.

(h) The defendant paid or was paid by another person or had agreed to pay or be paid by another person or had conspired to pay or be paid by another person for the killing of the victim.

(i) The defendant was previously convicted of another murder or manslaughter or of a felony involving the use of, or threat of, force or violence upon another person.

(j) The murder was committed while the defendant was engaged in the commission of, or attempt to commit, or flight after committing or attempting to commit any degree of rape, unlawful sexual intercourse, arson, kidnapping, robbery, sodomy, or burglary.

(k) The defendant's course of conduct resulted in the deaths of 2 or more persons where the deaths are a probable consequence of the defendant's conduct.

(l) The murder was outrageously or wantonly vile, horrible, or inhuman in that it involved torture, depravity of mind, use of an explosive device or poison, or the defendant used such means on the victim prior to murdering the victim.

(m) The defendant caused or directed another to commit murder or committed murder as an agent or employee of another person.

(n) The defendant was under a sentence of life imprisonment, whether for natural life or otherwise, at the time of the commission of the murder.

(o) The murder was committed for pecuniary gain.

(p) The victim was pregnant.

(q) The victim was severely handicapped or severely disabled.

(r) The victim was 62 years of age or older.
(s) The victim was a child 14 years of age or younger, and the murder was committed by an individual who is at least 4 years older than the victim.
(t) At the time of the killing, the victim was or had been a nongovernmental informant or had otherwise provided any investigative, law enforcement, or police agency with information concerning criminal activity, and the killing was in retaliation for the victim's activities as a nongovernmental informant or in providing information concerning criminal activity to an investigative, law enforcement, or police agency.
(u) The murder was premeditated and the result of substantial planning. Such planning must be as to the commission of the murder itself and not simply as to the commission or attempted commission of any underlying felony.
(v) The murder was committed for the purpose of interfering with the victim's free exercise or enjoyment of any right, privilege, or immunity protected by the First Amendment to the United States Constitution, or because the victim has exercised or enjoyed said rights, or because of the victim's race, religion, color, disability, national origin, or ancestry.

Florida – West's F.S.A. § 921.141. Sentence of death or life imprisonment for capital felonies; further proceedings to determine sentence

(5) Aggravating circumstances. Aggravating circumstances shall be limited to the following:
(a) The capital felony was committed by a person previously convicted of a felony and under sentence of imprisonment or placed on community control or on felony probation.
(b) The defendant was previously convicted of another capital felony or of a felony involving the use or threat of violence to the person.
(c) The defendant knowingly created a great risk of death to many persons.
(d) The capital felony was committed while the defendant was engaged, or was an accomplice, in the commission of, or an attempt to commit, or flight after committing or attempting to commit, any: robbery; sexual battery; aggravated child abuse; abuse of an elderly person or disabled adult resulting in great bodily harm, permanent disability, or permanent disfigurement; arson; burglary;

kidnapping; aircraft piracy; or unlawful throwing, placing, or discharging of a destructive device or bomb.
(e) The capital felony was committed for the purpose of avoiding or preventing a lawful arrest or effecting an escape from custody.
(f) The capital felony was committed for pecuniary gain.
(g) The capital felony was committed to disrupt or hinder the lawful exercise of any governmental function or the enforcement of laws.
(h) The capital felony was especially heinous, atrocious, or cruel.
(i) The capital felony was a homicide and was committed in a cold, calculated, and premeditated manner without any pretense of moral or legal justification.
(j) The victim of the capital felony was a law enforcement officer engaged in the performance of his or her official duties.
(k) The victim of the capital felony was an elected or appointed public official engaged in the performance of his or her official duties if the motive for the capital felony was related, in whole or in part, to the victim's official capacity.
(l) The victim of the capital felony was a person less than 12 years of age.
(m) The victim of the capital felony was particularly vulnerable due to advanced age or disability, or because the defendant stood in a position of familial or custodial authority over the victim.
(n) The capital felony was committed by a criminal gang member, as defined in § 874.03.
(o) The capital felony was committed by a person designated as a sexual predator pursuant to § 775.21 or a person previously designated as a sexual predator who had the sexual predator designation removed.

Georgia – Ga. Code Ann., § 17-10-30. Mitigating and aggravating circumstances; death penalty

(a) The death penalty may be imposed for the offenses of aircraft hijacking or treason in any case.
(b) In all cases of other offenses for which the death penalty may be authorized, the judge shall consider, or he shall include in his instructions to the jury for it to consider, any mitigating circumstances or aggravating circumstances otherwise authorized by law and any of the following statutory aggravating circumstances which may be supported by the evidence:
  (1) The offense of murder, rape, armed robbery, or kidnapping was committed by a person with a prior record of conviction for a capital felony;

(2) The offense of murder, rape, armed robbery, or kidnapping was committed while the offender was engaged in the commission of another capital felony or aggravated battery, or the offense of murder was committed while the offender was engaged in the commission of burglary or arson in the first degree;

(3) The offender, by his act of murder, armed robbery, or kidnapping, knowingly created a great risk of death to more than one person in a public place by means of a weapon or device which would normally be hazardous to the lives of more than one person;

(4) The offender committed the offense of murder for himself or another, for the purpose of receiving money or any other thing of monetary value;

(5) The murder of a judicial officer, former judicial officer, district attorney or solicitor-general, or former district attorney, solicitor, or solicitor-general was committed during or because of the exercise of his or her official duties;

(6) The offender caused or directed another to commit murder or committed murder as an agent or employee of another person;

(7) The offense of murder, rape, armed robbery, or kidnapping was outrageously or wantonly vile, horrible, or inhuman in that it involved torture, depravity of mind, or an aggravated battery to the victim;

(8) The offense of murder was committed against any peace officer, corrections employee, or firefighter while engaged in the performance of his official duties;

(9) The offense of murder was committed by a person in, or who has escaped from, the lawful custody of a peace officer or place of lawful confinement;

(10) The murder was committed for the purpose of avoiding, interfering with, or preventing a lawful arrest or custody in a place of lawful confinement, of himself or another; or

(11) The offense of murder, rape, or kidnapping was committed by a person previously convicted of rape, aggravated sodomy, aggravated child molestation, or aggravated sexual battery.

Idaho – I.C. § 19-2515. Sentence in capital cases—Special sentencing proceeding—Statutory aggravating circumstances—Special verdict or written findings

(9) The following are statutory aggravating circumstances, at least one (1) of which must be found to exist beyond a reasonable doubt before a sentence of death can be imposed:

(a) The defendant was previously convicted of another murder.

(b) At the time the murder was committed the defendant also committed another murder.
(c) The defendant knowingly created a great risk of death to many persons.
(d) The murder was committed for remuneration or the promise of remuneration or the defendant employed another to commit the murder for remuneration or the promise of remuneration.
(e) The murder was especially heinous, atrocious, or cruel, manifesting exceptional depravity.
(f) By the murder, or circumstances surrounding its commission, the defendant exhibited utter disregard for human life.
(g) The murder was committed in the perpetration of, or attempt to perpetrate, arson, rape, robbery, burglary, kidnapping, or mayhem and the defendant killed, intended a killing, or acted with reckless indifference to human life.
(h) The murder was committed in the perpetration of, or attempt to perpetrate, an infamous crime against nature, lewd and lascivious conduct with a minor, sexual abuse of a child under sixteen (16) years of age, ritualized abuse of a child, sexual exploitation of a child, sexual battery of a minor child sixteen (16) or seventeen (17) years of age, or forcible sexual penetration by use of a foreign object, and the defendant killed, intended a killing, or acted with reckless indifference to human life.
(i) The defendant, by his conduct, whether such conduct was before, during or after the commission of the murder at hand, has exhibited a propensity to commit murder which will probably constitute a continuing threat to society.
(j) The murder was committed against a former or present peace officer, executive officer, officer of the court, judicial officer or prosecuting attorney because of the exercise of official duty or because of the victim's former or present official status.
(k) The murder was committed against a witness or potential witness in a criminal or civil legal proceeding because of such proceeding.

Illinois – 730 ILCS 5/5-5-3.2. Factors in Aggravation

(a) The following factors shall be accorded weight in favor of imposing a term of imprisonment or may be considered by the court as reasons to impose a more severe sentence under Section 5-8-1:
(1) The defendant's conduct caused or threatened serious harm;

(2) The defendant received compensation for committing the offense;

(3) The defendant has a history of prior delinquency or criminal activity;

(4) The defendant, by the duties of his office or by his position, was obliged to prevent the particular offense committed or to bring the offenders committing it to justice;

(5) The defendant held public office at the time of the offense, and the offense related to the conduct of that office;

(6) The defendant utilized his professional reputation or position in the community to commit the offense, or to afford him an easier means of committing it;

(7) The sentence is necessary to deter others from committing the same crime;

(8) The defendant committed the offense against a person 60 years of age or older or such person's property;

(9) The defendant committed the offense against a person who is physically handicapped or such person's property;

(10) By reason of another individual's actual or perceived race, color, creed, religion, ancestry, gender, sexual orientation, physical or mental disability, or national origin, the defendant committed the offense against (i) the person or property of that individual; (ii) the person or property of a person who has an association with, is married to, or has a friendship with the other individual; or (iii) the person or property of a relative (by blood or marriage) of a person described in clause (i) or (ii). For the purposes of this Section, "sexual orientation" means heterosexuality, homosexuality, or bisexuality;

(11) The offense took place in a place of worship or on the grounds of a place of worship, immediately prior to, during, or immediately following worship services. For purposes of this subparagraph, "place of worship" shall mean any church, synagogue, or other building, structure, or place used primarily for religious worship;

(12) The defendant was convicted of a felony committed while he was released on bail or his own recognizance pending trial for a prior felony and was convicted of such prior felony, or the defendant was convicted of a felony committed while he was serving a period of probation, conditional discharge, or mandatory supervised release under subsection (d) of Section 5-8-1 for a prior felony;

(13) The defendant committed or attempted to commit a felony while he was wearing a bulletproof vest. For the purposes of this paragraph (13), a bulletproof vest is any device which is designed

for the purpose of protecting the wearer from bullets, shot, or other lethal projectiles;

(14) The defendant held a position of trust or supervision such as, but not limited to, family member as defined in Section 12-12 of the Criminal Code of 1961, teacher, scout leader, baby sitter, or day care worker, in relation to a victim under 18 years of age, and the defendant committed an offense in violation of Section 11-6, 11-11, 11-15.1, 11-19.1, 11-19.2, 11-20.1, 12-13, 12-14, 12-14.1, 12-15, or 12-16 of the Criminal Code of 1961 against that victim;

(15) The defendant committed an offense related to the activities of an organized gang. For the purposes of this factor, "organized gang" has the meaning ascribed to it in Section 10 of the Streetgang Terrorism Omnibus Prevention Act;

(16) The defendant committed an offense in violation of one of the following Sections while in a school, regardless of the time of day or time of year; on any conveyance owned, leased, or contracted by a school to transport students to or from school or a school related activity; on the real property of a school; or on a public way within 1,000 feet of the real property comprising any school: Section 10-1, 10-2, 10-5, 11-15.1, 11-17.1, 11-18.1, 11-19.1, 11-19.2, 12-2, 12-4, 12-4.1, 12-4.2, 12-4.3, 12-6, 12-6.1, 12-13, 12-14, 12-14.1, 12-15, 12-16, 18-2, or 33A-2 of the Criminal Code of 1961;

(16.5) The defendant committed an offense in violation of one of the following Sections while in a day care center, regardless of the time of day or time of year; on the real property of a day care center, regardless of the time of day or time of year; or on a public way within 1,000 feet of the real property comprising any day care center, regardless of the time of day or time of year: Section 10-1, 10-2, 10-5, 11-15.1, 11-17.1, 11-18.1, 11-19.1, 11-19.2, 12-2, 12-4, 12-4.1, 12-4.2, 12-4.3, 12-6, 12-6.1, 12-13, 12-14, 12-14.1, 12-15, 12-16, 18-2, or 33A-2 of the Criminal Code of 1961;

(17) The defendant committed the offense by reason of any person's activity as a community policing volunteer or to prevent any person from engaging in activity as a community policing volunteer. For the purpose of this Section, Section, "community policing volunteer" has the meaning ascribed to it in Section 2-3.5 of the Criminal Code of 1961;

(18) The defendant committed the offense in a nursing home or on the real property comprising a nursing home. For the purposes

of this paragraph (18), "nursing home" means a skilled nursing or intermediate long-term care facility that is subject to license by the Illinois Department of Public Health under the Nursing Home Care Act;

(19) The defendant was a federally licensed firearm dealer and was previously convicted of a violation of subsection (a) of Section 3 of the Firearm Owners Identification Card Act and has now committed either a felony violation of the Firearm Owners Identification Card Act or an act of armed violence while armed with a firearm;

(20) The defendant (i) committed the offense of reckless homicide under Section 9-3 of the Criminal Code of 1961 or the offense of driving under the influence of alcohol, other drug or drugs, intoxicating compound or compounds, or any combination thereof under Section 11-501 of the Illinois Vehicle Code or a similar provision of a local ordinance and (ii) was operating a motor vehicle in excess of 20 miles per hour over the posted speed limit as provided in Article VI of Chapter 11 of the Illinois Vehicle Code;

(21) The defendant (i) committed the offense of reckless driving or aggravated reckless driving under Section 11-503 of the Illinois Vehicle Code and (ii) was operating a motor vehicle in excess of 20 miles per hour over the posted speed limit as provided in Article VI of Chapter 11 of the Illinois Vehicle Code;

(22) The defendant committed the offense against a person that the defendant knew, or reasonably should have known, was a member of the Armed Forces of the United States serving on active duty. For purposes of this clause (22), the term "Armed Forces" means any of the Armed Forces of the United States, including a member of any reserve component thereof or National Guard unit called to active duty; or

(23) The defendant committed the offense against a person who was elderly, disabled, or infirm by taking advantage of a family or fiduciary relationship with the elderly, disabled, or infirm person.

Indiana – IC 35-50-2-9 Death sentence; life imprisonment without parole

(b) The aggravating circumstances are as follows:
(1) The defendant committed the murder by intentionally killing the victim while committing or attempting to commit any of the following:
(A) Arson (IC 35-43-1-1).

(B) Burglary (IC 35-43-2-1).
(C) Child molesting (IC 35-42-4-3).
(D) Criminal deviate conduct (IC 35-42-4-2).
(E) Kidnapping (IC 35-42-3-2).
(F) Rape (IC 35-42-4-1).
(G) Robbery (IC 35-42-5-1).
(H) Carjacking (IC 35-42-5-2).
(I) Criminal gang activity (IC 35-45-9-3).
(J) Dealing in cocaine or a narcotic drug (IC 35-48-4-1).
(2) The defendant committed the murder by the unlawful detonation of an explosive with intent to injure person or damage property.
(3) The defendant committed the murder by lying in wait.
(4) The defendant who committed the murder was hired to kill.
(5) The defendant committed the murder by hiring another person to kill.
(6) The victim of the murder was a corrections employee, probation officer, parole officer, community corrections worker, home detention officer, fireman, judge, or law enforcement officer, and either:
(A) the victim was acting in the course of duty; or
(B) the murder was motivated by an act the victim performed while acting in the course of duty.
(7) The defendant has been convicted of another murder.
(8) The defendant has committed another murder, at any time, regardless of whether the defendant has been convicted of that other murder.
(9) The defendant was:
(A) under the custody of the department of correction;
(B) under the custody of a county sheriff;
(C) on probation after receiving a sentence for the commission of a felony; or
(D) on parole; at the time the murder was committed.
(10) The defendant dismembered the victim.
(11) The defendant burned, mutilated, or tortured the victim while the victim was alive.
(12) The victim of the murder was less than twelve (12) years of age.
(13) The victim was a victim of any of the following offenses for which the defendant was convicted:
(A) Battery as a Class D felony or as a Class C felony under IC 35-42-2-1.
(B) Kidnapping (IC 35-42-3-2).

(C) Criminal confinement (IC 35-42-3-3).
(D) A sex crime under IC 35-42-4.
(14) The victim of the murder was listed by the state or known by the defendant to be a witness against the defendant and the defendant committed the murder with the intent to prevent the person from testifying.
(15) The defendant committed the murder by intentionally discharging a firearm (as defined in IC 35-47-1-5):
(A) into an inhabited dwelling; or
(B) from a vehicle.
(16) The victim of the murder was pregnant and the murder resulted in the intentional killing of a fetus that has attained viability.

Kansas – K.S.A. 21-4636. Same; aggravating circumstances

(a) The defendant was previously convicted of a felony in which the defendant inflicted great bodily harm, disfigurement, dismemberment, or death on another.
(b) The defendant knowingly or purposely killed or created a great risk of death to more than one person.
(c) The defendant committed the crime for the defendant's self or another for the purpose of receiving money or any other thing of monetary value.
(d) The defendant authorized or employed another person to commit the crime.
(e) The defendant committed the crime in order to avoid or prevent a lawful arrest or prosecution.
(f) The defendant committed the crime in an especially heinous, atrocious, or cruel manner. A finding that the victim was aware of such victim's fate or had conscious pain and suffering as a result of the physical trauma that resulted in the victim's death is not necessary to find that the manner in which the defendant killed the victim was especially heinous, atrocious, or cruel. In making a determination that the crime was committed in an especially heinous, atrocious, or cruel manner, any of the following conduct by the defendant may be considered sufficient:
(1) Prior stalking of or criminal threats to the victim;
(2) Preparation or planning, indicating an intention that the killing was meant to be especially heinous, atrocious, or cruel;
(3) Infliction of mental anguish or physical abuse before the victim's death;
(4) Torture of the victim;

(5) Continuous acts of violence begun before or continuing after the killing;
(6) Desecration of the victim's body in a manner indicating a particular depravity of mind, either during or following the killing; or
(7) Any other conduct in the opinion of the court that is especially heinous, atrocious, or cruel.
(g) The defendant committed the crime while serving a sentence of imprisonment on conviction of a felony.
(h) The victim was killed while engaging in, or because of the victim's performance or prospective performance of, the victim's duties as a witness in a criminal proceeding.

Kentucky – KRS 532.025 Presentence hearings; use of juvenile court records; aggravating or mitigating circumstances; instruction to jury

(2) In all cases of offenses for which the death penalty may be authorized, the judge shall consider, or he shall include in his instructions to the jury for it to consider, any mitigating circumstances or aggravating circumstances otherwise authorized by law and any of the following statutory aggravating or mitigating circumstances which may be supported by the evidence:
(a) Aggravating circumstances:
(1) The offense of murder or kidnapping was committed by a person with a prior record of conviction for a capital offense, or the offense of murder was committed by a person who has a substantial history of serious assaultive criminal convictions;
(2) The offense of murder or kidnapping was committed while the offender was engaged in the commission of arson in the first degree, robbery in the first degree, burglary in the first degree, rape in the first degree, or sodomy in the first degree;
(3) The offender by his act of murder, armed robbery, or kidnapping knowingly created a great risk of death to more than one person in a public place by means of a weapon of mass destruction, weapon, or other device which would normally be hazardous to the lives of more than one person;
(4) The offender committed the offense of murder for himself or another, for the purpose of receiving money or any other thing of monetary value, or for other profit;
(5) The offense of murder was committed by a person who was a prisoner and the victim was a prison employee engaged at the time of the act in the performance of his duties;
(6) The offender's act or acts of killing were intentional and resulted in multiple deaths;

(7) The offender's act of killing was intentional and the victim was a state or local public official or police officer, sheriff, or deputy sheriff engaged at the time of the act in the lawful performance of his duties; and

(8) The offender murdered the victim when an emergency protective order or a domestic violence order was in effect, or when any other order designed to protect the victim from the offender, such as an order issued as a condition of a bond, conditional release, probation, parole, or pretrial diversion, was in effect.

Louisiana – L.S.A-C.Cr.P. Art. 905.4. Aggravating circumstances

(1) The offender was engaged in the perpetration or attempted perpetration of aggravated rape, forcible rape, aggravated kidnapping, second-degree kidnapping, aggravated burglary, aggravated arson, aggravated escape, assault by drive-by shooting, armed robbery, first-degree robbery, second-degree robbery, simple robbery, cruelty to juveniles, second-degree cruelty to juveniles, or terrorism.
(2) The victim was a fireman or peace officer engaged in his lawful duties.
(3) The offender has been previously convicted of an unrelated murder, aggravated rape, aggravated burglary, aggravated arson, aggravated escape, armed robbery, or aggravated kidnapping.
(4) The offender knowingly created a risk of death or great bodily harm to more than one person.
(5) The offender offered or has been offered or has given or received anything of value for the commission of the offense.
(6) The offender at the time of the commission of the offense was imprisoned after sentence for the commission of an unrelated forcible felony.
(7) The offense was committed in an especially heinous, atrocious, or cruel manner.
(8) The victim was a witness in a prosecution against the defendant, gave material assistance to the state in any investigation or prosecution of the defendant, or was an eye witness to a crime alleged to have been committed by the defendant or possessed other material evidence against the defendant.
(9) The victim was a correctional officer or any employee of the Department of Public Safety and Corrections who, in the normal course of his employment was required to come in close contact with persons incarcerated in a state prison facility, and the victim was engaged in his lawful duties at the time of the offense.
(10) The victim was under the age of 12 years or 65 years of age or older.

(11) The offender was engaged in the distribution, exchange, sale, or purchase, or any attempt thereof, of a controlled dangerous substance listed in Schedule I, II, III, IV, or V of the Uniform Controlled Dangerous Substances Law.
(12) The offender was engaged in the activities prohibited by R.S. 14:107.1(C)(1) [ritualistic mutilation, dismemberment, or torture of a human as part of a ceremony, rite, initiation, observance, performance, or practice.

Maryland – MD Code, Criminal Law, § 2-303. First-degree murder—Sentencing procedure—Death penalty

(g) (1) In determining a sentence under subsection (b) of this section, the court or jury first shall consider whether any of the following aggravating circumstances exists beyond a reasonable doubt:
  (i) One or more persons committed the murder of a law enforcement officer while the officer was performing the officer's duties;
  (ii) The defendant committed the murder while confined in a correctional facility;
  (iii) The defendant committed the murder in furtherance of an escape from, an attempt to escape from, or an attempt to evade lawful arrest, custody, or detention by:
    (1) a guard or officer of a correctional facility; or
    (2) a law enforcement officer;
  (iv) The victim was taken or attempted to be taken in the course of an abduction, kidnapping, or an attempt to abduct or kidnap;
  (v) The victim was a child abducted in violation of § 3-503(a)(1) of this article;
  (vi) The defendant committed the murder under an agreement or contract for remuneration or promise of remuneration to commit the murder;
  (vii) The defendant employed or engaged another to commit the murder and the murder was committed under an agreement or contract for remuneration or promise of remuneration;
  (viii) The defendant committed the murder while under a sentence of death or imprisonment for life;
  (ix) The defendant committed more than one murder in the first degree arising out of the same incident; or

(x) The defendant committed the murder while committing, or attempting to commit:
  (1) arson in the first degree;
  (2) carjacking or armed carjacking;
  (3) rape in the first degree;
  (4) robbery under § 3-402 or § 3-403 of this article; or
  (5) sexual offense in the first degree.

Mississippi – Miss. Code Ann. § 99-19-101. Jury determination of death penalty

(5) Aggravating circumstances shall be limited to the following:
  (A) The capital offense was committed by a person under sentence of imprisonment.
  (B) The defendant was previously convicted of another capital offense or of a felony involving the use or threat of violence to the person.
  (C) The defendant knowingly created a great risk of death to many persons.
  (D) The capital offense was committed while the defendant was engaged, or was an accomplice, in the commission of, or an attempt to commit, or flight after committing or attempting to commit, any robbery, rape, arson, burglary, kidnapping, aircraft piracy, sexual battery, unnatural intercourse with any child under the age of 12, or nonconsensual unnatural intercourse with mankind, or felonious abuse and/or battery of a child in violation of subsection (2) of Section 97-5-39, Mississippi Code of 1972, or the unlawful use or detonation of a bomb or explosive device.
  (E) The capital offense was committed for the purpose of avoiding or preventing a lawful arrest or effecting an escape from custody.
  (F) The capital offense was committed for pecuniary gain.
  (G) The capital offense was committed to disrupt or hinder the lawful exercise of any governmental function or the enforcement of laws.
  (H) The capital offense was especially heinous, atrocious, or cruel.

Missouri – V.A.M.S. 565.032. Evidence to be considered in assessing punishment in first degree murder cases for which death penalty authorized

(1) The offense was committed by a person with a prior record of conviction for murder in the first degree, or the offense was committed by a person who has one or more serious assaultive criminal convictions;

(2) The murder in the first degree offense was committed while the offender was engaged in the commission or attempted commission of another unlawful homicide;

(3) The offender by his act of murder in the first degree knowingly created a great risk of death to more than one person by means of a weapon or device which would normally be hazardous to the lives of more than one person;

(4) The offender committed the offense of murder in the first degree for himself or another, for the purpose of receiving money or any other thing of monetary value from the victim of the murder or another;

(5) The murder in the first degree was committed against a judicial officer, former judicial officer, prosecuting attorney or former prosecuting attorney, circuit attorney or former circuit attorney, assistant prosecuting attorney or former assistant prosecuting attorney, assistant circuit attorney or former assistant circuit attorney, peace officer or former peace officer, elected official or former elected official during or because of the exercise of his official duty;

(6) The offender caused or directed another to commit murder in the first degree or committed murder in the first degree as an agent or employee of another person;

(7) The murder in the first degree was outrageously or wantonly vile, horrible, or inhuman in that it involved torture or depravity of mind;

(8) The murder in the first degree was committed against any peace officer or fireman while engaged in the performance of his official duty;

(9) The murder in the first degree was committed by a person in, or who has escaped from, the lawful custody of a peace officer or place of lawful confinement;

(10) The murder in the first degree was committed for the purpose of avoiding, interfering with, or preventing a lawful arrest or custody in a place of lawful confinement, of himself or another;

(11) The murder in the first degree was committed while the defendant was engaged in the perpetration or was aiding or encouraging another person to perpetrate or attempt to perpetrate a felony of any degree of rape, sodomy, burglary, robbery, kidnapping, or any felony offense in chapter 195, RSMo;

(12) The murdered individual was a witness or potential witness in any past or pending investigation or past or pending prosecution and was killed as a result of his status as a witness or potential witness;

(13) The murdered individual was an employee of an institution or facility of the department of corrections of this state or local correction agency and was killed in the course of performing his official duties, or the murdered individual was an inmate of such institution or facility;

(14) The murdered individual was killed as a result of the hijacking of an airplane, train, ship, bus, or other public conveyance;
(15) The murder was committed for the purpose of concealing or attempting to conceal any felony offense defined in chapter 195, RSMo;
(16) The murder was committed for the purpose of causing or attempting to cause a person to refrain from initiating or aiding in the prosecution of a felony offense defined in chapter 195, RSMo;
(17) The murder was committed during the commission of a crime which is part of a pattern of criminal street gang activity;

Montana – MCA 46-18-303. Aggravating circumstances

Aggravating circumstances are any of the following:

(1) (a) The offense was deliberate homicide and was committed:
   (i) by an offender while in official detention, as defined in 45-2-101;
   (ii) by an offender who had been previously convicted of another deliberate homicide;
   (iii) by means of torture;
   (iv) by an offender lying in wait or ambush;
   (v) as a part of a scheme or operation that, if completed, would result in the death of more than one person; or
   (vi) by an offender during the course of committing sexual assault, sexual intercourse without consent, deviate sexual conduct, or incest, and the victim was less than 18 years of age.
   (vii) The offense was deliberate homicide, as defined in 45-5-102(1)(a), and the victim was a peace officer killed while performing the officer's duty.
(2) The offense was aggravated kidnapping that resulted in the death of the victim or the death by direct action of the offender of a person who rescued or attempted to rescue the victim.
(3) The offense was attempted deliberate homicide, aggravated assault, or aggravated kidnapping committed while in official detention, as defined in 45- 2-101, by an offender who has been previously:
   (a) convicted of the offense of deliberate homicide; or
   (b) found to be a persistent felony offender pursuant to part 5 of this chapter, and one of the convictions was for an offense against the person in violation of Title 45, chapter 5, for which the minimum prison term is not less than 2 years.
(4) The offense was sexual intercourse without consent, the offender has a previous conviction of sexual intercourse without consent in this

state or of an offense under the laws of another state or of the United States that if committed in this state would be the offense of sexual intercourse without consent, and the offender inflicted serious bodily injury upon a person in the course of committing each offense.

Nebraska – Neb.Rev.St. § 29-2523. Aggravating and mitigating circumstances

(1) Aggravating Circumstances:
   (a) The offender was previously convicted of another murder or a crime involving the use or threat of violence to the person, or has a substantial prior history of serious assaultive or terrorizing criminal activity;
   (b) The murder was committed in an effort to conceal the commission of a crime, or to conceal the identity of the perpetrator of such crime;
   (c) The murder was committed for hire, or for pecuniary gain, or the defendant hired another to commit the murder for the defendant;
   (d) The murder was especially heinous, atrocious, cruel, or manifested exceptional depravity by ordinary standards of morality and intelligence;
   (e) At the time the murder was committed, the offender also committed another murder;
   (f) The offender knowingly created a great risk of death to at least several persons;
   (g) The victim was a public servant having lawful custody of the offender or another in the lawful performance of his or her official duties and the offender knew or should have known that the victim was a public servant performing his or her official duties;
   (h) The murder was committed knowingly to disrupt or hinder the lawful exercise of any governmental function or the enforcement of the laws; or
   (i) The victim was a law enforcement officer engaged in the lawful performance of his or her official duties as a law enforcement officer and the offender knew or reasonably should have known that the victim was a law enforcement officer.

Nevada – N.R.S. 200.033. Circumstances aggravating first degree murder

The only circumstances by which murder of the first degree may be aggravated are:

(1) The murder was committed by a person under sentence of imprisonment.

(2) The murder was committed by a person who, at any time before a penalty hearing is conducted for the murder pursuant to NRS 175.552, is or has been convicted of:
  (a) Another murder and the provisions of subsection 12 do not otherwise apply to that other murder; or
  (b) A felony involving the use or threat of violence to the person of another and the provisions of subsection 4 do not otherwise apply to that felony.

For the purposes of this subsection, a person shall be deemed to have been convicted at the time the jury verdict of guilt is rendered or upon pronouncement of guilt by a judge or judges sitting without a jury.

(3) The murder was committed by a person who knowingly created a great risk of death to more than one person by means of a weapon, device, or course of action which would normally be hazardous to the lives of more than one person.

(4) The murder was committed while the person was engaged, alone or with others, in the commission of, or an attempt to commit or flight after committing or attempting to commit, any robbery, arson in the first degree, burglary, invasion of the home or kidnapping in the first degree, and the person charged:
  (a) Killed or attempted to kill the person murdered; or
  (b) Knew or had reason to know that life would be taken or lethal force used.

(5) The murder was committed to avoid or prevent a lawful arrest or to effect an escape from custody.

(6) The murder was committed by a person, for himself or another, to receive money or any other thing of monetary value.

(7) The murder was committed upon a peace officer or firefighter who was killed while engaged in the performance of his official duty or because of an act performed in his official capacity, and the defendant knew or reasonably should have known that the victim was a peace officer or firefighter. For the purposes of this subsection, "peace officer" means:
  (a) An employee of the Department of Corrections who does not exercise general control over offenders imprisoned within the institutions and facilities of the Department, but whose normal duties require him to come into contact with those offenders when carrying out the duties prescribed by the Director of the Department.

(b) Any person upon whom some or all of the powers of a peace officer are conferred pursuant to NRS 289.150 to 289.360, inclusive, when carrying out those powers.
(8) The murder involved torture or the mutilation of the victim.
(9) The murder was committed upon one or more persons at random and without apparent motive.
(10) The murder was committed upon a person less than 14 years of age.
(11) The murder was committed upon a person because of the actual or perceived race, color, religion, national origin, physical or mental disability or sexual orientation of that person.
(12) The defendant has, in the immediate proceeding, been convicted of more than one offense of murder in the first or second degree. For the purposes of this subsection, a person shall be deemed to have been convicted of a murder at the time the jury verdict of guilt is rendered or upon pronouncement of guilt by a judge or judges sitting without a jury.
(13) The person, alone or with others, subjected or attempted to subject the victim of the murder to nonconsensual sexual penetration immediately before, during, or immediately after the commission of the murder. For the purposes of this subsection:
   (a) "Nonconsensual" means against the victim's will or under conditions in which the person knows or reasonably should know that the victim is mentally or physically incapable of resisting, consenting, or understanding the nature of his conduct, including, but not limited to, conditions in which the person knows or reasonably should know that the victim is dead.
   (b) "Sexual penetration" means cunnilingus, fellatio, or any intrusion, however slight, of any part of the victim's body or any object manipulated or inserted by a person, alone or with others, into the genital or anal openings of the body of the victim, whether or not the victim is alive. The term includes, but is not limited to, anal intercourse and sexual intercourse in what would be its ordinary meaning.
(14) The murder was committed on the property of a public or private school, at an activity sponsored by a public or private school or on a school bus while the bus was engaged in its official duties by a person who intended to create a great risk of death or substantial bodily harm to more than one person by means of a weapon, device, or course of action that would normally be hazardous to the lives of more than one person. For the purposes of this subsection, "school bus" has the meaning ascribed to it in NRS 483.160.
(15) The murder was committed with the intent to commit, cause, aid, further, or conceal an act of terrorism.

New Hampshire – N.H. Rev. Stat. § 630:5 Procedure in Capital Murder

(a) The defendant:
  (1) purposely killed the victim;
  (2) purposely inflicted serious bodily injury which resulted in the death of the victim;
  (3) purposely engaged in conduct which:
    (A) the defendant knew would create a grave risk of death to a person, other than one of the participants in the offense; and
    (B) resulted in the death of the victim.
(b) The defendant has been convicted of another state or federal offense resulting in the death of a person, for which a sentence of life imprisonment or a sentence of death was authorized by law.
(c) The defendant has previously been convicted of 2 or more state or federal offenses punishable by a term of imprisonment of more than one year, committed on different occasions, involving the infliction of, or attempted infliction of, serious bodily injury upon another person.
(d) The defendant has previously been convicted of 2 or more state or federal offenses punishable by a term of imprisonment of more than 1 year, committed on different occasions, involving the distribution of a controlled substance.
(e) In the commission of the offense of capital murder, the defendant knowingly created a grave risk of death to one or more persons in addition to the victims of the offense.
(f) The defendant committed the offense after substantial planning and premeditation.
(g) The victim was particularly vulnerable due to old age, youth, or infirmity.
(h) The defendant committed the offense in an especially heinous, cruel, or depraved manner in that it involved torture or serious physical abuse to the victim.
(i) The murder was committed for pecuniary gain.
(j) The murder was committed for the purpose of avoiding or preventing a lawful arrest or effecting an escape from lawful custody.

New Mexico – N. M. S. A. 1978, § 31-20A-5. Aggravating circumstances

(A) The victim was a peace officer who was acting in the lawful discharge of an official duty when he was murdered;

(B) The murder was committed with intent to kill in the commission of or attempt to commit kidnaping, criminal sexual contact of a minor, or criminal sexual penetration;
(C) The murder was committed with the intent to kill by the defendant while attempting to escape from a penal institution of New Mexico;
(D) While incarcerated in a penal institution in New Mexico, the defendant, with the intent to kill, murdered a person who was at the time incarcerated in or lawfully on the premises of a penal institution in New Mexico. As used in this subsection "penal institution" includes facilities under the jurisdiction of the corrections and criminal rehabilitation department [corrections department] and county and municipal jails;
(E) While incarcerated in a penal institution in New Mexico, the defendant, with the intent to kill, murdered an employee of the corrections and criminal rehabilitation department [corrections department];
(F) The capital felony was committed for hire; and
(G) The capital felony was murder of a witness to a crime or any person likely to become a witness to a crime, for the purpose of preventing report of the crime or testimony in any criminal proceeding, or for retaliation for the victim having testified in any criminal proceeding.

North Carolina – N.C.G.S.A. § 15A-2000. Sentence of death or life imprisonment for capital felonies; further proceedings to determine sentence

(e) Aggravating Circumstances. Aggravating circumstances which may be considered shall be limited to the following:
(1) The capital felony was committed by a person lawfully incarcerated.
(2) The defendant had been previously convicted of another capital felony or had been previously adjudicated delinquent in a juvenile proceeding for committing an offense that would be a capital felony if committed by an adult.
(3) The defendant had been previously convicted of a felony involving the use or threat of violence to the person or had been previously adjudicated delinquent in a juvenile proceeding for committing an offense that would be a Class A, B1, B2, C, D, or E felony involving the use or threat of violence to the person if the offense had been committed by an adult.
(4) The capital felony was committed for the purpose of avoiding or preventing a lawful arrest or effecting an escape from custody.

(5) The capital felony was committed while the defendant was engaged, or was an aider or abettor, in the commission of, or an attempt to commit, or flight after committing or attempting to commit, any homicide, robbery, rape or a sex offense, arson, burglary, kidnapping, or aircraft piracy or the unlawful throwing, placing, or discharging of a destructive device or bomb.
(6) The capital felony was committed for pecuniary gain.
(7) The capital felony was committed to disrupt or hinder the lawful exercise of any governmental function or the enforcement of laws.
(8) The capital felony was committed against a law-enforcement officer, employee of the Department of Correction, jailer, fireman, judge or justice, former judge or justice, prosecutor or former prosecutor, juror or former juror, or witness or former witness against the defendant, while engaged in the performance of his official duties or because of the exercise of his official duty.
(9) The capital felony was especially heinous, atrocious, or cruel.
(10) The defendant knowingly created a great risk of death to more than one person by means of a weapon or device which would normally be hazardous to the lives of more than one person.
(11) The murder for which the defendant stands convicted was part of a course of conduct in which the defendant engaged and which included the commission by the defendant of other crimes of violence against another person or persons.

Ohio – R.C. § 2929.04 Criteria for imposing death or imprisonment for a capital offense

(A) Imposition of the death penalty for aggravated murder is precluded, unless one or more of the following is specified in the indictment or count in the indictment pursuant to section 2941.14 of the Revised Code and proved beyond a reasonable doubt:
(1) The offense was the assassination of the president of the United States or person in line of succession to the presidency, or of the governor or lieutenant governor of this state, or of the president-elect or vice president-elect of the United States, or of the governor-elect or lieutenant governor-elect of this state, or of a candidate for any of the foregoing offices. For purposes of this division, a person is a candidate if he has been nominated for election according to law, or if he has filed a petition or petitions according to law to have his name placed on the ballot in a primary or general election, or if he campaigns as a write-in candidate in a primary or general election.

(2) The offense was committed for hire.
(3) The offense was committed for the purpose of escaping detection, apprehension, trial, or punishment for another offense committed by the offender.
(4) The offense was committed while the offender was a prisoner in a detention facility as defined in section 2921.01 of the Revised Code.
(5) Prior to the offense at bar, the offender was convicted of an offense an essential element of which was the purposeful killing of or attempt to kill another, or the offense at bar was part of a course of conduct involving the purposeful killing of or attempt to kill two or more persons by the offender.
(6) The victim of the offense was a peace officer, as defined in section 2935.01 of the Revised Code, whom the offender had reasonable cause to know or knew to be such, and either the victim, at the time of the commission of the offense, was engaged in his duties, or it was the offender's specific purpose to kill a peace officer.
(7) The offense was committed while the offender was committing, attempting to commit, or fleeing immediately after committing or attempting to commit kidnapping, rape, aggravated arson, aggravated robbery, or aggravated burglary, and either the offender was the principal offender in the commission of the aggravated murder or, if not the principal offender, committed the aggravated murder with prior calculation and design.
(8) The victim of the aggravated murder was a witness to an offense who was purposely killed to prevent his testimony in any criminal proceeding and the aggravated murder was not committed during the commission, attempted commission, or flight immediately after the commission or attempted commission of the offense to which the victim was a witness, or the victim of the aggravated murder was a witness to an offense and was purposely killed in retaliation for his testimony in any criminal proceeding.

Oklahoma – 21 Okl.St.Ann. § 701.12. Aggravating circumstances

(1) The defendant was previously convicted of a felony involving the use or threat of violence to the person;
(2) The defendant knowingly created a great risk of death to more than one person;
(3) The person committed the murder for remuneration or the promise of remuneration or employed another to commit the murder for remuneration or the promise of remuneration;

(4) The murder was especially heinous, atrocious, or cruel;
(5) The murder was committed for the purpose of avoiding or preventing a lawful arrest or prosecution;
(6) The murder was committed by a person while serving a sentence of imprisonment on conviction of a felony;
(7) The existence of a probability that the defendant would commit criminal acts of violence that would constitute a continuing threat to society; or
(8) The victim of the murder was a peace officer as defined by Section 99 of Title 21 of the Oklahoma Statutes, or guard of an institution under the control of the Department of Corrections, and such person was killed while in performance of official duty.

Oregon – O.R.S. 163.095. Aggravated murder

As used in ORS 163.105 and this section, "aggravated murder" means murder as defined in ORS 163.115 which is committed under, or accompanied by, any of the following circumstances:

(1) (a) The defendant committed the murder pursuant to an agreement that the defendant receive money or other thing of value for committing the murder.
 (b) The defendant solicited another to commit the murder and paid or agreed to pay the person money or other thing of value for committing the murder.
 (c) The defendant committed murder after having been convicted previously in any jurisdiction of any homicide, the elements of which constitute the crime of murder as defined in ORS 163.115 or manslaughter in the first degree as defined in ORS 163.118.
 (d) There was more than one murder victim in the same criminal episode as defined in ORS 131.505.
 (e) The homicide occurred in the course of or as a result of intentional maiming or torture of the victim.
 (f) The victim of the intentional homicide was a person under the age of 14 years.
(2) (a) The victim was one of the following and the murder was related to the performance of the victim's official duties in the justice system:
 (A) A police officer as defined in ORS 181.610;
 (B) A correctional, parole and probation officer or other person charged with the duty of custody, control or supervision of convicted persons;

- (C) A member of the Oregon State Police;
- (D) A judicial officer as defined in ORS 1.210;
- (E) A juror or witness in a criminal proceeding;
- (F) An employee or officer of a court of justice; or
- (G) A member of the State Board of Parole and Post-Prison Supervision.

(b) The defendant was confined in a state, county, or municipal penal or correctional facility or was otherwise in custody when the murder occurred.

(c) The defendant committed murder by means of an explosive as defined in ORS 164.055.

(d) Notwithstanding ORS 163.115 (1)(b), the defendant personally and intentionally committed the homicide under the circumstances set forth in ORS 163.115 (1)(b).

(e) The murder was committed in an effort to conceal the commission of a crime, or to conceal the identity of the perpetrator of a crime.

(f) The murder was committed after the defendant had escaped from a state, county, or municipal penal or correctional facility and before the defendant had been returned to the custody of the facility.

Pennsylvania – 42 Pa.C.S.A. § 9711. Sentencing procedure for murder of the first degree

(d) Aggravating circumstances—Aggravating circumstances shall be limited to the following:

(1) The victim was a firefighter, peace officer, public servant concerned in official detention, as defined in 18 Pa.C.S. § 5121 (relating to escape), judge of any court in the unified judicial system, the Attorney General of Pennsylvania, a deputy attorney general, district attorney, assistant district attorney, member of the General Assembly, Governor, Lieutenant Governor, Auditor General, State Treasurer, State law enforcement official, local law enforcement official, Federal law enforcement official or person employed to assist or assisting any law enforcement official in the performance of his duties, who was killed in the performance of his duties or as a result of his official position.

(2) The defendant paid or was paid by another person or had contracted to pay or be paid by another person or had conspired to pay or be paid by another person for the killing of the victim.

(3) The victim was being held by the defendant for ransom or reward, or as a shield or hostage.
(4) The death of the victim occurred while defendant was engaged in the hijacking of an aircraft.
(5) The victim was a prosecution witness to a murder or other felony committed by the defendant and was killed for the purpose of preventing his testimony against the defendant in any grand jury or criminal proceeding involving such offenses.
(6) The defendant committed a killing while in the perpetration of a felony.
(7) In the commission of the offense the defendant knowingly created a grave risk of death to another person in addition to the victim of the offense.
(8) The offense was committed by means of torture.
(9) The defendant has a significant history of felony convictions involving the use or threat of violence to the person.
(10) The defendant has been convicted of another Federal or State offense, committed either before or at the time of the offense at issue, for which a sentence of life imprisonment or death was imposable or the defendant was undergoing a sentence of life imprisonment for any reason at the time of the commission of the offense.
(11) The defendant has been convicted of another murder committed in any jurisdiction and committed either before or at the time of the offense at issue.
(12) The defendant has been convicted of voluntary manslaughter, as defined in 18 Pa.C.S. § 2503 (relating to voluntary manslaughter), or a substantially equivalent crime in any other jurisdiction, committed either before or at the time of the offense at issue.
(13) The defendant committed the killing or was an accomplice in the killing, as defined in 18 Pa.C.S. § 306(c) (relating to liability for conduct of another; complicity), while in the perpetration of a felony under the provisions of the act of April 14, 1972 (P.L. 233, No. 64), known as The Controlled Substance, Drug, Device and Cosmetic Act, and punishable under the provisions of 18 Pa.C.S. § 7508 (relating to drug trafficking sentencing and penalties).
(14) At the time of the killing, the victim was or had been involved, associated or in competition with the defendant in the sale, manufacture, distribution, or delivery of any controlled substance or counterfeit controlled substance in violation of The Controlled

Substance, Drug, Device and Cosmetic Act or similar law of any other state, the District of Columbia or the United States, and the defendant committed the killing or was an accomplice to the killing as defined in 18 Pa.C.S. § 306(c), and the killing resulted from or was related to that association, involvement or competition to promote the defendant's activities in selling, manufacturing, distributing, or delivering controlled substances or counterfeit controlled substances.

(15) At the time of the killing, the victim was or had been a nongovernmental informant or had otherwise provided any investigative, law enforcement, or police agency with information concerning criminal activity and the defendant committed the killing or was an accomplice to the killing as defined in 18 Pa.C.S. § 306(c), and the killing was in retaliation for the victim's activities as a nongovernmental informant or in providing information concerning criminal activity to an investigative, law enforcement, or police agency.

(16) The victim was a child under 12 years of age.

(17) At the time of the killing, the victim was in her third trimester of pregnancy or the defendant had knowledge of the victim's pregnancy.

(18) At the time of the killing the defendant was subject to a court order restricting in any way the defendant's behavior toward the victim pursuant to 23 Pa.C.S. Ch. 61 (relating to protection from abuse) or any other order of a court of common pleas or of the minor judiciary designed in whole or in part to protect the victim from the defendant.

South Carolina – Code 1976 § 16-3-20. Punishment for murder: separate sentencing proceeding to determine whether sentence should be death or life imprisonment

(a) Statutory aggravating circumstances:
  (1) The murder was committed while in the commission of the following crimes or acts:
    (a) criminal sexual conduct in any degree;
    (b) kidnapping;
    (c) burglary in any degree;
    (d) robbery while armed with a deadly weapon;
    (e) larceny with use of a deadly weapon;
    (f) killing by poison;

(g) drug trafficking as defined in Section 44-53-370(e), 44-53-375(B), 44-53-440, or 44-53-445;
(h) physical torture;
(i) dismemberment of a person; or
(j) arson in the first degree as defined in Section 16-11-110(A).
(2) The murder was committed by a person with a prior conviction for murder.
(3) The offender by his act of murder knowingly created a great risk of death to more than one person in a public place by means of a weapon or device which normally would be hazardous to the lives of more than one person.
(4) The offender committed the murder for himself or another for the purpose of receiving money or a thing of monetary value.
(5) The murder of a judicial officer, former judicial officer, solicitor, former solicitor, or other officer of the court during or because of the exercise of his official duty.
(6) The offender caused or directed another to commit murder or committed murder as an agent or employee of another person.
(7) The murder of a federal, state, or local law enforcement officer or former federal, state, or local law enforcement officer, peace officer or former peace officer, corrections officer or former corrections officer, including a county or municipal corrections officer or a former county or municipal corrections officer, a county or municipal detention facility employee or former county or municipal detention facility employee, or fireman or former fireman during or because of the performance of his official duties.
(8) The murder of a family member of an official listed in subitems (5) and (7) above with the intent to impede or retaliate against the official. "Family member" means a spouse, parent, brother, sister, child, or person to whom the official stands in the place of a parent or a person living in the official's household and related to him by blood or marriage.
(9) Two or more persons were murdered by the defendant by one act or pursuant to one scheme or course of conduct.
(10) The murder of a child eleven years of age or under.
(11) The murder of a witness or potential witness committed at any time during the criminal process for the purpose of impeding or deterring prosecution of any crime.
(12) The murder was committed by a person deemed a sexually violent predator pursuant to the provisions of Chapter 48, Title 44, or a person deemed a sexually violent predator who is released pursuant to Section 44-48-120.

South Dakota – SDCL § 23A-27A-1. Mitigating and aggravating circumstances considered by judge or jury

(1) The offense was committed by a person with a prior record of conviction for a Class A or Class B felony, or the offense of murder was committed by a person who has a felony conviction for a crime of violence as defined in subdivision 22-1-2(9);
(2) The defendant by the defendant's act knowingly created a great risk of death to more than one person in a public place by means of a weapon or device which would normally be hazardous to the lives of more than one person;
(3) The defendant committed the offense for the benefit of the defendant or another, for the purpose of receiving money or any other thing of monetary value;
(4) The defendant committed the offense on a judicial officer, former judicial officer, prosecutor, or former prosecutor while such prosecutor, former prosecutor, judicial officer, or former judicial officer was engaged in the performance of such person's official duties or where a major part of the motivation for the offense came from the official actions of such judicial officer, former judicial officer, prosecutor, or former prosecutor;
(5) The defendant caused or directed another to commit murder or committed murder as an agent or employee of another person;
(6) The offense was outrageously or wantonly vile, horrible, or inhuman in that it involved torture, depravity of mind, or an aggravated battery to the victim. Any murder is wantonly vile, horrible, and inhuman if the victim is less than thirteen years of age;
(7) The offense was committed against a law enforcement officer, employee of a corrections institution, or firefighter while engaged in the performance of such person's official duties;
(8) The offense was committed by a person in, or who has escaped from, the lawful custody of a law enforcement officer or place of lawful confinement;
(9) The offense was committed for the purpose of avoiding, interfering with, or preventing a lawful arrest or custody in a place of lawful confinement, of the defendant or another; or
(10) The offense was committed in the course of manufacturing, distributing, or dispensing substances listed in Schedules I and II in violation of § 22-42-2.

Tennessee – T. C. A. § 39-13-204. First-degree murder; sentencing; factors

(1) The murder was committed against a person less than twelve (12) years of age and the defendant was eighteen (18) years of age or older;

(2) The defendant was previously convicted of one (1) or more felonies, other than the present charge, whose statutory elements involve the use of violence to the person;

(3) The defendant knowingly created a great risk of death to two (2) or more persons, other than the victim murdered, during the act of murder;

(4) The defendant committed the murder for remuneration or the promise of remuneration, or employed another to commit the murder for remuneration or the promise of remuneration;

(5) The murder was especially heinous, atrocious, or cruel, in that it involved torture or serious physical abuse beyond that necessary to produce death;

(6) The murder was committed for the purpose of avoiding, interfering with, or preventing a lawful arrest or prosecution of the defendant or another;

(7) The murder was knowingly committed, solicited, directed, or aided by the defendant, while the defendant had a substantial role in committing or attempting to commit, or was fleeing after having a substantial role in committing or attempting to commit, any first degree murder, arson, rape, robbery, burglary, theft, kidnapping, aircraft piracy, or unlawful throwing, placing or discharging of a destructive device or bomb;

(8) The murder was committed by the defendant while the defendant was in lawful custody or in a place of lawful confinement or during the defendant's escape from lawful custody or from a place of lawful confinement;

(9) The murder was committed against any law enforcement officer, corrections official, corrections employee, probation and parole officer, emergency medical or rescue worker, emergency medical technician, paramedic or firefighter, who was engaged in the performance of official duties, and the defendant knew or reasonably should have known that the victim was a law enforcement officer, corrections official, corrections employee, probation and parole officer, emergency medical or rescue worker, emergency medical technician, paramedic or firefighter engaged in the performance of official duties;

(10) The murder was committed against any present or former judge, district attorney general or state attorney general, assistant district attorney general or assistant state attorney general, due to or because of the exercise of the victim's official duty or status and the defendant knew that the victim occupied such office;
(11) The murder was committed against a national, state, or local popularly elected official, due to or because of the official's lawful duties or status, and the defendant knew that the victim was such an official;
(12) The defendant committed "mass murder," which is defined as the murder of three (3) or more persons, whether committed during a single criminal episode or at different times within a forty-eight (48) month period;
(13) The defendant knowingly mutilated the body of the victim after death;
(14) The victim of the murder was seventy (70) years of age or older; or the victim of the murder was particularly vulnerable due to a significant handicap or significant disability, whether mental or physical, and at the time of the murder the defendant knew or reasonably should have known of such handicap or disability; or
(15) The murder was committed in the course of an act of terrorism.

Texas – V.T.C.A., Penal Code § 19.03. Capital Murder

(a) A person commits an offense if the person commits murder as defined under Section 19.02(b)(1) and:
  (1) The person murders a peace officer or fireman who is acting in the lawful discharge of an official duty and who the person knows is a peace officer or fireman;
  (2) The person intentionally commits the murder in the course of committing or attempting to commit kidnapping, burglary, robbery, aggravated sexual assault, arson, obstruction or retaliation, or terroristic threat under Section 22.07(a)(1), (3), (4), (5), or (6);
  (3) The person commits the murder for remuneration or the promise of remuneration or employs another to commit the murder for remuneration or the promise of remuneration;
  (4) The person commits the murder while escaping or attempting to escape from a penal institution;
  (5) The person, while incarcerated in a penal institution, murders another:
    (A) who is employed in the operation of the penal institution; or
    (B) with the intent to establish, maintain, or participate in a combination or in the profits of a combination;

(6) The person:
  (A) while incarcerated for an offense under this section or Section 19.02, murders another; or
  (B) while serving a sentence of life imprisonment or a term of 99 years for an offense under Section 20.04, 22.021, or 29.03, murders another;
(7) The person murders more than one person:
  (A) during the same criminal transaction; or
  (B) during different criminal transactions but the murders are committed pursuant to the same scheme or course of conduct;
(8) The person murders an individual under six years of age; or
(9) The person murders another person in retaliation for or on account of the service or status of the other person as a judge or justice of the supreme court, the court of criminal appeals, a court of appeals, a district court, a criminal district court, a constitutional county court, a statutory county court, a justice court, or a municipal court.

(b) An offense under this section is a capital felony.

Utah – U.C.A. 1953 § 76-5-202. Aggravated murder

(1) Criminal homicide constitutes aggravated murder if the actor intentionally or knowingly causes the death of another under any of the following circumstances:
  (a) The homicide was committed by a person who is confined in a jail or other correctional institution;
  (b) The homicide was committed incident to one act, scheme, course of conduct, or criminal episode during which two or more persons were killed, or during which the actor attempted to kill one or more persons in addition to the victim who was killed;
  (c) The actor knowingly created a great risk of death to a person other than the victim and the actor;
  (d) The homicide was committed incident to an act, scheme, course of conduct, or criminal episode during which the actor committed or attempted to commit aggravated robbery, robbery, rape, rape of a child, object rape, object rape of a child, forcible sodomy, sodomy upon a child, forcible sexual abuse, sexual abuse of a child, aggravated sexual abuse of a child, child abuse as defined in Subsection 76-5-109(2)(a), or aggravated sexual assault, aggravated arson, arson, aggravated burglary, burglary, aggravated kidnapping, or kidnapping, or child kidnapping;

(e) The homicide was committed incident to one act, scheme, course of conduct, or criminal episode during which the actor committed the crime of abuse or desecration of a dead human body as defined in Subsection 76-9-704(2)(e);

(f) The homicide was committed for the purpose of avoiding or preventing an arrest of the defendant or another by a peace officer acting under color of legal authority or for the purpose of effecting the defendant's or another's escape from lawful custody;

(g) The homicide was committed for pecuniary gain;

(h) The defendant committed, or engaged or employed another person to commit the homicide pursuant to an agreement or contract for remuneration or the promise of remuneration for commission of the homicide;

(i) The actor previously committed or was convicted of:
  (i) aggravated murder, Section 76-5-202;
  (ii) attempted aggravated murder, Section 76-5-202;
  (iii) murder, Section 76-5-203;
  (iv) attempted murder, Section 76-5-203; or
  (v) an offense committed in another jurisdiction which if committed in this state would be a violation of a crime listed in this Subsection (1)(i);

(j) The actor was previously convicted of:
  (i) aggravated assault, Subsection 76-5-103(2);
  (ii) mayhem, Section 76-5-105;
  (iii) kidnapping, Section 76-5-301;
  (iv) child kidnapping, Section 76-5-301.1;
  (v) aggravated kidnapping, Section 76-5-302;
  (vi) rape, Section 76-5-402;
  (vii) rape of a child, Section 76-5-402.1;
  (viii) object rape, Section 76-5-402.2;
  (ix) object rape of a child, Section 76-5-402.3;
  (x) forcible sodomy, Section 76-5-403;
  (xi) sodomy on a child, Section 76-5-403.1;
  (xii) aggravated sexual abuse of a child, Section 76-5-404.1;
  (xiii) aggravated sexual assault, Section 76-5-405;
  (xiv) aggravated arson, Section 76-6-103;
  (xv) aggravated burglary, Section 76-6-203;
  (xvi) aggravated robbery, Section 76-6-302; or
  (xvii) an offense committed in another jurisdiction which if committed in this state would be a violation of a crime listed in this Subsection (1)(j);

(k) The homicide was committed for the purpose of:
  (i) preventing a witness from testifying;
  (ii) preventing a person from providing evidence or participating in any legal proceedings or official investigation;
  (iii) retaliating against a person for testifying, providing evidence, or participating in any legal proceedings or official investigation; or
  (iv) disrupting or hindering any lawful governmental function or enforcement of laws;
(l) The victim is or has been a local, state, or federal public official, or a candidate for public office, and the homicide is based on, is caused by, or is related to that official position, act, capacity, or candidacy;
(m) The victim is or has been a peace officer, law enforcement officer, executive officer, prosecuting officer, jailer, prison official, firefighter, judge or other court official, juror, probation officer, or parole officer, and the victim is either on duty or the homicide is based on, is caused by, or is related to that official position, and the actor knew, or reasonably should have known, that the victim holds or has held that official position;
(n) The homicide was committed:
  (i) by means of a destructive device, bomb, explosive, incendiary device, or similar device which was planted, hidden, or concealed in any place, area, dwelling, building, or structure, or was mailed or delivered; or
  (ii) by means of any weapon of mass destruction as defined in Section 76-10-401;
(o) The homicide was committed during the act of unlawfully assuming control of any aircraft, train, or other public conveyance by use of threats or force with intent to obtain any valuable consideration for the release of the public conveyance or any passenger, crew member, or any other person aboard, or to direct the route or movement of the public conveyance or otherwise exert control over the public conveyance;
(p) The homicide was committed by means of the administration of a poison or of any lethal substance or of any substance administered in a lethal amount, dosage, or quantity;
(q) The victim was a person held or otherwise detained as a shield, hostage, or for ransom;
(r) The homicide was committed in an especially heinous, atrocious, cruel, or exceptionally depraved manner, any of which must be

demonstrated by physical torture, serious physical abuse, or serious bodily injury of the victim before death;
- (s) The actor dismembers, mutilates, or disfigures the victim's body, whether before or after death, in a manner demonstrating the actor's depravity of mind; or
- (t) The victim was younger than 14 years of age.
(2) Criminal homicide constitutes aggravated murder if the actor, with reckless indifference to human life, causes the death of another incident to an act, scheme, course of conduct, or criminal episode during which the actor is a major participant in the commission or attempted commission of:
- (a) child abuse, Subsection 76-5-109(2)(a);
- (b) child kidnapping, Section 76-5-301.1;
- (c) rape of a child, Section 76-5-402.1;
- (d) object rape of a child, Section 76-5-402.3;
- (e) sodomy on a child, Section 76-5-403.1; or
- (f) sexual abuse or aggravated sexual abuse of a child, Section 76-5-404. 1.

Virginia – Va. Code Ann. § 18.2-31. Capital murder defined; punishment

The following offenses shall constitute capital murder, punishable as a Class 1 felony:

(1) The willful, deliberate, and premeditated killing of any person in the commission of abduction, as defined in § 18.2-48, when such abduction was committed with the intent to extort money or a pecuniary benefit or with the intent to defile the victim of such abduction;

(2) The willful, deliberate, and premeditated killing of any person by another for hire;

(3) The willful, deliberate, and premeditated killing of any person by a prisoner confined in a state or local correctional facility as defined in § 53.1-1, or while in the custody of an employee thereof;

(4) The willful, deliberate, and premeditated killing of any person in the commission of robbery or attempted robbery;

(5) The willful, deliberate, and premeditated killing of any person in the commission of, or subsequent to, rape or attempted rape, forcible sodomy or attempted forcible sodomy, or object sexual penetration;

(6) The willful, deliberate, and premeditated killing of a law-enforcement officer as defined in § 9.1-101 or any law-enforcement officer of another state or the United States having the power to arrest for a felony under the laws of such state or the United States, when such

killing is for the purpose of interfering with the performance of his official duties;

(7) The willful, deliberate, and premeditated killing of more than one person as a part of the same act or transaction;

(8) The willful, deliberate, and premeditated killing of more than one person within a three-year period;

(9) The willful, deliberate, and premeditated killing of any person in the commission of or attempted commission of a violation of § 18.2-248, involving a Schedule I or II controlled substance, when such killing is for the purpose of furthering the commission or attempted commission of such violation;

(10) The willful, deliberate, and premeditated killing of any person by another pursuant to the direction or order of one who is engaged in a continuing criminal enterprise as defined in subsection I of § 18.2-248;

(11) The willful, deliberate, and premeditated killing of a pregnant woman by one who knows that the woman is pregnant and has the intent to cause the involuntary termination of the woman's pregnancy without a live birth;

(12) The willful, deliberate, and premeditated killing of a person under the age of fourteen by a person age twenty-one or older;

(13) The willful, deliberate, and premeditated killing of any person by another in the commission of or attempted commission of an act of terrorism as defined in § 18.2-46.4;

(14) The willful, deliberate, and premeditated killing of a justice of the Supreme Court, a judge of the Court of Appeals, a judge of a circuit court or district court, a retired judge sitting by designation or under temporary recall, or a substitute judge appointed under § 16.1-69.9:1 when the killing is for the purpose of interfering with his official duties as a judge; and

(15) The willful, deliberate, and premeditated killing of any witness in a criminal case after a subpoena has been issued for such witness by the court, the clerk, or an attorney, when the killing is for the purpose of interfering with the person's duties in such case.

Washington – West's RCWA 10.95.020. Definition

A person is guilty of aggravated first degree murder, a class A felony, if he or she commits first degree murder as defined by RCW 9A.32.030(1)(a), as now or hereafter amended, and one or more of the following aggravating circumstances exist:

(1) The victim was a law enforcement officer, corrections officer, or firefighter who was performing his or her official duties at the time of the

act resulting in death and the victim was known or reasonably should have been known by the person to be such at the time of the killing;
(2) At the time of the act resulting in the death, the person was serving a term of imprisonment, had escaped, or was on authorized or unauthorized leave in or from a state facility or program for the incarceration or treatment of persons adjudicated guilty of crimes;
(3) At the time of the act resulting in death, the person was in custody in a county or county-city jail as a consequence of having been adjudicated guilty of a felony;
(4) The person committed the murder pursuant to an agreement that he or she would receive money or any other thing of value for committing the murder;
(5) The person solicited another person to commit the murder and had paid or had agreed to pay money or any other thing of value for committing the murder;
(6) The person committed the murder to obtain or maintain his or her membership or to advance his or her position in the hierarchy of an organization, association, or identifiable group;
(7) The murder was committed during the course of or as a result of a shooting where the discharge of the firearm, as defined in RCW 9.41.010, is either from a motor vehicle or from the immediate area of a motor vehicle that was used to transport the shooter or the firearm, or both, to the scene of the discharge;
(8) The victim was:
  (a) A judge; juror or former juror; prospective, current, or former witness in an adjudicative proceeding; prosecuting attorney; deputy prosecuting attorney; defense attorney; a member of the indeterminate sentence review board; or a probation or parole officer; and
  (b) The murder was related to the exercise of official duties performed or to be performed by the victim;
(9) The person committed the murder to conceal the commission of a crime or to protect or conceal the identity of any person committing a crime, including, but specifically not limited to, any attempt to avoid prosecution as a persistent offender as defined in RCW 9.94A.030;
(10) There was more than one victim and the murders were part of a common scheme or plan or the result of a single act of the person;
(11) The murder was committed in the course of, in furtherance of, or in immediate flight from one of the following crimes:
  (a) Robbery in the first or second degree;
  (b) Rape in the first or second degree;
  (c) Burglary in the first or second degree or residential burglary;
  (d) Kidnapping in the first degree; or

(e) Arson in the first degree;
(12) The victim was regularly employed or self-employed as a newsreporter and the murder was committed to obstruct or hinder the investigative, research, or reporting activities of the victim;
(13) At the time the person committed the murder, there existed a court order, issued in this or any other state, which prohibited the person from either contacting the victim, molesting the victim, or disturbing the peace of the victim, and the person had knowledge of the existence of that order;
(14) At the time the person committed the murder, the person and the victim were "family or household members" as that term is defined in *RCW 10.99.020(1), and the person had previously engaged in a pattern or practice of three or more of the following crimes committed upon the victim within a five-year period, regardless of whether a conviction resulted:
(a) Harassment as defined in RCW 9A.46.020; or
(b) Any criminal assault.

Wyoming – W.S.1977 § 6-2-102. Presentence hearing for murder in the first degree; mitigating and aggravating circumstances; effect of error in hearing

(i) The murder was committed by a person:
(A) Confined in a jail or correctional facility;
(B) On parole or on probation for a felony;
(C) After escaping detention or incarceration; or
(D) Released on bail pending appeal of his conviction.
(ii) The defendant was previously convicted of another murder in the first degree or a felony involving the use or threat of violence to the person;
(iii) The defendant knowingly created a great risk of death to two (2) or more persons;
(iv) The murder was committed while the defendant was engaged, or was an accomplice, in the commission of, or an attempt to commit, or flight after committing or attempting to commit, any aircraft piracy or the unlawful throwing, placing or discharging of a destructive device or bomb;
(v) The murder was committed for the purpose of avoiding or preventing a lawful arrest or effecting an escape from custody;
(vi) The murder was committed for compensation, the collection of insurance benefits or other similar pecuniary gain;
(vii) The murder was especially atrocious or cruel, being unnecessarily torturous to the victim;

(viii) The murder of a judicial officer, former judicial officer, district attorney, former district attorney, defending attorney, peace officer, juror or witness, during or because of the exercise of his official duty or because of the victim's former or present official status;
(ix) The defendant knew or reasonably should have known the victim was less than seventeen (17) years of age or older than sixty-five (65) years of age;
(x) The defendant knew or reasonably should have known the victim was especially vulnerable due to significant mental or physical disability;
(xi) The defendant poses a substantial and continuing threat of future dangerousness or is likely to commit continued acts of criminal violence;
(xii) The defendant killed another human being purposely and with premeditated malice and while engaged in, or as an accomplice in the commission of, or an attempt to commit, or flight after committing or attempting to commit, any robbery, sexual assault, arson, burglary, kidnapping, or abuse of a child under the age of sixteen (16) years.

Appendix D: Statutorily Defined Mitigating Factors by State

Alabama – Ala.Code 1975 § 13A-5-51. Mitigating circumstances—Generally

(1) The defendant has no significant history of prior criminal activity;
(2) The capital offense was committed while the defendant was under the influence of extreme mental or emotional disturbance;
(3) The victim was a participant in the defendant's conduct or consented to it;
(4) The defendant was an accomplice in the capital offense committed by another person and his participation was relatively minor;
(5) The defendant acted under extreme duress or under the substantial domination of another person;
(6) The capacity of the defendant to appreciate the criminality of his conduct or to conform his conduct to the requirements of law was substantially impaired; and
(7) The age of the defendant at the time of the crime.

Ala. Code 1975 § 13A-5-52. Mitigating circumstances—Inclusion of defendant's character, record, etc.

In addition to the mitigating circumstances specified in Section 13A-5-51, mitigating circumstances shall include any aspect of a defendant's character or record and any of the circumstances of the offense that the defendant offers as a basis for a sentence of life imprisonment without parole instead of death, and any other relevant mitigating circumstance which the defendant offers as a basis for a sentence of life imprisonment without parole instead of death.

Arizona – A.R.S. § 13-703 Sentence of death or life imprisonment; aggravating and mitigating circumstances

(G) The trier of fact shall consider as mitigating circumstances any factors proffered by the defendant or the state that are relevant in determining whether to impose a sentence less than death, including any aspect of the defendant's character, propensities or record and any of the circumstances of the offense, including but not limited to the following:
   (1) The defendant's capacity to appreciate the wrongfulness of his conduct or to conform his conduct to the requirements of law was significantly impaired, but not so impaired as to constitute a defense to prosecution.
   (2) The defendant was under unusual and substantial duress, although not such as to constitute a defense to prosecution.
   (3) The defendant was legally accountable for the conduct of another under the provisions of § 13-303, but his participation was relatively minor, although not so minor as to constitute a defense to prosecution.
   (4) The defendant could not reasonably have foreseen that his conduct in the course of the commission of the offense for which the defendant was convicted would cause, or would create a grave risk of causing, death to another person.
   (5) The defendant's age.

Arkansas – A.C.A. § 5-4-605 Mitigating circumstances, inclusions; exclusions

A mitigating circumstance includes, but is not limited to, the following:

(1) The capital murder was committed while the defendant was under extreme mental or emotional disturbance;
(2) The capital murder was committed while the defendant was acting under an unusual pressure or influence or under the domination of another person;
(3) The capital murder was committed while the capacity of the defendant to appreciate the wrongfulness of his or her conduct or to conform his

or her conduct to the requirements of law was impaired as a result of mental disease or defect, intoxication, or drug abuse;
(4) The youth of the defendant at the time of the commission of the capital murder;
(5) The capital murder was committed by another person and the defendant was an accomplice and his or her participation was relatively minor; or
(6) The defendant has no significant history of prior criminal activity.

California – CA Penal Code § 190.3. Determination of death penalty or life imprisonment; evidence of aggravating and mitigating circumstances; considerations

(a) The circumstances of the crime of which the defendant was convicted in the present proceeding and the existence of any special circumstances found to be true pursuant to Section 190.1.
(b) The presence or absence of criminal activity by the defendant which involved the use or attempted use of force or violence or the express or implied threat to use force or violence.
(c) The presence or absence of any prior felony conviction.
(d) Whether or not the offense was committed while the defendant was under the influence of extreme mental or emotional disturbance.
(e) Whether or not the victim was a participant in the defendant's homicidal conduct or consented to the homicidal act.
(f) Whether or not the offense was committed under circumstances which the defendant reasonably believed to be a moral justification or extenuation for his conduct.
(g) Whether or not defendant acted under extreme duress or under the substantial domination of another person.
(h) Whether or not at the time of the offense the capacity of the defendant to appreciate the criminality of his conduct or to conform his conduct to the requirements of law was impaired as a result of mental disease or defect, or the affects of intoxication.
(i) The age of the defendant at the time of the crime.
(j) Whether or not the defendant was an accomplice to the offense and his participation in the commission of the offense was relatively minor.
(k) Any other circumstance which extenuates the gravity of the crime even though it is not a legal excuse for the crime.

Colorado – C.R.S.A. § 18-1.4-102. Imposition of sentence in class 1 felonies for crimes committed on or after July 1, 1995, and prior to July 12, 2002—appellate review

(4) For purposes of this section, mitigating factors shall be the following factors:
   (a) The age of the defendant at the time of the crime; or
   (b) The defendant's capacity to appreciate wrongfulness of the defendant's conduct or to conform the defendant's conduct to the requirements of law was significantly impaired, but not so impaired as to constitute a defense to prosecution; or
   (c) The defendant was under unusual and substantial duress, although not such duress as to constitute a defense to prosecution; or
   (d) The defendant was a principal in the offense which was committed by another, but the defendant's participation was relatively minor, although not so minor as to constitute a defense to prosecution; or
   (e) The defendant could not reasonably have foreseen that the defendant's conduct in the course of the commission of the offense for which the defendant was convicted would cause, or would create a grave risk of causing, death to another person; or
   (f) The emotional state of the defendant at the time the crime was committed; or
   (g) The absence of any significant prior conviction; or
   (h) The extent of the defendant's cooperation with law enforcement officers or agencies and with the office of the prosecuting district attorney; or
   (i) The influence of drugs or alcohol; or
   (j) The good faith, although mistaken, belief by the defendant that circumstances existed which constituted a moral justification for the defendant's conduct; or
   (k) The defendant is not a continuing threat to society; or
   (l) Any other evidence which in the court's opinion bears on the question of mitigation.

Connecticut–C.G.S.A. § 53a-46a. Imposition of sentence for capital felony. Hearing. Special verdict. Mitigating and aggravating factors. Factors barring death sentence

(h) The court shall not impose the sentence of death on the defendant if the jury or, if there is no jury, the court finds by a special verdict, as provided in subsection (e), that at the time of the offense:
   (1) The defendant was under the age of eighteen years, or

(2) The defendant was a person with mental retardation, as defined in section 1-1g, or
(3) The defendant's mental capacity was significantly impaired or the defendant's ability to conform the defendant's conduct to the requirements of law was significantly impaired but not so impaired in either case as to constitute a defense to prosecution, or
(4) The defendant was criminally liable under sections 53a-8, 53a-9, and 53a-10 for the offense, which was committed by another, but the defendant's participation in such offense was relatively minor, although not so minor as to constitute a defense to prosecution, or
(5) The defendant could not reasonably have foreseen that the defendant's conduct in the course of commission of the offense of which the defendant was convicted would cause, or would create a grave risk of causing, death to another person.

Delaware – 11 Del.C. § 4209 Punishment, procedure for determining punishment, review of punishment, and method of punishment for first-degree murder

(e) (*Aggravating factors statutorily defined; no mitigating factors statutorily defined*)

Florida – West's F.S.A. § 921.141(6) Mitigating circumstances

(a) The defendant has no significant history of prior criminal activity.
(b) The capital felony was committed while the defendant was under the influence of extreme mental or emotional disturbance.
(c) The victim was a participant in the defendant's conduct or consented to the act.
(d) The defendant was an accomplice in the capital felony committed by another person and his or her participation was relatively minor.
(e) The defendant acted under extreme duress or under the substantial domination of another person.
(f) The capacity of the defendant to appreciate the criminality of his or her conduct or to conform his or her conduct to the requirements of law was substantially impaired.
(g) The age of the defendant at the time of the crime.
(h) The existence of any other factors in the defendant's background that would mitigate against imposition of the death penalty.

Georgia – Ga. Code Ann., § 17-10-30.1. Mitigating and aggravating circumstances; sentence of life imprisonment without parole

(Aggravating factors statutorily defined in 17-10-30; no mitigating factors statutorily defined)

Idaho – ID ST § 19-2515. Sentence in capital cases—Special sentencing proceeding—Statutory aggravating circumstances—Special verdict or written findings

(Aggravating factors statutorily defined; no mitigating factors statutorily defined)

Illinois – IL ST CH 720 § 5/9-1(c) Consideration of factors in Aggravation and Mitigation

The court shall consider, or shall instruct the jury to consider any aggravating and any mitigating factors which are relevant to the imposition of the death penalty. Aggravating factors may include but need not be limited to those factors set forth in subsection (b). Mitigating factors may include but need not be limited to the following:

(1) The defendant has no significant history of prior criminal activity;
(2) The murder was committed while the defendant was under the influence of extreme mental or emotional disturbance, although not such as to constitute a defense to prosecution;
(3) The murdered individual was a participant in the defendant's homicidal conduct or consented to the homicidal act;
(4) The defendant acted under the compulsion of threat or menace of the imminent infliction of death or great bodily harm;
(5) The defendant was not personally present during commission of the act or acts causing death;
(6) The defendant's background includes a history of extreme emotional or physical abuse;
(7) The defendant suffers from a reduced mental capacity.

Indiana – IC 35-50-2-9. Death sentence; life imprisonment without parole

(c) The mitigating circumstances that may be considered under this section are as follows:
   (1) The defendant has no significant history of prior criminal conduct.

(2) The defendant was under the influence of extreme mental or emotional disturbance when the murder was committed.
(3) The victim was a participant in or consented to the defendant's conduct.
(4) The defendant was an accomplice in a murder committed by another person, and the defendant's participation was relatively minor.
(5) The defendant acted under the substantial domination of another person.
(6) The defendant's capacity to appreciate the criminality of the defendant's conduct or to conform that conduct to the requirements of law was substantially impaired as a result of mental disease or defect or of intoxication.
(7) The defendant was less than eighteen (18) years of age at the time the murder was committed.
(8) Any other circumstances appropriate for consideration.

Kansas – K.S.A. § 21-4626. Persons convicted of capital murder; mitigating circumstances

Mitigating circumstances shall include, but are not limited to, the following:

(1) The defendant has no significant history of prior criminal activity.
(2) The crime was committed while the defendant was under the influence of extreme mental or emotional disturbances.
(3) The victim was a participant in or consented to the defendant's conduct.
(4) The defendant was an accomplice in the crime committed by another person, and the defendant's participation was relatively minor.
(5) The defendant acted under extreme distress or under the substantial domination of another person.
(6) The capacity of the defendant to appreciate the criminality of the defendant's conduct or to conform the defendant's conduct to the requirements of law was substantially impaired.
(7) The age of the defendant at the time of the crime.
(8) At the time of the crime, the defendant was suffering from post-traumatic stress syndrome caused by violence or abuse by the victim.
(9) A term of imprisonment is sufficient to defend and protect the people's safety from the defendant.

Kentucky – KRS § 532.025(2)(b) Mitigating circumstances

(1) The defendant has no significant history of prior criminal activity;

(2) The capital offense was committed while the defendant was under the influence of extreme mental or emotional disturbance even though the influence of extreme mental or emotional disturbance is not sufficient to constitute a defense to the crime;
(3) The victim was a participant in the defendant's criminal conduct or consented to the criminal act;
(4) The capital offense was committed under circumstances which the defendant believed to provide a moral justification or extenuation for his conduct even though the circumstances which the defendant believed to provide a moral justification or extenuation for his conduct are not sufficient to constitute a defense to the crime;
(5) The defendant was an accomplice in a capital offense committed by another person and his participation in the capital offense was relatively minor;
(6) The defendant acted under duress or under the domination of another person even though the duress or the domination of another person is not sufficient to constitute a defense to the crime;
(7) At the time of the capital offense, the capacity of the defendant to appreciate the criminality of his conduct to the requirements of law was impaired as a result of mental illness or retardation or intoxication even though the impairment of the capacity of the defendant to appreciate the criminality of his conduct or to conform the conduct to the requirements of law is insufficient to constitute a defense to the crime; and
(8) The youth of the defendant at the time of the crime.

Louisiana – L.S.A-C.Cr.P. Art. 905.5. Mitigating circumstances

(a) The offender has no significant prior history of criminal activity;
(b) The offense was committed while the offender was under the influence of extreme mental or emotional disturbance;
(c) The offense was committed while the offender was under the influence or under the domination of another person;
(d) The offense was committed under circumstances which the offender reasonably believed to provide a moral justification or extenuation for his conduct;
(e) At the time of the offense the capacity of the offender to appreciate the criminality of his conduct or to conform his conduct to the requirements of law was impaired as a result of mental disease or defect or intoxication;
(f) The youth of the offender at the time of the offense;
(g) The offender was a principal whose participation was relatively minor;
(h) Any other relevant mitigating circumstance.

Maryland – MD Code, Criminal Law, § 2-303 Murder in the first degree—Sentence of imprisonment for life without the possibility of parole

(h) (2) If the court or jury finds beyond a reasonable doubt that one or more of the aggravating circumstances under subsection (g) of this section exist, it then shall consider whether any of the following mitigating circumstances exists based on a preponderance of the evidence:
  (i) The defendant previously has not:
     (1) been found guilty of a crime of violence;
     (2) entered a guilty plea or a plea of nolo contendere to a charge of a crime of violence; or
     (3) received probation before judgment for a crime of violence;
  (ii) The victim was a participant in the conduct of the defendant or consented to the act that caused the victim's death;
  (iii) The defendant acted under substantial duress, domination, or provocation of another, but not so substantial as to constitute a complete defense to the prosecution;
  (iv) The murder was committed while the capacity of the defendant to appreciate the criminality of the defendant's conduct or to conform that conduct to the requirements of law was substantially impaired due to emotional disturbance, mental disorder, or mental incapacity;
  (v) The defendant was of a youthful age at the time of the murder;
  (vi) The act of the defendant was not the sole proximate cause of the victim's death;
  (vii) It is unlikely that the defendant will engage in further criminal activity that would be a continuing threat to society; or
  (viii) Any other fact that the court or jury specifically sets forth in writing as a mitigating circumstance in the case.

Mississippi – § 99-19-101. Jury determination of death penalty

(6) Mitigating circumstances shall be the following:
  (a) The defendant has no significant history of prior criminal activity.
  (b) The offense was committed while the defendant was under the influence of extreme mental or emotional disturbance.
  (c) The victim was a participant in the defendant's conduct or consented to the act.
  (d) The defendant was an accomplice in the capital offense committed by another person and his participation was relatively minor.

(e) The defendant acted under extreme duress or under the substantial domination of another person.
(f) The capacity of the defendant to appreciate the criminality of his conduct or to conform his conduct to the requirements of law was substantially impaired.
(g) The age of the defendant at the time of the crime.

Missouri – V.A.M.S. 565.032. Evidence to be considered in assessing punishment in first-degree murder cases for which death penalty authorized

(1) The defendant has no significant history of prior criminal activity;
(2) The murder in the first degree was committed while the defendant was under the influence of extreme mental or emotional disturbance;
(3) The victim was a participant in the defendant's conduct or consented to the act;
(4) The defendant was an accomplice in the murder in the first degree committed by another person and his participation was relatively minor;
(5) The defendant acted under extreme duress or under the substantial domination of another person;
(6) The capacity of the defendant to appreciate the criminality of his conduct or to conform his conduct to the requirements of law was substantially impaired;
(7) The age of the defendant at the time of the crime.

Montana – MT ST 46-18-304. Mitigating circumstances

(1) Mitigating circumstances are any of the following:
   (a) The defendant has no significant history of prior criminal activity.
   (b) The offense was committed while the defendant was under the influence of extreme mental or emotional disturbance.
   (c) The defendant acted under extreme duress or under the substantial domination of another person.
   (d) The capacity of the defendant to appreciate the criminality of the defendant's conduct or to conform the defendant's conduct to the requirements of law was substantially impaired.
   (e) The victim was a participant in the defendant's conduct or consented to the act.
   (f) The defendant was an accomplice in an offense committed by another person, and the defendant's participation was relatively minor.

(g) The defendant, at the time of the commission of the crime, was less than 18 years of age.
(2) The court may consider any other fact that exists in mitigation of the penalty.

Nebraska – NE ST § 29-2523. Aggravating and mitigating circumstances

(2) Mitigating Circumstances:
   (a) The offender has no significant history of prior criminal activity;
   (b) The offender acted under unusual pressures or influences or under the domination of another person;
   (c) The crime was committed while the offender was under the influence of extreme mental or emotional disturbance;
   (d) The age of the defendant at the time of the crime;
   (e) The offender was an accomplice in the crime committed by another person and his or her participation was relatively minor;
   (f) The victim was a participant in the defendant's conduct or consented to the act; or
   (g) At the time of the crime, the capacity of the defendant to appreciate the wrongfulness of his or her conduct or to conform his or her conduct to the requirements of law was impaired as a result of mental illness, mental defect, or intoxication.

Nevada – N.R.S. 200.035. Circumstances mitigating first-degree murder

Murder of the first degree may be mitigated by any of the following circumstances, even though the mitigating circumstance is not sufficient to constitute a defense or reduce the degree of the crime:

(1) The defendant has no significant history of prior criminal activity.
(2) The murder was committed while the defendant was under the influence of extreme mental or emotional disturbance.
(3) The victim was a participant in the defendant's criminal conduct or consented to the act.
(4) The defendant was an accomplice in a murder committed by another person and his participation in the murder was relatively minor.
(5) The defendant acted under duress or under the domination of another person.
(6) The youth of the defendant at the time of the crime.
(7) Any other mitigating circumstance.

New Hampshire – N.H. Rev. Stat. § 630:5. Procedure in Capital Murder

(VI) In determining whether a sentence of death is to be imposed upon a defendant, the jury shall consider mitigating factors, including the following:
   (a) The defendant's capacity to appreciate the wrongfulness of his conduct or to conform his conduct to the requirements of law was significantly impaired, regardless of whether the capacity was so impaired as to constitute a defense to the charge.
   (b) The defendant was under unusual and substantial duress, regardless of whether the duress was of such a degree as to constitute a defense to the charge.
   (c) The defendant is punishable as an accomplice (as defined in RSA 626:8) in the offense, which was committed by another, but the defendant's participation was relatively minor, regardless of whether the participation was so minor as to constitute a defense to the charge.
   (d) The defendant was youthful, although not under the age of 18.
   (e) The defendant did not have a significant prior criminal record.
   (f) The defendant committed the offense under severe mental or emotional disturbance.
   (g) Another defendant or defendants, equally culpable in the crime, will not be punished by death.
   (h) The victim consented to the criminal conduct that resulted in the victim's death.
   (i) Other factors in the defendant's background or character mitigate against imposition of the death sentence.

New Mexico – N. M. S. A. 1978, § 31-20A-6. Mitigating Circumstances

The mitigating circumstances to be considered by the sentencing court or the jury pursuant to the provisions of Section 3 of this act shall include but not be limited to the following:

(A) The defendant has no significant history of prior criminal activity;
(B) The defendant acted under duress or under the domination of another person;
(C) The defendant's capacity to appreciate the criminality of his conduct or to conform his conduct to the requirements of the law was impaired;
(D) The defendant was under the influence of mental or emotional disturbance;

(E) The victim was a willing participant in the defendant's conduct;
(F) The defendant acted under circumstances which tended to justify, excuse, or reduce the crime;
(G) The defendant is likely to be rehabilitated;
(H) The defendant cooperated with authorities; and
(I) The defendant's age.

North Carolina – N.C.G.S.A. § 15A-2000. Sentence of death or life imprisonment for capital felonies; further proceedings to determine sentence

(f) Mitigating Circumstances. Mitigating circumstances which may be considered shall include, but not be limited to, the following:
(1) The defendant has no significant history of prior criminal activity.
(2) The capital felony was committed while the defendant was under the influence of mental or emotional disturbance.
(3) The victim was a voluntary participant in the defendant's homicidal conduct or consented to the homicidal act.
(4) The defendant was an accomplice in or accessory to the capital felony committed by another person and his participation was relatively minor.
(5) The defendant acted under duress or under the domination of another person.
(6) The capacity of the defendant to appreciate the criminality of his conduct or to conform his conduct to the requirements of law was impaired.
(7) The age of the defendant at the time of the crime.
(8) The defendant aided in the apprehension of another capital felon or testified truthfully on behalf of the prosecution in another prosecution of a felony.
(9) Any other circumstance arising from the evidence which the jury deems to have mitigating value.

Ohio – R.C. § 2929.04. Criteria for imposing death or imprisonment for a capital offense

(B) If one or more of the aggravating circumstances listed in division (A) of this section is specified in the indictment or count in the indictment and proved beyond a reasonable doubt, and if the offender did not raise the matter of age pursuant to section 2929.023 of the Revised Code or

if the offender, after raising the matter of age, was found at trial to have been eighteen years of age or older at the time of the commission of the offense, the court, trial jury, or panel of three judges shall consider, and weigh against the aggravating circumstances proved beyond a reasonable doubt, the nature and circumstances of the offense, the history, character, and background of the offender, and all of the following factors:
(1) Whether the victim of the offense induced or facilitated it;
(2) Whether it is unlikely that the offense would have been committed, but for the fact that the offender was under duress, coercion, or strong provocation;
(3) Whether, at the time of committing the offense, the offender, because of a mental disease or defect, lacked substantial capacity to appreciate the criminality of the offender's conduct or to conform the offender's conduct to the requirements of the law;
(4) The youth of the offender;
(5) The offender's lack of a significant history of prior criminal convictions and delinquency adjudications;
(6) If the offender was a participant in the offense but not the principal offender, the degree of the offender's participation in the offense and the degree of the offender's participation in the acts that led to the death of the victim;
(7) Any other factors that are relevant to the issue of whether the offender should be sentenced to death.
(C) The defendant shall be given great latitude in the presentation of evidence of the factors listed in division (B) of this section and of any other factors in mitigation of the imposition of the sentence of death.

Oklahoma – 21 Okl.St.Ann. § 701.10. Sentencing proceeding—
Murder in the first degree

(C) In the sentencing proceeding, evidence may be presented as to any mitigating circumstances or as to any of the aggravating circumstances enumerated in Section 701.7 et seq. of this title. Only such evidence in aggravation as the state has made known to the defendant prior to his trial shall be admissible. In addition, the state may introduce evidence about the victim and about the impact of the murder on the family of the victim.

(Aggravating factors statutorily defined in 701.7; no mitigating factors statutorily defined)

Oregon – O.R.S. § 163.150. Sentencing; aggravated murder

(c) (A) The court shall instruct the jury to consider, in determining the issues in paragraph (b) of this subsection, any mitigating circumstances offered in evidence, including but not limited to the defendant's age, the extent and severity of the defendant's prior criminal conduct and the extent of the mental and emotional pressure under which the defendant was acting at the time the offense was committed.

Pennsylvania – 42 Pa.C.S.A. § 9711. Sentencing procedure for murder of the first degree

(e) Mitigating circumstances. Mitigating circumstances shall include the following:
 (1) The defendant has no significant history of prior criminal convictions.
 (2) The defendant was under the influence of extreme mental or emotional disturbance.
 (3) The capacity of the defendant to appreciate the criminality of his conduct or to conform his conduct to the requirements of law was substantially impaired.
 (4) The age of the defendant at the time of the crime.
 (5) The defendant acted under extreme duress, although not such duress as to constitute a defense to prosecution under 18 Pa.C.S. § 309 (relating to duress), or acted under the substantial domination of another person.
 (6) The victim was a participant in the defendant's homicidal conduct or consented to the homicidal acts.
 (7) The defendant's participation in the homicidal act was relatively minor.
 (8) Any other evidence of mitigation concerning the character and record of the defendant and the circumstances of his offense.

South Carolina – Code 1976 § 16-3-20. Punishment for murder: separate sentencing proceeding to determine whether sentence should be death or life imprisonment

(b) Mitigating circumstances:
 (1) The defendant has no significant history of prior criminal conviction involving the use of violence against another person.

(2) The murder was committed while the defendant was under the influence of mental or emotional disturbance.
(3) The victim was a participant in the defendant's conduct or consented to the act.
(4) The defendant was an accomplice in the murder committed by another person and his participation was relatively minor.
(5) The defendant acted under duress or under the domination of another person.
(6) The capacity of the defendant to appreciate the criminality of his conduct or to conform his conduct to the requirements of law was substantially impaired.
(7) The age or mentality of the defendant at the time of the crime.
(8) The defendant was provoked by the victim into committing the murder.
(9) The defendant was below the age of eighteen at the time of the crime.
(10) The defendant had mental retardation at the time of the crime. "Mental retardation" means significantly subaverage general intellectual functioning existing concurrently with deficits in adaptive behavior and manifested during the developmental period.

South Dakota – SDCL § 23A-27A-1. Mitigating and aggravating circumstances considered by judge or jury

Pursuant to §§ 23A-27A-2 to 23A-27A-6, inclusive, in all cases for which the death penalty may be authorized, the judge shall consider, or shall include in instructions to the jury for it to consider, any mitigating circumstances and any of the following aggravating circumstances which may be supported by the evidence...

(Aggravating factors statutorily defined; no mitigating factors statutorily defined)

Tennessee – T. C. A. § 39-13-204. First-degree murder; sentencing; factors

(j) In arriving at the punishment, the jury shall consider, pursuant to the provisions of this section, any mitigating circumstances, which shall include, but are not limited to, the following:
(1) The defendant has no significant history of prior criminal activity;
(2) The murder was committed while the defendant was under the influence of extreme mental or emotional disturbance;

(3) The victim was a participant in the defendant's conduct or consented to the act;
(4) The murder was committed under circumstances that the defendant reasonably believed to provide a moral justification for the defendant's conduct;
(5) The defendant was an accomplice in the murder committed by another person and the defendant's participation was relatively minor;
(6) The defendant acted under extreme duress or under the substantial domination of another person;
(7) The youth or advanced age of the defendant at the time of the crime;
(8) The capacity of the defendant to appreciate the wrongfulness of the defendant's conduct or to conform the defendant's conduct to the requirements of the law was substantially impaired as a result of mental disease or defect or intoxication, which was insufficient to establish a defense to the crime but which substantially affected the defendant's judgment; and
(9) Any other mitigating factor that is raised by the evidence produced by either the prosecution or defense, at either the guilt or sentencing hearing.

Texas – Vernon's Ann.Texas C.C.P. Art. 37.071. Procedure in capital case

(e) (1) The court shall instruct the jury that if the jury returns an affirmative finding to each issue submitted under Subsection (b), it shall answer the following issue:

Whether, taking into consideration all of the evidence, including the circumstances of the offense, the defendant's character and background, and the personal moral culpability of the defendant, there is a sufficient mitigating circumstance or circumstances to warrant that a sentence of life imprisonment without parole rather than a death sentence be imposed.

Utah – U.C.A. 1953 § 76-3-207. Capital felony—Sentencing proceeding

(2) (a) In capital sentencing proceedings, evidence may be presented on:
    (i) The nature and circumstances of the crime;

(ii) The defendant's character, background, history, and mental and physical condition;
(iii) The victim and the impact of the crime on the victim's family and community without comparison to other persons or victims; and
(iv) Any other facts in aggravation or mitigation of the penalty that the court considers relevant to the sentence.

. . .

(4) Mitigating circumstances include:
  (a) The defendant has no significant history of prior criminal activity;
  (b) The homicide was committed while the defendant was under the influence of mental or emotional disturbance;
  (c) The defendant acted under duress or under the domination of another person;
  (d) At the time of the homicide, the capacity of the defendant to appreciate the wrongfulness of his conduct or to conform his conduct to the requirement of law was impaired as a result of a mental condition, intoxication, or influence of drugs, except that "mental condition" under this Subsection (4)(d) does not mean an abnormality manifested primarily by repeated criminal conduct;
  (e) The youth of the defendant at the time of the crime;
  (f) The defendant was an accomplice in the homicide committed by another person and the defendant's participation was relatively minor; and
  (g) Any other fact in mitigation of the penalty.

Virginia – Va. Code Ann. § 19.2-264.4. Sentence proceeding

(B) Evidence which may be admissible, subject to the rules of evidence governing admissibility, may include the circumstances surrounding the offense, the history and background of the defendant, and any other facts in mitigation of the offense. Facts in mitigation may include, but shall not be limited to, the following:
  (i) The defendant has no significant history of prior criminal activity,
  (ii) The capital felony was committed while the defendant was under the influence of extreme mental or emotional disturbance,
  (iii) The victim was a participant in the defendant's conduct or consented to the act,

(iv) At the time of the commission of the capital felony, the capacity of the defendant to appreciate the criminality of his conduct or to conform his conduct to the requirements of law was significantly impaired,
(v) The age of the defendant at the time of the commission of the capital offense, or
(vi) Even if § 19.2- 264.3:1.1 is inapplicable as a bar to the death penalty, the subaverage intellectual functioning of the defendant.

Washington– West's RCWA 10.95.070. Special sentencing proceeding—Factors which jury may consider in deciding whether leniency merited

In deciding the question posed by RCW 10.95.060(4), the jury, or the court if a jury is waived, may consider any relevant factors, including but not limited to the following:

(1) Whether the defendant has or does not have a significant history, either as a juvenile or an adult, of prior criminal activity;
(2) Whether the murder was committed while the defendant was under the influence of extreme mental disturbance;
(3) Whether the victim consented to the act of murder;
(4) Whether the defendant was an accomplice to a murder committed by another person where the defendant's participation in the murder was relatively minor;
(5) Whether the defendant acted under duress or domination of another person;
(6) Whether, at the time of the murder, the capacity of the defendant to appreciate the wrongfulness of his or her conduct or to conform his or her conduct to the requirements of law was substantially impaired as a result of mental disease or defect. However, a person found to be mentally retarded under RCW 10.95.030(2) may in no case be sentenced to death;
(7) Whether the age of the defendant at the time of the crime calls for leniency; and
(8) Whether there is a likelihood that the defendant will pose a danger to others in the future.

Wyoming–W.S.1977 § 6-2-102. Presentence hearing for murder in the first degree; mitigating and aggravating circumstances; effect of error in hearing

(j) Mitigating circumstances shall include the following:
   (i) The defendant has no significant history of prior criminal activity;
   (ii) The murder was committed while the defendant was under the influence of extreme mental or emotional disturbance;
   (iii) The victim was a participant in the defendant's conduct or consented to the act;
   (iv) The defendant was an accomplice in a murder committed by another person and his participation in the homicidal act was relatively minor;
   (v) The defendant acted under extreme duress or under the substantial domination of another person;
   (vi) The capacity of the defendant to appreciate the criminality of his conduct or to conform his conduct to the requirements of law was substantially impaired;
   (vii) The age of the defendant at the time of the crime;
   (viii) Any other fact or circumstance of the defendant's character or prior record or matter surrounding his offense which serves to mitigate his culpability.

Appendix E: State Differences in Clemency Procedure

(Death Penalty Information Center)

Governor Has Sole Authority to Grant Clemency

Alabama, California,* Colorado, Kansas, Kentucky, New Jersey, New Mexico, New York, North Carolina, Oregon, South Carolina, Virginia, Washington, Wyoming

Clemency Granted by Governor on Recommendation From a Board or Advisory Group

Arizona, Delaware, Florida, Louisiana, Montana, Oklahoma, Pennsylvania, Texas

Non-Binding Clemency Recommendations Made to Governor by Board or Advisory Group

Arkansas, Illinois, Indiana, Maryland, Mississippi, Missouri, New Hampshire, Ohio, South Dakota, Tennessee

Board or Advisory Group Determines Clemency Without Governor Involvement

Connecticut, Georgia, Idaho

Governor Sits on the Board or Advisory Group That Collectively Determines Clemency

Nebraska, Nevada, Utah

*The governor may not grant a pardon or commutation to a person twice convicted of a felony except on recommendation of the state Supreme Court, with at least four judges concurring.

3

Death Penalty Jurisprudence

Introduction

"Death is different." In the landmark decision *Gregg v. Georgia* (1976), the U.S. Supreme Court upheld the death penalty as constitutional but emphasized that it remains unique from all other forms of criminal punishments (p. 188). Since this 1976 decision, the theme that a death sentence is qualitatively different from all other forms of criminal punishment has been an enduring feature of the Supreme Court's death penalty jurisprudence (see, e.g., Abramson, 2004; Acker, 2009; Cunningham & Goldstein, 2003; Reisner, Slobogin, & Rai, 2004; Slobogin, Rai, & Reisner, 2009; see also *Atkins v. Virginia*, 2002; *Lockett v. Ohio*, 1978; *McCleskey v. Kemp*, 1987; *Ring v. Arizona*, 2002; *Roper v. Simmons*, 2005; *Spaziano v. Florida*, 1984; *Wainwright v. Witt*, 1985; *Woodson v. North Carolina*, 1976). The Supreme Court has also emphasized that the unique and irreversible nature of a death sentence requires special precautions to protect against judicial error and to ensure that death sentences are neither arbitrary nor capricious. As a result, death penalty sentencing schemes, and other procedural and substantive aspects of the capital punishment process, have been the subject of intense political and judicial scrutiny over the past 35 years.

Given the judicial scrutiny of death penalty cases, there is a large and growing body of case law addressing various aspects of capital punishment. Some of these cases have focused broadly on the overall appropriateness of the death penalty as a criminal punishment, generating both controversy and debate in legal, political, religious, and social circles over the past few decades. Other cases have focused broadly on the constitutionality of the death penalty, or taken a more circumscribed look at specific procedural and substantive due process issues. Given that many issues relating to capital punishment are governed largely at the state level, capital punishment jurisprudence can be complex and vary considerably among the states.

Of particular interest for this chapter are the Supreme Court cases that have addressed which categories of offenders are eligible—and not eligible—for a death sentence. Some cases from the U.S. Supreme Court have focused on the age of the offender at the time of the offense and the nature of the criminal offense when determining eligibility for the death penalty. Mental health professionals have no expertise to offer on these issues. However, other cases have focused on the mental health functioning of the offender, either at the time of the offense or closer to the date of the scheduled execution. In some of these cases, the Supreme Court has simply reinforced and refined previous holdings in a particular area, with very little meaningful substantive change. However, in other cases, the Supreme Court has reversed its previous holdings and created new substantive standards intended to be implemented by the states. These cases have obvious relevance for forensic mental health professionals.

This chapter begins with a brief historical overview of death as a punishment. We then detail death penalty jurisprudence in the United States, with a particular focus on cases decided since 1972, which is the beginning of the modern era of death penalty jurisprudence. Next, we discuss cases that are particularly relevant for forensic mental health professionals who are involved in capital cases. To this end, we examine cases that address whether certain classes of offenders, such as those with mental retardation, are eligible for the death penalty. Although the focus of this chapter will be predominantly on cases decided by the U.S. Supreme Court, we will also mention several influential and informative cases from lower federal and state courts. The purpose of this chapter is to establish a solid foundation that will set the stage for a more detailed examination of these issues—particularly as they apply to forensic mental health assessments—in later chapters.

History of the Death Penalty

Although a detailed history of the death penalty as a punishment is beyond the scope of this book, we provide a very brief historical overview. The use of death as a punishment dates back several thousand years (see Banner, 2002, and Randa, 1997, for informative discussions of the history of the death penalty). For example, the Code of King Hammurabi of Babylon, which dates back to the 18th century BC, prescribed death as a penalty for 25 different offenses. Several centuries later, early Greek and Roman laws also provided that death was an appropriate punishment for certain offenses. For example, the Draconian Code of Athens, which dates to the 7th century BC, prescribed death as a punishment for every crime, while the Roman Law of the Twelve Tables, which was established in the 5th century BC, prescribed death as a punishment for only certain types of offenses.

The death penalty in Britain can be traced back to at least 450 BC, and it became an enduring feature of British law for many centuries thereafter. In the early 1700s, the use of the death penalty was quite commonplace in Britain, with over 220 offenses punishable by death, including several offenses that would appear to be minor by today's standards. When the first colonists made their way from England to settle the first colonies in the early 1600s, the death penalty came with them. The first recorded execution in the English American colonies dates back to 1608, when George Kendall was executed in Virginia for allegedly plotting to betray the British to the Spanish. Since that time, with several notable exceptions, the death penalty has remained an enduring feature of the law in the United States.

Modern Death Penalty Jurisprudence in the United States

The modern era of death penalty jurisprudence in the United States began in 1972 when the U.S. Supreme Court temporarily abolished the death penalty. The most well known of the 1972 cases abolishing the death penalty is *Furman v. Georgia*. By a narrow five-to-four vote, the Supreme Court in *Furman* (along with two companion cases that were consolidated[1]) held that the capital punishment statutes of Texas and Georgia violated two provisions of the U.S. Constitution: the Eighth Amendment's prohibition against cruel and unusual punishment and the Due Process Clause of the Fourteenth Amendment. The Supreme Court announced its decision in *Furman* via a brief unsigned *per curiam* opinion, and then each of the nine Justices wrote separate opinions to detail their reasoning. Although *Furman* held that the death penalty is unconstitutional, it is important to note that seven Justices did not object to the constitutionality of the death penalty per se, but instead expressed concerns that the absence of sentencing guidelines would result in the arbitrary imposition

---

1. The two cases consolidated with *Furman* were *Jackson v. Georgia* (1972) and *Branch v. Texas* (1972).

of the death penalty. In the characteristically colorful words of Justice Potter Stewart, capital punishment is a unique penalty that was "wantonly" and "freakishly" imposed (*Furman*, 1972, p. 310). The nine Supreme Court Justices ultimately offered several rationales for striking down the capital punishment statutes at issue, but the *Furman* decision is typically interpreted as prohibiting all capital punishment statutes that leave the sentencing decision to the unguided discretion of the sentencing judge or jury.

The Supreme Court's decision in *Furman* effectively led to a moratorium on capital punishment in the United States. In the several years following the *Furman* decision, 35 states rewrote their death penalty statutes in an attempt to make those statutes constitutionally acceptable. Broadly speaking, the states took one of two approaches. Approximately half of the states removed jury discretion by making the death penalty mandatory in specified circumstances. For example, North Carolina prescribed death as the punishment for all first-degree murder convictions. Most of the remaining states permitted jurors to exercise considerable discretion in sentencing a defendant, but they established guidelines to assist juries in making more consistent and less arbitrary sentencing decisions. The guidelines in these states typically instructed the jury to consider a variety of aggravating and mitigating factors when reaching a sentencing decision.

The moratorium on capital punishment that followed *Furman* lasted approximately 4 years. In 1976, the U.S. Supreme Court again considered the constitutionality of capital punishment in a series of cases decided together, including *Gregg v. Georgia*, *Jurek v. Texas*, and *Proffitt v. Florida*. In *Gregg*, by a seven-to-two vote, the Supreme Court concluded that capital punishment would be constitutional under certain defined circumstances. The 1976 cases, as well as several subsequent Supreme Court decisions, were instrumental in clarifying the distinction between constitutional and unconstitutional death penalty sentencing statutes. In these cases, the Supreme Court held unconstitutional the sentencing statutes that imposed mandatory death sentences in response to certain offenses, such as that established in North Carolina in the wake of *Furman*. The Supreme Court concluded that mandatory death sentences are unconstitutional because they do not provide for the individualized consideration of the defendant's character, the defendant's criminal record, and the circumstances surrounding the offense (see *Roberts v. Louisiana*, 1976; *Woodson v. North Carolina*, 1976).

In contrast, the Supreme Court upheld the sentencing statutory schemes that required sentencing juries to consider aggravating and mitigating factors when deciding on a sentence of life or death. The Supreme Court concluded that Georgia's capital sentencing procedure, which required the jury to consider a combination of aggravating and mitigating factors relating to the offense and offender, was constitutionally acceptable (see *Gregg v. Georgia*, 1976;

Zant v. Stephens, 1983). The 1976 Supreme Court cases reinstating the death penalty stand for the proposition that although sentencing juries could not be given unbridled discretion when making their sentencing decisions, they must be permitted to consider all relevant information relating to the offense and offender as a way of individualizing the sentence (see Cunningham & Goldstein, 2003; Latzer, 1998; Reisner et al., 2004).

Several Supreme Court cases decided after *Gregg* in 1976 provided additional clarification regarding constitutionally acceptable practice in death penalty sentencing decisions. For example, in *Lockett v. Ohio* (1978), the Supreme Court struck down a death penalty statute that required the sentencing jury to impose a death sentence unless the defendant proved at least one of three specified mitigating factors. The Supreme Court held that the Ohio sentencing statute improperly prevented the jury from making an individualized sentencing decision (as required by *Gregg*), and it reiterated that the sentencing jury must be permitted to consider all mitigating evidence related to the defendant's character, the defendant's history, and the circumstances surrounding the capital offense. As a result, any mitigating evidence related to the defendant's history is typically considered admissible during the sentencing phase of capital cases, and judges in capital cases are understandably reluctant to exclude any mitigating evidence for fear of having their decision reversed on appeal.

Several years later, in *Eddings v. Oklahoma* (1982), the Supreme Court reversed the death sentence imposed on a 16-year-old defendant because the sentencing judge had failed to consider evidence of the defendant's turbulent family history, which included abuse and mental health problems. In *Eddings*, the Supreme Court emphasized that sentencing juries must be permitted to consider *all* relevant mitigating evidence relating to the defendant's character and the circumstances of the offense. Although the sentencing body can decide how much weight should be accorded to mitigating evidence, the court cannot exclude mitigating evidence from consideration (see also *Skipper v. South Carolina*, 1986). With these rulings, the Supreme Court attempted to make the death penalty less arbitrary and narrow the class of persons eligible for the death penalty.

Cases Relevant to Forensic Mental Health Assessments

Several cases decided by the U.S. Supreme Court are important for forensic mental health professionals involved in capital cases. In fact, several cases decided by the Supreme Court within the past 10 years have modified standards or even created new standards that guide evaluators in some death penalty evaluations. Most of these cases considered whether particular offenders with mental disabilities or mental health problems should be considered eligible for the death penalty. Because the Supreme Court cases are typically binding in all jurisdictions, understanding the implications of these cases for forensic mental health practice is essential.

The first set of cases we discuss in this chapter address the relationship between mental retardation and an offender's eligibility for a death sentence. The U.S. Supreme Court has addressed this issue twice in the past few decades, and a recent Supreme Court decision reversed its previous position on this issue and created a new type of FMHA. The second set of cases address the concept of competence to face execution. The Supreme Court's most recent ruling on this issue was handed down in 2007, but it failed to alleviate some of the confusion that resulted from its earlier decision regarding competence for execution. This chapter focuses on the legal rulings and reasoning in these influential cases, whereas Chapters 5 and 6 address the implications of these cases for forensic mental health professionals who conduct evaluations in capital contexts.

Mental Retardation and the Death Penalty

Over the past 25 years, the U.S. Supreme Court has addressed the relationship between mental retardation and eligibility for a death sentence in two highly influential and much-discussed decisions. Given the higher-than-average rates of intellectual disabilities among criminal offenders, particularly among those sentenced to death (see Cunningham & Vigen, 1999, 2002; Ellis, 2002), these cases are important for forensic mental health professionals who conduct evaluations in capital contexts. The Supreme Court's most recent pronouncement on this issue reversed its previous position and effectively created a new type of FMHA in which the clinical issue (i.e., absence/presence of mental retardation) is largely synonymous with the legal issue.

In its most recent decision on this issue, the Supreme Court established a bright-line constitutional rule holding that offenders with mental retardation are not eligible for a death sentence (see *Atkins v. Virginia*, 2002). Although the rule appears to be straightforward, at least in terms of the Supreme Court's stated intention to further narrow the class of offenders eligible for a death sentence, the subsequent implementation of the rule among death penalty states has been anything but straightforward. It has been nearly a decade since this case was decided and states are still struggling to implement the rule set out in that case, both in terms of proper procedural mechanisms and meaningful substantive standards. But to understand the *Atkins* decision, it is important to begin with the Supreme Court decision that set the stage for *Atkins*.

Penry v. Lynaugh (1989)

In October 1979, 22-year-old Pamela Mosely Carpenter was raped, beaten, and stabbed to death with scissors by a man who broke into her Texas home. Before succumbing to her fatal injuries, Carpenter provided a detailed description of her attacker. Local law enforcement authorities later identified her attacker as 22-year-old Johnny Paul Penry. At the time of the offense, Penry was on parole for a rape conviction. After being apprehended, Penry confessed to the murder of Carpenter in two separate statements that he made to the police, and he was eventually charged with capital murder.

At the conclusion of his trial, a Texas trial court jury rejected Penry's proffered insanity defense and found him guilty of capital murder. During the sentencing phase of the proceedings, Penry's defense team argued that the imposition of the death penalty would be constitutionally inappropriate—in violation of the Eighth Amendment's prohibition against cruel and unusual punishment—because of Penry's mental functioning. The defense argued that Penry had organic brain damage resulting from a breach birth, and asserted that his Full Scale IQ score was somewhere between 50 and the low 60s. Nevertheless, the sentencing jury concluded that the presence of aggravating factors justified the imposition of the death penalty, and Penry was sentenced to death.

On appeal, the Texas Court of Criminal Appeals affirmed the trial court's conviction and sentence of death. Among other findings, the state appellate court affirmed that the death penalty was not prohibited based solely on Penry's level of mental functioning. Penry's attorneys subsequently filed a petition for *habeas corpus* in federal district court challenging the constitutionality of the death sentence. The U.S. District Court for the Eastern District of Texas denied Penry's petition for relief, and Penry subsequently appealed to the federal circuit court. On appeal, the U.S. Court of Appeals for the Fifth Circuit affirmed Penry's death sentence. The court specifically rejected Penry's claim that executing an offender who is mentally retarded would violate the Eighth Amendment's prohibition against cruel and unusual punishment. After losing on appeal again, Penry's attorneys appealed to the U.S. Supreme Court.

The U.S. Supreme Court granted certiorari to determine whether the Eighth Amendment's prohibition against cruel and unusual punishment prohibits the execution of a defendant who is mentally retarded. This was the first time in the modern era of the death penalty that the Supreme Court addressed this question. Penry's defense attorney offered two arguments: *(1)* executing a criminal offender who is mentally retarded would violate the Eighth Amendment's prohibition against cruel and unusual punishment because such individuals are not morally culpable to an extent that would justify a death sentence; and *(2)* there is an emerging national consensus against executing offenders who are mentally retarded.

The prosecution countered the defense's arguments by asserting that existing procedural safeguards adequately protected the legal interests of defendants who are mentally retarded. In particular, the prosecution noted that safeguards related to competence to stand trial and mental state defenses (e.g., insanity, diminished capacity) function sufficiently to protect the interests of offenders who have intellectual and cognitive disabilities. According to the prosecution, there was no need for additional procedural or substantive protections. The prosecution also argued that there is insufficient evidence of a national consensus against executing offenders who are mentally retarded.

In evaluating the constitutionality of a law or practice under the Eighth Amendment, the Supreme Court draws guidance from a prior Supreme Court case and follows a somewhat predictable approach. In *Trop v. Dulles* (1958), Chief Justice Warren stated that the Eighth Amendment must draw its meaning "from evolving standards of decency that mark progress of a maturing society" (p. 101). Relying on Chief Justice Warren's guidance, the Supreme Court typically looks to objective factors, such as state statutes, to discern such "evolving standards of decency." Statutes are considered the strongest objective evidence of contemporary standards of decency because legislatures are supposed to respond to the will and moral values of the people when enacting laws. Therefore, in Eighth Amendment cases, the Supreme Court examines state statutes to determine whether a national consensus exists that is sufficient to support a constitutional ruling in the matter being decided.

In *Penry*, by a narrow five-to-four vote, the Supreme Court rejected the defense's arguments and held that executing offenders who are mentally retarded is not a per se violation of the Eighth Amendment. In an opinion written by Justice O'Connor, the Supreme Court stated that mental retardation does not categorically exclude an offender from the reach of capital punishment, but the Court acknowledged that it should be considered as a mitigating factor during the sentencing phase of a capital trial. According to the Court, this adequately ensures the individualized sentencing determinations required by prior Supreme Court decisions (e.g., *Gregg v. Georgia*, 1976; *Roberts v. Louisiana*, 1976). The Court also agreed with the prosecution that existing procedural safeguards, such as the insanity defense, would likely protect severely and profoundly mentally retarded offenders from being executed.[2] Finally, the Court concluded that there was no national consensus against executing offenders who are mentally retarded, because only the federal

---

2. This, of course, does not speak to the procedural protections that would be available to offenders with mild or moderate mental retardation, who comprise the majority of criminal offenders with intellectual disabilities.

jurisdiction and two states (Georgia and Maryland) had prohibited executing such offenders at that time. Accordingly, based on *Penry*, mental retardation was viewed as a mitigating factor during capital sentencing, but it was not considered a constitutional basis for excluding a defendant from the reach of capital punishment. The 1989 *Penry* decision remained the Supreme Court's position on this issue for the next 13 years.

Atkins v. Virginia (2002)

In *Atkins v. Virginia*, the Supreme Court reversed the position it announced in *Penry* and held that the Eighth Amendment's prohibition against cruel and unusual punishment does indeed prohibit the execution of a defendant who is mentally retarded. This reversal of position was largely based on changes that occurred in the national legislative landscape and public opinion since *Penry* was decided. With this decision, a new type of FMHA was created.

On August 16, 1996, Daryl Renard Atkins and William Jones carjacked Eric Nesbitt, an airman from Langley Air Force Base, as he walked out of a convenience store near midnight. Armed with a semi-automatic handgun, Atkins and Jones robbed Nesbitt of $60, drove him to an automated teller machine, and ordered him to withdraw more money. Nesbitt withdrew $200 at gunpoint. After driving Nesbitt to a secluded area and debating his fate, Atkins and Jones eventually ordered Nesbitt out of the truck and shot him eight times. Nesbitt was killed instantly. Testimony from both Atkins and Jones largely agreed on the key elements of the offense, with the notable exception that each defendant stated that the other had actually pulled the trigger and killed Nesbitt.

In 1998, a Virginia trial court found Atkins guilty of capital murder and related offenses. During the sentencing phase, the prosecution introduced evidence of two aggravating factors: future dangerousness (due to Atkins's lengthy history of 16 prior felony convictions) and the vileness of the current offense. The defense presented the testimony of a clinical psychologist, Dr. Evan Nelson, who diagnosed Atkins as being mildly mentally retarded. After weighing the aggravating and mitigating factors, the sentencing jury recommended a sentence of death for Atkins.

On appeal, the Virginia Supreme Court ordered a second sentencing hearing because the trial court had used a misleading verdict form. During the second sentencing hearing, Dr. Nelson reiterated his testimony that Atkins was mildly mentally retarded. The prosecution countered with testimony from Dr. Stanton Samenow, who opined that Atkins was not mentally retarded and instead met diagnostic criteria for Antisocial Personality Disorder. Following this testimony, the jury again sentenced Atkins to death.

Atkins' attorneys appealed the decision to the Virginia Supreme Court. The defense argued that executing a criminal defendant with an IQ of 59 (as measured by Dr. Nelson using the WAIS-III) was a disproportionate punishment and, therefore, unconstitutional. Relying on the Supreme Court's decision in *Penry*, the prosecution argued that it does not violate the Eighth Amendment's prohibition against cruel and unusual punishment to execute a defendant who is mentally retarded. Using *Penry* as precedent, the Virginia Supreme Court rejected the defense's argument and affirmed the death sentence. In a last effort, Atkins' attorneys appealed to the U.S. Supreme Court.

The U.S. Supreme Court granted certiorari to address the same question it had addressed 13 years earlier in *Penry*—that is, whether executing an offender who is mentally retarded violates the Eighth Amendment's prohibition against cruel and unusual punishment. The Supreme Court noted that it granted certiorari because of concerns expressed by the dissenting judges in the Virginia Supreme Court and the dramatic shifts that had occurred in the state legislative landscape since *Penry* was decided. In a six-to-three decision, the Supreme Court reversed its holding in *Penry* and held that executing an offender who is mentally retarded is excessive in light of evolving standards of decency and therefore violates the Eighth Amendment. Writing for the majority, Justice Stevens stated that although the deficiencies associated with mental retardation do not exempt one from punishment, they diminish personal culpability to the point where death is no longer a constitutionally appropriate punishment. The Court concluded that significant disabilities in the areas of reasoning, judgment, and impulse control render offenders who are mentally retarded less culpable than other offenders. Furthermore, the Court emphasized that executing an offender who is mentally retarded would not further the primary goals of capital punishment—that is, retribution and deterrence.

Finally, the Court noted that there was a national consensus against executing offenders who are mentally retarded that did not exist at the time *Penry* was decided. The Court found evidence of a national consensus because 18 states and the federal jurisdiction prohibited executing offenders who are mentally retarded, numerous secular and religious organizations opposed capital punishment for such individuals, and public opinion surveys suggested that the American public opposed executing offenders who are mentally retarded. According to the Court, these were notable changes in state legislation and public opinion since *Penry* was decided 13 years earlier, and they provided evidence of a national consensus.[3]

---

3. In a dissenting opinion, Justice Scalia questioned the existence of a national consensus against the execution of offenders who are mentally retarded. He noted, for example, that the prohibition against executing offenders who are mentally retarded existed in only 18 of the 38 states that permitted capital punishment at that time. He questioned whether a prohibition endorsed by less than half of the death penalty states actually constituted a national consensus for Eighth Amendment purposes.

Despite the seemingly straightforward constitutional rule articulated in *Atkins*, the Supreme Court's decision left several important substantive and procedural questions either partially or completely unanswered. For example, the Court did not specify when the question of mental retardation should be decided in capital cases (i.e., pretrial vs. posttrial vs. postsentencing), the burden of proof that must be met to entitle a claim of mental retardation to an evidentiary hearing, the burden of proof that must be satisfied when establishing mental retardation, which party bears the burden of proof, and whether the question of mental retardation must be decided by a judge or jury (see Blume, Johnson, & Seeds, 2009; Reisner et al., 2004; Tobolowsky, 2003). As a result, states have been left to craft their own procedural law to implement *Atkins* and, perhaps not surprisingly, there is considerable variability among the states (see, e.g., Duvall & Morris, 2006; and Chapter 5 of this text).

An important aspect of *Atkins* was the Supreme Court's decision not to provide a definition of mental retardation. Although the Supreme Court could have supported, adopted, endorsed, or presumably even imposed a uniform definition of mental retardation to be used by the states, the Court instead elected to charge each state with "the task of developing appropriate ways to enforce the constitutional restriction" against executing offenders with mental retardation (*Atkins v. Virginia*, 2002, p. 317). As a result, each state was left to develop its own definition of mental retardation, with very little meaningful guidance from the Supreme Court. This was the same approach the Supreme Court took in *Ford v. Wainwright* (1986) (discussed later in this chapter) with respect to the substantive legal standard that should be used when determining whether a prisoner is competent to face execution (see Farringer, 2001; Orpen, 2003).

The Supreme Court's only guidance in *Atkins* was that the definitions of mental retardation adopted by the states must be consistent with "a national consensus" (*Atkins v. Virginia*, 2002, p. 317). In footnotes, the Supreme Court referenced the definitions of mental retardation promulgated by the American Association of Mental Retardation (AAMR) and the American Psychiatric Association (in the *Diagnostic and Statistical Manual of Mental Disorders, 4th edition [DSM-IV]*), but it did not specifically endorse either definition or require that states adopt either definition. This gave the states considerable substantive leeway, and they have responded by enacting widely varying definitions of mental retardation (see DeMatteo, Marczyk, & Pich, 2007, for a review of the state legislation; see also Dowling, 2003). Although some of the states chose to adopt accepted clinical criteria to define mental retardation (such as the *DSM-IV* or AAMR criteria), other states strayed quite far from accepted clinical standards and developed definitions of mental retardation that have little resemblance to standard clinical definitions.

Consistent with the Supreme Court's intent, the *Atkins* decision effectively narrowed the class of offenders who are eligible for the death penalty by categorically excluding all offenders who are mentally retarded. Given recent estimates suggesting that perhaps as many as 10% of all death row inmates are mentally retarded (see, e.g., Ellis, 2002), and research suggesting that death row inmates disproportionately suffer from intellectual limitations (see, e.g., Cunningham & Vigen, 1999, 2002), the *Atkins* decision could have a significant effect on the death row population in the United States. But because many states are continuing to struggle with implementing *Atkins* (see Blume et al., 2009, DeMatteo et al., 2007, and Chapter 5), the full effects of the *Atkins* decision may not be clear until procedural rules and case law develop further. Moreover, as discussed in Chapter 5, the *Atkins* decision poses some unique clinical challenges for forensic mental health professionals who conduct *Atkins*-type evaluations.

Several federal and state cases decided after *Atkins* have added to the jurisprudence surrounding mental retardation and the death penalty. For example, in *Tennard v. Dretke* (2004), the U.S. Supreme Court held that a low IQ, regardless of whether it is in the range that defines mental retardation (i.e., typically <70), is a relevant mitigating factor at capital sentencing even if the offender's low intellectual functioning was not directly related to the capital offense. To clarify, per *Tennard*, a low IQ (if not below 70) is a relevant mitigator, but not a basis for a categorical exclusion from the death penalty. As more states continue to grapple with the interpretation and implementation of *Atkins*, additional cases will no doubt further refine the *Atkins* ruling.

Competence to Face Execution

Even if a criminal offender is ostensibly eligible for the death penalty at the time of trial (i.e., there is no evidence of mental retardation that would preclude the prosecution from mounting a capital case, or there is no evidence of a severe mental health disorder that would reduce the offender's culpability for the offense), there are constitutional restrictions that prohibit the government from carrying out an execution on an incompetent prisoner. The prohibition against executing incompetent offenders dates back at least several hundred years (see Ackerson, Brodsky, & Zapf, 2005; Blackstone, 1978; Broderick, 1979; Ward, 1986). Both English common law and early American law prohibited executing incompetent offenders based on a variety of rationales, most of which involved religious, humane, and societal considerations (Radelet & Barnard, 1986; Zapf, 2008).

In a series of decisions dating back many years, the U.S. Supreme Court addressed some procedural due process issues related to the disposition or execution of incompetent offenders (e.g., *Caritativo v. California*, 1958; *Nobles v. Georgia*, 1897; *Phyle v. Duffy*, 1948; *Solesbee v. Balkcom*, 1950).

But *Ford v. Wainwright*, in 1986, was the first Supreme Court decision to directly address the constitutionality of executing incompetent offenders. *Ford* addressed the concept of dignitarian competency (see Reisner et al., 2004), which is more commonly referred to as competence to be executed or competence to face execution. Some scholars have referred to competence to be executed as the "last competency" because of its late temporal placement in the criminal adjudication process (see, e.g., Brodsky, Zapf, & Boccaccini, 2005; Zapf, 2008). As detailed later in this chapter, the Supreme Court's decision in *Ford* left unanswered several important questions that have direct implications for forensic mental health professionals who conduct evaluations in capital cases. In particular, *Ford* did not address the appropriate substantive legal standard that should be used when determining whether an offender is competent to face execution. A more recent decision—*Panetti v. Quarterman* (2007)—resolved some of the confusion that resulted from *Ford*, but left important questions unanswered.

Ford v. Wainwright (1986)

In December 1974, Alvin Bernard Ford was convicted on a capital murder charge for killing a police officer, and he was sentenced to death in January 1975. Although Ford's defense team did not raise any concerns about Ford's mental health during the guilt-innocence phase or sentencing phase of the proceedings, Ford began to exhibit symptoms that were consistent with a severe and persistent mental health disorder several years after he was sentenced to death. In 1982, for example, Ford began experiencing paranoid and grandiose delusions. He developed an obsession with the Ku Klux Klan, began referring to himself as Pope John Paul III, and explained that he had appointed nine new justices to the Florida Supreme Court. Around this same time, Ford also began threatening others and harming himself.

Based on Ford's deteriorating mental health, his attorneys retained a psychiatrist to evaluate his mental health and make treatment recommendations. The psychiatrist, Dr. Jamal Amin, determined that Ford was suffering from schizophrenia, which affected his ability to assist counsel in his own defense. Ford's lawyers asked the court for a determination of whether Ford was competent to face execution. Pursuant to Florida statutory law, the Governor of Florida appointed three psychiatrists to evaluate Ford to determine whether he had the mental capacity to understand the nature of the death penalty and the reasons it was being imposed upon him. The three psychiatrists conducted a joint interview of Ford for a total of 30 minutes. Although all three psychiatrists arrived at different psychiatric diagnoses, they all agreed that he was competent to face execution according to the standard set forth in Florida statutory law. Accordingly, the Governor signed a death warrant for Ford's execution on April 30, 1984. The execution order was later stayed as Ford's case weaved its way through the appellate process and ultimately to the U.S. Supreme Court.

The central question in *Ford* was whether the Eighth Amendment's prohibition against cruel and unusual punishment prohibited the execution of incompetent offenders.[4] Although there was a common law prohibition against such executions, the Supreme Court had not yet directly addressed the constitutionality of executing incompetent offenders (see Pastroff, 1986). As an Eighth Amendment case, the Supreme Court drew guidance from *Trop v. Dulles* (1958) and looked to objective factors to discern the "evolving standards of decency that mark the progress of a maturing society" (p. 101). As previously noted, the most relevant "objective factors" examined in Eighth Amendment cases are state statutes.

The Supreme Court began its analysis by reviewing the common law reasons for excluding incompetent offenders from the death penalty. One potential justification, according to the Court, is that mental illness is a sufficient punishment by itself. The Court also noted that the common law prohibition existed because executing incompetent offenders would offend humanity without furthering the primary goals of punishment (retribution and deterrence). Another explanation for the common law prohibition is religious sentiment. Turning to more recent practices, the Court noted that no state permitted the execution of incompetent offenders at that time, which is an important consideration in an Eighth Amendment case.

In a four-Justice plurality opinion by Justice Marshall, the Supreme Court held that the Eighth Amendment prohibits states from executing incompetent offenders. The Court's decision rested primarily on the historical underpinnings of such a prohibition and current practices among states that have addressed the issue. Specifically, the Court reasoned that executing incompetent offenders would, among other problems, offend humanity and fail to serve the goal of deterrence. The Court also questioned the retributive value of "executing a person who has no comprehension of why he has been singled out and stripped of his fundamental right to life" (*Ford v. Wainwright*, 1986, p. 409). Finally, the Court cited the "natural abhorrence" that civilized societies experience when "killing one who has no capacity to come to grips with his own conscience or deity" (*Ford*, 1986, p. 409). Based on these considerations, the Supreme Court held that it is unconstitutional to execute incompetent offenders.

---

4. Somewhat inexplicably, the Supreme Court used the term "insane" throughout the *Ford* opinion, even though the case clearly centered on competence to face execution, not mental state at the time of the offense. To avoid confusion with mental state at the time of the offense, which is a concept relevant to criminal responsibility as opposed to fitness for execution, we use the more appropriate term "competence for execution" throughout this chapter.

Importantly, however, the Supreme Court's plurality opinion in *Ford* provided neither a substantive legal standard nor meaningful guidelines for determining whether an offender is competent to face execution.[5] Although the Court has often been criticized for not providing a legal standard in its decision, the *Ford* case did not present this specific issue to the Court (see Melton, Petrila, Poythress, & Slobogin, 2007; Winick, 1992). The specific issue in *Ford* was whether it was constitutional to execute incompetent offenders, not the particular standard that should be used to determine such competence.

Although the plurality opinion in *Ford* (1986) did not identify a substantive legal standard for competence to face execution, an influential concurring opinion by Justice Powell stated that the Eighth Amendment should prohibit the "execution only of those who are unaware of the punishment they are about to suffer and why they are to suffer it" (p. 422). Justice Powell asserted that the test for competence to face execution should be whether the offender understands the nature, pendency, and purpose of the impending execution. Justice Powell also stated that "the retributive goal of the criminal law is satisfied" only if the defendant "perceives the connection between his crime and his punishment" (*Ford*, 1986, p. 422). Finally, Justice Powell noted that states were free to adopt a more expansive view of competence to face execution which might include the requirement that the defendant be able to assist counsel in his or her own defense.[6] Justice Powell's concurring opinion proved to be influential among courts seeking to develop/adopt a standard for competence for execution.

Instead of providing a uniform legal standard for states to use when determining whether an offender is competent to face execution, the Supreme Court charged each state with developing procedures to ensure that incompetent offenders would be excluded from the death penalty. After *Ford*, most courts that addressed the issue adopted some variation of Justice Powell's rationale as the basis for excluding incompetent offenders from capital punishment (see Otto, 2009; Reisner et al., 2004). At the time *Ford* was decided in 1986, 37 states authorized the death penalty and had laws, either statutory or case law, relating to competence to face execution. Shortly after *Ford* was decided, Heilbrun (1987) examined the standards used by the 23 states that had statutory provisions prohibiting the execution of incompetent offenders. He found that of the 23 states, 2 states used an

---

5. The *Ford* decision also failed to address the procedures that should be followed to enforce *Ford*'s mandate. As a result, some courts have been forced to create procedural guidelines in the context of deciding specific cases (see, e.g., *Ex parte Clarence Curtis Jordan*, 1988).

6. At least one U.S. court, the Supreme Court of Washington, accepted Justice Powell's suggestion in *Ford* and adopted an "ability to assist" test (see *Washington v. Harris*, 1990; *Washington v. Rice*, 1988).

"understand" standard (focusing on the offenders' factual understanding of the reasons the death penalty was being imposed in that particular case), 6 states used an "understand and assist" standard (similar to the standard articulated by the Supreme Court in *Dusky v. United States* (1960) for competence to stand trial), and the remaining states used short and vague definitions of competence to face execution that simply excluded "insane" and "mentally ill" offenders from capital punishment (Heilbrun, 1987; see also Miller, 1988). The confusion among the states that followed *Ford* is similar to the confusion among the states in the aftermath of *Atkins* (see Chapter 5 of this text).

Post-Ford Cases and Developments

Several years after the Supreme Court's ruling in *Ford*, the American Bar Association (ABA) adopted a standard for competence to face execution (see Zapf, 2008, for an informative discussion of the ABA's standard). Specifically, in the *American Bar Association Criminal Justice Mental Health Standards* (American Bar Association, 1989), the ABA stated that "[c]onvicts who have been sentenced to death should not be executed if they are currently mentally incompetent" (p. 290). As noted by Zapf (2008), this standard "reflects both the constitutional and common-law prohibition against executing any defendant currently judged to be incompetent" (p. 243). The ABA (1989) recommended that executions should be stayed if an offender is determined to be "mentally incompetent" as a way of protecting the integrity of the criminal justice system (p. 290). The ABA also offered the following test for determining competence to face execution:

> A convict is incompetent to be executed if, as a result of mental illness or mental retardation, the convict cannot understand the nature of the pending proceedings, what he or she was tried for, the reasons for the punishment, or the nature of the punishment. A convict is also incompetent if, as a result of mental illness or mental retardation, the convict lacks sufficient capacity to recognize or understand any fact which might exist which would make the punishment unjust or unlawful, or lacks the ability to convey such information to the court. (p. 290)

The standard articulated by the ABA is similar to the "understand and assist" standard identified by Heilbrun (1987) in his review of state statutory laws relating to competence to face execution. Of course, the ABA standard is not binding law unless it is adopted in a particular jurisdiction.

Following *Ford*, relatively few reported court decisions addressed the appropriate standard that should be used when determining whether an offender is competent to face execution, largely because the issue of competence to face execution is so infrequently raised. Nevertheless, a few court decisions in the wake of *Ford* did address relevant issues.

In *Barnard v. Collins* (1994), the U.S. Court of Appeals for the Fifth Circuit adopted Justice Powell's proposed standard in upholding the state court's determination that Harold Barnard was competent to face execution. Barnard demonstrated a sufficient factual understanding that he was sentenced to death by lethal injection because he was convicted of killing a 16-year-old boy during a robbery, but he apparently maintained a delusional belief that his death sentence was also attributable to a conspiracy among Asians, Jews, African Americans, homosexuals, and organized crime. The Fifth Circuit concluded that Barnard comprehended the nature, pendency, and purpose of the execution (mirroring Justice Powell's language in *Ford*), which provided a sufficient factual basis for the state court's conclusion that Barnard was competent to face execution. Interestingly, the Fifth Circuit conceded that Barnard's perception of the reason for his conviction and pending execution was at times "distorted by a delusional system" (p. 876), but it nevertheless upheld the lower court's determination because it was based on Barnard's factual understanding.

Several other courts have also followed Justice Powell's standard when determining whether an offender is competent to face execution (see, e.g., *Coe v. Bell*, 2000; *Fearance v. Scott*, 1995; *Walter v. Angelone*, 2003). Interestingly, some courts have both adopted Justice Powell's standard and explicitly rejected the defense's efforts to make a distinction between a defendant's factual and rational understanding of the reasons for the execution (see, e.g., *Martin v. Florida*, 1987).

A few courts, however, adopted a standard for competence to face execution that is more stringent than the standard Justice Powell proposed in *Ford*. For example, the Supreme Court of Washington has twice held that competence to face execution requires the offender to demonstrate not only a factual understanding of the pending execution, but an ability to assist counsel in defense efforts (see *Washington v. Harris*, 1990; *Washington v. Rice*, 1988). Other cases have held that competence to face execution requires more from defendants than a purely factual understanding. In *Walton v. Johnson* (2005), for example, the U.S. Court of Appeals for the Fourth Circuit concluded that the purely factual standard used by the lower courts was too narrow and restrictive. Although the Fourth Circuit's ruling in *Walton* was later vacated when the case was heard en banc, the court's reasoning is noteworthy because it foreshadows some of the reasoning used by the Supreme Court in *Panetti v. Quarterman* (2007).

Panetti v. Quarterman (2007)

In *Panetti v. Quarterman*, which was decided more than 20 years after *Ford*, the Supreme Court again addressed the question of whether the execution of incompetent offenders violates the Eighth Amendment's prohibition against cruel and unusual punishment. Given the confusion that followed *Ford*, the Supreme Court's decision in *Panetti* was eagerly anticipated by scholars and professionals in law and the social sciences. Although *Panetti* addressed a few of the questions left open by *Ford*—and therefore offered a degree of additional guidance to states and forensic mental health professionals—it still left some important questions unanswered (see Appelbaum, 2007, for a discussion). In fact, *Panetti* raised some additional questions that did not exist in relation to the *Ford* decision, which added to the confusion surrounding competence for execution.

Scott Louis Panetti was convicted of capital murder and sentenced to death in a Texas state trial court after shooting his estranged wife's parents. Panetti had a well-documented history of mental illness and mental health treatment, including more than a dozen psychiatric hospitalizations over the previous 10 years. On September 8, 1992, Panetti woke up before dawn, shaved his head, dressed himself in combat fatigues, sawed off the barrel of a shotgun, broke into the home of his wife's parents, and shot them to death in the kitchen in front of his estranged wife and 3-year-old daughter. Panetti held his wife and daughter hostage for several hours before showering, putting on a suit, and surrendering himself to local law enforcement authorities.

Three years later, after a court determined Panetti was competent to stand trial and competent to waive counsel, Panetti was permitted to represent himself at trial. He pleaded not guilty by reason of insanity. During the trial, Panetti exhibited some odd behaviors, such as wearing a purple cowboy outfit, posing incomprehensible questions to witnesses, and attempting to subpoena John F. Kennedy, Jr., Anne Bancroft, Pope John Paul II, and Jesus Christ. At the conclusion of the trial, the jury rejected Panetti's insanity plea, convicted him of two counts of capital murder, and sentenced him to death.

Two months after his conviction and sentencing, a Texas appellate court determined that Panetti was not competent to waive counsel in his appeal. His attorney raised various objections related to trial procedures, but the appellate court denied relief and affirmed the conviction and death sentence. At that point, Panetti's attorney petitioned for a writ of habeas corpus in federal district court raising a variety of challenges related to the constitutionality of the criminal proceedings. The U.S. District Court for the Western District of Texas denied Panetti's petition for relief, and on appeal the U.S. Court of Appeals for the Fifth Circuit affirmed his death sentence. Panetti appeared to be out of legal recourse when the U.S. Supreme Court declined to hear the case.

Shortly before his scheduled execution, Panetti's lawyers alleged that Panetti was not competent to face execution because he reportedly did not understand the reasons and rationale for his sentence. Interestingly, this was the first time that Panetti or his lawyers raised any concerns regarding Panetti's competence to face execution. The state court denied relief without holding a hearing, but the federal district court subsequently stayed Panetti's execution and remanded the case to the state court. The state trial court appointed a psychiatrist and clinical psychologist to evaluate Panetti. Both mental health professionals acknowledged that Panetti displayed symptoms of a severe mental health disorder, but they nevertheless concluded that he was competent to be executed according to the standard set forth under Texas law. Most notably, Panetti was aware that he was being executed for killing his wife's parents. After reviewing the reports of the mental health professionals, the state court dismissed Panetti's claim without holding a hearing.

Panetti's attorneys petitioned for a writ of habeas corpus in federal district court to challenge how the Texas state court had handled his assertion of incompetence. The U.S. District Court for the Western District of Texas refused to defer to the state court's competency determination because the state court did not hold a competency hearing, which was required by *Ford* (see *Panetti v. Dretke*, 2004). After receiving testimony from four mental health experts for the defense and two mental health experts for the State of Texas, the district court concluded that although Panetti suffered from "some form of mental illness," he was aware that he was being sentenced to death for the two murders he committed (*Panetti*, 2004, p. 707). In September 2004, based on these findings, the district court held that Panetti was competent to face execution.

In May 2006, the U.S. Court of Appeals for the Fifth Circuit affirmed the district court's judgment (see *Panetti v. Dretke*). The Fifth Circuit's decision rested on its interpretation of the Supreme Court's decision in *Ford*, and it rejected Panetti's arguments that he needed to have more than a factual understanding of the reasons for his execution. The Fifth Circuit concluded that Justice Powell's articulated standard for competence to face execution did not require the offender to have a "rational understanding" of the reasons for his or her execution; rather, the offender only needed to be "aware" of the reasons for the execution, which the court interpreted as a factual awareness. Based on this interpretation of *Ford*, the Fifth Circuit concluded that the district court's findings were sufficient to establish that Panetti was competent to face execution. In particular, the Fifth Circuit cited the lower court's findings that Panetti was aware that he killed his in-laws, aware that he was scheduled to be executed, and aware that he was being executed because of the murders he committed. The Fifth Circuit determined that Panetti's factual awareness provided a sufficient basis for concluding that he was competent to face execution.

In January 2007, the U.S. Supreme Court granted certiorari to determine whether the Eighth Amendment permits the execution of an offender who has a factual awareness of the reasons for his or her execution, but who because of severe mental illness has a delusional belief regarding the reasons why the execution is taking place. According to Panetti's defense attorneys, Panetti possessed a factual understanding that he was sentenced to death for committing two murders, but he lacked a sufficient rational understanding because he held a delusional belief he was being executed for preaching the Gospel. Panetti's attorneys also argued that the Fifth Circuit's interpretation of *Ford* was unconstitutionally narrow and prevented the Eighth Amendment from offering any constitutional protection from execution for offenders suffering from severe forms of mental illness.

By contrast, the State of Texas argued that Panetti's erroneous belief about the basis for his impending execution did not negate the lower court's determination that he possessed a sufficient factual understanding of the reasons for his execution. Moreover, the State of Texas pointed out that Panetti perceived a logical connection between his criminal behavior and the pending punishment. The State of Texas argued that Panetti's demonstrated factual understanding provided a constitutionally sufficient basis pursuant to *Ford* for concluding that Panetti was competent to be executed. The defense and prosecution had made their arguments, and the stage was now set for the Supreme Court to weigh in on the matter and resolve the controversy that resulted from *Ford*.

The *Panetti* case attracted a great deal of attention from a variety of religious and secular organizations, several of which filed amicus curiae briefs in support of either the State of Texas or Panetti. In an amicus brief filed in support of the State of Texas, the Criminal Justice Legal Foundation (CJLF) argued that the "awareness" standard from *Ford* is constitutionally sufficient to determine whether an offender is competent to face execution (see Brief Amicus Curiae of the CJLF in Support of Respondent, 2007). The American Bar Association (ABA) filed an amicus brief on Panetti's behalf arguing that to be competent to face execution, an offender must not only be aware of the nature and purpose of the punishment, but must appreciate its personal application in the offender's own case (see Brief Amicus Curiae of the ABA, 2007).

In a jointly filed amicus brief filed in support of Panetti, the American Psychological Association (APA), the American Psychiatric Association, and the National Alliance on Mental Illness (NAMI) asserted that a criminal offender is not competent to face execution if the offender has a mental health disorder that significantly impairs his or her capacity to understand the nature and purpose of the punishment, or to appreciate the reason for its imposition in the offender's own case (see Brief for Amici Curiae APA, American Psychiatric Association, and NAMI in Support of Petitioner, 2007; see also Schopp, 2009a). In the brief, the amici recommended excluding from the death penalty all offenders who show evidence of severe and persistent mental illness before the offense or those offenders who have a severe mental health disorder at the time of the offense.

The position taken by the amici was the same position initially advanced by the Task Force on Mental Disability and the Death Penalty, which was a 24-member panel convened in April 2003 by the Individual Rights and Responsibilities Section of the ABA. The Task Force, which included representatives from the ABA, APA, American Psychiatric Association, and NAMI, was commissioned to address how courts should sentence criminal offenders with mental health problems in those jurisdictions that impose the death penalty. After several revisions, the APA's Council of Representatives officially approved the Task Force's recommendations in February 2006 (Task Force on Mental Disability and the Death Penalty, 2006).

The Supreme Court began by addressing some procedural questions (summarized in Slobogin, 2007) before turning its attention to Panetti's substantive claims. The Supreme Court first held that because the Texas state court failed to hold a hearing when determining whether Panetti was competent to face execution, which was required by *Ford*, the court's competency determination should not be given any judicial deference. Next, the Court concluded that the Fifth Circuit's interpretation of the standard articulated in *Ford* was too restrictive to provide mentally ill prisoners with the protections meant to be conferred by the Eighth Amendment. In *Panetti*, by a narrow five-to-four vote, the Court held that the factual understanding standard from *Ford* was not constitutionally sufficient, and it concluded that a prisoner must have both *(1)* a factual understanding of the offense, the impending execution, and the state's reason for ordering the execution; and *(2)* a rational understanding of the connection between the offense and the impending execution.[7]

The Supreme Court based its decision largely on the perception that an offender's mental illness would frustrate the retributive purpose of the death penalty. The Court noted that mental illness may limit an inmate's understanding and appreciation that he or she is being executed and why the execution is taking place. The Court also noted that the lower court should have examined the relationship between Panetti's delusions and his appreciation of his impending execution when determining whether he was competent to be executed. If an offender does not appreciate the reasons for the impending execution, then the death sentence is not fulfilling its objective of making the

---

[7]. After the Supreme Court issued its ruling in *Panetti*, the case was remanded to the federal district court for a determination of whether Panetti had both a factual and rational understanding of why the death penalty was being imposed on him. On remand in March 2008, the U.S. District Court for the Western District of Texas concluded that Panetti was competent to face execution. Specifically, the district court concluded that although Panetti was mentally ill, he had a factual and rational understanding of his offense, his impending execution, and the causal connection between the two (*Panetti v. Quarterman*, 2008).

offender and community see the seriousness of the offense, which has both specific and general deterrent effects.[8]

Although *Panetti* went one step beyond *Ford* and clarified that the U.S. Constitution requires that offenders have both a factual and rational understanding of the reasons for the execution for a court to determine they are competent to face execution, the Supreme Court somewhat inexplicably declined to define a specific standard for courts to follow (see Appelbaum, 2007; Blanks & Pinals, 2007). Writing for the majority, Justice Kennedy claimed that the factual record from the lower courts was not developed sufficiently to permit the Supreme Court to define a standard for competence to face execution. Moreover, the Supreme Court acknowledged that defining "rational understanding" could be challenging. As a result, lower courts will likely be forced to engage in some degree of interpretation when implementing the *Panetti* decision, much as they were forced to do after the Supreme Court decided *Ford*. Moreover, forensic mental health professionals will likely continue to grapple with the appropriate standard that should be used when conducting an evaluation to determine whether an offender is competent to face execution (see Chapter 6).

Conclusion

The Supreme Court has handed down several decisions that are relevant for forensic mental health professionals involved in capital cases. In this chapter, we focused on two issues: the relationship between mental retardation and eligibility for the death penalty, and competence for execution. Although the Supreme Court's intentions are clear in these cases, implementing the Supreme Court's intent has not been a straightforward process. Moreover, these rulings have created several ethical and clinical challenges for forensic mental health professionals who conduct *Atkins*-type evaluations and evaluations of competence for execution, which will be discussed in the next few chapters.

---

8. In a vigorous dissent, Justice Thomas (joined by Chief Justice Roberts and Justices Scalia and Alito) called the majority's decision a "half-baked holding that leaves the details of the insanity standard for the District Court to work out" (*Panetti v. Quarterman*, 2007, p. 978).

4

Ethical Considerations in Death Penalty Assessments

Ethical considerations are central to any forensic mental health assessment (FMHA; see Connell, 2008), but they take on increased salience in the context of death penalty cases. The consequences of poor practice or unethical conduct may be lethal and irreversible. Furthermore, subpar practice or unethical conduct may be more visible because death penalty cases are often highly publicized and intensely scrutinized. The procedures, results, and products (e.g., written reports, testimony) of evaluations conducted in death penalty contexts—and the forensic mental health professionals themselves—must be able to withstand intense scrutiny from opposing counsel and the court. This requires maintaining the highest standards of ethical practice.

This chapter addresses the ethical considerations that are most relevant across all types of FMHAs conducted in death penalty cases. In later chapters, we discuss the ethical considerations as they relate to specific types of assessments in capital cases.

Ethics Codes

Any discussion of professional ethics starts by examining the applicable ethics codes. We therefore examine the ethics codes that govern the behavior of psychologists and psychiatrists, who conduct the majority of FMHAs.[1] Following the review of the general ethics codes in psychiatry and psychology, we discuss the ethical guidelines specific to psychiatrists and psychologists in forensic practice.

Ethics Codes for Psychologists

The American Psychological Association developed and published their first ethics code, the *Ethical Standards of Psychologists*, in 1953. Since that original publication, the ethics code was revised and republished nine times, with the most recent iteration, *Ethical Principles of Psychologists and Code of Conduct* [hereinafter "Ethics Code"], published in 2002. The Ethics Code explicitly states that compliance with the code is required by members and student affiliates of the American Psychological Association, although not all provisions in the Ethics Code are enforceable. The Ethics Code is intended to be a broad guide for psychologists in fulfilling their roles as scientists, educators, supervisors, therapists, and evaluators. It also seeks to protect those with whom psychologists work, including students, clients, research participants, and the general public. Toward those ends, the Ethics Code attempts to guide psychologists through ethically challenging situations.

The Ethics Code includes a Preamble, General Principles, and Ethical Standards. The *Preamble* describes the goals of those in the field of psychology and introduces the remainder of the Ethics Code. The *General Principles* are aspirational principles that, although not enforceable, reflect the highest standards of the field. Violating a General Principle is typically not cause for sanctions because the code describes those principles as nonenforceable.[2] The *Ethical Standards* are the more specific and enforceable rules addressing competence, human relations while functioning in a professional role, privacy and confidentiality, public statements, record keeping and fees, education and training, research and publication, assessment, and therapy. Although there is a section of the Ethics Code that pertains to forensic activities, most of the

---

1. Licensed social workers also perform certain roles in FMHAs, including mitigation investigations at capital sentencing. But social workers do not perform evaluations, per se, with the same frequency as psychologists and psychiatrists.
2. Although the American Psychological Association describes the General Principles as nonenforceable, states are free to make these provisions enforceable. States may attach sanctions to these violations by enacting statutes in the state code, through judicial decisions imposing civil liability or criminal sanctions, or through regulations promulgated by the State Board of Psychology.

ethical guidance is not specific enough to address the unique ethical challenges that arise in forensic contexts.

Therefore, in 1991, the Committee on Ethical Guidelines for Forensic Psychologists published the *Specialty Guidelines for Forensic Psychologists* [hereinafter "Specialty Guidelines"] as a complement to the Ethics Code. The Specialty Guidelines was developed to provide ethical guidelines specific to the practice of forensic psychology in response to a perceived lack of such guidelines in the Ethics Code. The Specialty Guidelines specifies the conduct expected of psychologists who engage in the practice of forensic psychology, which it broadly defines as taking the role of "a psychological expert on explicitly psycholegal issues" (Committee on Ethical Guidelines for Forensic Psychologists, 1991, p. 657). Although this publication is designed for psychologists who regularly practice forensic psychology, it also provides some guidance for psychologists who occasionally engage in more limited forensic activities. The Specialty Guidelines consists of an introduction, a description of the Specialty Guidelines' purpose and scope, and several ethical guidelines categorized by topic. The Specialty Guidelines addresses forensic psychologists' responsibility for their conduct and services, competence, relationships with the parties they serve, confidentiality and privilege, methods and procedures in providing services, and public and professional communications. The Specialty Guidelines is currently undergoing extensive revision (see Committee on the Revision of the Ethical Guidelines for Forensic Psychologists, 2006).

Ethics Codes for Psychiatrists

The Principles of Medical Ethics (American Medical Association, 2001) applies to all physicians, including psychiatrists. However, due to the difficulty of applying some of the principles to the practice of psychiatrists, which differs from the practice of most other subspecialties in medicine, the American Psychiatric Association developed *The Principles of Medical Ethics with Annotations Especially Applicable to Psychiatry* [hereinafter "Annotated Principles"], with the most recent version published in 2009. The ethical principles delineated in the Annotated Principles are considered binding on all American psychiatrists (American Psychiatric Association, 2009). The principles define the physicians' and psychiatrists' responsibilities to patients, society, and other health care professionals. In addition, the Annotated Principles specifies, with a reasonable degree of precision, what is considered ethical or unethical behavior by psychiatrists (American Psychiatric Association, 2009). The Annotated Principles consists of the Principles of Medical Ethics, and it includes specific notes with each principle that make the medical principle more clearly applicable to psychiatrists' behavior. It starts with a Preamble, followed by several sections of ethical standards that include professionalism, the best interests of the patient, rights to privacy and confidentiality, continuing education, provision of patient care, and procedures for ethical complaints. The Annotated Principles also includes an addendum that specifies additional guidelines for the application of ethical rules to practice in organized settings, and a question-and-answer section regarding ethical complaint procedures (American Psychiatric Association, 2009).

The field of psychiatry has also developed guidelines for psychiatrists who engage in forensic practice. The most recent *Ethics Guidelines for the Practice of Forensic Psychiatry* [hereinafter "Ethics Guidelines"] was adopted in 2005 by the American Academy of Psychiatry and the Law. The subset of American psychiatrists who provide forensic services and identify as forensic psychiatrists are expected to abide by these principles. These guidelines are intended to supplement the American Psychiatric Association's more general Annotated Principles (American Academy of Psychiatry and the Law, 2005). Much like the Specialty Guidelines applicable to forensic psychologists, the Ethics Guidelines was developed to address the unique ethical concerns that result from practicing at the intersection of psychiatry and the law, and to help psychiatrists navigate differences in the procedures, vocabulary, and expectations of the two fields while maintaining the highest standards of psychiatric practice (American Academy of Psychiatry and the Law, 2005).

Similar to the Annotated Principles, the Ethics Guidelines consists of a stated ethical standard followed by individualized commentary on the applicability of the standard. However, unlike the more general guidelines found in the Annotated Principles, each ethical standard in the Ethics Guidelines is written specifically to guide forensic psychiatric practice. The Ethics Guidelines addresses confidentiality, consent to evaluation, honesty and objectivity, qualifications, and the process of handling ethical complaints (American Academy of Psychiatry and the Law, 2005).

Ethical Practice in Death Penalty Assessments

Forensic mental health professionals in capital cases face several unique challenges. Some of these challenges are clinical and relate to the evaluation procedures, interpretative strategies, and written report. Other challenges are ethical and stem from the ethical guidelines that govern the behavior of forensic mental health professionals (see Bersoff, 2008; Marczyk, Knauss, Kutinsky, DeMatteo, & Heilbrun, 2008, for an overview). Despite general ethical guidelines for mental health professionals, there are many ethical questions in capital cases for which the field offers no clear answer.

The debates about capital cases highlight the ethical dilemmas found at the intersection of mental health and the law (Stone, 2002). Mental health professionals who work within the legal system are obligated to respect the rights and well-being of the individuals they examine, and they must also serve the interests of greater society (Bloche, 1993; Schopp, 2009b; Stone, 2002). They must satisfy the needs of the legal system while adhering to the ethical standards of their professions (Ewing, 1987). In certain situations, balancing public and individual needs risks violating the ethical principles and rules that underlie forensic mental health practice (Ferris, 1997). Some mental health professionals claim that there is a duty to the accused, and any work that facilitates the execution of the defendant is a violation of the ethical obligation to avoid harm. Others state that the mental health professional's duty is only to the client, typically an attorney or the court, and not to the defendant (e.g., Kermani & Drob, 1988).

Over the past several decades, there has been much discussion about the ethics of mental health professionals' involvement in death penalty cases, given that these professions proscribe doing harm to those they serve. Many of these discussions address physicians because their specialized knowledge has the potential to assist in executions directly. The American Medical Association declared in its *Code of Medical Ethics* (2001) that physicians should not participate in executions. The *Code of Medical Ethics* defined participation in executions as directly causing the death of the condemned, assisting another in directly causing the condemned's death, or automatically causing an execution to occur (e.g., by monitoring an execution to determine the point at which the condemned dies) (American Medical Association, 2001; Council on Ethical and Judicial Affairs, 1993). The *Code of Medical Ethics* also barred physicians from rendering treatment to a prisoner found incompetent to be executed for the purpose of restoring competency, unless the prisoner's sentence has been commuted prior to the beginning of treatment (American Medical Association, 2001). Notably, the *Code of Medical Ethics* also defined professional conduct *not* considered unethical, which includes evaluation of a defendant's competence to stand trial in a capital case, testimony about aggravating or mitigating factors in capital sentencing hearings, certification of the death of a condemned prisoner after other nonmedical personnel have pronounced the prisoner dead, witnessing an execution in a nonprofessional capacity, and taking steps to alleviate the acute suffering of a condemned prisoner (American Medical Association, 2001).

Psychiatrists, psychologists, and other mental health professionals are not involved in the physical process of execution. So guidance intended for physicians in the context of capital punishment is not adequate for mental health professionals in the same context (see Bloche, 1993). To assist psychiatrists, the American Psychiatric Association (2008) issued a position statement outlining the American Medical Association's official stance in the context of capital cases. However, no authoritative body has developed ethical guidelines for psychologists that deal explicitly and specifically with professional behavior in capital cases. Compared with physicians, mental health professionals have less direct guidance regarding participation in death penalty litigation (Ferris, 1997). This lack of formal guidelines contributes to the active and longstanding debate about whether mental health professionals' involvement in death penalty cases is ethically appropriate. However, even if formal guidelines are developed, the debate about the ethics of being involved in death penalty cases will no doubt continue.

Views about mental health professionals' involvement in capital cases vary as much as views about capital punishment itself. At one end of the spectrum, some mental health professionals argue that participating in capital proceedings at any point is akin to active participation in an execution and is therefore incompatible with the ethical principle of doing no harm (see Bonnie, 1990; Kermani & Drob, 1988). Some argue that assisting in sentencing hearings in which the death penalty is a possibility is unethical, particularly if retained by the prosecution (Reid, 2001; see Diamond, 1992). Others have argued only against psychological testimony addressing future dangerousness during capital sentencing. Indeed, at an earlier stage in death penalty jurisprudence, professional guilds for both psychiatry and psychology attempted to prohibit this practice (see *Barefoot v. Estelle*, 1983). Arguing that mental health practitioners cannot predict future violence with sufficient accuracy, they maintained that testifying about a particular defendant's future behavior exceeds the boundaries of professional knowledge and competence and is consequently unethical (see, e.g., Ewing, 1987; see Chapter 8 for further discussion).

Other mental health professionals consider the risk that the defendant will be sentenced to death an extra-clinical harm that lies outside of the control of mental health professionals. They point out that harm is not certain because the defendant may be acquitted or sentenced to something less than death (Ferris, 1997; Schopp, 2009b). According to this view, the risk is similar to the risk of negative outcomes in other FMHAs; such risks may include a lengthy prison term following a standard presentence evaluation or the denial of worker's compensation following an independent medical examination (Ferris, 1997). As such, so the argument goes, forensic mental health professionals should not avoid conducting these evaluations any more than they would avoid other types of FMHAs.

At the furthest end of the spectrum (opposite those who oppose any participation in capital proceedings) are those who argue that conscientious, qualified participation by mental health professionals may enhance accuracy and justice in capital proceedings. They argue that mental health evidence can help the law generate just outcomes by assisting the court's efforts to uncover the truth and by providing information about the defendant's circumstances and mental health (Bonnie, 1990; Kermani & Drob, 1988; Reid, 2001). Participation in these cases may be necessary in the interest of fairness to all players in the case, including the defendant and the state (Reid, 2001). If mental health professionals opt out of testifying in capital cases, the court makes decisions about the defendant's future dangerousness and amenability to treatment without access to relevant mental health data. From this perspective, an absence of mental health evaluations would particularly hinder the defense's ability to build a compelling case for leniency, and it may in fact *increase* the number of defendants who are ultimately sentenced to death (Ferris, 1997; Kermani & Drob, 1988).

Some mental health practitioners propose that rather than issuing a profession-wide ban on participation in capital cases, mental health professionals who feel strongly against the death penalty should only testify on behalf of the defendant (Diamond, 1992; Weinstock, Leong, & Silva, 1992). Although this approach may have appeal for some forensic mental health professionals, such a compromise may be problematic because strong partisan beliefs would likely weaken professional objectivity and weaken the quality of services rendered (Bonnie, 1990).

The debate over mental health professionals' roles in capital proceedings becomes particularly intense when it comes to evaluating and restoring competence for execution. Some argue that this type of work is inconsistent with the ethical foundation of helping professions because a finding of competence removes the final hurdle to execution. There may also be a risk that involvement in the execution phase will link the mental health professions to the death penalty in the eyes of the public and decrease public trust in the mental health fields (as discussed by Bonnie, 1990). Some also express concern that conducting competence to face execution evaluations may lead the legal system to depend heavily on the opinions of expert witnesses, who would then possess and exercise the power to facilitate or delay executions as per their judgments and beliefs (e.g., Bonnie, 1990).

Other practitioners argue that evaluating or restoring competence to face execution remains ethically appropriate because mental health professionals are not directly involved with the execution and do not make the final decision of whether to execute a condemned prisoner. Schopp (2009b) argued that although having to choose between suffering from a serious mental illness and undergoing execution is a difficult decision, prisoners do not have a constitutionally protected interest in avoiding a legal sanction. Some assert that competence to face execution evaluations have the potential to help legal practitioners make informed choices (see Bonnie, 1990). Some also believe that treatment to restore competence works in the broader interest of justice. Perhaps banning professional involvement in the evaluation and treatment of condemned prisoners may ultimately deprive mentally ill death row prisoners of access to mental health care (Bloche, 1993; Bonnie, 1990). Deprivation of health care services is a legal issue as well as an ethical one, because prison inmates—even on death row—are constitutionally entitled to adequate treatment (Ewing, 1987).

Mental health professionals face other ethical challenges that stem from an unavoidable conflict between the legal system's demand for precision and the less precise nature of mental health evaluation and diagnosis. For example, as discussed in Chapter 3, the U.S. Supreme Court held that it is unconstitutional to execute a criminal offender who is mentally retarded (see *Atkins v. Virginia*, 2002). From a legal perspective, this is a bright-line rule that clearly delineates constitutional and unconstitutional punishments. But the application of the rule may be less straightforward from a clinical perspective. First, states have adopted several different definitions of mental retardation (see Chapter 5), with some definitions straying quite far from accepted clinical definitions of mental retardation. Second, diagnosing mental retardation, even if one uses clearly defined clinical criteria, may not be as simple as many judges and attorneys may presume it to be. Although a diagnosis of mental retardation may be clear in some cases, particularly those involving severe intellectual deficits, other cases may require "judgment calls" that tip the balance of case data toward or away from assigning a diagnosis.

The debate about the appropriateness of mental health professionals being involved in capital proceedings is unlikely to be resolved any time soon. However, one conclusion is quite clear: Those mental health professionals who opt to participate in capital proceedings have a responsibility to adhere to the highest standards of professionalism and follow best practices. Obviously, a first step is closely following the ethical guidelines applicable to their discipline. Next, we discuss the general ethical guidelines most relevant to forensic mental health professionals involved in capital cases.

Boundaries of Competence

A fundamental principle of ethical conduct requires mental health professionals to practice solely within the boundaries of their own professional competence. Standard 2.01(a) of the American Psychological Association's (2002) Ethics Code limits a psychologist's scope of practice "based on their education, training, supervised experience, consultation, study, or professional experience." Psychologists are ethically obligated to refer a case to a more competent professional when they lack sufficient education, training, and experience to provide the service themselves (see Ethics Code Standard 2.01(b), American Psychological Association, 2002). Applied to death penalty contexts, this principle appears to prohibit mental health professionals from becoming involved in capital cases unless they are adequately trained and have sufficient experience. Of course, what constitutes adequate education, training, and experience remains unspecified in the Ethics Code and is open to debate.

The Specialty Guidelines also requires practitioners to attend vigilantly to the boundaries of their own competence (Committee on Ethical Guidelines for Forensic Psychologists, 1991). As with the Ethics Code, the Specialty Guidelines suggests that practitioners recognize and practice within their professional experience and training (Committee on Ethical Guidelines for Forensic Psychologists, 1991, Section III). The Specialty Guidelines also holds that a forensic psychologist who plans to testify as an expert witness must be able to demonstrate the relevant factual bases (knowledge, skill, experience, training, and education) of his or her qualifications as an expert (Committee on Ethical Guidelines for Forensic Psychologists, 1991, Section III(b)). Forensic psychologists also have an obligation to understand the legal context in which they work. For example, forensic psychologists should *(1)* possess a fundamental and reasonable level of knowledge and understanding of the legal and professional standards that govern their participation as experts in legal proceedings; *(2)* understand the civil rights of parties in legal proceedings in which they participate; *(3)* manage their professional conduct in a manner that does not diminish or threaten those civil rights; and *(4)* maintain current knowledge of scientific, professional, and legal developments within their claimed areas of competence (Committee on Ethical Guidelines for Forensic Psychologists, 1991, Sections III(b, c, and d), Section IV(a)).

Although staying within one's scope of competence is important in all types of forensic cases, it arguably becomes more important in the context of capital cases. Two reasons merit discussion. First, the nature of capital cases raises the competence bar. Defendants may have limited opportunities to rectify the serious consequences of an inadequate or inappropriate FMHA. Also, courts may be unresponsive even when poor practice does come to their attention. For example, the Supreme Court appeared unswayed by an apparent professional consensus, including an amicus brief from the American Psychiatric Association, against an evaluator's inappropriate and unscientific violence risk assessment at capital sentencing in *Barefoot v. Estelle* (1983; see *United States v. Fields*, 2007, and the related Brief Amicus Curiae of the American Psychological Association, 2005).

Second, the challenges in many death penalty evaluations highlight the need for competent practice. Complex clinical presentations, co-occurring mental health disorders, chronic substance abuse, and the possibility of malingering complicate assessments in capital contexts. Some types of capital case evaluations (e.g., capital mitigation) require evaluators to have a greater *breadth* of knowledge than required for "typical" forensic evaluations. Other types of capital case evaluations require evaluators to have a greater *depth* of knowledge in a specialized type of assessment (e.g., diagnosing mental retardation, assessing risk of violence in prison). So mental health professionals considering involvement in a capital case must closely scrutinize their training and experience beforehand to ensure they are working within the bounds of their competence.

Do No Harm

An oft-cited principle of the Hippocratic Oath taken by physicians is to "do no harm." Similarly, General Principle A of the American Psychological Association's (2002) Ethics Code states: "Psychologists strive to benefit those with whom they work and take care to do no harm. In their professional actions, psychologists seek to safeguard the welfare and rights of those with whom they interact professionally. . ." (p. 1062). This and the other General Principles of the Ethics Code are aspirational in nature and meant to guide and inspire psychologists toward the highest ethical ideals of the profession. As such, the "do no harm" principle does not impose an enforceable obligation upon psychologists.

Two questions stem from this principle in death penalty contexts, and these questions illustrate the complexity underlying this seemingly straightforward principle. The first question is whether involvement in death penalty proceedings, by definition, runs afoul of the do-no-harm principle (see Ewing, 1987, for a discussion). As discussed, the principle of "do no harm" has been cited to oppose the involvement of psychologists in death penalty evaluations. However, the counterargument is that well-trained and experienced forensic mental health professionals who choose *not* to become involved in capital cases may inadvertently be causing more harm by allowing their less-qualified counterparts to perform the tasks or allowing proceedings to progress without the benefit of mental health expertise (Bonnie, 1990; Leong, Weinstock, Silva, & Eth, 1993). We cannot resolve the debate here, but we believe it is important for forensic mental health professionals to be aware of the primary arguments on both sides of the debate.

The second question relates to the procedures forensic mental health professionals use. To "do no harm," psychologists should use appropriate evaluation procedures, following best practices whenever possible (see Heilbrun, DeMatteo, Marczyk, & Goldstein, 2008). The obvious problem is that the field has not agreed upon minimum standards of practice, let alone best practices, for many evaluations conducted in death penalty cases (see Cunningham, 2010, for a recent, important exception).

Although these concepts are often used interchangeably, there are important distinctions between "standards of practice" and "standards of care," and both concepts are relevant in forensic contexts (see Heilbrun et al., 2008, for a discussion). First, standards of practice are defined as either the customary way of doing things (i.e., the "industry standard") or as best practices in a specific field (Caldwell & Seamone, 2007). In contrast, standards of care are defined as judicial, legislative, or administrative determinations that establish minimally acceptable standards of professional conduct in a particular context (see American Law Institute, Restatement (Second) of Torts § 282, 1965). Whereas standards of practice is a clinical/practice concept established internally by the field, standards of care is a legal concept established judicially, legislatively, or administratively.

Second, adherence to a standard of care should be viewed as mandatory because such standards carry the force of law, whereas adherence to standards of practice is viewed as an aspirational goal, but not necessarily mandatory. Standards of practice articulated by a professional committee or organization may identify "best practices," but adhering to such guidelines is often strongly suggested rather than mandatory. This distinction is directly relevant to the consequences (or lack of consequences) for violating either standards of care or standards of practice.

Finally, failing to adhere to a standard of care may constitute legal negligence and potentially expose one to civil liability, which typically consists of monetary fines (American Law Institute, Restatement (Second) of Torts § 282, 1965). By contrast, deviating from a standard of practice does not result in legal liability, although it may result in sanctions from the profession itself (e.g., monetary fines or expulsion from professional organizations), or sanctions imposed by an administrative law body, such as a state psychology licensure board (e.g., monetary fines, limitations on the ability to practice independently, or the loss of one's professional license).

Informed Consent

Informed consent refers to the requirement that mental health professionals make available to their patients or clients any and all information that might reasonably affect their decision to seek services from the mental health professional. This information must be delivered in a way that is reasonably understandable to the client, and it must be provided to the client prior to providing any services (American Psychological Association, 2002, Standard 3.10). These explanations must be provided even if the person being assessed is legally unable to give consent (American Psychological Association, 2002, Standard 3.10(b)). Informed consent disclosures must include an explanation of the nature and purpose of the assessment, fees, involvement of third parties, and limits of confidentiality, and there must be sufficient opportunity for the individual to ask questions and receive answers prior to receiving services (American Psychological Association, 2002, Standard 9.03(a)).

In forensic settings, the psychologist must also inform the individual being evaluated of the nature of the anticipated services, including whether the services are court ordered and the limits to confidentiality (American Psychological Association, 2002, Standard 3.10(c)). In addition, the Specialty Guidelines suggests that forensic psychologists are obligated to ensure that prospective examinees are informed of their legal rights with respect to the anticipated forensic service, the purposes of any evaluation, the nature of the procedures to be employed, the intended uses of any product of their services, and the party who has employed the forensic psychologist (Committee on Ethical Guidelines for Forensic Psychologists, 1991, Section IV(e)). Clinicians evaluating a defendant in a forensic context must make it clear that they are not providing therapy or advocating on the defendant's behalf, but instead acting as objective evaluators (see, e.g., Heilbrun, 2001). Of course, the specific informed consent requirements necessary in a particular case may vary along with the specifics of the case, and the forensic mental health professional is responsible for providing informed consent that is adequate to each case.

Authorization to conduct an FMHA comes from the court or an attorney for one of the parties, and the source of the authorization determines whether the evaluator should provide a notification of purpose to the defendant or seek informed consent from the defendant. If the evaluation is court ordered, there is no legal requirement that the defendant consent to the evaluation. In these contexts, the defendant is not free to decline the evaluation.[3] Although consent is not required, the evaluator should provide a notification of purpose that includes the evaluator's name and profession, who requested the evaluation, why the evaluation was requested, the purpose(s) for which the evaluation might be used, the distinction between a forensic assessment and clinical treatment, and the associated limits on confidentiality. If an evaluation is requested by the defense or prosecution, the defendant has a legal right to refuse to participate in the evaluation. A mental health professional retained by the prosecution should not attempt to evaluate the capital defendant without first obtaining the agreement of the defense counsel (and perhaps after

---

3. The defendant could, of course, simply decline to answer questions or meaningfully participate in the evaluation. Depending on the context, the defendant's refusal could have important legal consequences. For example, a defendant seeking to offer an affirmative defense based on his or her mental state at the time of offense may be prohibited from proffering that defense if he or she does not meaningfully participate in an evaluation requested by the prosecution. Similarly, some jurisdictions prevent the defense from entering mitigation testimony from a mental health professional if the defendant declined to participate in an evaluation with the prosecution-retained mental health professional.

seeking confirmation from the court that the defense was given proper notice and agreed to the evaluation). In two cases, the U.S. Supreme Court addressed the situation in which a prosecution-retained mental health expert evaluated capital defendants without the knowledge of defense counsel (see *Estelle v. Smith*, 1981; *Satterwhite v. Texas*, 1988). In both cases, the Supreme Court recognized the Sixth Amendment right of a criminal defendant charged with a capital crime to consult with an attorney before submitting to an FMHA addressing the defendant's risk of future danger.

In many forensic contexts, psychologists must clarify the limits of their professional role with the attorneys and other parties involved in the case. The prohibition against dual roles is relevant in this discussion. A psychologist may function as a nonobjective consultant or an impartial expert, but he or she should avoid filling both roles within the same case (Heilbrun, 2001). A psychologist-consultant may assist the defense or prosecution in developing a general trial strategy, but in doing so he or she loses the ability to act as an impartial and objective expert evaluator. It is also important to note that any psychologist called as an expert witness is ethically required to deliver the results of his or her evaluation in an objective and impartial manner, regardless of who is paying for the psychologist's services (Committee on Ethical Guidelines for Forensic Psychologists, 1991, Section VI). Psychologists should make these considerations known to the individual being evaluated, either through informed consent or notification of purpose.

Although informed consent always requires transparency and forethought on the part of a forensic mental health professional, Cunningham and Reidy (2001) identify three other considerations that heighten ethical expectations related to informed consent in death penalty cases. First, they assert that the greater magnitude of the potential harm involved in death penalty contexts calls for a greater need for the individual to be fully informed of the procedures, limits on confidentiality, and other key aspects related to the mental health professional's involvement in the case. Second, the complexity and sheer number of factors under assessment in death penalty cases can lead to an array of highly significant, but not readily apparent, repercussions. Finally, because of the wide range of possible issues relevant to a capital mitigation assessment, there is a correspondingly wide breadth of matters that could conceivably affect an individual's decision to agree to such an assessment. Thus, according to Cunningham and Reidy, the ethical requirement that mental health professionals provide thorough and understandable informed consent disclosures is never greater than in the death penalty context (see also Connell, 2003).

Cunningham (2006a) agrees that the "ultimate gravity of death penalty determinations," combined with the complexity of FMHAs conducted in capital cases, requires careful attention to informed consent procedures (p. 452).

However, Cunningham suggests that informed consent in capital cases should be discussed with defense counsel more than the defendant. Although the defendant should be informed of basic information, Cunningham conceptualizes this disclosure as more of a warning than a traditional informed consent. Defense counsel is responsible for protecting the defendant's constitutional rights, better equipped to do so, and better prepared to make strategic decisions in a given case. Thus, Cunningham argues defense counsel is the primary participant, and has primary authority, in informed consent procedures.

Although Cunningham (2006a) asserts that defense counsel should be the primary target for informed consent in capital cases, he notes that the informed consent obligations differ for prosecution-retained and defense-retained experts. In addition to providing basic information, such as who retained the expert and the purpose and parameters of the evaluation, prosecution-retained experts have an obligation to provide meaningful notice to the defense attorney (see *Estelle v. Smith*, 1982; *Satterwhite v. Texas*, 1988). Notice must be given with sufficient time to allow the defendant to consult with counsel prior to the evaluation. Cunningham identifies several "fundamental elements of notice" (p. 453) that should be provided to defense counsel, including the purpose of the evaluation and issues that will be addressed, the dates and duration of the evaluation, who will be present/observing, how the evaluation will be memorialized (e.g., notes, recorded), whether the defendant will be asked about the capital offense or any unadjudicated criminal conduct, the procedures that will be used, when and how the findings will be reported, and any pending complaints or adverse findings against the psychologist by professional associations or licensing boards. Cunningham suggests that informed consent provided to defense counsel by a defense-retained expert should encompass considerations related to the psychologist (e.g., experience in capital cases, expertise in case-specific areas of assessment, attitudes about capital punishment), logistics of the evaluation (e.g., fees, how the evaluation will be memorialized, whether a report will be issued), and the parameters and process of the evaluation.

Psychometric Considerations

The use of psychological tests and measures has become a core feature of almost every type of FMHA (see Archer, 2006; Lally, 2003). Among other benefits, nomothetically derived psychometric instruments *(1)* allow for systematic comparison of the individual being evaluated to similar individuals from the normative group, *(2)* often provide the evaluator with an indication of the individual's response style, *(3)* help ensure that the evaluator uses standardized assessment procedures, and *(4)* often increase an assessment's perceived legitimacy and usefulness in the eyes of the court and/or jury (see, e.g., Cunningham & Reidy, 2001; Heilbrun, 2001; Heilbrun, Marczyk, & DeMatteo, 2002; Melton, Petrila, Poythress, & Slobogin, 2007). However, using psychometric instruments in an FMHA, or any clinical context for that matter, requires considering several relevant ethical issues (see generally Messick, 1980).

A key consideration is the requirement that any instruments used in an evaluation demonstrate adequate psychometric properties. Key psychometric properties include reliability (meaning the instrument has limited measurement error and provides consistent results) and validity (meaning the instrument measures what it purports to measure). Generally speaking, both the Ethics Code and the Specialty Guidelines require that all assessment tools selected for an evaluation be anchored by empirical research that establishes their sufficiency and appropriateness for the specific question under consideration (American Psychological Association, 2002, Standards 9.01 and 9.02; Committee on Ethical Guidelines for Forensic Psychologists, 1991, Section VI). More specifically, the Ethics Code requires that assessment techniques be administered, adapted, scored, and interpreted in a manner and for purposes that are appropriate in light of the research or evidence regarding the usefulness and proper application of the techniques (Standard 9.02(a)).

Psychologists should also choose assessment instruments that have been psychometrically tested among the population from which the examinee comes. For example, if an instrument was developed primarily with members from one racial group or one gender, the validity of the instrument may be compromised if it is used with individuals who differ from the normative group. When validity or reliability has not been established, psychologists are obligated to describe the strengths and limitations of their test results and associated interpretation (American Psychological Association, 2002, Standard 9.02(b)). These requirements are part of a larger obligation that any psychological assessment, as a whole, be based upon accepted scientific and professional knowledge (American Psychological Association, 2002, Standard 2.04).

The use of psychological testing in death penalty contexts is well established (see Marczyk et al., 2008). In fact, courts seem to have an expectation that forensic mental health professionals will use at least some testing in their evaluations, and some evaluations could not be performed properly without psychological testing. For example, in the *Atkins* context, formal testing of intellectual functioning is essential. In some states, IQ testing is required as a matter of law before a diagnosis of mental retardation can be made in an *Atkins* context (see DeMatteo, Marczyk, & Pich, 2007; see also Chapter 5).

The ethical use of these instruments, however, requires a thorough understanding of each instrument's proper uses and limitations, along with close attention to accuracy and precision when describing and interpreting the results. This is particularly true in death penalty contexts, where life-or-death consequences may hinge on the results of a particular test. Unfortunately, most psychometric instruments were not developed/normed on an incarcerated population. Even instruments that were developed specifically for use in forensic contexts were not developed specifically for use with a death-eligible population. As such, the validity and generalizability of psychometric test results may be somewhat limited in death penalty cases. Even when using well-established measures, it is possible that the meaning and accuracy of particular test results may change over time. For example, there is a tendency for IQ scores to increase naturally over time, which is known as the Flynn effect (see, e.g., Flynn, 1998, 2006). This suggests that some IQ scores may slightly overestimate intellectual functioning (see Chapter 5).

Test results may be only loosely connected to many of the questions at the focus of capital sentencing hearings. Psychometric measures provide only inferential data on the types of adverse developmental factors that are often the focus of death penalty mitigation arguments. In addition, psychological tests may identify the presence of certain mental health disorders, such as antisocial personality disorder or psychopathy, that may be influential but unrelated to the legal issues at stake (see Cunningham & Reidy, 2001; Edens, Colwell, Desforges, & Fernandez, 2005; Edens, Desforges, Fernandez, & Palac, 2004).[4] Given these considerations, forensic mental health professionals must seek to uphold the highest scientific standards when selecting their psychometric instruments, interpreting test results, connecting those results to legally relevant questions, and describing the limitations of the results.

Cultural Fairness of Psychological Measures

Mental health professionals have an obligation to ensure that psychological instruments are culturally fair. This obligation is implied in the Ethics Code, which requires psychologists to respect the dignity and worth of all people, and the rights of individuals to privacy, confidentiality, and self-determination

---

4. Several courts have held that psychopathy evidence is inadmissible in capital proceedings because it is unduly prejudicial against the defendant. For example, in *United States v. Taylor* (2004), the U.S. District Court for the Northern District of Indiana excluded psychopathy evidence as part of a substance use evaluation in a capital sentencing proceeding, concluding that its relevance to the main issue before the court was questionable. In *United States v. Lee* (2000), the U.S. District Court for the Eastern District of Arkansas held that psychopathy evidence admitted during the penalty phase of a capital case improperly emphasized the defendant's potential for future dangerousness. Given concerns about the prejudicial impact of the psychopathy evidence, the court excluded the psychopathy evidence and ordered a new sentencing hearing.

(see General Principle E). Special attention is given to the importance of individual differences (e.g., age, gender, gender identity, race, ethnicity, culture, national origin, religion, sexual orientation, disability, language, and socioeconomic status) and the need to consider these factors when working with members of such groups. Finally, this aspirational guideline suggests that psychologists attempt to eliminate the effect of biases in their professional work, and not knowingly participate in or condone activities of others based upon such prejudices (General Principle E).

General Principle E is aspirational and, therefore, not enforceable. However, there are several ethical principles related to cultural fairness in the Ethics Code (in the Code of Conduct) that are indeed enforceable. Generally, the Ethics Code specifically prohibits discrimination based upon the individual differences listed earlier, and it notes that an understanding of these factors is an important aspect of training and effective psychological practice (Standards 2.01(b) & 3.01). The Ethics Code specifically addresses the importance of cultural fairness when it comes to assessment practices by emphasizing that the interpretation of test results should take into account the various test factors, test-taking abilities, and other characteristics of the person being assessed, such as situational, personal, linguistic, and cultural differences, that might affect the psychologists' judgments or reduce the accuracy of their interpretations (Standard 9.06). Moreover, psychologists must clearly indicate any culturally based interpretive limitations on their data (Standard 9.06).

A similar principle was included in the most recent revision of the Specialty Guidelines (Committee on the Revision of the Ethical Guidelines for Forensic Psychologists, 2006). These guidelines closely mirror the language and spirit of the Ethics Code by noting that forensic mental health professionals should be aware of and respect cultural, individual, and role differences, and they should consider these factors when working with members of such groups (Section 4.08). Similarly, the Revised Specialty Guidelines states that forensic psychologists take steps to correct or limit the effects of such cultural/ individual factors on their work, or decline participation if they are not able to account for these factors (Section 4.08).

The concern over cultural fairness, along with the ethical principles related to that concern, is particularly relevant in capital contexts. The Ethics Code requires that all assessment methods be appropriate to an individual's language preference and competence. The cultural fairness of the psychological instruments typically used in death penalty assessments has long been a controversial topic. In fact, Kane (2003) described concerns about cultural fairness as the most enduring controversy in the measurement of intelligence.

For individuals whose native language is English, well-validated and properly administered IQ tests and personality inventories probably provide a valid and reliable measure of intellectual and personality functioning. But there is evidence suggesting that these measures are less valid and reliable when used with nonnative English speakers, poorly educated individuals, or individuals raised in non-Western or third-world cultures (see, e.g., Kaufman, 1994). Although some IQ and personality measures have been translated into foreign languages, other factors may contribute to the cultural insensitivity of such measures even when foreign language differences are taken into account. Some IQ items are drawn from White, middle-class culture, and the forms of spoken English used by African American or Latino children may not correspond to the language used in IQ tests and personality measures (Kaufman, 1994). Measures of intellectual functioning may systematically underreport the IQ of African Americans and Latinos because of the cultural biases inherent in IQ test construction. As a result, individuals from these minority groups may be more likely than their White, English-speaking counterparts to be classified as mentally retarded using one of the standard measures of intellectual functioning. These same minority groups are also disproportionately more likely to be convicted of a capital crime and are therefore overrepresented in America's death row populations.

Forensic mental health professionals must use culturally sensitive measures and interpret test results in culturally appropriate ways. Indeed, several legally relevant diagnostic criteria sets contained in the *Diagnostic and Statistical Manual of Mental Disorders, 4th Edition, Text Revision* (*DSM-IV-TR*), including mental retardation and antisocial personality disorder, specifically demand that clinicians consider cultural and environmental factors when providing a diagnosis (American Psychiatric Association, 2000). Similarly, the American Association of Mental Retardation's definition of mental retardation requires consideration of cultural, community, and peer contexts (see American Association of Mental Retardation, 2002; Luckasson et al., 2002).

Malingering

Authorities emphasize the importance of assessing response style in any FMHA (see, e.g., Heilbrun, 1992, 2001; Heilbrun et al., 2002; McCann, 1998; Rogers, 1984, 1997), but the assessment of malingering is a top priority in capital case FMHAs (Brodsky & Galloway, 2003). The Ethics Code indirectly addresses the importance of assessing the accuracy of response style by noting that psychologists take into account the various test factors and characteristics of the person being assessed that might affect the psychologists' judgments or reduce the accuracy of their interpretations (see Standard 9.02(c)). Similarly, the Specialty Guidelines emphasizes the importance of third-party and other sources of information, noting that forensic mental health professionals should actively seek information that will allow them to differentially test plausible rival hypotheses (Section VI). Put simply, in a capital context, malingering is always a rival hypothesis that must be tested.

Unfortunately, detecting malingering is easier said than done. Distinguishing between simulated and real psychopathology (including mental retardation) is one of the most challenging tasks facing forensic mental health professionals. However, the use of multiple measures, specialized measures, and multiple sources of information provide valuable ways for forensic mental health professionals to identify genuine mental illness and mental retardation. Several commonly used psychological measures—include measures of response style the Minnesota Multiphasic Personality Inventory-II (Butcher, Dahlstrom, Graham, Tellegen, & Kaemmer, 1989), the Millon Clinical Multiaxial Inventory-III (Millon, 1994), and the Personality Assessment Inventory (Morey, 1991)—which may be helpful in assessing malingering (see Greene, 1997, for review). In addition, several instruments have been developed expressly to identify malingered psychopathology, such as the Structured Inventory of Reported Symptoms, which is now in its second edition (SIRS & SIRS-2; Rogers, 1992; Rogers, Sewell, & Gillard, 2010). Finally, the value of using multiple sources of information in terms of assessing response style has been addressed by numerous researchers and commentators (see, e.g., Coons, 1989; Goodman-Delahunty & Foote, 1995; Grisso, 1998; Heilbrun & Collins, 1995; Heilbrun et al., 2002). Seeking convergent validity across multiple sources of information, including self-report, official records, and third-party interviews, is essential to assess the validity of psychological symptoms.

Conclusion

We view the material presented in this chapter as foundational and broadly applicable to the many roles psychologists and other mental health professionals may play in death penalty cases. The ethical practice of mental health professionals in death penalty cases will no doubt continue to be debated. Perhaps the result of such debate will be improved guidance for forensic mental health professionals. In future chapters, we highlight ethical considerations related to specific types of FMHAs conducted in death penalty contexts.

5

Eligibility for the Death Penalty—Part 1: *Atkins*-Type Evaluations

Introduction

Throughout its long jurisprudence, the U.S. Supreme Court has occasionally decided that it is constitutionally inappropriate to impose the death penalty on specific offenders or even entire categories of offenders. For example, in *Roper v. Simmons* (2005), the Supreme Court categorically excluded from the death penalty offenders who were juveniles at the time of the offense.[1] Other offenders may be excluded from the death penalty based on their mental

---

1. Prior to *Roper*, the U.S. Supreme Court addressed the constitutionality of executing juvenile offenders in two cases. In *Thompson v. Oklahoma* (1988), the Court held that the Eighth Amendment prohibited executing offenders who were under 16 years old at the time of the offense. The Court found that a national consensus existed because all 18 states with a minimum age in their death penalty statutes required defendants to be at least 16 years old at the time of the offense for the death penalty to be imposed. One year later, in *Stanford v. Kentucky* (1989), the Court held that executing offenders who were 16 or 17 at the time of the offense did not violate the Eighth Amendment, because the majority of death penalty states permitted the death penalty for 16- or 17- year-old offenders. *Roper* effectively ended the debate, at least for now, regarding the execution of juvenile offenders by holding that it is unconstitutional to execute offenders who were under 18 years old at the time of the offense.

health functioning, either at the time of the offense, at the time of the trial and sentencing, or postconviction closer to the date of the scheduled execution.

Increasingly, forensic mental health professionals provide data to courts that are considering whether capital punishment is appropriate in a particular case. Some of these forensic mental health assessments (FMHAs) are conducted at the pretrial stage (front-end evaluations) to determine whether it is appropriate for the prosecution to seek the death penalty. Other evaluations are conducted to inform the sentencing phase, or even postsentencing closer to the date of the scheduled execution, to determine whether the offender should be executed (back-end evaluations). In this chapter, we discuss front-end evaluations for determining whether an offender is eligible for the death penalty. In light of a recent decision from the U.S. Supreme Court (*Atkins v. Virginia*, 2002), the discussion focuses on the assessment of mental retardation in capital contexts.[2]

Atkins v. Virginia

In 2002, the U.S. Supreme Court decided *Atkins v. Virginia*, which categorically prohibited imposing the death penalty on offenders who are mentally retarded. The Court concluded that executing offenders who are mentally retarded would violate the constitutional prohibition against cruel and unusual punishment found in the Eighth Amendment to the U.S. Constitution. The *Atkins* decision came after several states had already legislatively prohibited the execution of offenders with mental retardation, and it reversed the Supreme Court's position on the question of whether mental retardation rendered an offender ineligible for the death penalty. In its previous decision on this issue, *Penry v. Lynaugh* (1989), the Supreme Court concluded that a diagnosis of mental retardation should be considered as a mitigating factor during the sentencing phase of a capital case, but that it was not a per se violation of the Eighth Amendment to execute an offender who was mentally retarded. In the 13 years between *Penry* and *Atkins*, the legislative landscape had changed enough for the Supreme Court to conclude that a national consensus existed against executing offenders who are mentally retarded. Given estimates that

---

2. Nomenclature is slowly shifting from "mental retardation" to "intellectual disability," following the lead of the American Association on Intellectual and Developmental Disabilities (formerly the American Association of Mental Retardation). The U.S. Supreme Court used the term "mental retardation" in *Atkins*, and "Mental Retardation" remains the diagnostic term in the most recent edition of the American Psychiatric Association's *Diagnostic and Statistical Manual of Mental Disorders* (2000). So, we too use the term "mental retardation" in this text to remain consistent with these two sources that are so influential in capital proceedings. Our use of this term reflects an effort to maximize clarity for readers, rather than any political or philosophical position. We anticipate that the term "intellectual disability" will increasingly replace "mental retardation."

approximately 10% of death row inmates are mentally retarded (Ellis, 2002), the effects of the *Atkins* decision are significant.

As a direct result of *Atkins*, the diagnosis of mental retardation has taken on increased importance—literally, constitutional significance—in capital contexts. Forensic mental health professionals involved in capital cases must be familiar with *Atkins* and, perhaps more important, the manner in which *Atkins* has been implemented in their particular state. The bright-line rule established in *Atkins* makes it clear that a diagnosis of mental retardation excludes an offender from capital punishment. Although this constitutional prohibition is straightforward and seemingly clear, the implementation of the constitutional rule articulated in *Atkins* has presented a number of challenges for the states. States have handled these challenges in widely disparate ways, which means that *Atkins*-type evaluations can differ significantly both in content and procedure from state to state.

Implications of *Atkins* for Forensic Mental Health Professionals

The *Atkins* decision is noteworthy in two respects relevant for our purposes. First, *Atkins* is the only Supreme Court decision that categorically excludes an entire class of offenders from the death penalty based on a specific psychiatric diagnosis. To be clear, the Supreme Court has created other categorical exclusions from the death penalty. For example, in *Roper v. Simmons* (2005), the Supreme Court excluded from the death penalty offenders who were under age 18 years old at the time of the offense. Although *Roper* and *Atkins* are based on similar premises—that is, both juvenile offenders and offenders with mental retardation are less culpable than other offenders, and the death penalty is unlikely to serve retributive and deterrent purposes with either group—the *Atkins* decision stands alone in terms of a categorical exclusion based on a psychiatric diagnosis. In essence, *Atkins* turned a specific clinical diagnosis into the ultimate legal issue.

As a result, *Atkins* stands in stark contrast to previous decisions from the Supreme Court relating to the appropriateness of capital punishment for offenders with mental illness. The Supreme Court's decision in *Ford v. Wainwright* (1986) excluded incompetent offenders from being executed (as least while they remain incompetent), but a finding of incompetence to be executed could be premised on the effects of a variety of psychiatric disorders. Although some psychiatric disorders are certainly more likely to be associated with a finding of incompetence to be executed (e.g., psychotic disorders and other types of severe and persistent mental illness), the Supreme Court has never specified that a particular psychiatric diagnosis must inevitably lead to a finding of incompetence to be executed. Similarly, the Supreme

Court has never held that the presence of a particular mental health disorder must lead to a finding of incompetence to stand trial or a finding of not guilty by reason of insanity.

Perhaps more important, it has never been the psychiatric diagnosis itself that renders an offender incompetent to be executed, but rather the nexus between the offender's psychiatric symptoms and the required functional legal capacities. Mental health law rarely focuses solely on a mental health disorder, but rather the functional abilities related to the relevant legal question, and the strength of the causal connection between the mental health disorder and those functional abilities related to the legal question (Morse, 1978a, 1978b; see Greenspan & Switzky, 2003). For example, determinations of incompetence to stand trial and not guilty by reason of insanity are (or should be) based on the relationship between the offender's mental health symptoms and the relevant functional legal capacities, and not on the offender's specific psychiatric diagnosis (see Melton, Petrila, Poythress, & Slobogin, 2007). A diagnosis by itself may convey little meaningful information about the nature of the individual's legally relevant deficits. Moreover, Bonnie and Gustafson (2007) recently noted that although "clinical diagnoses often serve as a threshold requirement in legal 'tests' of incompetence, non-responsibility, and disability, they are almost never sufficient to establish that the legal criteria are satisfied" (p. 813). By excluding an entire category of people from the death penalty based exclusively on a psychiatric diagnosis, *Atkins* occupies a unique position in the Supreme Court's death penalty jurisprudence, and in mental health law generally.

The second noteworthy aspect of *Atkins* is that the Supreme Court did not define mental retardation and instead charged each state with developing appropriate definitions.[3] Some legal scholars have expressed concern that the Supreme Court's failure to define mental retardation will leave some intellectually impaired offenders at risk of not receiving the protections intended by the Eighth Amendment (e.g., Meany, 2004; Orpen, 2003). The only guidance provided by the Court in *Atkins* was that the definition of mental retardation must be consistent with "a national consensus" (*Atkins v. Virginia*, 2002, p. 317). In footnotes, the Supreme Court referenced the definitions of mental retardation established by the American Association of Mental Retardation

---

3. Interestingly, not all legal commentators agree that the *Atkins* decision left the states completely free to define mental retardation. For example, Bonnie and Gustafson (2007) argue that although "the Supreme Court in Atkins left it to the states to enforce the constitutional rule, Atkins did not leave each state free to define mental retardation" (p. 818). They go on to assert that the Supreme Court clearly intended for the states to embrace a "clinical definition of mental retardation, as a diagnosable disorder, rather than a legally constructed definition focusing on functional impairments and bearing on diminished culpability" (pp. 818–819).

(AAMR)[4] and the American Psychiatric Association (in the *Diagnostic and Statistical Manual of Mental Disorders*, or *DSM*), but it did not endorse either—or any—specific definition of mental retardation.[5]

The definitions of mental retardation established by the American Association on Intellectual and Developmental Disabilities (AAIDD, formerly the American Association on Mental Retardation, or AAMR) and American Psychiatric Association are widely used in clinical practice. The *DSM-IV-TR* (American Psychiatric Association, 2000, p. 49) defines mental retardation using the following tripartite criteria set:

(1) Significantly subaverage intellectual functioning: an IQ of approximately 70 or below on an individually administered IQ test . . .
(2) Concurrent deficits or impairments in present adaptive functioning . . . in at least two of the following areas: communication, self-care, home living, social/interpersonal skills, use of community resources, self-direction, functional academic skills, work, leisure, health, and safety.
(3) The onset is before age 18 years.

The definition of mental retardation provided in the *DSM-IV-TR* makes an allowance for the five-point standard error of measurement found in well-established IQ tests, such as the Wechsler instruments. Specifically, the *DSM-IV-TR* provides that individuals with Full Scale IQ scores between 70 and 75 can be diagnosed with mental retardation if they exhibit significant deficits in adaptive functioning and satisfy the criterion regarding age of onset (American Psychiatric Association, 2000).

The AAMR (now AAIDD) first defined mental retardation in 1908, and it has revised its definition on numerous occasions since that time (see Stevens & Price, 2006, for a description of the key diagnostic changes). AAIDD defines mental retardation using the same three elements as the *DSM-IV-TR*, but there are some differences between the *DSM* and AAIDD definitions of mental retardation. Specifically, AAIDD defines mental retardation as a disability characterized by significant limitations both in intellectual functioning and in adaptive behavior as expressed in conceptual, social, and practical adaptive skills (Luckasson et al., 2002). "Significant limitations in intellectual functioning" is defined as a Full Scale IQ score of up to 75 on a standardized intelligence test, which mirrors the *DSM* approach and takes into account the five-point standard error of measurement found in well-established IQ tests (Luckasson et al., 2002; see Fabian, 2005). "Adaptive behavior" is defined as

---

4. In 2006, several years after the Supreme Court decided *Atkins*, the AAMR changed its name to the American Association on Intellectual and Developmental Disabilities (AAIDD).

5. Some have suggested that the Supreme Court "tacitly signal[ed] its approval" of the AAMR and *DSM* definitions of mental retardation (see Weithorn, 2008, p. 1209).

the collection of conceptual, social, and practical skills necessary for day-to-day functioning in the home and community (Luckasson et al., 2002); this aspect of the definition differs a bit from the *DSM* definition. The AAIDD definition also states that impairment in adaptive functioning should be identified through standardized testing. Finally, according to the AAIDD, the disability must originate before age 18 years, which is consistent with the age of onset criterion in the *DSM-IV-TR*.

The *DSM-IV-TR* and AAIDD definitions of mental retardation are widely employed in clinical practice, but other organizations have also offered definitions of mental retardation. The American Psychological Association defines mental retardation in terms of significant limitations in general intellectual functioning, significant concurrent limitations in adaptive functioning, and age of onset prior to age 22 years (see Jacobson & Mulick, 1996). According to this definition, "significant limitations in general intellectual functioning" include IQ scores that are two or more standard deviations below the mean IQ score on a valid and comprehensive individual measure of intelligence. This corresponds with an IQ score of 70 or less on the Wechsler intelligence measures, but could extend slightly higher considering the standard error of measurement.

The results of recent research suggest that states have adopted widely varying definitions of mental retardation following *Atkins* (see DeMatteo, Marczyk, & Pich, 2007; Dowling, 2003; Duvall & Morris, 2006). DeMatteo et al. (2007) conducted a national survey of state legislation defining mental retardation after *Atkins*. They identified each state's statutory definition of mental retardation and grouped the definitions based on their degree of consistency with the clinical definitions of mental retardation put forth by the American Psychiatric Association (2000) in the *DSM-IV-TR*, the AAIDD (Luckasson et al., 2002), and the American Psychological Association (Jacobson & Mulick, 1996). The definitions of mental retardation used in each state are presented in Table 5.1. Although approximately one-quarter of the states defined mental retardation using accepted clinical standards—*DSM-IV-TR* (5 states), AAIDD (6 states), or APA (1 state)—the large majority of states either failed to mention all three elements common to accepted clinical definitions of mental retardation or failed to operationally define some or all of the diagnostic elements in any meaningful manner.

In their survey, DeMatteo et al. (2007) found that all of the states included subaverage intellectual functioning as a definitional element of mental retardation, but that the majority of states did not provide any cutoff either in terms of a specific IQ score or number of standard deviations below the normative mean IQ score. They also noted that some statutory definitions of mental retardation provided that a low IQ score, by itself and in the absence of other evidence of functional impairment, gave rise to a rebuttable presumption of mental retardation. For example, the statutory definitions of mental

Table 5.1 State Statutory Definitions of Mental Retardation

State	Statutory Provision	Relevant Language Defining Mental Retardation
Alabama	Ala. Code § 15-24-2 (LexisNexis 2010)	"A person with significant subaverage general intellectual functioning resulting in or associated with concurrent impairments in adaptive behavior and manifested during the developmental period, as measured by appropriate standardized testing instruments."
Alaska	Alaska Stat. § 12.47.130 (2010)	"[A] significantly below average general intellectual functioning that impairs a person's ability to adapt to or cope with the ordinary demands of life."
Arizona	Ariz. Rev. Stat. § 13-753 (2010)	"[A] condition based on a mental deficit that involves significantly subaverage general intellectual functioning, existing concurrently with significant impairment in adaptive behavior, where the onset of the foregoing conditions occurred before the defendant reached the age of eighteen." "Significant subaverage general intellectual functioning" is defined as "a full scale intelligence quotient of seventy or lower . . . [taking] into account the margin of error for the test administered."
Arkansas	Ark. Code Ann. § 5-4-618 (2010)	"[A] Significantly subaverage general intellectual functioning accompanied by significant deficits or impairments in adaptive functioning manifest in the developmental period, but no later than age eighteen (18); and (B) A deficit in adaptive behavior . . . There is a rebuttable presumption of mental retardation when a defendant has an intelligence quotient of sixty-five (65) or below."
California	Cal. Penal Code § 1376 (2009)	"[T]he condition of significantly subaverage general intellectual functioning existing concurrently with deficits in adaptive behavior and manifested before the age of 18."
Colorado	Colo. Rev. Stat. § 18-1.3-1101 (2009)	"[S]ignificantly subaverage general intellectual functioning existing concurrently with substantial deficits in adaptive behavior and manifested and documented during the developmental period."
Connecticut	Conn. Gen. Stat. § 1-1g (2010)	"[S]ignificantly subaverage general intellectual functioning existing concurrently with deficits in adaptive behavior and manifested during the developmental period." "General intellectual functioning" is defined as "results obtained by assessment with one or more of the individually administered general intelligence tests developed for that purpose and standardized on a significantly adequate population and administered by a person or persons formally trained in test administration." "Significantly subaverage" is defined as "an intelligence quotient more than two standard deviations below the mean for the test." "Adaptive behavior" is defined as "the effectiveness or degree with which an individual meets the standards of personal independence and social responsibility expected for the individual's age and cultural group." "Developmental period" is defined as "the period of time between birth and the eighteenth birthday."

Table 5.1 State Statutory Definitions of Mental Retardation (Continued)

State	Statutory Provision	Relevant Language Defining Mental Retardation
Delaware	Del. Code Ann. Tit. 11, § 4209 (2010)	"[S]ignificantly subaverage intellectual functioning that exists concurrently with substantial deficits in adaptive behavior and both the subaverage intellectual functioning and the deficits in adaptive behavior were manifested before the individual became 18 years of age." "Significantly subaverage intellectual functioning" is defined as "an intelligent [*sic*] quotient of 70 or below obtained by assessment with 1 or more of the standardized, individually administered general intelligence tests developed for the purpose of assessing intellectual functioning." "Adaptive behavior" is defined as "the effectiveness or degree to which the individual meets the standards of personal independence expected of the individual's age group, sociocultural background and community setting, as evidenced by significant limitations in not less than 2 of the following adaptive skill areas: communication, self-care, home living, social skills, use of community resources, self-direction, functional academic skills, work, leisure, health or safety."
Florida	Fla. Stat. Ann. § 921.137 (2010)	"[S]ignificantly subaverage general intellectual functioning existing concurrently with deficits in adaptive behavior and manifested during the period from conception to age 18." "Significantly subaverage general intellectual functioning" is defined as "performance that is two or more standard deviations from the mean score on a standardized intelligence test specified in the rules of the Agency for Persons with Disabilities." "Adaptive behavior" is defined as "the effectiveness or degree with which an individual meets the standards of personal independence and social responsibility expected of his or her age, cultural group, and community."
Georgia	Ga. Code Ann. § 17-7-131 (2010)	"[S]ignificantly subaverage general intellectual functioning resulting in or associated with impairments in adaptive behavior which manifested during the developmental period."
Hawaii	Haw. Rev. Stat. § 333F-1 (2010)	"[S]ignificantly subaverage general intellectual functioning resulting in or associated with concurrent moderate, severe, or profound impairments in adaptive behavior and manifested during the developmental period."
Idaho	Idaho Code Ann. § 19-2515A (2010)	"[S]ignificantly subaverage general intellectual functioning that is accompanied by significant limitations in adaptive functioning in at least two (2) of the following skill areas: communication, self-care, home living, social or interpersonal skills, use of community resources, self-direction, functional academic skills, work, leisure, health and safety. The onset of significant subaverage general intelligence functioning and significant limitations in adaptive functioning must occur before age eighteen (18) years." "Significantly subaverage general intellectual functioning" is defined as "an intelligence quotient of seventy (70) or below."

(*Continued*)

Table 5.1 State Statutory Definitions of Mental Retardation (Continued)

State	Statutory Provision	Relevant Language Defining Mental Retardation
Illinois	725 Ill. Comp. Stat. 5/114-15 (2010)	"Mental retardation must have manifested itself by the age of 18. . . . A low IQ must be accompanied by significant deficits in adaptive behavior in at least 2 of the following skill areas: communication, self-care, social or interpersonal skills, home living, self-direction, academics, health and safety, use of community resources, and work. An intelligence quotient (IQ) of 75 or below is presumptive evidence of mental retardation."
Indiana	Ind. Code Ann. § 35-36-9-2 (LexisNexis 2010)	"[A]n individual who, before becoming twenty-two (22) years of age, manifests: (1) significantly subaverage intellectual functioning; and (2) substantial impairment of adaptive behavior that is documented in a court ordered evaluative report."
Iowa	Iowa Code § 222.2 (2010)	"[C]hildren and adults who as a result of inadequately developed intelligence are significantly impaired in ability to learn or to adapt to the demands of society."
Kansas	Kan. Stat. Ann. § 21-4623 (2009); Kan. Stat. Ann. § 76-12b01 (2009)	"'[M]entally retarded' means having significantly subaverage general intellectual functioning, as defined by K.S.A. 76-12b01 and amendments thereto, to an extent which substantially impairs one's capacity to appreciate the criminality of one's conduct or to conform one's conduct to the requirements of law" (Kan. Stat. Ann. § 21-4623). "'Mental retardation' means significantly subaverage general intellectual functioning existing concurrently with deficits in adaptive behavior and manifested during the period from birth to age 18." "'Significantly subaverage general intellectual functioning' means performance which is two or more standard deviations from the mean score on a standardized intelligence test specified by the secretary." "'Adaptive behavior' means the effectiveness or degree with which an individual meets the standards of personal independence and social responsibility expected of that person's age, cultural group and community" (Kan. Stat. Ann. § 76-12b01).
Kentucky	Ky. Rev. Stat. Ann. § 532.130 (LexisNexis 2010)	"[S]ignificant subaverage intellectual functioning existing concurrently with substantial deficits in adaptive behavior and manifested during the developmental period . . ." "Significantly subaverage general intellectual functioning" is defined as "an intelligence quotient (I.Q.) of seventy (70) or below."
Louisiana	La. C. Cr. P. § 905.5.1 (2010)	"[A] disability characterized by significant limitations in both intellectual functioning and adaptive behavior as expressed in conceptual, social, and practical adaptive skills. The onset must occur before the age of eighteen years."
Maine	Me. Rev. Stat. Ann. tit. 34-B, § 5001 (2009)	"[A] condition of significantly subaverage intellectual functioning resulting in or associated with concurrent impairments in adaptive behavior and manifested during the developmental period."

Table 5.1 State Statutory Definitions of Mental Retardation (Continued)

State	Statutory Provision	Relevant Language Defining Mental Retardation
Maryland	Md. Code Ann., Criminal Law § 2-202 (2010)	"[S]ignificantly below average intellectual functioning, as shown by an intelligence quotient of 70 or below on an individually administered intelligence quotient test and an impairment in adaptive behavior; and . . . manifested before the age of 22 years."
Massachusetts	Mass. Gen. Laws ch. 123B, § 1 (LexisNexis 2010)	"[A] person who, as a result of inadequately developed or impaired intelligence . . . is substantially limited in his ability to learn or adapt, as judged by established standards available for the evaluation of a person's ability to function in the community."
Michigan	Mich. Comp. Laws Serv. § 330.1100b (LexisNexis 2010)	"[A] condition manifesting before the age of 18 years that is characterized by significantly subaverage intellectual functioning and related limitations in 2 or more adaptive skills . . ."
Minnesota	Minn. Stat. § 252A.02 (2009)	"'Developmentally disabled person' refers to any person age 18 or older who has been diagnosed as having significantly subaverage intellectual functioning existing concurrently with demonstrated deficits in adaptive behavior such as to require supervision and protection for the person's welfare or the public welfare."
Mississippi	Miss. Code Ann. § 41-21-61 (2010)	"[A]ny person (i) who has been diagnosed as having substantial limitations in present functioning, manifested significantly subaverage intellectual functioning, existing concurrently with related limitations in two or more of the following applicable adaptive skill areas: communication, self-care, home living, social skills, community use, self-direction, health and safety, functional academics, leisure and work, and (ii) whose recent conduct is a result of mental retardation and poses a substantial likelihood of physical harm to himself or others in that there has been (A) a recent attempt or threat to physically harm himself or others, or (B) a failure and inability to provide necessary food, clothing, shelter, safety, or medical care for himself."
Missouri	Mo. Rev. Stat. § 565.030 (2010)	"[A] condition involving substantial limitations in general functioning characterized by significantly subaverage intellectual functioning with continual extensive related deficits and limitations in two or more adaptive behaviors such as communication, self-care, home living, social skills, community use, self-direction, health and safety, functional academics, leisure and work, which conditions are manifested and documented before eighteen years of age."
Montana	*None available	*None available

(Continued)

Table 5.1 State Statutory Definitions of Mental Retardation (Continued)

State	Statutory Provision	Relevant Language Defining Mental Retardation
Nebraska	Neb. Rev. Stat. Ann. § 28-105.01 (LexisNexis 2010)	"[S]ignificantly subaverage general intellectual functioning existing concurrently with deficits in adaptive behavior. An intelligence quotient of seventy or below on a reliably administered intelligence quotient test shall be presumptive evidence of mental retardation."
Nevada	Nev. Rev. Stat. Ann. § 174.098 (LexisNexis 2010)	"[S]ignificant subaverage general intellectual functioning which exists concurrently with deficits in adaptive behavior and manifested during the developmental period."
New Hampshire	N.H. Rev. Stat. Ann. § 171-A:2 (LexisNexis 2010)	"[S]ignificantly subaverage general intellectual functioning existing concurrently with deficits in adaptive behavior, and manifested during the developmental period."
New Jersey	N.J. Rev. Stat. § 30:4-25.1 (2010)	"[S]ignificant subaverage general intellectual functioning existing concurrently with deficits in adaptive behavior which are manifested during the development period."
New Mexico	N.M. Stat. § 31-9-1.6 (2010)	"[S]ignificantly subaverage general intellectual functioning existing concurrently with deficits in adaptive behavior. An intelligence quotient of seventy or below on a reliably administered intelligence quotient test shall be presumptive evidence of mental retardation."
New York	N.Y. Criminal Procedure Law § 400.27 (Consol. 2010)	"[S]ignificantly subaverage general intellectual functioning existing concurrently with deficits in adaptive behavior which were manifested before the age of eighteen."
North Carolina	N.C. Gen. Stat. § 15A-2005 (2010)	"[S]ignificantly subaverage general intellectual functioning, existing concurrently with significant limitations in adaptive functioning, both of which were manifested before the age of 18." "Significantly subaverage general intellectual functioning" is defined as an "intelligence quotient of 70 or below." "Significant limitations in adaptive functioning" is defined as "significant limitations in two or more of the following adaptive skill areas: communication, self-care, home living, social skills, community use, self-direction, health and safety, functional academics, leisure skills, and work skills."
North Dakota	N.D. Cent. Code § 25-03.3-01 (2010)	"'Mental retardation' means mental retardation as defined in the 'Diagnostic and Statistical Manual of Mental Disorders,' American psychiatric association, fourth edition, 1994."
Ohio	Ohio Rev. Code Ann. § 5123.01 (LexisNexis 2010)	"[S]ignificantly subaverage general intellectual functioning existing concurrently with deficiencies in adaptive behavior, manifested during the developmental period."

Table 5.1 State Statutory Definitions of Mental Retardation (Continued)

State	Statutory Provision	Relevant Language Defining Mental Retardation
Oklahoma	Okla. Stat. tit. 10, § 1408 (2010)	"[S]ignificantly subaverage functioning, IQ of less than 70, manifested before age 18 and existing concurrently with related limitations in two or more of the following applicable adaptive skill areas: 1. Communication; 2. Self-care; 3. Home living; 4. Social skills; 5. Use of community resources; 6. Self-direction; 7. Health and safety; 8. Functional academics; 9. Leisure; and 10. Work."
Oregon	Or. Rev. Stat. § 427.005 (2010)	"[S]ignificantly subaverage general intellectual functioning existing concurrently with deficits in adaptive behavior and manifested during the developmental period. Persons of borderline intelligence may be considered to have mental retardation if there is also serious impairment of adaptive behavior. Definitions and classifications shall be consistent with the 'Manual on Terminology and Classification in Mental Retardation' of the American Association on Mental Deficiency. Mental retardation is synonymous with mental deficiency." "Significantly subaverage" is defined as "a score on a test of intellectual functioning that is two or more standard deviations below the mean for the test." "Significantly subaverage" has been interpreted to mean an IQ test score of below 67 on the Stanford-Binet test, or 69 on the Weschler Adult Intelligence Scale, and persons with IQs of up to 10 points above the significantly subaverage levels may be so impaired in their adaptive behavior that they can be classified as mentally retarded (*In re Grandy*, 623 P.2d 666 (Or. Ct. App. 1981)). "Adaptive behavior" is defined as the "effectiveness or degree with which an individual meets the standards of personal independence and social responsibility expected for age and cultural group." "Developmental period" is defined as "the period of time between birth and the 18th birthday."
Pennsylvania	50 Pa. Cons. Stat. § 4102 (2010)	"[S]ubaverage general intellectual functioning which originates during the developmental period and is associated with impairment of one or more of the following: (1) maturation, (2) learning and (3) social adjustment."
Rhode Island	R.I. Gen. Laws § 40.1-21-4.3 (2010)	"[A] person eighteen (18) years old or older and not under the jurisdiction of the department for children, youth, and families, with significant subaverage, general intellectual functioning two (2) standard deviations below the norm, existing concurrently with deficits in adaptive behavior and manifested during the developmental period."
South Carolina	S.C. Code Ann. § 16-3-20 (2009)	"[S]ignificantly subaverage general intellectual functioning existing concurrently with deficits in adaptive behavior and manifested during the developmental period."

(*Continued*)

Table 5.1 State Statutory Definitions of Mental Retardation (Continued)

State	Statutory Provision	Relevant Language Defining Mental Retardation
South Dakota	S.D. Codified Laws § 23A-27A-26.1 (2010); S.D. Codified Laws § 23A-27A-26.2 (2010)	"[S]ignificant subaverage general intellectual functioning existing concurrently with substantial related deficits in applicable adaptive skill areas. An intelligence quotient exceeding seventy on a reliable standardized measure of intelligence is presumptive evidence that the defendant does not have significant subaverage general intellectual functioning." Mental retardation must be "manifested and documented before the age of eighteen years."
Tennessee	Tenn. Code Ann. § 39-13-203 (2010)	"(1) Significantly subaverage general intellectual functioning as evidenced by a functional intelligence quotient (I.Q.) of seventy (70) or below; (2) Deficits in adaptive behavior; and (3) The mental retardation must have been manifested during the developmental period, or by eighteen (18) years of age."
Texas	Tex. Health & Safety Code § 591.003 (2010)	"[S]ignificantly subaverage general intellectual functioning that is concurrent with deficits in adaptive behavior and originates during the developmental period." "Subaverage general intellectual functioning" is defined as "measured intelligence on standardized psychometric instruments of two or more standard deviations below the age-group mean for the tests used." "Adaptive behavior" is defined as "the effectiveness with or degree to which a person meets the standards of personal independence and social responsibility expected of the person's age and cultural group." According to case law, capital defendants in Texas must meet AAMR criteria for mental retardation to be exempt from the death penalty (*Morris v. Dretke*, 379 F.3d 199 (5th Cir. 2004)).
Utah	Utah Code Ann. § 77-15a-102 (2010)	"(1) the defendant has significant subaverage general intellectual functioning that results in and exists concurrently with significant deficiencies in adaptive functioning that exist primarily in the areas of reasoning or impulse control, or in both of these areas; and (2) the subaverage general intellectual functioning and the significant deficiencies in adaptive functioning . . . are both manifested prior to age 22."
Vermont	Vt. Stat. Ann. tit. 18, § 7101 (2010)	"[S]ignificantly subaverage general intellectual functioning existing concurrently with deficits in adaptive behavior."
Virginia	Va. Code Ann. § 19.2-264.3:1.1 (2010)	"[A] disability, originating before the age of 18 years, characterized concurrently by (i) significantly subaverage intellectual functioning as demonstrated by performance on a standardized measure of intellectual functioning administered in conformity with accepted professional practice, that is at least two standard deviations below the mean and (ii) significant limitations in adaptive behavior as expressed in conceptual, social and practical adaptive skills."

Table 5.1 State Statutory Definitions of Mental Retardation (Continued)

State	Statutory Provision	Relevant Language Defining Mental Retardation
Washington	Wash. Rev. Code Ann. § 10.95.030 (LexisNexis 2010)	"(i) Significantly subaverage general intellectual functioning; (ii) existing concurrently with deficits in adaptive behavior; and (iii) both significantly subaverage general intellectual functioning and deficits in adaptive behavior were manifested during the developmental period." "Significantly subaverage general intellectual functioning" is defined as an "intelligence quotient seventy or below." "Adaptive behavior" is defined as "the effectiveness or degree with which individuals meet the standards of personal independence and social responsibility expected for his or her age." "Developmental period" is defined as "the period of time between conception and the eighteenth birthday."
Wisconsin	* None Available	*None available
West Virginia	W. Va. Code Ann. § 27-1-3 (LexisNexis 2010)	"[S]ignificantly subaverage intellectual functioning which manifests itself in a person during his developmental period and which is characterized by his inadequacy in adaptive behavior."
Wyoming	Wyo. Stat. Ann. § 25-5-102 (2010)	"[S]ignificantly subaverage general intellectual functioning with concurrent deficits in adaptive behavior manifested during the developmental period." "Adaptive behavior" is defined as "the collection of conceptual, social and practical skills that have been learned by people in order to function in their everyday lives."

retardation in four states (Arkansas, Nebraska, New Mexico, and Illinois) provided that an IQ score below a specific cutoff—65 in Arkansas, 70 in Nebraska and New Mexico, and 75 in Illinois—constituted presumptive evidence of mental retardation. This presumption of mental retardation applies regardless of age of onset and the presence (or absence) of concurrent deficits in adaptive behavior, which is not consistent with clinically accepted definitions of mental retardation.

DeMatteo et al. (2007) also documented ambiguities in how states defined deficits in adaptive functioning and age of onset. Although some states used well-defined criteria, such as deficits in two or more areas of adaptive functioning in specific areas, many states did not indicate how many deficits in adaptive functioning were required or in what areas of functioning. With respect to age of onset, some states specified particular age cutoffs (typically age 18 but occasionally age 22), while other states failed to identify a specific age cutoff and instead simply noted that the impairment must have been evident during the "developmental period." Interestingly, one state's definition of mental retardation included cognitive and volitional elements that are most typically found in definitions of insanity. The Kansas statute requires that the intellectual and adaptive deficits impair the defendant's capacity to appreciate the criminality of his or her conduct or to conform his or her conduct to the requirements of the law.

In addition to examining the definitions of mental retardation in all states, DeMatteo et al. (2007) took a closer look at the statutory definitions of mental retardation enacted in the states that permitted the death penalty. Of the 38 states that permitted the death penalty at the time of the legislative survey, fewer than one-third defined mental retardation using accepted clinical standards: four states used *DSM-IV-TR* criteria, six states used AAIDD criteria, and one state used APA criteria. The remaining death penalty states used definitions of mental retardation that were much less well defined, in which some or all of the definitional elements of the disorder were either not present in the statute or not operationalized in any meaningful way.

Finally, DeMatteo et al. (2007) noted that prior to *Atkins* 18 of the 38 states that permitted the death penalty had legislatively protected offenders who are mentally retarded. After *Atkins*, at least 10 other states legislatively excluded offenders who are mentally retarded (Duvall & Morris, 2006). However, as of 2006, several states that permitted the imposition of the death penalty had still not complied with *Atkins* by enacting legislation that prohibited the execution of offenders who are mentally retarded (Duvall & Morris, 2006).

The use of well-defined criteria for diagnosing mental retardation has benefits and drawbacks. Perhaps the primary benefit is that there is less ambiguity in applying the diagnostic criteria, which may make the diagnosis more reliable. In short, this means that the constitutional prohibition against executing offenders who are mentally retarded could be applied in a more straightforward, even-handed, and consistent manner.

The primary drawback of using a well-defined diagnostic criteria set is that it encourages an overemphasis on a particular IQ cutoff, and any cutoff score is inevitably somewhat arbitrary. Certainly, mental retardation has a widely varying and heterogeneous presentation, and it may make little sense from a clinical standpoint to provide a diagnosis of mental retardation when an individual has an IQ of 69, but not provide that diagnosis when an individual has an IQ of 71, assuming the presence of similar deficits in adaptive functioning. This might place too much emphasis on the IQ score, which is subject to measurement error and other sources of variability.

There has been considerable controversy regarding the use of a strict upper-boundary cutoff score, which Everington and Olley (2008) referred to as "the tyranny of the single score" (p. 6). Commentators have criticized the "artificiality" of using a single IQ score as the boundary for diagnosing mental retardation (e.g., Baroff, 2003). Furthermore, the use of 70 as a cutoff score for a diagnosis of mental retardation primarily reflects a statistical convention rather than a natural boundary (i.e., a score of 70 is two standard deviations below the normative mean of roughly 100), and it promotes the mistaken belief that a one-point difference in scores (i.e., 69 vs. 70) reflects a significant difference in cognitive capacities (Mossman, 2003). Clinicians continue to grapple with these issues, so it is not surprising that courts have similarly struggled when determining whether an offender meets diagnostic criteria for mental retardation. Because a diagnosis of mental retardation excludes an offender from the death penalty, while the absence of the diagnosis leaves one eligible for a death sentence, issues relating to IQ cutoffs and diagnostic criteria are more than academic.

If an individual's IQ score falls a little above 70, the diagnosis may ultimately be determined by the presence (or absence) of deficits in adaptive functioning.[6] In fact, some commentators have asserted that it is erroneous to rule out a diagnosis of mental retardation simply because someone has an IQ score slightly above 70 "without first considering context and deficits in adaptive functioning" (Blume, Johnson, & Seeds, 2009, p. 12). This approach is consistent with the definition of mental retardation in the *DSM-IV-TR*.

The primary concern expressed by both supporters and detractors of the *Atkins* decision centers on the inclusiveness of its effects. Regarding the potential for under-inclusiveness, the Supreme Court's decision not to define mental retardation may leave some intellectually impaired offenders at risk of missing the protections afforded by the Eighth Amendment. Given the differing definitions of mental retardation among the states, this concern may be materializing. An offender diagnosed as mentally retarded in one state may not qualify for that diagnosis in a neighboring state due to definitional differences.

There is also an over-inclusiveness concern related to *Atkins*, because there will inevitably be some criminal offenders with mental retardation who demonstrate the reasoning and culpability that appear sufficient to justify a death sentence. Bersoff (2002) argued that some individuals who are mentally retarded likely have the capacity to carry out murder with the requisite intent or foresight that is required to justify a death sentence. Despite vigorous opposition to the death penalty, Bersoff expressed concern about the effects of a blanket exclusion from capital punishment for all offenders who are mentally retarded. The core of this concern is that the class of people with mental retardation is

---

6. Some court decisions appear to reflect a rather heavy emphasis on deficits in adaptive functioning in the diagnosis of mental retardation, particularly in cases of mild mental retardation. For example, one case from an Oregon appellate court held that individuals with Full Scale IQ scores of up to 10 points above significantly subaverage levels (i.e., above 80) may be so impaired in their adaptive functioning that they can nevertheless be diagnosed as mentally retarded (see *In re Grandy*, 1981).

heterogeneous, with widely varying levels of maturity, judgment, reasoning ability, and, ultimately, legal culpability (Bersoff, 2002, 2004).

Procedural, Clinical, and Ethical Considerations Relevant to *Atkins*-type Evaluations

The *Atkins* decision required states to establish their own procedures for determining if an offender is mentally retarded, and states have adopted differing procedures regarding when these evaluations can be conducted, who can conduct them, and how they must be conducted (Orpen, 2003; Tobolowsky, 2003). Besides procedural considerations, there are clinical and ethical considerations related to the assessment and diagnosis of mental retardation in capital contexts, including the inherent variability and instability of IQ scores, the impact of repeated intelligence testing on the validity of test results, and the difficulties in assessing deficits in adaptive functioning among incarcerated populations. These topics have generated a good deal of attention in the wake of *Atkins* (see Duvall & Morris, 2006; Knauss & Kutinsky, 2004; Marczyk, Knauss, Kutinsky, DeMatteo, & Heilbrun, 2008; and Young, Boccaccini, Conroy, & Lawson, 2007, for discussions of these issues).[7] To be clear, some concerns related to IQ testing and IQ scores are relevant in a variety of clinical contexts, but they take on greater importance—perhaps even constitutional significance—in an *Atkins* context. Many states have statutorily defined mental retardation with reference to a specific IQ cutoff score, so factors that affect the stability of IQ scores warrant close attention.

Procedural Issues Relevant to *Atkins*-type Evaluations

The Supreme Court's decision in *Atkins* left several important questions unanswered. Besides not defining mental retardation, the *Atkins* decision failed to address a host of relevant procedural issues, such as when the question of mental retardation should be decided in capital cases (i.e., pretrial vs. guilt/innocence phase vs. sentencing phase vs. postsentencing), the burden of proof

---

7. There are other issues related to the diagnosis of mental retardation that have important implications but may be beyond the scope of this discussion. For example, the criteria for mental retardation have not been static over time, and the changing diagnostic criteria have implications with respect to the proportion of individuals who will be diagnosed as mentally retarded. Both the AAMR and *DSM* definitions of mental retardation have been revised fairly frequently (see Ceci, Sculllin, & Kanaya, 2003, for a discussion). The AAIDD has revised its definition nine times over the last century, and the effects have occasionally been notable. For example, a lowering of the IQ cutoff score in 1973 changed the proportion of the U.S. population classified as mentally retarded from roughly 16% to roughly 3% (Ceci et al., 2003). In the contexts of capital cases, such a boundary change could have dramatic consequences.

that must be met to entitle a claim of mental retardation to an evidentiary hearing,[8] the burden of proof that must be satisfied when establishing mental retardation, which party has the burden of proof, and whether the question of mental retardation must be decided by a judge or jury (see Blume et al., 2009; Tobolowsky, 2003). As a result, states have been forced to address these issues either through legislation or case law, and there are notable differences across states. These are *legally* relevant procedural questions and, therefore, perhaps less important for forensic mental health professionals.

However, several *clinically* relevant procedural questions also went unaddressed in *Atkins*. For example, questions relating to how these evaluations must be conducted, how many evaluations are permissible, and who can perform them were not addressed. Apparently, only a few states have statutorily specified the procedures for conducting these types of evaluations. Duvall and Morris (2006) noted that only Arizona, California, Nevada, and Virginia provided statutory guidance regarding *Atkins*-type evaluations. In Arizona, for example, the governing statute permits up to four assessments of intellectual functioning within 68 to 90 days. In contrast, in Nevada, only one evaluation is permitted by an expert selected by the prosecution. In capital cases in Virginia involving indigent defendants, the court appoints a mental health professional to determine whether the defendant is mentally retarded and to assist the defense in preparing its case with respect to the issue of mental retardation. Duvall and Morris (2006) concluded that in the remaining states, the procedures for determining whether a defendant is mentally retarded are determined by the presiding judge on an ad hoc basis.

Several states specified the types of intelligence tests that can or must be used in capital cases (Arizona, Connecticut, Florida, Illinois, North Carolina, South Dakota, and Virginia; see Duvall & Morris, 2006). For example, Connecticut requires the use of an individually administered intelligence test that was standardized on an adequate population. Florida and Virginia provide a list of appropriate tests from which evaluators can choose. Virginia statutory law also provides that the intelligence test must be appropriate for the defendant taking into account cultural, linguistic, sensory, motor, behavioral, and other individual factors.

Finally, several states provide guidance regarding who can conduct these types of evaluations. Only a few states expressly require licensure as a prerequisite for conducting these evaluations, and some states specify that these evaluations can be performed by psychologists or psychiatrists. Some states,

---

8. Several courts have begun to address the question of how much evidence is needed to trigger an *Atkins* hearing. For example, in *Rivera v. Quarterman* (2007), the U.S. Court of Appeals for the Fifth Circuit held that states must give a hearing to prisoners who show a prima facie case of mental retardation (see Widroff & Watson, 2008).

such as Florida, Illinois, and Kansas, require that the mental health professional have specific expertise in the area of mental retardation. Most of the states, however, do not provide any guidance regarding the qualifications that are needed to perform these types of evaluations.

This section was intended to highlight some of the more relevant procedural considerations related to *Atkins*-type evaluations. Because the guiding literature is sparse and laws can change, forensic mental health professionals should take steps to become familiar with the laws in their particular jurisdiction.

In addition to the procedural issues just described, *Atkins* raises many clinical issues for evaluators. Indeed, the Supreme Court embraced a clinical definition of mental retardation, rather than a legal definition that focuses on functional impairments and their bearing on diminished culpability (Bonnie & Gustafson, 2007). So clinical challenges in assessing mental retardation deserve close scrutiny. In particular, we address the variability of IQ scores (including measurement error and the Flynn effect), the problems with repeated intelligence testing, and the difficulty of assessing adaptive functioning among prisoners.

Variability of IQ Scores: Measurement Error and the Flynn Effect

Measurement Error

As with any measurement tool, measures of intelligence, including the well-established Wechsler and Stanford-Binet measures, exhibit some degree of measurement error. Measurement error in intelligence testing can result from a variety of sources, including the manner in which the test is administered, the environment in which the test is taken, the mood of the individual being evaluated, timing mistakes, and properties of the test instrument itself. "There is no finite score that can represent one's intellectual functioning with 100% accuracy. There is always measurement error" (Everington & Olley, 2008 p. 6). Any observed IQ score is an estimate of true intellectual functioning, combined with some degree of measurement error. Even though the Wechsler and Stanford-Binet measures are well-developed, well-validated measures with excellent psychometric properties, some degree of measurement error is inevitable.

The Wechsler and Stanford-Binet measures of intelligence have a measurement error of between three and five points for the Full Scale IQ score (e.g., Koocher, 2003), depending on the specific version of the test. The most recent edition of the Wechsler Adult Intelligence Test (WAIS) reports standard errors of measurement (SEM) to assist with the interpretation of IQ results. The SEM provides an estimate of the amount of error present in an individual's observed IQ test score. In more technical terms, the SEM is the standard deviation (SD) of the distribution of measurement error.[9] The WAIS-IV technical and interpretive manual reports SEMs for each subtest score and each composite score, and it provides SEMs for various age groups (Wechsler, 2008).

The SEM can then be used to calculate a confidence interval, which is a band of scores around the observed IQ score in which the individual's true IQ score is most likely to fall. When calculating the confidence interval, an evaluator can either use the overall average SEM or use the SEM for the specific age group in which the individual being evaluated falls. The overall average SEM for the WAIS-IV Full Scale IQ score is 2.16. The formula for calculating a 95% confidence interval is the following: *IQ score ± 1.96 x SEM* (using either 2.16 as the SEM value or the SEM value for the specific age group of the individual being evaluated). The formula for calculating a 90% confidence interval is *IQ score ± 1.65 x SEM* (again, using either 2.16 as the SEM value or the SEM value for the specific age group of the individual being evaluated).

Consider an example. If an individual obtains a Full Scale IQ score of 73, the evaluator can be 95% confident that the individual's true IQ score falls within the range of 68.8 to 77.2 (i.e., 73 ± 4.2), and 90% confident that the individual's true IQ score falls within the range of 69.4 to 76.6 (i.e., 73 ± 3.6). There is an inverse relationship between the size of the confidence interval and the range of scores included within the interval, so that a 95% confidence interval will have a larger range of scores than a 90% confidence interval. As the level of confidence increases, the precision of the estimate decreases. For a more precise estimate (arguably ideal for the court), confidence in that estimate must decrease.

Courts have not always appeared sensitive to measurement error. For example, in *Cherry v. Florida* (2007), the defendant obtained a Full Scale IQ score of 72, which the state argued disqualified him from the protection provided by *Atkins*. Relying on the concept of measurement error, Cherry argued that his true IQ should be viewed as falling somewhere between 67 and 77, which might exclude him from the death penalty. The Supreme Court of Florida cited the IQ cutoff score of 70 set by Florida statutory law, rejected Cherry's argument, and dismissed his *Atkins* claim without considering his adaptive functioning or the age of onset of his alleged impairments.

---

9. In this context, it is important to remember that the WAIS-IV has a mean score of 100 and SD of 15 points, while the fourth edition of the Stanford-Binet IQ test has a mean score of 100 and a SD of 16. If a variable is approximately normally distributed within a population, knowledge of the normal distribution curve allows one to estimate the proportion of the population that falls within each segment of the distribution. IQ scores on the Wechsler measures tend to be normally distributed, so we can reliably estimate that 68% of the population falls within ± 1 SD of the mean population IQ score of 100 (i.e., between 85 and 115), 95% of the population falls within ± 2 SDs of the mean population IQ score (i.e., between 70 and 130), and 99% of the population falls between ± 3 SDs of the mean population IQ score (i.e., between 55 and 145).

Arguments based on the SEM can cut both ways. The concept of SEM can be used by the defense to argue that the defendant's score may actually be lower than measured, but the SEM can also be used by the prosecution to argue the opposite. Bonnie and Gustafson (2007) make the point that courts may decide to consider SEM in only one direction based on a societal value. In other words, courts may decide to err on the side of concluding that a defendant may be within the range of mental retardation and therefore ineligible for the death penalty. For example, if a defendant's IQ is measured at 72, the court may recognize measurement error and acknowledge that the defendant's "true" IQ may be less than 70.

Clearly, measurement error must be considered in the context of capital cases, in which one or two IQ points can have significant consequences. Because eliminating measurement error is not an option, the safest course of action is reporting an IQ score in a proper context. Simply reporting an individual's IQ score, with no mention of measurement error or confidence intervals, is misleading and falls short of professional practice standards regarding test interpretation.

Practically, evaluators can most accurately convey an individual's true IQ score using a confidence interval. It is important to note that the audience for a forensic report or testimony is likely not familiar with the concept of measurement error or confidence intervals, and a responsible evaluator will take appropriate steps to avoid providing incomplete, misleading, or incomprehensible information. Evaluators should frankly explain that the observed IQ score is an *estimate* of the defendant's true intellectual functioning, and discuss measurement error and confidence intervals in nontechnical, jargon-free, lay language.

The Flynn Effect

Besides measurement error, a phenomenon often referred to as the "Flynn Effect" deserves attention in capital contexts. The Flynn effect refers to the gradual, systematic, and population-wide improvement in intelligence test performance over time that causes IQ test norms to become obsolete approximately every 20 years (Flynn, 1985, 1998, 2006). Most sources report an increase of about 0.3 IQ points per year between renorming periods (see, e.g., Flynn, 1984, 1999), although several more recent sources note that the factors underpinning the changes in average IQ scores over time are more complex than previously believed (see Hagan, Drogin, & Guilmette, 2008).[10]

---

10. In a recent article, Hagan et al. (2008) noted the differential impact of several factors on IQ scores, including gender, ethnicity, age, culture, level of industrial and technological development, type of cognitive task being measured (i.e., fluid vs. crystallized), and where the scores fall along the distribution curve. It is also important to note that some research has found that IQ scores actually *decrease* over time, a so-called reverse Flynn effect (e.g., Shayer, Ginsburg, & Coe, 2007). Moreover, some researchers speculate that the Flynn effect may be coming to an end in developed countries

(*Continued*)

The Wechsler and Stanford-Binet intelligence measures have a roughly uniform rate of increase in IQ scores between norming periods (Flynn, 2006).

The Flynn effect can affect the validity and stability of determinations of mental retardation. The result is that IQ tests need to be renormed so the scores more closely reflect the population's true level of intellectual functioning. Each time an IQ test is renormed there is a generalized lowering of IQ scores because the new norms recalibrate the average IQ to remove the increases that accumulated over the previous norming cycle. As a result, there is typically a well-documented appreciable increase in mental retardation diagnoses each time new IQ norms are published (Ceci et al., 2003; Flynn, 2006; Scullin, 2006). This spike in mental retardation diagnoses can have effects across a variety of contexts, including the number of children classified as mentally retarded and eligible for special education and other services.

Obviously, the Flynn effect could potentially play an integral role in capital contexts (Cunningham & Tasse, 2010; Duvall & Morris, 2006; Young et al., 2007). It may be particularly prominent—and problematic—in situations in which a defendant was administered an intelligence test at the end of a renorming period. If, for example, an offender is tested 10 years after a particular IQ test was normed, the Flynn effect suggests that the offender's measured IQ will be artificially increased by 3 points (i.e., 0.3 points per year). Needless to say, this could make a dramatic difference for an offender functioning near the IQ cutoff for mental retardation.

The Flynn effect may also be evident when an offender is tested twice, but at different phases in the renorming period (see Kanaya, Scullin, & Ceci, 2003, for a discussion of this issue). For example, it is possible for an offender's IQ to be measured at slightly above 70 at one administration (which, all things being equal, would make the offender eligible for the death penalty), but then measured at slightly below 70 at the time of the FMHA when new IQ norms came into use (which yield slightly lower IQ scores, on average). This slight shift in scores could have considerable constitutional implications. The reverse scenario is, of course, also possible (i.e., the offender scores below 70 at one administration and then above 70 on subsequent testing with a renormed version of the IQ test). Of course, IQ scores can vary across repeated testing for many reasons, with the Flynn effect being only one such reason.

Given evidence for the Flynn effect, and the constitutional implications it could have, the key question is how forensic mental health professionals should deal with the Flynn effect in the context of FMHA in a capital case.

(*Continued*)
(e.g., Teasdale & Owen, 2005, 2008). On balance, however, the Flynn effect appears to be a generally accepted phenomenon, supported by a sufficient body of empirical research (e.g., Kanaya, Scullin, & Ceci, 2003), that warrants attention in capital cases.

Unfortunately, no state statute specifically addresses the Flynn effect (Duvall & Morris, 2006), and the field has not identified a universally agreed upon method of dealing with the Flynn effect in evaluations (forensic or clinical).

Although there is a lack of statutory guidance related to the Flynn effect, several courts have advanced positions. For example, in *Walker v. True* (2005), the U.S. Court of Appeals for the Fourth Circuit held that a Virginia trial court erred by not considering the defendant's proffered evidence regarding the Flynn effect. In *People v. Superior Court* (2005), a state appeals court in California concluded that the Flynn effect must be considered when determining a defendant's IQ score. Other courts at both the state and federal levels have advanced similar positions.[11]

Other courts have been skeptical or downright dismissive of the Flynn effect. For example, in *Neal v. Texas* (2008), a Texas appellate court dismissed the Flynn effect as an "unexamined scientific concept that does not provide a reliable basis for concluding that an appellant has significant sub-average general intellectual functioning" (p. 273). In *Ledford v. Head* (2008), the U.S. District Court for the Northern District of Georgia concluded that the Flynn effect is a "theory that is used solely for the purpose of lowering IQ scores in a death penalty context" (p. 20). In *Green v. Johnson* (2008), the U.S. Court of Appeals for the Fourth Circuit noted that neither *Atkins* nor Virginia law required consideration of the Flynn effect.

There have been several proposals for addressing the Flynn effect in practice. In fact, Flynn himself has advanced several views on this point over the past 20 years (see Hagan et al., 2008, for a discussion). In a 2006 article, Flynn argued that adjusting IQ scores to counter the Flynn effect was acceptable because it would create no greater harm than failing to adjust the scores. He provided a formula for adjusting IQ scores to counter the Flynn effect (2006)[12] and explained that the formula converts IQ scores to a common metric—that is, the norms current at the time the test was administered. The basic score adjustment involves reducing an individual's IQ score by 0.3 points per year since the test was most recently normed. Based on the results of their empirical research, Kanaya et al. (2003) argued that score adjustments were appropriate, and Greenspan (2006) asserted that adjusting IQ scores is essential.

---

11. Flynn (2006) provides a list of several additional U.S. courts, both state and federal, that have discussed the relevance of the Flynn effect.

12. In a 2006 article, Flynn offered the following formula for adjusting IQ scores: *Intelligence: Test Score* $- (I \times 0.3) = IQ$, where "I" is the time interval between when the measure was normed and when the measure was administered. Flynn stated that this formula should be used with IQ scores derived from a Wechsler or Stanford-Binet instrument that is administered in the United States. Moreover, Flynn suggested that an extra 2.34 points should be deducted from an individual's IQ score if the IQ score is derived using the WAIS-III, because the WAIS-III was shown to give inflated IQ scores even in the year in which it was normed.

Perhaps most influentially, guidelines from the AAIDD argue that clinicians should consider score inflation when reviewing historical testing, and consider adjustments for the Flynn effect when interpreting IQ scores from tests with outdated norms (Schalock et al., 2010).

On the other hand, adjusting IQ scores is not common clinical practice (Moore, 2006). The issue of adjusting scores to counter the Flynn effect is simply not addressed in the administration and technical manuals for the Wechsler IQ tests (Wechsler, 1997, 2003, 2008). But a more recent report from Harcourt Assessments, the test publisher, "does not endorse the recommendation made by Flynn to adjust WAIS-III scores" (Weiss, undated, p. 1). Generally, sources of authority caution against score adjustments because they are "subject to misinterpretation" (American Educational Research Association, American Psychological Association, and National Council on Measurement in Education, 1999, p. 58).

Recently, Hagan and colleagues (2008) surveyed program directors from APA-approved clinical, counseling, and school psychology doctoral programs, and school psychologists who achieved Diplomate status in school psychology by the American Board of Professional Psychology. Among the program directors, only a minority reported they were very familiar with the Flynn effect. However, most of the Diplomates in School Psychology reported being moderately familiar or very familiar with the Flynn effect. Hagan et al. (2008) also systematically reviewed IQ technical manuals, contemporary textbooks on intelligence testing, federally regulated IQ testing protocols, and various sources of legal and ethical guidance. Based on their review, they concluded that adjusting IQ scores downward to counter the Flynn effect is not consistent with prevailing standards of psychological practice. Further, they concluded that "recalculating an individual's actual data likely violates standardization procedures and departs from training practices, prevailing canons, guidelines, most treatises, and test instructional manuals" (Hagan et al., 2008, p. 623).

Hagan and colleagues are almost certainly correct when they observe that reporting Flynn-adjusted IQ scores is not common in routine clinical practice, even in fields such as school psychology that emphasize IQ testing. Of course, common practice in routine assessment, and best practices in capital-case FMHA, are not necessarily the same. Cunningham and Tasse (2010) criticized the conclusions from Hagan et al. (2008) and emphasized that experts in capital proceedings are bound to apply the most rigorous and recent science (i.e., data regarding the Flynn effect); they are not bound to procedures common in routine (non-forensic) clinical practice. Whereas some consider Flynn adjustment skeptically, because these seem to occur primarily in the unusual context of capital proceedings (e.g., *Ledford v. Head*, 2008), Cunningham and Tasse (2010) suggest that Flynn adjustments should be common in capital proceedings precisely because this unusual context requires the most scientifically advanced approach available.

So how common are Flynn effect considerations among forensic evaluators who perform capital cases? Young and colleagues (2007) surveyed 20 evaluators (13 psychologists and 7 psychiatrists) who had conducted at least one evaluation of mental retardation in a capital case in Texas to gauge their awareness of the Flynn effect and how they address it in evaluations. The sample was small, but it comprised the small subset of evaluators who actually perform assessments of mental retardation in Texas capital cases. The researchers found that 69.2% of the psychologists, but none of the psychiatrists, were aware of the Flynn effect by name. They also found that 76.9% of the psychologists and 28.6% of the psychiatrists were aware of the concept of the Flynn effect, if not the name itself. But nearly one-quarter of the psychologists (23.1%) and nearly three-quarters of the psychiatrists (71.4%) were unaware of the Flynn effect, either by concept or by name. The qualitative survey results did not quantify practices, but it appeared that at least a few evaluators considered the Flynn effect as one possible explanation for varied IQ scores across a defendant's historical records. But responses suggested that few evaluators consistently adjusted scores to account for the Flynn effect. The researchers concluded that there is "no agreed-upon method for how diagnostic conclusions should be influenced" by the Flynn effect (Young et al., 2007, p. 176).

The question, therefore, remains: How should forensic mental health professionals deal with the Flynn effect when conducting evaluations in capital contexts? An obvious first step is for evaluators to become educated regarding the Flynn effect, and the range of perspectives on the issue. Most capital litigators are increasingly attuned to the issue and forensic evaluators should expect to field questions on the topic. More importantly, to the extent that credible research documents any phenomena that could influence the interpretation of IQ scores, evaluators are ethically obligated to consider that data objectively.

Should forensic evaluators report IQ scores adjusted to account for the Flynn effect? Recently, Cunningham proposed that best practice in *Atkins*-type evaluations should indeed give substantial attention to the Flynn effect (Cunningham & Tasse, 2010; Macvaugh & Cunningham, 2009). In a recent publication, Macvaugh and Cunninghman (2009) stated:

> Though recognizing that there is debate among forensic practitioners regarding this issue, as well as inconsistent court rulings, we believe that the Flynn Effect has gained sufficient scientific acceptance that this factor should be described in *Atkins* assessments and that Flynn-corrected IQ scores (including the 2.34 adjustment of WAIS-III Full Scale IQ score) should be reported in addition to observed scores. This recommendation is consistent with providing the court with scientific perspectives that will facilitate a more complete understanding of IQ scores. (p. 151).

This recommendation is new, and likely to be met with some resistance. We expect the debate to continue, and there will be no consensus that this reflects "best practice" in the near future. But, for practical reasons, we suspect that evaluators should probably be prepared to perform each one of the steps Cunningham and colleagues propose. Capital litigators are rapidly becoming—if not already—familiar with the Flynn effect and arguments for and against adjusting IQ scores to counter the Flynn effect. Any evaluator who considers IQ scores during capital proceedings—whether retained by the prosecution or defense, and regardless of individual perspective on Flynn effect issues—should probably expect some questions about the Flynn effect. These questions might address when IQ scores (whether from historical records or more recent testing) were obtained, when the IQ test was renormed, and how the observed IQ score might change under the most commonly proposed adjustments to counter the Flynn effect.

We suggest, however, that an emphasis on "adjusting scores" might be misplaced. Evaluators who discuss IQ scores in capital proceedings should contextualize these scores with an understandable discussion of intelligence estimates and measurement error, and should report scores with respect to the SEM and related confidence intervals (see earlier in this chapter; see Macvaugh & Cunningham, 2009). Although evaluators should make every effort to minimize measurement error in tests they administer, they should openly acknowledge the potential sources of error and test scores obtained through collateral sources. By all accounts, one potential source of error—or factor influencing the validity of an IQ estimate—is the Flynn effect.

When conducting testing in an evaluation, the evaluator's goal is not to assign and defend the "exact score." Rather, the evaluator's goal is to administer testing in a way that minimizes error and yields the most valid estimate, and then convey these findings in a way that helps the court understand their strengths and limitations, including some inevitable measurement error. When addressing a historical IQ score in collateral records, the goal is not to attack or defend a particular IQ score (or adjusted score). Rather, the goal is to report the score with enough contextual information to help the court understand its value and limitations. This will include the usual discussion of SEM, confidence intervals, and sources of measurement error (including any measurement error that may have been attributable to idiosyncratic administration or scoring). One source of measurement error is the Flynn effect. None of this contextualizing test results is an effort to dismiss the value of formal IQ testing; indeed, contextualizing test results might require emphasizing the rigor and standardization of formal IQ testing, and the ways these are superior to unstructured clinical judgment. But even the most rigorous measures include some measurement error. Evaluators should comfortably discuss this error because their goal is to provide adequate, and adequately clear, information to inform the court's decision, not simply to provide an IQ score.

Test-Retest Effects

It is not uncommon for a criminal offender to undergo multiple evaluations as different mental health experts conduct assessments at different points in the legal proceedings. Unfortunately, however, some of the more commonly used intelligence measures are subject to practice effects, whereby repeated administrations of the same IQ test within a certain period of time can lead to artificial elevations in the Full Scale IQ score (Wechsler, 1997).

The practice effect is strongest over short test-retest intervals. For example, the technical manual for the third edition of the Wechsler Adult Intelligence Scale reports that the mean Full Scale IQ score for adults between the ages of 30 and 54 years increases by approximately 5 points if those adults retake the same test within 12 weeks of the first test administration (Wechsler, 1997). Therefore, a Full Scale WAIS-III IQ score of 75 could be masking a more accurate IQ score of 70 if practice effects are present. To prevent such an artificial inflation of IQ scores, the WAIS-III administration manual recommends that a minimum interval of 1 to 2 years lapse between test administrations (Wechsler, 1997).

The Administration and Scoring Manual for the newest version of the WAIS—the WAIS-IV—acknowledges research has not yet identified the shortest test-retest time interval that will not result in practice effects on the WAIS-IV (Wechsler, 2008). However, based on research with previous editions of the WAIS, the manual recommends an interval of 1 to 2 years between test administrations (Wechsler, 2008). Of note, practice effects appear to have a differential impact on the Performance and Verbal subtests of the WAIS. Based on research with previous editions of the Wechsler measures, researchers have found that the practice effects on the Performance subtests are minimized after an interval of 1 to 2 years, while practice effects on the Verbal subtests are minimized after 1 year (Canivez & Watkins, 1998; Wechsler, 2008).

Test-retest effects may be particularly troublesome in *Atkins*-type evaluations, because it is likely that an offender in a capital context would undergo more than one mental health evaluation. In most states, the defense expert assesses the offender first and, if the expert finds a score suggestive/indicative of mental retardation, the prosecution expert would conduct a second evaluation of the offender, which could produce an artificially inflated IQ score due to practice effects. The danger of test-retest effects is obviously dependent on the length of time between evaluations and the types of testing measures being used, but it is something that all forensic mental health evaluators should keep in mind if the offender has undergone previous evaluations.

The *Atkins* case itself illustrates what may be the unfortunate consequences of test-retest effects. Atkins obtained a Full Scale WAIS-III IQ score of 59 when initially tested in 1998, and this IQ score was the impetus for his constitutionally based arguments against imposing the death penalty on offenders who are mentally retarded. After the Supreme Court decided *Atkins v. Virginia* in 2002, Atkins underwent additional FMHAs in 2004 and 2005. He obtained a Full Scale IQ score of 74 in 2004 and a Full Scale IQ score of 76 in 2005. As a result of these test scores, a Virginia jury found that he did not meet the diagnostic criteria for mental retardation, at least in terms of his intellectual functioning, and was therefore eligible for the death penalty. As of this writing, Atkins remains on death row.

Intelligence Testing: Recommendations for Evaluators

First, use a standardized measure of intelligence. We mention this obvious starting point because most state statutes relevant to *Atkins*-type evaluations do not require any specific measure of intelligence, although a few states explicitly require the use of standardized measures or refer to a list of state-approved measures. Standardized measures of intelligence include normative data and meet evidentiary laws regarding the admissibility of expert evidence in either a *Daubert* or *Frye* jurisdiction (see *Daubert v. Merrell Dow Pharmaceuticals, Inc.*, 1993; *Frye v. United States*, 1923).

Second, acknowledge the inherent variability of IQ scores. Even the most well-established measures of intellectual functioning, including the Wechsler and Stanford-Binet measures, have some degree of measurement error that introduces variability into the results. Therefore, as previously noted, a defendant's observed IQ score is as an *estimate* of intellectual functioning. Reporting a confidence interval that contains the defendant's "true" IQ score acknowledges measurement error and helps place the results of intelligence testing in a proper perspective. Evaluators must also be cognizant of the Flynn effect as a source of error and be knowledgeable about current research related to the specific intelligence test they are using.

Finally, if an offender's intellectual functioning has been previously evaluated, evaluators must be aware of test-retest effects. Evaluators should determine whether an offender's intellectual functioning has previously been tested and, if so, how recently. If the most recent previous test administration occurred within the time frame proscribed by the administration manual, then a different measure of intellectual functioning should be used or (if possible) the assessment must be delayed until the appropriate time interval has lapsed.

If not properly understood and acknowledged, measurement error, the Flynn effect, and test-retest effects have the potential to distort the outcome of intelligence testing and lead to erroneous legal conclusions regarding whether the offender is mentally retarded. Given the Supreme Court's bright-line rule established in *Atkins*, a minor distortion in IQ scores can have dramatic and constitutionally significant consequences.

Adaptive Functioning

The *DSM-IV-TR*, AAIDD, and APA definitions of mental retardation all indicate that mental retardation should not be diagnosed based solely on the presence of subaverage intellectual functioning (AAMR, 2002; American Psychiatric Association, 2000; Jacobson & Mulick, 1996).[13] Rather, individuals must also exhibit significant concurrent deficits in adaptive functioning (and, of course, satisfy the definitional element relating to age of onset). In fact, in the context of capital cases, questions surrounding an offender's level of adaptive functioning and how the offender's level of adaptive functioning was measured often generate more controversy than questions regarding the offender's intellectual functioning (see, e.g., Everington & Keyes, 1999; Fabian, 2006; Scullin, 2008; Stevens & Price, 2006). This may be particularly true when a defendant has mild mental retardation (see Collins, 2009). For defendants with IQ scores measured near 70, courts appear to place more emphasis on deficits in adaptive functioning when determining whether the defendant satisfies the criteria for mental retardation. For defendants with moderate, severe, or profound mental retardation, the deficits in adaptive functioning will typically be much more obvious and require less scrutiny by experts or the court (see Bonnie & Gustafson, 2007).

Adaptive functioning generally refers to how well individuals cope with the routine demands of life and whether they are able to achieve a level of independence that is consistent with their age and social or cultural background. As previously noted, there are slight differences in the definition and description of adaptive deficits among the diagnostic criteria sets from the *DSM*, AAIDD, and APA, although the general content appears consistent. Deficits in adaptive functioning can be assessed through a variety of means, including interviewing and testing the defendant, firsthand observation, record reviews (e.g., educational, employment, medical, mental health), and collateral interviews with family members or caregivers. Best-practice standards suggest that

---

13. However, as previously noted, several states have enacted statutes that conflict with traditional clinical thinking regarding mental retardation. The statutory definitions of mental retardation in several states provide that an IQ score below a specific cutoff—ranging from 65 in Arkansas to 75 in Illinois—constitutes *presumptive* evidence of mental retardation, regardless of age of onset and the presence (or absence) of concurrent significant deficits in adaptive behavior. These statutes are clearly at odds with currently accepted clinical thinking regarding the nature of mental retardation, which recognizes the tripartite criteria for mental retardation, though perhaps they are most cautious from a legal perspective.

evaluators should not rely on one assessment strategy to assess for deficits in adaptive functioning, but instead should gather information from multiple sources (see Brodsky & Galloway, 2003; Harrison & Raineri, 2008).

Despite the availability of some standardized measures, it is important to acknowledge that assessing adaptive functioning often involves some degree of clinical judgment by the evaluator, and there may be some latitude in determining the point at which deficits in adaptive functioning become so clinically significant as to support a diagnosis of mental retardation. The assessment of adaptive functioning is open to interpretation. For example, in *Williams v. Quarterman* (2008), the U.S. Court of Appeals for the Fifth Circuit supported the lower court's determination that the defendant's adaptive deficits, which included a failure to secure housing, live independently, cook, hold a job, maintain basic hygiene, dress appropriately, and follow rules in a game, were better explained by antisocial personality than mental retardation.

Assessing deficits in adaptive functioning can be particularly challenging with prisoners. The structure provided by the correctional facility can reduce or alter the environmental demands placed upon inmates (Everington & Keyes, 1999), which changes the conceptualization of what is "adaptive," normative, or even possible behavior. This issue was raised by defense attorneys in *Atkins* who argued that the structured environment of the prison gave the erroneous impression that Atkins was functioning at a higher level than he actually was. As noted by Young et al. (2007), some death row inmates and capital case defendants have spent much of their lives in a correctional environment, which means they may not have had the opportunity to display deficits in various areas of adaptive functioning.

Assessing deficits in adaptive functioning among prisoners is also complicated because no measures of adaptive functioning have been designed or normed for use with prisoners (see Brodksy & Galloway, 2003; Tasse, 2009; Taylor, 1997). As such, the AAIDD's recommendation to establish the existence of deficits in adaptive functioning through the use of standardized measures places forensic mental health professionals in a difficult position. Everington and Keyes (1999) argued that standardized measures of adaptive functioning should not be used with individuals who have been incarcerated for lengthy periods of time because "the individual has had no opportunity to perform in most of the skill domains" measured by these instruments (p. 33). It is also important to note that some behaviors considered maladaptive in a community setting may not be considered maladaptive in a correctional setting, because the expectations and normative behavior differ considerably between these two diverse environments (see, e.g., Fabian, 2006).

In their survey of 20 experienced capital evaluators, Young and colleagues (2007) found that the evaluators reported using similar procedures for assessing deficits in adaptive functioning among both death row inmates and pretrial defendants. But the evaluators were somewhat more likely to report using standardized measures of adaptive functioning for pretrial defendants than for death row inmates. Although the small, Texas-specific sample may limit the generalizability of their findings, their results suggest that standardized measures of adaptive functioning may not be the accepted standard of practice in Texas capital cases that address mental retardation. It is possible that the forensic evaluators chose not to use existing measures of adaptive functioning due to concerns related to the validity of those instruments when used with incarcerated individuals.

Other researchers have also examined standards of practice among forensic mental health professionals in terms of assessing deficits in adaptive functioning among offender populations. In her survey of more than 300 psychologists, Salekin (2004) found that approximately 80% believed that *(1)* existing measures of adaptive functioning were appropriate for use in correctional contexts, *(2)* using standardized measures of adaptive functioning is necessary, and *(3)* obtaining a detailed history of the defendant is required. Salekin (2004) also found that roughly 50% of the psychologists believed that using correctional personnel as raters was beneficial. Based on these results, she concluded that no standard of practice exists for assessing deficits in adaptive functioning in capital cases.

Should information relating to the offender's criminal behavior and behavior while incarcerated be used as evidence of adaptive functioning? Not surprisingly, there are cogent arguments on both sides of the debate (see Blume et al., 2009, and Young et al., 2007, for interesting discussions). On the one hand, criminal behavior, like many other types of behavior, can often reflect adaptive or maladaptive functioning. This arguably makes criminal behavior a valuable source of information regarding adaptive functioning. Furthermore, there is often more substantial documentation of the offender's criminal behavior (e.g., arrest reports, statements by the defendant, victim statements, witness statements) than collateral documentation of routine, day-to-day functioning.

On the other hand, some argue that evidence relating to criminal behavior may be unreliable due to some offenders' tendencies to be highly suggestible and/or highly acquiescent to law enforcement personnel (Greenspan & Switzky, 2003). Also, addressing criminal behavior raises concerns about bias, and simple criminal behaviors may be perceived as planned or calculated (in ways that imply greater adaptive behavior than is truly present). Furthermore, there are no accepted approaches for how to use information related to criminal behavior and behavior while incarcerated in making clinical determinations about an offender's level of adaptive functioning. Some commentators also argue that focusing on an inmate's behavior while incarcerated inevitably inflates inmate's strengths because prison provides too much structure for deficits to become noticable (Blume et al., 2009), while other commentators assert that conducting adaptive behavior assessments in prison makes it impossible to assess adaptive behavior in a manner that is consistent with AAIDD standards (Everington & Olley, 2008). Finally, using correctional personnel as sources of information has generated a good deal of controversy (e.g., Stevens & Price, 2006).

Several courts have weighed in on this debate and concluded that criminal behavior is relevant when determining whether the offender meets criteria for mental retardation (see Fabian, 2006). In *Clemons v. Alabama* (2005), an Alabama appellate court noted that Alabama courts have traditionally looked at various factors when determining whether an offender is mentally retarded and, therefore, ineligible for the death penalty, including extensive involvement in criminal activity and the offender's post-conviction behavior. In *Ex parte Briseno* (2004), a Texas appellate court concluded that various factors relating to criminal behavior should be examined when determining whether an offender is mentally retarded, including whether the offender formulated plans and carried them through, whether the offender's criminal behavior showed evidence of leadership skills, and whether the commission of the offense required forethought and planning. Finally, in *Ex parte Smith* (2003), the Supreme Court of Alabama considered various crime-related behaviors when determining whether the defendant had deficits in adaptive functioning. Other courts have most certainly addressed the issue, and some legislatures have apparently debated whether to include reference to the offender's criminal behavior when defining mental retardation (Blume et al., 2009).

Some courts have also expressly considered an inmate's behavior while incarcerated when determining the validity of a claim of mental retardation. In *Clark v. Quarterman* (2006), for example, the U.S. Court of Appeals for the Fifth Circuit relied on an inmate's prison behavior as the basis for dismissing his claim of mental retardation. Among other factors, the Fifth Circuit focused on the inmate's complaints regarding his broken television set (which referenced a coaxial cable and jack), his handwritten diet plan, handwritten puzzles, and complaints about delays in approving his request for a legal visit with another inmate. Undoubtedly, other courts have scrutinized an inmate's behavior while incarcerated when evaluating the inmate's claim of being mentally retarded.

Finally, some courts have used a defendant's behavior during the trial to find an absence of deficits in adaptive functioning and ultimately dismiss the defendant's claim of being mentally retarded. In *Rodriguez v. Florida* (2005), the Supreme Court of Florida concluded that the defendant, who obtained a Full Scale IQ score of 64, was not mentally retarded based on his awareness and understanding of what was happening in the courtroom during his trial. In this case, the court dismissed the results of standardized testing and relied almost exclusively on the defendant's behavior at trial when determining whether the defendant was mentally retarded.

Recommendations for Evaluators Relevant to the Assessment of Adaptive Functioning

Given the ambiguities and complexities involved in the assessment of adaptive deficits in capital cases, it is important that forensic mental health professionals carefully choose their assessment strategies. As a starting point, if one chooses to use standard measures of adaptive functioning, it is important to use measures that have solid psychometric properties, with the explicit recognition that these measures were not developed for use with offender populations. The AAMR (2002) lists several measures of adaptive functioning that meet the organization's standards, including the Vineland Adaptive Behavior Scales, the AAMR Adaptive Behavior Scales, the Scales of Independent Behavior (from the Woodcock-Johnson), the Comprehensive Test of Adaptive Behavior-Revised, and the Adaptive Behavior Assessment System. Another assessment approach would be to avoid using measures of adaptive functioning, and instead assess an offender's adaptive functioning through other means, including self-report, behavioral observation, and information from third-party and collateral sources. The third-party informants should be individuals who have had significant and recent contact with the defendant in a variety of settings. This will help ensure the relevancy of the information in terms of actual deficits in adaptive functioning in multiple domains. Finally, as with all assessment approaches, it is important for evaluators to openly acknowledge the limitations of their chosen assessment strategy, and present a balanced interpretation of the results (see generally Heilbrun, 2001; Heilbrun, Grisso, & Goldstein, 2009).

Age of Onset

The requirement that the disorder first manifest during the developmental period is found in the *DSM-IV-TR*, AAIDD, and APA diagnostic criteria sets for mental retardation, although these sources do not take a uniform approach to this criterion. Both the *DSM-IV-TR* and AAIDD require that the disorder manifest before age 18 years, while the APA criterion for age of onset specifies a cutoff of age 22 years. The age cutoff was intended to distinguish between mental retardation and other deficits in intellectual functioning, such as those typically attributable to brain injuries and dementia.

The age cutoff has interesting implications when applied in an *Atkins* context. If strictly interpreted, offenders who exhibit the same deficits in intellectual functioning and adaptive behavior as individuals who are mentally retarded will not receive the Eighth Amendment protection afforded by *Atkins* if their deficits did not exist prior to age 18 (or 22). Presumably, a capital offender with adaptive deficits and an IQ of 59 due to brain damage following a motorcycle accident or stroke can be executed as long as the brain damage and deficits occurred *after* the developmental period ended. It is difficult to justify this seemingly contradictory outcome based on some of the Supreme Court's language in *Atkins*.

The basis of the *Atkins* decision is that offenders who are mentally retarded are less culpable due to their deficits. The age at which impairments first appear does not seem relevant to the legal question of whether the defendant is legally culpable for his or her acts. Therefore, it arguably makes little sense to execute similarly impaired offenders who happened to have the misfortune of suffering organic brain damage after the developmental period has ended. Although other procedural protections, such as incompetence to stand trial or incompetence to face execution, could provide protection from execution for these individuals, the Eighth Amendment protections provided via *Atkins* to offenders who are mentally retarded would not be available to offenders who are similarly impaired and therefore similarly less culpable if their deficits appeared after the developmental period ended. To this end, Slobogin (2000, 2003) has argued that states which prohibit the execution of offenders with mental retardation may be violating the Equal Protection Clause of the U.S. Constitution if they continue to execute other people with serious mental illnesses who are no more culpable or deterrable than offenders who are mentally retarded.

In a similar vein, four leading professional organizations endorsed policies recommending that offenders with severe mental illness be categorically excluded from the death penalty. In April 2003, the Individual Rights and Responsibilities Section of the American Bar Association (ABA) convened representatives from the ABA, American Psychological Association, American Psychiatric Association, and National Alliance on Mental Illness (NAMI) to form the Task Force on Mental Disability and the Death Penalty (Packer, 2007). The 24-member task force met regularly over a 2-year period to determine how courts should sentence people with severe mental illness in jurisdictions that impose the death penalty. The Task Force concluded that several groups of offenders should be excluded from the death penalty: *(1)* offenders who have persistent mental disability or mental retardation that began before the offense; *(2)* defendants who, at the time of the offense, had a severe mental disorder; and *(3)* offenders who, once convicted and sentenced, become incompetent to face execution because of a mental disorder (Task Force on Mental Disability and the Death Penalty, 2006). The American Psychological Association Council of Representatives approved the Task Force's recommendations as initial policy in February 2005. The American Psychiatric

Association adopted a slightly amended policy in December 2005, and the American Psychological Association approved the revised language as amended policy in February 2006 (Task Force on Mental Disability and the Death Penalty, 2006). Subsequently, the ABA and NAMI endorsed the amended the version of the policy, thus achieving consensus among the four professional organizations.

The specification of an age of onset does, however, serve some practical purposes in an *Atkins* context. Perhaps most notably, it reduces the likelihood of malingering. Even if it were possible for an offender to feign intellectual and adaptive deficits suggestive of mental retardation (see Doane & Salekin, 2009; Salekin & Doane, 2009; Shandera et al., 2010), the requirement that the disorder manifest during the developmental period means that the disorder must have been present before there was an incentive to feign mental retardation.

The age of onset is typically determined by reviewing educational, mental health, and other records with information relevant to intellectual and adaptive deficits. Interviews with parents, teachers, other caregivers, and peers are also an important source of information. As with other aspects of FMHAs, the use of multiple sources of information is recommended (see Heilbrun, 2001).

Of note, the age of onset criterion does not require that a *diagnosis* of mental retardation have been made prior to age 18 (or 22) years; rather, there simply needs to be some evidence that sufficient impairment was present. Also, age of onset does not need to be established by referring to standardized test scores from the developmental period. Not all children have the same level of access to intellectual testing, even if there are indications of a learning disability or mental retardation. According to Blume et al. (2009), some school districts have prohibited intelligence testing because it may result in disparate treatment of racial groups. Bonnie and Gustafson (2007) argue that requiring the existence of standardized test scores from the developmental period to make a present diagnosis of mental retardation would be unconstitutional, because it would be discriminatory against those who did not have access to adequate clinical or social services as a child.

Several courts have strictly interpreted the age of onset criterion as requiring "definitive" or "concrete" evidence of subaverage intellectual functioning and adaptive deficits prior to age 18. In *Ohio v. Stallings* (2004), an offender challenged the trial court's ruling that he was not mentally retarded as defined by Ohio statutory law. The Ohio trial court had concluded that Michael Stallings had subaverage intellectual functioning and significant limitations in two or more adaptive skills, but it held that he failed to establish that these impairments were present before he reached the age of 18. As such, the trial court held that Stallings did not satisfy the criteria for mental retardation. Stallings appealed, and an Ohio appellate court affirmed the trial court's holding. On federal habeas review, the U.S. District Court for the Northern District of Ohio affirmed, albeit reluctantly, the state court's holding (*Stallings v. Bagley*, 2008). Despite recognition that the trial court may have imposed "an impossible burden" on Stallings—and a standard of proof that is higher than that required by *Atkins*—it concluded that the deference to state court rulings precluded granting relief to Stallings. The court also held that the trial court's interpretation of the age of onset criterion was not an objectively unreasonable interpretation of *Atkins*. Other courts have also strictly interpreted the age of onset criterion as requiring concrete evidence of impairment during the developmental period.[14]

Conclusion

The Supreme Court's mandate in *Atkins v. Virginia* (2002) to exclude offenders with mental retardation from the reach of the death penalty has imposed constitutional significance on clinical assessments of mental retardation. The interpretation and implementation of the Court's decision by the states has resulted in different definitions of mental retardation and different procedural frameworks for addressing offenders' *Atkins* claims. As states continue to grapple with the many substantive and procedural issues related to these types of claims, the laws governing these procedures will continue to develop. As such, it is imperative that forensic mental health evaluators stay current on the law in their jurisdiction. Moreover, as with other evaluations conducted in capital contexts, evaluators should follow the best-practice standards outlined in this chapter and elsewhere.

---

14. For example, in *Rosales v. Quarterman* (2008), the U.S. Court of Appeals for the Fifth Circuit rejected an *Atkins* claim because the offender failed to present any concrete evidence of deficits in adaptive behavior that had an onset before the age of 18 years.

6

Eligibility for the Death Penalty—Part 2: Competence for Execution Evaluations

Introduction

The U.S. Supreme Court has created categorical exclusions from the death penalty based on certain offenses (e.g., rape) and categories of offenders (e.g., juveniles). As with other exclusions from the death penalty, these decisions were primarily intended to narrow the class of criminal offenders who are eligible for a death sentence to those considered most deserving of the legal system's ultimate penalty. The Supreme Court has also recognized that some offenders may be excluded from the death penalty based on their mental state, either at the time of the offense, during the trial and sentencing stage of the criminal proceedings, or closer to the date of the scheduled execution. These death penalty eligibility determinations are made on a case-by-case basis depending on the defendant's mental functioning and associated deficits. There are several points during capital proceedings at which a court may be asked to determine whether a criminal offender is eligible for the death penalty, and the procedural and constitutional protections available to defendants differ based on *when* the issue of death-penalty eligibility is addressed in the course of the legal proceedings. Some of these procedural and constitutional protections were discussed earlier in this text (see Chapters 2 and 3).

In some contexts, a court may be asked to determine whether a defendant is eligible for the death penalty during pretrial proceedings. In Chapter 5, we discussed front-end forensic mental health assessments (FMHAs) conducted to determine whether a criminal defendant is mentally retarded and, therefore, not eligible for the death penalty based on the U.S. Supreme Court's decision in *Atkins v. Virginia* (2002).[1] A pretrial determination of death penalty eligibility has a couple of potential benefits. First, a pretrial determination that a defendant is not eligible for a death sentence due to mental retardation spares the prosecution from expending the heavy resources and enormous financial expenses necessary for a capital case. Second, taking the possibility of a death sentence off of the table might influence the nature of the defense put forth. In other words, a defense lawyer may be more likely to gamble with a less certain defense if there is no possibility that the defendant will be sentenced to death if the defense is not successful.[2] Finally, if it is not a capital case, the concerns related to empanelling a potentially biased death-qualified jury are obviated.

In other contexts, the issue of whether an offender is eligible for the death penalty is not raised until the guilt-innocence phase of the trial has been completed and the offender has been sentenced to death. There may be several legal grounds upon which a challenge to a death sentence can be based. Although some of these challenges are based on various aspects of the legal proceedings (e.g., procedural error), other challenges are based on the offender's mental health functioning.

The etiology and course of mental illness are complex, multidetermined, and likely influenced by a variety of individual and environmental factors. It is possible, for example, that an offender who has been sentenced to death will

---

1. *Atkins* shares similarities with previous cases from the U.S. Supreme Court involving categorical exclusions from the death penalty, but it also stands alone in some respects. Although *Atkins* is similar to *Coker*, *Roper*, and *Kennedy* in the sense that it created a categorical exclusion from capital punishment, unlike those other cases, *Atkins*-type cases are dissimilar in that the court addresses the legal issue (i.e., whether a criminal offender is mentally retarded) on a case-by-case basis. Moreover, *Coker*, *Roper*, and *Kennedy* are based on clear-cut static characteristics – the age of the offender at the time of the offense (*Roper*) and the category of the criminal offense (*Coker*, *Kennedy*) – that rarely require intense debate. By contrast, although mental retardation is a static characteristic (in the sense that it does not go into remission like some other psychiatric disorders), determining whether a defendant is mentally retarded in an *Atkins*-type case can be a point of controversy vigorously contested by opposing attorneys. As discussed in Chapter 5, a diagnosis (or no diagnosis) of mental retardation can be challenged on various grounds relating to the assessment measures and procedures used by the forensic mental health professional. Finally, as discussed in Chapter 5, the exclusion created by *Atkins* is based entirely on a psychiatric diagnosis, which represents a clear break from the Supreme Court's typical approach when it comes to the relationship between functional deficits and psycholegal abilities.

2. As an example, if a death sentence is no longer an option, a defense lawyer might take a somewhat riskier approach in seeking a full acquittal rather than more conservatively seeking a manslaughter verdict.

develop a mental health disorder that is unrelated to his or her incarceration. The prevalence of some types of mental health disorders, such as major depressive disorder and some types of anxiety disorders, are relatively high, which means it is likely that some portion of criminal offenders will suffer from these disorders. Moreover, the age of onset (i.e., late adolescence and early adulthood) for some forms of severe and persistent mental illness overlaps to a great extent with the age range of many criminal offenders.

For some offenders who have been sentenced to death, the psychological stress of being incarcerated on death row may exacerbate pre-existing mental health disorders or perhaps trigger the development of new disorders. In either situation, the result may be a general deterioration in the offender's mental health functioning (see Cunningham & Goldstein, 2003; Mathias, 1988). Furthermore, most offenders on death row are housed in solitary confinement and only briefly permitted out of their cells. According to research spanning several decades, solitary confinement can have negative effects on offenders' mental health functioning (see, e.g., Grassian & Friedman, 1986; Haney, 2003; Toch, 1975). Therefore, it seems reasonable to believe that awaiting one's execution in solitary confinement likely involves substantial psychological distress.

Regardless of the etiology of an offender's mental health symptoms, the U.S. Supreme Court has held that prisoners must be competent to be executed (see *Ford v. Wainwright*, 1986; *Panetti v. Quarterman*, 2007). The issue of whether a prisoner is competent for execution can be raised by, or on behalf of, any prisoner who has been sentenced to death and who is suffering from a serious mental health disorder (see Zapf, 2008, 2009).[3] If the issue is raised, forensic mental health professionals may be called upon to assist legal decision makers in determining whether an offender who has been sentenced to death is, in fact, eligible for the death penalty (Melton, Petrila, Poythress, & Slobogin, 2007).

Of course, competence for execution evaluations are not common, particularly when compared with other types of FMHAs conducted in criminal contexts, such as competence to stand trial. But the high-stakes nature of the evaluations makes them theoretically and practically important. As with other FMHAs conducted in capital contexts, evaluators must possess a thorough understanding of the relevant legal standards and "best practices" associated with evaluations for competence for execution. Unfortunately, when it comes to these evaluations, there is a limited research base and limited agreement as to what constitutes "best practices."

---

3. In fact, the issue of competence to be executed can be raised even in the absence of a mental health disorder, but such a claim is unlikely to get very far on its merit.

Although the U.S. Supreme Court first addressed the constitutionality of executing incompetent offenders nearly 25 years ago in *Ford v. Wainwright* (1986), the Court's decision left unanswered several important questions. Most notably, *Ford* did not address the appropriate substantive legal standard that should be used when determining whether a prisoner is competent to be executed. A more recent decision from the U.S. Supreme Court, *Panetti v. Quarterman* (2007), answered some of the questions left open by *Ford*, but it has perhaps raised a few more questions along the way.

Cases Relevant to Competence for Execution

As discussed in Chapter 3, the prohibition against executing incompetent offenders dates back several hundred years (see Ackerson, Brodsky, & Zapf, 2005; Blackstone, 1978; Broderick, 1979; Ward, 1986), but the U.S. Supreme Court's decision in *Ford v. Wainwright* (1986) was the first Supreme Court case to directly address the constitutionality of executing incompetent offenders. The central issue decided in *Ford* was whether the Eighth Amendment's prohibition against cruel and unusual punishment prohibited the execution of incompetent offenders. The Supreme Court answered in the affirmative and concluded that executing incompetent offenders would offend humanity and fail to serve the traditional punishment goals of deterrence and retribution.

Importantly, the U.S. Supreme Court's plurality opinion in *Ford* did not provide a substantive legal standard for courts to apply when determining whether a prisoner is competent to be executed. Instead, much like the approach it took over 15 years later in *Atkins v. Virginia* (2002) when it came to defining mental retardation, the Supreme Court charged each state with developing appropriate procedural safeguards to ensure that incompetent offenders would be excluded from the death penalty. This left states and courts in the difficult position of needing to provide meaningful substance to the Supreme Court's stated intent, which has proved to be much easier said than done. The failure to provide a substantive legal standard for competence for execution has been a much criticized aspect of the Court's decision in *Ford*.

Fortunately, however, the *Ford* decision provided some degree of guidance, although not in the plurality opinion. In a highly influential and often-cited concurring opinion, Justice Powell stated that the Eighth Amendment should prohibit the "execution only of those who are unaware of the punishment they are about to suffer and why they are to suffer it" (*Ford*, 1986, p. 422). Justice Powell's proposed standard requires that the offender have a factual understanding of the capital proceedings, and he stated that the test for competency should be whether the offender understands the nature, pendency, and purpose of the impending execution. After *Ford*, most courts that addressed the issue adopted some variation of Justice Powell's rationale as the basis for excluding incompetent offenders from capital punishment (see Otto, 2009; Reisner, Slobogin, & Rai, 2004; see also *Barnard v. Collins*, 1994; *Coe v. Bell*, 2000; *Fearance v. Scott*, 1995; *Walter v. Angelone*, 2003). Some courts, however, elected to use more stringent standards when making determinations regarding the eligibility of incompetent offenders for the death penalty (e.g., *Walton v. Johnson*, 2005).[4]

A little over 20 years after *Ford* was decided, the U.S. Supreme Court re-examined the issue of competence for execution in *Panetti v. Quarterman* (2007). In *Panetti*, the Supreme Court addressed the specific question of whether the Eighth Amendment permits the execution of an offender who has a factual awareness of the reasons for his or her execution, but who because of severe mental illness also has a delusional belief regarding the reasons why the execution is taking place. Panetti's attorneys conceded that he had a sufficient *factual* awareness of the reasons for his execution (because he acknowledged that he was facing execution for murdering two people), but they argued that he lacked an adequate *rational* understanding (because he also held the delusional belief that he was being executed for preaching the Gospel).

By a narrow five-to-four vote, the U.S. Supreme Court held that the factual understanding standard articulated by Justice Powell in *Ford* was not constitutionally sufficient. The Court held that a prisoner must have *both* a factual understanding of the offense, the impending execution, and the state's reason for ordering the execution, *and* a rational understanding of the connection between the offense and the impending execution. In reaching its decision, the Court focused mostly on how an offender's mental illness would frustrate the retributive and deterrent purposes of the death penalty.

By adding a requirement that prisoners must have both a factual and rational understanding of the reasons for the impending execution, the *Panetti* decision provided a degree of guidance above and beyond what it initially provided in *Ford*. However, for various reasons, the U.S. Supreme Court again declined to define a specific standard for courts to use when determining when an offender is competent for execution (see Appelbaum, 2007; Blanks & Pinals, 2007). Writing for the majority, Justice Kennedy stated that the factual record was not developed sufficiently to permit the Court to define a standard for competence for execution. The Court also conceded that defining "rational understanding" could be challenging. As a result, much like states were forced

---

4. As in other areas of the law, states were free to adopt more stringent standards that would provide greater protection from the death penalty for a larger group of offenders, but they could not adopt a more lenient standard that provided constitutional protection to a group smaller than the Supreme Court intended to protect.

to do after *Ford* (in terms of the standard for competence for execution) and *Atkins* (with respect to defining mental retardation), states and courts will likely need to engage in some degree of interpretation when implementing the *Panetti* decision.

Ethical and Clinical Considerations Relevant to Evaluations for Competence for Execution

Competence for execution evaluations raise a variety of ethical and clinical considerations. As a starting point, some forensic mental health professionals and legal scholars have questioned whether it is appropriate for forensic clinicians to conduct evaluations of competence for execution. The root of this concern is that if the forensic clinician assists the court in determining that the offender is competent, the offender will most likely be executed. The clinician, they argue, is too close to the punishment process and violating the ethical imperative to "do no harm."

In addition to ethical concerns, there are obvious questions relating to the legal standard to be used in these types of evaluations. In light of the U.S. Supreme Court's decisions in *Ford* and *Panetti*, and the resulting ambiguity regarding the appropriate legal standard for competence for execution, it is perhaps not surprising that forensic mental health professionals have struggled to identify appropriate clinical procedures in these types of evaluations. Limited literature addresses appropriate evaluation procedures, which makes the task of forensic mental health professionals even more difficult.

Ethical Considerations

The debate surrounding the ethical appropriateness of forensic mental health professionals evaluating offenders for competence for execution is not new. Indeed, the ethical aspects of participating in these evaluations have been much debated in the social science and legal literatures for well over 25 years (see, e.g., Appelbaum, 1986; Bonnie, 1990; Brodsky, 1990; Brodsky, Zapf, & Boccaccini, 2001, 2005; Cunningham & Goldstein, 2003; Deitchman, Kennedy, & Beckham, 1991; Ewing, 1987; Foot, 1990; Heilbrun, 1987; Heilbrun & McClaren, 1988; Radelet & Barnard, 1986; Small & Otto, 1991; Weinstock, Leong, & Silva, 2010). Given the visceral reaction that often surrounds all things related to capital punishment, it is unlikely that the ethical debate will be resolved any time soon. We make no effort to resolve this debate, but we suggest that evaluators become familiar with the arguments on both sides.

At base, the key ethical question is whether forensic mental health professionals should be involved in evaluations that are so closely linked with the potential execution of a criminal offender. The central concern is that such involvement may conflict with the ethical principle of nonmaleficence (i.e., "do no harm") for mental health professionals (see, e.g., Ewing, 1987).[5] As with most issues relating to capital punishment, this question has had a polarizing effect among legal and social science professionals, and strong views have been offered on both sides of the debate. Once the issue of *whether* forensic mental health professionals should be involved in competence for execution evaluations is addressed, the next important question pertains to *how* those evaluations should be conducted.

The pro-involvement position rests on the premise that capital punishment, at least for now, is a constitutional punishment in the United States. Criminal offenders are routinely sentenced to death, and in several states offenders are executed with some regularity. In a small proportion of these cases, questions are likely to arise as to whether the offender is competent for execution. Pro-involvement proponents argue that when the issue of an offender's competence for execution is raised, evaluations should be performed by forensic mental health professionals who are well trained, highly skilled, and sufficiently experienced. They argue that if conscientious and well-qualified clinicians refrain from participating in these evaluations, based on ethical considerations or otherwise, the evaluations will be conducted by poorly qualified clinicians. The result would be that prisoners who are indeed not competent may nevertheless be executed because their deficits were not properly evaluated and documented (see Leong et al., 1993). Of course, the reverse scenario is also possible, in which prisoners who are competent may be determined by a court to be incompetent based on the results of an improper evaluation. Arguably, however, the former context is more troubling because it ends in the execution of a prisoner who should have been excluded from the death penalty (at least while his or her deficits persisted).

The anti-involvement position rests on several interrelated arguments. The most common argument is that evaluating prisoners for competence for execution places mental health professionals in unacceptably close proximity to the administration of a criminal punishment. The close relationship between mental health professionals and execution can have two unintended effects.

---

5. Similar ethical concerns have been expressed with regard to the involvement of forensic mental health professionals in treating prisoners found to be incompetent to face execution, because the restoration of competence would most likely result in the offender's execution. (For a discussion of the ethical concerns related to the restoration of competency to be executed, see Cunningham & Goldstein, 2003; Ferris, 1997; Heilbrun, Radelet, & Dvoskin, 1992; Hensl, 2005; Leong, Silva, Weinstock, & Ganzini, 2000; Leong, Weinstock, Silva, & Eth, 1993; and Mossman, 1987, 1995.) However, our focus is on assessments, not treatment, in capital contexts.

First, participating in evaluations that may result in the execution of a prisoner may conflict with the ethical obligation of mental health professionals to do no harm (Ewing, 1987). Second, any participation in the execution process, even if far removed from the actual execution of the prisoner, may ultimately change the public's perception of mental health professionals as being in the business of helping people.[6]

Along these lines, Freedman and Halpern (1998, 1999) have argued that participating in competence for execution evaluations is unethical because it provides mental health professionals with an integral role in the final legal obstacle to the execution of an offender. For example, testimony that a prisoner is, in fact, competent to be executed would likely result in the prisoner's execution. Freedman and Halpern (1998, 1999) believe that participating in this causal chain is not ethical. In contrast, Bonnie (1990) has asserted that well-performed evaluations for competence for execution may ultimately increase the court's ability to make a well-informed decision, which could potentially spare incompetent offenders from execution. Based on this reasoning, Bonnie concluded that participating in these types of evaluations is not inherently unethical. Bonnie cautioned, however, that if an evaluator's beliefs preclude conducting an objective evaluation, the evaluator should decline participation, or discontinue his or her involvement if the evaluation has already begun.

In addition to concerns about nonmaleficence, anti-involvement constituents have focused on the lack of a clear substantive legal standard for competence for execution and the lack of appropriate assessment measures for these types of evaluations. Brodsky (1990) voiced concerns about the absence of a clear legal standard nearly 20 years ago, well before the U.S. Supreme Court's recent decision in *Panetti*, but they remain relevant today. The essence of Brodsky's concern is that evaluators will be more likely to rely on their own values when the legal criteria are vague, compromising the evaluator's neutrality and objectivity. Similarly, Radelet and Barnard (1986) argued that extraneous factors are more likely to influence the evaluator's judgment and thereby reduce evaluator objectivity when the legal criteria are vague.

---

6. The same arguments have been raised with respect to physicians and other medical professionals participating in executions. Of course, medical professionals can have more direct involvement in the actual execution, particularly in those states that use lethal injection. The involvement of medical professionals can consist of administering the cocktail of drugs, monitoring the inmate's vital signs during the execution, and making the official pronouncement of death. The American Medical Association's *Code of Medical Ethics* (2008) prohibits physicians from participating directly in executions, and it defines participation as *(1)* an action that would directly cause the death of the prisoner; *(2)* an action that would assist, supervise, or contribute to the ability of another individual to directly cause the death of the prisoner; and *(3)* an action that could automatically cause an execution to be carried out on a prisoner.

They cited such extraneous factors as the mental health professional's opinion on capital punishment, the seriousness of the underlying criminal offense, and the likeability of the offender.

A key question is whether evaluator opinions in these cases are more influenced by personal values than by legal criteria. This is an empirical question. Unfortunately, the available research can not adequately answer it. Perhaps because competence for execution evaluations are so rare, few researchers have examined clinician attitudes in the context of these evaluations, and the few available studies rely on survey methodology (see Zapf, 2008, for a summary). Given the small body of available research, summarizing the key findings from each study is not a difficult task.

In 1982, White surveyed 72 psychologists attending the annual conference of the Ohio Psychological Association in an effort to gauge their level of agreement with guidelines for participating in capital cases being promulgated by several organizations, including the American Psychological Association.[7] Results revealed that 72% of the psychologists surveyed supported the participation of psychologists in death penalty cases as long as appropriate practice guidelines were implemented. By contrast, 18% of the psychologists surveyed were categorically opposed to the participation of psychologists in death penalty cases. It is interesting to note that White's study was published several years before the U.S. Supreme Court decided *Ford*.

In another early study, Deitchman and colleagues (1991) surveyed 222 forensic psychologists and psychiatrists to examine whether mental health professionals who choose to participate in evaluations for competence for execution are different from their colleagues who choose not to participate in such evaluations. They found that these two groups differed significantly in their attitude toward capital punishment, with the clinicians willing to conduct competence for execution evaluations showing considerably more support for the death penalty. The two groups also differed significantly in the extent to which they viewed participation in competence for execution evaluations as a violation of their professional ethics; willing clinicians were less likely to perceive their professional ethics as precluding participation.

Interestingly, Deitchman et al. (1991) found that the proportion of willing clinicians did not differ considerably between psychiatrists and psychologists, with 69% of psychiatrists and 60% of psychologists reporting a willingness to conduct evaluations for competence for execution. Moreover, there was no significant difference between the psychiatrists and psychologists in their views regarding the ethics of being involved in these evaluations. Deitchman et al. interpreted these findings as supporting the belief that

---

7. Importantly, White (1982) found that 90% of the survey respondents reported having forensic experience, so the survey sample appeared to be an appropriate target group.

evaluator self-selection plays a decisive role in which mental health professionals become involved in competence for execution evaluations. They also emphasized the concern that clinician characteristics may influence the results of these evaluations.

In a later study, Leong and colleagues (2000) surveyed 290 board-certified forensic psychiatrists regarding their views on capital punishment and involvement in capital cases. Unlike the results reported by Deitchman et al. (1991), Leong et al. found little agreement among their sample on these issues. In addition to differences regarding the acceptability of capital punishment as a social practice, the psychiatrists expressed significantly different levels of support regarding the involvement of psychiatrists in capital cases based on *when* in the proceedings the evaluation was being conducted. For example, a few psychiatrists (8.5%) believed that it was unethical to conduct an evaluation in *any* phase of capital proceedings. More psychiatrists (22.3%) believed that evaluations of competence to stand trial conducted either pretrial or during the trial were ethically appropriate, but that evaluations of competence for execution should be avoided. Nonetheless, most psychiatrists saw no ethical dilemma in conducting evaluations of competence for execution. Interestingly, Leong and colleagues found no significant relationship between any demographic variables and psychiatrists' views on capital punishment, although the older psychiatrists were somewhat more likely to support the involvement of psychiatrists in restoring prisoners' competence for execution.

In a more recent study, Pirelli and Zapf (2008) surveyed 231 forensic psychologists regarding their attitudes and practices related to death penalty proceedings. They reported that less than half of the psychologists surveyed (46%) endorsed a willingness to conduct competence for execution evaluations, even though the majority of the responding psychologists did not oppose participating in other types of FMHAs in capital proceedings. Pirelli and Zapf also found that opposition to other types of FMHAs in capital contexts (e.g., competence to waive *Miranda* rights, competence to stand trial, competence to waive counsel) could be reliably predicted by the participants' religiosity, their views on the death penalty, their personal values, and the adequacy of training and experience relevant to conducting evaluations in capital contexts.

Taken together, the results of this small body of research suggest that views are split when it comes to the ethics of participating in competence for execution evaluations. Although there is no direct prohibition against such participation in the ethics codes that govern psychologists, this small body of research suggests that some psychologists oppose such participation. The appropriateness of participating in competence for execution evaluations will no doubt continue to be debated.

Clinical Considerations

In light of the ambiguity surrounding the appropriate substantive legal standard that should be used when determining whether an offender is competent for execution, forensic mental health professionals have struggled with identifying appropriate evaluation procedures and techniques. Although competence for execution evaluations are quite rare when compared to all other types of criminal FMHAs (see Zapf, 2008, 2009), the stakes are arguably higher because the evaluation is typically the final hurdle before the execution of the offender. In this respect, Brodsky, Zapf, and Boccaccini (2001) referred to competence for execution evaluations as "low demand, high impact evaluations" (p. 21).

Several researchers and practitioners have offered guidelines, recommendations, and even general advice for conducting evaluations of competence for execution. But this literature is limited and widespread agreement on "best practices" for these types of evaluations still does not exist. Because competence for execution evaluations are so rare, data regarding these types of evaluations are simply not available in the same quantity as with other types of FMHAs. Nevertheless, some attempts have been made to identify current practices among forensic mental health professionals who conduct these types of evaluations (see, e.g., Young, Boccaccini, Lawson, & Conroy, 2008; Zapf, Boccaccini, & Brodsky, 2003).

In this section, we review the available clinical literature addressing evaluations of competence for execution. We begin by briefly describing the various guidelines and recommendations provided by researchers and scholars over the past 25 years. Following that discussion, we synthesize the practice literature by focusing more specifically on the evaluation procedures and techniques that appear to have gained the strongest support across multiple sources. Most evaluators—even those routinely involved in capital cases—will never evaluate an individual's competence for execution. Thus, the rarity of these evaluations makes practice guidelines *practically* important for only a few evaluators, and perhaps for the few attorneys who retain (or challenge) them. However, the gravity of competence for execution evaluations makes practice guidelines *theoretically* important to the fields of forensic mental health and capital litigation. But neither field has clearly defined how we should assess one's factual and rational understanding of impending execution, which is the standard set by the U.S. Supreme Court in *Panetti*.

Early efforts at describing assessments for competence for execution (i.e., Heilbrun, 1987; Heilbrun & McClaren, 1988) were published shortly after the U.S. Supreme Court decided *Ford*. Heilbrun (1987) raised several considerations including the qualifications of the evaluators (i.e., objective, well-trained evaluators with experience and demonstrated skill in both clinical and clinical-legal areas), the notification of purpose given to the offender (i.e., regarding the nature and purpose of the evaluation, taking into consideration any deficits that may prevent the offender from understanding the notification elements), the comprehensiveness of the evaluation itself (i.e., collecting historical and descriptive information from the offender and collaterals; assessing psychopathology, intellectual functioning, personality characteristics, motivation, and response style), the context and circumstances of the evaluation (i.e., physical environment, individuals who are present), and the sufficiency of the written report (which should be detailed enough to permit the attorneys and court to understand the evaluation procedures and the reasoning process behind the evaluator's conclusions). Despite being published over 20 years ago, and prior to the U.S. Supreme Court's decision in *Panetti*, these considerations remain relevant.

After addressing the ethical considerations most relevant to competence for execution evaluations, Heilbrun and McClaren (1988) discussed clinical procedures and considerations in both preadjudication and postadjudication evaluation contexts. Preadjudication evaluations occur after the issue of competence for execution has been raised, but before the court has issued a formal judgment regarding the offender's competence. Postadjudication evaluations take place after an offender has been declared incompetent and transferred to another facility for additional assessment and treatment. Of course, very few offenders have ever been found incompetent to be executed, so preadjudication evaluations are much more common (Zapf, 2008). Therefore, we focus on preadjudication evaluations of competence for execution (readers interested in postadjudication evaluations should consult Heilbrun and McClaren, 1988).

Heilbrun and McClaren (1988) identified several minimum components of competence for execution evaluations. For example, evaluators should provide a notification of purpose that describes the purpose of the evaluation, the evaluation procedures, and the possible consequences of the evaluation. Evaluators should also make some effort to determine whether the offender understood the key elements of the notification. Heilbrun and McClaren recognized that the environment and surroundings for these types of evaluations may be less than ideal, but they suggested seeking at least "minimally adequate" conditions (i.e., private and distraction free) (p. 209). Consistent with other types of FMHAs, Heilbrun and McClaren emphasized the importance of obtaining third-party information, particularly relating to the offender's history and current functioning. Such independent information can help the evaluator assess the offender's response style and determine whether the offender is exaggerating or minimizing his or her deficits. Response style can also be assessed using several well-validated measures (see Rogers, 2008). Many of these aspects of competence for execution evaluations are discussed in more detail in Chapter 9.

In addition to general considerations, Heilbrun and McClaren (1988) offered a number of specific recommendations for the evaluation itself. Of central importance, the evaluator must be familiar with the specific legal standard for competence for execution used in the relevant jurisdiction. Recognizing that the legal standard was vague in some states, they recommended considering the standard in its broadest form, which would allow the legal decision maker to make a determination as to which aspects of the evaluation are applicable. They also recommended conducting the evaluation over the course of several meetings so the evaluator would be able to obtain more observational data on the offender's mental functioning. In terms of evaluation content, Heilbrun and McClaren recommended assessing motivation (or response style), intellectual functioning, personality characteristics, psychopathology, and whether the offender satisfies the relevant legal criteria for competence for execution. Traditional psychological tests can be helpful in terms of gathering information in several of these areas, though they cannot address directly competence for execution.

Several years later, Small and Otto (1991) offered guidance for clinicians who conduct evaluations of competence for execution. Small and Otto recognized the importance of the clinical interview. Among other things, they recommended that the forensic mental health professional should evaluate the offender's understanding of the reasons for his or her incarceration and impending execution, and (if jurisdictionally relevant) evaluate whether the offender is capable of assisting his or her attorney. Small and Otto placed somewhat less emphasis on traditional psychological testing, and instead focused more on assessing the offender's functional abilities. Consistent with other sources of authority, they emphasized the importance of obtaining collateral information. Finally, Small and Otto recommended that evaluators avoid answering the ultimate legal question in their reports and testimony, and instead focus on functional abilities related to the relevant legal standard.

Conducting Competence for Execution Evaluations

More recent contributions to the literature include specific frameworks, guidelines, and instrumentation to assist evaluators when conducting competence for execution evaluations. In several publications, Zapf and colleagues have identified guiding frameworks and professional standards for these evaluations (Zapf, 2008, 2009; Zapf et al., 2003). In doing so, they were careful to distinguish between *minimum* standards, which would enable an evaluator to conduct the evaluation in a basic yet adequate way, and *professional* standards, which are more stringent than minimal standards and similar to "best practices."

Looking across existing sources, both historical and more current, we believe it is possible to discern a set of recommendations and guidelines that can be used to assist clinicians who conduct evaluations of competence for execution. The vast majority of resources relevant to competence for execution evaluations were published prior to the U.S. Supreme Court's 2007 decision in *Panetti* (with notable exceptions being Otto, 2009, and Zapf, 2009). So we are expanding upon previous work in this area by synthesizing the existing literature, and by providing recommendations and guidelines that have gained the most support across multiple sources *and* appear most consistent with the U.S. Supreme Court's decisions in both *Ford* and *Panetti*.

Competence

As with any type of FMHA, evaluators should be competent to conduct evaluations of competence for execution. According to the American Psychological Association's (2002) *Ethical Principles of Psychologists and Code of Conduct*, "competence" is based on relevant "education, training, supervised experience, consultation, study, or professional experience" (p. 1063). Of course, the Ethics Code does not provide any guidelines regarding what constitutes minimum thresholds in these areas. For example, it is not clear how much "education," "training," or "supervised experience" is sufficient for an evaluator to be considered competent. Given that competence for execution evaluations are rarely conducted, few clinicians will have any experience with these evaluations. However, at a minimum, clinicians should have previous forensic experience, and preferably a good deal of such experience, before conducting competence for execution evaluations (or any FMHAs in capital contexts). The Ethics Code only requires a minimum degree of competence, but forensic evaluators are encouraged to have substantially more experience and training if they work in capital contexts. As recommended by Heilbrun (1987), competence for execution evaluations should be conducted by objective and well-trained evaluators who have experience and demonstrated skill in both clinical and clinical-legal areas. We suggest that evaluators who conduct competence for execution evaluations have substantial experience assessing other types of competence (e.g., competence to stand trial, competence to waive *Miranda* rights).

Substantive and Procedural Legal Knowledge

Beyond possessing a minimum degree of competence (and preferably a much higher level), evaluators must be knowledgeable about the substantive and procedural aspects of competence for execution evaluations. Such knowledge would include the appropriate legal standard in the evaluator's jurisdiction, and procedural issues relating to when and how the evaluation should be conducted. Referring to governing statutes in one's jurisdiction would be an important first step in obtaining the necessary substantive and procedural information needed to conduct the evaluation. Confirming the statutory requirements through discussions with experienced colleagues is strongly recommended. If statutory guidance is vague or lacking in one's jurisdiction, conceptualizing competence for execution in its broadest form may be most appropriate (see Heilbrun & McClaren, 1988). In this regard, it would be important to keep in mind the guidance, albeit somewhat limited, provided by the *Ford* and *Panetti* decisions.

Informed Consent or Notification of Purpose

At the beginning of the evaluation, the clinician should obtain informed consent from the offender (if the evaluation was requested by an attorney) or provide a notification of purpose (if the evaluation was court ordered). At a minimum, the clinician should describe the nature and purpose of the evaluation, who requested the evaluation, what the evaluation will involve (e.g., review of records, interview, testing, collateral interviews), the potential consequences of the evaluation, and the relevant limits on confidentiality. If the evaluation is requested by the defense attorney (which is the most typical scenario), the offender should be informed that participation in the evaluation is voluntary. This would, of course, not be the case if the evaluation is court ordered because the offender is required to participate. However, it is often the case that a defense-requested evaluation results in a court order (perhaps to facilitate payment of the evaluator through public funds in an *Ake* context, or facilitate the evaluator's entry into the prison), and in this limited context the prisoner should be given the option to refuse to participate in the evaluation. Clinicians should also make an effort to determine whether the offender understood the key elements of the notification, taking into account any deficits that may prevent the offender from understanding the notification elements.

Clinical Interview

The clinical interview is considered the most important component of a competence for execution evaluation. This is particularly true because there are few measures developed specifically for these evaluations. The evaluator should gather information about the offender's past and current psychological functioning and the course (if any) of mental health treatment, including the use of psychotropic medications. Because competence for execution, like other competencies (e.g., stand trial, waive *Miranda* rights), is a present-focused concept, focusing on the offender's *current* psychological functioning is essential. Consistent with recommendations from several authorities (e.g., Heilbrun, Grisso, & Goldstein, 2009; Heilbrun & McClaren, 1988; Small & Otto, 1991), the evaluator should seek information from a wide range of sources, including the offender, knowledgeable collaterals (individuals from a variety of contexts who know the offender), and archival records. Obtaining information from multiple sources can help the evaluator to assess the offender's response style (e.g., truthful responding vs. exaggeration/minimization of deficits), reduce the error associated with any single source of information, and highlight inconsistencies between the offender's self-report and more objective sources of information. Conducting the evaluation over the course of more than one meeting, as recommended by Heilbrun and McClaren (1988), is a useful way for evaluators to observe the presentation and stability of the offender's mental health functioning.

The central component of the clinical interview is assessing the degree to which the offender understands his or her pending execution and the reasons for it. Such understanding lies at the heart of the concept of competence for execution and thus constitutes the key inquiry in these types of evaluations. Unfortunately, this is also the aspect of these evaluations that leads to some confusion among evaluators, because the U.S. Supreme Court provided very little guidance on this issue.

In light of *Panetti*, it is no longer acceptable simply to assess whether the offender has a sufficient factual understanding of the nature, pendency, and purpose of the impending execution, which was the standard gleaned from Justice Powell's concurrence in *Ford*. After *Panetti*, the key inquiry is whether the offender has both a factual understanding of the offense, the impending execution, and the state's reason for ordering the execution, *and* a rational understanding of the connection between the offense and the impending execution. The requirement that offenders possess both a factual and rational understanding should guide evaluators' inquiries in these types of evaluations.

Unfortunately, assessing an offender's rational understanding may be tricky. Even the U.S. Supreme Court in *Panetti* conceded that defining rational understanding could be challenging. Fortunately, Otto (2009) provided a detailed discussion of how four categories of mental health problems can affect competence-related abilities, including rational understanding. First, Otto noted that *impaired thought content*, such as grandiose delusions, paranoid delusions, and religious delusions, may affect the competence-related abilities of understanding and appreciating the death sentence. Given the relatively high base rate of psychotic symptoms reported by death row inmates (e.g., Cunningham & Vigen, 2002), evaluators should be particularly conscientious about looking for these symptoms. Although the presence of psychotic symptoms, by itself, does not ipso facto lead to a finding of incompetence to face execution, it is possible that such symptoms can affect an offender's rational understanding of the reasons for the pending execution. Recall that Scott Panetti possessed a sufficient factual understanding of the reasons he was being executed, but he held a delusional belief that he was also being executed for preaching the Gospel. Second, *impaired thought process or form* can affect competence-related abilities. For example, it is possible that disordered thinking, tangentiality, or circumstantiality could affect an offender's understanding or appreciation of the death sentence. Third, *cognitive impairment*, broadly defined to include deficits in memory, attention/concentration, orientation, executive functioning, and intellectual functioning, could lead to a finding of incompetence for execution. Finally, Otto noted that *mood disorders*, if sufficiently severe, may affect an offender's ability to understand or appreciate the death sentence.

In addition to assessing the offender's factual and rational understanding of the offense and the reasons for his or her incarceration and pending execution, it may be important to evaluate whether the offender is capable of assisting his or her attorney in the appellate process or more generally assisting in efforts to avoid execution. Importantly, not all jurisdictions require offenders to have this ability. If the ability to assist counsel is required, the evaluator would want to assess, at a minimum, whether the offender can disclose relevant information to the attorney and communicate with the attorney in a reasonably effective manner. Some sources recommend observing interactions between the offender and attorney (e.g., Small & Otto, 1991; Zapf, 2008). The ability to assist counsel in this context can be conceptualized as similar to the "assist" prong from the "understand and assist" standard for competence to stand trial (see *Dusky v. United States*, 1960).

Traditional Psychological Measures

Traditional psychological measures can be helpful in terms of identifying functional deficits. For example, an evaluator can use measures of psychopathology, intellectual functioning, and personality characteristics to get a more comprehensive and detailed picture of the offender's current functioning. Traditional psychological testing has at least three benefits. First, these measures can be used to identify mental health symptoms or intellectual impairments that may be interfering with the offender's ability to understand the reasons for the impending execution. Second, some widely used psychological measures, such as the Minnesota Multiphasic Personality Inventory (MMPI), may be useful in assessing the offender's response style, which provides an indication of whether the offender is responding genuinely or attempting to exaggerate/minimize his or her mental health symptoms. Third, these measures can be helpful in identifying treatment targets if the offender appears incompetent for execution and requires restorative treatment (see Small & Otto, 1991). Despite the benefits of traditional psychological testing, it is important to remember that the focus of the evaluation should be squarely on the offender's *functional abilities and deficits* as they relate to competence for execution. In this respect, traditional psychological measures may not be particularly helpful.

Competence-Specific Instruments

In recent years, several checklists and measures have been developed to assist evaluators in conducting competence for execution evaluations. This is a welcome development. Among other benefits, checklists may help evaluators to assess the relevant psycholegal criteria in a structured and replicable manner (see Zapf, 2008). However, one limitation of the few available measures is that they were developed prior to the U.S. Supreme Court's ruling in *Panetti*.

Ebert (2001) made an early attempt to develop a checklist for competence for execution evaluations. Ebert generated a list of 12 items, with 8 assessing functional legal abilities and 4 more clinical in nature, that could be rated on a 6-point Likert scale: 0 (no incapacity), 1 (some incapacity), 2 (mild incapacity), 3 (moderate incapacity), 4 (severe incapacity), and 5 (severe incapacity) (scores of 4 and 5 are both labeled "severe incapacity"). The 12 items were: *(1)* ability to identify what is about to happen, *(2)* ability to understand and conceptualize that the person is housed on death row, *(3)* ability to understand the meaning of the term and concept of punishment, *(4)* ability to work with attorney, *(5)* ability to understand the sentence of death, *(6)* ability to understand the reason for the punishment of death, *(7)* ability to conceptualize what will happen when the punishment is carried out, *(8)* ability to describe the role of key people involved in the punishment, *(9)* ability to provide recent facts that may be helpful to deal with the issue of current competency, *(10)* ability to voluntarily control thoughts, *(11)* ability to perceive reality in the present, and *(12)* self-serving versus self-defeating motivation. Unfortunately, as noted by Zapf (2008), Ebert did not provide information for determining how the level of incapacity is determined or how the item ratings can be combined for making an overall determination of competence for execution. Moreover, Ebert did not provide sample questions for all items or present any data on the measure's psychometric properties.

Zapf and colleagues (2003) developed the *Interview Checklist for Evaluations of Competency for Execution* "to serve as an aide memoire to assist professionals in conducting the interview portion" of competence for execution evaluations (p. 115). They developed the checklist after reviewing the literature on criminal competencies, reviewing relevant case law, and consulting with professionals who conduct competence for execution evaluations. The checklist is divided into four sections that assess an offender's *(1)* understanding of the reasons for punishment, *(2)* understanding of the punishment, *(3)* appreciation and reasoning, and *(4)* ability to assist the attorney. Zapf et al. selected these topic areas as representing the legal criteria for competence for execution in many states. Although this measure was developed several years before the U.S. Supreme Court decided *Panetti*, it is interesting to note that Zapf et al. recognized the importance of going beyond a simple assessment of whether the offender possesses a sufficient factual understanding of the punishment. Specifically, they recommended (in Section 3 of the checklist) assessing the offender's appreciation and reasoning abilities, which goes beyond what *Ford* requires. This foresight resulted in a checklist that remains relevant post *Panetti*.

Several years later, researchers developed the *Competency for Execution Research Rating Scales* (CERRS) (Ackerson et al., 2005) to assist mental health professionals in the evaluation of competence for execution. Ackerson et al. developed the CERRS after surveying 113 judges with authority to give death penalty sentences about content areas that they considered important when determining competence for execution. The measure was developed following accepted procedures for developing legal competence assessment instruments (see Grisso, 1986). The CERRS has four sections: *(1)* understanding and appreciating punishment (eight items), *(2)* understanding and appreciating death (two items), *(3)* capacity to work with counsel (four items), and *(4)* relevant clinical information (three items). Each of the 17 items is scored on a 5-point Likert scale ranging from 1 = severe incapacity to 5 = no incapacity, and item descriptions are provided in an accompanying manual.

To our knowledge, the CERRS is the only competence for execution instrument that has been the subject of empirical research. Ackerson et al. (2005) asked 90 forensic psychologists to make assessments of competence for execution based on nine fictional vignettes. To examine the utility of the CERRS, 41 of the psychologists were asked to use the CERRS when making their determinations of competence, and 49 psychologists were asked to make their competence determinations without using the CERRS. The results revealed that when the legal criteria for competence for execution were ambiguous in the vignettes, the CERRS group was significantly more likely to be influenced by legal information contained in the vignettes. Ackerson et al. also found that 48% of the variance in the competence determinations made by the CERRS group was explained by legal criteria (34%) and diagnostic symptomatology (14%), compared to 37% of the variance in the determinations for the non-CERRS group (26% legal criteria; 11% diagnostic symptomatology). Ackerson et al. concluded that the CERRS appears to guide evaluators to consider both legal and clinical factors when making determinations of competence for execution.

As the foregoing discussion illustrates, evaluators who wish to make use of competence-specific measures when evaluating an offender's competence for execution have limited options. Perhaps because competence for execution evaluations are unusual and controversial, few researchers have attempted to carefully study them or develop assessment measures. Nevertheless, much of the writing on these evaluations occurred in the immediate aftermath of *Ford* in the mid to late 1980s, so perhaps the U.S. Supreme Court's recent decision in *Panetti* will lead to a resurgence of research and scholarship in this important area.

Response Style

Criminal defendants and civil litigants may have incentives to provide false, misleading, or distorted information in a forensic evaluation. Offenders facing the death penalty may have an incentive to "fake bad" by feigning or exaggerating mental health symptoms in an effort to avoid being executed, and the temporal placement of competence for execution evaluations in the criminal justice process means that such evaluations may represent the last chance for an offender to avoid execution. Therefore, forensic evaluators should have a low threshold for suspecting inaccurate responding by the offender and they should have a well-developed strategy for assessing the offender's response style.

There are several useful approaches for assessing response style that have gained support in the literature. The use of archival and third-party information can assist an evaluator to assess the validity/accuracy of the offender's self-report and the likelihood that the offender is exaggerating his or her legally relevant deficits. Such sources of information might include historical records (e.g., medical, mental health, educational, criminal justice, employment) and collateral interviews with knowledgeable third parties (e.g., family members, close friends, significant others, coworkers, supervisors, correctional officers). In the report and accompanying testimony, the evaluator should describe the degree of consistency between the offender's self-report and the archival or third-party information. Documenting inconsistencies is useful for the evaluator to clarify reasoning and conclusions, and it is also useful for the court to see such inconsistencies when reaching the ultimate determination regarding whether the offender is competent to be executed.

There are also several well-validated instruments that are helpful in assessing an offender's response style. Some of these are specialized measures designed specifically to assess an individual's response style, whereas others are more general measures that are nevertheless sensitive to response style (see generally Rogers, 2008, for a discussion of response styles). Some useful measures include the Structured Interview of Reported Symptoms (Rogers, Bagby, & Dickens, 1992; Rogers, Sewell, & Gillard, 2010), the Miller Forensic Assessment of Symptoms Test (Miller, 2001), the Validity Indicator Profile (Frederick, 1997), and the Test of Memory Malingering

(Tombaugh, 1997). Measures such as the MMPI-2 (Butcher, Dahlstrom, Graham, Tellegen, & Kaemmer, 1989) and the Personality Assessment Inventory (Morey, 1991) are not exclusively designed to assess exaggerated or fabricated symptom presentations, but both instruments contain well-validated validity indicators and can therefore prove useful when assessing an offender's response style.

Reports

There is a relatively well-developed body of literature on report writing in FMHA contexts (see, e.g., Grisso, 2010; Heilbrun, 2001; Heilbrun et al., 2009; Heilbrun, Marczyk, & DeMatteo, 2002; Melton et al., 2007; Witt, 2010). Reports describing the results of competence for execution evaluations are likely to be the subject of considerable scrutiny. The prosecution and state officials may be seeking to have the death sentence carried out in response to a variety of pressures (e.g., political, economic), and the defense may be seeking to avert the death sentence just as vigorously. So evaluators must ensure that the report (and the evaluation on which it is based) reflects best practices in the field of FMHA. Heilbrun (2001) offered several recommendations that are applicable across different types of FMHA reports. For example, he recommends attributing information to sources, using plain language and avoiding technical jargon, and writing the report in sections. The report should clearly identify/describe the referral question, legal issue being addressed, evaluation procedures, evaluation results, supportive reasoning, and conclusions. The legal decision maker should be presented with all historical and current information relevant to the ultimate determination of whether the offender is competent to be executed. Additional recommendations relating to report writing in capital contexts will be discussed in Chapter 9.

Ultimate Legal Issue

There is an ongoing and oftentimes vigorous debate in the fields of forensic psychology and forensic psychiatry regarding whether forensic mental health professionals should answer the "ultimate legal question" in their report and/or testimony. The core of the debate is that the ultimate question being decided by the court is a legal question. For example, whether a criminal offender is competent to stand trial or insane is a legal determination that is ultimately made by the court. Although some scholars have argued that forensic mental health professionals should avoid answering such legal questions (see, e.g., Grisso, 2003; Tillbrook, Mumley, & Grisso, 2003), others have argued that answering the ultimate legal question does not present a problem because many judges and attorneys anticipate that the evaluator will answer the ultimate legal question in the course of the evaluation (see, e.g., Rogers & Ewing, 1989; Rogers & Shuman, 2000). The debate will no doubt continue, and any attempts at resolving this debate are well beyond the scope of this discussion and book.

The ultimate legal issue in relation to our present topic is whether the offender is competent for execution. We believe evaluators should limit their conclusions to the functional capacities of the offender, without addressing the ultimate legal issue of whether the offender is in fact competent for execution. This viewpoint is consistent with the recommendation of Small and Otto (1991), who recommended that evaluators avoid answering the ultimate legal question in their reports and testimony, and instead focus on functional abilities as they relate to the relevant legal standard. Additional discussion relating to the ultimate legal issue debate is presented in Chapter 9.

Conclusion

Competence for execution evaluations remain one of the most rare and ill-defined types of evaluations conducted by forensic mental health professionals. The U.S. Supreme Court has addressed the constitutionality of executing incompetent offenders twice in the past 25 years, but both decisions left important questions unanswered. The Supreme Court's decision not to provide a substantive legal standard in *Ford* left states, courts, and forensic mental health professionals in a difficult position. Although *Panetti* clarified that offenders must possess both a factual and rational understanding of the punishment and why it is being imposed, the Supreme Court again declined to define a specific standard for courts to use when determining when an offender is competent for execution.

In this chapter, we discussed the ethical and clinical considerations most relevant to competence for execution. We also identified a set of recommendations and guidelines designed to assist clinicians who conduct these types of evaluations. As noted, these recommendations and guidelines appear to have gained the most support across multiple sources, and they appear to be consistent with the Supreme Court's decisions in *Ford* and *Panetti*.

Despite a recent Supreme Court decision, advances in the relevant literature, the development of instrumentation for use in these evaluations, and our attempt to identify a core set of recommendations and guidelines, it is likely that assessments of competence for execution will continue to generate some level of controversy and confusion. Although these evaluations are so rare that developing a large body of research is unlikely, we hope some researchers will invest effort in this important area. Continued discussion of this topic in the literature and other forums, combined with empirical research and the refining/developing of relevant instrumentation, should result in developments that will assist evaluators and courts who consider an offender's competence for execution.

7

Evaluations Addressing Mitigation in Capital Sentencing

No other type of forensic mental health assessment (FMHA) requires the depth and breadth of focus that is necessary for mitigation evaluations in capital cases. Most FMHAs address one narrowly defined psycholegal construct. Legal insanity, for example, addresses whether a defendant was impaired by a specific condition (i.e., serious psychiatric illness) in a specific manner (i.e., so as not to understand the nature, character, consequences, or wrongfulness of a particular offense) at a specific moment (i.e., when committing the offense). Even other types of FMHAs in capital litigation address narrowly defined questions; for example, assessing whether a defendant meets criteria for mental retardation or determining what risk of violence a defendant poses if serving a life sentence in prison. But mitigation evaluations, by definition, address a concept that is expansive and even subjective. The U.S. Supreme Court has defined mitigation as "any aspect of a defendant's character or record, or any of the circumstances of the offense that the defendant proffered as a basis for a sentence less than death" (*Lockett v. Ohio*, 1978, p. 604). This requires an evaluation with a far broader scope than examining a defendant's behavior or capacities at a particular time.

So what, exactly, is mitigation? Anything jurors might consider mitigating. Tautological or not, the U.S. Supreme Court has consistently conveyed that mitigation is, in some ways, in the eye of the beholder. Consequently, the Court has emphasized that the defense team should have the opportunity to present almost any case-specific information that might prompt a jury to better understand the defendant and assign a sentence of less than death. In practical terms, mitigating evidence tends to be either *explanatory and contextualizing*, in that it sheds light on the defendant's experiences and deficits that may have shaped the defendant into someone who eventually committed a capital offense, or *counterbalancing*, in that it sheds light on more positive aspects of the defendant that were not evident in that capital offense (Connell, 2003). But even these broad categories do not capture all evidence that might be mitigating. Therefore, clinicians who evaluate mitigation in the context of capital sentencing approach an unusually comprehensive task.

Legal Background: Case Law Defining Mitigation

Recall from Chapter 3 that modern death penalty jurisprudence began to take shape after the U.S. Supreme Court held that the death penalty—as applied at the time—violated the Eighth Amendment's prohibition against cruel and unusual punishment and the Fourteenth Amendment's guarantee of due process of law (*Furman v. Georgia*, 1972). The Court's decision was based, at least in part, on evidence of disparate sentencing across defendants and inconsistent sentencing procedures across jurisdictions. Reacting to the Court's reasoning in *Furman*, state legislatures modified their relevant statutes, typically in one of two ways. New statutes either *(1)* imposed the death penalty automatically for certain offenses, or *(2)* added guidelines and protections to capital case procedure. Although both of these approaches attempted to remedy inconsistent and disparate sentencing, only the latter approach eventually went on to pass constitutional muster.

In 1976, the U.S. Supreme Court re-examined the death penalty and essentially lifted the moratorium it had imposed 4 years earlier in *Furman*. In its decision in *Gregg v. Georgia* (1976)—which consolidated several other cases (*Jurek v. Texas*, 1976; *Proffitt v. Florida*, 1976; *Roberts v. Louisiana*, 1976; *Woodson v. North Carolina*, 1976)—the Supreme Court identified a constitutionally permissible framework for imposing the death penalty. The Court concluded that *(1)* there must be objective criteria to direct sentencing and limit sentencing discretion, and *(2)* criteria must allow the sentencer[1] to give

---

1. "Sentencer" in this context refers to the judge or the jury because, in these early cases, jurisdictions handled the sentencing process somewhat differently. Technically, the jury makes sentencing

(Continued)

"particularized consideration" to the character and record of the convicted (*Woodson v. North Carolina*, 1976, p. 303). In ruling on the five cases that came before it, the Supreme Court held that Georgia, Florida, and Texas satisfied these requirements, while North Carolina and Louisiana did not. Whereas a variety of death penalty states had adjusted their statutes independently between 1972 and 1976, this affirmative ruling suggested a framework that would satisfy the U.S. Supreme Court and its interpretation of the U.S. Constitution.

Since the *Gregg v. Georgia* ruling in 1976, death penalty statutes and the procedures they prescribe have become increasingly similar across jurisdictions. Generally, the process consists of a bifurcated trial, with the first phase devoted to determining the defendant's guilt and, if the first phase yields a guilty verdict, a second phase devoted to determining the appropriate sentence. The sentencing phase must "direct and limit" the sentencer's decision, while still allowing for "particularized consideration" through aggravating and mitigating evidence (*Woodson v. North Carolina*, 1976, p. 303).

Mitigation plays a crucial role during the sentencing phase. *Furman v. Georgia* (1972) and *Gregg v. Georgia* (1976) set the stage for formal attention to mitigating evidence in capital sentencing,[2] but the U.S. Supreme Court periodically re-examined the issue to limit, clarify, or expand mitigating evidence. The principal case guiding mitigation came only 2 years after *Gregg*, with the Supreme Court's decision in *Lockett v. Ohio* (1978). In *Lockett*, the Court held that "the Eighth and Fourteenth Amendments require that the sentencer . . . not be precluded from considering, *as a mitigating factor*, any aspect of a defendant's character or record and any of the circumstances of the offense that the defendant proffers as a basis for a sentence less than death" (p. 604).

The practical effect of *Lockett* has been that defense attorneys can cast a wide net to search for mitigating evidence (American Bar Association, 2003; Melton, Petrila, Poythress, & Slobogin, 2007) and judges tend to be deferential in allowing potentially mitigating evidence. After all, if a judge were to exclude evidence that the defense considers mitigating, the defense may have

---

(*Continued*)
recommendations, while the judge decides upon the actual sentence. This provided a loophole for the judge to depart from the jury's recommendation, although such departures were rare. However, after the Supreme Court's decision in *Ring v. Arizona* (2002), juries, not the judge, must find the aggravating factors necessary to impose a death sentence.

2. Actually, a preview of the U.S. Supreme Court's later approach to mitigation came in 1971 *before* the moratorium and return of the death penalty. The Supreme Court ruled in *McGautha v. California* (1971) that evidence of a defendant's history of childhood trauma and abuse was relevant for the jury to consider in its sentencing recommendation. Though it preceded the modern death penalty era, the case was consistent with a general trend toward broad inclusion of mitigating evidence, even when the evidence was essentially irrelevant to a defendant's factual guilt or innocence.

grounds to appeal the case outcome by arguing that the exclusion violated *Lockett*. Since *Lockett*, then, mitigating evidence is understood in the broadest terms by both defense counsel and judges.

A second landmark U.S. Supreme Court decision addressing mitigating evidence was handed down 4 years after *Lockett*. In *Eddings v. Oklahoma* (1982), the Supreme Court reviewed a case in which an Oklahoma trial judge sentenced a defendant to death following a guilty verdict for first-degree murder. During sentencing, the prosecution put forth three aggravating factors (i.e., the murder was especially heinous, atrocious, or cruel; the crime was committed to avoid arrest; the defendant was likely to constitute a continuing threat to society). The trial judge later concluded that the prosecution proved these three aggravating factors beyond a reasonable doubt. In contrast, the defense put forth mitigating evidence regarding the defendant's young age at the time of the offense and his turbulent childhood (including an alcoholic mother and a physically abusive father). Regarding mitigating evidence, the judge concluded that the defendant's age at the time of the offense (16 years) had mitigating value, but evidence of his turbulent childhood did not. The trial judge explained that he could not "in following the law . . . consider the fact of [the] young man's violent background" (*Eddings*, p. 108). The trial judge concluded that the mitigating evidence of the defendant's youth had not outweighed the aggravating evidence, and he sentenced the defendant to death.[3] However, on review of this case by the Supreme Court, Justice Powell explained that, "Because the [sentencer's] failure to consider all of the mitigating evidence risks erroneous imposition of the death sentence, in plain violation of *Lockett*, it is our duty to remand this case for resentencing" (*Eddings*, p. 117).[4]

At first glance, it might appear that the trial court's decision in *Eddings* was overturned simply because it did not follow the U.S. Supreme Court's holding in *Lockett*. However, *Eddings* also broke important new ground. Whereas *Lockett* suggests that any and all mitigating evidence must be *allowed into evidence*, *Eddings* demands that any and all mitigating evidence must be *considered by the sentencer*. Of course, the sentencer has flexibility in deciding how much weight (if any) to assign to mitigating evidence. But the judge must allow the defense to put forth any mitigating evidence (*Lockett*) and the

---

3. Since more recent U.S. Supreme Court decisions, most notably *Ring v. Arizona* (2002), judges are no longer allowed to act as the sentencer for the purposes of weighing aggravating and mitigating evidence.

4. Ironically, Chief Justice Burger, who authored the *Lockett* decision, filed a dissenting opinion in *Eddings*, although mostly on technical grounds. In his dissent, Chief Justice Burger argued that the issue on which the Supreme Court was overturning the lower ruling was not the issue for which certiorari had been granted.

sentencer must consider that evidence (*Eddings*) before rendering a sentence. *Lockett* and *Eddings* established the framework for presenting and considering mitigating evidence in capital cases.

After the U.S. Supreme Court defined mitigating evidence broadly, and required the sentencer to consider it, the next landmark case addressed the minimum acceptable standard for a defense attorney representing a capital defendant, lest a death sentence result from a failure to explore mitigating evidence. In *Strickland v. Washington* (1984), the defendant pled guilty to three capital murder charges, and relying on the defendant's admission of responsibility and assertion that he lacked any prior criminal record, defense counsel chose not to present any additional mitigating evidence. The defense attorney had not sought any character witnesses or requested a psychiatric examination of the defendant, partly for fear of the state putting forth its own psychiatric evidence and cross-examining defense witnesses.

On appeal, the U.S. Supreme Court examined whether Strickland's Sixth Amendment right to effective assistance of counsel had been violated. In its holding, the Court explained that the standard for defense counsel in a capital case is that of "reasonably effective assistance." To show that this standard is not met (or that the defendant was "prejudiced" in his or her ability to receive a fair trial), the defendant must demonstrate a reasonable probability that, but for counsel's shortcomings, the outcome of the trial would have been different. This type of "but for" standard is common in effective assistance of counsel cases in other contexts, too. In Strickland's case specifically, the Supreme Court concluded that Strickland's attorney had not acted unreasonably, and that even had he acted differently the outcome of the case would not necessarily have been any different. Thus, although the Supreme Court refused to set aside Strickland's death sentence, the Court did use this case to identify the standard of practice for defense in capital litigation. Later decisions about defense practice in capital litigation (discussed later in this section) have clear implications for forensic mental health professionals who conduct mitigation evaluations.

Though *Lockett* defined mitigating evidence, the U.S. Supreme Court continued to revisit the issue of mitigation over the next several decades. Just 4 years after *Eddings*, the Supreme Court heard an appeal from a South Carolina defendant who had been sentenced to death after a trial judge refused to allow certain character witnesses to testify on his behalf (*Skipper v. South Carolina*, 1986). Skipper's defense attorney had attempted to introduce character evidence in the form of testimony from visitors to the defendant and the correctional officers who oversaw the defendant during his incarceration. The trial judge did not allow any of the individuals to testify, concluding that their testimony would not be legally relevant. In the Supreme Court's ruling on Skipper's appeal, Justice White explained:

> [T]he only question . . . is whether the exclusion from the sentencing hearing of the testimony [Skipper offered] regarding his good behavior during the over seven months he spent in jail awaiting trial deprived [him] of his right to place before the sentencer relevant [mitigating evidence]. It can hardly be disputed that it did. (*Skipper*, p. 4)

Thus, the U.S. Supreme Court had ruled in *Lockett* and *Eddings* that all mitigating evidence is admissible for consideration, and *Skipper* marked the first in a series of cases that reiterated this theme by identifying a specific type of admissible evidence. In Skipper's case, it was clear that evidence of behavior during incarceration preceding the trial could indeed be offered as mitigating evidence.

Across these rulings, two major themes have recurred. Based on the U.S. Supreme Court's decisions regarding mitigating evidence, the first theme addresses the scope of mitigation (*Lockett*, *Eddings*, *Skipper*), while the second theme addresses the behavior of courtroom players (*Strickland*). A third theme in Supreme Court decisions addresses mitigating factors not found in state statutes. In *Hitchcock v. Dugger* (1987), Hitchcock had been sentenced to death in Florida following the trial judge's instruction to the jury that they may consider only statutorily defined mitigating factors—that is, only those factors actually written in the Florida death penalty statute.[5] The Supreme Court overturned Hitchcock's death sentence after it concluded that denying the jury the opportunity to weigh nonstatutory mitigating factors was a clear violation of *Lockett* and *Eddings*. Considering *Hitchcock* alongside prior Supreme Court rulings suggests that the scope of mitigation includes evidence not enumerated in the relevant statute. Therefore, statutes addressing mitigating factors are not exhaustive and the judge may not limit a jury's opportunity to weigh any relevant mitigating evidence.

Of course, if the judge cannot limit a jury's opportunity to weigh mitigating evidence, then the judge's instructions to the jury become particularly important and serve as a common basis for appeal. In *Mills v. Maryland* (1988), the U.S. Supreme Court reviewed a case in which the trial judge's instructions to the jury were misinterpreted. One juror had interpreted the judge's instructions as indicating that, in sentencing the defendant, a given mitigating factor could only be assigned weight if *all* jurors were in agreement on it.

---

5. Recall from Chapter 2 that some mitigating and some aggravating factors appear in states' respective death penalty statutes. Although *Gregg* has been interpreted as requiring the finding of at least one statutorily defined aggravating factor to allow imposition of the death penalty, *Lockett* demands that any mitigating evidence that the defense deems relevant be admissible, and *Eddings* demands that it be allowed due consideration by the sentencer.

Upon review of the instructions, the Supreme Court concluded that there was "a substantial probability that reasonable jurors, upon receiving the judge's instructions in this case . . . may have thought they were precluded from considering any mitigating evidence unless all 12 jurors agreed on the existence of a particular such circumstance" (*Mills*, p. 384). The Court further stated that "the possibility that a single juror could block such consideration, and consequently require the jury to impose the death penalty . . ." was not acceptable (*Mills*, p. 384).

The U.S. Supreme Court reviewed a similar case from North Carolina only 2 years later. In *McCoy v. North Carolina* (1990), the Supreme Court identified in the jury instructions an expressed limitation of mitigating value to those factors upon which all of the jurors agreed.[6] In other words, the trial judge's instructions had not been *misinterpreted* as limiting jury consideration (as in *Mills*); the judge's instructions *explicitly stated* that the jury would have to agree on each factor to which it wanted to assign weight, whether mitigating or aggravating. On appeal, the Supreme Court concluded that in light of the Eighth Amendment and the recent *Mills* decision, "[A] State may not limit a sentencer's consideration of mitigating evidence merely because it places the same limitation on consideration of aggravating circumstances" (*McCoy*, p. 442).

Despite having ruled on mandatory death penalty statutes in 1976, the U.S. Supreme Court would go on to revisit the issue in 1990 in a case that addressed a *lack* of mitigating evidence. In *Blystone v. Pennsylvania* (1990), the Supreme Court addressed the constitutionality of Pennsylvania's variation on mandatory death penalty statutes, whereby a defendant would automatically be sentenced to death if the jury found at least one of the requisite aggravating factors and no mitigating factors. The Supreme Court granted an appeal in which the defendant asserted that his Eighth Amendment rights had been violated under the Pennsylvania sentencing framework. In upholding the defendant's death sentence, the Court explained that the statute was not "impermissibly 'mandatory' as . . . understood in *Woodson* or *Roberts*. Death is . . . imposed only after a determination that the aggravating circumstances outweigh the mitigating circumstances . . . or that there are no such mitigating circumstances" (*Blystone*, p. 305). Thus, although mandatory imposition of the death penalty for certain offenses is unconstitutional (*Woodson*, *Roberts*), mandatory imposition of the death penalty *following certain conclusions about aggravating and mitigating evidence* is constitutional (*Blystone*).

Between the 1976 *Gregg* decision and 2002, all death penalty jurisdictions required some weighing of aggravating and mitigating evidence, but there was no requirement regarding who did that weighing. In many cases, a jury of

---

6. As detailed in Chapter 2, the presiding judge gives the jury specific instructions regarding how to weigh sentencing evidence and arrive at a sentencing recommendation.

peers weighed aggravating and mitigating factors to make a sentence recommendation; in other cases, a judge handled the entire sentencing phase. Although the Sixth Amendment guarantees a defendant a right to *trial* by jury, there is no explicit constitutional guarantee for *sentencing* by jury. In fact, outside the realm of capital sentencing, the jury is largely uninvolved in most criminal sentencing. Jury involvement in capital sentencing is more a function of judicial construction following *Gregg* and the statutory modifications thereafter.

However, the task of capital sentencing fell solely to juries after the 2002 U.S. Supreme Court decision in *Ring v. Arizona*. The facts of the case were complex, but in brief, Ring was found guilty of felony murder, a capital offense, because the victim of Ring's armed robbery had been killed during the commission of the robbery. The jury had deadlocked on whether Ring was guilty of premeditated murder, suggesting that they could not agree on whether he personally had killed the victim. At the time in Arizona, two procedural facts were important: first, a defendant convicted of felony murder could be sentenced to death only if the sentencer concluded that the defendant personally killed the victim; and second, the judge was the sole sentencer. This meant that for the judge to sentence Ring to death, he had to essentially go one step further than the jury and conclude that Ring was the physical killer of the victim, not just an accomplice guilty of felony murder. After finding that aggravating evidence outweighed the mitigating evidence, the trial judge did just that and sentenced Ring to death.

On review of *Ring*, the U.S. Supreme Court concluded that the Sixth Amendment right to trial by jury should extend to capital sentencing. Thus, the judge's weighing of aggravating and mitigating evidence and subsequent sentencing of Ring to death was unconstitutional, and Ring's death sentence was set aside. Since *Ring*, aggravating and mitigating factors must be evaluated by a jury, not a judge.[7] Initially, it was unclear whether the Court's decision would apply retroactively to defendants who had been sentenced to death by a judge. The immediate reaction to *Ring* was that over 100 defendants on death rows across the United States appealed their judge-imposed death sentences. In *Summerlin v. Stewart* (2003), the U.S. Court of Appeals for the Ninth Circuit addressed those appeals by interpreting *Ring* to apply retroactively, commuting 111 appealed judge-imposed death sentences to life imprisonment. However, that interpretation was corrected by the U.S. Supreme Court 1 year later in *Schiro v. Summerlin* (2004). As a result, the commuted death sentences would remain life imprisonment sentences, but other death

---

7. An important caveat is that statutory frameworks which permit the judge to treat the jury's sentence as *advisory*, though still requiring that the jury make the findings regarding aggravators and mitigators, have thus far survived constitutional challenge.

row inmates who had failed to appeal their judge-imposed sentences would go without redress.

Shortly after *Ring*, the U.S. Supreme Court again addressed the standard of practice for defense attorneys working on capital cases. Recall that *Strickland* set the standard for defense counsel as "reasonably effective assistance." To show that defense counsel failed to meet this standard, a defendant must show a reasonable probability that, but for defense counsel's shortcomings, the outcome of the trial would have been different. In *Wiggins v. Smith* (2003), the Supreme Court reviewed a death sentence after defense counsel had not expanded the mitigation inquiry or research beyond the presentence investigation. In its decision examining whether this fell below acceptable standards of practice, the Supreme Court reversed and remanded the death sentence, citing counsel's limited investigation. Quoting the American Bar Association (ABA) Guidelines for the Appointment and Performance of Counsel in Death Penalty Cases, the Court emphasized that investigation into mitigating evidence "should comprise efforts to discover *all reasonably available* mitigating evidence and evidence to rebut any aggravating evidence that may be introduced by the prosecutor" (*Wiggins*, citing ABA Guidelines, 1989, 11.4.1(c), p. 93). Thus, prior decisions defined the scope of mitigation broadly, and *Wiggins* indicated that defense counsel had a duty to *actively pursue potentially mitigating evidence*. The *Wiggins* decision has clear implications for forensic mental health professionals who conduct mitigation evaluations.

The year before *Wiggins*, the U.S. Supreme Court ruled in *Atkins v. Virginia* (2002) that execution of a mentally retarded offender is unconstitutional under the Eighth Amendment. The *Atkins* decision, which was discussed in Chapter 5, has certainly increased the salience of mental retardation to capital sentencing, but it is important in the mitigation context primarily because it set the stage for *Tennard v. Dretke* (2004). Tennard was sentenced to death after his defense team presented evidence that his IQ was approximately 67, a score consistent with a diagnosis of mild mental retardation.[8] The case was remanded following the *Atkins* decision, but the U.S. Court of Appeals for the Fifth Circuit concluded that Tennard was not mentally retarded and therefore remained eligible for the death penalty.

On appeal to the U.S. Supreme Court, the defense argued that Tennard's low IQ was ignored during the sentencing for being—in the words of the trial judge—"constitutionally irrelevant." In its review, the Supreme Court concluded that the jury should have been able to consider Tennard's low IQ,

---

8. An IQ of 67 falls within the "Extremely Low" level of intellectual functioning. An IQ of less than 70 is a necessary—but not sufficient—element of a diagnosis of mental retardation using the diagnostic criteria in the *Diagnostic and Statistical Manual of Mental Disorders, 4th edition, text revision* (*DSM-IV-TR*; American Psychiatric Association, 2000).

particularly because the prosecution had highlighted his intelligence when arguing that he posed a risk of future dangerousness. Thus, the implication of *Tennard* is that evidence of low IQ, even if not amounting to evidence of mental retardation, still has mitigating value and should be considered by the jury. The decision echoes themes from *Lockett* and *Eddings*—emphasizing that all potentially mitigating evidence should be considered by the sentencer.

The U.S. Supreme Court has also recently addressed Texas capital sentencing proceedings (*Smith v. Texas*, 2004) much like it had considered Pennsylvania proceedings in the 1990 *Blystone* decision. The Texas capital sentencing statute requires the jury to consider not only aggravating factors, but to address two special issues. Regardless of the jury's interpretation of the mitigating and aggravating factors, the judge in *Smith* had instructed the jury that if it wished to sentence the defendant to life imprisonment rather than death, it would have to answer "no" to at least one of the special issue questions. When the jury answered the special issue questions in the affirmative (i.e., that the offense was "deliberate" and that the defendant would constitute a "future danger"), the defendant was sentenced to death. In overturning the sentence, the Supreme Court explained that the "jury was essentially instructed to return a false answer to a special issue in order to avoid a death sentence," which failed to allow full weight to be assigned to the mitigating evidence (*Smith*, p. 48).

In sum, the U.S. Supreme Court decisions addressing mitigation have conveyed three themes. First, rulings concerning the admissibility of mitigating evidence have shown that admissibility is largely deferential. If defense counsel thinks that evidence regarding a defendant's history or character could be interpreted by the jury as mitigating, then the judge is likely to admit that evidence (e.g., *Lockett*, *Eddings*, *Tennard*).

A second theme in the U.S. Supreme Court decisions addresses the roles of courtroom players, particularly defense counsel. At a minimum, defense counsel must provide "reasonable assistance" (*Strickland*), and reasonable assistance includes proactive efforts to present any evidence that might have mitigating value (*Wiggins*). When it comes to considering mitigating evidence and assigning a sentence of death, the jury—rather than the judge—carries the responsibility (*Ring*).

Finally, the third type of U.S. Supreme Court decision related to mitigation has attempted to interpret death penalty statutes. These decisions seem somewhat split. In some cases, the Court clearly adopts a liberal stance in allowing for consideration of any mitigating evidence that may benefit the defendant (e.g., *Hitchcock*). On the other hand, some of the cases seem to convey that, so long as certain protections were afforded, no extra protections need be extended (e.g., *Blystone*).

Mitigation in State Statute

Each state that allows the death penalty has adopted a statute to define or guide mitigation. States may list somewhat different mitigating factors or phrase these factors somewhat differently. Generally, however, statutes are more similar than dissimilar. Common statutorily defined mitigating factors include:

- The defendant's age (or "youth") at the time of the offense.
- The defendant had little or no history of prior offending.
- The defendant was one of several offenders committing the capital offense, and the defendant played a less active role in the offense than others.
- The victim somehow participated in, or consented to, the defendant's behavior that resulted in the capital offense.
- The defendant acted under circumstances that he or she reasonably believed provided a moral justification or rationale for the capital offense.
- The defendant acted under extreme duress, pressure, or domination by others when committing the capital offense.
- The defendant acted under severe mental or emotional disturbance at the time of the capital offense.
- The defendant acted with some degree of impairment that limited his or her capacity to appreciate the nature, character, consequences, or wrongfulness of the capital offense.
- The defendant acted with some degree of impairment that limited his or her ability to conform behavior to the law.

Some of these common mitigating factors are straightforward facts (i.e., age at offense, prior criminal record). But as the list progresses, the mitigating factors become increasingly complex and more likely to require input from mental health professionals. Indeed, the last two factors in the list are nearly identical to the common criteria for legal insanity, albeit slightly relaxed.

Finally, in addition to specifically defined mitigating factors, most statutes include a final, open-ended mitigating factor that allows for any other potentially mitigating evidence. Consistent with U.S. Supreme Court case law (i.e., *Lockett*, *Eddings*, *Wiggins*), this defines mitigation in the most expansive terms. Examples of typical "catchall" mitigating factors include:

- "In addition to the mitigating circumstances specified in Section 13A-5-51, mitigating circumstances shall include any aspect of a

defendant's character or record and any of the circumstances of the offense that the defendant offers as a basis for a sentence of life imprisonment without parole instead of death, and any other relevant mitigating circumstance which the defendant offers as a basis for a sentence of life imprisonment without parole instead of death." (Ala. Code § 13A-5-52, 2010)
- "Any other evidence of mitigation concerning the character and record of the defendant and the circumstances of his offense" (42 Pa. Cons. Stat. Ann. § 9711(e)(8), 2010)
- "Any other circumstance which extenuates the gravity of the crime even though it is not a legal excuse for the crime" (Cal. Penal Code § 190.3(k), 2010)
- "The existence of any other factors in the defendant's background that would mitigate against imposition of the death penalty" (Fla. Stat. § 921.141(6)(h), 2010)
- "Any other circumstances appropriate for consideration" (Ind. Code Ann. § 35-50-2-9(c)(8) West, 2010)

Overall, state statutes, like U.S. Supreme Court jurisprudence, have clearly articulated several issues that must be explored as potentially mitigating. But perhaps even more important, both sources of law have emphasized that the realm of mitigating evidence is potentially boundless. Thus, capital defense attorneys face a daunting task, because they are bound to make reasonable efforts to present any evidence that might be mitigating (*Strickland, Wiggins*; see also American Bar Association, 2003). Prosecutors who view mitigation evidence skeptically also face a difficult challenge, albeit in a different way. Therefore, both groups tend to seek mental health professionals to provide formal evaluation and consultation related to capital mitigation.

Forensic Mental Health Assessment Addressing Capital Mitigation

Forensic mental health professionals who perform capital mitigation evaluations face the task of seeking a broadly defined range of data that is important because it *might* prove mitigating. What are the practical implications of such an expansive job description?

Mitigation evaluations adopt a broad scope, as we emphasize throughout this chapter. Evaluators are not simply comparing a defendant's particular functional capacities to a particular legal standard, as in most FMHAs (Grisso, 2003). Rather, evaluators must consider all aspects of the defendant's character and capacities, and the people and experiences that shaped the defendant's character and capacities. The U.S. Supreme Court once mentioned that mitigating evidence could include any of "the diverse frailties of humankind" (*Woodson v. North Carolina*, 1976, p. 304). It is hard to imagine a more broadly defined scope of inquiry.

But mitigation evaluations are not simply a matter of accumulating more data. The case law and statutes reviewed earlier not only shape the *scope* of a mitigation evaluation, but the *focus* of mitigation evaluations and the nature of the mental health expertise that evaluators are expected to offer. The U.S. Supreme Court has consistently emphasized that a death sentence requires an individualized consideration of each defendant, including mitigation in the defendant's background, character, or offense. So the task of a forensic mental health professional approaching a mitigation evaluation in capital sentencing is usually to provide the court with *(1)* a thorough and objective evaluation of the salient characteristics of an individual defendant, including his or her formative experiences; and *(2)* a scientifically based perspective on the ways in which these characteristics and experiences may be mitigating.

Themes and Frameworks in Mitigation Evaluations

Given this complex task, there are certain concepts and theoretical frameworks that are important for mental health professionals to understand when approaching a mitigation evaluation. We discuss two that we consider particularly important: the concept of *moral culpability*, and the field of *developmental psychopathology*. These are certainly not the only concepts or frameworks relevant to mitigation evaluations (nor are the labels and concepts we emphasize the only way to understand some of these themes). But the concept of *moral culpability* is a crucial consideration underlying much of mitigation (Cunningham, 2008; Cunningham & Goldstein, 2003; Cunningham & Reidy, 2001), and mental health expertise may help the court to better consider a defendant's moral culpability for a capital offense. In addition, mental health professionals with a rich understanding of developmental psychopathology may be particularly well suited to articulate a *scientifically based* description of the interplay among the biological, psychological, social, and contextual factors that influence an individual's behaviors and life course.

Moral Culpability

Recall that capital sentencing involves a bifurcated process. The first stage addresses criminal responsibility; that is, whether all of the necessary elements of the criminal offense were proven by the prosecution beyond a reasonable doubt. *Only if* the defendant is found criminally responsible will a second trial stage address sentencing, which encompasses a deliberation between a sentence of death or life in prison. So only during this second stage, *after* the court has found the defendant criminally responsible, does the defense formally present—and the prosecution formally rebut—mitigating evidence, which may include testimony from a forensic mental health professional. Thus, mitigating evidence (including expert reports and testimony) never disputes that a capital offender is criminally responsible for the capital offense of which he or she was convicted. By definition, mitigating evidence is offered only for the jury to consider whether the offender, who has already been found criminally responsible for a capital offense, deserves a sentence less than death.

As the jury weighs the mitigating evidence to determine a sentence, a crucial consideration is *moral culpability* (Cunningham, 2008; Cunningham & Goldstein, 2003; Cunningham & Reidy, 2001), or the extent to which an offender is morally blameworthy for the capital offense he or she committed. Whereas criminal responsibility is typically dichotomous (the court finds a defendant guilty or not guilty), moral culpability can be understood as a continuum. Even among a group of offenders who are criminally responsible of a capital offense, some may be more morally culpable—worthy of more blame—than others. Indeed, the assumption that moral culpability might vary even among offenders who committed the same crime underlies the U.S. Supreme Court's rationale when it required a particularized consideration of each defendant and ruled against assigning the death sentence automatically for certain crimes (*Roberts v. Louisiana*, 1976; *Woodson v. North Carolina*, 1976).

In general terms, our moral culpability for wrong decisions or wrong behavior appears greater to the extent that we have the resources, capacities, influences, and experiences that allow us to consider a range of options, yet we knowingly and independently chose a wrong behavior with minimal pressure to do so. Our moral culpability appears lesser to the extent that we lack the resources, capacities, influences, or experiences that allow us to consider a range of options, or to the extent that our options have been shaped and limited by influences or experiences we did not choose. Cunningham (2006b; 2008) and colleagues (Cunningham & Goldstein, 2003; Cunningham & Reidy, 2001) have repeatedly discussed moral culpability as related to capital sentencing:

> The concept of moral culpability acknowledges an elementary psychological reality: we do not all arrive at our choices out of equivalent raw material. More specifically, the nature and quality of understanding, perception, impulse control, judgments, and values that underlie choice—even choice that results in heinous violence—are influenced by developmental, cognitive, neuropsychological, relationship, cultural, community, and situational factors. (Cunningham & Reidy, 2001, p. 475)

Thus, careful attention to moral culpability requires careful attention to the internal and external factors that shaped a person's particular behavior.

Is Addressing Moral Culpability Just a Matter of Defending Criminal Behavior?

If considering moral culpability requires considering the factors that led to a capital offense, is a focus on moral culpability just a matter of defending, excusing, or "explaining away" criminal behavior? Cunningham (2006b; 2008) and colleagues (Cunningham & Goldstein, 2003; Cunningham & Reidy, 2001) observed that the concept of moral culpability appears more congruent with the arguments defense attorneys often put forth about a capital defendant (i.e., the offense was the culmination of past adverse experiences interacting with current adverse circumstances) and much less congruent with the arguments prosecutors often put forth (i.e., the offense was the result of an autonomous choice that reflects only the defendant's moral character). At first glance, the concept of moral culpability might look suspiciously "partisan" if it appears more congruent with defense arguments than prosecution. But at least two factors reveal clearly that the concept of moral culpability itself is "nonpartisan."

First, an emphasis on moral culpability is rooted in the case law and statutes surrounding capital sentencing. For example, in two recent decisions that limited the scope of capital punishment, the U.S. Supreme Court specifically identified culpability as a primary consideration. In *Atkins v. Virginia* (2002), the Court explained: "[T]he severity of the appropriate punishment necessarily depends on the offender's culpability. If the culpability of the average murderer is insufficient to justify imposition of death . . . the lesser culpability of the mentally retarded offender surely does not merit that form of retribution" (p. 319). Similarly, in *Roper v. Simmons* (2005), the Court echoed the theme: "Capital punishment must be limited to those offenders . . . whose extreme culpability makes them 'the most deserving of execution'" (p. 568).

Moral culpability is also emphasized in some statutes that guide capital sentencing. For example, in the state that performs more executions than any other, the capital procedure statute instructs the court to "consider mitigating evidence to be evidence that a juror might regard as reducing the defendant's moral blameworthiness" (Tex. Code Crim. Proc. art. 37.071, 2010). Likewise, the statute directs jurors to decide on a sentence after considering "the personal moral culpability of the defendant." Other states have similar statutory provisions relating to the defendant's moral culpability. Thus, the law itself is clear that moral culpability is a critical factor in capital sentencing decisions, and there seems little reason to believe that considering moral culpability (versus criminal responsibility alone) reflects a defense advocacy position. Indeed, a focus on moral culpability is not always helpful to the defense.

This is the second reason that the concept of moral culpability is "nonpartisan." Careful analysis *often* reveals that a defendant's capital offense was deeply intertwined with adverse experiences, influences, or deficits over which the defendant had little control. So *most* capital cases feature considerations that jurors may perceive as reducing moral culpability. However, in a few capital cases, careful analysis reveals that relatively less external influence shaped the decision to commit a capital offense. Prosecutors might argue that the absence of certain mitigating factors enhances, rather than reduces, a defendant's moral culpability, which would argue in favor of a death sentence.

It is important that forensic evaluators understand the concept of moral culpability in capital sentencing because this concept, in this context, is ripe for confusion. Cunningham (2006b) warns that the prosecution sometimes "mis-characterizes the relevant psycho-legal issue" at sentencing and "routinely frames its arguments and examinations of mental health experts in terms of criminal responsibility rather than moral culpability" (p. 209; see also Cunningham, 2008). For example, questions regarding criminal responsibility (e.g., Did the defendant intentionally commit the offense? Could the defendant understand that his or her behavior was wrong? Could the defendant have resisted impulses to behave that way?) were settled with a guilty sentence in the first stage of trial. If the answers to questions about criminal responsibility were clearly negative, the defendant would have been found not guilty, or not guilty by reason of insanity (Cunningham & Goldstein, 2003; Cunningham & Reidy, 2001). Re-examining criminal responsibility does little to "individualize" the sentencing decisions, because all defendants who reach the sentencing stage have been found criminally responsible (Cunningham, 2008). Rather, the sentencing process is more likely to reach an individualized decision by considering the defendant's experiences, influences, and capacities as they relate to moral culpability.

Regardless of whether the prosecution "mis-characterizes the relevant psycho-legal issue" (Cunningham, 2006b, p. 209) in a given case, there still remains room for confusion among forensic evaluators (and the jurors who hear their testimony) when it comes to moral culpability. One source of confusion is philosophical. Addressing the factors that influenced a defendant's choice to commit an offense can be perceived as *deterministic*, and even misperceived as a claim that a defendant lacked the free will to choose among various behaviors. But considering moral culpability never requires one to accept a strict deterministic perspective, and it never denies that a defendant had some degree of choice in his or her offense behavior. An emphasis on moral culpability only considers the psychological, social, and biological factors that *influenced*, not *determined*, a particular behavior. It is because the court considers these factors (i.e., psychological, social, biological, and related influences on behavior) that forensic mental health professionals have a role in sentencing deliberations that consider moral culpability.

What Do Mental Health Experts Know About Moral Culpability Anyway?

Obviously, forensic mental health professionals are not involved in capital proceedings to offer *judgments* about an offender's moral culpability. Forensic clinicians have no specialized knowledge regarding morality. Indeed, authorities in forensic psychology (e.g., Melton et al., 2007) have long emphasized that forensic mental health professionals must steer clear of offering "ultimate issue" moral and philosophical judgments about guilt and culpability, because such judgments are reserved for the judge or jury. So why involve forensic mental health professionals *at all* in sentencing proceedings that consider moral culpability?

Examining moral culpability requires examining the developmental, cognitive, psychological, neurological, social, and contextual factors that may have shaped an offender's particular behavior or pattern of behaviors. Forensic mental health professionals offer unique clinical expertise in identifying and assessing these factors, and mental health research reveals the well-established ways in which these factors tend to influence development and behavior. So forensic mental health professionals are not involved in sentencing proceedings to answer the question: "Was the defendant morally culpable for his or her offense?" But the forensic mental health professional may have genuine expertise to help answer related questions, including the following:

- What neurological and psychological factors might have influenced this defendant's judgment, decision making, and impulse control?
- What does research reveal about the judgment, decision making, and impulse control of others who manifest similar neurological and psychological factors?
- What developmental, familial, and social experiences shaped this defendant's value system and his or her day-to-day decisions?
- What does research suggest are common outcomes among others who experience similar developmental, familial, and social experiences?
- What adverse experiences and contextual factors may have constrained this defendant's range of opportunities and general life course?
- What does research suggest are common outcomes among others who have been exposed to similar experiences and contexts?

Answering questions like these typically requires clinical skills and scientific knowledge that are "beyond the ken" of most laypersons.[9] Therefore, forensic

---

9. "Beyond the ken" of the average layperson is the typical standard used by courts to determine whether expert testimony is necessary. If a particular topic is, in the court's opinion, within the ken of the jury, the court will typically exclude expert testimony on that topic.

mental health professionals may have a unique role to play as forensic experts who help inform capital sentencing decisions that consider moral culpability.[10]

Developmental Psychopathology

Recall that the task of a forensic mental health professional approaching a mitigation evaluation in capital sentencing is usually to provide the court with *(a)* a thorough and objective evaluation of the salient characteristics of an individual defendant, including his or her formative experiences; and *(b)* a scientifically based perspective on the ways in which these characteristics and experiences may or may not be mitigating. Thus, evaluators must have the clinical skills necessary to elicit and investigate a defendant's developmental history and clinical status. But the evaluator must also have the scientific or empirical knowledge regarding how these developmental, social, and clinical factors interact to influence a defendant's development and behavior. Mitigation evaluations typically require evaluators to draw upon data from medical, behavioral, and social sciences. Thus, the tasks in a mitigation evaluation are particularly congruent with the field of Developmental Psychopathology, a scientific discipline that studies the interplay among biological, psychological, and social-contextual influences that shape development and behavior (Cicchetti, 2006). Indeed, a seminal article defined the field of developmental psychopathology in terms that sound remarkably similar to the clinical task an evaluator faces in a mitigation evaluation: "[T]he study of the origins and the course of individual patterns of behavioral maladaptation, whatever the age of onset, whatever the causes . . . and however complex the course of the developmental pattern may be" (Sroufe & Rutter, 1984, p. 18).

Developmental psychopathology can be informative to forensic mental health professionals (and the jurors who consider their input) because the field emphasizes the interaction between the individual and the environment over the course of development (Cicchetti & Aber, 1998). Furthermore, the field applies scientific methodology to the types of questions that routinely emerge in capital sentencing. For example: How do certain adverse experiences tend to shape development? Why do these adverse experiences seem to influence

---

10. Again, not all mitigating evidence addresses moral culpability. Although moral culpability is a crucial underlying focus in mitigation, the concept of mitigation (see *Lockett, Eddings*) is certainly broad enough to include evidence that is not directly related to moral culpability, yet which may still lead jurors to assign a sentence less than death. Forensic mental health professionals may, of course, have a substantial role to play in addressing mitigating evidence that is not linked to moral culpability. But this subsection emphasizes that their role in mitigation that addresses moral culpability is to clarify what may seem a murky concept, and to underscore the rationale behind—and some limits of—the forensic mental health professional's potential contributions.

different people in different ways? Why do some individuals seem resilient in the face of adversity, while others seem vulnerable? What are the adult outcomes associated with childhood risk factors, and how do multiple risk factors interact to influence outcomes?

Of course, evaluators will need to be fluent in the specific research most relevant to the mitigating factors in a given case. But across many cases, key concepts and principles from developmental psychopathology (Cicchetti, 2006; Cicchetti & Cohen, 1995) may be relevant to capital mitigation (see Salekin, 2007). For example, consider the following principles from developmental psychopathology.

Risk Factors

"Risk factors," a concept common to many fields, are simply those factors that correspond with a negative outcome (e.g., violence or criminality). Some "risk factors" are better understood as *risk markers*, in that they co-occur with a negative outcome but do not directly *cause* that outcome (Kraemer et al., 1997). However, true *causal risk factors* actually influence the negative outcome. The scientific literature documents numerous risk markers and causal risk factors related to the outcomes most relevant in capital sentencing evaluations (e.g., delinquency, criminality, violence, homicide). Most capital defendants have been exposed to many of these well-documented risk factors. Considering risk factors is a crucial aspect of mitigation evaluations, not because these risk factors might elicit sympathy, but because these risk factors bear a strong empirical relationship to poor outcomes (regardless of whether a person chooses to manifest them).

Developmental scholars have long emphasized that the cumulative effect of multiple risk factors contributes to negative outcomes more so than any one specific risk factor (see generally Sameroff, 2000). In short, the presence of more risk factors is associated with a worse long-term outcome. For example, in the prospective Pittsburgh Youth Study of over 1,500 urban boys, those with four or more risk factors for homicide were 14 times more likely to later commit homicide than boys with fewer than four risk factors, regardless of *which* risk factors were considered (Loeber et al., 2005). Considering capital mitigation requires considering the cumulative effect of risk factors.

Protective Factors

Of course, risk factors should be considered alongside protective factors, that is, those processes or influences that buffer the negative impact of risk and increase the likelihood of competent development and positive outcomes (Luthar, Cicchetti, & Becker, 2000). Most capital defendants have been exposed to both protective factors and risk factors, so it becomes important to examine how the defendant fared when protective factors were present and how the defendant fared when protective factors were absent.

Equifinality

At the time of capital sentencing, all capital defendants have reached the same point, but they have reached that point via very different pathways. "*Equifinality* refers to the observation that in any open system, a diversity of pathways, including chance events . . . may lead to the same outcome" (Cicchetti, 2006, p. 13; see also Cicchetti & Rogosh, 1996). Obviously, there is no one path that leads to capital murder.

Multifinality

Conversely, even individuals who appear to follow very similar life pathways may arrive at very different outcomes, which is a concept known as *multifinality* (Cicchetti, 2006). "Not everyone with this background goes on to commit capital murder!" some listeners may respond after considering a capital defendant's troubled background. They are correct. In human development, the same adverse experience rarely leads to precisely the same negative outcome. Just as not everyone exposed to a virus becomes ill (or ill in the same way or to the same degree), not everyone with adverse early experiences commits a serious criminal offense.

Multifinality is the norm because even when people step into the same set of experiences or influences, they never do so with the same intellect and temperament, or the same set of strengths, capacities, vulnerabilities, and deficits. Differences can be substantial even among those we might expect to share similar "raw materials" and a similar environment; that is, biological siblings raised in the same home. Developmental scholars have long emphasized that family experiences vary greatly among siblings because of differences in their genetic makeup, birth order, age, gender, and idiosyncratic experiences (Hoffman, 1991). For example, a natural genetic difference in one sibling (e.g., a fussy temperament as an infant, or hyperactivity as a young child) often elicits a different approach from parents (e.g., impatience, frustration, physical abuse), leading to a different environment for one sibling as compared to the other. Of course, individual choices also lead to different environments and different outcomes, but conscious choice is only one of the *many* ways that children evoke different environments and are then differently shaped by those environments (Scarr & McCartney, 1983).

Resilience

Multifinality is the norm also because people vary in resilience, which is the capacity for adapting successfully, and functioning well, despite adversity or trauma (Cicchetti, 2006; Luthar et al., 2000). Resilient individuals "turn out well," despite early adversity that might lead us to expect poor outcomes.

In popular conversation, resilience is sometimes described as a personal attribute similar to moral fortitude, willpower, or self-discipline. Certainly personal attributes (themselves influenced by the environment) play some role in individual responses to adversity. But science suggests that resilience has less to do with strength of character, and more to do with normal human adaptation and common resources accessible to most children (Masten, 2001). Even in the seminal studies that popularized the concept of resilience by following a cohort of impoverished Hawaiian children (Werner & Smith, 1982, 1992), those children who turned out to be "resilient" tended to have better parents, better access to adult role models and religious programming, better intellectual skills, and an "easy temperament" as infants. In other words, resilience was largely related to hidden assets in an otherwise impoverished environment, or to common genetically based strengths.

A comprehensive review of resilience research emphasized that several commonplace factors supported resilience (e.g., competent and caring adults in the family and community, cognitive and self-regulation skills) and suggested that resilience tends to be the norm unless "important adaptive systems, such as cognition and parenting, are compromised" (Masten, 2001, p. 232). Of course, these important adaptive systems have indeed been compromised among many—though not all—capital defendants, who tend to have had abusive or absent parents (Haney, 1995) and substantial cognitive limitations (Cunningham & Vigen, 2002). Thus, it becomes important for forensic evaluators who conduct capital mitigation evaluations to understand the concept of resilience and factors that leave children more or less likely to respond in a resilient manner.

Overall, these concepts from developmental psychopathology are never enough to answer the particular questions that arise in any particular capital case. But they do provide a science-based framework for addressing some of the general questions and general themes, such as individual differences and pathways toward disastrous outcomes, that emerge in most capital cases. As such, evaluators should remain vigilant to the themes discussed in this section when they conduct mitigation evaluations.

Roles for Forensic Mental Health Professionals Addressing Mitigation

Generally, attorneys ask a forensic mental health professional to address mitigation in capital sentencing when they believe he or she may have expertise in identifying mitigating evidence or helping others understand that mitigating evidence. This generality is true of defense teams retaining a forensic mental health professional to address mitigation, and for prosecutors retaining a forensic mental health professional to provide a second opinion on evidence of mitigation. Of course, mitigating evidence need not be *presented* by an expert witness. Indeed, some of the most compelling mitigation evidence is presented through testimony by the defendant's family or friends, who can convey firsthand accounts of the defendant's life experiences. But regardless of whether a forensic mental health professional presents evidence in court, attorneys may retain forensic mental health professionals to help identify and explain mitigating evidence that is beyond the knowledge base of laypersons. Because mitigating evidence can vary greatly, forensic mental health professionals might fill different roles, depending on the nature of the mitigating evidence they are addressing. In fact, many defense teams retain more than one forensic mental health professional, with each filling a different expert role with respect to mitigating evidence. Generally, roles for forensic mental health professionals can be considered *consulting* roles or *expert* (testifying) roles.

The "Mitigation Specialist" Consulting Role

Defense teams typically include an investigator-like role, often labeled "mitigation specialist." These investigators need not be mental health professionals—a few have professional backgrounds in law or even law enforcement—but most have a background in social work or, occasionally, psychology. The mitigation specialist serves as a social historian who investigates the defendant's background to identify potentially mitigating data and themes (Leonard, 2003). Typically, mitigation specialists invest hundreds of hours in a detailed mitigation investigation. They compile relevant historical records and identify historical contacts (family members, friends, teachers, clergy, coaches, employers, neighbors, treatment providers) who can provide input regarding the defendant. These materials are then available to the defense team, and any forensic clinician who serves in a formal evaluation role at the request of the defense.

The mitigation specialist role involves straightforward advocacy, with no pretense of objectivity or neutrality. As a crucial member of the defense team, the mitigation specialist interprets information in the manner most sympathetic to the defendant, and then works closely with defense attorneys to strategize presentation of mitigation evidence. In this respect, the specialists' stance is different from the stance necessary for most other roles that forensic mental health professionals fill, which usually require considering information the mitigation specialist has gathered, but retaining an objective stance and "an arms-length relationship with the defense team" (Connell, 2003, p. 342; see also Goldstein, 2001).

Other Consulting Roles

Attorneys occasionally seek mental health professionals to serve in a consulting role for a variety of reasons. As with the mitigation specialist, this role is explicitly partisan with the goal of helping the attorneys identify, understand, and communicate mitigation in the manner most helpful to their case. Generally, consultants help attorneys become familiar with the psychological issues or concepts likely to emerge in a particular case (Goldstein, Goldstein, & Kalbeitzer, 2006). Consultants may review relevant records or even interview the defendant to identify further issues that the attorney may ask an additional mental health professional serving as forensic evaluator to address. Or consultants might require no clinical contact with the defendant but simply educate an attorney about the research most relevant to a case and the limits of the research an opposing expert is likely to present. Consultants may assist with broad strategic tasks, such as identifying witnesses who are likely to present the most compelling mitigating evidence. Or consultants may assist with narrow strategic tasks, such as critiquing an opposing expert, or that expert's report and/or testimony, and preparing cross-examination questions that highlight weaknesses. Mental health professionals or social scientists may even serve as consultants in jury selection (Lieberman & Sales, 2006), although this tends to be a specialty distinct from other types of consultation in a capital case.

The "Teaching Expert"

As in most litigation, attorneys in capital cases can retain an expert to educate the court regarding scientific or technical knowledge that is unfamiliar to laypersons. The "teaching expert," sometimes called a "topic expert" (Goldstein et al., 2006), offers testimony about a circumscribed topic, usually a mitigating factor that is complex or poorly understood by laypersons. Often teaching experts are scholars who can summarize research regarding the typical effects of a particular experience or risk factor (e.g., abuse, trauma, parental neglect, or family dysfunction) relevant to a particular defendant. When attorneys believe that a medical or psychiatric condition may reduce the defendant's moral culpability for a crime, they may retain medical or mental health teaching experts who can describe the research and medical/psychological/ cognitive implications related to the defendant's condition (e.g., brain injury, attention-deficit/hyperactivity disorder, posttraumatic stress disorder). The teaching expert may or may not directly examine the defendant, but the focus is on providing scientifically sound data that help jurors better understand the nature and likely implications of a given mitigating factor. It remains up to the jury, of course, to decide "how mitigating" the factor may be, giving whatever weight to the teaching expert's testimony they deem appropriate. A teaching expert is bound by the relevant ethical codes or guidelines to present relevant research and clinical knowledge in an accurate and objective manner that acknowledges relevant limitations (e.g., American Academy of Psychiatry and the Law, 2005; American Psychiatric Association, 2009; American

Psychological Association, 2002; Committee on Ethical Guidelines for Forensic Psychologists, 1991; Committee on the Revision of the Ethical Guidelines for Forensic Psychologists, 2006). Although teaching experts should advocate for the strengths or quality of the data they present (Committee on Ethical Guidelines for Forensic Psychologists, 1991), they do not alter or misrepresent those data to further the interests of the party that retained them. In one sense, teaching experts represent the knowledge base of their field more than they represent the retaining party.

The Evaluating Expert

The most common—and most comprehensive—role for a forensic mental health professional at capital sentencing involves serving as the evaluating expert. As we stress throughout this chapter, the task of a mitigation evaluation is vast in scope and more comprehensive than any other FMHA (see Connell, 2003; Cunningham 2006b, 2008, 2010; Cunningham & Goldstein, 2003; Cunningham & Reidy, 2001; Eisenberg, 2004; Goldstein et al., 2006, for discussion of mitigation evaluations). In short, the role of the evaluating expert is to examine the defendant and his or her history to identify potentially mitigating data or themes. Ideally, evaluators then rely on scientific knowledge and empirical research to illuminate ways in which this potentially mitigating data (e.g., severe abuse, cognitive deficits) can, indeed, be understood as mitigating (e.g., it has well-documented links to adult criminality, it impairs judgment and reasoning). The evaluating expert then presents these findings via written report and/or courtroom testimony.

Despite this general description of evaluator duties, aspects of the evaluation content—and even the evaluation process—will vary depending on the case and the evaluator's preference. Whatever the format, no mitigation evaluation is brief. Any mitigation evaluation will require dozens of hours of interview (with the defendant and others), and many more hours reviewing collateral records. Mitigation evaluations often require many months, although it is not uncommon for case delays or continuances to stretch the entire process over the course of a year or more. Indeed, evaluators may reasonably decline to conduct an evaluation when presented with an insufficient time frame.

Mitigation evaluations specifically require a search for mitigating evidence. Some statutes even clearly suggest that evaluators work as active members of the defense team (see, e.g., Va. Code Ann. § 19.2-264.3:1(A), 2010). Yet the evaluator's role remains objective. Connell (2003) explains this unusual arrangement:

> Mitigation evaluation differs substantially from most kinds of forensic assessment in that the outcome is anticipated to provide whatever support may exist for one side of

a legal argument. The question is "What are the mitigating factors?" rather than "Are there any mitigating factors?" We do not search for aggravating and for mitigating factors, determine the weight to give each, and then render an opinion about the ultimate issue. Rather, we focus our attention on mitigating factors, with attention to aggravating factors only to acquaint ourselves fully with the case. (p. 326)

This mitigation emphasis is based directly on the case law and statute that demand a search for any mitigating evidence. Because the jury—not the evaluator—ultimately decides the extent to which evidence is mitigating and influential, the evaluator's task is to gather all *potentially* mitigating information. The emphasis requires vigorously *searching* for evidence that may be mitigating, *but not distorting* evidence to make it seem more mitigating. Likewise, the task often requires some teaching to convey a science-based perspective on how some findings may be mitigating, but not a distortion of the relevant science.

But the unusual focus of a mitigation evaluation:

[D]oes not represent an absence of neutrality or objectivity on the part of the evaluator: in fact, it is essential to approach each potential mitigating factor with a posture of receptivity to evidence of its existence or absence. Whatever is learned to support either position is to be disclosed in a candid and forthcoming manner. (Connell, 2003, p. 327)

Overall, forensic mental health professionals who conduct mitigation evaluations—whether retained by the defense or the prosecution—objectively investigate for evidence that, by definition, is more consistent with the goals of the defense than the prosecution.

Conducting Mitigation Evaluations for Capital Sentencing

Methodology: How Do Evaluators Gather Data?

Interview

For many mental health professionals, an interview seems like the nonnegotiable foundation of any evaluation. But there may be a few reasons to thoughtfully consider the utility of direct interview in a capital mitigation evaluation. For example, Cunningham (2006a) cautions that participating in an interview may begin to jeopardize some Fifth Amendment rights that the defendant might otherwise protect, particularly the right against self-incrimination. For example, some jurisdictions require that for a defense-retained evaluator to testify on the basis of interview with the defendant, the defendant must also submit to interview with a prosecution-retained evaluator, if the prosecution requests it. In other instances, a defendant's participation in an interview—particularly if the evaluator addresses details specific to the alleged offense—may create dilemmas with respect to defense counsel's trial strategy at the guilt/innocence phase of trial. Mitigation evaluations almost always take place well before the defendant has entered a plea or faced trial for the capital offense. At this point, some defendants may be maintaining that they are not guilty of the charges against them, so discussing the offense during a pretrial evaluation may interfere with the defense's intended trial strategy. An attorney cannot ethically claim that a defendant did not commit a specific offense if the attorney has clear evidence to the contrary (which may be contained in the mitigation report). So the defendant's acknowledgment of factual guilt at the pretrial stage may limit the defenses available to the attorney.[11]

On a more practical level, much of the mitigating evidence in any given case comes from sources other than the defendant (Cunningham, 2006a). Although an interview may be crucial for questions about psychiatric diagnosis or mental state, it may not be essential for questions about the defendant's early experience and other history. Overall, Cunningham (2006a) does not argue against all interviews in mitigation evaluations, but simply emphasizes the need for a delicate process of "balancing the basis of the evaluation against the Constitutional rights of the defendant. This balance will shift depending on the focus of the capital sentencing evaluation, the nature of the mitigating factors under consideration, and the adequacy of alternative sources of data" (p. 456). Of course this balancing act is one for defense counsel, not the evaluator. But defense counsel requires help from the clinician to appreciate the clinical basis and limits to any clinical interview and alternate data-gathering approaches.

Cunningham's (2006a) perspective provides a helpful reminder that evaluators should not simply "default" into interviewing a defendant without carefully considering the implications and discussing those implications with counsel. In practice, a direct interview still tends to be the norm in capital mitigation evaluations. Indeed, including a direct interview often appears preferable for a variety of reasons. For example, the defendant is often the only source for certain types of information. Also, the defendant's behavior during the interview may be a "data sample" relevant to some topics the evaluator is investigating (e.g., psychiatric symptoms, interpersonal style).

When evaluators do conduct an interview, the process is lengthy. Typically, the interview spans several visits, each lasting many hours. The lengthy process is necessary for several reasons. First, there is much ground to cover. Mitigating data may emerge in discussions of the defendant's childhood, adulthood, capital offense, and many more narrow subtopics. Second, because

---

11. Anecdotally, some defense attorneys do not look at the mitigation report unless/until the defendant is found guilty.

a mitigation evaluation involves constantly amassing information from various sources, it is often necessary to revisit the defendant to inquire about new data that have emerged from other sources. An evaluator cannot simply schedule one comprehensive interview after all collateral data are available, because it is the interview itself that also helps identify essential collateral data sources (for example, the defendant mentions relatives and associates whom the evaluator decides to interview, or the defendant mentions prior contact with an agency from which the evaluator then requests records). Finally, repeated interviews are often necessary because mitigating evidence tends to be sensitive. Few capital defendants come from contexts that foster emotional vulnerability or a trust of clinicians, yet a thorough mitigation evaluation requires evaluators to elicit information about delicate topics such as sexual abuse, physical abuse, failed relationships, and family dysfunction. Multiple interviews are often necessary if evaluators are to develop the rapport and insight to probe such sensitive topics.

Of course, many people are understandably suspicious that capital defendants may be *too* forthcoming with sensitive topics, exaggerating or even fabricating experiences that they perceive as mitigating. Certainly this is a possibility to which experienced forensic evaluators are always attuned. This is why collateral data are essential in every evaluation. But surprisingly often, defendants appear to underreport, rather than overreport, mitigating data. In some instances the data may be sensitive or shameful enough that the defendant intentionally neglects to mention it (e.g., sexual abuse). In other instances, defendants may lack insight to the data (e.g., psychiatric symptoms) or be unaware that certain data are meaningful to mental health professionals (e.g., a loss of consciousness following a head injury). In other instances, the defendant simply may not recognize that particular experiences were unusual, let alone mitigating. Evaluators often discover through collateral sources details about a defendant's family life (e.g., severe violence, parent support for illegal or damaging behavior) that the defendant failed to mention because he or she did not consider them atypical or noteworthy.

Collateral Records

Forensic mental health professionals regard collateral records as essential to forensic evaluation because these often provide a more objective source of data that can be compared against defendant or witness recollections (Heilbrun, 2001; Heilbrun, Warren, & Picarello, 2003). Indeed, some authorities emphasize that retrospective forensic evaluations are better understood as "investigations" than "evaluations" because they are primarily based on collateral data such as records (Melton et al., 2007). This holds particularly true in capital sentencing evaluations. Mitigating data are more often found in historical records than in a defendant's first statements to an evaluator, and mitigation found in historical records always appears more objective and credible than statements from the defendant.

As Cunningham and Goldstein (2003) emphasized, "The extent of record retrieval and review is uniquely comprehensive in capital mitigation evaluations. Not uncommonly, efforts are made to recover virtually *all* records associated with a defendant's life" (p. 424). Put simply, the evaluator's task usually requires reviewing any records that address the defendant, regardless of when they were created. Often defense counsel or a mitigation specialist has gathered the records, but the evaluator remains responsible for reviewing them and actively pursuing any missing records.

Collateral records can contribute to the evaluation in countless ways, but some are particularly common. First, as so often emphasized in forensic training, collateral records provide a point of comparison to reports from the defendant and his or her family, which may be suspect because of their potential for self-serving bias. Second, collateral records reveal new information that may have been unknown to the defendant or other sources. The professionals who first created collateral records may have been attuned to details—such as formal psychiatric symptoms and diagnoses, medical conditions, or home conditions—to which the defendant may have been unattuned, or otherwise unable to describe accurately in retrospect. Finally, it is not uncommon for collateral records to include detailed narratives that describe mitigating data in rich and poignant ways. For example, some records reveal statements from professionals who lament that the child (and future capital defendant) fares well with intervention but falters when returned to a chaotic home. Others reveal speculation about how a child will fare if he or she does not receive certain interventions. When reviewed in the context of capital litigation years later, some statements in records appear tragically prescient, and many articulate mitigation themes in poignant detail.

Although the range of collateral records for review is potentially limitless, some common sources of collateral records are listed in Table 7.1.

Collateral Interviews

Collateral interviews are essential for many of the same reasons as collateral records. "Third parties" such as family members, friends, romantic partners, and professionals have data and perspectives on the defendant and the defendant's history that may be unknown to the defendant or more credible than those from the defendant. For example, family members are often a better source of information about the defendant's early developmental history and histories of their extended family. Of course, the closer the emotional connection a third party has to the defendant, the more we might consider the possibility of bias. But bias does not always take the form we might expect. Rather than exaggerating pathology or hardship in an effort to enhance mitigation,

Table 7.1 Potential Sources for Collateral Records in Mitigation Evaluation

Stage	Medical and Psychiatric	Educational	Legal
Multigenerational	• Family medical records • Family records of psychiatric care, including hospitalizations and medication		• Family correctional records • Family social service records
Prenatal through early childhood	• Prenatal visit records • Birth records • Early check-up, immunization contact	• Special-needs education assessments and records	• Parent's criminal records • Social service records for the defendant or other siblings
Childhood and adolescence	• Counseling records • Psychiatrist notes	• Report cards • Standardized testing • School entrance and exit forms • Disciplinary reports • Special education records and evaluations	• Juvenile justice contact • Probation records • Foster care or residential treatment records
Early adulthood to adulthood	• Counseling records • Psychiatrist notes	• Military records, testing • Vocational assessments • Higher education records	• Police records, including witness statements, warrants, summons • Court transcripts • Correctional records, including disciplinary infractions • Prior probation records

family members sometimes minimize problems, present their family in the most positive light, and distance themselves from the defendant (see Cunningham, 2008, and Dekleva, 2001, for similar observations). Consider the mother who laments, "I did everything I could for that boy . . . I can't tell you why he went bad," though records reveal she severely beat her child and neglected him during her own lengthy periods of drug addiction. Even when family members are not concerned about making a good impression, they may be blind to their family pathology for the same reasons the defendant is. That is, they may be so immersed in their family patterns that they lack the perspective necessary to identify their patterns or problems as unusual ("I thought that's just how families worked"). For these reasons, it is important to interview third parties using specific questions rather than vague ones that may be answered differently depending on family values and expectations (e.g., "Was your father an alcoholic?" or "Was his mother abusive?"). It is also important to consider the reports from collateral interviews alongside collateral records.

Testing

For psychologists, psychological testing is a standard component of almost any assessment. But in capital mitigation, general personality testing is less common. Why? The first reason is practical. Although any deficit or vulnerability can be considered mitigating, mitigation evaluations more often consider a long-term developmental pathway rather than a snapshot of psychological symptoms at a given moment (particularly a moment that is months or years after the capital offense). So traditional personality testing may be helpful to bolster evidence of long-term psychiatric illness, but this is not the most common focus of mitigation. The primary criterion for deciding whether to employ psychological testing in a forensic evaluation is whether the test offers data that are relevant to the legal question being addressed (Heilbrun, 1992, 2001). Even though questions about mitigation may be broad, most address issues of a defendant's background and character, which psychological tests may not be well suited to address.

The second reason personality testing is inconsistently employed in mitigation evaluations is a strategic reason. Many authorities seem to argue that personality testing is often more prejudicial than probative (Cunningham, 2006a, 2008). For example, most capital defendants will elevate test scales related to antisocial personality or behavior. Such scale elevations are almost unremarkable from a clinical perspective, because they are so commonplace among most prison inmates or criminal offenders, but they may appear inflammatory to those less familiar with the psychological tests, their properties, and implications.

Overall, the type of broad, multipurpose personality and pathology testing that psychologists typically employ should not be considered a "default component" of a mitigation evaluation, nor should it be precluded from all mitigation evaluations. Again, the purpose of psychological testing in an FMHA is to gather reliable data relevant to the legal question being addressed (Heilbrun, 1992). If the legal question about mitigation involves secondary questions about clinical diagnosis, personality style, and reported symptoms, evaluators might reasonably administer a well-established psychological test to help inform these questions. If, however, the primary focus of a mitigation evaluation involves the type of data that psychological testing does not provide, there is certainly no reason to administer testing and there may be some reasons not to (i.e., the potential for misleading or prejudicial data).

Specialized Cognitive or Neuropsychological Testing

The type of testing to which most psychologists are most accustomed (i.e., broad-scale personality inventories) need not be a regular component of mitigation evaluations. However, cognitive and specialized neuropsychological testing is more commonplace, because these tests are more often relevant to questions about mitigation. Obviously, *Atkins* precludes the execution of individuals with a diagnosis of mental retardation (which requires formal cognitive testing to diagnose), but the *Tennard* decision suggests impaired cognitive skills may be considered mitigating, regardless of whether they fall within the range of mental retardation. Furthermore, the high rates of cognitive and neuropsychological deficits among death-row inmates (e.g., Cunningham & Vigen, 2002) suggest that many capital defendants are likely to manifest deficits that could be understood as mitigating.

Of course, formal cognitive or neuropsychological testing may not be necessary in *every* mitigation evaluation; other collateral data may seem to rule out the need for further testing in a given case. However, this type of testing is probably a component of mitigation evaluations more often than not. The mitigation evaluator need not perform this testing directly; referral to a specialist may be feasible or even preferable.

Content: What Areas Do Evaluators Explore?

Evaluators rely on the combination of methods described earlier (i.e., interview, collateral records, collateral interview, some testing) because the content of mitigation evaluations tends to be so broad. One authority aptly labeled mitigation evaluations "psychobiographical," in that they require amassing comprehensive and detailed biographies and using psychological expertise to shed light on any people, experiences, and capacities that shaped a defendant's life course (Connell, 2003). Although the precise areas of inquiry will vary by case, evaluators must consider every stage of a defendant's life. Table 7.2 suggests more specific areas for inquiry in each of these stages.

A Multigenerational Family History

Understanding a defendant usually requires some understanding of the defendant's family, including events and long-standing patterns that may have influenced his or life trajectory, even before birth. A defendant's problems often echo long-standing intergenerational patterns. In the context of a mitigation evaluation, information on a defendant's family history may reveal familial patterns of thinking and behavior that could potentially shed some light on the defendant's antisocial behavior.

Early Development

For good reason, most comprehensive psychological evaluations consider developmental history. Early development often reveals the first signs of neurological or biological deficits that influence a person's learning and behavior throughout the rest of his or her life. From a mitigation perspective, early development may be particularly relevant in that it reflects something about a defendant's "raw materials" or natural capacities, before the defendant's own choices played any role.

Table 7.2 Sample Mitigating Factors

Life Stage	Medical, Psychiatric, and Neurological Influences	Individual	Family/ Relationship	Community
Generational	• Family history of mental illness or substance abuse		• History of violence or domestic violence in extended family • History of legal contact, incarceration in extended family	
Prenatal and perinatal	• Maternal substance use • Access to prenatal care • Birth complications, premature birth • Chromosomal abnormalities or other birth defects		• Number of children in the home • Mother's age at onset of childbearing • Mother experience of domestic violence	• Toxin exposure
Early childhood	• Early trauma, accidents • Delays in developmental milestones	• Childhood temperament	• Exposure to family conflict or violence • Insufficient supervision	• Poverty • Community violence and criminality
Childhood	• Attention-deficit/hyperactivity disorder or problems with hyperactivity and concentration • Learning disabilities • Conduct or oppositional defiant disorder	• Involvement in early antisocial behavior • Repeating grades, poor school performance	• Father absence • Unstable living arrangements, frequent school transitions • Multiple caregivers • Disrupted attachments • Loss of family member or peer • Childhood abuse, neglect	• Gang presence and recruitment • Availability of drugs and firearms • Underprivileged educational system • Racial prejudice • Community disorganization, derelict environment

Table 7.2 Sample Mitigating Factors (Continued)

Life Stage	Medical, Psychiatric, and Neurological Influences	Individual	Family/ Relationship	Community
Adolescence	• Psychiatric disorders or symptoms • Substance use and abuse • Head injuries from vehicle accidents, sports	• Contact with juvenile justice • Relative immaturity, impulsiveness	• Sexually traumatic experiences • Socialization to criminal lifestyle • Delinquent peers or siblings	
Early adulthood to adulthood	• Psychotic experiences • Lingering effects of substance abuse • Availability of health care	• Prior adjudications, incarceration • Gang involvement • Poor job skills • Inability to live independently or care for self	• Marital or relationship conflict • Substance abuse, criminality in romantic relationship or social network	• Workplace prejudice, conflict • Poor availability of housing, poor housing conditions • High-crime neighborhood

Childhood

During childhood, trauma and adverse experiences may be particularly influential to the subsequent life course. Family influences are especially pronounced because children are malleable and unable to extract themselves from damaging environments. Sometimes a defendant's childhood experiences are noteworthy precisely because they occurred in childhood, rather than later in life; for example, early exposure to criminal behaviors, sexuality, and severe violence.

Adolescence

During adolescence, youth are shaped more by peer influence. Sexuality and substance use may play prominent roles. For youth who have started down a delinquent pathway, adolescence may be the period in which they progress further, or interventions steer them toward better outcomes. However, families continue to play an influential role, such that family pathology or parent absence may remain important.

Early Adulthood and Adulthood

During early adulthood, family influence may decrease. It is also during this time that individuals struggle to establish independence and adult relationships.

Certain serious psychiatric illnesses are often not evident until early adulthood, and other forms of mental illness may become more influential when individuals receive less support and monitoring from family and school.

For all of the life stages described thus far, *evaluators should investigate mitigating evidence in light of the available scientific research*. Several authors (e.g., Cunningham, 2008; Eisenberg, 2004; Fabian, 2009; Salekin, 2007) emphasize the importance of considering the comprehensive documents that federal agencies publish to summarize the risk factors for violence and delinquency (e.g., Howell, 1995). These summary documents—many of which are available through the Office of Juvenile Justice and Delinquency Prevention website—report results from numerous, comprehensive, federally funded studies designed to better understand, and further reduce, youth violence and criminality. Although evaluators should not use this research in a rigid "checklist" manner, the studies do provide a helpful reminder of areas to explore. They also help demonstrate to jurors that the link between early experiences and subsequent violence is not simply a defense theory, but a pattern of human development so well recognized that it has become the basis of government-funded violence-prevention efforts. Of course, evaluators should not limit their use of research to these documents. Most cases will require the evaluator to explore more specialized literature addressing unique mitigating factors in each case.

The Capital Offense

In addition to the life-course overview described earlier, most mitigation evaluations require a careful examination of the alleged capital offense. Indeed, most state statutes that delineate mitigation describe circumstances that fall just short of meeting the criteria for an insanity defense, but nevertheless appear closely intertwined with the offender's mental health (for example, the defendant acted under severe mental or emotional distress; the defendant had impaired capacity to appreciate the nature, character, consequences, or wrongfulness of the capital offense). Of course, evaluators may not always interview the defendant about the actual offense (see Connell, 2003; Cunningham, 2006a, 2008), but the offense is usually within the scope of a mitigation evaluation.

Communication: How Do Evaluators Present Findings?

Reports

Most mitigation evaluations result in a formal, written report of findings. Indeed, many state statutes require that the evaluator prepare a written report as part of any mitigation evaluation. One purpose of the written report is to provide the retaining party with an overview of the evaluator's findings and the bases for these findings—usually to be further elucidated during courtroom testimony. However, reports do not always remain with the retaining party. Sometimes defense counsel may voluntarily share a copy of the report with the prosecution, as part of their efforts to pursue a plea agreement. Typically, defense counsel *must* share a copy of the report with the prosecution if defense counsel plans to introduce evidence from the mitigation evaluator. If the prosecution retains a second opinion evaluation, they too, typically, must provide the evaluation report to opposing counsel. Although jurors may never read the evaluation report, the report is often crucial as attorneys consider the case and prepare their direct and cross-examination of the evaluator. Thus, evaluators prepare these reports with considerable care.

Evaluation reports vary dramatically among evaluators. Evaluators make countless clinical, stylistic, and strategic decisions as they draft a report, so even reports from the same evaluator may vary from case to case. Typically, there seem to be at least two general approaches to drafting a report for a mitigation evaluation.

Broad narrative reports tend to be lengthy, and biographical, in that they describe the defendant's history and life course in considerable detail. Of course, these reports focus primarily on data that are potentially mitigating, but they also include narrative to weave together the mitigating data, usually in a chronological format. Some evaluators tend to prefer this format because it allows the flexibility to "tell the defendant's story" and document the defendant's psychosocial history in rich detail.

However, this broad narrative format carries some drawbacks. In attempting to draft a comprehensive psychosocial history, evaluators must make decisions about what content to include and how much detail to provide. Although evaluators are tasked with identifying potentially mitigating data, creating a comprehensive psychosocial history might require addressing all major life events, regardless of whether they are potentially mitigating. Evaluators who focus primarily on creating a comprehensive biography may be straying from their role of specifically identifying mitigating data. On the other hand, evaluators who draft a biographical narrative comprised only of mitigating details—neglecting other important events or perspectives—may be accused of "cherry-picking" data or misrepresenting a defendant's history. Nevertheless, some evaluators prefer the flexibility of comprehensive narrative, and at least for certain cases, consider it preferable to the alternative.

Narrow statute-based reports attempt only to answer the evaluation questions identified in the guiding statute, without attempting to present these in a chronological narrative. A typical statute-based report might simply list—and provide findings relevant to—each element of the relevant statute. For example: Did the defendant act under extreme mental or emotional disturbance at the time of the offense? Did the defendant have an impaired capacity to appreciate the criminality of his or her conduct or to conform such conduct to the law? Are there other mitigating factors related to the history and character of the defendant or his or her mental condition at the time of offense? The nature and quantity of content will vary for each statutory factor, but evaluators typically have the most content to report for the "catchall" factor that addresses any other mitigation.

Using this statute-based format, evaluators need not list their findings in chronological order or describe them with a comprehensive narrative. This format, too, may carry some challenges. Done poorly, it may come to resemble a checklist of disjointed facts or events. However, many evaluators are able to balance the structure of a statute-based format with the narrative necessary to explain and contextualize findings.

Testimony

Testimony is the other common method through which evaluators convey their findings. Although expert testimony is common, it is not always necessary. Some attorneys find that mitigating evidence may be presented (or rebutted) in a more compelling manner by fact witnesses, such as friends and family, or lay witnesses, such as teachers and probation officers. In many cases, attorneys are able to craft a compelling presentation of mitigating evidence by interweaving testimony from an expert witness with testimony from lay witnesses, who can often better illuminate some of the specifics introduced in expert testimony (Sundby, 1997).

Guidance on expert testimony is far beyond the scope of this chapter, and it is available elsewhere (e.g., Brodsky, 1991, 1999, 2004; Dvoskin & Guy, 2008; Kwartner & Boccaccini, 2008; Melton et al., 2007). But it is worth emphasizing a caution about expert testimony in capital mitigation: There is tremendous potential for jurors to misunderstand the concept of mitigation and the role of the forensic mental health professional. It may be helpful, early in testimony, to define the concept of mitigation and explain that the statute specifically demands that evaluators seek mitigating information. Some evaluators (Cohen, 2010) even arrange for initial direct-examination questions along these lines:

- Attorney: First, are you aware that Mr. D has been convicted of _____?
- Evaluator: Yes
- Attorney: Are you here to testify that Mr. D is not responsible for his actions in committing those crimes?
- Evaluator: No
- Attorney: Are you here to testify that Mr. D should be excused for these crimes?

- Evaluator: No
- Attorney: Are you here to testify that Mr. D should not be punished for his crimes?
- Evaluator: No
- Attorney: What was the purpose of your evaluation?
- Evaluator: (Reviews the statutory language describing the evaluation requirements)

In short, even more so than in other instances of expert testimony, evaluators likely need to clarify the nature and purpose of their evaluation.

Another way jurors may misunderstand expert testimony became clear in a study from the capital jury project (Sundby, 1997; see Salekin, 2007). Jurors—already skeptical that expert witnesses tend to be biased—complained that experts often painted a sympathetic picture of the defendant without linking the mitigating data from a defendant's history to the defendant's capital offense itself. Of course, from a legal perspective, data need not be directly related to the offense to be mitigating. But jurors clearly suggested that experts sometimes failed to make the link between early experience and adult outcome. Salekin (2007) argues that these jury complaints underscore the need for evaluators to take a developmental perspective and rely on scientific data that address childhood risk factors for negative outcomes in adulthood. Likewise, we argue that some concepts from developmental psychopathology and some attention to relevant research—*if conveyed in an easily accessible manner*—may help jurors better understand the rationale for presenting certain types of information. Specifically, evaluators are not primarily "telling sad stories," but rather identifying experiences and influences known to shape development and behavior.

Conclusion

Overall, evaluations of mitigation at capital sentencing remain some of the most comprehensive and difficult evaluations to conduct and for which to summarize and convey findings. Nevertheless, capital jurisprudence clearly and consistently underscores that jurors should be allowed to consider a range of mitigating evidence. Thus, the evaluations are demanding, but the findings are important.

8

Evaluations of Violence Risk in Capital Sentencing

To those unfamiliar with capital sentencing, the idea of requesting a violence risk assessment in this context may not make immediate sense. After all, those individuals convicted of capital murder have presumably demonstrated the capacity for lethal violence in the community. They have also lost any opportunity to return to the community in the foreseeable future. At first glance, then, it may seem hard to imagine what decisions a violence risk assessment might inform.

Nevertheless, questions about violence risk underlie capital sentencing, and expert testimony about violence risk may influence whether a defendant receives a sentence of death or life in prison. Two states (Oregon and Texas) explicitly *require* jurors to consider the defendant's likelihood of future criminal violence as a "special issue" in all capital determinations (Ore. Rev. Stat. § 163.150, 2010; Tex. Code Crim. Proc. art. 37.071, 2010). Four other states (Idaho, Oklahoma, Virginia, Wyoming) include risk for future violence as a statutorily defined aggravating factor (Idaho Code Ann. § 19-2515, 2010; Okla. Stat. Ann. Tit. 21, § 701.12, 2010; Va. Code Ann. § 19.2-264.2, 2010; Wyo. Stat. Ann. § 6-2-101, 2010), and more than a dozen other states allow jurors to consider risk for future violence as a nonstatutory aggravating factor (see Keesler, DeMatteo, Murrie, & Anumba, 2010). Only a few states, such as Florida, explicitly *preclude* any consideration of violence risk (see *Knight v. Florida*, 1998). Overall, of the 35 states that currently have the death penalty, at least 21 allow or require juries to consider a defendant's risk for future violence when assigning a sentence (Dorland & Krauss, 2005; Keesler et al., 2010).

In many jurisdictions, considering future violence risk is not only allowed but commonplace. Shapiro (2009) reviewed allegations of violence risk in capital proceedings and reported that among the three states that have led the nation in executions since *Furman v. Georgia* (1972), a defendant's perceived risk for future violence played a prominent role in most death sentences. The possibility of future violence was an aggravating factor in most Oklahoma death sentences (65 of 89) and most Virginia death sentences (74 of 103); of course, all 436 Texas death sentences followed a conclusion that the defendant posed a risk of future violence (Shapiro, 2009). In federal capital cases, prosecutors alleged a risk of future violence in 21 of 37 (57%) capital trials prior to 1995, and in 75 of 84 (89%) of cases between 1995 and 1999 (Cunningham & Goldstein, 2003; Cunningham & Reidy, 1999).

But even if neither the statute nor the prosecutor *explicitly* raise questions of violence risk, capital jurors nevertheless consider whether a defendant might pose a risk of future violence (see juror surveys conducted through the Capital Jury Project [Blume, Garvey, & Johnson, 2001; Bowers & Steiner, 1999; Eisneberg & Wells, 1993] as well as other research [e.g., Costanzo & Costanzo, 1994]). Thus, questions about a capital defendant's risk for violent reoffense are "always at issue" (Blume et al., 2001, p. 403) and they are often addressed explicitly through testimony by a forensic mental health professional.

Legal Background: Case Law and Statute Addressing Violence Risk in Capital Sentencing

Generally, the emphasis on violence risk results from an emphasis on *individualized consideration* of capital defendants. Recall from Chapter 2 that modern death penalty jurisprudence took shape after the U.S. Supreme Court held the death penalty was unconstitutional as applied at the time (*Furman v. Georgia*, 1972). The Court was particularly concerned about the "unbridled discretion" allowed to jurors and the evidence of disparate sentencing across defendants and jurisdictions. Reacting to the *Furman* decision, state legislatures modified their capital sentencing statutes, typically in one of two ways. New statutes either *(1)* imposed the death penalty automatically for certain offenses, or *(2)* added guidelines and protections to capital case procedure. Texas reportedly considered both strategies (Cunningham, 2006b, 2006c) but eventually settled on an approach that ostensibly required individualized consideration of each defendant: Texas explicitly required jurors to consider the defendant's likelihood of future violence (Kuhn, 1974). The new statute identified violence risk as one of three "special issues,"[1] and instructed jurors to assign the death penalty only "if there was a probability that the defendant would commit criminal acts of violence that would constitute a continuing threat to society" if not executed (Tex. Code Crim. Proc. art. 37.0711).

In 1976, the U.S. Supreme Court re-examined the death penalty and essentially lifted the moratorium it had imposed 4 years earlier in *Furman*. In *Jurek v. Texas* (1976), the Court declared constitutional the recrafted Texas law and its emphasis on considering a defendant's risk of future violence. Although the Justices acknowledged that estimating the risk of future violence is difficult, they reasoned that doing so is crucial to many legal decisions and, therefore, should not present unique problems in capital sentencing. Along with the *Jurek* decision, the Supreme Court ruled on four other new state statutes that addressed capital sentencing (i.e., *Gregg v. Georgia*, 1976; *Proffitt v. Florida*, 1976; *Roberts v. Louisiana*, 1976; and *Woodson v. North Carolina*, 1976), and their opinions on these cases suggested a constitutionally permissible framework for imposing the death penalty. The Court required that *(1)* objective criteria direct sentencing and limit discretion, and *(2)* the criteria must allow the sentencer to give "particularized consideration" to the character and record of the convicted (*Woodson v. North Carolina*, 1976, p. 303). The Court's decisions in 1976 left room for Oregon to draft a capital sentencing statute modeled after the Texas statute, and for several other states to include violence risk as one of the aggravating factors that guides sentencing.

Even after *Jurek*, the Supreme Court continued to consider violence risk assessment in capital sentencing procedures, each time addressing Texas cases. In *Estelle v. Smith* (1981), the Court ruled that a psychiatrist's violence risk assessment—such as it was—should have been preceded by proper notice to the defendant and defense counsel. Another consequence

---

1. Although the probability of future violence was only one of three special issues defined in Article 37.0711 of the Texas Code of Criminal Procedure (which applies to capital offenses committed before Sept. 1, 1991), it is the *only* special issue about which there tends to be any debate or discussion. The first and third special issues are already affirmed in most capital cases. These address:

"1. whether the conduct of the defendant that caused the death of the deceased was committed deliberately and with the reasonable expectation that the death of the deceased or another would result," and, if raised by the evidence,
"3. . . . whether the conduct of the defendant in killing the deceased was unreasonable in response to the provocation, if any, by the deceased."

Because these first and third questions are a given in nearly all cases, "it is the prediction of future dangerousness that is the determining factor between a life and a death sentence in Texas" (Marquart, Ekland-Olson, & Sorensen, 1989, p. 451).

of the Court's decision, Cunningham (2006c) notes, was introducing the phrase "future dangerousness" as a shorthand phrase for the more lengthy special issue #2 defined in Texas Code: "whether there is a probability that the defendant would commit criminal acts of violence that would constitute a continuing threat to society." Thereafter, "future dangerousness" was the commonplace, but imprecise, term that courts and legal scholars usually used to describe the violence risk a capital defendant might pose if not executed.

Shortly after *Estelle v. Smith* (1981), the U.S. Supreme Court issued a decision with tremendous implications for violence risk assessment, particularly in capital proceedings (*Barefoot v. Estelle*, 1983). A Texas jury sentenced Thomas Barefoot to death based, at least in part, on psychiatrist James Grigson's testimony regarding future dangerousness. Dr. Grigson, who had not interviewed the defendant but responded to extended hypothetical questions from the prosecutor, opined that whether in the community or in prison, there was a "one hundred percent and absolute chance" that Barefoot would commit future acts of criminal violence that would pose a continuing threat to society (*Barefoot v. Estelle*, 1983, p. 919). Barefoot's counsel argued that psychiatric testimony about future dangerousness should not have been admitted. Most of the mental health field agreed. The American Psychiatric Association submitted an *amicus curiae* brief to the Court, emphasizing that Grigson's statements were improper and arguing that psychiatric predictions of dangerousness were notoriously inaccurate (i.e., wrong as often as two out of three times) (see Brief Amicus Curiae of the American Psychiatric Association, 1983). The Justices acknowledged the *amicus* brief, as well as Monahan's (1981) influential review of the shortcomings in violence prediction, but they nevertheless upheld the Texas statute. Justice White explained:

> [Barefoot argues] that his death sentence must be set aside because the Constitution of the United States barred the testimony of the two psychiatrists who testified against him at the punishment hearing... [Barefoot] urged that psychiatrists, individually and as a group, are incompetent to predict with an acceptable degree of reliability that a particular criminal will commit other crimes in the future and so represent a danger to the community... The suggestion that no psychiatrist's testimony may be presented with respect to a defendant's future dangerousness is somewhat like asking us to disinvent the wheel. In the first place, it is contrary to our cases. If the likelihood of a defendant's committing further crimes is a constitutionally acceptable criterion for imposing the death penalty, which it is, *Jurek v. Texas*, 428 U.S. 262 (1976), and if it is not impossible for even a lay person sensibly to arrive at that conclusion, it makes little sense, if any, to submit that psychiatrists, out of the entire universe of persons who might have an opinion on the issue, would know so little about the subject that they should not be permitted to testify. (*Barefoot v. Estelle*, 1983, pp. 896–897)

Thus, the U.S. Supreme Court upheld the admissibility of psychiatric testimony addressing "future dangerousness." The Court did not convey much faith that violence risk assessments were accurate, but it instead conveyed more of a resignation that violence risk assessments were inevitable. Apparently, it reasoned that risk assessment was so tightly woven into criminal justice and mental health systems, it seemed unreasonable and impractical to disallow it in this particular context (i.e., capital sentencing) by these particular professionals (i.e., mental health professionals). The Court's majority opinion also conveyed a faith in juries to "sort out the reliable from the unreliable evidence and opinion" (*Barefoot v. Estelle*, 1983, p. 929) that mental health experts present.

The U.S. Supreme Court's decision in *Barefoot* has not been popular. Even at the time of the ruling, Justice Blackmun wrote a vigorous dissent. He emphasized the "overwhelming" evidence of unreliability in psychiatric predictions of violence, the potential for jurors to give too much credit to expert witness testimony, and the need for heightened standards of reliability in capital cases. Since the 1983 *Barefoot* ruling, legal scholars have tended to echo and add to Justice Blackmun's critiques, whether addressing the *Barefoot* case or assertions of "future dangerousness" at capital sentencing more generally (see, e.g., Beecher-Monas, 2003; Dorland & Krauss, 2005; Faigman, Kaye, Saks, & Sanders, 2009; Regnier, 2004; Shapiro, 2009). Nevertheless, courts have tended to remain receptive to expert testimony that a capital defendant poses a high risk of future violence.

Key rulings regarding the admissibility of expert testimony (e.g., *Daubert v. Merrell Dow Pharmaceuticals, Inc.*, 1993; *Kumho Tire Co. v. Carmichael*, 1999) have the potential to constrain some of the violence risk testimony that has been historically presented at capital sentencing. Many scholars argue that the testimony in *Barefoot*, or similar expert testimony asserting that a capital defendant poses a high risk of future violence, should be rejected under the heightened admissibility standard of *Daubert* (e.g., Regnier, 2004).[2] But so far, to our knowledge, no court has initiated a *Daubert* analysis of violence risk testimony at capital sentencing (Faigman et al., 2009) and some courts

---

2. Ten years after *Barefoot*, the U.S. Supreme Court decided *Daubert v. Merrell Dow Pharmaceuticals, Inc.* (1993), which established general standards for the admissibility of expert testimony in federal courts. In short, the Supreme Court offered five factors to assist trial court judges in deciding whether to admit expert testimony. The courts, they suggested, should examine: *(1)* whether the theory or technique underlying testimony has been tested; *(2)* whether this theory or technique has been subjected to peer review and publication; *(3)* the known or potential rate of error of this technique; *(4)* whether there are standards to control the operation of this technique; and *(5)* the degree to which this theory or technique has been generally accepted by the scientific community. Although *Daubert* only addressed the admissibility standards for "scientific" expert testimony, a subsequent Supreme Court decision extended the *Daubert* criteria to all forms of expert testimony (*Kumho Tire Co. v. Carmichael*, 1999). Moreover, *Daubert* is only binding in federal courts (because it addressed admissibility under the Federal Rules of Evidence), although the majority of states have since adopted the *Daubert* standard either through case law or statute.

have flatly rejected defense appeals that they do so (*United States v. Fields*, 2007).[3]

Of course, it is not clear that all contemporary testimony about violence risk would (or should) fail such a *Daubert* challenge. The field of violence risk assessment has changed dramatically since the 1983 *Barefoot* case. For example, in contrast to the earlier summary that clinician predictions were wrong more often than not (Monahan, 1981), later research found that clinicians could predict violence with modest, or better than chance, accuracy (e.g., Lidz, Mulvey, & Gardner, 1993; Mossman, 1994; see generally Monahan, 2003; Otto & Douglas, 2010). The field has amassed detailed data on base rates of violence among special populations, including the population of men sentenced for capital murder (e.g., Cunningham & Sorensen, 2007; Edens, Buffington-Vollum, Keilen, Roskamp, & Anthony, 2005; Marquart, Ekland-Olson, & Sorensen, 1989; Marquart & Sorensen, 1989). Finally, risk assessment "technology," including approaches to violence risk assessment at capital sentencing (e.g., Cunningham, 2006c; 2010; Cunningham & Sorensen, 2010) has improved substantially since the *Barefoot* era (Borum, 1996; Monahan, 1996; Monahan et al., 2001). So what might be an appropriate approach to violence risk assessment at capital sentencing?

Forensic Mental Health Assessment Addressing Violence Risk in Capital Proceedings

Violence risk assessments at capital sentencing are appropriate to the extent that they are firmly rooted in empirical data, particularly base rate data, regarding the contexts and forms of violence that are relevant to capital sentencing decisions. Thus, many traditional forms of "dangerousness prediction" or violence risk assessment are clearly *in*appropriate (see Brief Amicus Curiae of the American Psychological Association, 2005). But current science and best-practice standards also offer an approach that may indeed be appropriate in

---

3. In *United States v. Fields* (2007), the defendant appealed his capital conviction, which was based, at least in part, on a psychiatrist's testimony that that the defendant was at risk for violence to others, even in prison. The defense urged the court to examine this violence risk testimony in light of *Daubert*, and the American Psychological Association submitted an *amicus curiae* brief urging the court to formally adopt the *Daubert* reliability factors for determining the admissibility of expert evidence in federal death penalty sentencing hearings (see Brief Amicus Curiae of the American Psychological Association, 2005). Nevertheless, the U.S. Court of Appeals for the Fifth Circuit rejected the defendant's claim that *Daubert* should apply to expert testimony on violence risk, and it rejected the defense's claim that the psychiatric testimony on violence risk was so unreliable that the district court abused its discretion by admitting it. In short, courts have been reluctant to apply *Daubert* criteria to expert testimony from forensic mental health professionals, particularly when they testify to the probability of future violence (Slobogin, 2006).

capital sentencing contexts. To understand approaches to risk assessment that appear ethically and scientifically reasonable, it becomes important to review the practice of violence risk assessment generally, and as applied to capital sentencing contexts specifically.

Violence Risk Assessment: An Overview

As the U.S. Supreme Court emphasized in *Barefoot v. Estelle* (1983), capital sentencing proceedings are just one of many legal proceedings that consider violence risk. Questions about violence risk are commonplace in both criminal justice and mental health contexts (Skeem & Monahan, in press; see Shah, 1978, for an illustrative list). In fact, Grisso and Tomkins (1996) referred to the assessment of violence risk as "a required professional ability for every clinical psychologist" (p. 928). Courts often call upon clinicians to provide estimates of violence risk when considering civil commitment to a psychiatric facility or when making noncapital sentencing decisions for criminal defendants. Parole boards or other criminal justice administrators may request risk assessments when considering an offender facing parole, probation, or early release. In some respects, violence risk assessment may vary greatly depending on the legal context, the precise referral question, and the population of which the examinee is part. But nearly every scientifically sound violence risk assessment must include certain key components (Conroy & Murrie, 2007). Following are those most crucial to violence risk assessment in capital sentencing:

- *Defining the question of risk.* All risk assessment is context specific. The "referral question" that guides a risk assessment must specify what risk behavior shall be assessed, over what time span, and across what settings.
- *Consider normative data and population base rates.* Once the risk assessment question is appropriately defined, evaluators must begin forming a risk estimate by relying on empirically derived data. The field has long recognized that an assessment of violence risk must begin by considering relevant bases rates; that is, the known rate of violence among a particular population (Shah, 1978). Monahan (1981) emphasized "knowledge of the appropriate base rate is the most important single piece of information necessary to make an accurate (violence) prediction" (p. 60). Base rates serve as a starting point for subsequent evaluation of probability (Borum, Otto, & Golding, 1993; Monahan, 1981). With a base rate as an anchor, evaluators can then cautiously adjust their appraisal of violence risk based on assessment data, such as relevant violence risk factors.

- *Assess empirically demonstrated risk and protective factors.* Over the past two decades, researchers have created a vast literature detailing factors that correspond with particular types of violence or offending among particular populations (for summaries, see Bonta, Law, & Hanson, 1998; Gendreau, Goggin, & Law, 1997; Gendreau, Little & Goggin, 1996; Hanson & Morton-Bourgon, 2005). Thus, evaluators can consider whether the characteristics an examinee presents (particularly the static, historical characteristics) are empirically associated with violence. Indeed, the state of violence research has advanced to the point that any ethically or scientifically sound risk assessment should consider empirically demonstrated risk factors.
- *Risk communication.* A well-conducted and empirically sound risk assessment is useless if evaluators cannot convey findings in an honest and understandable manner. Generally, the task of evaluators is to communicate clearly, while also candidly acknowledging the limits to their assessments and avoiding the pull to speculate beyond what available data can support.

Violence Risk Assessment as Applied to Capital Sentencing

Despite the complexity of capital cases, the general model of violence risk assessment summarized in the previous section fits well (Conroy & Murrie, 2007). Indeed, the research data relevant to risk assessments in capital contexts, such as base rates and empirically supported risk factors, are probably more consistent and better documented than the data that underlie violence risk assessment in many other contexts.

Defining the Question of Risk in Capital Sentencing: Context Is Crucial

Violence risk assessments are legally irrelevant in the guilt/innocence phase of a capital trial; thus, attorneys request violence risk assessments to inform the sentencing phase. Sentencing, of course, occurs only if the defendant has been convicted of a capital offense. Although logic might suggest mental health professionals become involved only after sentencing has begun, this leaves inadequate time to complete a thorough and detailed evaluation.

Recall that at the capital sentencing stage, the jury usually deliberates between sentencing the individual to death or life in prison. In the vast majority of cases, release to the community is not an option in the foreseeable future. *Therefore, questions about violence risk in capital contexts are primarily questions about prison violence, or violence risk while incarcerated* (see Brief Amicus Curiae of the American Psychological Association, 2005; Cunningham, 2006c, 2008; Edens, Buffington-Vollum, et al., 2005). This important distinction might not be immediately obvious to jurors, but it remains crucial to understanding the question of violence risk. Indeed, in jurisdictions where the only option other than death is life imprisonment without the possibility of parole (LWOP), the U.S. Supreme Court has ruled that juries must be explicitly instructed on the defendant's parole ineligibility (see *Simmons v. South Carolina*, 1994).

Many courts have explicitly recognized that violence risk assessments in capital cases are specific to the prison context when parole is not an option (e.g., *Simmons v. South Carolina*, 1994; *Sterling v. Texas*, 1992; *United States v. Sablan*, 2007; *United States v. Sampson*, 2004; see also Cunningham, Sorensen, & Reidy, 2009, for discussion). But even when courts do not explicitly acknowledge the specific context, evaluators must. Modern scholarship and practice guidelines emphasize that violence risk assessment is *context specific* (Borum & Veerhagen, 2006; Conroy & Murrie, 2007; Heilbrun, 1992). One well-documented flaw in the early research on "dangerousness prediction" was the tendency to perceive "dangerousness" as a fixed trait of an individual (see Melton, Petrila, Poythress, & Slobogin, 2007, for discussion). But modern scholarship emphasizes what probably should have been acknowledged from the start: Violence is more likely in some contexts than others. Violence risk is a function of an individual *and* a context. Thus, forensic mental health professionals must approach violence risk assessment at capital sentencing not as a question of whether a particular defendant is generally "dangerous,"[4] but as a question about the degree of violence risk the defendant poses in a secure prison over many decades.

In *a few* capital cases, attorneys may ask that violence risk assessments address risk for violence if and when the offender is released to the community *decades into the future*. Though all states now allow sentences of LWOP, a few also allow for capital sentences with the possibility of release or parole in the distant future. Recall that attorneys in capital cases must typically request violence risk assessments (or any mental health evaluations) well before the guilt-innocence phase of proceedings if results are to be available for the sentencing phase. So attorneys who are pursuing plea agreements for sentences less than LWOP *may* request that evaluations address risk in the

---

4. Not only are assessments of vaguely defined "dangerousness" inconsistent with modern standards of practice, but they also fail to serve the rationale behind risk assessment at capital sentencing (Cunningham, 2006b). If the goal of assessment at capital sentencing is to help jurors determine who is most deserving of the death penalty, the broad descriptor of "dangerousness" fails (Cunningham, 2008). After all, Cunningham argues, every violent felon has already demonstrated "dangerousness" by committing a violent offense. On the other hand, assessments that address varying levels of violence risk during incarceration may be more helpful to individualizing decisions about sentencing.

context of a release to the community at a point the attorney perceives to be the soonest conceivable release date. A small minority of cases may require that an evaluator consider data relevant to community release decades into the future, but such situations are rare. The vast majority of violence risk assessments at capital sentencing must consider only the prison context. Thus, there is never a scenario in which a violence risk assessment for capital sentencing would address risk of violence in the community in the *near* future. Indeed, addressing risk for violence in the community in the near future is at best irrelevant, and at worst, disingenuous.

So the context for potential violence is clear (i.e., prison), but other aspects of the violence risk question may be less clearly defined for the forensic mental health professional (and the jury). For example, Texas—the jurisdiction in which this issue is most frequently addressed—requires jurors to consider whether there is a "probability that the defendant would commit criminal acts of violence that would constitute a continuing threat to society" (Tex. Code Crim. Proc. art. 37.071), but it offers no operational definition for important concepts such as "probability," "criminal acts," or "continuing threat" (Cunningham, 2008; Edens, Buffington-Vollum, et al., 2005). Likewise, other states that consider violence risk in capital sentencing tend not to operationally define violence or concepts related to risk. How do forensic mental health professionals proceed when important aspects of the risk assessment "referral question" are ill defined?

Cunningham, a psychologist who specializes in capital case scholarship and practice, has extensively addressed violence risk assessment at capital sentencing, including the ambiguity in statute and case law (e.g., 2006c, 2008, 2010; Cunningham & Goldstein, 2003). He emphasizes that violence risk assessments at capital sentencing are premised on the post-*Furman* goal of *individualizing* death penalty decisions, so ambiguities should be interpreted with this broad goal in mind. Thus, when the Texas statute specifies a "probability" of violence, Cunningham (2008) argues that the statute cannot mean "any possibility," because this would hold true for *any* defendant (indeed, virtually *anyone* might have "any possibility" of some violent behavior). Thus, "probability" in the Texas statute must connote something greater than "any possibility." Similarly, Cunningham (2008, p. 216) explains:

> The rationale of an individualized determination of death-worthiness also informs an understanding of the severity and context of the future violent acts that are contemplated by "criminal acts of violence that constitute a continuing threat to society." Because shoving another inmate, occasional belligerence with staff, and even a mutual fistfight are routine if not ubiquitous acts among prison inmates, these behaviors are of little value in individualizing or narrowing the application of the death penalty. Additionally, reasonable proportionality would require that "threat to society" be limited to acts of sufficient severity that a sanction of death is a reasonable preventive intervention.

Cunningham's examples address statutory law in Texas, a state in which capital sentencing (and violence risk assessment at capital sentencing) is quite common. But his general logic—that is, interpreting ambiguity with an eye toward post-*Furman* goals of individualizing capital sentencing—seems applicable in any death penalty state. Of course, courts may ultimately define "violence" or "probability" (or other key concepts in other jurisdictions) in ways different from what Cunningham (2008) suggests. But in the meantime, his approach offers a consistent and conceptually reasonable approach to these types of ambiguities.

Considering Base Rates of Violence Relevant to Risk Assessment in Capital Sentencing

Knowledge of relevant base rates is important in any forensic evaluation (Borum et al., 1993), particularly violence risk assessment (Monahan, 1981). Base rates allow us to tether risk estimates to known facts—in the form of group data—rather than to intuition or assumptions. In capital case risk assessments, considering base rates might be even more crucial (Cunningham & Goldstein, 2003; Cunningham & Reidy, 1999), because our intuition and assumptions tend to be so misleading. Prisons are crowded with men who have been violent in the community, so we reasonably assume that prison violence is commonplace and lethal. But government data reveal just the opposite. For example, the U.S. Department of Justice (Mumola, 2005) reports that rates of homicide within state correctional facilities (4 per 100,000 inmates, or a rate of 0.004%) are less than one-eighth the rate of homicides within the community when demographics are held constant (35 per 100,000 people, or a rate of 0.035%). These rates of prison violence have declined steadily and sharply since 1980 (Mumola, 2005), and rates of serious violence remain quite low, even when measured by inmate self-report (Lahm, 2008). In terms of inmate homicides on correctional staff in state prisons, the base rate is less than 1 per 1 million inmates per year, nationally. In short, prison violence tends to be less common and less severe than we typically assume.

Of course, broad rates of prison violence are not specific to prisoners who have committed murder, a group we might expect to be more violent than other prisoners. But again, empirical data prove surprising. For example, one study of over 51,000 inmates in the Florida correctional system found no differences in the prevalence rates of prison violence between inmates convicted of first-degree murder versus inmates convicted of property offenses versus all other inmates; the prevalence of assault ranged from 2% to 3% regardless of group (Sorensen & Cunningham, 2010). In fact, murderers demonstrated lower rates of disciplinary infractions and potentially violent offenses (Sorensen & Cunningham, 2010). In a study that provided prison violence base rate data for 6,390 convicted murderers incarcerated in Texas, Sorensen and Pilgrim (2000) reported an inmate-on-inmate homicide base rate of 0.2 per 1,000 inmates per year (no prison staff were murdered during the study period), and a base rate of 1.1 assaults on guards per 1,000 inmates per year. The total base rate of violence (including potentially violent acts, such as possessing a weapon) was 24 per 1,000 (or 2.4%) inmates per year.

Of course, capital sentencing proceedings require base rate data on the even smaller group of prisoners convicted of capital murder. Fortunately, research since the 1980s has carefully documented the base rates of violence among capital offenders. Indeed, because the population of capital offenders is small (relative to other offenders) and closely supervised (homicide in prison rarely goes undetected), the violence base rate data for this population is probably more comprehensive and detailed than the violence base rate data underlying any other form of violence risk assessment that forensic mental health professionals perform.

Base Rates of Postconviction Prison Violence by Death-Sentenced Capital Offenders

Recall that the U.S. Supreme Court's ruling in *Furman v. Georgia* (1972) not only caused a brief moratorium on death sentencing in the United States but also invalidated death sentences for hundreds of inmates awaiting execution across 31 jurisdictions. By commuting their sentences of death to sentences of life imprisonment among the general prisoner population, *Furman* created a natural experiment ideal for examining issues surrounding violence risk at capital sentencing. Marquart and colleagues (Marquart et al., 1989; Marquart & Sorensen, 1988) used the *Furman* natural experiment to document rates of violence among death-sentenced offenders after their sentences were commuted.

First, Marquart and Sorensen (1988) followed 47 Texas inmates from 1973 to 1986, after the *Furman* decision commuted their death sentences. Over 13 years in the general prison population, their violent offenses included a total of three weapons offenses and two assaults on correctional staff. During this period of incarceration, 93% were not sanctioned for any violent behavior, and none committed homicide. Marquart and Sorensen concluded that the rates of prison violence were much lower than anticipated among the death-sentenced offenders.

Next, Marquart and Sorensen (1989) performed a nationwide study of death-sentenced inmates who had their sentence commuted by *Furman*. Examining data on 558 commutees from 30 jurisdictions, they found that during the 15 years following commutation, 6 murders and 59 serious violent offenses took place. Stated as base rates, 30% of the offenders committed *any* serious rule violations. Half of these (i.e., 15.8% of the overall sample) committed only one, suggesting that "most serious infractions were one-time events or situations" (p. 20). But a few offenders (7.4% of the entire sample) committed three or more violations each. This small group of chronic offenders accounted for most of the serious infractions in the sample overall.

After examining the *Furman* commutees, Marquart et al. (1989) examined a post-*Furman* sample and described their study as a test of whether Texas jurors are accurate when they sentence capital defendants to death based on "future dangerousness." The authors identified 92 Texas capital murderers who were sentenced after 1973 (i.e., after Texas statute required jurors must find that the defendant posed a probability of future "criminal acts of violence that would constitute a continuing threat to society" to assign a death sentence) but were released from death row because their death sentences were commuted, retried, or dismissed. The authors then compared these 92 (whom jurors had anticipated to be dangerous) with 107 life-sentenced murderers (whom jurors had not anticipated to be dangerous), as well as a sample of Texas inmates in a high-security prison, and the population of Texas inmates overall.

Generally, the 92 capital offenders who had death sentences commuted had lower rates of violent rule infractions than the comparison groups. When calculated as an annual base rate (i.e., number of violent rule infractions per 100 inmates per year), the 92 death-sentenced capital murders had a rate of 1.61, compared to 2.60 for the life-sentenced capital murderers, 11.66 for Texas inmates overall, and 19.54 for inmates in a high-security facility. Stated differently, the annual violence base rate among death-sentenced-but-commuted capital murderers was around one-seventh the rate among Texas inmates overall. Some serious prison violence occurred: One of the 92 death-sentenced murderers committed a homicide in prison (reportedly related to prison gang activity), as did three inmates in the general prison sample. But overall, rates of violent infractions among the 92 death-sentenced murderers were lower than rates among each of the comparison groups, and apparently lower than anticipated by jurors (who must "predict" future violence to assign a death sentence): Only 10% engaged in serious prison violence and 1% committed a prison homicide.

Since the Marquart studies, researchers have continued to document the base rates of prison violence among death-sentenced murderers. For example, among 39 Indiana death row inmates who were transferred to the general population, 36% were involved in any documented violence during a follow-up period that averaged 16 years. In terms of assaults causing serious injuries, a total of six inmates committed a total of seven serious assaults, for a 15.4% prevalence rate, or an annual rate of 1.1 serious assaults per 100 inmates per year (Reidy, Cunningham, & Sorensen, 2001).

In a similar study, Sorensen and Cunningham (2009) examined 80 capital offenders in Arizona who had their death sentences commuted and served subsequent time (13 years, on average) in the general prison population. As in all studies of prison violence, base rates grew smaller as the types of violence grew more serious. Almost 24% of the inmates committed some form of assault, while 16.3% committed an assault categorized as serious, and 3.8% committed an assault that caused serious injury to the victim. One inmate (1.3%) committed murder, killing two other inmates.

Edens, Buffington-Vollum, Keilen, Roskamp, and Anthony (2005) studied the prison disciplinary records of Texas inmates who had been sentenced to death following "future dangerousness" testimony during sentencing. These inmates had been on Texas Death Row for an average of 9.5 years, including a period when death row functioned as an open population and a more recent period in which death row was "locked down," to segregate death-sentenced inmates from others. Overall, 32% of the inmates committed minor assault, 5.2% committed a serious assault (defined as an assault that required more than first aid), and none committed a homicide. More than 20% of the sample had no disciplinary infractions of any sort.

Base Rates of Postconviction Prison Violence by Other Capital Offenders

Researchers who collect base rate data relevant to capital sentencing decisions often compare various capital sentencing arrangements to address some questions that might arise at capital sentencing (for example, "Does a sentence of life without parole encourage prison violence because it leaves an inmate with 'nothing to lose'?") or questions about existing studies (for example, "Did inmates on death row commit little violence because of stricter supervision?"). Although no single study can provide base rate data for all questions at capital sentencing, several studies can shed light on common questions. For example, in a study of all inmates convicted of capital murder in Missouri since 1977, Sorensen and Wrinkle (1996) compared 93 capital offenders sentenced to death and 323 capital offenders sentenced to LWOP to a comparison sample of 232 men who were convicted of second-degree murder and eligible for parole. All three groups were housed in the general prison population—an arrangement unique to the Missouri system—allowing similar opportunity to commit violence. Results revealed no significant differences across groups in the rate or number of assaultive behaviors. In terms of base rates, the prevalence rate of assault was around 20%, and the rate of prison homicide was 1.2%, regardless of sentencing arrangements. In short, the study suggested that capital murderers, regardless of their sentence, tend to be no more violent in prison than other murderers.

Cunningham and Sorensen (2007) analyzed records from 136 capital murderers who entered Texas prisons after 2001, serving a sentence *less than* death. Unlike recently death-sentenced inmates, this sample was not housed under segregated "lock down" conditions and therefore had greater opportunity to commit violence. The study followed the inmates during their initial period of incarceration, the time at which violence is most likely. Of these capital inmates, 37% were involved in conduct that could be *potentially* violent, 19% were involved in a fight, 14% were involved in some form of assault (including behaviors such as throwing waste at others), and 5% committed a serious assault that required medical attention for the victim. None of the 136 inmates committed a homicide during the period covered by the study. Thus, even when sentenced to less restrictive conditions, rates of serious assault remained fairly low among capital offenders.

In a similar study of federal inmates, researchers reviewed disciplinary infractions among 145 capital offenders who had been sentenced to the federal equivalent of LWOP (Cunningham, Reidy, & Sorensen, 2008). Over a period averaging 6 years, 21% committed any assault, 9% committed more serious assaults, and 1% committed an assault resulting in moderate injury. None committed an assault resulting in major injury, a serious assault on staff, an escape, or murder of another inmate. As a group, the LWOP inmates did not commit disproportionate rates of assault compared to other federal inmates in high-security facilities. Among the LWOP inmates, prevalence rates of assault were similar, regardless of whether prosecutors had alleged "future dangerousness" as a nonstatutory aggravating factor (see Cunningham, Sorensen, & Reidy, 2009, for a similar analysis of *juror* predictions of future dangerousness compared to subsequent rates of violence among federal capital defendants).

Implications of Base Rates of Violence Among Capital Offenders

The base rates reviewed earlier are illustrative rather than exhaustive. Forensic mental health professionals involved in capital proceedings must review new base rate data as it becomes available and seek base rate data from the correctional systems most appropriate to their jurisdiction. Nevertheless, a fair read of the available base rate data suggests several broad conclusions that are relevant to violence risk assessments at capital sentencing:

- Rates of serious prison violence appear no higher among murderers than among other types of offenders (e.g., Cunningham, Reidy, & Sorensen, 2005; Marquart et al., 1989; Sorensen & Cunningham, 2010).
- Rates of prison violence appear no higher among capital murderers sentenced to death than among capital murderers sentenced to LWOP (e.g., Cunningham, Reidy, & Sorensen, 2005; Sorensen & Wrinkle, 1996).
- Rates of prison violence among capital murderers sentenced to LWOP appear no higher than among inmates convicted of lesser degrees of murder (e.g., Sorensen & Wrinkle, 1996) or other inmates serving

long-term sentences (e.g., Cunningham et al., 2008). Likewise, capital murderers who are eligible for parole in the distant future appear no more likely (indeed, they appear less likely) to commit violence than capital murderers eligible for parole in the nearer future (Morris, Longmire, Buffington-Vollum, & Vollum, 2010).
- Most capital murderers—at least two-thirds depending on jurisdiction and definition of violence—are never sanctioned for physical violence in prison (e.g., Edens, Buffington-Vollum, et al., 2005; Marquart et al., 1989; Marquart, Ekland-Olson, & Sorensen, 1994; Marquart & Sorensen, 1989).
- Rates of serious prison violence among capital offenders appear low—around 10% or below—with lower rates for more serious forms of violence (e.g., Cunningham et al., 2008; Edens, Buffington-Vollum, et al., 2005; Marquart & Sorensen, 1988; Marquart et al., 1989)
- Rates of prison homicide among capital murderers are quite low—around 1% or below—and appear no higher than rates among noncapital inmates (e.g., Cunningham et al., 2008; Cunningham & Sorensen, 2007; Edens, Buffington-Vollum, et al., 2005; Marquart & Sorensen, 1988; Marquart et al., 1989; Sorensen & Cunningham, 2009).

What do these low base rates mean for forensic mental health professionals who are involved in capital sentencing evaluations? Authorities on forensic mental health assessment (FMHA) describe the role of base rates in forensic evaluations this way:

> The evaluator should use the base rate to set the starting point for subsequent evaluation of probability. That is, higher frequency events will be seen as more likely, and low frequency events will be seen as less likely. With the base rates as a starting point, the examiner can then consider assessment data and (cautiously) modify these rates accordingly to make a judgment about the individual case. (Borum et al., 1993, p. 46)

Thus, in violence risk assessment at capital sentencing, our starting point is to acknowledge that low frequency events such as serious violence are relatively unlikely, and lower frequency events such as homicide are quite unlikely. Predicting that a capital defendant will commit serious prison violence is, colloquially speaking, betting against the odds. Therefore, assertions that a capital offender is likely to commit serious violence in prison often prove to be erroneous (Cunningham et al., 2009; Edens, Buffington-Vollum, et al., 2005; Marquart et al., 1989), whereas assertions that a capital offender is unlikely to commit serious violence in prison usually prove to be accurate (Cunningham & Sorensen, 2010).

These low base rates do not indicate that *no* capital defendant will commit serious violence in prison, only that very few will. These base rates also reveal that a small minority of capital defendants *do* commit serious prison violence. Fortunately, research reveals a few risk factors that tend to correspond with this violence. Forensic mental health professional tasked with violence risk assessment at capital sentencing may identify which of the research-demonstrated risk factors for prison violence are present for a particular defendant. Then, depending on the extent to which these well-established risk factors are present or absent, the forensic mental health professional may cautiously infer that the defendant's risk for violence is above or below the base rates of serious violence among similar offenders. Of course, any deviations from the base rate "starting point" must be made cautiously (Borum et al., 1993). Even among offenders who manifest several of the empirically supported risk factors, serious violence remains the exception rather than the rule (Sorensen & Cunningham, 2009; Sorensen & Pilgrim, 2000). For this reason, Cunningham describes violence risk assessment at capital sentencing as delineating "various degrees of *im*probability" of prison violence (Cunningham & Sorensen, 2010, p. 71, emphasis added).

This process of beginning with base rates and then considering empirically supported risk factors is a process of *individualizing* the violence risk estimate. Courts have sometimes rejected violence risk testimony that they perceive to be group data detached from the defendant facing trial (e.g., *Porter v. Virginia*, 2008).[5] But examining the empirically supported risk factors in a particular case is indeed an individualized scrutiny of a unique defendant. Just as in other science-based clinical work, this scrutiny is guided by research: Forensic mental health professionals know which risk factors are most relevant precisely because they have proven relevant to violence in studies of similar offenders in similar contexts. Prioritizing risk factors that have proven relevant across group data is no less individualized, but it does lead to risk estimates that tend to be more accurate than the unaided, impressionistic, clinical predictions made without the benefit of group data (see, e.g., Brief Amicus Curiae of the American Psychological Association, 2005, for discussion).[6]

---

5. In *Porter v. Virginia* (2008), the Virginia Supreme Court held that the trial court had not erred when it excluded a capital defendant's expert testimony that was based on "statistical projection on future violent acts of an inmate who may be similarly situated to [the defendant]" (p. 440). The court concluded that statistical speculation was inadmissible without showing that the expert's opinions were particularized to the defendant's own case. The court explained that "nothing in [the defendant's] motion is a proffer of an "individualized" or "particularized" analysis of [the defendant's] "prior criminal record," "prior history," his prior or current incarceration, or the circumstances of the crime for which he had been convicted" (*Porter v. Virginia*, 2008, p. 440). Legal scholars lamented that the Virginia Supreme Court appeared to welcome subjective clinical judgment, but reject empirically derived data because it might be considered "statistical" (Faigman et al., 2009).

6. Consider an analogy from medical practice. If I ask a physician about my risk of heart disease, the physician may begin by considering my gender, weight, and age. The physician may then ask about my family history of heart disease, my diet, my exercise habits, and other lifestyle variables such as

(*Continued*)

Considering Empirically Demonstrated Risk Factors

Age

The factor most consistently and robustly related to prison violence is the prisoner's age, with younger prisoners being more likely to commit violence than older prisoners (Gendreau et al., 1997). This finding has held true across diverse samples spanning several decades (e.g., Flanagan, 1980; Hirschi & Gottfredson, 1983; Mabli, Holley, Patrick, & Walls, 1979) up to the present day (e.g., Cunningham & Sorensen, 2007; Kuanliang, Sorensen, & Cunningham, 2008; Lahm, 2008). The finding also holds true in samples restricted to murderers (e.g., Sorensen & Pilgrim, 2000) and even capital murderers (e.g., Cunningham et al., 2008; Morris et al., 2010; Sorensen & Cunningham, 2009; Sorensen & Wrinkle, 1996).

Sorensen and Pilgrim (2000) provided the most detailed findings related to age when they developed an actuarial model to assess violence risk among capital defendants. The researchers examined 6,390 Texas inmates who had been convicted of murder, and followed them for an average of 4.55 years. They reported violence base rate data (described above), estimated a 16.4% likelihood of any violence among an "average" capital offender across a 40-year span, and examined factors that increased or decreased this average violence risk in their sample. Ultimately they reported that, "Clearly the most influential indicator of prison violence is the age of the defendant upon entry into prison" (p. 1266). In their actuarial model, Sorensen and Pilgrim (2000) identified the average age category as 21–25 years, and reported that violence risk was higher by 5.5% among offenders below 21 years of age:

> Risk of violence among offenders decreased as the age of the inmates increased, with those aged 26 through 30 years being 7.2 percentage points less likely to be violent than those 21 through 25 years of age. The risk of violence among inmates aged 31

(Continued)
smoking and stress. In short, the physician would gauge the extent to which I manifested the risk factors that have been empirically linked to heart disease in large-scale medical studies. When other patients ask this physician questions about *their* risk for heart disease, the physician probably asks them the same questions about the same risk factors. But none of us, if we were genuinely interested in our risk of heart disease, would complain that the physician failed to conduct an individualized assessment. We would appreciate that the physician considered the most relevant risk factors and provided an individualized estimate of our risk for heart disease based on the extent to which each of us manifested those risk factors. If we learned that the physician was so concerned about individualizing patient care that he or she asked each patient detailed and personalized questions addressing factors with no known relationship to heart disease risk, we would not commend the physician for providing individualized care. Nor would we trust the physician's appraisal of our risk for heart disease. Instead, we would look for a new physician who used better methods of assessing risk.

through 35 years old decreased by 12.3 percentage points while the risk decreased by 14.4 percentage points for those over the age of 35. (p. 1266)

The precise values reported in the Sorensen and Pilgrim (2000) model may not perfectly generalize to other samples. But for purposes of violence risk assessment at capital sentencing, age remains the best-documented and strongest risk factor.

Prior Prison Violence

Not surprisingly, prior prison violence is associated with subsequent prison violence, whether among capital offenders (Sorensen & Cunningham, 2009; Sorensen & Pilgrim, 2000) or other inmates (Cunningham & Sorensen, 2007). "Simply put, although violence in the free world is not indicative of violence in prison, prior violent acts in prison are a good indicator of future violence in an institutional setting" (Cunningham & Sorensen, 2007, p. 248). For forensic mental health professionals conducting violence risk assessments at capital sentencing, considering prior prison violence is crucial. But, of course, this is not possible among capital defendants who have not served prior prison terms (although a history of violence while awaiting trial in jail may be relevant).

Prior Prison Terms

Several studies suggest that inmates who have served a prior prison term show somewhat higher rates of prison violence, a finding that appears to hold true among capital offenders and other high-security inmates (Cunningham & Sorensen, 2006; Cunningham, Sorensen, & Reidy, 2005; Sorensen & Pilgrim, 2000). On the other hand, one of these studies (Cunningham, Sorensen, & Reidy, 2005) also found that inmates who had previously completed a probated sentence had slightly lower rates of violence.

Education

Criminologists have long reported that higher educational achievement is associated with better adjustment to prison (Gendreau et al., 1997; Toch & Adams, 1986). Likewise, greater educational achievement (often operationalized as a high school diploma or GED versus none) appears to be associated with lower rates of prison violence (Cunningham & Sorensen, 2006; Cunningham, Sorensen, & Reidy, 2005), even among capital offenders (Cunningham, Reidy, & Sorensen, 2008). Thus, failing to complete high school or earn a GED may be considered a risk factor for prison violence, whereas completing high school or beyond may be considered a protective factor.

Prison Gang Membership

Prison gang membership emerged as the second strongest predictor of serious prison violence, after age, in the large study of Texas inmates convicted of murder (Sorensen & Pilgrim, 2000). Prison gang membership has also been strongly associated with prison violence in other large-scale studies of state prison inmates (e.g., Cunningham & Sorensen, 2007; Griffin & Hepburn, 2006; Huebner, 2003), though these have not been specific to capital defendants. In a recent Texas study, gang membership was associated with some forms of misconduct, but not serious violence, among capital inmates (Morris et al., 2010), suggesting gang membership may not be as clear a risk factor as previously assumed.

Offense Characteristics

Several studies suggest that certain characteristics of the capital offense itself correspond with higher rates of violence among capital offenders. In the large Sorensen and Pilgrim (2000) study, offenders who had been involved in a contemporaneous robbery or burglary as part of their capital murder conviction, had multiple victims in their capital murder conviction, or had additional murder or assault attempts as part of their capital conviction were more likely to commit violent infractions in prison. In a study of federal capital defendants, the group of "LWOP inmates whose capital offenses involved robberies, carjacking, or kidnapping/abductions were more likely to be involved in disruptive prison conduct" (Cunningham et al., 2008, p. 60). The reasons these offense characteristics correspond with prison violence are unclear; perhaps capital murders that included other criminal behaviors more often involve offenders who used murder for instrumental goals as part of a broader criminal lifestyle.[7] The generalizability of these risk factors is also somewhat unclear. A study of 136 Texas capital defendants (Cunningham & Sorensen, 2007) failed to replicate the earlier finding that men whose capital offenses included multiple murder victims or contemporaneous attempted murder or assault showed higher rates of prison violence (Sorensen & Pilgrim, 2000).

---

7. Also, recall from the Chapter 2 appendices that murder as part of a course of criminal conduct appears as a statutorily defined aggravating factor.

Factors Unrelated to Violence in Prison

The finding that few offense characteristics correspond to prison violence illustrates the surprising nature of research on prison violence. The crimes for which an inmate is incarcerated are poor predictors of whether that inmate will commit violence in prison (Alexander & Austin, 1992; Marquart et al., 1989; Sorensen & Pilgrim, 2000). When they do predict prison violence, it is often in a manner that seems counterintuitive. For example, a large study of Missouri inmates found that men incarcerated for property offenses were much more likely to be involved in violent prison misconduct than men incarcerated for murder (Cunningham, Sorensen, & Reidy, 2005). Indeed, several studies have found that groups of inmates facing longer sentences, who have committed more serious offenses, show lower rates of prison misconduct, including violent misconduct (e.g., Cunningham, Reidy, & Sorensen, 2005; Cunningham & Sorensen, 2006, 2007; Flanagan, 1980; Marquart et al., 1989).

Research on prison violence is surprising also because many variables strongly related to violence risk in the community appear unrelated to violence risk in prison. For example, substance abuse is among the strongest risk factors for violence in the community (Gendreau et al., 1996; Harris, Rice, & Quinsey, 1993; Monahan et al., 2001; Swanson, 1994), and many inmates were under the influence of substances at the time they committed the crimes for which they are incarcerated (Zhang, 2004). In fact, substance abuse appears to play a role in at least half of violent crimes in the community (National Institute on Drug Abuse, 1993; National Institute of Justice, 2000). But violence is context specific. Prisons greatly reduce an inmate's access to drugs and alcohol, and thus greatly reduce the opportunity for substance abuse to play a role in prison violence (Cunningham & Reidy, 1999).

Of course, a history of substance abuse also fails to predict prison violence because of the base rates reviewed earlier. Although most inmates have some history of substance abuse, most do not go on to commit serious prison violence. In short, characteristics that are commonplace among prisoners cannot reliably predict behaviors that are rare among prisoners (see generally, Cunningham, 2006c; Cunningham & Reidy, 1999).

For similar reasons, a diagnosis of Antisocial Personality Disorder (APD)—though sometimes addressed during capital sentencing (Edens & Cox, 2010)—is virtually useless as a predictor of violent misconduct while incarcerated. Because APD is diagnosed primarily on criminal behavior, the diagnosis is pervasive in prisons (Cunningham & Reidy, 1998), applicable to the vast majority of capital defendants, and therefore adds no new information to help identify the few inmates most likely to be violent in prison. A feature common to most of a population does little to help identify the small percentage of that population likely to commit acts of violence.

Psychopathy, as formally measured by Hare's (2003) Psychopathy Checklist-Revised, may initially appear more relevant as a risk factor. After all, high psychopathy scores are less common than APD diagnoses, and psychopathy scores correspond with a variety of antisocial behaviors, including violence, across a variety of populations (Leistico, Salekin, deCoster, & Rogers, 2008). But regarding prison violence specifically, the predictive value of the PCL-R is poorer. In the most comprehensive meta-analysis of PCL-R scores and institutional violence, PCL-R scores corresponded only modestly ($r_w = .17$) with measures of physically violent misconduct, and these effects were weakest in samples from the United States (Guy, Edens, Anthony, & Douglas, 2005; see Walters, 2003). Given these data, several authorities have argued against considering the PCL-R as a risk factor for violence at capital sentencing (see, e.g., DeMatteo, Edens, & Hart, 2010; Edens, Buffington-Vollum, et al., 2005; Edens, Petrila, & Buffington-Vollum, 2001; Guy et al., 2005), and evaluators would find it difficult to justify relying on the PCL-R when conducting a violence risk assessment in capital cases. Nevertheless, research suggests that the PCL-R continues to be used in capital sentencing proceedings (DeMatteo & Edens, 2006; Walsh & Walsh, 2006).

Like the PCL-R, many measures that are appropriate in other FMHAs are inappropriate to address the narrow question of violence risk at capital sentencing (for reviews, see Cunningham & Reidy, 1999; and Edens, Buffington-Vollum, et al., 2005). Broad, multiscale personality inventories do not provide data specific to risk of prison violence. Even commonly used risk assessment measures that were developed to predict community violence with samples of psychiatric patients, forensic psychiatric patients, or even criminal offenders released to the community cannot adequately assess risk of prison violence among capital defendants.

Recently, scholars have studied large correctional samples to develop actuarial measures specifically to predict violence *in prison* (i.e., Cunningham, Sorensen, & Reidy, 2005; Cunningham & Sorensen, 2006; Sorensen & Pilgrim, 2000). Each of these has shown more promise for predicting prison violence than some of the general risk instruments (mis)applied for that purpose, and each may be refined to a condition suitable for applied use. But at present each remains suitable for research only. One effort to replicate the Sorensen and Pilgrim (2000) model concluded that "it seems premature—and unwise—for experts to be introducing the Sorensen and Pilgrim model into their testimony at capital sentencing" (Buffington-Vollum, Edens, & Keilen, 2008, p. 21). To be clear, the studies from which these instruments were developed provide important information about base rates of prison violence and empirically supported risk factors, which evaluators may use to inform forensic evaluations. But applying the actual research measures to individual cases in other jurisdictions is probably not yet appropriate.

Risk Communication

The point of any FMHA is to contribute information that helps someone make a well-informed legal decision. So even the most rigorous risk assessment and research data are useless if evaluators cannot communicate clearly the relevant findings. The relevant findings may vary as a function of the forensic mental health professional's role in a particular case. Forensic mental health professionals who have accepted a "teaching expert" role will explain broad information about base rates of prison violence and, perhaps, empirically supported risk factors for prison violence. In the strictest form of the "teaching expert" role, the forensic mental health professional will know nothing specific about the defendant and will not need to relate any of the general scientific data to the defendant at trial.

For forensic mental health professionals who accept an "evaluator" role, the risk communication involves much more. Some forms of risk communication might occur at the earliest stages of the evaluation process. For example, in an initial discussion with an attorney seeking a violence risk assessment at capital sentencing, the forensic mental health professional might provide some general education about base rates of prison violence and empirically supported risk factors. This helps orient the attorney to the forensic mental health professional's approach (i.e., rooted in empirical data rather than unstructured clinical impressions), the data the forensic mental health professional must access, and the potential range of conclusions. Depending on the nature of the case and attorney preferences, forensic mental health professionals may prepare a written report detailing conclusions about risk. Ultimately, the retaining attorney may call the forensic mental health professional to testify to a jury regarding the violence risk assessment.

In a broad guide to violence risk assessments, Conroy and Murrie (2007) provided several suggestions for risk communication. Some of these general suggestions are particularly applicable to violence risk assessment at capital sentencing. The overall goal of these suggestions is to make the evaluation and opinion-formation process *transparent*. In other words, evaluators convey clearly how they gathered and considered data to arrive at a reasonable opinion.

1. *Clearly reiterate the specific risk assessment referral question, and boundaries of the evaluation.*

Violence risk assessments at capital sentencing are unusually narrow, in that they address potential violence only in the prison context. Few laypersons will naturally anticipate this narrow focus, or the fact that this narrow focus requires considering a different set of risk factors than those considered in other violence risk assessments. Explaining the unique, narrowly focused referral question helps orient listeners to the unique, narrowly focused evaluation procedures.

2. *Assume the role of educator.*

Without condescending, good evaluators communicate the rationale and science behind risk assessment procedures. Because jurors tend to prefer risk messages that are more impressionistic than data based (Krauss & Lee, 2003; Krauss, Lieberman, & Olson, 2004; Krauss & Sales, 2001), evaluators who plan to express opinions rooted in group data must adopt the role of educator. One approach might be to guide jurors through the risk assessment procedure, specifying how group data help us consider a specific defendant in the context of accumulated scientific data from similar defendants. Evaluators should make clear that they consider carefully case-specific data as well as the broad data from empirical research.[8] Ideally, jurors understand that group data are not research results detached from a particular defendant, but rather a crucial starting point for understanding that particular defendant.

3. *Emphasize context.*

To what extent does any defendant pose a risk of violence? It depends on context. This holds especially true for capital defendants, who (in most cases) face the remainder of their lives in prison. As emphasized earlier, forensic mental health professionals focus solely on the prison context when considering relevant base rates and risk factors. But risk communication, too, requires understanding (and explaining) the context-specific nature of violence risk assessment in capital cases.

4. *Clearly delineate the data considered, the procedures used, and the reasoning underlying the conclusions.*

Describing the evaluation procedure is a "transparent" practice that allows others to examine how the evaluator obtained and considered data, and arrived at an opinion. A federal district court once emphasized that an evaluator's opinion "rises no higher than the reasons on which it is based" (*United States v. Horowitz,* 1973, p. 777). So it becomes important for evaluators to make clear how the data they considered led to the risk estimate they offer. A clear articulation of reasoning should be even handed. That is, forensic mental

---

8. After reviewing research on expert witness testimony, Kwartner and Boccaccini (2008) identified "case-specific testimony" as a primary factor in effective courtroom communication.

health professionals should acknowledge conflicting data or unavailable data that would have better informed their conclusions.

5. *Communicate risk with a point of reference.*

In capital contexts, terms like "high risk" or "low risk" for violence are potentially misleading. Should a juror infer that "high risk" means the defendant is more likely than not to commit violence? Or does it only mean that the defendant appears to be at higher risk than other capital defendants, who as a group have less than a 1% rate of homicide in prison? The best way to reduce ambiguity is to communicate risk estimates relative to a base rate reference point. Some risk conclusions may include little more than base rate data for a particular population and a conclusion that the risk assessment revealed no data that would raise or lower the risk estimate relative to the population base rate. Other times, a risk communication message might describe how risk factors place a defendant at somewhat higher or lower risk than the population base rate for violence.

6. *Acknowledge limits.*

By definition, risk assessment involves developing an opinion in the context of some uncertainty. Even in a well-conducted risk assessment, some questions may remain unanswered, or an evaluator cannot offer a risk estimate that is as precise as others request (Conroy & Murrie, 2007). Evaluators are bound to openly acknowledge these limits. Psychologists communicating their assessment results "indicate any significant limitations of their interpretations" (American Psychological Association, 2002 p. 14). Authorities on forensic evaluation consistently emphasize the need to discuss in a straightforward manner the limits to data and opinions (Brodsky, 1991, 1999; Heilbrun, 2001; Heilbrun, Marczyk, & DeMatteo, 2002; Melton et al., 2007; Shuman & Greenberg, 2003).

Conclusion

Risk assessments require addressing uncertain outcomes. However, in capital cases, ample data help shed light on likely outcomes. These data reveal low base rates of prison violence and a few risk factors associated with that violence. Forensic mental health professionals who perform violence risk assessments at capital sentencing must not only be familiar with these data but also be able to apply them to a given case and communicate to a lay audience how and why they did so.

9

Principles of Forensic Mental Health Assessment Applied to Death Penalty Cases

Introduction

As the preceding chapters illustrate, several types of forensic mental health assessments (FMHAs) can be conducted in capital contexts. Throughout the discussion of these evaluations, we have attempted to identify the key legal issue (e.g., the presence/absence of mental retardation in *Atkins*-type evaluations, or the absence of a factual and rational understanding in competence for execution evaluations), highlight the complex clinical and procedural considerations, and (whenever possible) present empirically supported best-practice approaches for conducting these evaluations.

Despite the substantial differences among the various capital case evaluations we have discussed, common principles underlie all of them. FMHAs in capital cases are, first and foremost, FMHAs. But authorities correctly emphasize that capital case evaluations require higher standards of practice than FMHAs conducted in other contexts. We suggest that meeting these high standards in capital case evaluations begins with following the same best practices that underlie all FMHAs.

Principles of Forensic Mental Health Assessment

In 2001, Heilbrun detailed a set of 29 principles of FMHA that were theoretically applicable across a wide range of FMHAs.[1] Heilbrun's (2001) principles are organized sequentially around the four broad steps within FMHAs: *(1)* preparation, *(2)* data collection, *(3)* data interpretation, and *(4)* communication. Heilbrun discussed each principle in terms of the support that it received from law (relevant statutory law, case law, and administrative regulations affecting standards and procedure), ethics (professional ethics codes applicable to mental health professionals, including psychologists and psychiatrists), science (theory and empirical evidence), and standards of practice (professional literature offering guidelines and recommendations for best practices). After analyzing these sources of authority, Heilbrun classified each of the 29 principles as either *established* (i.e., the principles are largely supported by research, accepted in practice, and consistent with ethical and legal standards) or *emerging* (i.e., the principles are supported in some areas, but with mixed or absent evidence from others, or supported by some evidence, but with continuing disagreement among professionals regarding their application).

After Heilbrun (2001) identified these principles, Heilbrun, Marczyk, and DeMatteo (2002) illustrated how these principles could be applied to FMHAs in criminal, civil, juvenile, and family law contexts. Subsequent efforts demonstrated how these principles could improve the overall quality of forensic practice (Heilbrun, DeMatteo, & Marczyk, 2004) and apply to specific offender populations (including sexual offenders; Heilbrun, 2003) and tasks (including neuropsychological evaluations; Heilbrun et al., 2003).

More recently, Heilbrun slightly revised several of his original principles (see Heilbrun, Grisso, & Goldstein, 2009) and provided an integrated principle-based framework that combines his original principles with principles, guidelines, and maxims developed by other authorities (see Brodsky, 1991, 1999, 2004; Melton et al., 2007; Simon & Gold, 2004). As Table 9.1 indicates, the 38 integrated principles fall into the following categories (which expand upon Heilbrun's initial categories): General, Preparation, Data Collection, Data Interpretation, Written Communication, and Testimony.

---

1. Several authorities have offered guidelines for conducting FMHAs (see, e.g., Melton, Petrila, Poythress, & Slobogin, 2007; Shapiro, 1991, 1999). However, Heilbrun's (2001) principles are unique in that they were designed to apply to all types of FMHAs.

Table 9.1 Principles of Forensic Mental Health Assessment

General

1. Be aware of the important differences between clinical and forensic domains.
2. Obtain appropriate education, training, and experience in one's area of forensic specialization.
3. Be familiar with the relevant legal, ethical, scientific, and practice literatures pertaining to forensic mental health assessment.
4. Be guided by honesty and striving for impartiality, actively disclosing the limitations on as well as the support for one's opinions.
5. Control potential evaluator bias in general through monitoring case selection, continuing education, and consultation with knowledgeable colleagues.
6. Be familiar with specific aspects of the legal system, particularly communication, discovery, deposition, and testimony.
7. Do not become adversarial, but present and defend your opinions effectively.

Preparation

8. Identify relevant forensic issues.
9. Accept referrals only within area of expertise.
10. Decline the referral when evaluator impartiality is unlikely.
11. Clarify the evaluator's role with the attorney.
12. Clarify financial arrangements.
13. Obtain appropriate authorization.
14. Avoid playing the dual roles of therapist and forensic evaluator.
15. Determine the particular role to be played within forensic assessment if the referral is accepted.
16. Select the most appropriate model to guide data gathering, interpretation, and communication.

Data Collection

17. Use multiple sources of information for each area being assessed. Review the available background information and actively seek important missing elements.
18. Use relevance and reliability (validity) as guides for seeking information and selecting data sources.
19. Obtain relevant historical information.
20. Assess clinical characteristics in relevant, reliable, and valid ways.
21. Assess legally relevant behavior.
22. Ensure that conditions for evaluation are quiet, private, and distraction-free.
23. Provide appropriate notification of purpose and/or obtain appropriate authorization before beginning.
24. Determine whether the individual understands the purpose of the evaluation and the associated limits on confidentiality.

Data Interpretation

25. Use third party information in assessing response style.
26. Use testing when indicated in assessing response style.
27. Use case-specific (idiographic) evidence in assessing clinical condition, functional abilities, and causal connection.
28. Use nomothetic evidence in assessing clinical condition, functional abilities, and causal connection.

(Continued)

Table 9.1 Principles of Forensic Mental Health Assessment (Continued)

Data Interpretation

29. Use scientific reasoning in assessing causal connection between clinical condition and functional abilities.
30. Carefully consider whether to answer the ultimate legal question. If it is answered, it should be in the context of a thorough evaluation clearly describing data and reasoning, and with the clear recognition that this question is in the domain of the legal decision maker.
31. Describe findings and limits so that they need change little under cross examination.

Written Communication

32. Attribute information to sources.
33. Use plain language; avoid technical jargon.
34. Write report in sections, according to model and procedures.

Testimony

35. Base testimony on the results of the properly performed FMHA.
36. Prepare.
37. Communicate effectively.
38. Control the message. Strive to obtain, retain, and regain control over the meaning and impact of what is presented in expert testimony.

Sources: Heilbrun, 2001; Heilbrun, Grisso, & Goldstein, 2009.

Applying the Integrated Principles of Forensic Mental Heath Assessment in Capital Contexts

Previous practice guidelines and recommendations targeted specific legal questions (see, e.g., Weiner & Hess, 2006), including competence to stand trial (Grisso, 1988), criminal responsibility (Rogers, 1986; Rogers & Shuman, 2000; Shapiro, 1999), competence to consent to treatment (Grisso & Appelbaum, 1998), and child custody (Ackerman & Kane, 1998; Gould & Martindale, 2007; Martindale & Gould, 2007). Guidelines that focus on specific types of FMHAs have obvious importance. But a strength of Heilbrun's integrated principles is their broad applicability across various types of FMHAs, including those in capital contexts. Several papers have applied Heilbrun's (2001) original principles to *Atkins*-type and capital mitigation evaluations (see, e.g., Heilbrun et al., 2005; Heilbrun, Marczyk, DeMatteo, & Mack-Allen, 2007; Marczyk, Heilbrun, DeMatteo, & Bell, 2003; Marczyk, Knauss, Kutinsky, DeMatteo, & Heilbrun, 2008). In this chapter, we summarize and expand upon those efforts by applying the more recent integrated principles of FMHA identified in Heilbrun et al. (2009) to evaluations in capital cases.

Applying these integrated principles is consistent with the guidelines and substantive criteria for capital mitigation first articulated by the U.S. Supreme Court in *Furman v. Georgia* (1972). In response to *Furman*, which held that the capital punishment statutes of Texas and Georgia violated the Eighth and Fourteenth Amendments to the U.S. Constitution, modern death penalty statutes specify aggravating and mitigating factors that are designed to assist juries in reaching a sentencing decision in a capital case (as discussed in Chapter 2). Applying integrated principles of FMHA should help minimize arbitrariness in the decision-making process by promoting thoroughness, consistency, clarity, and impartiality.

Principle 1: *Be aware of the important differences between clinical and forensic domains.* Evaluators must clearly understand the differences between an FMHA (which is conducted to assist a legal decision maker or attorney) and a therapeutic assessment (which is conducted for diagnostic or treatment-planning purposes) (see Greenberg & Shuman, 1997, 2007; Heilbrun, 2001; Melton et al., 2007; Simon & Gold, 2004). This basic distinction is often overlooked or blurred in ways that undermine the quality of forensic evaluation. As detailed in Chapter 1, Heilbrun (2001) described several key distinctions between these two types of assessments, including the purpose of the evaluation (to diagnose and treat symptoms of mental health disorders in a therapeutic assessment, or to assist a legal decision maker or attorney in a forensic assessment), the entity served (the individual patient in a therapeutic assessment, or the court, attorney, or client in a forensic assessment), the response style of the examinee (assumed to be reliable in a therapeutic assessment but not assumed to be reliable in a forensic assessment), the written report (brief and conclusory in a therapeutic assessment but often detailed in a forensic assessment), and the resulting court testimony (not expected in a therapeutic context but often expected in forensic contexts).

Understanding the forensic versus therapeutic distinction is essential in capital contexts, and this distinction must be clear to the examinee, the attorneys, and the evaluator. However, several aspects of the capital context make misunderstanding likely. First, many capital defendants and death row inmates have intellectual deficits that leave them less likely to appreciate subtle distinctions in the evaluator role (a distinction that is often confusing even to laypersons and experienced attorneys). Those referred for an *Atkins*-type evaluation or a competence for execution evaluation are particularly likely to have substantial deficits in communication and understanding. Second, evaluations in capital contexts often involve prolonged contact with an examinee during an intensely stressful period. Mitigation evaluations require an evaluator to develop the rapport necessary to elicit personal information about sensitive topics (e.g., abuse, family dysfunction, criminal behavior) over a series of interviews that may span many months. This ongoing relationship is likely to feel therapeutic, particularly when a defendant understands that the evaluator is, in some respects, working as part of "the defense team." Nevertheless, evaluators remain responsible for ensuring that examinees—and attorneys—understand the important distinctions between therapeutic and forensic assessment. The distinction is not simply academic. Defendants themselves may feel treated unfairly when their (perceived) relationship with a "helpful doctor" ends abruptly or ends in testimony that may convey unflattering details, or otherwise conflicts with an examinee's preferences. In the context of FMHAs, clear boundaries, explained to all involved parties, are the best protection.

Principle 2: *Obtain appropriate education, training, and experience in one's area of forensic specialization*. This principle emphasizes the importance of combining formal education, training, and experience to develop competence in forensic practice. As increased opportunities for more specialized forensic training become available at the graduate and postgraduate levels (see DeMatteo, Marczyk, Krauss, & Burl, 2009; Hall, Cook, & Berman, 2010), there will likely be increased expectations that evaluators complete specialized training. Dabbling in forensic practice will likely be a thing of the past. Consistent with the ethics codes that govern psychology and psychiatry (discussed in Chapter 4), professionals should not engage in any practice that is outside of their competence and expertise.

Competence takes on increased importance when it comes to evaluations in capital contexts. Forensic mental health professionals with minimal training and experience should not "cut their forensic teeth" on a complicated, high-stakes capital case. Yet the rarity of capital evaluations (and experienced capital evaluators) creates some challenges to gaining the necessary experience to develop competence and expertise. For example, competence for execution evaluations are so rare that few evaluators have any experience with them. In jurisdictions that rarely pursue the death penalty, even experienced forensic evaluators may have little experience with capital cases. Thus, evaluators may pursue training by assisting or collaborating with more experienced evaluators and by completing formal continuing education workshops. Several entities offer continuing education specifically on capital cases, including the American Board of Forensic Psychology (part of the American Board of Professional Psychology) and the University of Virginia's Institute of Law, Psychiatry, and Public Policy.

Evaluators in capital contexts should have considerable experience with forensic populations similar to the population from which the examinee comes. For example, in an *Atkins*-type evaluation, evaluators should have specific expertise with the assessment of intellectual disabilities and mental retardation, preferably among a criminal population. A minimum degree of competence is required, and forensic evaluators should have substantially more experience and training if they work in capital contexts.

Principle 3: *Be familiar with the relevant legal, ethical, scientific, and practice literatures pertaining to forensic mental health assessment.* When Heilbrun (2001) identified his original set of principles, he classified each one as either *established* or *emerging* based on the degree of support it received from four sources of authority: law, ethics, science, and standards of practice. On a broad level, forensic evaluators should have knowledge of each of these four areas as they relate to the practice of FMHA in general. Even some forensic training programs neglect these domains in their training curricula (see DeMatteo et al., 2009), so some degree of continuing education is essential. For example, evaluators should know the admissibility standards for expert testimony (e.g., *Daubert, Frye*, Rules of Evidence) and how these should shape their selection of tests and evaluation procedures. Broadly, evaluators must know the ethics codes that govern their profession and stay abreast of emerging law and research related to their practice areas.

Although Heilbrun et al. (2009) identified this as a general principle of competent forensic practice, it also applies well at the level of individual cases. Forensic mental health professionals should have a basic knowledge of the law, ethics, science, and standards of practice relevant to the case at hand. Among other benefits, knowledge in these areas will help to ensure that the forensic evaluator is providing a "relevant" assessment and addressing the appropriate legal standard in an empirically defensible manner (see Grisso, 1986, 2003). For example, a few states have requirements, either specified by statute or case law, regarding the minimal qualifications to conduct evaluations in *Atkins*-type contexts and how these evaluations should be conducted (see Chapter 5). Evaluators must be familiar with these requirements before accepting a referral for an *Atkins*-type evaluation. Moreover, as discussed in Chapter 5, states have adopted several different statutory definitions of mental retardation (see DeMatteo, Marczyk, & Pich, 2007), and an informed evaluator needs to be familiar with the definition used in his or her jurisdiction.

To take another example, the literature base for mitigation evaluations is tremendously broad. Although "the relevant legal, ethical . . . and practice literatures" may require knowing relevant law and forensic literature, knowing the "relevant . . . science" might require knowledge of developmental psychopathology, childhood abuse, delinquency, addiction, neuropsychology, and other research literatures. Some of the necessary science may fall beyond the knowledge base common to forensic evaluators who assess only adults (e.g., developmental psychopathology), and some may fall beyond the knowledge base of any clinician other than a specialist in the topic area (e.g., particular forms of addiction, brain injury, or medical disease). Evaluators should therefore consider their competence on a case-by-case basis. An evaluator might be competent for many capital evaluations, but not all. Fortunately, capital contexts often allow for greater flexibility to retain specialists.

For example, because of the serious consequences of a conviction, the court might allow a defense team to retain both a neuropsychologist and an addictions specialist. But in any case, evaluators remain responsible for accepting referral questions only within their area of competence.

Principle 4: *Be guided by honesty and striving for impartiality, actively disclosing the limitations on as well as the support for one's opinions.* This principle emphasizes the importance of recognizing and limiting possible evaluator bias, and actively disclosing limitations and inconsistent data when providing opinions in a forensic report or expert testimony (see Shuman & Greenberg, 2003). The death penalty is a polarizing practice that evokes a wide range of emotions, and many people—both lay and professional—have strong views on the topic. Forensic evaluators are no different in this respect, and they must examine their own biases related to capital punishment. If they are unable to set aside those biases, or if they are concerned that their biases will affect their ability to be objective, they should refuse to conduct evaluations in capital contexts. This is one way to ensure the impartiality of the evaluation.

Evaluators who conduct capital evaluations should consider all available data from multiple perspectives and in light of rival hypotheses (Specialty Guidelines for Forensic Psychologists, 1991). In reports, evaluators should document the evidence that supports their opinions, as well as evidence that appears to contradict it. In short, evaluators should provide "transparent" reports that allow readers to follow the evaluator's reasoning and consider the potential for bias and alternate interpretations of the data.

Principle 5: *Control potential evaluator bias in general through monitoring case selection, continuing education, and consultation with knowledgeable colleagues.* On a broad level, forensic evaluators can help manage potential bias by monitoring the types of cases they accept (e.g., all defense-requested evaluations vs. a mix of defense-requested and prosecution-requested), consulting with colleagues about trouble spots that arise in their evaluations, and staying abreast of current developments in their area of expertise. Clinicians who conduct evaluations in capital contexts should periodically monitor the types of cases they accept and the referral sources for those cases. For example, an evaluator who is retained exclusively by one side (defense or prosecution) in adversarial proceedings should probably examine the reasons underlying the apparent inequity. There may be a reasonable explanation for the imbalance, and a tendency to testify primarily for one side does not necessarily reflect evaluator bias.[2] But cross-examining attorneys might reasonably suspect that it does.

---

2. For example, a researcher who studies rates of violence within correctional institutions would typically be called to testify by defense attorneys hoping to convey to juries the low likelihood of
(*Continued*)

Of course, performing evaluations for both sides does not rule out the possibility that an evaluator is vulnerable to bias in a given case. A core ethical challenge in forensic evaluation involves pursuing impartial and accurate opinions, rather than pursuing data to support the retaining party's theory of the case. Although many perceive forensic experts as "hired guns" who consciously craft opinions to suit the party who retained them (see commentary by Hagen, 1997, or public survey results from Hans, 1986), we suspect a more common problem is that forensic experts are vulnerable to the same well-known human decision-making processes that can produce biased opinions in other contexts. For example, evaluators often accept a case after hearing a one-sided perspective from an attorney, which potentially primes the evaluator to interpret subsequent case material in a particular direction. In a form of confirmation bias, evaluators might then seek information that is consistent with their initial hypothesis and avoid searching for information that is inconsistent with the hypothesis. These processes are rarely intentional, but they are potentially powerful and potentially harmful to evaluator objectivity.

How do evaluators guard against unintentional bias? The literature offers some suggestions for evaluators to monitor their patterns of forensic opinions across cases. For example, Brodsky (1991, 1999) described calculating an "objectivity quotient" related to Colbach's (1981) "contrary quotient." In these procedures, the forensic evaluator calculates the percentage of cases in which the evaluator's opinion is consistent with the employing attorney and the percentage of cases in which the evaluator's opinion is contrary to the employing attorney. Other suggestions include comparing one's rate of forensic opinions (e.g., opinions supporting an insanity defense) to the base rate of such opinions in large-scale samples of forensic evaluations (Murrie & Warren, 2005). Generally, these self-monitoring strategies appear reasonable for forensic evaluations that yield an easy-to-code dichotomous outcome (e.g., meets criteria for legal sanity or not; meets criteria for mental retardation or not). But the procedures apply less well to many capital-case evaluations in which the resulting forensic opinion is more descriptive than dichotomous. For example, it is difficult to quantify a pattern of evaluator findings in capital mitigation evaluations.

But not all strategies for minimizing bias require evaluators to quantify their patterns of findings. In discussing ways to guard against bias in forensic

---

(*Continued*)
violence in prison. Likewise, a specialist in child abuse would likely be retained primarily by defense attorneys hoping to demonstrate the long-term negative outcomes associated with early abuse. Even among clinicians who perform FMHAs, it would not be surprising to do so at the request of the defense, more often than the prosecution, simply because defense attorneys tend to initiate more FMHAs than prosecutors.

neuropsychological assessments, Sweet and Moulthrop (1999) suggest that the evaluator ask, "Have I taken a position, in very similar cases, when retained by an attorney from one side that I did not take when retained by the opposite side?" (p. 77). They also suggest asking whether one applies the same decision rules regardless of the "side" retaining his or her services. In a broad review of clinical judgment errors, Borum, Otto, and Golding (1993) encouraged evaluators to avoid confirmation bias by specifically seeking evidence that would disconfirm their hypotheses. They also emphasized the need to consider base rates and other empirical data that may anchor opinions and reduce bias.

Another approach for limiting bias is for evaluators to limit what they hear from the retaining attorney at the time of the initial referral. Evaluators certainly need to know the legal issue being addressed, and behavioral observations by the attorney can prove useful. But evaluators may want to avoid hearing the attorney's "theory of the case" or legal strategy.

Finally, as in most types of clinical practice, consultation is crucial. Consulting with knowledgeable colleagues about forensic evaluations can reveal evaluator biases or error, highlight alternative ways of conducting evaluations or interpreting the data, and ultimately improve the evaluator's final work product (the report and/or testimony). Of course, it is important to solicit consultation in a way that minimizes the chances of confirmation bias and groupthink, so seeking objective guidance is a high priority.

Principle 6: *Be familiar with specific aspects of the legal system, particularly communication, discovery, deposition, and testimony.* Principle 3 emphasized the importance of being familiar with the relevant legal, ethical, scientific, and practice literatures relating to FMHAs in general. Principle 6 is more specific in its focus on substantive and procedural *legal* knowledge (see generally Haas, 1993). For example, evaluators must be aware of the rules governing communications with attorneys and judges (e.g., rules prohibiting ex parte communication), the standards governing discovery (e.g., which evidence must be turned over to the defense and which evidence can justifiably be withheld), the process of being deposed, and the admissibility rules that govern expert testimony (e.g., *Daubert*, *Frye*, Rules of Evidence). This type of knowledge allows the evaluator to make appropriate requests and responses in a particular case, and it likely instills a degree of confidence in the attorneys and judges with whom the evaluator interacts. In the context of a capital case, one misstep along the way can have notable consequences for the individual being evaluated and the evaluator, so it is particularly important for evaluators to have a basic knowledge of the procedural and substantive laws that govern the conduct of evaluations in capital contexts.

Principle 7: *Do not become adversarial, but present and defend your opinions effectively.* When providing expert testimony during cross-examination, forensic evaluators can be most effective when they focus on presenting their findings, reasoning, and conclusions, while avoiding a tug of war with the opposing attorney. Of course, this is easier said than done, particularly in the high-stress atmosphere of capital cases. In several publications, Brodsky (1991, 1999, 2004) presents numerous substantive and stylistic maxims that represent best practice in expert testimony. These guidelines apply equally well in capital and noncapital contexts.

Principle 8: *Identify relevant forensic issues.* This principle focuses on citing the capacities and abilities underlying the ultimate legal question. It draws a distinction between the legal question, which is decided by the court, and the forensic issues, which are the functional capacities, skills, and abilities relevant to the legal question. This is an important distinction, and one that is basic to all FMHAs. Forensic mental health professionals have a long-standing history of failing to address the relevant functional legal capacities. A major criticism of forensic psychology identified by Grisso (1986, 2003) over 20 years ago is "irrelevance," which he defined as performing an evaluation without reference to the legally relevant abilities.

In any FMHA conducted in a capital case, the evaluator should clearly articulate, early in the report, the specific legal question and forensic issues addressed. In an evaluation of competence for execution, the legally relevant abilities are usually described in case law. In the most recent U.S. Supreme Court decision addressing competence for execution, the Court held that prisoners must have both a factual and rational understanding of the reasons for the impending execution (*Panetti v. Quarterman*, 2007). In a capital sentencing evaluation, the legally relevant "abilities" are typically the mitigating factors that can be identified by a forensic mental health professional. As discussed in Chapter 5, the Supreme Court's decision in *Atkins v. Virginia* (2002) created the need for a forensic evaluation that is solely diagnostic, because the key (and indeed only) legal issue in an *Atkins*-type evaluation is whether the offender is mentally retarded.

Principle 9: *Accept referrals only within area of expertise.* On a general level, this principle highlights the need for the evaluator to have clinical and didactic forensic training and experience with populations similar to the person evaluated, and then to thoughtfully apply that training and experience in actual forensic contexts. Some state statutes that govern evaluations specify minimum qualifications for an evaluator to be appointed, but not all states provide such guidance. For example, only a few states have delineated the minimum qualifications required for evaluators to conduct *Atkins*-type evaluations. When state statutes do not specify the minimum qualifications for an evaluator, an evaluator can demonstrate expertise in several ways. At a minimum, an evaluator can cite terminal degree, licensure status, and board certification status to demonstrate a basic level of competence. However, basic competence is not sufficient in capital cases. The complexity of some evaluations conducted in capital contexts, and the intense scrutiny forensic reports and testimony may face, demand a heightened level of evaluator expertise. The evaluator's curriculum vitae should clearly reflect professional experience with forensic evaluation generally, and the specific issues present in the capital case (e.g., developmentally disabled individuals for *Atkins*-type evaluations). The evaluator should anticipate discussing his or her qualifications and experience during testimony.

Principle 10: *Decline the referral when evaluator impartiality is unlikely.* Evaluator objectivity is crucial across all types of FMHAs. Evaluators should avoid involvement in cases in which there is a substantial incentive—either personal, financial, or professional—for the evaluator to reach a certain conclusion or for the case to be decided in a particular direction. Ideally, evaluators assess their biases beforehand and decide whether to accept or reject a particular referral. If, during the course of an evaluator's involvement in a case, the evaluator becomes concerned that his or her impartiality has become compromised for any reason, the evaluator should discuss these concerns with the referral source. Having similar discussions with trusted colleagues (who are presumably more objective than the referral source) is also recommended. Although withdrawing from a case can lead to delays in the adjudication or disposition processes, and frustration for all involved, it may be a necessary step if evaluator impartiality cannot be maintained.

Evaluator impartiality has obvious importance in capital contexts, and even the appearance of partiality can be damaging in several respects. In capital cases, evaluators are often paid hourly fees that appear high (and indeed are higher than in most other evaluations for indigent defendants). Because capital cases typically require many hours of work, such evaluations can appear lucrative (and may in fact be lucrative sometimes). As with other types of evaluations in forensic contexts, evaluators should ensure that they are being compensated for their time, and not for their case-specific conclusions. A potentially more problematic scenario arises when an evaluator has strong feelings—pro or con—regarding capital punishment. Although such feelings are not necessarily problematic in the absolute, they can become problematic if the evaluator's objectivity becomes compromised, or even if it appears to be compromised. If an evaluator is unable to separate his or her personal or political views on capital punishment from the evaluation at hand, he or she is advised to avoid conducting evaluations in capital contexts.

The value and necessity of remaining objective and impartial is partially dependent on the role being assumed by the forensic mental health professional. When functioning as an evaluator, objectivity is essential. However, impartiality is less important when a mental health professional is functioning as a consultant hired to assist an attorney. For example, a mitigation consultant/specialist is hired to assist the defense with the gathering and, sometimes, presenting of mitigating evidence during the sentencing phase of a capital case (see Leonard, 2003). The goal of the consultant's involvement is clearly partisan—that is, to avoid a death sentence for the defendant—so the expectation of impartiality is not present. With that said, a mitigation consultant/ specialist can be most valuable by helping the attorney to maintain a balanced view of the proceedings and evidence. Even a consultant hired to critique a prior evaluator's work or provide a second opinion should perform these functions objectively, and convey accurately the relevant science and best practices.

Principle 11: *Clarify the evaluator's role with the attorney.* The American Psychological Association's *Ethical Principles of Psychologists and Code of Conduct* (2002) strongly cautions against assuming "dual roles" in the same case (as discussed in Chapter 4). Within the context of a forensic case, it is usually problematic to assume more than one forensic role. Mental health professionals must determine a priori whether they will be serving as an expert, consultant, or fact witness. Then, they must maintain the integrity of that role throughout their involvement in the case. This principle applies to all types of FMHAs conducted in capital contexts.

In *Ake v. Oklahoma* (1985), the U.S. Supreme Court held that a capital defendant is entitled to the services of an expert, compensated at state expense, to assist the defense on the issue of mental state at the time of the offense and at capital sentencing. The *Ake* expert could serve as an impartial evaluator or as a consultant, but the expert must not serve in both of these roles in the same case.

Principle 12: *Clarify financial arrangements.* Payment for the services of mental health professionals in capital cases can come from several sources. For example, a mental health professional may be privately retained by the defense attorney to conduct an *Atkins*-type, capital mitigation, or competence for execution evaluation. In these circumstances, the financial arrangements are agreed upon by the parties and governed by market forces, typically with no oversight by the court. Financial arrangements in these contexts should be established at the time the forensic mental health professional becomes involved in the case.

However, private pay is the exception in capital cases. In the vast majority of capital cases, evaluations are publicly funded and governed by state statute or administrative regulations. In these instances, it may not be necessary to clarify the terms of payment if an evaluator is retained by one of the attorneys or ordered by the court to conduct an evaluation and the the compensation is determined by statute or regulation. If evaluators think that the fee necessary to reasonably compensate them for their time will exceed the limit set by statute, one option is obtaining a court order authorizing payment up to an agreed-upon limit in excess of the statutory limit. This would eliminate the risk that a court will not approve a postevaluation compensation request that exceeds the statutorily imposed limit. In some states, evaluations are paid for by the court, but at the rate set by the evaluator (although the amount is typically still capped by the court).

Principle 13: *Obtain appropriate authorization.* Authorization to conduct an FMHA can come from two sources: the court or an attorney for the prosecution or defense. If the forensic mental health professional is court appointed, the clinician needs authorization from the court, which is typically provided in the form of a court order. If the forensic mental health professional is retained by the defense or prosecution, authorization to conduct the evaluation comes from the retaining party and the examinee. Of note, when the evaluation is prosecution requested, it is usually then ordered by the court. The source of the authorization determines whether the evaluator should provide a notification of purpose or seek informed consent from the examinee, and we discuss that distinction under Principle 23.

Principle 14: *Avoid playing the dual roles of therapist and forensic evaluator.* As detailed in Chapters 1 and 4, a mental health professional should not serve as a therapist and forensic evaluator in the same case. The traditional form of this ethical problem almost never arises in a capital context (i.e., a therapist is asked to assume a forensic role). It is possible, however, that a mental health professional who works as a therapist in a correctional facility may be asked to provide an opinion regarding whether the defendant is mentally retarded (in an *Atkins*-type evaluation) or suffering from a serious mental health disorder (in a competence for execution evaluation). Clinicians should make every effort to avoid this type of dual role. If avoiding involvement is not possible, it may be possible for the mental health professional to serve as a fact witness, rather than an expert witness.

Even when a clinician assumes an evaluator role, there is some potential for the capital defendant to become confused about this role. Mitigation evaluations typically require months of intense interview about sensitive topics (e.g., physical/sexual abuse, drug use, family dysfunction), and often during a period of time when a defendant may be experiencing substantial emotional distress. This ongoing relationship—which may involve more personal disclosure than any other relationship the defendant has ever experienced—may certainly feel therapeutic to the defendant, despite clear explanations by the evaluator to the contrary. Evaluators therefore face a balancing act. They must develop the rapport and working relationship to elicit necessary information from the defendant. But they must also clearly acknowledge the time-limited nature of the relationship, and reiterate as needed that the relationship has not been established for traditional therapeutic purposes.

Principle 15: *Determine role to be played within forensic assessment if the referral is accepted.* In a capital case, as in other forensic assessment contexts, a mental health professional should decide whether he or she will be functioning as an impartial expert (retained by either party or appointed by the court) or as a consultant hired to assist the attorney for a particular task. In either situation, the mental health professional should only assume one of these roles and then maintain that role throughout his or her involvement in the case. Heilbrun et al. (2002) note one potential exception to this principle, which involves moving from the role of expert to the role of consultant. In this situation, the mental health professional is moving from a role that requires impartiality (i.e., expert) to a role that does not (i.e., consultant). Heilbrun et al. emphasize that this role change is only acceptable "if it is clear from the results of the evaluation that the attorney would not ask for a report or testimony" (p. 9). They also note that moving in the other direction—that is, from consultant to impartial expert—is inappropriate. The application of this principle is the same in *Atkins*-type, capital sentencing, and competence for execution evaluations.

Principle 16: *Select the most appropriate model to guide data gathering, interpretation, and communication.* The use of a model to guide data gathering, interpretation and reasoning, and the communication of results can be helpful in conducting an evaluation in any forensic context, but it may be particularly helpful in capital cases (see Marczyk et al., 2003). Two models are helpful in this respect. The Morse (1978a, 1978b) model is applicable across different types of evaluations, and it contains the following three elements: whether there is a mental health disorder (or symptoms), the functional abilities related to the tasks that are part of the legal question being addressed, and the causal connection (or nexus) between the mental health disorder and the functional legal abilities.

The other model, first proposed by Grisso in 1986 and revised in 2003, has five components (set in the context of a competence evaluation): *(1)* functional (what an individual can do or accomplish, and the knowledge, understanding, and beliefs that are necessary), *(2)* causal (describing the relationship between an individual's functional abilities or deficits and the legal competence question being addressed), *(3)* interactive (congruence or incongruence between the individual's functional abilities and the demands of the situation), *(4)* judgmental (whether the incongruence is sufficient to warrant a legal finding of incompetence), and *(5)* dispositional (the consequences of the legal determination). As noted by Heilbrun (2001), the Morse and Grisso models share two components: *(1)* the functional legal capacities underlying the legal question, and *(2)* the causal connection between the deficits in such functional legal capacities and the potential sources of those deficits.

The Morse and Grisso models should be applied in different ways in an *Atkins*-type evaluation versus capital sentencing evaluations and competence for execution evaluations. The only legally relevant question in an *Atkins*-type evaluation is whether the defendant meets diagnostic criteria for mental retardation. There is no need to describe the functional legal capacities underlying the legal question, because the diagnosis *is* the legal question in this context. By contrast, the diagnostic/symptomatic criteria are distinct from the functional legal criteria in all other types of FMHAs, including capital sentencing evaluations and competence for execution evaluations. In these types of evaluations, using the Morse or Grisso model can help to maintain this distinction.

Principle 17: *Use multiple sources of information for each area being assessed. Review the available background information and actively seek important missing elements.*[3] Individuals undergoing FMHAs often have an incentive to distort information or provide misleading information to achieve a desired result. An effective way to reveal such distortions in self-report information is by obtaining information from multiple sources. Multiple sources of information provide a more complete picture of the defendant's history and functioning across multiple domains. Seeking multiple sources of information and gauging the consistency across those sources tends to reduce the error associated with any single source of information (Heilbrun, Warren, & Picarello, 2003; Otto, Slobogin, & Greenberg, 2007; Shapiro, 1991). Indeed, some authorities describe forensic evaluations as "investigations" (more so than assessments) to emphasize the importance of seeking collateral data beyond the tests and interviews on which clinicians typically rely (see, e.g., Melton et al., 2007).

Forensic evaluators may rely on a defendant's self-report, psychological testing, specialized forensic testing, a review of records, and interviews with knowledgeable third parties. Sometimes there may be notable gaps or missing information in the documents that an evaluator receives. In these instances, the evaluator must take steps to obtain the needed information (typically through requests to the referring attorney). If the evaluator is not successful in obtaining the information, the report should convey that important information was sought but not obtained, and clearly describe the resulting limitations.

Although this principle applies to all types of evaluations conducted in capital contexts, the scope of the information used by evaluators can differ substantially. For example, the legal question in an *Atkins*-type evaluation is circumscribed to a diagnostic consideration of mental retardation. So only sources relevant to the diagnosis need to be consulted (e.g., mental health records, educational records, interviews with teachers and other caretakers).

---

3. As originally developed by Heilbrun (2001), this principle only consisted of the first sentence. In Heilbrun et al. (2009), this principle was revised by adding the second sentence regarding background materials.

By contrast, capital mitigation evaluations are quite broad in scope and usually involve many mitigating factors. This requires consulting many, many more sources (see Chapter 7).

Principle 18: *Use relevance and reliability (validity) as guides for seeking information and selecting data sources.* The concepts of relevance and reliability, which guide evidentiary law on the admissibility of expert testimony, should guide an evaluator's choice of which sources of information to use and which psychological instruments to administer. Information should be reliable (in both the general sense and the psychometric sense) and relevant to the question being addressed. Using standardized psychological tests and specialized forensic assessment instruments generally puts an evaluator on safe ground if these measures have their psychometric properties described in a published manual (see Heilbrun, Rogers, & Otto, 2002). It is unlikely that the admissibility of such standardized measures would be successfully challenged in either a *Frye* or *Daubert* jurisdiction. However, even well-developed and reliable measures may not be relevant for particular questions in particular cases. Evaluators too often administer tests that are not directly relevant to the legal question at hand (see, for example, Chapter 7 for a discussion of how standard personality measures are rarely directly relevant to questions of mitigation), or not appropriate to the unique context of capital sentencing (see Chapter 8 for a discussion of how popular violence risk measures are rarely relevant to questions of risk at capital sentencing).

As with the previous principle, applying Principle 18 depends on the scope of the evaluation. An *Atkins*-type evaluation is present focused and narrow in scope, and it calls for the use of traditional measures used for diagnosing mental retardation. Evaluators can choose from several well-validated measures of intellectual functioning, although they probably cannot choose a measure of adaptive functioning suitable for offenders who have been incarcerated for years (as discussed in Chapter 5). Similarly, competence for execution evaluations are present focused and narrow in scope, with the evaluation focusing primarily on the offender's understanding (rational and factual) of the impending execution and the reasons for it. Formal psychological testing may be conducted, but it is often not the primary method of assessment in these evaluations. Capital sentencing evaluations are broader in scope and require considering data related to history and mental state at the time of the offense. There are fewer standardized instruments that can be used in this context. As recommended by Heilbrun (2001), evaluators will need to use more sources of information, judge the credibility of the sources that have no formal validation (e.g., third-party interviews), and gauge the consistency of findings across sources rather than relying heavily on a few well-validated sources.

Principle 19: *Obtain relevant historical information.* The application of this principle is largely dependent on the type of evaluation being conducted.

In an *Atkins*-type evaluation, historical information can serve two (related) purposes. First, to diagnose mental retardation using either the *DSM-IV-TR* or AAIDD criteria, it is necessary to document that impairments existed prior to age 18. As such, obtaining historical information about the offender, from a review of historical records (e.g., medical, mental health, school, occupational) or interviews with knowledgeable third parties, is essential to making a proper diagnosis. Second, obtaining historical information regarding an offender's intellectual functioning can help evaluators determine whether an offender is malingering. The absence of any historical records documenting impaired functioning would cast doubt on a current claim of mental retardation.

In a capital sentencing evaluation, obtaining historical information is essential in terms of providing a coherent and complete longitudinal description of the offender's functioning. For example, the offender's description of the current offense and his or her mental state at the time of the offense can be initially assessed through self-report and then corroborated through a review of historical information corresponding with the time period. The assessment of some mitigating and aggravating factors may be enhanced by obtaining historical information (preferably from multiple sources), including information related to childhood abuse or neglect, school problems, mental health problems, peer relationships, living environment, and drug use.

Principle 20: *Assess clinical characteristics in relevant, reliable, and valid ways.* In forensic assessment contexts, it is important to use psychological measures that are reliable (i.e., they measure consistently, with limited measurement error), valid (i.e., they measure what they purport to measure), and relevant to the question addressed in the case. In an *Atkins*-type assessment, it is important to use measures of intellectual functioning and adaptive behaviors that are well validated and psychometrically sound. As discussed, this presents no problem when it comes to measures of intellectual functioning, but the application of this principle becomes more complicated when it comes to assessing adaptive deficits among offenders who have been incarcerated for many years.

In capital sentencing evaluations, the scope of the assessment is much broader, which provides forensic evaluators with more choices in terms of psychological tests and measures. But it remains important for evaluators to choose well-validated measures that have empirical support for use with offender populations. Several measures commonly used in FMHAs provide normative data for correctional populations. For example, although the MMPI-2 is not a specialized forensic instrument, it provides norms applicable to correctional populations.

Principle 21: *Assess legally relevant behavior.* In reviewing a litany of historical problems with FMHAs, Grisso (1986, 2003) specifically noted "irrelevance" as a common criticism. Principle 21 applies with equal weight to all evaluations conducted in capital contexts.

If the sole legal question in an *Atkins*-type evaluation is whether the offender is mentally retarded, the assessment of legally relevant behavior is synonymous with diagnosing (or not) mental retardation. In a capital sentencing evaluation, however, there are many potential mitigating factors, including whether the offense was committed while the defendant was under the influence of extreme mental or emotional disturbance, whether the defendant acted under extreme duress or under the substantial domination of another person, and whether at the time of the offense the capacity of the defendant to appreciate the criminality of his or her conduct or to conform his or her conduct to the requirements of law was impaired as a result of mental disease or defect. The assessment of these factors is not as straightforward as diagnosing mental retardation. As a result, Heilbrun et al. (2009) recommend combining multiple sources of information and reaching conclusions that are supported by consistent findings across the sources.

A capital sentencing evaluation becomes more challenging when the defendant chooses not to report on his or her mental state at the time of the offense by way of a categorical denial of involvement in the offense. Capital sentencing evaluations are typically conducted pretrial, which increases the chances that a defendant would deny involvement in the offense, so establishing the presence of mitigating factors relating to the defendant's mental state becomes much more difficult. It may be possible, however, to establish the existence of some mitigating factors through reliance on collateral information. Historical information pertaining to the offender's mental state at the time of the offense may be helpful (perhaps gleaned from arrest records and other sources contemporaneous with the arrest), as would information regarding the defendant's mental health functioning throughout his or her life (which might indicate the presence of a stable and enduring form of mental illness, or perhaps provide some reason for believing that the defendant is malingering).

Principle 22: *Ensure that conditions for evaluation are quiet, private, and distraction-free*. This is a basic principle of psychological assessment, but it often becomes more challenging to apply in FMHAs contexts. Evaluators must often conduct capital case evaluations in correctional facilities, and some distractions may be present (e.g., background noise, the presence of uninvited third parties, low/high temperature). Heilbrun (2001) emphasizes the importance of conducting FMHAs in conditions that are reasonably quiet (limited noise), sufficiently private (so conversations can not be overheard by staff or other inmates/residents), and otherwise distraction-free to the extent that is reasonably possible.

Poor testing conditions in an *Atkins*-type evaluation can have dramatic consequences for the offender. When assessing an individual's level of intellectual functioning, the testing environment should be amenable to producing valid results. The presence of third parties (i.e., not part of the evaluation, such as other inmates/residents or staff), poor lighting, high noise levels, and awkward testing conditions (e.g., administering an IQ test over a half-wall or Plexiglas partition separating the evaluator from the offender) can adversely affect the offender's performance. For offenders with IQs around 70, the difference of a few IQ points can make a substantial difference in case outcome.

Applying this principle in a capital sentencing evaluation is also important. For example, the evaluation typically involves a discussion of sensitive information when focusing on the offender's mental state at the time of an offense. The information may be particularly sensitive if the evaluation takes place, as it typically does, while the offender is still pre-adjudication. It could be damaging for such information to be overheard by staff or other inmates/residents, both from a legal standpoint and a safety standpoint. Therefore, the privacy of the testing conditions is paramount.

Principle 23: *Provide appropriate notification of purpose and/or obtain appropriate authorization before beginning.* If an FMHA is court ordered, an evaluator is not legally required to obtain informed consent from the individual being evaluated because the examinee does not have a legal right to refuse participation. Nevertheless, evaluators should provide a notification of purpose that contains basic information about the evaluator, reasons for the evaluation, associated limits on confidentiality, and how the information will be used. All of this should be conveyed using simple language that can be easily understood.

When an evaluation is requested by the defense or prosecution, the defendant is not required to participate in the evaluation. As such, the evaluator should obtain the examinee's informed consent before the evaluation begins. There are, however, some differences depending on whether the defense or prosecution requests the evaluation. If the evaluation was requested by the defense, the evaluator should obtain informed consent from the defendant. Given the complexity of capital cases, defense counsel (rather than the defendant) should probably be the primary participant in discussions of informed consent (Cunningham, 2006a). When the prosecution requests an evaluation, they usually do so because they have a right to a second-opinion evaluation following a defense-initiated evaluation on the same issue. So most evaluations initially requested by the prosecution are subsequently ordered by the court. Defendants can certainly refuse to cooperate with a prosecution-retained evaluator, but not without substantial consequences. In many jurisdictions, defendants who refuse to cooperate with a prosecution-initiated second-opinion evaluation are barred from introducing results from the defense-initiated evaluation on the same issue. Of course, regardless of whether a defendant chooses to participate in an interview or testing, evaluators may proceed with the evaluation using other collateral sources (e.g., review of records, collateral interviews) that inform forensic opinions, recognizing that this approach is more feasible for some types of evaluations (e.g., mitigation) than others (i.e., *Atkins*-type).

Although Principle 23 holds true across all evaluations, the details differ depending on the type of evaluation, context, and role. An *Atkins*-type evaluation is predominantly present focused. These evaluations seek to determine whether the defendant is mentally retarded, which primarily requires an assessment of the offender's present intellectual functioning and deficits in adaptive behavior. Information concerning the defendant's mental state at the time of the offense is not relevant in an *Atkins*-type evaluation and typically does not need to be obtained. Discussion of the defendant's involvement in the capital offense is usually unnecessary. Because *Atkins*-type evaluations are focused exclusively on the issue of mental retardation, there is a reduced likelihood that the defendant will make self-incriminating statements, particularly when compared to a mitigation evaluation that focuses on past behavior, including behavior during the alleged offense. So the statement of disclosure in an *Atkins*-type evaluation, like the evaluation itself, is more narrow in scope.

Evaluations for competence for execution are also predominantly present focused. The purpose of these evaluations is to determine whether the prisoner has *(1)* a sufficient factual understanding of the offense, the impending execution, and the state's reason for ordering the execution, and *(2)* a sufficient rational understanding of the connection between the offense and impending execution (see *Panetti v. Quarterman*, 2007). So there is typically no need to discuss the offender's mental state at the time of the offense. Perhaps more important, these evaluations take place after the offender has been convicted and sentenced, and often close to the date of the scheduled execution, so most concerns regarding whether the individual will make self-incriminating statements are moot.

However, when conducting a mitigation evaluation, the evaluator typically addresses several factors associated with the offender's mental state at the time of the offense (see Cunningham & Goldstein, 2003). Factors relevant to the defendant's mental state at the time of the offense include extreme mental and emotional disturbance, extreme duress or domination by another, and substantial impairment in the defendant's capacity to appreciate the criminality of the behavior or conform that behavior to the requirements of the law. In most mitigation evaluations, an evaluator must obtain information about the defendant's thinking, emotions, perceptions, and behavior at and around the time of the offense.

Importantly, capital sentencing evaluations are often conducted *pretrial* to allow enough time to gather information, perform the evaluation, and write the report. In many states, the time period between conviction and sentencing is short, so there would not be sufficient time to conduct a capital sentencing evaluation after the defendant is convicted. But conducting these evaluations pretrial may make it difficult for evaluators to obtain the information they need (at least from the defendant's self-report) about the defendant's mental state at the time of the offense because many defendants may deny or minimize their culpability. Perhaps understandably, defendants may be hesitant to admit their role in the offense at the pretrial stage of proceedings. As a result, during a capital sentencing evaluation, it is important for the evaluator to draw the complex distinction between the defendant's legal right to assert innocence until proven guilty, which is exercised pre-adjudication, versus the defendant's interest in providing information regarding mental state at the time of the offense, which is potentially useful in mitigation *if* the defendant has been convicted of a death-eligible offense (see Cunningham, 2006a). The absence of relevant information regarding the defendant's mental state at the time of the offense leaves evaluators in the position of having to draw more limited conclusions regarding applicable mitigating factors, which could work against the defendant once the proceedings reach the sentencing phase.

Principle 24: *Determine whether the individual understands the purpose of the evaluation and the associated limits on confidentiality.* After the defendant receives a notification of purpose or provides informed consent, the evaluator should make some immediate and concrete attempt to determine whether the defendant understands the basic points that were conveyed. One useful approach is asking the defendant several open-ended questions regarding key points, including the purpose of the evaluation, who maintains control of the report, limits on confidentiality, and so on. The notification given in an *Atkins*-type context is relatively simple and straightforward—that is, the defendant is being evaluated (at the request of his or her attorney or the court) to determine whether the defendant is mentally retarded. Even the presence of intellectual deficits, if relatively mild, should not interfere with the defendant's ability to understand this basic information. Capital sentencing evaluations are more complex in terms of scope, procedures, the sensitive nature of the material, and the circumstances under which the results of the evaluation may be used (Cunningham, 2006a). This makes it more important for the evaluator to provide a clear explanation about the nature and purpose of the evaluation, and to ensure that the defendant understands the key points.

An important question is how to proceed if it becomes clear that the defendant does not fully understand the notification provided by the evaluator. Importantly, a defendant's failure to fully comprehend the essential elements of the notification does not inevitably require terminating the evaluation. The absence of informed consent, or the lack of fully informed consent, is not a sufficient basis to discontinue the evaluation if the defendant's attorney wants the evaluation to proceed and the defendant is still willing to participate in the evaluation. In this circumstance, the defendant is essentially providing assent rather than consent. It is also important for the evaluator to describe the attempt at notification/consent, indicate what aspects of the notification/consent were and were not understood by the individual, and discuss the defendant's deficits that appeared to interfere with his or her understanding of the notification/consent.

A defendant's failure to understand notification/consent rarely halts an evaluation for competence for execution. In an evaluation to determine whether a prisoner is competent to be executed, the same deficits that interfere with the prisoner's ability to understand the notification/consent may be the same deficits that ultimately render the prisoner incompetent to be executed. Heilbrun et al. (2009) note that stopping the evaluation based on these deficits would create a Catch-22 in which the prisoner's deficits prevent the evaluation from taking place, which essentially results in an inability to show that the prisoner is incompetent to be executed. With permission from the attorney, it may be preferable to proceed with the evaluation so that the prisoners' deficits can be properly documented.

Principle 25: *Use third party information in assessing response style.* As previously noted, individuals evaluated in a forensic context often have an incentive to provide inaccurate or misleading information in an effort to achieve a desired result. Certainly, in a capital context, an offender might have a substantial incentive to provide distorted or misleading information that presents him or her in particular light. In an *Atkins*-type context, there are often concerns that the defendant may be exaggerating intellectual or adaptive deficits to secure a diagnosis of mental retardation and thereby avoid a death sentence. It is important to emphasize that a misleading response style may not be sophisticated, and in some cases is not even self-serving. For example, in capital sentencing evaluations, defendants with a guarded or suspicious personality style may deny emotional difficulties or painful historical events, even though these are mitigating factors that are potentially helpful to their defense. Using third-party information can help an evaluator assess the validity/accuracy of the offender's self-report and the likelihood that the offender is distorting legally relevant history or symptoms.

Third-party information can come in the form of historical records (e.g., medical, mental health, educational, criminal justice, employment) or collateral interviews with knowledgeable third parties (e.g., parents, significant others, employers, parole/probation officers, correctional officers). The evaluator should describe the degree of consistency between the offender's self-report and third-party information. If the self-report information is significantly different from reliable third-party information, the evaluator should detail relevant inconsistencies in the report and exercise caution in relying on defendant self-report. Obviously, third-party interviewees can also provide misleading or inaccurate information, as can collateral records. There may be obvious (or at least understandable) reasons for doing so (e.g., parents may selectively recall positive aspects of their child, while "forgetting" or suppressing negative aspects; relatives may not discuss family dysfunction because they are genuinely unaware that aspects of their family were out of the ordinary). Therefore, it is equally important for the evaluator to assess the validity of the information provided by third parties.

Principle 26: *Use testing when indicated in assessing response style.* Because the defendant's response style shapes the information the defendant provides, the evaluator may choose to assess the defendant's response style via formal testing. There are some specialized measures designed specifically to assess an individual's response style, and there are other measures that are sensitive to response style (see generally Rogers, 2008, for a discussion of response styles). For example, several tools are useful for measuring exaggerated or fabricated symptoms, including the Structured Interview of Reported Symptoms (Rogers, Bagby, & Dickens, 1992; Rogers, Sewell, & Gillard, 2010), the Validity Indicator Profile (Frederick, 1997), the Test of Memory Malingering (Tombaugh, 1997), and the Miller Forensic Assessment of Symptoms Test (Miller, 2001). Other measures are broader in scope (i.e., not exclusively designed to assess exaggerated or fabricated symptom presentations) but contain well-validated validity indicators, including the MMPI-2 (Butcher, Dahlstrom, Graham, Tellegen, & Kaemmer, 1989). Given the broad scope of capital sentencing evaluations, a measure of response style is recommended. If measures provide convergent evidence that the defendant is, for example, exaggerating or fabricating mental health symptoms, then the defendant's self-report concerning those symptoms should carry less weight in the interpretation of the data.

Principle 27: *Use case-specific (idiographic) evidence in assessing clinical condition, functional abilities, and causal connection.* It is particularly helpful to legal decision makers when evaluators obtain information specific to the case and the defendant's present functioning, and then compare it to the defendant's capacities and functioning at other times. In an *Atkins* context, this requires evaluating the defendant's present intellectual and adaptive functioning, comparing his or her functioning with previous levels of functioning (if available), and providing case-specific details and examples for clarity. Likewise, in competence for execution evaluations, evaluators must provide case-specific details illustrating how the offender understands—or fails to understand—the nature of his or her pending execution and the reasons for it. As with several other principles already discussed, Principle 27 applies more broadly in the context of capital sentencing evaluations. Consistent with the U.S. Supreme Court's mandate of individualized consideration of aggravating and mitigating factors, an evaluator should detail the unique, case-specific aspects of the defendant's history and character, and mental state during the capital offense.

Principle 28: *Use nomothetic evidence in assessing clinical condition, functional abilities, and causal connection.* Case-specific data have obvious value in forensic contexts, but an evaluator also obtains important information from group data. The field has derived empirical data from groups that have similar characteristics to many defendants in capital cases, and it has also developed several measures that have been validated on comparable populations. Using such measures allows the forensic evaluator to compare the measured capacities of the defendant to those in "known groups" using the norms developed from those groups. The known groups provide a reference point, or point of comparison, against which the defendant can be evaluated. Of course, any time an evaluator uses tests to assess a defendant's clinical condition and functional legal capacities, the evaluator needs to select the tests carefully. Validity is not a static property of a test, but rather a property of the inferences that may be drawn from test scores for a particular purpose (Messick, 1995). The accuracy of such inferences depends largely on whether the test has been validated on populations similar to the population from which the defendant comes, and for purposes similar to the purpose for which the defendant is evaluated.

Applying Principle 28 is straightforward when assessing intellectual functioning in an *Atkins*-type evaluation, because well-developed IQ measures allow evaluators to compare the defendant's IQ to large normative samples. These tests are well-validated for assessing individuals with mental retardation of varying severities. Unfortunately, the same cannot be said for measures of adaptive functioning, which have not been developed for use with offenders and incarcerated populations.

Nomothetic, or group, data are also important in capital sentencing evaluations, though this might initially appear incongruent with the goal of an "individualized" understanding of a particular defendant. But group data often allow us to quantify ways in which a defendant was unique compared to others (e.g., scoring far lower than other adults on measures of certain skills, or scoring far higher than other adults on measures of certain problems or psychiatric symptoms). Also, as detailed in Chapter 7, group data from the social sciences often help illustrate the risks or outcomes associated with life experiences that may be considered mitigating. In this way, group data often suggest a well-established, empirically supported link between a defendant's prior experiences (e.g., early abuse, exposure to violence) and subsequent behavior (e.g., crime, violence, or psychiatric symptoms). When evaluators offer opinions about mitigating evidence in light of rigorous research, based on group data, their opinions are more likely to reflect reasonable inferences.

When evaluators offer opinions about mitigating evidence, but cannot identify relevant research or group data, their opinions may appear more speculative and idiosyncratic. Of course, there is not sufficient research to address *every* experience or issue that might be considered mitigating—every capital defendant has unique experiences—but research does address many common mitigating factors (see Chapter 7).

Similarly, nomothetic data are essential in capital sentencing evaluations that address violence risk (see Chapter 8). Indeed, risk assessment must be rooted in reliable nomothetic data from relevant groups (i.e., prison inmates, particularly capital offenders) in relevant contexts (i.e., in prisons). Evaluators who offer risk opinions without a clear link to relevant nomothetic data—particularly data addressing violence base rates in prison and risk factors for prison violence—are likely relying more on speculation than on science or best practices.

Principle 29: *Use scientific reasoning in assessing causal connection between clinical condition and functional abilities.* This principle applies equally well to all evaluations conducted in capital contexts. Heilbrun (2001) noted that the process of conducting an FMHA is similar in some ways to a scientific investigation. For example, information from one source can be treated as hypotheses to be verified through information from other sources (see Heilbrun, 1992). Accepting hypotheses that account for the most information using the simplest explanation is consistent with the scientific principle of parsimony (and captured by the principle Ockham's Razor). Of course, just as in science, evidence in an FMHA may appear mixed, and there may be alternative explanations that account for the information equally well. Evaluators should use scientific reasoning to identify the connection between clinical data and legal opinion, and acknowledge those instances in which the data are inconclusive.

Principle 30: *Carefully consider whether to answer the ultimate legal question. If it is answered, it should be in the context of a thorough evaluation clearly describing data and reasoning, and with the clear recognition that this question is in the domain of the legal decision maker.*[4] Despite years of scholarly debate, there continues to be disagreement within the fields of forensic psychology and forensic psychiatry over whether forensic evaluators should answer the "ultimate legal question" to be decided by the court. Some commentators have asserted that answering the ultimate legal question is not problematic because many judges and attorneys anticipate that the

---

4. As originally developed by Heilbrun (2001), this principle was a blanket prohibition on evaluators answering the ultimate legal question. More recent guidance has revised this principle to reflect certain limited circumstances under which the ultimate legal question could be answered (see Heilbrun et al., 2009).

forensic evaluator will answer the ultimate legal question in the course of the evaluation (e.g., Rogers & Ewing, 1989; Rogers & Shuman, 2000). Others assert that forensic mental health professionals should stay focused on forensic capacities and avoid answering the ultimate legal question (e.g., Grisso, 1986, 2003; Tillbrook, Mumley, & Grisso, 2003). In most jurisdictions, forensic experts are permitted to offer opinions on the ultimate legal question (Goldstein, Morse, & Shapiro, 2003).[5]

Although Heilbrun (2001) initially recommended not answering the ultimate legal question, he later identified conditions in which the evaluator could choose to answer the ultimate legal question, and remain consistent with best-practice standards. Heilbrun stated that the ultimate legal question could be answered in the larger context of having conducted a thorough evaluation, with data and reasoning carefully described, so the legal consumer could separate such data and reasoning from the additional political and moral values embedded in some ultimate legal questions (see Heilbrun et al., 2009). The appropriateness of capital punishment is certainly a legal issue that has political and moral overtones. Heilbrun also suggested that the report or testimony should include explicit recognition that the evaluator is aware that the ultimate legal question is properly in the domain of the court.

The ultimate legal issue in an *Atkins*-type evaluation is whether the defendant should be excluded from a death sentence due to mental retardation. Because a finding of mental retardation ipso facto leads to the offender's exclusion from the death penalty, there is little meaningful distinction between the clinical issue (i.e., presence/absence of mental retardation) and the legal issue (i.e., whether the defendant should be excluded from the death penalty based on the presence of mental retardation). In fact, the diagnostic/symptomatic criteria and the functional legal criteria are synonymous in an *Atkins*-type evaluation. With that said, an evaluator should limit his or her conclusions to the circumscribed issue of whether the defendant is a person with mental retardation, without specifically addressing the legal consequences that flow directly from such a diagnosis (i.e., exclusion from the death penalty). On balance, this principle presents little difficulty in the context of *Atkins*-type evaluations.

The ultimate legal issue in a capital sentencing evaluation is whether the defendant should receive a sentence of death or life in prison. The sentencing jury is responsible for reaching findings related to aggravating and mitigating factors (see *Ring v. Arizona*, 2002), many of which are fact based and

---

5. According to the Federal Rules of Evidence, which apply in all federal courts, testimony on the ultimate issue is generally permitted (FRE 704(a)), although "an expert witness testifying with respect to the mental state or condition of a defendant in a criminal case can not state an opinion or inference as to whether the defendant did or did not have the mental state or condition constituting an element of the crime charged or of a defense thereto" (FRE 704(b)). Many states have adopted evidentiary rules that are based on (or identical to) the FRE.

therefore outside of the limited purview/expertise of forensic mental health professionals. Therefore, in a capital sentencing context, this principle suggests that evaluators should limit their report/testimony to a discussion of the relevant aggravating and mitigating factors, without expressing an opinion about the appropriateness, or lack thereof, of a death sentence. The same reasoning would apply in an evaluation for competence for execution. The evaluator should limit his or her conclusions to the functional capacities of the prisoner (i.e., whether the prisoner has a factual and rational understanding of the reasons for his or her impending execution), without addressing the ultimate legal issue of whether the prisoner is in fact competent to be executed (see Small & Otto, 1991).

Principle 31: *Describe findings and limits so that they need change little under cross-examination.* The data and reasoning in the FMHA report should be described impartially, thoroughly, and with an appropriate acknowledgment of relevant limitations (e.g., based on missing data, conflicting findings, poor testing conditions). An *impartial* report will be objective and contain both supporting and nonsupporting information related to the evaluator's opinions. A *thorough* report will include a sufficient history of the offender (which will differ in scope and detail depending on the type of evaluation), a clear description of the evaluation procedures and findings, and a full discussion of the relevant functional legal capacities. Acknowledging the *limitations* can take several forms, including noting missing data and inconsistent data. It is also helpful to anticipate challenges that may be raised during cross-examination and preemptively dispel them in the report. This principle applies to all FMHAs, and it applies similarly in all capital evaluations.

Principle 32: *Attribute information to sources.* Conducting an FMHA often involves the review of many legal, clinical, and other historical and contemporary documents. This may be particularly true in capital mitigation evaluations because many capital defendants have lengthy histories in several domains (e.g., criminal, educational, medical, mental health, substance use), and the scope of the evaluation is broad in comparison to other types of evaluations in capital contexts. Attributing all factual information in the report to a specific source is important. An evaluator should expect that some of his or her findings and conclusions may be challenged during cross-examination, and it becomes easier for the evaluator to defend his or her position if there is a clear attribution of information to sources. When challenged, the evaluator can more easily pinpoint the source of the findings (e.g., records, self-report, collateral report). Attributing information to sources can also highlight when there is convergent or discriminant evidence for a finding. For example, if a particular finding, such as the presence of mental retardation, is supported across several sources of information (e.g., private mental health evaluations, school-based evaluations, interviews with third parties), the finding is more difficult to challenge, which strengthens the conclusions based on those findings. This is a basic principle of FMHA that applies to all evaluations performed in capital contexts.

Principle 33: *Use plain language; avoid technical jargon.* As with any written product, it is important to remember the reader. Judges and attorneys read written FMHA reports, and they rarely have extensive psychological or medical training. It is therefore important to minimize technical language and jargon, and to define any technical terms that remain necessary to include. In an *Atkins*-type evaluation, for example, it would be important to define terms such as "subaverage intellectual functioning" (perhaps with reference to normative data or percentiles in easy-to-understand terms) and "deficits in adaptive functioning" (by describing examples of such deficits). The recommendation to use plain language and avoid technical jargon also applies to expert testimony delivered to court personnel and layperson jurors. This principle applies well across all evaluations performed in capital contexts.

Principle 34: *Write report in sections, according to model and procedures.* FMHAs often result in a written report, and the report may be the only "product" of the evaluation when testimony is not required. So forensic mental health professionals should strive to write reports that are clear, relevant, informative, and defensible (Weiner, 2006). Fortunately, there is a growing literature on writing forensic reports (see, e.g., Gagliardi & Miller, 2008; Grisso, 2010; Heilbrun, 2001; Heilbrun et al., 2002; Nicholson & Norwood, 2000; Weiner, 2006; Witt, 2010).

Forensic reports should include sections and headings to communicate information in a clear, user-friendly manner. Reports that result from evaluations conducted in a capital context may be quite lengthy, so using headings is an effective way to present the material in an organized manner and orient the reader to the material presented in each section. Using headings can also make it easier to apply many of the principles already discussed. Heilbrun (2001) suggested that forensic reports should include the following headings: *(1) Referral* (with identifying information concerning the individual being evaluated [e.g., name, date of birth], his or her characteristics [e.g., gender, age, race], the nature and purpose of the evaluation [e.g., competence for execution], and the party that requested or ordered the evaluation [e.g., requested by one of the attorneys, court ordered]); *(2) Procedures* (dates and location of the evaluation, tests or procedures used, records reviewed, third-party interviews conducted, documentation of notification of purpose or informed consent, and documentation of the degree to which the information was apparently understood by the individual being evaluated); *(3) Relevant History* (integrating information from multiple sources relating to different areas of the individual's history, including family, school, medical, mental health, social, substance use, occupational, and criminal); *(4) Current Clinical*

Condition (information related to the individual's appearance, mood, behavior, sensorium, intellectual functioning, thinking, and personality); *(5) Forensic Capacities* (these will differ based on the legal question being addressed); and *(6) Conclusions and Recommendations* (addressing the relevant functional and behavioral capacities as opposed to the ultimate legal question, except under limited circumstances; see Principle 30).

Reports based on capital sentencing evaluations and evaluations for competence for execution can use all of the sections just identified. An *Atkins*-type evaluation would include all of the sections noted except Forensic Capacities. An *Atkins*-type evaluation is focused on the individual's current clinical condition, and not on the relationship between the individual's current clinical condition and any specific forensic capacities, so that section of the report does not need to be included.

Principle 35: *Base testimony on the results of the properly performed forensic mental health assessment.* A properly performed forensic evaluation and well-written report provide a foundation for subsequent expert testimony. As noted by Heilbrun (2001), performing an evaluation in a manner that is consistent with the previously discussed principles and carefully documenting the evaluation in a thorough and impartial report provides a solid basis for expert testimony; this allows the presenting attorney to use these findings in a more effective manner, the opposing attorney to prepare to challenge them, the judge and jury to understand them, and the evaluator to communicate them. This principle can be summed up nicely in the words of Joel Dvoskin (2006)—"Show your work"—and it applies equally well to all evaluations performed in capital contexts.

Principle 36: *Prepare.* The final three principles relate to expert testimony. Principle 36 in particular emphasizes the importance of being prepared to provide testimony during both direct examination and cross-examination. To prepare for direct examination, evaluators should, at a minimum, know their written report. This may seem basic, but keep in mind that many months may lapse between when the evaluator writes the report and when the evaluator finally testifies. Working with the attorney who will be conducting the direct examination is also an effective way of preparing. This enables the evaluator to become more comfortable with the types of questions that will be asked, as well as the phrasing, ordering, and pacing of the questions. To prepare for cross-examination, evaluators should anticipate the most likely challenges that will be raised to their evaluation procedures, findings, opinions, and so on, and then prepare answers that adequately address or rebut those challenges. Of course, acknowledging limitations stemming from missing or contradictory data is often necessary and should be done as needed.

Relative to other types of FMHAs, evaluations in capital cases are more likely to receive intense scrutiny, and to result in testimony. During direct examination, it is important for the evaluator to clearly describe the evaluation procedures, results, reasoning, and conclusions. Because findings relating to aggravating and mitigating factors in capital cases must be made by the jury, it is important for the expert to convey this information in a manner that is understandable to a lay audience. During cross-examination, attorneys will most certainly challenge aspects of the evaluation and the expert's findings, and the expert should be prepared to meet those challenges. Brodsky (1991, 1999, 2004) offers a number of maxims that can help prepare mental health experts to provide effective testimony.

Principle 37: *Communicate effectively.* The effectiveness of expert testimony is a function of the substantive and stylistic aspects of the testimony. The substantive component of expert testimony concerns the evaluation procedures, results, reasoning, and conclusions, whereas the stylistic component concerns how the expert presents as credible, interesting, understandable, and likeable through speech, dress, and other aspects of behavior. This principle applies equally well to expert testimony provided in all types of capital assessments.

Principle 38: *Control the message. Strive to obtain, retain, and regain control over the meaning and impact of what is presented in expert testimony.* This principle applies mostly to expert testimony provided during cross-examination. In a capital case, any expert will be challenged during cross-examination. Despite being challenged, an expert must be able to convey findings effectively while staying within the bounds of the evaluation and report. Seasoned attorneys are often adept atderailing an expert's testimony during cross-examination, and it is important for the evaluator to maintain control of the testimony and regain control if it is lost during the questioning.

Although testimony may feel adversarial, the goal of "controlling the message" is not simply to win an argument. Rather, expert witnesses "control the message" to avoid providing testimony that may mislead the listener. Forensic evaluators should present testimony that is accurate, candid, and free from manipulation ("the truth, the whole truth, and nothing but the truth"). This requires that they assertively correct any efforts to mischaracterize their testimony, whether those efforts come from the retaining counsel or opposing counsel.

Conclusion

As noted at the outset of this chapter, a principles-based approach can provide a useful framework for conducting FMHAs in capital contexts. These principles can help evaluators to work effectively with the referral source, conduct the evaluation, structure the report, and convey the results effectively during testimony. Although the effectiveness of these principles in improving judicial decision making in capital cases is an empirical question, applying best practice principles may be one way forensic mental health professionals can help minimize arbitrariness in the judicial decision-making process, which is an important concern in light of the U.S. Supreme Court's mandate that capital sentencing be individualized to the offense and offender.

10

Sample Reports

Throughout this book, we have discussed the many clinical, legal, ethical, and practical considerations related to different types of forensic mental health assessments (FMHAs) conducted in capital contexts. Whenever possible, we have attempted to highlight what the practice literature reflects as "best practices." We hope this will prove useful for clinicians who perform FMHAs in capital cases and attorneys who retain those clinicians. After discussing several specific types of FMHAs in death penalty cases, we also presented a principles-based approach that we believe provides clinicians with a useful conceptual and practical framework.

To illustrate the various ways in which forensic practitioners conduct FMHAs in capital contexts, this chapter presents actual sample reports provided by forensic mental health professionals. Given differences in training, education, and perspective among forensic practitioners, it is not surprising that forensic reports often differ considerably in content, style, and length. Despite these differences, we believe that the reports included in this chapter reflect "best practices" in FMHAs conducted in capital contexts. We solicited reports from well-respected colleagues who have specialized expertise with death penalty assessments.

Using actual forensic reports raises concerns about confidentiality. To protect privacy, we asked contributors to ensure that their reports were sanitized (i.e., devoid of identifying information), hybridized (i.e., a combination of elements of several actual cases into a composite case), or both. An exception to this policy was made for a report that is in the public domain and, therefore, readily obtainable by anyone willing to pay the copying fees charged by the court clerk's office. Although we occasionally edited reports for formatting reasons, we have preserved the substantive content of the reports.

These reports reflect several different types of evaluations in death penalty cases, including *Atkins*-type, capital mitigation, and competence for execution. For some types of evaluations, we included reports from multiple contributors, to illustrate differences in approach, content, and style among evaluators. Finally, we asked the contributors to provide short introductions to their reports to help readers to better understand the case and the evaluator's approach.

Report 1: *Atkins*-type Evaluation

Contributor Introduction (Mary Alice Conroy, Ph.D.): The evaluation of mental retardation in *Atkins* cases raises numerous unsettled controversies. A diagnosis of mental retardation is based upon three criteria: *(1)* reduced level of intellectual functioning, *(2)* limitations in adaptive behavior, and *(3)* limitations identified during the developmental period. The following sample report is based on two controversial positions related to the assessment of adaptive behavior. First, I contend that current standardized measures of adaptive behavior are generally inappropriate for capital defendants or convicted inmates who have been incarcerated for lengthy periods. Second, I suggest that behavior commonly considered "maladaptive behavior" can be a critical element to this type of evaluation.

Some have argued that standardized measures of adaptive behavior are essential to evaluating mental retardation (American Association on Mental Retardation, 2002). Yet these measures are not widely used by experienced evaluators in *Atkins* cases (Young, Boccaccini, Conroy, & Lawson, 2007). Popular measures of adaptive behavior may be inappropriate in this context because they are based on samples of people in the community, whereas inmates subject to long-term incarceration may have no opportunity to demonstrate the behaviors specified in these measures (Everington & Keyes, 1999). In addition, behavior that is adaptive in a general community population (e.g., volunteering for extra work assignments, being truthful, avoiding hurting another's feelings) may not be at all adaptive in a prison or in a population disposed to chronic criminal activity (Young et al., 2007). Deficits in certain adaptive behaviors among inmates may have no relationship to intellectual functioning, but rather reflect a conscious choice, given the environment. Currently, the American Association of Intellectual and Developmental Disabilities (2010) (formally AAMR) has stressed that evaluators must take "factors into account, such as community environment typical of the individual's peers and culture." To date, no measure has been validated with inmates, or similar populations. Therefore, I take the position that it is preferable to use no standardized instrument than to provide information to the court that could be seriously misleading—particularly given the gravity of these cases.

Regarding the second controversial position, some have argued that behavior generally defined as "maladaptive," or criminal, should not be considered in these assessments (Everington & Keyes, 1999; Greenspan & Switzky, 2003). However, "maladaptive" is often defined by mainstream cultural practices and not by specific environments or circumstances. Additionally, for many persons who have a lengthy history of chronic criminal activity, the primary behavioral record available involves maladaptive or criminal behavior. Although reliability is certainly an issue, it is no more of an issue than in considering conventional prosocial behaviors. As described in this sample report, antisocial behavior may be very illustrative of how the individual functions, and, I believe, should be considered by the trier of fact.

Name: H. Q.
DOB: _____,1953
Date of Evaluation: _____,2004

Identification and Reason for Referral: H. Q. is a 50-year-old African American male, currently incarcerated on the Texas Department of Criminal Justice (TDCJ)'s Death Row for the murders of his employers. This evaluation was requested by his attorney to determine whether Mr. Q. is a person with mental retardation.

Evaluation Procedures: Mr. Q. was seen for approximately 4 hours on _____, 2004. This included an interview and the administration of the Wechsler Adult Intelligence Scale–Third Edition (WAIS-III). Prior to beginning the interview, Mr. Q. was informed of the nature and scope of the evaluation, as well as the limits of confidentiality. He gave informed consent.

Ms. W. X., mother of Mr. Q., was subsequently interviewed by telephone for approximately 1 hour. In addition, the following documents were reviewed:

(1) Subsequent Application for Writ of Habeas Corpus Seeking Relief from Death Penalty, prepared by _____, which included:

TDCJ Mentally Retarded Offender Program Comprehensive D & E, Dated 1989

Brief for the State in H. Q. v. State of Texas, Filed _____,1995

Excerpted testimony from Mr. Q.'s 1994 trial

_____Independent School District Psychological Report, Dated _____, 1963

_____Independent School District Special Education Screening, Dated ____, 1963

_____Independent School District Psychological Report, Dated _____,1968

Memorandum from Military Commander_____, Dated _____,1973

Vineland Adaptive Behavior Scales protocol, dated_____,1989

SSSQ protocol, dated_____,1989

(2) Transcript of testimony of H. Q. in State of Texas v. H. Q.

(3) Confession of H. Q., dated_____,1974

(4) Confession of H. Q., dated_____,1974

Background Information: Mr. Q.'s mother was just 17 when he was born. She described her pregnancy and his birth as normal. She said his biological father and several of his family members were "mentally slow;" however, she was unaware of any similar problems on her side of the family.

Mr. Q. spent the early years of his life in Louisiana. His parents divorced when he was 3 years old. Ms. X. said she noticed he was "a little goofy" as a very young child. She had him examined at a charity hospital and said doctors indicated he was having chronic ear infections and was "growing too fast." She said he was prescribed medication to slow the growth, but she did not remember what kind.

Shortly after Mr. Q. began elementary school, the family moved to the _____ area. He was raised primarily by his mother and grandmother in a household that included four sisters, one brother, and six half-siblings. His mother worked as a nurse. She married twice more, and Mr. Q. said he had difficulties with both of his stepfathers. During childhood, Mr. Q. suffered from asthma, chronic ear infections, and a significant speech impediment. There are no indications he was ever treated for a mental illness nor did he receive any type of psychotropic medication.

Following the move to Texas, significant academic problems were identified by the school. Although beginning the school year in second grade, Mr. Q. was placed back in the first. In 1963, he underwent intelligence and achievement testing. School reports indicate he scored an IQ of 54 on the Stanford-Binet and his achievement scores were at minimal levels. He was subsequently placed in Special Education and assigned to the EMR (Educable Mentally Retarded) program. Despite academic difficulties, no significant behavioral problems were noted. Problems with peers were described by his mother, specifically that he could not stand up for himself and was only "tolerated" by other children.

Ms. X. said her son was very upset by the placement. Other children teased him and called him "crazy." On some days he was released from school early to avoid these problems. His mother worried that he had very poor judgment about people, thinking everyone was his friend and not realizing when he was being used. He did take part in the special education baseball program, and, at some point during his school years, began to learn boxing.

In 1968, Mr. Q. was retested, this time achieving an IQ of 62 on the Wechsler Intelligence Scale for Children (WISC). It was recommended that his further education be focused on vocational rehabilitation. Ms. X.'s understanding was that he had progressed as far as he could academically. For the rest of his time in school he received on-the-job training that included restaurant work, janitorial services, and cleaning oil tanks. After completing 12 years of school, he was given a special education diploma.

Following graduation, a social worker encouraged Mr. Q. to enroll in the Job Corps for additional training. However, he wanted to enlist in the military. His initial efforts were unsuccessful, because he was unable to pass the necessary tests for any branch of the service. The social worker finally recommended that the family take him to see a specific recruiter who would "work with him." After a day spent with that recruiter, H. Q.'s eligibility was changed from 4F to 1D. Mr. Q. said the recruiter helped him with the testing materials, even altering some scores. He suggested this may have been because bonuses were offered for successful recruiting.

H. Q. was sworn into the Reserve, which made him eligible for regular service. He said at first life in the military was very good. He continued amateur boxing and was reportedly knocked out on three occasions. However, as he began receiving more complex assignments, often involving paperwork, he found he needed to cajole or bribe fellow soldiers for assistance. He received numerous disciplinary reports that his commander described as "petty and irritating offenses" that seemed to come more from "stupidity and ignorance than by design." This created escalating peer problems as the whole platoon was often punished "when I messed up." In 1973, Mr. Q. was discharged from the military due to mental inability to function in this service.

Following discharge, Mr. Q. returned home to live with his family. His stepfather had strong objections to this arrangement. However, his mother did not believe her son was capable of living independently. She finally made an agreement with a cousin to rent a small house on the cousin's property. Her understanding was that her cousin would "keep watch" over him. His mother agreed to supplement any rent due beyond what her son could earn. She also provided many of his meals. When not eating with his mother, Mr. Q. often got meals at the_____ Restaurant, where Ms. X. had an agreement with the owner not to allow her son to spend more that $10 at a time. Given that Mr. Q. had never succeeded in obtaining a driver's license, his mother was his primary source of transportation, taking him to various unskilled jobs such as mowing lawns. Ms. X. said her son never had a serious girlfriend and, even as an adult, was very naïve in selecting friends. He never had an independent checking account. She generally managed all of his money, keeping a ledger of earnings and expenditures that she used as a teaching tool.

In 1974, Mr. Q. managed to secure a job at a hardware store operated by M. E. and F. E. They had been seeking someone to drive a truck, but since Mr. Q. had no driver's license, he was assigned other menial duties. He described this as one of the best jobs he ever had. However, after less than 2 months, he and a coworker were involved in an accident that damaged the employer's truck. Mr. Q. was fired.

In 1974, H. Q. was arrested for the murders of M. E. and F. E. He had three prior altercations with police for failing to produce identification, vagrancy, and forgery. He signed two confessions giving differing accounts of the crime.

He was convicted of the murder of M. E., sentenced to death, and sent to Death Row. However, that sentence was ultimately commuted. He was then tried for the murder of F. E., convicted, sentenced to death, and returned to Death Row. He was later retried, secondary to the second *Penry* decision, so that the jury might consider mental retardation as a mitigating circumstance. Apparently, the state was not contesting the diagnosis. However, he was once again sentenced to death.

Mr. Q. spent the majority of his 29 years on Death Row at the Ellis Unit, which operated as open population. Records indicate that during the first 15 years he received only two disciplinary reports. He worked regularly in the institution laundry and the garment factory. TDCJ records are complementary of his job performance, describing him as very dependent and compliant when given instructions. However, records noted that these same traits left him open to exploitation and manipulation. While in prison he was able to make some improvement in his basic academic skills; however, he was unable to pass the GED test. He maintained good relationships with his family. However, the only time he phoned his mother was when TDCJ staff members helped him place a call after the unexpected death of his brother.

In 1989, H. Q. was evaluated by a team from TDCJ's Mentally Retarded Offender Program. He was given the Wechsler Adult Intelligence Scale—Revised (WAIS-R) on which he obtained a Full Scale IQ score of 58. Records refer to an earlier WAIS-R score (estimated) of 59, but the protocol was not included. Staff made attempts to formally assess his adaptive functioning. The Street Survival Skills Questionnaire (SSSQ) yielded scores in the profoundly mentally retarded range on knowledge of adaptive behavior. A Vineland Adaptive Behavior Scale was also completed and scores were very low. However, the protocol notes that the scale was completed based on records, without any additional information, which is not standard procedure. The MROP team concluded that Mr. Q. was functionally illiterate. No evidence of mental illness or substance abuse was found. However, both the psychiatrist and the psychologist diagnosed mild mental retardation. In 1994, Mr. Q.'s intelligence was again tested. This time a clinical psychologist reported a Full Scale IQ score on the WAIS-R of 69.

Mental Status Examination: At the time of the current evaluation, H. Q. was oriented to time, place, person, and situation. He was polite and cooperative, and we easily established rapport. Despite a slight stutter, his speech was normal in rate and tone. No unusual movements or mannerisms were apparent. He maintained good eye contact and appeared spontaneous in response to questions.

There was no evidence of confusion, disorganization, or poor reality testing that would indicate any thought disorder. No bizarre or unusual ideas were expressed. He said that sometimes he thought he heard someone calling his name, but this did not bother him and he did not answer. The description was not consistent with a psychotic hallucination. His thinking was very concrete, but not illogical. Although he had some difficulty remembering exact times and dates, both recent and remote memory seemed grossly intact.

Mr. Q.'s affect was flexible and appropriate throughout the interview. Although understandably unhappy about his current circumstances, there was no evidence of clinical depression. He reported eating and sleeping well. His energy level appears to be adequate. He denied any thoughts of suicide.

Psychological Testing: During the evaluation, the WAIS-III was administered. Circumstances and facilities provided for the testing were adequate. Mr. Q. seemed to concentrate well and put forth maximum effort. He achieved a Full Scale IQ score of 65, with a Verbal score of 66 and a Performance score of 70.

Case Formulation: There was no evidence that H. Q. has ever suffered from a significant mental illness, nor has he experienced a problem with substance abuse. Evidence does support a diagnosis of mild mental retardation. This diagnosis requires three elements: *(1)* subaverage general intellectual functioning, *(2)* significant limitations in adaptive functioning, and *(3)* and onset before the age of 18 years.

Records of cognitive functioning, dating from 1963 until the present, all substantiate reduced cognitive functioning. All Full Scale IQ scores, from testing administered over the past decades, fell in the range of mild mental retardation.

Significant deficits in adaptive functioning have been identified across time and across situations. Sources of information include school personnel, military personnel, and TDCJ officials, as well as Mr. Q. and his mother. Overall, Mr. Q could not succeed in a regular school environment, had difficulty relating to peers throughout his life, never managed his own money, and never held a job over a significant period or held a skilled job of any kind. He was unable to function at the most basic level in the structured environment of the military and required assistance in meeting his most basic needs as a civilian adult (e.g., obtaining food and lodging). Finally, well-documented offense behavior reflected significant limitations in adaptive functioning. For example, following the incident, he was confused as to how to return home, so he called the cab company that his mother had him use routinely, and asked that they pick him up at the scene of the crime. He took a checkbook from the victims' premises and the following day attempted to cash an improperly written check at the bank where the victims had an account. Deficits in both cognitive functioning and adaptive behavior were identified when he was in elementary school.

Diagnostic Impressions:

Axis I: V71.09 No Diagnosis

Axis II: 317 Mild Mental Retardation

Conclusion: In my professional opinion, H. Q. is a person with mild mental retardation.

Mary Alice Conroy, Ph.D.   Date
Diplomate in Forensic Psychology
American Board of Professional Psychology

Report 2: *Atkins*-type Evaluation

Contributor Introduction (Karen Salekin, Ph.D.): On the surface, the assessment of intellectual disability (ID) seems to be straightforward. Indeed, there are only three criteria: *(1)* an IQ score, *(2)* an assessment of adaptive behavior, and *(3)* a determination that any deficits noted in intelligence and adaptive behavior originated before the age of 18 years. How hard can this be? Mental health professionals have been assessing this disorder for years and there is nothing in the literature to indicate that these assessments are more complex than any other. However, the case of *Atkins v. Virginia,* 536 U.S. 304 (2002), and many since, have demonstrated that these evaluations are anything but straightforward, and ID status, whether present or absent, can be difficult to prove.

The evaluation of intellectual disability in the context of an *Atkins* hearing is unlike evaluations in a community setting, or even one conducted for the purposes of mitigation in a capital case. In fact, in *Bobby v. Bies,* 129 S. Ct. 2145 (2009), the Supreme Court of the United States (SCOTUS) opined that a finding of intellectual disability [mental retardation] at the trial level is not sufficient to satisfy the requirements of *Atkins*. According to SCOTUS:

> Mental retardation as a mitigator and mental retardation under *Atkins* and *Lott* are discrete legal issues. The *Atkins* decision itself highlights one difference: "[R]eliance on mental retardation as a mitigating factor can be a two-edged sword that may enhance the likelihood that the aggravating factor of future dangerousness will be found by the jury." 536 U.S., at 321, 122 S.Ct. 2242, 153 L. Ed. 2d 335. This reality explains why prosecutors, pre-*Atkins,* had little incentive vigorously to contest evidence of retardation. (*Bobby v. Bies*, 129 S. Ct. at 2153)

The job for all clinicians who agree to conduct these evaluations, regardless of whether hired by the court, prosecution, or defense, is to conduct an evaluation that is comprehensive enough to provide the trier of fact with *all* relevant information, so they can make a fully informed decision. Collateral sources should not be limited to a handful, but should cover as many realms of functioning as possible. Evaluators must attempt to contact family members (immediate and extended), prior employers, coworkers, teachers, neighbors, friends, among others, to evaluate the defendant's adaptive behavior. Current functioning is relevant and as such, fellow inmates, correctional officers, and other individuals in the correctional setting should be interviewed and asked about their experiences with, and observations of, the defendant. Record review should not be limited to the obvious (i.e., defendant's school records), but instead must span as many realms as possible (e.g., employment, Department of Social Services, military, medical, mental health, Department of Corrections). While recognizing that there is no "perfect" evaluation, when the outcome is life or death, clinicians must be certain that they have done all that they can to obtain data sufficient to make a fully informed decision. Opinions based on suppositions and partial information are simply not acceptable.

The following report provides one example of the time commitment required to obtain data for such an evaluation. The report mentions that 16 hours were spent with the defendant and 23 hours were spent with collateral sources. Some people might argue that 16 hours is excessive, but this writer would argue otherwise. The defendants themselves provide the springboard from which an evaluation can proceed. They provide names of collateral sources, clues to the location of records, and behavioral observations that cannot be obtained any other way. The perception of the offender with ID as being uncommunicative, without knowledge, without memory, and incapable of participating in the evaluation is simply false and part of the stereotype that has plagued individuals with ID for decades. As for 23 hours with collateral sources, the time was more than well spent and the importance of these meetings is detailed in the report. Appendix A provides a list of the records that were provided to this writer; each page was read, and important data were culled and presented to the Court in the written document.

SUMMARY OF PSYCHOLOGICAL ASSESSMENT

Case Name: Munroe, Steven Edward   **Date of Report:** **-**-**
Case #: ******************   **D.O.B:** **-**-**

Respondent	**Age**	**Race/Gender**
Steven Edward Munroe	56-2	Caucasian/Male

Evaluation Procedures

Clinical interview and test administration

Mr. Steven Munroe	In-person interview	07/17/** (6.5 hours)
	In-person interview	07/23/** (5.75 hours)
	In-person interview	08/10/** (2.75 hours)

Total time with respondent = 16 hours

Third-Party Contacts[1]:

Mr. Jeffery Munroe		
(respondent's brother)	In-person interview	07/19/** (2.0 hour)
	Telephone interview	08/14/** (3.25 hours)

---

1. All correctional officers worked at Prescott Correctional Facility, where Mr. Munroe has resided for the past 16 years. Mr. Munroe has always resided on death row while at this facility.

Mr. Grant Munroe (respondent's brother)	In-person interview	08/09/** (3.0 hours)
Ms. Chandra Bell (respondent's sister)	In-person interview	08/09/** (3.5 hours)
Ms. Tonya Gray (respondent's sister)	Telephone interview	07/19/** (1.25 hours)
Correctional Officer Jonathon Carr	In-person interview	08/06/** (45 minutes)
Correctional Officer Richard Williams	In-person interview	08/06/** (30 minutes)
Correctional Officer Philip Lendall	In-person interview	08/06/** (15 minutes)
Sergeant Stuart Carmichael	In-person interview	08/06/** (55 minutes)
Mr. James Henderson, social worker at Prescott Correctional Facility	In-person interview	08/06/** (20 minutes)
Ms. Sammie Boden, nurse at Prescott Correctional Facility	In-person interview	08/06/** (15 minutes)
Mr. Lennie Brooks, attorney (trial)	Telephone interview	07/22/** (1.5 hour)
Robert Hall, attorney (current appeal)	In-person interview	07/10/** (1.0 hour)
Mr. Edwin Jemison, friend	Telephone interview	08/10/** (1.5 hours)
Mr. Ben Duncan, half-brother of ex-wife	Telephone interview	08/10/** (30 minutes)
Mr. Joe Reed, friend & death row inmate	In-person interview	07/23/** (2.5 hours)
Mr. Joe Reed, friend & death row inmate	Letter received	08/08/** (N/A)

Total time with third-party contacts: 23 hours

Review of Records
See Appendix A

Psychological Testing/Procedures–Respondent
Mini-Mental Status Exam (modified) X3 (07/17/**; 07/23/**; 08/10/**)

The Stanford-Binet Intelligence Scale–5th edition (07/23/**)

Woodcock-Johnson Test of Achievement (selected subtests only) (08/10/**)

Psychological Testing/Procedures–Collateral Sources
Mr. Jeffery Munroe–Scales of Independent Behavior Revised (SIB-R) completed for Mr. Steven Munroe in relation to his adaptive skills at the age of 17 years (07/19/**).

Mr. Grant Munroe–Scales of Independent Behavior Revised (SIB-R) completed for Mr. Steven Munroe in relation to his adaptive skills at the age of 13 years (08/09/**).

Submitted To
Honorable Judge Jeffrey D. Robinson
Middle District Court of Illinois

Prepared By
Karen Salekin, Ph.D., Psychologist
Illinois License #****

Reason for Referral

Mr. Munroe is a 55-year-old Caucasian male who was referred to this examiner for an evaluation of intellectual disability. The request for evaluation was put forth by Mr. Robert Hall, attorney for the respondent, and was approved by the Honorable Judge Jeffery D. Robinson on June 16, **** Mr. Munroe currently resides on death row at Prescott Prison in Red Plain, Illinois. As of 07/17/**; the respondent has resided at this location for 12 years, 3 months, and 12 days (as per "Illinois Department of Corrections Inmate Log Sheet"). Mr. Munroe was convicted of two counts of capital murder in the shooting deaths of two individuals.

Notification

Prior to any discussion with this evaluator, Mr. Munroe and all third-party informants were informed of the limits of confidentiality. Specifically, all individuals were informed that the information obtained during discussions with this examiner (telephone or in-person) was not confidential, and that any or all of this information could be presented to the Court in either written and/or oral format (i.e., via a report that would be submitted to the Court, via testimony, or both). All individuals were informed that they did not have to participate in the evaluation process and should they choose to participate, they had the right to end the discussion at any time. In addition, all individuals were told that they had a right to refuse to answer any question that was posed to them. With the exception of Ms. Shannon Blevins and Charlese Kincaid (both ex-wives of Mr. Munroe), all the individuals contacted stated that they understood the limits of confidentiality and chose to participate. Messages were left for Mr. Peter Hammond (respondent's friend) and Ms. Charlotte Green (friend of respondent's mother), but contact with these individuals had not been made by the time of writing.

Defining Mental Retardation

Intellectual disability (ID; formerly mental retardation) is a diagnostic term that refers to an impairment in the level at which an individual typically functions. Individuals with ID demonstrate limitations in one or more areas of day-to-day functioning and have a measured intelligence that is approximately two standard deviations below the mean of the general population (FIQ = 70 +/− 5). Deficits in measured intelligence and adaptive behavior must be present before the age of 18 years. The two most commonly used definitions of MR are those of the American Association on Intellectual and Developmental Disabilities ([AAIDD]; AAIDD, 2010) and the American Psychiatric Association ([APA]; APA, 2000).

Though similar with regard to age of onset and the requirement of deficits in both measured intelligence and adaptive behavior, the definitions put forth by the AAIDD and the APA differ in two ways. First, they view the construct of adaptive behavior differently, and second, the AAIDD has focused its attention on systems of support and removed the levels of ID (i.e., mild, moderate, severe, and profound) from their definition. Of note, the APA follows the 1992 definition put forth by AAIDD with the requirement that an individual demonstrate deficits in adaptive behavior in 2 of 10 categories (i.e., communication, self-care, home living, social/interpersonal skills, use of community resources, self-direction, functional academic skills, work, leisure, and health and safety). In contrast, the AAIDD no longer requires impairments in 2 of 10 categories, but instead requires that an individual display significant impairments that are at least two standard deviations below the mean, in either *(a)* conceptual, social, or practical skills, or *(b)* an overall score that includes the domains of conceptual, social, and practical skills (AAIDD, 2010).

In addition to the aforementioned signs/symptoms, intellectual disability is often associated with poor self-confidence and impaired moral reasoning. Certain characteristics such as poor memory, poor transference and generalization of skills, impaired judgment, and a tendency to acquiesce to those in authority are related to the adaptive functioning of individuals with intellectual disability and deficits in these areas are common within this population (Everington & Keyes, 1999). Individuals with intellectual disability tend to develop compensatory behaviors or appearances to offset their deficits in social and intellectual functioning, often making it difficult to detect whether someone has the condition; this is particularly true if the level of impairment falls in the mild range (Keyes, Edwards, & Derning, 1998).

Summary of Findings

Background Information

The following historical information should be considered a *summary* of personal data pertaining to Mr. Munroe's upbringing and life experiences.

Mr. Steven Munroe is the fourth child born to the union of Mr. Reginald Munroe and Ms. Carmen Munroe, both of whom are deceased. He is fourth in a sibship of twelve, with four of his siblings still living. According to hospital records, Mr. Munroe was born in breach position during a home delivery. At the time of his birth, his mother had been a long-standing alcoholic who had been in and out of rehabilitation programs for 5 years prior to his birth. Records indicate that Ms. Munroe may have been in recovery during her pregnancy; however, the presence or absence of substance use could not be verified.

Information provided from multiple sources (e.g., the respondent, the Department of Social Services, Mr. Grant Munroe, Mr. Jeffery Munroe, Ms. Chandra Bell) indicated the respondent was raised in Rafferty, Illinois, in a very chaotic and dangerous home environment. The family resided in a government-assisted housing project and had limited resources to meet basic needs such as food and clothing. According to a Supplementary Court Report found within Department of Social Services records (DSS; date not reported), the Munroe family became known in the Department in June of **** and continued their involvement for 20 years. In these records were numerous reports with varied allegations, including but not limited to: child abuse, spousal abuse, "excessive drinking on the part of Ms. Munroe, desertion on the part of Ms. Munroe, and delinquency on the part of six of the children." Mr. Munroe himself, as well as his four siblings, corroborated a history of frequent and sometimes severe physical abuse by Ms. Munroe toward the respondent. Moreover, the progress notes included in the DSS records suggested that there was a need for intervention for the "adequate care and treatment" of all of the

Munroe children. With regard to the respondent, there were numerous notations made regarding problems with the legal system, difficulties succeeding in the school system, and the "need for special services" within the education system (these notations began after his second year of the first grade). As detailed in a separate section of the DSS file, Mr. Munroe was not provided with any such services until he was approximately 13 years of age, at which time he was 2 years behind his same-aged peers (*see "Education" section for more details*).

Other notes from DSS indicate that the Munroe children were often left unsupervised and would be observed to be unkempt and playing in the streets. Both the respondent and his brother Grant report spending time playing on the railroad tracks, hopping on slow-moving rail cars, or standing in front of trains and jumping off the track at the last minute. Of import, however, was that Mr. Munroe did not limit his behavior to jumping on the moving rail cars but also chose to crawl under the moving rail cars in order to get to the other side (as per report from Mr. Grant Munroe).

Due to continued problems with the care and treatment of the Munroe children, DSS found them to be "dependent and neglected" (*see note dated ****, signed by Katherine Johnson*), and removed them from the home in January of ****. Initial placement of all children was in the home of their paternal cousin and his wife, but due to problems with Mr. Munroe's behavior, the couple requested that he be placed elsewhere. As a result, Mr. Munroe was transferred to a boarding home for delinquent and dependent children, where he stayed for 2 days, and then to another one where he remained for a period of 2 months. The respondent's behavior at the first boarding home was reported to be a problem (e.g., he had a belligerent attitude, did not get along with other residents, did not obey direct commands) and his response to discipline essentially negligible. Mr. Munroe ran away from this placement and once found (length of elopement not known to this examiner), he was informed by a family court judge that his behavior must improve or he would be sent to the "training school." At this time, the respondent was 14 years of age.

Throughout the records (e.g., Exhibits 5, 9, and 10; DSS), there are references to the possibility that Mr. Munroe received head injuries one or more times in his life. It was reported that the respondent was "knocked unconscious" after falling off the roof of a house (age 5 years), was in a "couple of car wrecks" (details not noted in the records), was "beaten unconscious" in a gang attack while in the Larson County Jail (11-16-**), and was once struck on the back of the head with a tire iron.[2] Over the past 17 years, there have been numerous recommendations to have Mr. Munroe evaluated for

---

2. Notation was made by Lance Carillol, M.D.; undated; Department of Social Services records *see* Exhibit 4.

brain injury[3]; however, there is no documentation to indicate that this evaluation was ever completed.

According to multiple sources, Mr. Munroe was married three times, with all relationships ending in divorce. His first marriage occurred when he was approximately 17 years of age at which time he married Ms. Shannon Blevins (*see Exhibit 12 for marriage certificate*). The marriage lasted approximately 18 months and their union resulted in the birth of a daughter. According to Mr. Munroe, he did not want to marry Ms. Blevins and stated that he did so because people told him that he should (Ms. Blevins was pregnant at the time). When asked about the reason behind the divorce, Mr. Munroe stated that his wife left him after he was arrested, incarcerated, and ultimately court ordered to participate in a sex offender treatment program at Deardon State Hospital (DSH; court-ordered participation confirmed by records; convicted of sexual abuse, first degree). When asked about the incident that led to his incarceration, he stated that it related to "a run in with a girl . . . you know it's been a long time. . . I think it was at a skating rink and I think I tried to kiss her or did kiss her and I got in trouble, but not then." Mr. Munroe volunteered that prior to the aforementioned act he had engaged in other deviant sexual behavior, specifically voyeurism and attempted sexual intercourse with animals. When asked about his relationship with his wife, Mr. Munroe stated that it was "fine," and could not elaborate further. Ms. Blevins refused to speak with this examiner; thus, little is known to this examiner about his functioning in this relationship or the nature of the relationship.

Mr. Munroe's second marriage occurred approximately 3 years later at which time he married Charlese Kincaid, a woman 17 years his senior. According to the respondent, she was a "mean woman" and the two did not get along at all. Their marriage ended after 2 years. Mr. Munroe provided little information regarding this marriage and Ms. Kincaid refused to speak with this examiner; thus, nothing is known about his functioning in this relationship or the nature of their relationship.

Mr. Munroe was married to his third wife, Linda Graham, for approximately 3 years (date of marriage not known to this examiner or Mr. Munroe). According to the respondent, he did not want to get married, but was simply "going with the flow." The couple resided together for only 4 months before Mr. Munroe was arrested, and ultimately convicted, for rape in the second degree (see Exhibits 10, 13, and 15). As was typical for the respondent, following his release from prison, he stated that he had trouble finding employment and remained in trouble with the law (confirmed by Department of Corrections records). The divorce was reported to have been final in ****,

---

3. See Exhibits 9, 10, 18, and 19.

but according to Mr. Munroe, he and Ms. Graham had ongoing sexual relations until she was killed in an automobile accident in November ****.

Available information suggests that Mr. Munroe has never lived by himself. According to his brothers and sisters, Mr. Munroe did not have the skills to obtain a job (all jobs were obtained for him), cook for himself (though he could cook simple meals such as scrambled eggs), or otherwise live independently (e.g., pay rent/mortgage; locate a doctor when ill; pay bills that arrive in the mail; use the services at a bank). Mr. Munroe concurred with these statements, but added that, while he had limitations, he also had the ability to do some things on his own. He stated that he could drive his car in a familiar town and on freeways, could pay for small things at a store or a bill at a motel, and could complete some tasks at work. All tasks reported required only manual labor without independent thinking or problem solving (e.g., stacking boxes; toting shingles). With regard to finances, multiple sources (e.g., all siblings; Mr. Jemison) stated that Mr. Munroe depended on his wives and other family members to take care of paying his bills, purchasing necessities (e.g., clothes), and cashing his paychecks. Mr. Munroe did not have a bank account.

Education

Review of available school records suggests that Mr. Munroe had trouble learning and functioning in the school environment. He failed the both the first and second grade and, with the exception of a C- in arithmetic (grade 3, end of year grade), earned F's in all academic subjects.

Though sparse, records indicate that in addition to having trouble learning and succeeding in the school environment, Mr. Munroe was also disruptive in the classroom. For example, in a note dated 06-10-**, the following statement was written: "Steven, age 13, is somewhat of a retarded child, according to school authorities. Although he has been promoted to the seventh grade, it is doubtful that he will be able to do anything except present a problem in the classroom." In a report to the court (dated 06-22-**; age 13 years), it was noted that the principal of Brantford Elementary School stated that Mr. Munroe was "definitely mentally retarded and that efforts had been made to have him attend Stramm Street Special School." At that time, he had earned F's in all of his classes, had been absent 40 days, and had caused "continual disturbance in the classroom." The principal further stated that he viewed Mr. Munroe as "a follower who was easily led." In a letter to written to Mrs. Bennett Shell "of Stramm Street Special Classroom" (05-10-**)[4], it was again stated that the principal of Brantford Middle School, in concert with Mr. Munroe's

---

4. The letter was written by Ms. Linda Gabriel, counselor at Brantford Elementary School.

teacher, believed that "he did not have the ability to learn on the level of an average child" and both were requesting his placement in Stramm Street Special School. In response to this request, Ms. Shell wrote a letter to the respondent's mother in which she stated that, despite meeting eligibility requirements, Mr. Munroe could not be admitted to Stramm School at that time. She further stated that he was "number one on the eligibility list," but due to lack of space, his chances of admission were extremely poor. As such, Ms. Shell recommended that Mr. Munroe be placed in the special education class at Madison High School.

Records indicate that Mr. Munroe was eventually placed in the "special class for retarded children" at Madison High School (date of admission not available to this examiner). Available information suggests that he enjoyed attending this school, and he told his counselor that he thought that he would function better there, and would learn more, because of the way that they were teaching him. One of his teachers reported that he was succeeding in this placement and commented that it was her belief that his problems in learning may have been the result of conflict within the home environment, rather than serious intellectual limitations. His teacher supported this supposition by her observation that he had "some successes in math" and "could say back to her some of the things that she read to him." At the time that this statement was written Mr. Munroe was 15 years of age and could not read or write.

Due to his involvement in criminal activity, Mr. Munroe also attended school at the Indiana Boys Industrial School (09-10-**; age 15 years). In a letter from his counselor, Ms. Linda Gabriel, to one of the directors of the program (Mrs. Stevens), a request was made for Mr. Munroe to be placed in trade school; the rationale for the request was that his impaired cognitive ability would prevent him from succeeding elsewhere. There are no records to suggest that this request was acted upon, and according to the respondent, he never attended a trade school. Upon his release from IBIS Mr. Munroe quit school; he was 17 years of age and was in the seventh grade.

Employment History

The following chronology of employment is created solely on the basis of statements made to this examiner by Mr. Munroe, and statements made by Mr. Munroe to other individuals, as documented in the records reviewed for this case (see Table 10.1). There were no employment records available nor, with the exception of Mr. Jeffery Munroe, were individuals available to discuss the respondent's ability to function in the workplace.

Though listed in order from first to last job, the list should not be taken as an exact chronology, or a complete listing, of work experiences. As previously mentioned, Mr. Munroe was often incarcerated, and as such, some lapses in employment may be related to his physical inability to obtain a job.

When asked about his behavior postrelease, his siblings stated that he would not seek employment, but instead counted on family members and friends to take care of all of his physical and financial needs. According to both the respondent and Mr. Jeffery Munroe, none of the jobs in the following list were secured by Mr. Munroe, but instead were obtained with assistance of friends or family members.

Legal History

A. Delinquency

Available information indicates that Mr. Munroe was adjudicated delinquent on two occasions. His first adjudication occurred on June 22, **** (age 13 years) at which time he was arrested for placing rocks and spikes and other items on the L&N Railroad track. The outcome of this case was Mr. Munroe's placement on "indefinite probation"; information regarding his ability to function under this sanction was not included in available documents. However, his second adjudication occurred 2 years later, at which time he was charged with crimes that were conducted over the course of at least 1 year. As such, it is safe to say that the longest period of time that he could have been compliant with the legal system is 1 year, though there is no data to support that he was ever compliant with probation.

Mr. Munroe's second adjudication occurred on August 26, *** (age 15 years) at which time he was charged with stealing a motor vehicle (X3), burglary, and shoplifting (X5) in the city of Rafferty, Indiana. Mr. Munroe reportedly confessed to all crimes and when asked by authorities the reasons for the burglaries, he stated, "I don't know," but added that he did not believe that his parents gave him enough money. In response to his adjudication, and his inability to function well in his home and community, Mr. Munroe's counselor (Ms. Linda Gabriel) considered it to be in his best interests that he be placed at the Indiana Boys Industrial School (IBIS). As previously mentioned, Mr. Munroe was placed at this school on September 10, ***. A preparole report stated that upon release from IBIS he was ordered to return to his family home and that "due to his known retardation," his parents were encouraged to enroll him in trade school (see Exhibit 4, note not dated, written by James Farety).

B. Adult Legal History

Criminal Record: Records provided by the Indiana Department of Corrections indicate that Mr. Munroe has been incarcerated for the majority of his adult life and has been convicted of both violent and nonviolent offenses. His record reflects charges of Assault and Battery, Sexual Abuse 1st degree, Buying and Receiving Stolen Property, Peeping Tom, Sexual Abuse, Rape,

Table 10.1 Employment History

Job (Age)	Responsibilities	Approx. Length of Employment	Place of Employment (If Known)	Reason for Leaving
Service station ("in my 20s")	Pumped gas—stopped fill on the even dollar	3 months	Rafferty, IN	Could not do the job because could not work the cash register and could not read or write—all were reported to be necessary for the job
Chicken plant ("in my 20s")	Loaded boxes on trucks	4 months	Bowden, IL	To earn more money at "a warehouse." Left without telling them—just did not show up
"A warehouse" ("in my 20s")	Loaded trucks	9 months	Bowden, IL	Unclear (laid off and/or due to divorce and need to return home)
Bakery ("in my 20s")	Stacked boxes in a cooler	3 or 4 months	Rafferty, IN	Quit because felt that he was being overworked
Assistant to a mason ("in my 30s")	Toted bricks and tools	"Off and on"	Rafferty, IN	N/A
Service stations ("in my 30s")	Could only pump gas—ended the fill on the even dollar	"Never lasted too long"	Rafferty, IN	Lack of education and impaired ability to do the work
"I call it a self-job" (many times over the course of his life)	Picked up cans, bottles, and other junk with another person. The other person "knew what to get" and sold the goods	"Off and on"	Rafferty, IN	N/A
Assisting father with painting (many times over the course of his life)	Only the "big stuff" (meaning painting things that required only gross motor movements)	"Off and on"	Rafferty, IN	N/A

Escape, Attempted Escape, Kidnapping, Attempted Murder, various firearms charges, and Capital Murder.

Regarding the charges of Escape, legal documents indicate that Mr. Munroe eloped from the Larson County Jail. Mr. Munroe's first attempt to escape was unsuccessful. According to records, Mr. Munroe attempted to escape by climbing over a 10-foot fence. As part of his plan, he had tied a series of sheets together to make a rope. These sheets came undone during the attempted escape and he fell to the ground, breaking both of his feet. With respect to his second charge, available documentation indicates that he and another inmate assaulted two correctional officers, and subsequently took their weapons and locked them in a cell. In order to flee from the area, the two kidnapped a man and stole his truck for use as a getaway car. According to Mr. Munroe, he did not plan the escape, but he did participate in the commission of the crime. No other information is known to this examiner about the planning of this event, nor the difficulty level of such an escape. At the time of his arrest for capital murder, Mr. Munroe had a warrant out for his arrest in relation to this escape charge.

Functioning within correctional institutions: Records obtained from the Indiana Department of Corrections (IDOC) indicate that, over the course of his many incarcerations, Mr. Munroe had exhibited violent and threatening behavior toward staff and inmates. For example, a note written on July 20, **** indicates that Mr. Munroe would pick fights with other death row inmates and would do so without provocation. On a separate document it was noted that on August 3, **** he was found guilty on three charges: *(1)* making threats to an officer, *(2)* failure to obey a direct order, and *(3)* destruction of state property. IDOC records suggest that Mr. Munroe's disruptive behavior eventually ceased and he began to function well within the system. Discussions with correctional officers who currently work with Mr. Munroe indicate that he is a "model inmate" who does not cause problems and interacts well with both staff and inmates. These sentiments were consistent with those of Sergeant Carmichael, a former death row officer who had close contact with him for approximately 10 years.

There is ample evidence in the files provided by the IDOC regarding Mr. Munroe's ability to seek and receive medical attention. There are numerous slips pertaining to his need for care in response to a variety of ailments, perhaps the most serious being diabetes for which he receives chronic care. According to Mr. Munroe and Mr. Reed, a fellow death row inmate, other death row inmates have completed all current and past medical request forms. Mr. Reed stated that he has written many of these requests and noted that his requests for medical attention are always detailed and specific. For example, he stated that he might write, "My kidney is hurting. I would like to get an X-ray and or a CAT scan." When asked if the respondent would know what was written on the request form, Mr. Reed stated that he would have no idea and added that "Steve has to trust us to do the right thing." With regard to care and treatment for diabetes, Nurse Sammie Boden stated that Mr. Munroe is compliant with treatment, and he has learned to administer his finger sticks and to interpret the numeric values obtained on the blood sugar monitor (i.e., he understands if his level is high, low, or fine based on the number obtained).

By all reports, Mr. Munroe functions well within the structure of the Prescott Correctional Facility (PCF). According to multiple sources,[5] a day on death row is quite simple and may include a trip to the library or the church, 1 hour for exercise, and attendance to daily needs such as eating, dressing, and sleeping. In short, all basic needs are taken care of by others and there is little room for independent activity. When asked, Mr. Henderson, a social worker at PCF, stated that the behaviors required to function on death row are not difficult and in his opinion could easily be carried out by people with low intellectual functioning.

Based on record review and discussions with IDOC personnel, it appears that Mr. Munroe has learned to function adequately on death row and does so with the assistance of others. For example, he has learned to update his visiting log, place orders from the canteen, and update his phone log. Mr. Reed shared with this examiner the method by which he and Mr. Munroe work together to complete his canteen order. In brief, completing the canteen order requires that Mr. Munroe ask Mr. Reed for the number that coincides with the desired item, and then Mr. Munroe writes that number down on the form. According to Mr. Reed, Mr. Munroe would not know how much he could order with a particular amount of money, nor would he know if he were shorted on items that he ordered (*Note:* this statement was corroborated by Sergeant Carmichael). When asked about updating his visiting log, Mr. Munroe stated that he sometimes requires assistance, but he can now copy names and numbers from one sheet to the next in order to make the changes necessary to update his log.

When asked about Mr. Muroe's ability to interact with inmates and staff, information obtained from Mr. Reed suggests that Mr. Munroe exhibits problems, even within the highly structured setting of death row. For example, Mr. Reed noted that the respondent cannot use the phone on his own, has impaired social skills (e.g., frequently interrupts people), has a poor memory, and when in conversations with others, he begins to talk about topics that are unrelated to the subject matter. According to this source, the respondent has no insight into his poor social skills. In addition to this, Mr. Reed stated that

---

5. All officers interviewed, Mr. Reed, and Mr. Henderson.

he views Mr. Munroe as a person that is gullible and easily led by others. To support this statement he provided one example in which a reporter contacted Mr. Munroe and asked that he speak publically about the murders that resulted in his placement on death row. Apparently, Mr. Munroe wanted to speak with this individual because he thought that he wanted to be his pen pal.

With regard to his ability to maintain appropriate hygiene, multiple sources[6] stated that Mr. Munroe is able to dress himself, shower, and present in a generally neat and clean manner. Sgt. Carmichael indicated that Mr. Munroe was not the tidiest of inmates (also noted by Mr. Reed and Officers Carr, Williams, and Lendall) and noted that he would have to be reminded to sweep the floors and conduct general cleaning of his cell. That said, Sgt. Carmichael suggested that his ability to deal with certain situations is not the same as other people, and in one incident, resulted in behaviors that he noted to be physically dangerous and "disgusting." Specifically, Sgt. Carmichael described an incident in which Mr. Munroe took it upon himself to self-administer a self-made enema (made out of plastic bottles). The outcome of this action was reported to be an "explosion" of feces that resulted in Mr. Munroe, the bed, the commode, and other objects in the near vicinity being covered in human excrement. What was surprising to Sgt. Carmichael was that Mr. Munroe seemed to have no awareness that this occurrence was problematic, nor that such an event may be offensive to others. Instead, Mr. Munroe reportedly stood there waiting for assistance, as if nothing had really happened. Of import, Mr. Munroe required medical treatment for this incident.

In addition to the aforementioned, Sgt. Carmichael stated that you could "see that he is different" and described him as man of "limited mental capability" and "not an asset to anybody." He explained further that Mr. Munroe would not be an asset because he does not have many skills and "probably doesn't have the ability to acquire these skills." He further commented that he believed that Mr. Munroe would have the ability to conduct simple tasks and engage in menial labor jobs, but that he would "not be of much value in the workforce." When asked about his ability to communicate, Sgt. Carmichael noted that he did not have trouble understanding Mr. Munroe, but that he had noticed that Mr. Munroe would sometimes have trouble understanding him. In order to maximize the likelihood that the respondent would understand what was being said, Sgt. Carmichael purposely spoke in simple language and at a very slow pace. All correctional officers interviewed noted that Mr. Munroe was extremely talkative and, in the opinion of Sgt. Carmichael, this was an attempt to portray himself as "smarter than he actually is."

---

6. Mr. Reed, Sergeant Carmichael, and Officers Carr, Williams, and Lendall.

Information obtained from Officers Carr and Williams was similar to that provided by Sgt. Carmichael. While neither officer considered himself to be completely knowledgeable about Mr. Munroe, both reported him to be slow with regard to intellectual functioning. Officer Carr stated that he considers Mr. Munroe to be a nice person who loves to talk and who will talk about things he does not know anything about. This same officer reported having frequently observed Mr. Munroe assisting a fellow inmate in the yard and also commented that he "really likes animals and will often save some of his food to feed them." In contrast, Officer Lendall, repeatedly stated his belief that Mr. Munroe "knows right from wrong," that he gets along with others, and that he "does not cause trouble." He further stated that the respondent does not appear to be different from other inmates, but he prefaced this statement by noting his lack of personal familiarity with Mr. Munroe.

With regard to the diagnosis of mental retardation, there are notations in various legal documents that suggest that Mr. Munroe has either mild mental retardation (see Exhibit 10 for notes written by Mr. Henderson), or can be best described as a person who is "slow" (see Exhibit 10 for multiple segregation forms). In addition, during the sentencing phase of the criminal proceedings against Mr. Munroe, the Court found him to be "slightly mentally retarded" and used mental retardation as a mitigating circumstance.[7]

Data from legal documents pertaining to offense of capital murder and Mr. Munroe's functioning during trial: In brief, Mr. Munroe was charged with, and convicted of, capital murder after having shot and killed two people. At the time of the murders, Mr. Munroe was on escape from the Larson County Jail and had been living in a motel in Kentucky. According to the respondent, he did not intend to murder anyone, but he had gone to Ms. Graham's (victim and ex-girlfriend of 1 month) place of employment to talk with her about her intimate relationship with Craig Patton (victim and boyfriend of Ms. Graham). According to police reports, Mr. Munroe's behavior "suggested that he acted with intent because he hid his vehicle so that the victims would not know that he was there." When asked about the events of that evening, Mr. Munroe stated that his first activity was to look through the windows of the convenience store to see who was in there; he said that he saw Mr. Patton, who he noted had a gun in his rear pant pocket. While Mr. Munroe was peering through a window, he saw Mr. Patton reach toward the gun and in response he ran into the store and shot Mr. Patton. When asked why he did this, he stated that he felt he had no option but to shoot him, because he firmly believed that Mr. Patton saw him and was intending to short him first. He then proceeded to short Ms. Graham and then fled the scene in her vehicle (unlocked and parked behind the store).

---

7. Details related to the assessment of cognitive functioning within the department of corrections are covered in the section titled "History of Psychological Evaluation."

When asked why he killed Ms. Graham, he stated that he didn't really know because his recollection for the event was not good. Records indicate that Mr. Munroe made a similar statement at the time of his arrest. He remained at large for a period of 6 weeks before he was arrested at a motel in Ashton, Kentucky.

Of particular import to the current evaluation were observations made by this examiner in relation to the ability of Mr. Munroe to function during his trial and deposition in June of ****. With respect to his deposition, review of the transcript indicates that Mr. Munroe frequently became confused during questioning and on numerous occasions looked to his counsel for guidance as to whether he should answer certain questions. An example from page 19 of the deposition illustrates both problems, while at the same time providing a concrete example of poor judgment; specifically Mr. Munroe's decision to answer questions against the advice of his attorney.

> Ms. Harper (state attorney): Mr. Munroe, do you understand the question, "Where did you live just before you were arrested?"
> Mr. Munroe: Before I was arrested?
> Ms. Harper: Yes, sir.
> Mr. Brooks (defense attorney): Do you understand the question? It calls for your answer.
> Mr. Munroe: Yeah.
> Ms. Harper: Could you tell me, please, sir?
> Mr. Munroe (to his attorney): Can I answer that?
> Mr. Brooks: I'm advising you not to answer that, Steven.
> Mr. Munroe (to Ms. Harper): Well, I don't really recall to be honest with you about it.

The pattern of responding can be observed throughout the deposition, as can his tendency to answer questions concretely and his seeming inability to understand and follow the advice of his attorney (e.g., p. 135). Though the formerly described response style is prevalent throughout the deposition, there are also many instances in which Mr. Munroe appeared to understand the questions posed and was able to respond appropriately.

Telephone contact and discussion with Mr. Brooks (defense attorney for Mr. Munroe) supported the noted observations made by this examiner. Specifically, Mr. Brooks recalled that Mr. Munroe did not readily understand even simple information and because of this, he spent a lot of time explaining very basic information. Mr. Brooks remembered preparing Mr. Munroe for deposition and did so by using very concrete instructions. An example that he provided was, "if I say "X" you need to respond this way because it is in your best interests." Despite numerous hours of preparation, Mr. Brooks felt that Mr. Munroe was not able to function well as a defendant and that he often responded in ways that were "not in his best interests." In addition, Mr. Brooks recalled the respondent having been embarrassed that he was unable to use the vending machine (a skill that he has since learned), but noted that he was not embarrassed when talking about his sexual experiences with farm animals. Apparently, Mr. Munroe spoke freely with Mr. Brooks about these sexual experiences and did not appear to understand that this behavior would be something most people would try to hide.

Of interest, Mr. Munroe decided to testify during the guilt phase of his capital murder trial. Not only did he testify against the advice of his attorney, but he did so after having heard cautionary instructions provided to him by the judge and after the District Attorney clearly recommended against it (i.e., "And as a matter of fairness, Mr. Munroe, as far as the State is concerned, it is in your best interest not to testify"). Upon review of the transcript, it is clear that Mr. Munroe was a poor liar and had no insight into the significant limitations he had with regard to lying in a convincing manner. For example, on page 1921 of the trial transcript, Mr. Munroe stated that he had never been in the vehicle in which the name and number of a witness was found. The state informed Mr. Munroe that his fingerprints were found in the car, yet he continued to adamantly deny ever having been in the car. Instead, he offered a somewhat less convincing argument that perhaps someone had "borrowed" his fingerprints. When asked by this examiner why he had made the decision to testify at trial, Mr. Munroe could not provide a reason.

History of Psychological Evaluation

Available information indicates that Mr. Munroe has undergone numerous mental health evaluations. There is information in his records indicating that, during one or more incarcerations, he had reported experiencing hallucinations. Review of records indicates that the treatment with Mellaril, Thorazine, and/or Stelazine[8] was initiated on self-report data, in the absence of any external corroboration (e.g., there were no observations consistent with the presence of psychosis or prior treatment for a psychotic disorder). While in the Department of Corrections, Mr. Munroe has been diagnosed with antisocial personality disorder, organic personality disorder, voyeurism, anxiety disorder, and depression. Due to the limited focus of the evaluation, the following discussion will pertain solely to information relevant to the evaluation of mental retardation.

---

8. All three of these medications are used to treat psychosis; however, they are also used to control agitation and assist with insomnia, among other pharmacologic uses. The purpose of treatment with these medications was not indicated in the record and, as such, the reason for administration to Mr. Munroe is unknown to this examiner.

Assessment of Cognitive Functioning

Mr. Munroe's first known evaluation of cognitive functioning occurred on July 15, **** (age 6 years) and prior to the current evaluation, his most recent evaluation was conducted on January 8, **** (age 42). For ease of review, the results of the intelligence tests that have been conducted over a period of approximately 36 years have been put together in table format and can be found in Appendix B, Table 1, of this document (see Appendix B, Table 2, for Flynn-adjusted scores). Information pertaining to the results of tests such as the Slosson, The Quick Test, and the Beta are not included in the table, nor will they be discussed, as they are inappropriate instruments for the purposes of diagnosing mental retardation.

A. Assessment of Cognitive Functioning—Prior to 18 years of age: Review of the summary and recommendations section of the psychological report dated July 15, **** indicates that Dr. Hughes, a clinical psychologist, assessed Mr. Munroe using the Wechsler Intelligence Scale for Children (WISC; Mr. Munroe was 6 years of age). The results of this evaluation showed Mr. Munroe's verbal IQ to be 60, his performance IQ to be 47, and his full scale IQ to be 51. Dr. Hughes reported that in his opinion, ". . . this boy is of borderline Intelligence in handling verbal problems and that he should be able to proceed in regular school, if he is placed in a grade below the level of his chronological age. I would suggest first grade placement now with plans to pass him each year until he is 16 or through the sixth grade. He needs encouragement to do his best rather than give up." As noted previously, Mr. Munroe failed two grades, was placed in special education, and quit school after completing the sixth grade. The respondent was also assessed using the WISC at the age of 8 years (01/15/**) and 13 years (05/13/**); unfortunately, information regarding the outcomes of his assessments was sparse and included only face sheets with raw and scaled scores for the measures (see Appendix B, Table 1).

B. Assessment of Cognitive Functioning and/or Adaptive Behavior—Post 18 years of age: With the exception of the following five evaluations, the reader is directed to Table 1 of Appendix B to review information pertaining to the results of intelligence testing conducted on Mr. Munroe after the age of 18 years. Some detailed information pertaining to his evaluations at Deardon State Hospital (DSH), Kindle Correctional Facility (KCF), Harrison Secure Medical Facility (HSMF), and those conducted by Dr.'s Carillo and Raynor are provided in the paragraphs that follow.

With regard to the findings of Mr. Munroe's first evaluation as an adult, the results of his assessment at DSH show a discharge diagnosis of mild mental retardation and voyeurism (i.e., "The behavioral observations and test results most nearly resemble the diagnostic category of mild mental retardation, with sexual deviation, voyeurism."). Information provided in this same report indicates that staff considered Mr. Munroe to be "functioning well within the borderline or dull normal range of intelligence." Support for this functional assessment was limited to one statement that detailed their belief that Mr. Munroe had been able to "hold responsible jobs and adequately support his family." Of note, at the time of his commitment to DSH, he was 21 years of age and had been convicted of molestation and of being a peeping tom.

During Mr. Munroe's incarceration in **** (age 25 years) he was evaluated by Jennifer Gardner, Ed.D. At that time, the respondent was being reevaluated for transfer from B-Dorm (a unit at Kindle Correctional Facility in Indiana that housed inmates with mild cognitive impairment) back to general population. Dr. Gardner opined that Mr. Munroe was appropriate for return to general population and, based on the scores of the WAIS (e.g., FIQ = 67), recommended that he be evaluated for a learning disability and/or suspected brain damage. Based on review of the information available, these evaluations were never conducted. It is important to note that Dr. Gardner did not make a statement as to whether the respondent did or did not have mental retardation.

On January 27, **** (age 27), Mr. Munroe was admitted to Harrison Secure Medical Facility (HSMF) for an evaluation of competence to stand trial and mental state at the time of the offense. Review of documents indicates that Mr. Munroe functioned well at the facility and did not demonstrate problems related to maintaining hygiene, assisting with maintaining cleanliness of the living environment, and ability to communicate with staff. At the conclusion of the 1 month evaluation at HSMF, Mr. Munroe was determined to be competent to stand trial and to be without "substantial evidence of psychological abnormality" at the time of the alleged crime. Though formal assessment of mental retardation was not completed at HSMF (i.e., no formal assessment of adaptive functioning with one or more raters or an interview based assessment of adaptive behavior in multiple settings over multiple years), Dr. Gerald Morrow proffered an opinion regarding the appropriateness of the diagnosis. According to Dr. Morrow, "IQ scores from the WAIS-R were 68 (verbal), 81 (performance), and 73 (full scale), respectively. These scores suggest intellectual functioning in the borderline range, though the defendant's level of speech and history of autonomous living in the community suggest that he is a rather streetwise individual and, apart from well-documented criminal tendencies, not the kind of person who would require extensive supervision on the basis of intellectual dysfunction" (see p. 2 of Psychological Evaluation Report dated March 29, ****).

On May 23, **** (age 37) Mr. Munroe was evaluated by Marc F. Carillo, M.D. Dr. Carillo was hired by the defense for the purpose of evaluating mental retardation for use at the postconviction hearing. Dr. Carillo reviewed file information and met with Mr. Munroe for 7 hours. Dr. Carillo is not a psychologist; thus, he did not conduct psychological tests to support or refute the diagnoses of mild mental retardation and organic personality disorder, both of which he made. Among other things, Dr. Carillo reported that Mr. Munroe was often tangential in speech and would relate information in a very disjointed manner. The respondent informed Dr. Carillo that he began having sexual relations with farm animals around the age of 21 years, having had one failed attempt at the age of 12 or 13 years. Record review and interview with the respondent revealed to Dr. Carillo a history of alleged head injury, a tumultuous and difficult upbringing, and IQ tests with scores in the range of mild mental retardation. The doctor reported that he used all of this information in arriving at these diagnoses, but as previously mentioned, he did not conduct a standardized assessment of possible brain damage (e.g., neuropsychological testing; medical imaging).

In October of **** (age 42), Dr. Frank Raynor, a neuropsychologist, conducted an evaluation of mental retardation regarding Mr. Munroe. His evaluation consisted of an interview of the respondent and the administration of six psychological measures: *(1)* Wechsler Adult Intelligence Scale-Revised (WAIS-R), *(2)* the Bender-Visual Motor Gestalt, *(3)* House-Tree-Person Test, *(4)* Aphasia Screening Test, *(5)* Sentence Completion Test, and *(6)* Trails A&B. On the basis of IQ scores and deficits in adaptive functioning (e.g., problems maintaining employment, poor social skills, inability to function for any extended period of time without getting into legal trouble, poor communication skills), Dr. Raynor diagnosed Mr. Munroe as having mild mental retardation (FIQ = 66). He further opined that Mr. Munroe would likely be able to do well in an institutional setting, but that his deficits in adaptive functioning would impair his ability to function in a typical real-world setting.

The Current Evaluation

Observations/Mental Status

Mr. Munroe was evaluated for a total of 15 hours over a period of 3 days. Prior to beginning each meeting, this examiner administered a modified version of the Mini-Mental Status Exam (MMSE). The modifications made were in response to the respondent's inability to read and write, as well as the lack of fit between some of the orientation questions and the current living arrangements of Mr. Munroe. Because of these modifications, the MMSE was not scored, and interpretations were based on qualitative review of the responses and observations made by this examiner.

Mr. Munroe's responses to all administrations of the modified MMSE were similar. He was oriented to time, place, and person, and he demonstrated adequate attention and concentration as measured by the tasks required of this screening instrument. During the process of evaluation, the respondent was alert, adequately groomed, and exhibited interest and motivation in completing the tasks required of him. His speech was judged to be simple with respect to word choice and content, and his comprehension was judged to be limited. These limitations were first identified on the modified MMSE and became more obvious when asked to complete tasks of increasing complexity such as those on the Stanford-Binet, 5th edition (SB5) and the Woodcock-Johnson Tests of Achievement (WJ-III). Despite the observed limitations in communication and comprehension, Mr. Munroe provided this examiner with information about his life history and appeared to complete the assessment measures to the best of his ability. Mr. Munroe was always polite and courteous, and his demeanor was judged to be positive.

Throughout the interviews, Mr. Munroe demonstrated marked inability to maintain a cohesive train of thought. After being asked a question, the respondent would typically begin to answer the question posed, but would soon talk about topics or events that were either completely unrelated or related, but only tangentially. As previously mentioned, information from third-party sources (i.e., Dr. Carillo, Dr. Raynor, and Mr. Brooks) indicates that this style of communicating has been long-standing. This examiner periodically redirected Mr. Munroe to answer the specific question posed, but at times allowed him to speak freely in order to obtain a more complete picture of his ability to communicate. An example of one of the many examples of tangential speech is provided below:

> Examiner: Tell me about the trouble that you mentioned.
> Steven: Oh, the girl . . .

NOTE: *The question posed referred to the trouble that was not at all related to this topic.*

> Steven: well . . . there was more trouble.
> Examiner: Tell me about that.
> Steven: See . . . she was pregnant and . . . her dad had been in trouble and he told me about this lawyer . . . [he spoke too quickly on this tangent—all words were not recorded]—and I got on a bus. I always said it was a straight shot to Bloomington.
> Examiner: *[He was asked to clarify what he was talking about.]*
> Steven: I'm looking for the lawyer . . . and where we lived at, the bus took you right there. I remember I went up there and I remember getting into some more trouble and when I was there I went in the wrong bathroom . . . because I can't read . . . I needed to go to the bathroom. . . I don't remember any women, but then they came in. I got in a little trouble for that because I couldn't read . . . you know on account that I can't read. . . Oh ya, that other girl said something about me hanging out in bathrooms. I don't hang out in no bathrooms. I had to use the bathroom. I don't think she understood.

In addition to these problems with communication, Mr. Munroe at times demonstrated an apparent inability to understand the viewpoints of other people. For example, during the interview with Mr. Munroe he volunteered that he had a history of having sexual relations with animals (notably cows and horses with attempted sexual relations with sheep and dogs). During this conversation, he did not appear to be self-conscious or embarrassed and stated directly that he sees nothing wrong with the behavior because animals were his best friends. Furthermore, Mr. Munroe reported to have done little to hide this behavior and, on at least one occasion, had attempted intercourse with an animal in the middle of an open field. There were other examples of lack of insight during the evaluation, including his sudden raising of his shirt to show this examiner scars from gunshot wounds and the lack of embarrassment when discussing the previously mentioned incident in which he found himself covered in his own excrement and having to be cleaned by persons employed by the Indiana Department of Corrections.

Results of Psychological Tests/Procedures[9]

1. Stanford-Binet Intelligence Scale–5th Edition (SB-5)

The following descriptive information was obtained from the SB5 Technical Manual (Roid, 2003). The Stanford-Binet 5 is an individually administered measure for the assessment of intelligence and cognitive abilities. "The Full Scale IQ is derived from the administration of 10 subtests and is considered the standard measure of global intellectual ability" (Roid, 2003, p. 2). This edition of the Stanford-Binet includes extensive high-end items designed to measure the highest level of gifted performance. It also includes improved low-end items for better measurement of young children, low-functioning older adults, or adults with mental retardation. The measure was normed on a representative U.S. sample of 4,800 individual, ages 2–85+ (based on the U.S. Census Bureau, 2001). In one test of predictive validity, the SB5 was correlated the Woodcock-Johnson Tests of Achievement (WJIII–also used in this evaluation) and the all of the correlations between SB5 factor scores and IQ scores and the WJIII were found to be in the average range consistent with the overall expectation of .60 found by Sattler (1988).

The results of Mr. Munroe's evaluation with the SB5 are presented in Table 10.2. Of note, testing resulted in a Full Scale IQ = 57, a Nonverbal IQ = 63, and a Verbal IQ = 56. These scores were not significantly different from each other.

---

[9]. All raw test scores have been changed, but the resulting interpretation of the data remains the same.

Table 10.2 SB5 Results

	Sum of Scaled Scores	Standard Score	Percentile	95% Confidence Interval–Score Range	95% Confidence Interval–Percentile
IQ Scores					
Full Scale	35	**57**	0.3	54–62	<0.1–1
Nonverbal IQ	24	**63**	1	56–71	0.3–3
Verbal IQ	15	**56**	0.3	52–65	<0.1–1
Factor Index Scores					
Fluid Reasoning	1	48	<0.1	45–58	<0.1–1
Knowledge	2	55	<0.1	46–66	<0.1–1
Quantitative Reasoning	13	80	9	74–89	2–23
Visual Spatial	16	84	14	75–93	4–29
Working Memory	4	55	0.5	50–67	<0.1–1

Note. All standard scores have been changed; the original values fall in the same descriptive category of mild mental retardation.

Table 10.3 Subtest Scores

Nonverbal Subtests

	Raw Scores	Scaled Scores	Percentile
Fluid Reasoning	12	1	0.1
Knowledge	14	1	0.6
Quantitative Reasoning	15	7	7
Visual Spatial	19	8	14
Working Memory	10	2	1

Verbal Subtests

	Raw Scores	Scaled Scores	Percentile
Fluid Reasoning	8	1	0.2
Knowledge	11	2	0.1
Quantitative Reasoning	12	5	8
Visual Spatial	18	6	15
Working Memory	10	1	0.1

2. Woodcock-Johnson Tests of Achievement–3rd Edition (WJ-III)

The following information was obtained from the Examiner's Manual for the Woodcock-Johnson III (WJIII, 2001). The WJIII is a comprehensive set of norm-referenced tests for the measurement of academic achievement. Normative data are based on a national sample of 8,000 individuals ranging in age from 2 to over 90 years. The demographic and community characteristics closely match the general U.S. population. The tests in the Standard Battery combine to form 10 cluster scores, including a Total Achievement score. Cluster interpretation results in higher validity because more than one broad component of a broad ability comprises the score and serves as the best interpretation.

Due to illiteracy, Mr. Munroe was not administered the following subtests: Reading Fluency, Writing Samples, Word Attack, Editing, Reading Vocabulary, Spelling of Sounds, and Punctuation and Capitalization. Mr. Munroe was unable to understand the instructions for the administration of Sound Awareness and as a result, this subtest could not be administered. Additionally, the use of audio equipment at Prescott Correction Facility was not allowed and as such, the tests that required this equipment were administered verbally by this examiner (as per WJIII protocol).

As evident from the results depicted earlier, Mr. Munroe shows broad-based deficits in achievement as measured by the WJIII. All Cluster Scores fell in the 4–4 to 7–9 age range (lowest score obtained on Academic Knowledge). As compared to other Cluster Scores, the respondent demonstrated relative strengths on the following Cluster Scores: Oral Language Expression (EXT.), Oral Expression, and Listening Comprehension (see Table 10.4).

3. Scales of Independent Behavior- Revised (SIB-R)

The following information was obtained from the SIB-R Comprehensive Manual (Bruininks, Woodcock, Weatherman, & Hill, 1996). "The SIB-R is a comprehensive measure of adaptive and problem behaviors. It is primarily a measure of functional independence and adaptive functioning in school, home, employment, and community settings. These functions are evaluated using objective assessment procedures that allow users to compare one individual to others" and has been normed on individuals from early infancy to mature adult levels (80 years and older). "The SIB-R Full Scale is a broad measure of adaptive behavior comprised of 14 subscales organized into four adaptive behavior clusters (Motor, Social Interaction and Communication, Personal Living, and Community Living)." Cluster Score interpretation provides the primary and substantial basis for normative interpretations as it minimizes the

Table 10.4 WJ-III Results

CLUSTER/Test	Age Equivalent	Percentile Rank	Standard Score (68% Band)	Grade Equivalent
Oral Language (Ext.)	6–10	5	76 (76–78)	K.6
Oral Expression	7–1	7	73 (71–74)	1.7
Listening Comp.	6–11	6	77 (76–780)	1.2
Broad Math	7–9	1	62 (60–64)	1.9
Math Calc. Skills	7–5	0.6	57 (55–59)	1.5
Math Reasoning	6–10	3	71 (69–74)	2.3
Academic Skills	5–11	<0.1	42 (40–44)	K.9
Academic Knowledge	4–4	.04	58 (56–60)	<K.0
Form A–Tests	Age Equivalent	Percentile Rank	Standard Score (68% band)	Grade Equivalent
Letter-Word Recognition	5–4	<0.1	43 (40–48)	K.6
Story Recall	7–4	12	84 (74–94)	2.1
Understanding Directions	5–11	13	82 (80–85)	1.7
Calculation	7–8	0.4	58 (55–64)	2.1
Math Fluency	6–7	0.5	63 (59–65)	1.3
Spelling	5–8	<0.1	47 (43–51)	K.4
Passage Comprehension	7–2	2	67 (64–70)	1.7
Applied Problems	7–8	4	74 (71–76)	2.3
Story Recall– Delayed	7–3	17	85 (76–99)	2.3
Picture Vocabulary	6–11	4	74 (72–76)	K.2
Oral Comprehension	6–10	7	77 (75–82)	K.2
Quantitative Concepts	6–7	2	69 (67–73)	1.8
Academic Knowledge	4–5	1	61 (59–63)	<K.0

danger inherent in "generalizing from a single narrow measure of behavior to a broad, multifaceted ability."

The SIB-R is intended for administration to informants who know the person of interest well (preferably a parent or caretaker). While there is no requirement regarding recency of contact between the person of interest and the rater for the SIB-R, it is safe to assume that information obtained from individuals who have been in recent contact with the person of interest would produce more valid results. Furthermore, the SIB-R is used to assess an individual's current level of functioning, rather than that of the past. Test-retest reliabilities have been documented for a maximum of 4 weeks.

Due to his prolonged incarceration, there is no way to assess Mr. Munroe's current adaptive behavior in a community setting. Moreover, in order to assess his functioning prior to the age of 18 years, measures of adaptive behavior require retrospective administration. That is, administration of the interview for time periods in the distant past. As such, the SIB-R was administered to two of Mr. Munroe's family members, his brothers Jeffery and Grant Munroe, each of whom completed the measure for a different time period (17 years and 13 years, respectively). The goal was to obtain quantitative information related to their memories of Mr. Munroe when they were last in contact with him for any substantial period of time.

A word of caution is required regarding this unorthodox administration of the SIB-R. As already stated, the scores obtained from the measure are being used as a means to objectively evaluate the rater's memory for specific abilities related to overall adaptive functioning. The examiner is well aware of the problems related to memory of life events and the absence of studies determining the validity of this type of administration. As such, the scores obtained from the following two SIB-R protocols are *not* intended to reflect true scores.

The results of the retrospective SIB-R administrations suggest that Mr. Munroe demonstrated deficits in adaptive behavior at the ages of 13 and 17 years (see Tables 10.5A and 10.5B). Both brothers reported deficits that were present across multiple areas with particular impairments noted in Motor Skills and Social and Community Interactions. Review of the protocols indicates that, with age, Mr. Munroe's adaptive functioning improved in the majority of domains. At the age of 17 years, his highest score was observed in be in the area of Personal Living and the lowest Motor Skills.

Conclusions

In the opinion of the examiner, Mr. Munroe meets criteria for intellectual disability as delineated in the *DSM-IV- TR* (2000) and the AAIDD (2010). Record review demonstrates that he was identified to have subaverage intellectual functioning (less than or equal to 70+/−5) with concomitant deficits in adaptive behavior before the age of 18 years. In addition, there are no data to indicate that Mr. Munroe has not moved beyond this designation, as some individuals previously identified as having intellectual disability do (AAIDD, 2010).

With regard to measured intelligence, Mr. Munroe's record is replete with data to support the notion that Mr. Munroe's IQ has always fallen in the descriptive category of mild intellectual disability as delineated by the *DSM-IV-TR* (2000). This designation is also true for the current evaluation, which found Mr. Munroe's Nonverbal IQ to be 63, his Verbal IQ to be 56, and his Full Scale IQ to be 57 (SB5), and it is true when taking into consideration the widely accepted standard error of measurement (70+/− 5). In addition, with

Table 10.5A SIB-R Completed by Mr. Grant Munroe with reference to his memory of Steven Munroe's abilities at the age of 13 years

CLUSTER/Subscale	Age Equivalent	Percentile Rank	Standard Score	Relative Mastery Index	Skill with Age-Level Tasks
BROAD INDEPENDENCE	6–9	0.1	53 (51–57)	46/90	Limited
MOTOR SKILLS	7–5	.1	63 (58–72)	45/90	Limited
Gross-Motor	8–6				Limited
Fine-Motor	5–2				Limited to very limited
SOCIAL/COMM	4–9	0.3	48 (44–54)	22/90	Limited to very limited
Social Inter.	6–8				Limited
Language Comp.	5–10				Limited to very limited
Language Expr.	5–4				Very limited
PERSONAL LIVING	11–3	24	92 (87–97)	85/90	Age appropriate
Eating	11–1				Limited to age appropriate
Toileting	11–11				Age appropriate
Dressing	9–9				Limited
Self-Care	10–5				Limited to age appropriate
Domestic Skills	14–3				Age appropriate
COMMUNITY LIVING	7–9	0.4	53 (50–57)	38/90	Limited
Time & Punc.	5–6				Very limited
Money & Value	6–4				Limited
Work Skills	8–1				Limited
Home-Community	12–3				Age appropriate

the exception of Mr. Munroe's score on the Visual-Spatial Index (low average range), all of his index scores placed him in the SB5 descriptive category of delayed (borderline, mild or moderate). There were no significant differences noted between his nonverbal IQ and his verbal IQ and, as such, the FIQ of 57 best represents his cognitive ability at this time. In the opinion of this examiner, the respondent's low scores on the aforementioned subtests are not unexpected because his incarceration has likely impacted his ability to learn new information. In addition, both fluid reasoning and working memory have consistently been found to decline with age (even when controlled for level

Table 10.5B SIB-R Completed by Mr. Jeffery Munroe with reference to his memory of Steven Munroe's abilities at the age of 17 years

CLUSTER/Subscale	Age Equivalent	Percentile Rank	Standard Score	Relative Mastery Index	Skill with Age-Level Tasks
BROAD INDEPENDENCE	9–7	0.3	53 (50–56)	45/90	Limited
MOTOR SKILLS	5–11	0.3	34 (30–42)	16/90	Very limited
Gross-Motor	5–4				Limited to very limited
Fine-Motor	5–2				Very limited
SOCIAL/COMM	8–4	0.7	59 (55–65)	36/90	Limited
Social Inter.	7–6				Limited to very limited
Language Comp.	6–10				Limited to very limited
Language Expr.	11–5				Limited
PERSONAL LIVING	13–10	18	84 (80–90)	79/90	Limited to age appropriate
Eating	13–0				Limited
Toileting	58[80]				Age appropriate to advanced
Dressing	11–11				Limited
Self-Care	14–10				Limited to age appropriate
Domestic Skills	120				Age appropriate
COMMUNITY LIVING	10–8	1	65 (60–70)	49/90	Limited
Time & Punc.	7–8				Limited to very limited
Money & Value	8–9				Limited
Work Skills	10–6				Limited
Home-Community	17–11				Age appropriate

of education; see Kaufman & Lichtenberger, 2002 and Kaufman, 1990 for specific studies conducted over the past 30 years).

As previously mentioned, the results of the WJIII suggest broad-based deficits in cognitive ability. In light of Mr. Munroe's limited educational background and his history of repeated and extended incarceration, it would be expected for scores on the WJIII to be lower than those which may have been obtained in his childhood and adolescent years. However, the scores obtained during this administration are consistent with school documents that clearly identified him as a person who required placement in special education classes, who had low IQ scores (often identified as having mental retardation), and who demonstrated a general inability to learn in the classroom. Review of the Cluster Scores shows extreme deficits in both Academic Skills and Academic Knowledge; these scores are considered to be accurate with respect to his current abilities and are likely to have been negatively impacted by the effects of his prolonged incarceration. In addition, these results are consistent with the current administration of the SB5, which indicates that his cognitive ability is quite limited.

The diagnosis of mental retardation requires evidence of deficits in adaptive functioning prior to the age of 18 years in relation to their age group, sociocultural background, and community setting. Record review, evaluation of Mr. Munroe, and information provided from collateral sources provide information to support the presence of these deficits in adaptive functioning prior to the age of 18 years. Specifically, he demonstrated deficits in the areas of communication, social-interpersonal skills, use of community resources, home living, self-direction, functional academic skills, work, and safety.

As was discussed in the body of the report, the respondent currently functions relatively well within the institutional setting, with observed deficits related to communication, functional academic skills, and social/interpersonal skills. Mr. Munroe has demonstrated the ability to adjust and work within the system and does so by enlisting the help of others (e.g., he has learned to manage his visiting log and phone log). Two of the three correctional officers interviewed stated that Mr. Munroe does not function similarly to other inmates and noted that his problems likely stem from lower intellectual ability. Sgt. Carmichael's description of the respondent as a man of "limited mental capability" seems to capture the essence of the correctional staff interviewed. As noted by Mr. Henderson, functioning on death row does not require much skill or effort, and in his opinion, a person with cognitive deficits would be able to meet the minimal demands.

Information provided by third-party sources (i.e., record review and interviews with individuals who have interacted with Mr. Munroe prior to his current incarceration) supports the presence of adaptive behavior deficits prior to and after the age of 18 years. This finding is true in the areas of communication (e.g., poor comprehension; tangential speech), social skills (e.g., poor peer relations; bestiality), community use (e.g., unable to live independently; only a basic understanding of money concepts), functional academics (e.g., repeated first and second grades; earned almost all F's in the third grade; special education), and work (e.g., unskilled labor; unable to meet the demands of some very simple tasks). The reader is referred back to the body of the report for more examples of such deficits.

In closing, based on all available information, it is the opinion of this examiner that Mr. Munroe currently meets the diagnostic criteria for mild intellectual disability, and did so prior to the age of 18 years. It is my further opinion that the record revealed substantial information regarding the possibility that Mr. Munroe has suffered organic impairment. While the finding of organic impairment would not change the opinion of this examiner, the findings would have provided more information from which to render an opinion.

Respectfully Submitted,
Karen L. Salekin, Ph.D.

Appendix A

Memorandum: From: Robert Golden
To: Denny Martin
Date: ****
Re: Interview with Munroe Family

Memorandum: From Carole Hanson
To: Robert Hall
Date: ****
Re: Meeting the Munroe Family

Notes taken by Mr. Robert Hall during interviews with the following people:
Peter Hammond (03-10-**)
Tonya Gray, Chandra Bell, and Grant Munroe (group meeting; 03-10-**)
Jeffery Munroe (03-10-**)

Forensic Evaluation Report completed by William Davis (*date*)

Index of Documents Produced by Petitioner to William Davis (*date*) as provided to this examiner:

- Exhibit 1 Birth Certificate
- Exhibit 2 Photographs of Petitioner and Family
- Exhibit 3 School Records
- Exhibit 4 Department of Social Services Records
- Exhibit 5 Juvenile Court Records
- Exhibit 6 IQ test results from 1958 and 1963
- Exhibit 7 Deardon State Hospital Records (Jasper, Missouri)
- Exhibit 8 Peterson Memorial Hospital Records
- Exhibit 9 Jasper Kline Hospital Records
- Exhibit 10 Department of Corrections Records
- Exhibit 11 Wanted Poster of Petitioner
- Exhibit 12 Harrison Secure Medical Facility Records
- Exhibit 13 Trial Record and Trial Transcript
- Exhibit 14 Judgment of the Court Sentencing the Petitioner to Death
- Exhibit 15 State Post-Conviction Clerk's Record and Evidentiary Hearing Transcripts
- Exhibit 16 Deposition of Steven Munroe–January 18, 2001
- Exhibit 17 Deposition of Steven Munroe–April 19, 2001
- Exhibit 18 Deposition of Lance Carillo, M.D.

- Exhibit 19 Deposition of R. Frank Raynor, Ph.D.
- Exhibit 20 Affidavit of Hank M. Cowden, Ed.D.
- Exhibit 21 Petition for Writ of Certatori to the Alabama Court of Criminal Appeals
- Exhibit 22 Petition for Writ of Certatori to the Alabama Supreme Court
- Exhibit 23 Petition for Writ of Habeas Corpus by a Prisoner in State Custody Under the Sentence of Death
- Exhibit 24 Petitioner's Motion for Withdrawal of the Magistrate's Report And Recommendation Denying Habeas Corpus Relief in a Death Penalty Case
- Exhibit 25 Petitioner's Objections to the Magistrate's Report and And Recommendation Denying Habeas Corpus Relief in a Death Penalty Case
- Exhibit 26 Petition for Writ of Certiorari to the Eleventh Circuit Court U.S. Court of Appeals
- Exhibit 27 Successive Petition for Writ of Habeas Corpus
- Exhibit 28 Answer of the Respondent
- Exhibit 29 Petitioner's Reply to the Respondent's Answer
- Exhibit 30 Identity of Individuals Knowledgeable of Petitioner's Mental Retardation

Appendix B

Table 1

Adm #	Name of Test	Age (Date of Admin.)	Verbal Intelligence Quotient	Performance Intelligence Quotient	Full Scale Intelligence Quotient	Full Scale Descriptive Classification	Opinion regarding Mental Retardation
1	WISC*	9 years 09-09-58	62	44	49	Mental Defective	None noted
2	WISC*	9 years 09-29-58	75	44	56	Mental Defective	None noted. Interpreted VIQ as most valid
3	WISC*	14 years 9-11-63	57	58	54	Mental Defective	None noted
4	WAIS	19 years March 1969	**	**	66	Mental Defective	Mild Mental Retardation
5	Presumed to be the WAIS	20 years 11-06-69	**	**	73	Borderline Mental Retardation	Unknown
6	WAIS	28 years January 1978	64	81	69	Mild Mental Retardation	Unknown
7	WAIS	29 years March 16, 1979 (Kindle Correctional Facility)	69	80	72	Borderline Mental Retardation	Rule out learning disability and organic brain injury
8	WAIS-R*	37 years January 1987	69	75	71	Borderline Mental Retardation	Not available
9	Presumed to be WAIS-R	41 years April 1991	74	61	65	Mild Mental Retardation	Mild Mental Retardation

*Full battery was not administered—IQ scores based on prorating procedure.
**IQ scores could not be located.
WISC, Wechsler Intelligence Scale for Children; WAIS, Wechsler Adult Intelligence Scale; WAIS-R, Wechsler Adult Intelligence Scale–Revised.

Table 2

Admin. No.	Name of Test	Year Normed	Age (Date of Administration)	Increase in IQ in Relation to the Flynn Effect	Full Scale Intelligence Quotient	Adjusted Full Scale Intelligence Quotient	Full Scale Descriptive Classification
1	WISC*	Normed 1949	1959	3.0	51	48.0	Mental Defective
2	WISC*	Normed 1949	1960	3.3	54	50.7	Mental Defective**
3	WISC*	Normed 1949	1964	4.5	56	51.5	Mental Defective
4	WAIS	Normed 1955	1970	4.5	64	59.5	Mental Defective
5	?? Presumed to be the WAIS	Normed 1955	1971	4.8	74	69.2	Mild Mental Retardation
6	WAIS	Normed 1955	1979	7.2	67	59.8	Mild Mental Retardation
7	WAIS	Normed 1955	1980	7.5.	73	65.5	Mild Mental Retardation
8	WAIS-R*	Normed 1981	1987	1.8	70	68.2	Mild Mental Retardation
9	Presumed to be WAIS-R	Normed 1981	1992	3.3	66	62.7	Mild Mental Retardation

Note. Flynn adjustment was based on publication date rather than the initiation of the norming cycle of the test. This method provides the most conservative approach to the adjustment. Dr. Flynn advocates adjusting from the time of initiation of the norming cycle, which is typically 2 years prior to publication.
*Full battery was not administered; IQ scores based on prorating procedure.
**Psychologist interpreted the VIQ rather than FIQ as being representative of his abilities at the time of testing. VIQ is susceptible to the Flynn effect, but the magnitude of effect has not been as well studied as that of the FIQ. Even without adjustment, a VIQ of 75 falls within the acceptable range for mild mental retardation.
WISC, Wechsler Intelligence Scale for Children; WAIS, Wechsler Adult Intelligence Scale; CFIT, Culture Fair Intelligence Test; WAIS-R, Wechsler Adult Intelligence Scale–Revised.

Report 3: Capital Mitigation Evaluation

Contributor Introduction (Kirk Heilbrun, Ph.D.): The evaluation of capital sentencing offers the broadest focus of any form of FMHA. The mitigators set forth in state statute typically provide a structure that requires the evaluator to address several questions. (Aggravating factors, because they are almost always fact based, do not require expert opinion and hence are typically not incorporated into capital sentencing evaluations.) Consider the following mitigating factors in Pennsylvania:

1. The defendant has no significant history of prior criminal convictions.
2. The defendant was under the influence of extreme mental or emotional disturbance.
3. The capacity of the defendant to appreciate the criminality of his conduct or to conform his conduct to the requirements of the law was substantially impaired.
4. The age of the defendant at the time of the crime.
5. The defendant acted under extreme duress as to constitute a defense to prosecution . . . or acted under the substantial domination of another person.
6. The victim was a participant in the defendant's homicidal conduct or consented to the homicidal acts.
7. The defendant's participation in the homicidal act was relatively minor.
8. Any other evidence of mitigation concerning the character and record of the defendant and the circumstances of his offense.

Factors 2, 3, and 5 clearly require expert mental health opinion. In addition, they each refer to some aspect of the defendant's mental state at the time of the offense—so the evaluator must conduct a reconstructive evaluation to address them properly. Factor 4 has been the subject of a good deal of empirical research during the last 15 years; as the field learns more about the relationship between human development and offending, it has become even more important to consider the possibility that developmental immaturity affected the defendant's conduct in a capital homicide.

Finally, Factor 8 makes it clear that there is little about the defendant's life that need be excluded from this evaluation—assuming that the evaluator can describe some potential relationship between other influences seen in the history and functioning of the defendant and the offense with which the defendant is charged. What Factor 8 encourages is the provision of a detailed, multisourced, accurate account of the defendant's life. Juries making a decision as important as imposing a death sentence deserve no less.

Forensic Evaluation
September 20, 2009

Re: Karl LaHaney
PP#: 123456

Referral Information

Karl LaHaney is a 21-year-old African American male (D.O.B.: 9-18-88) who is charged with three counts of Murder. Mr. LaHaney's attorney (Carl Stanton, Esq.) requested a mental health evaluation to provide the defense with information, pursuant to 42 Pa. C.S.A. § 9711(e), relevant to capital sentencing.

Procedures

Mr. LaHaney was evaluated for a total of approximately 6 hours on June 15, 2009, at the Pittsburgh Correction Center (PCC). In addition to a clinical interview, Mr. LaHaney was administered a standard screening instrument for symptoms of mental and emotional disorder experienced both currently and at the time of the offense (Brief Symptom Inventory or BSI), a standard objective measure of risks and needs information relevant to offender treatment planning and assigning levels of freedom and supervision (Level of Service/Case Management Inventory, or LS/CMI), a standard test of current functioning in relevant academic areas (the Wide Range Achievement Test, 4th Edition, or WRAT-4), a measure of overall intellectual functioning (the Wechsler Adult Intelligence Scale–3rd Edition, or WAIS-III), and a standard measure of adult psychopathology and personality functioning (the Minnesota Multiphasic Personality Inventory, 2nd Edition, or MMPI-2).

Attempts were made to conduct collateral interviews with Mr. LaHaney's mother, Dorothy LaHaney, and his cousin, Christine LaHaney. The phone number Mr. LaHaney provided for Dorothy LaHaney was no longer in service. The phone number Mr. LaHaney provided for Christine LaHaney was a wrong number.

The following documents, obtained from Mr. Stanton's office, were reviewed as part of the evaluation:

1. Pittsburgh Police Department Activity Sheets (dated 9-11-08 to 11-30-08)
2. Witness statement of Dominique Howard (dated 9-12-08)
3. Witness statement of (witness 1) (dated 9-12-08)
4. Witness statement of (witness 2) (dated 9-12-08)

5. Witness statement of (witness 3) (dated 9-12-08)
6. Witness statement of (witness 4) (dated 9-12-08)
7. Witness statement of (witness 5) (dated 9-12-08)
8. Witness statement of (witness 6) (dated 9-12-08)
9. Witness statement of (witness 7) (dated 9-12-08)
10. Witness statement of (witness 8) (dated 11-25-08)
11. Witness statement of (witness 9) (dated 9-12-08)
12. Witness statement of (witness 10) (dated 9-12-08)
13. Witness statement of (witness 11) (dated 9-12-08)
14. Witness statement of (witness 12) (dated 9-12-08)
15. Witness statement of (witness 13) (dated 9-12-08)
16. Witness statement of (witness 14) (dated 9-12-08)
17. Witness statement of (witness 16) (dated 9-12-08)
18. Witness statement of (witness 17) (dated 9-12-08)
19. Pittsburgh Police Department Neighborhood Survey (dated 9-15-08)
20. Pittsburgh Police Department Ballistics Reports (dated 9-26-08 and 12-11-08)
21. Pittsburgh Police Department Incident Report (dated 11-25-08)
22. Witness statement of Karl LaHaney (dated 11-30-08)
23. Witness statement of (witness 18) (dated 3-23-09)
24. First Judicial District Court Summary for Karl LaHaney (dated 6-1-09)

Prior to the evaluation, Mr. LaHaney was notified about its purpose and the associated limits of confidentiality. He appeared to understand the purpose, reporting back his understanding that he would be evaluated and that a written report would be submitted to his attorney. He further understood that the report could be used in the sentencing hearing and, if it were, copies would be provided to the prosecution and the court.

Relevant History

Historical information was obtained from the collateral sources described earlier as well as from Mr. LaHaney himself. Whenever possible, we have assessed the consistency of self-reported information with that obtained from collateral sources. If additional information is obtained prior to Mr. LaHaney's hearing, a supplemental report will be filed.

Family History

Mr. LaHaney was born in Pittsburgh, PA. He reported that his parents were "not together" and he lived with his mother throughout his childhood. Mr. LaHaney reported that the family moved approximately 15 or 16 times during his childhood because his mother "wanted to move back and forth, back and forth." He stated that he did not see his biological father until he was 16 years old. At that time, he said, he began to see his father approximately once a week. Mr. LaHaney reported that his mother did not have a partner during his childhood. He stated that he has two half-brothers on his mother's side who are 13 and 19 years old, and one half-sister on his father's side who is 13 years old. He reported that his brothers live with him and his mother, and that he visits his sister approximately once every 2 weeks. When asked about his relationship with his siblings, Mr. LaHaney replied that they all get along "good." When asked about his relationship with his mother, he replied "it's cool . . . she visited me in jail." He stated that he can turn to his mother for help and that they do not argue because "we (are) like brother and sister, best friends and all that."

When asked about family strengths, Mr. LaHaney replied "nothing." Family challenges, he said, involved the family "always arguing, fighting . . . (it's) why we never went to family outings and stuff like that." He reported that his mother would fight with his youngest brother's father. He stated that on at least one occasion his brother's father hit his mother. Mr. LaHaney reported that his mother also fought with his aunt concerning where his grandmother should live. Mr. LaHaney denied the presence of physical or sexual abuse of himself or his siblings.

Mr. LaHaney stated that he has a 3-month-old daughter. He reported that he has not yet seen his daughter because she was born while he was incarcerated. He stated that he is still in a relationship with his daughter's mother, adding that he has been involved with his daughter's mother since June 2008 and that they got along "good." He added, however, that "the only reason I'm still with her is because she's got my daughter." Mr. LaHaney reported that he has a second girlfriend, whom he has been dating since they were both approximately 13 years old.

Educational History

Mr. LaHaney reported that he attended four or five elementary schools. He stated that he changed schools because he was expelled for fighting and because his family moved. He reported that his attendance was regular with the exception of days he missed for suspensions. Mr. LaHaney reported that he fought "a lot" in elementary school and was suspended and expelled for fighting. He stated that he fought because "I got a short temper and people talk . . . (if they were) getting smart, talking back, disrespecting my mom (I would fight)." He reported that he received Bs, Cs, and occasional As. He stated that he did not repeat any grades, was not enrolled in special education classes, and did not have an Individualized Education Plan (IEP). Mr. LaHaney reported that he attended two middle schools because he was expelled from one school for fighting. He stated that his attendance was regular during middle school. He reported that he was involved in approximately 10 fights in middle school and that he received suspensions for fighting. Mr. LaHaney said that his grades in middle school were mostly Ds and Fs. He stated that he did not repeat any grades, was not enrolled in special education classes, and did not have an IEP during this time. Mr. LaHaney indicated that attended one high school, but he left as a result of being incarcerated for 2 years. He reported that he completed his schooling in Community Education Partners (CEP). He stated that he was "sent away and graduated (high school while) in placement." Mr. LaHaney reported that his attendance was good because he "liked CEP . . . I had to go." He reported that he fought "a lot . . . but knew the teachers, so there weren't no suspensions." He stated that he received Bs and Cs.

Employment History

Mr. LaHaney reported that he has no formal job history. He reported that he completed high school in January 2007 and has not been employed since then. He stated that he is interested in working with computers as a possible career.

Medical and Psychiatric History

Mr. LaHaney described limited medical and psychiatric histories. He did not report a history of injuries or illnesses, nor did he indicate that he received treatment (medication or therapy/counseling) for mental or emotional disorders. When asked whether any family members have a history of mental illness, he replied that he was not aware of any.

Substance Abuse History

Mr. LaHaney reported that he has used alcohol, marijuana, and prescription drugs that were not prescribed for him. He stated that he has used Promethazine (an antihistamine used to prevent allergy symptoms and motion sickness, which also has sedative effects), codeine (a narcotic used for pain relief and cough suppression, sometimes combined with Promethazine to treat cold or allergy symptoms), Xanax (a drug used to treat anxiety symptoms), Percocet (also called oxycodone, a narcotic drug used to treat pain), and Seroquel (an antipsychotic). When asked how often he used such drugs, Mr. LaHaney replied, "every day." He reported that he smoked marijuana "a little bit." He stated that his drug use impaired his school performance because he would "sleep the whole day away" in school. He reported that his family has not complained about his drug use, but he stated, "Even if they did (complain), I wouldn't listen."

Social History

Mr. LaHaney reported that he enjoys working with computers, playing video games, listening to music, and playing sports. He stated that he played basketball and football in his neighborhood and played baseball while in placement. He stated that he also enjoys watching hockey "because they fight." Mr. LaHaney reported that he spends his spare time smoking marijuana, going to movies, and working on laptops. He stated that many of his friends are involved in criminal activities. He reported that he has a friend "doing double life for murder" and other friends who sell drugs.

Offense and Incarceration History

Mr. LaHaney reported a history of criminal involvement beginning in 2004. He stated that he was first arrested when he was 15 years old, when he was charged with assault. He reported that he pled guilty and was given probation that he did not complete because he was arrested again for assault a second time in 2004. Mr. LaHaney said that he was arrested once more in 2004 for possession of crack cocaine with intent to deliver. He stated that he was sent to boot camp for 6 months and completed the program. Mr. LaHaney reported that his first adult arrest occurred in 2007, for drug possession and possession of an instrument of crime (a gun). Mr. LaHaney reported that he was arrested and charged with murder in 2008 for the murder of Cam Edwards. He stated that his present charge for the murders of Darnell Smith and Mark Lawson also occurred in 2008.

Current Clinical Condition

Mr. LaHaney is a 21-year-old African American male of short height who appeared his stated age. He displayed a medium build, good posture, and normal eye contact. He wore institutional garb, and was adequately groomed. Mr. LaHaney reported that he has no scars and does not have his ears pierced. He stated that he has a tattoo of the letter "K" for Karl on his right hand and the letter "L" for LaHaney on his left hand. He stated that he has a third tattoo on his right forearm that reads "RIP Peaches 29." He reported that "Peaches" refers to his grandmother who passed away in 2005, and that "29" refers to 29th Street, where his grandmother lived. Mr. LaHaney reported that he requires glasses for distance. He denied auditory and motor problems. Mr. LaHaney was cooperative throughout the evaluation. He displayed appropriate affect, and his speech was clear and coherent. His attention and concentration appeared adequate. Therefore, it would appear that this evaluation provides a reasonably good estimate of Mr. LaHaney's current functioning.

Mr. LaHaney's basic academic skills, as measured by the WRAT-4, showed deficits in Word Reading (grade equivalent = 10.8), Sentence Comprehension (grade equivalent = 7.7), Spelling (grade equivalent = 7.7), and Arithmetic Skills (grade equivalent = 5.4). His academic skills in these areas should be considered in need of remediation.

Mr. LaHaney completed a standard test of current intellectual functioning (WAIS-III) as part of the current evaluation. On the WAIS-III, Mr. LaHaney was measured with a Full Scale IQ of 84, placing him in the Low Average range. His score ranks him at the 14th percentile when compared to his peers. Mr. LaHaney also achieved a Verbal IQ score of 86 (Low Average, 18th percentile) and a Performance IQ score of 83 (Low Average, 13th percentile).

Mr. LaHaney appears to meet diagnostic criteria for Attention-Deficit/ Hyperactivity Disorder. According to his self-report, he fails to give close attention to details; has difficulty sustaining attention; does not listen when spoken to directly; does not follow through on instructions; has difficulty organizing tasks; avoids, dislikes, or is reluctant to engage in tasks that require sustained mental effort; loses things necessary for tasks; is easily distracted by extraneous stimuli; and is often forgetful in daily activities. Mr. LaHaney reported that he fidgets or squirms in his seat; has difficulty playing or engaging in leisure activities quietly; is often "on the go;" often talks excessively; blurts out answers before questions are completed; has difficulty awaiting his turn; and interrupts others. Mr. LaHaney stated that impairment from these symptoms has occurred in at least two settings (home and school). He could not recall whether his symptoms were present before he was 7 years old.

Mr. LaHaney also completed two versions of a structured inventory of symptoms of mental and emotional disorders, the Brief Symptom Inventory (BSI). The first concerns his present functioning (discussed here) and the second describes his thoughts and feelings during the period of events for which he is currently charged (discussed in the sentencing section of this evaluation). On the BSI, Mr. LaHaney reported currently being "extremely" distressed on three of the 53 items. He reported that he was extremely distressed by feeling easily annoyed or irritated, feeling that most people cannot be trusted, and having difficulty falling asleep. Mr. LaHaney reported currently being "quite a bit" distressed on seven items: having difficulty remembering things; having a poor appetite; having to check and double-check what he does; feeling hopeless about the future; having difficulty concentrating; having urges to beat, injure, or harm someone; and having urges to break or smash things.

Compared to nonpatient adult males, Mr. LaHaney's scores were significantly elevated (i.e., greater than two standard deviations above the mean) on two of the nine scales (Obsessive-Compulsive and Hostility).

When asked to elaborate on the symptoms he endorsed, Mr. LaHaney's explanations indicated that they are related to his drug use, his temper, and his current legal situation. Mr. LaHaney stated that he is distressed by having difficulty remembering things because "I just forget a lot . . . it's probably (because of) drugs (I used)." He stated that he feels easily annoyed or irritated because "people just get me irritated. . . I get irritated for nothing, just every day." He reported that he is distressed by feeling that most people cannot be trusted because "people can't be trusted . . . one minute they are trying to be your friend, next they're trying to stab you." He stated that he has a poor appetite because "(I) just don't have a feeling to eat food in this joint . . . sometimes (because I) be feeling down, sometimes (the quality of) the food." He reported that he has difficulty falling asleep because "it's been going on for awhile. . . . I'll be up all night thinking." He stated that he began having difficulty sleeping when he was 12 or 13 years old. Mr. LaHaney reported having to check and double-check what he does because "if (I'm) filling something out, sometimes I forget to fill a bubble." He reported feeling hopeless about the future because "it's like I'm never going to get out of jail." He stated that he has trouble concentrating because "(it's) just me not paying attention." He described having urges to beat, injure, or harm someone because of "my temper." Mr. LaHaney reported having urges to break or smash things because "the same thing . . . I get frustrated in this place."

Mr. LaHaney completed the MMPI-2 in approximately 1.5 hours, and he appeared to be distracted during portions of the test. His clinical profile (Welsh Code 382"417'+0-695/F*"L'+-K/) appears to be invalid. Mr. LaHaney's validity profile was significantly elevated on four scales (VRIN T = 88; F T = 92; F_B T = 116; F_P T = 120), indicating he endorsed items in a random fashion, he endorsed items that 10% or fewer normal participants typically endorse, and he endorsed items that 20% or fewer of psychiatric inpatients typically endorse. Therefore, Mr. LaHaney's validity profile suggests that he responded without attention to item content, which could reflect his difficulty in understanding some items or also his problems in paying attention over the 1.5 hour period it took to complete this measure.

On the LS/CMI, Mr. LaHaney scored in the Very High risks/needs category (raw score = 31). Approximately 89.2% of community offenders and 79.6% of prison inmates scored lower than Mr. LaHaney on the LS/CMI. The LS/CMI has eight domains; each domain may reflect a particular problem area for an individual. Mr. LaHaney has deficits in eight areas: Criminal History, Education/Employment, Family/Marital, Leisure/Recreation, Companions, Alcohol/Drug Problem, Procriminal Attitude/Orientation, and Antisocial Pattern. Specifically, Mr. LaHaney's reponses indicated that he has history of criminal activity. He indicated that he had three dispositions as a youth and three open charges as an adult. He stated that he was first arrested before the age of 16 years, had his probation revoked, and has been punished for institutional misconduct. Mr. LaHaney reported that he has never been employed and was often suspended or expelled from school. He reported that having a job is not important to him. He stated that he has two girlfriends, and he is staying in a relationship with one woman solely because she is the mother of his daughter. He reported having frequent arguments, having communication problems, and arguing about money, parents, leisure time, and ex-partners. Mr. LaHaney reported that two of his family members have criminal records. He stated that he does not belong to any organizations and spends his free time smoking marijuana, going to movies, and working on laptops. He reported that he knows many people involved in crime, and he does not know many people who are not involved in crime. Mr. LaHaney reporting using alcohol, marijuana, and multiple prescription drugs for recreational use. He stated that his drug use may have contributed to his law violations and impaired his performance in school. When asked if he would like to lead a life without crime, he replied, "yeah, somewhat . . . the money is fast from that life (but) I would like to live a straight life for my daughter." Mr. LaHaney's responses throughout the LS/CMI indicate early antisocial behavior and an orientation toward offending.

Sentencing Considerations

According to 42 Pa. C.S.A. § 9711(a)(2), any evidence relating to mitigating circumstances can be presented at the sentencing hearing. The following factors, as enumerated in 42 Pa. C.S.A. § 9711(e), can be considered as mitigating factors:

1. The defendant has no significant history of prior criminal convictions.
2. The defendant was under the influence of extreme mental or emotional disturbance.
3. The capacity of the defendant to appreciate the criminality of his conduct or to conform his conduct to the requirements of law was substantially impaired.
4. The age of the defendant at the time of the crime.
5. The defendant acted under extreme duress, although not such duress as to constitute a defense to prosecution . . . or acted under the substantial domination of another person.
6. The victim was a participant in the defendant's homicidal conduct or consented to the homicidal acts.
7. The defendant's participation in the homicidal act was relatively minor.
8. Any other evidence of mitigation concerning the character and record of the defendant and the circumstances of his offense.

The mitigating factors that can be addressed through forensic mental health assessment are factors 2, 3, 5, and 8. Because Mr. LaHaney denied any involvement in the alleged offense, it was not possible to assess the application of factors 2, 3, or 5. Information related to factor 8 is discussed in this section.

When asked about the circumstances surrounding the offense for which he is currently charged, Mr. LaHaney stated "I told them I didn't know Young Boy, never met him. I kept telling them I didn't shoot nobody." Mr. LaHaney stated that he did not know the victims personally, but that "I think he (Young Boy) had (was selling) weed or something like that up around Dexter Street." Mr. LaHaney denied any involvement in the crime.

(8) *Any other evidence of mitigation concerning the character and record of the defendant and the circumstances of his offense.*

Mr. LaHaney has faced some difficulties throughout his life, as his parents did not maintain a relationship and Mr. LaHaney did not see his biological father until he was 16 years old. He stated that his mother raised him and his siblings as a single parent. Mr. LaHaney reported that his family moved approximately 15 to 16 times throughout his childhood. He could not describe a family strength, and he added that his family members often fought and argued. Mr. LaHaney reported that his mother fought with his younger brother's father, and his brother's father once struck Mr. LaHaney's mother. Mr. LaHaney reported that attended multiple schools through his childhood because of expulsions for fighting and his family's frequent moves. Mr. LaHaney reported that he has abused alcohol, marijuana, and prescription drugs, stating that he used drugs "every day." He stated that many of his friends are involved in criminal activity.

Mr. LaHaney also has some strengths, as he has completed high school and expressed interest in being a good father for his daughter. He reported an interest in working with computers as a possible career path. Mr. LaHaney stated that he has a good relationship with his siblings, and that he can turn to his mother for help. He reported that he and his mother do not argue and are close, "like brother and sister."

Conclusions

In the opinion of the undersigned, based on all of the above:

1. Mr. LaHaney's considerations relevant to mitigation include significant substance abuse problems, his problems in his early family life, and his father's absence from the home. He also has positive strengths in his life. He completed high school, expresses interest in working with computers, and a desire to conduct himself so he can remain a part of his daughter's life.

Thank you for the opportunity to evaluate Karl LaHaney.

Kirk Heilbrun, Ph.D.
Consulting Psychologist

Heather Zelle, M.S.
Clinical Psychology Graduate Student

Report 4: Capital Mitigation Evaluation

Contributor Introduction (Daniel Murrie, Ph.D.): Capital mitigation evaluations are distinct from nearly every other form of forensic mental health evaluation. They are unusually broad in scope, yet their focus is exclusively on mitigating information, or information that might prompt a jury to offer a sentence less than death (*Lockett v. Ohio*, 1978). For example, section 19.2-264.3:1 of the Code of Virginia, the statute guiding this sample report, requires the evaluator to prepare a report that includes opinions on the following:

1. Whether the defendant acted under extreme mental or emotional disturbance at the time of the offenses
2. Whether the defendant was significantly impaired with respect to his appreciation of the criminality of his conduct or his capacity to conform his conduct to the requirements of the law
3. Whether there are other factors in mitigation relating to the history or character of the defendant or the defendant's mental condition at the time of the offenses

As detailed in Chapter 7, the broad scope and the mitigation-specific focus create some challenges for forensic mental health professionals who offer written reports of capital mitigation evaluations. Should an evaluator attempt a comprehensive narrative of the defendant's life and capital offense (even if this must include much information that is not mitigating)? Or should the evaluator only offer detailed responses to the mitigation questions listed in statute (even if doing so lacks a coherent narrative or "life story")? Each approach has pros and cons, and there are competent evaluators who prefer each. Some evaluators even select format on a case-by-case basis.

This report sample adopts a narrow, statute-specific format. As in many cases, there was little mitigation to describe regarding the capital offense itself (i.e., items 1 and 2 in the Virginia statute above), but there was much more to describe regarding the broad category "relating to the history or character of the defendant" (i.e., item 3 in the Virginia code). All capital mitigation statutes have a similar "catchall" category (remember *Lockett v. Ohio*, 1978), so evaluators often must prepare lengthy reports that detail a variety of mitigating factors. In this report, it seemed most parsimonious to group these mitigating factors according to "history of the defendant" and "character of the defendant." The former included many themes of abuse, trauma, and instability. The latter included many of the defendant's attempts at stability and attempts to establish healthy relationships, which would not have been evident to jurors considering the capital offense in isolation.

Defense counsel may share the reports from a mitigation evaluation with the court and the prosecution if they chose to introduce testimony from the mental health professional. Testimony often includes many of the data and themes detailed in the report, but it does not necessarily include all of them. Conversely, testimony may also include additional information not detailed in the report (e.g., social science research). In other instances, defense counsel may share mitigation reports with opposing counsel as part of their efforts to pursue a plea agreement and avoid trial. Again, the content and format of mitigation reports vary by state and by evaluator. But all require that evaluators conduct a broad, comprehensive evaluation and present any available data that may be perceived as mitigating.

Commonwealth v. Johnson Doe

Name:	John Doe	Court Order Code:	§ 19.2-264.3:1
Age:	23	Commonwealth's Attorney:	_____
DOB:	February 29, 1987	Defense Attorneys:	_____
Report Date:	July 31, 2010		_____

Referral

This report is submitted in accordance with my appointment under § 19.2-264.3:1 of the Code of Virginia. This code section requires the evaluator to prepare a report regarding the history and character of the defendant and the defendant's mental condition at the time of the alleged offenses. The report is to include opinions as to *(1)* whether the defendant acted under extreme mental or emotional disturbance at the time of the offenses, *(2)* whether the defendant was significantly impaired with respect to his appreciation of the criminality of his conduct or his capacity to conform his conduct to the requirements of the law, and *(3)* whether there are other factors in mitigation relating to the history or character of the defendant or the defendant's mental condition at the time of the offenses.

Sources of Information

This report is based on a broad range of information and evaluation procedures. This broad approach is standard practice in capital sentencing evaluations, because the Code of Virginia requires the evaluator to develop a comprehensive understanding of the defendant's history, character, and mental condition. The present evaluation relied upon the following sources:

Direct and Collateral Interviews:

1. Interviews with the defendant on May 7 and May 10, 2010, and July 3, 2010, totaling 17.5 hours
2. Telephone interview of _____ (Mr. Doe's mother) on June 25, 2010, approximately 1.5 hours in length
3. Collateral interview with Mr. and Mrs. _____ (Mr. Doe's aunt and uncle) on June 20, 2010, approximately 1.5 hours in length
4. Collateral interview with Mr. _____ (Mr. Doe's grandfather), approximately 1 hour in length
5. Collateral interview with Jenny and _____ Girlfriend (Mr. Doe's girlfriend and her mother, respectively) approximately 2 hours in length
6. Second collateral interview with Jenny Girlfriend (Mr. Doe's girlfriend) on May 27, 2010 and June 16, 2010, totaling approximately 4.5 hours
7. Collateral interview with Mary Teacher (Mr. Doe's teacher from Structured High School), on June 9, 2010, 1 hour in length
8. Neuropsychological testing of defendant, by David Colleague, Ph.D., on June 13, 2010, approximately 5 hours in length

Collateral Records Reviewed:

1. Copy of the videotaped police interrogation of the defendant, Mr. Doe
2. Copy of the Order for Appointment of Mental Health Expert, dated May 2, 2010
3. Letter from _____, Esq. from the Office of the Commonwealth's Attorney, dated May 1, 2010
4. Copies of interdisciplinary and psychiatric progress notes from Anytown Regional Jail dated November 16, 2008 through April 21, 2010
5. Request for and copies of records from the Department of Juvenile Justice and the Juvenile and Domestic Relations District Court, including all available petitions, adjudications, and dispositions for Mr. Doe, dated February 1, 1992 through January 8, 2010
6. Copy of the Case Supplemental Report provided by the Anytown Police Department, dated December 13, 2008
7. Transcript of telephone conversation between Mr. Doe and his mother, recorded when Mr. Doe was in Anytown Jail, dated November 14, 2008.
8. Copy of Emergency Department Record of the Virginia State University, dated July 7, 2002

9. Copies of academic, disciplinary, and psychological records from Anytown High School, dated October 27, 1998 through June 6, 2002
10. Copies of Academic, Disciplinary, and Psychological records from Anytown Public Schools dated March 11, 1999 through March 11, 2002
11. Copies of records from Virginia Standards of Learning Assessments dated Spring, 2002
12. Copies of Academic, Behavioral, and Psychological records from New Beginnings Residential Center dated July 2, 1999 through August 11, 2000
13. Copy of Quarterly Summary Report from Family Preservation Services, dated February 14, 2000
14. Copies of records from the Commonwealth of Virginia Department of Social Services, dated February 18, 1999 through July 26, 1999
15. Copies of records from the Education Program at the Anytown Juvenile Detention Home dated March 17, 1999 through June 4, 1999
16. Copies of Academic, Disciplinary, and Psychological records from Anytown Middle School dated November 13, 1998 through May 17, 1999
17. Copies of records from the Anytown Community Mental Health Center, dated October 18, 1993 through January 13, 1999
18. Copies of Virginia Literacy Testing Program results, dated 1997 through 1998
19. Copy of Cognitive Abilities Test Results and Interpretation, dated October 1991
20. Copies of records from the Outpatient Department at Anytown Children's Center of the Virginia State University, dated April 15, 1991 through April 23, 1991

Confidentiality Statement

Before beginning the evaluation, I provided Mr. Doe with clear notice that I would not be acting as a therapist, but rather conducting a forensic evaluation consistent with Virginia statute governing capital sentencing evaluations. Mr. Doe also received clear notice that although this evaluation would be protected by attorney–client privilege, a copy of the report could be released to the Court and to the Commonwealth's attorney if he and his attorneys choose to do so. After opportunities to ask questions, Mr. Doe demonstrated an understanding of the nature of the evaluation and limits to confidentiality. He agreed to proceed with the interview. Over the course of subsequent interviews, I provided Mr. Doe with additional reminders of the purpose of the evaluation and limits to confidentiality. Similarly, when initiating collateral interviews with others who knew Mr. Doe, I described the purpose of the interview and the limits of confidentiality.

Circumstances Surrounding the Offenses

Commonwealth's version: According to a letter dated May 1, 2010, and signed by Assistant Commonwealth's Attorney _____, Mr. Doe and his friend John Codefendant participated in a robbery and homicide. Specifically,

> Doe and codefendant forced their way into the Smith residence, where they ransacked the house, taking valuables. During this process, the victim arrived home. He was startled and began to confront Doe and codefendant. Doe and codefendant held the victim at gunpoint until Doe shot him twice, in the chest, at close range. He and the codefendant left the residence with the victim's wallet and other valuables, and they took the victim's car. The stolen vehicle was hidden on a dirt road behind the codefendant's home.

Defendant's version: The defendant's statements about the time period surrounding the alleged offenses are protected against disclosure unless and until such disclosure is compelled, or until the defendant waives his privilege.

Opinions

i) Whether the defendant acted under extreme mental or emotional disturbance at the time of the offenses.

The available evidence suggests that Mr. Doe was under the influence of marijuana throughout the evening of the alleged offense. Although marijuana may compromise judgment and reasoning, the effects of marijuana intoxication are typically not considered extreme mental or emotional disturbance. Mr. Doe also has a long-standing history of mood disorder symptoms, particularly depression. Although neither of these factors is typically sufficient to grossly distort a person's understanding of reality, they may have had some influence on his mental state around the time of the offense.

ii) Whether the capacity of the defendant to appreciate the criminality of his conduct or to conform his conduct to the requirements of the law were significantly impaired.

There is no information available at this time to indicate that Mr. Doe was unable to appreciate the criminality of his conduct. Regarding his ability to conform his conduct to the requirements of the law, Mr. Doe's marijuana intoxication may have left him with poorer perception, reasoning, and judgment than he would manifest in a sober state. However, marijuana intoxication alone is rarely sufficient to grossly impair one's capacity to appreciate the criminality of an act, or conform one's conduct to the law.

iii) *Whether there are other factors in mitigation relating to the history and character of the defendant or the defendant's mental condition at the time of the offenses.*

Overall, several factors in Mr. Doe's developmental history and personal character are typical of those factors considered mitigating at capital sentencing. In capital sentencing, mitigating factors often reflect adverse experiences and reduced opportunities for healthy emotional development. They also reflect more positive behaviors and decisions that were not evident in the offense for which a defendant was charged. A comprehensive review of Mr. Doe's history revealed many potentially mitigating details regarding his history and character. Key factors are summarized in the following text, beginning with Mr. Doe's chaotic childhood and proceeding through Mr. Doe's efforts to establish a more stable adulthood.

Mitigation Related to *History* of the Defendant

During early development, and before Mr. Doe was capable of exercising individual control over his circumstances, he experienced substantial trauma, abuse, and neglect. These experiences are typical of risk factors that social science research has linked to adverse outcomes in adulthood.

- *Prenatal risk factors*: Mr. Doe was born to Mr. Doe and Ms. Doe, who were aged 17 and 14, respectively, at the time Ms. Doe became pregnant. Collateral interviews and the available records (including a 1991 report from Anytown Children's Center) consistently reported that Ms. Doe abused marijuana during her pregnancy with John Doe, and they speculated that she may have abused other drugs as well. Mr. Doe's exposure to drugs in utero is noteworthy because research has linked such prenatal drug exposure to later intellectual problems, impulsivity, and a vulnerability to substance abuse.
- *Early abuse and neglect:* Mr. Doe lived with his mother, Ms. Doe, until approximately the age of 4 years. He had occasional contact with his biological father during this period as well. However, neither his mother nor father was well equipped to parent. Records consistently describe his father as absent, due to his cocaine addiction and chronic trouble with the legal system; he was incarcerated for most of Mr. Doe's childhood. Most accounts also suggest that when he was present in the home, he was emotionally and physically abusive to his wife and son. His mother emphasized that she was ill equipped to parent Mr. Doe because of her

own history of substantial abuse and neglect. Indeed, her account of her physical abuse by her father suggests that Mr. Doe was born into a multigenerational cycle of physical abuse and neglect.

Consistent with this multigenerational pattern, Mr. Doe described substantial physical abuse during his early years living with his biological mother. Specifically, he explained that his mother beat him with "switches, belts, and extension cords . . . she left marks . . . [he] had to wear pants so nobody could see." For example, Mr. Doe discussed one memory in which his mother beat him after he spilled a pot of hot dogs in boiling water on himself.

Mr. Doe reported that, during early childhood, the family often had insufficient food and therefore went to the nearby home of his maternal aunt. Mr. Doe explained that the relationship with this aunt served a protective function, reducing the impact of neglect and poverty that the children otherwise experienced.

When Mr. Doe was around the age of 5 years, his mother placed him and one sister in the care of their maternal grandparents. Most official records, which often relied on Ms. Doe's self-report, indicated that she made this decision based on her own difficulty caring for the children while she was relatively young and under financial strain. During our interview she explained, "there was no way in the world I could take care of three kids." Collateral interview with another family member shed further light on this transition. Ms. Doe's sister explained that when Mr. Doe was 4 years old and his younger sister was 2 years old, their mother placed both children in a small bedroom and locked it with a padlock. Ms. Doe's sister became aware of this situation and informed her mother. Subsequently, the grandmother went to Ms. Doe's house to release the children from the bedroom. Reportedly, Ms. Doe warned her mother that if she released the children from the room, her mother would "have to raise them herself." According to Ms. Doe's sister, this was the point at which their grandmother accepted responsibility for the Doe children; Mr. Doe and his sister then went to live with their grandmother.

Mr. Doe's early experiences of abuse and neglect are noteworthy because research has demonstrated ways in which abuse and neglect damage the developing brain and increase the likelihood of poor outcomes in adulthood. Amid early abuse and neglect, Mr. Doe had little opportunity for the stable and nurturing caretaking that tend to support healthy development and healthy adult relationships.

- ***Early instability and trauma:*** One aspect of the neglect Mr. Doe experienced while living with his biological parents involved exposure to adult substance abuse and adult sexuality from an early age. For example, Mr. Doe recalled that his mother regularly took him to a neighbor's home in the Providence Drive housing development of Anytown. He reported that the children were "left in the living room, supposed to play video games and be quiet" while "the grownups partied in the kitchen." He recalled that adults drank heavily, consumed illegal drugs, and sometimes fought (he recalled one instance of a fight that resulted in a stabbing). He also recalled a few examples of exposure to adult sexuality during these visits. In the instance that he identified as most disturbing, Mr. Doe overheard his father exchange money with a man, and later—when looking for his mother—walked into a bedroom to find the man having aggressive sexual intercourse with Mr. Doe's mother. Mr. Doe recalled that the man threw an object at him, and threatened him. Once locked out, Mr. Doe reportedly waited outside the room, confused and concerned for his mother's safety. Mr. Doe explained that after reflecting on the incident years later, and speaking to other adults who had been involved in that social circle, he was told that his father had sold opportunities for sexual contact with his mother, in exchange for money to support his drug addiction. Mr. Doe speculated that this incident contributed to the general sense of instability and vulnerability he felt during childhood.

Other early traumatizing experiences involved witnessing domestic violence. Mr. Doe's mother reported that she lived with a romantic partner during Mr. Doe's early childhood years. She described this partner as aggressive and physically abusive. Thus, during periods when Mr. Doe was in the home as a child, he witnessed his mother physically abused by her romantic partner.

- *Poor bonding and early separation from biological parents:* As the instability reviewed earlier suggests, Mr. Doe had little opportunity to form healthy attachments to his biological parents. According to records from Anytown Children's Center—documented when Mr. Doe was around the age of 5 years—he was raised in a "very chaotic family . . . with a single mother who [was] experiencing significant stressors including minimal parenting skills, minimal support from her own parents, and her own personal emotional and psychological issues." These records reported that Ms. Doe had "trouble coping with her children," and difficulty bonding with her son. A psychological evaluation of Mr. Doe at the age of 5 years, conducted at Anytown Children's Center, characterized Mr. Doe as an "emotionally needy boy who (was) experiencing strong unmet nurturance needs, leading to feelings of sadness and anger at a mother who is rarely available or interested in parenting him."

These records also indicated that Ms. Doe failed to recognize that she contributed to her son's difficulties. Records noted,

> John's mother has had some difficulty accepting that the problems John is experiencing may be connected to her, and the ways she disciplines or treats John. She has had to be encouraged to examine her role in his difficulties. But this has proven difficult because Ms. Doe maintains the expectation that John will not change, and she has little motivation to change her own behavior towards him.

To summarize, records suggest that Ms. Doe perceived her son primarily as a stressor and demonstrated little desire to establish an emotional bond with him, even when he was an infant and toddler. Although Mr. Doe's move from his mother's home to his grandmother's home was probably in his best interests, Mr. Doe perceived the move as further evidence that his mother felt no desire to care for him and had essentially abandoned him.

Whereas Mr. Doe described feeling that his mother was disinterested in him, he described even less opportunity for attachment to his biological father. Mr. Doe's father left the home early in Mr. Doe's childhood, reportedly due to cocaine addiction and incarceration. Mr. Doe described a few disappointing encounters with his father during later childhood. For example, around the age of 8 years, he reportedly attempted to leave his grandmother's home (in response to a severe beating from his grandfather) and run to his father's nearby home. He described arriving in his father's disheveled home, which was marked by evidence of substance abuse, and asking to stay. His father reportedly told Mr. Doe he "didn't give a [expletive] and slammed the door in [Mr. Doe's] face." Similarly, Mr. Doe recalled that when he was 14 years old he saw his father at a town fair, but his father did not recognize him. Mr. Doe described this as a disappointing and humiliating encounter. He also recalled an incident a few years later, when his father apparently attempted to contact Mr. Doe, but Mr. Doe again was disappointed when he realized his father was heavily intoxicated and confused.

Overall, Mr. Doe reported little contact—and no nurturing relationship—with his father. Mr. Doe's account appeared consistent with (though perhaps more subdued than) accounts from other family members. During collateral interviews, other family members used words such as "pitiful" to characterize Mr. Doe's approach to his father; they detailed ways in which Mr. Doe often discussed or pursued a relationship with his biological father, who avoided or actively rejected Mr. Doe on the few occasions Mr. Doe did find him.

Mr. Doe's lack of bonding with his biological parents appeared to shape his emotional life even during late adolescence. For example, a report from a school psychologist who counseled Mr. Doe during his high school years summarized,

> John appears to be experiencing a great deal of emotional turmoil and uncertainty with regard to several issues including when, if, and how his father will return to his life, his lack of relationship with his mother, and his own unmet need for support.

- *Ongoing abuse as a child:* As detailed earlier, Mr. Doe began living with his grandparents around the age of 5 years, when his mother asked her own mother to assume responsibility for Mr. Doe. Although most accounts suggest that Mr. Doe's experience living with his grandparents was less difficult than his experience living with his mother and her partners, Mr. Doe's experience with his grandparents was also marked by neglect and substantial abuse.

All collateral sources reported that Mr. Doe's grandfather was an alcoholic who often became violent with the children in the home. Even the grandfather, who has reportedly abstained from alcohol more recently, characterized himself as an aggressive alcoholic during Mr. Doe's childhood. Mr. Doe described incidents in which his grandfather beat him with belts and sticks, sometimes as he crawled under the bed to escape such beatings. Family members, during collateral interviews, described other instances of abusive behaviors, such as when his grandfather threw a beer bottle that struck Mr. Doe in the head. Ms. Doe (mother of the defendant) explained that her father was "real hateful" to Mr. Doe, and in addition to physical abuse, directed other cruel behaviors at Mr. Doe, such as destroying his favorite possessions.

In addition to experiencing abuse from his grandfather, Mr. Doe also observed his grandfather abuse his grandmother, the adult to whom Mr. Doe was closest. All sources I interviewed reported that Mr. Doe was exposed to substantial domestic violence within their home. To take one example, Ms. Doe explained, "My mom went to her grave with no teeth in her mouth because my dad took them out with his fist." In sum, Mr. Doe experienced significant abuse, and he also observed significant abuse against his primary caretaker, when he lived in his grandparent's home.

Simultaneous with the abuse, Mr. Doe also described periods of deprivation in his grandparents' home. For example, Mr. Doe and other family members reported that the children were limited to one bath per week. They reportedly had no toothpaste, resulting in long-term dental problems. They also reportedly had no deodorant or hygiene products, resulting in teasing from peers. Although this type of deprivation was probably preferable to the problems in his early childhood home, several family members suggested the deprivation was substantial, and the lack of basic toiletries led to ostracism from peers.

- *Loss of primary caretaker:* Despite significant abuse in his grandparents' home, Mr. Doe described his grandmother as his primary caretaker. He explained, "In my heart grandma is mom because she's the only mom I know." Regarding his transition from his mother's custody to his grandmother's, he recalled,

> I was happy to finally go to grandma's. She gave me things I never had. . . . I never knew attention. She played with me, loved me . . . she didn't beat me. She didn't do no cussing or no drinking. . .she made me feel safe, for once.

However, his grandmother became terminally ill when Mr. Doe was around 12 years old, at which point it was necessary for him to return to his mother's home. Nevertheless, he maintained contact with his grandmother, visiting her in the hospital. Indeed, school records describing instances of truancy indicate that Mr. Doe left the school building to visit his grandmother in the hospital. His grandmother died in March 2000 when Mr. Doe was 13 years old.

Both Mr. Doe and collateral records suggested that his grandmother's death marked a pivotal event in Mr. Doe's development. According to school records, shortly after his grandmother's death, school staff requested that Mr. Doe receive treatment through Anytown Community Mental Health Center. In April 2000, 1 month after her death, the school determined that Mr. Doe qualified for special education services on the basis of emotional disturbance.

In addition to Mr. Doe himself, objective collateral sources characterized his grandmother's death as a substantial disruption. For example, a quarterly report from Family Preservation Services, dated April 14, 2001, summarized,

> My impression is that John's problems were a result of his grandmother's illness and subsequent death and his life being turned upside down after leaving his grandmother and having to return to live with his own mother, who was openly frustrated by his return and hostile to him.

Mr. Doe experienced another significant loss during late adolescence, when his aunt died, reportedly due to complications related to methamphetamine abuse. Mr. Doe reportedly became close to his aunt when they both resided in his grandparents' home. Indeed, all sources we interviewed reported that Mr. Doe was much closer to his aunt than to his biological mother. Mr. Doe explained that he became close to his aunt because she "gave (him) love and attention," despite her own unstable lifestyle.

Reflecting on the deaths of his aunt and grandmother, Mr. Doe's mother speculated, "everybody that John got close to passed away." Consistent with Mr. Doe's report, his mother explained that her son was much closer to his grandmother and aunt than to his own mother. His mother explained, "me and John . . . were more like a fighting brother and sister than a mother and son." Although not particularly sympathetic to her son, Ms. Doe frankly acknowledged that his aunt's death had a substantial impact on Mr. Doe, comparable to losing a nurturing mother.

- ***Instability in home and family, but progress when in stable circumstances:*** When his grandmother's terminal illness became severe, it was necessary for Mr. Doe to return to his mother's home. At first, his mother resided with a romantic partner whom she described as physically abusive, particularly later in the relationship when Mr. Doe was present to witness the violence. Soon after this relationship ended, Ms. Doe began to reside with Jimmy Partner, a new romantic partner with whom she has since cohabitated. All sources we interviewed explained that Mr. Partner and Mr. Doe were in conflict whenever Mr. Doe lived in the home. Although Ms. Doe described Mr. Partner in very favorable terms, all other sources described him as volatile and highly aggressive. For example, several described instances in which he threatened family members, including Mr. Doe, with firearms.

Mr. Doe attributed much of the instability in his home life to his mother's relationship with romantic partners such as Mr. Partner. For example, Mr. Doe explained that he sometimes had conversations with his mother when her partners were not at home, but that he had minimal interaction with his mother once her partner returned home from work. Similarly, several family members observed that Ms. Doe, "always let her boyfriend control her," in a way that further damaged her relationship with her son.

After a few months living with his mother and Mr. Partner, Mr. Doe was charged with *destruction of property* when he destroyed belongings in his room, following a conflict with Mr. Partner. Subsequently, Mr. Doe changed residences again at the age of 14 years, as he was placed at New Beginnings Residential Center on July 28, 2000, where he remained until August 11, 2001.

Mr. Doe described this placement at New Beginnings as "the best thing that happened to me after grandma died." Consistent with his report, records written by New Beginnings staff described Mr. Doe in positive terms, as a youth who responded well to the structure and supervision in their group home. For example, one summary from the Director of Education concluded,

> John displayed no behavioral problems at the school. He related well to the staff and interacted with them in an appropriate manner. John engaged in conversation with adults and was always polite and cooperative. John provided leadership to his peers and offered meaningful feedback to other residents in the program. . . . He had good insight into his own circumstances and was realistic about what needed to be done to improve his performance.

Although other records documented some later instances of misbehavior at New Beginnings, at least one staff member speculated that Mr. Doe's misbehavior was an effort to sabotage his discharge plan, and remain at New Beginnings, rather than be discharged back to his mother's home. For example, one counselor wrote,

> John is afraid of being abandoned again and fearful of his mother's health problems. He is afraid she will die like his grandmother did. Though John states he wants to go home, I have confronted John that maybe unconsciously his misbehaving at New Beginnings is due to his fears that perhaps it is safer for him to be at New Beginnings rather than to go home.

Nevertheless, Mr. Doe returned from New Beginnings to live with his mother and Mr. Partner. Upon return, his home life was marked by instability and conflict. For example, records from the Department of Social Services dated December 2001 observed,

> John seems to be the scapegoat in the family in some circumstances, particularly if there is conflict between Ms. Doe and Mr. Partner.

In short, Mr. Doe apparently responded well to the structured, supportive environment in New Beginnings, but he fared poorly when he lived in a high-conflict home with his mother and her partner.

Another instance in which Mr. Doe made progress in a structured setting involved attending Structured High School, the alternative educational program in which he enrolled after New Beginnings. Although his home life remained tumultuous, school records described him as thriving in the structured and supportive setting. For example, a school record from May 2000 summarized,

> John is responding well to the structure of his different placement and has few behavioral issues. He would be appropriate for consideration in a vocational program while taking regular education classes at the public high school. John has the ability to succeed in the regular classroom environment but continues to have issues with his own self-confidence, and low expectations for his future opportunities.

Consistent with school records, Mr. Doe's former teacher, Ms. Mary Teacher, recalled his performance in positive terms. During our interview she explained that Mr. Doe,

> Worked real hard . . . and was diligent. . . Anything I'd suggest, he would try. He was pretty amicable about receiving help, which isn't always the case for adolescent boys.

Ms. Teacher acknowledged several instances in which Mr. Doe became agitated at school (punching a wall on one occasion). However, she also explained that he

> . . . took responsibility when he did something wrong, and offered an apology when an apology was warranted. He took initiative in making amends; it would come from him, but wasn't manipulative.

In short, Ms. Teacher characterized Mr. Doe as a boy who worked diligently to thrive in the supportive school, despite what she understood to be difficulties in Mr. Doe's home life.

Eventually, Mr. Doe moved from his mother's home due to his conflict with her partner, Mr. Partner. He began residing in a trailer park with his aunt. However, she was addicted to illicit drugs, and Mr. Doe's time living in her trailer was marked by substantial stress, such as a physical assault (described later), efforts to provide for her children (also described later), and eventually, his aunt's death due to substance abuse (described previously).

- ***Lack of suitable role models or supervision during adolescence:*** Frequent transitions in living arrangements may not be particularly problematic for a child *if* these transitions are accompanied by consistent relationships with supportive adults. However, during Mr. Doe's unstable adolescent years, he apparently had no consistent supervision or consistent relationship with a stable adult.

Although Mr. Doe described himself as emotionally close to his aunt, her influence was probably not a stabilizing one. Mr. Doe recalled family stories about his aunt helping him smoke marijuana when he was around 7 years old. He explained, "me and her hung real tight. . . I watched her party and buy drugs. I knew she was a mess, but she was real kind to me, and I'd do anything for that." During later adolescence, when Mr. Doe lived in his aunt's trailer, he reportedly attempted to care for her children (described later), while she was engaged in substance abuse elsewhere in the neighborhood.

Like his aunt, Mr. Doe's mother also failed to serve as a constructive role model or source of supervision. The only times that Mr. Doe recalled his mother interacting pleasantly were those times when they smoked marijuana together. Mr. Doe explained that he began smoking marijuana with his mother when he moved in with her when we was around 13 years old, near the time of his grandmother's death. He recalled that they smoked marijuana together when he came home from school, after dinner, and before bedtime on nearly a daily basis. He recalled that during weekends, "we smoked the whole time." Mr. Doe described smoking marijuana with his mother in fairly positive terms. These were apparently the only instances he spent time alone with his mother; at other times her partner was present and conflict ensued. But it was also clear that these experiences with his mother did not provide the structure, support, and discipline parents typically provide to young adolescents.

Although Mr. Doe had contact with his grandfather and with Mr. Partner (his mother's romantic partner), the family members we interviewed described both men as volatile and aggressive. Neither man provided a stabilizing influence in Mr. Doe's development. The discipline they provided was more haphazard and abusive, as opposed to thoughtful or constructive.

- *Head injury during late adolescence:* Mr. Doe reported that he sustained substantial injuries during an incident when he was "jumped" by several peers in the trailer park when he lived in his aunt's trailer. Mr. Doe reportedly confronted a peer who had previously assaulted Mr. Doe's younger cousin, and he was then attacked by at least two other males. He reported that his head struck a sidewalk, his jaw was injured, and the peers attempted to strike him with a car, before his aunt intervened by moving him. He reported that others told him he was unconscious for several hours following the assault.

    Medical records from the Virginia State University (VSU) Hospital Emergency Department dated July 22, 2002, confirm that Mr. Doe suffered broken teeth and a fractured jaw. Records also indicate that he was instructed to return later in the week for jaw repair, but Mr. Doe reportedly declined to do so. Medical staff apparently did not conduct testing to determine the nature or extent of any traumatic brain injury Mr. Doe might have experienced during the assault.

Both Mr. Doe and his girlfriend, Jenny Girlfriend, reported that he demonstrated substantial changes following the assault. Ms. Girlfriend summarized that he "became a different person" who appeared depressed, isolated, suspicious of others, and prone to frustration. She described changes in his self-care, such as poorer hygiene and requests for assistance with dressing himself and other simple tasks. She also recalled instances after the assault when Mr. Doe appeared to faint after periods of anger or intense emotional arousal.

Ms. Girlfriend, Mr. Doe, and others close to him were consistent in reporting that his personality and behavior changed following the assault. However, it is impossible to determine what caused any changes. One possibility is that he suffered a traumatic brain injury, resulting in physiological damage that has consequences for personality and behavior. However, there is no testing from the VSU Emergency Department to support or exclude this possibility.

Neuropsychological testing (described later) may be suggestive, but it is far from conclusive, particularly because similar testing was not conducted shortly before and/or after the assault. A second possible explanation for Mr. Doe's reported changes following the accident is psychological. It may be that an experience he described as frightening and humiliating—he was reportedly beaten by peers while relatives and friends declined to intervene—left him ashamed, depressed, and distrustful. Finally, it is possible that both physiological and psychological factors contributed to the changes he and Ms. Girlfriend observed after the assault.

- *Mild neurocognitive problems*: Records dating back to Mr. Doe's early childhood describe him as manifesting problems with attention, concentration, and hyperactivity, to the extent that doctors prescribed Ritalin when he was a young child. Records also suggest that he was prescribed Ritalin again years later. More recently, neuropsychological testing conducted as part of this evaluation by Dr. Colleague of the University of Virginia Medical Center revealed some mild deficits. Although Dr. Colleague found no evidence of severe neuropsychological impairments, he concluded results provided "some suggestion of mild cerebral dysfunction." This mild dysfunction appeared consistent with Mr. Doe's risk factors for neuropsychological problems (e.g., substance abuse, childhood attention problems, head trauma, etc.), according to Dr. Colleague.

- *Symptoms of mood disorder:* Mr. Doe and his family described long-standing symptoms consistent with a mood disorder. For example,

Mr. Doe reportedly demonstrated symptoms of depression during childhood. Some of these symptoms, and his general pattern of mood instability, reportedly became more severe following the assault described earlier. Considering Mr. Doe's history of instability, loss, and poor family support, it is not surprising that he has demonstrated symptoms of depression. More recently, Mr. Doe has received mood-stabilizing medication as part of his psychiatric treatment in the jail, and he described this medication as helpful.

To summarize, Mr. Doe's history is notable for several adverse influences—such as poor parental care, abuse, neglect, and loss—dating back to the earliest stages of his life. Even as he entered adolescence, the adults and circumstances to which he was exposed were marked by substantial instability, conflict, and substance abuse. Although Mr. Doe fared better during the few instances in which he experienced structure and supervision (i.e., residing with his grandmother before her death, residing in New Beginnings residential facility as a young adolescent), he struggled more when he returned to live with family members, whose homes were marked by violence and other instability.

Mitigation Related to *Character* of the Defendant

Virginia Code § 19.2-264.3:1 requires evaluators to address "other factors in mitigation relating to the *history*" of the defendant; these historical factors were described earlier. The code also requires evaluators to address "factors in mitigation relating to the . . . *character* of the defendant." Therefore, the observations that follow address positive aspects of Mr. Doe's character that were not evident in the capital offense for which he was charged. Indeed, these mitigating characteristics appear more striking in light of Mr. Doe's difficult developmental history, which exemplified many well-known risk factors for adult crime and violence.

- *Minimal violence or criminal history prior to current charges*: Mr. Doe has no record of violent crime prior to his recent charges. Criminal records reveal only a juvenile charge of destruction of property, which followed the instance when he damaged his own room. Although not reflected on his criminal record, Mr. Doe also has a history of criminal behavior related to possession and sale of marijuana.

    Even regarding noncriminal violence, a review of school records revealed no fistfights or similar violence to peers. For example, his former teacher, Ms. Mary Teacher, recalled no violence even when

Mr. Doe attended an alternative educational program that included many other students with substantial discipline problems. Rather, Ms. Teacher emphasized that Mr. Doe was "never violent towards a person," even when he became frustrated and harmed himself by punching a wall. Mr. Doe himself denied any history of fistfights, and Ms. Girlfriend explained that Mr. Doe tended to avoid aggressive peers.

- *Efforts to establish stability and family:* As detailed earlier, Mr. Doe's history was notable for chronic instability and a minimal family support. Nevertheless, Mr. Doe spent much of his late adolescence and early adulthood attempting to establish a stable family, of sorts. These efforts were most clear in two examples:
  - First, when Mr. Doe moved to his aunt's trailer during late adolescence, he reportedly adopted a parental role with her children, because she was often away from the home due to severe substance abuse. Both Mr. Doe and Ms. Girlfriend described a period in which Mr. Doe moved into the trailer and began attempting to care for his younger cousins. He reportedly used his wages to purchase food, and he urged the children to attend school. However, he reported that he struggled in these efforts and soon asked Ms. Girlfriend to move into the trailer and assist. He asked her to contribute both her wages from a veterinary assistant job and her time to help care for the children. Ms. Girlfriend described instances when she and Mr. Doe purchased clothes for the children, provided food, directed them to school, and otherwise provided parent-like support. Of course, the makeshift family they established was not ideal. For example, Mr. Doe and Ms. Girlfriend allowed alcohol and marijuana in the home, and they were probably less than ideal parent-figures in other respects. Nevertheless, all accounts suggest that their actions reflected a genuine effort to provide a more stable, family-like context for the children. Indeed, all accounts also suggested that the children fared better under their care than without it. However, these arrangements reportedly ended when the Department of Social Services (DSS) became aware of their mother's methamphetamine use and removed the children from the home.
  - A second, clearer example of Mr. Doe's efforts to establish stability and family involve his own children and his partner, Jenny Girlfriend. Mr. Doe reportedly dated Ms. Girlfriend since 1999, when they attended high school together. One of Mr. Doe's high school teachers, Ms. Teacher, characterized him as demonstrating a "tender heart for his girlfriend" as an adolescent, despite his guarded exterior and chaotic background.

Mr. Doe and Ms. Girlfriend have maintained their relationship—including some brief periods of separation—since 1999. For much of that time, the two have lived together, though they have also lived apart, with their respective families, reportedly in an effort to save money for a home together. There was also a period in which Mr. Doe lived with Ms. Girlfriend and her family, who reportedly welcomed Mr. Doe into the home (though they forbade their daughter from visiting Mr. Doe's home, based on their prior knowledge of his mother and other family members).

Mr. Doe and Ms. Girlfriend's first child, Jane, was born in August of 2003. Because she experienced several birth complications and infant health problems, the family remained in the hospital throughout her first year of life. Ms. Girlfriend described Mr. Doe as a conscientious father during this time in the hospital with Jane. She explained that he "did whatever it took" to support her and Jane, both emotionally and financially.

In 2006, Ms. Girlfriend gave birth to a second child, who was not fathered by Mr. Doe, but rather, a man she dated briefly during a period of separation from Mr. Doe. Nevertheless, Mr. Doe and Ms. Girlfriend reunited when she was 4 months pregnant. Mr. Doe remained with Ms. Girlfriend thereafter, and took a paternal role to the child, Angela, with whom she was pregnant. Indeed, Mr. Doe joined her in the delivery room and through the hospital stay. He described Angela as his daughter and described her in entirely positive terms (indeed, issues regarding her paternity did not emerge until substantial, specific questioning during the evaluation).

Regarding recent parenting efforts, Ms. Girlfriend cited numerous ways in which Mr. Doe attempted to maintain contact with his daughters from jail (e.g., sending notes and drawings, placing phone calls). In sum, the family members with whom we spoke tended to describe Mr. Doe as an invested father to two daughters.

Conclusion

A review of Mr. Doe's history and character—through interviews and review of collateral records—reveals a number of experiences and characteristics typical of those introduced as mitigation during capital sentencing. Examples detailed earlier relate to Mr. Doe's tumultuous and abusive childhood, which provided little opportunity to establish stable relationships and healthy goals. Despite this background, Mr. Doe tended to thrive in structured settings (such as a residential program during adolescence) and made several efforts to establish a more stable adulthood with more healthy relationships. Despite a history of experiencing violence and abuse, Mr. Doe has no record of criminal violence prior to the present case.

The opinions presented in this report are based upon information available at the time of this writing. In the event that new information becomes available from any source prior to trial, my opinions are subject to review and modification.

Respectfully submitted,

Daniel Murrie, Ph.D.
Director of Psychology,
Institute of Law, Psychiatry, and Public Policy
Associate Professor of Psychiatry and Neurobehavioral Sciences
University of Virginia School of Medicine

Report 5: Capital Mitigation Evaluation

Contributor Introduction (Eileen Ryan, D.O.): As detailed in Chapter 7, and as demonstrated in other sample reports, capital mitigation evaluations are remarkably comprehensive in scope, and mitigating evidence may vary greatly from case to case. Just as mitigation varies, attorney strategy varies across cases. Some attorneys request that evaluators prepare a lengthy and highly detailed narrative report that allows readers to examine the defendant's life course and the mitigation present at each point. This strategy seems particularly common when attorneys intend to share a report with opposing counsel prior to sentencing, perhaps to pursue a plea agreement. In contrast, other attorneys request a report that addresses only the briefest summary of findings. This strategy seems particularly common when attorneys intend to present detailed mitigation findings via expert testimony, and they suspect that a detailed report will better prepare opposing counsel to aggressively cross-examine their expert. Evaluators tend to respect attorneys' preferences regarding the length and level of detail in a report, and doing so is usually ethically appropriate. In fact, the Virginia statute that guided the evaluation report presented here (§ 19.2-264.3:1 of the Code of Virginia) specifies that the evaluator's job is to "*assist the defense in the preparation and presentation of information* concerning the defendant's history, character, or mental condition. . ." (emphasis added). Of course, there is a difference between report length and report content. Although evaluators may quite reasonably follow an attorney's preferences about length and level of detail in a report, they do not follow attorney's preferences about report content. The findings and opinions are attributable to the evaluator only.

In the de-identified report sample that follows, there was much mitigating evidence related to each of the three domains put forth in the Virginia statute: "(i) whether the defendant acted under extreme mental or emotional disturbance at the time of the offense; (ii) whether the capacity of the defendant to appreciate the criminality of his conduct or to conform his conduct to the requirements of the law was significantly impaired at the time of the offense; and (iii) whether there are any other factors in mitigation relating to the history or character of the defendant or the defendant's mental condition at the time of the offense" (§ 19.2-264.3:1 of the Code of Virginia). However, defense counsel requested a very brief, summative report. Therefore, the report only includes brief, summative findings. More detail was presented during expert testimony, and these details corresponded with testimony from lay witnesses who could speak directly about the defendant's history and experiences.

CAPITAL SENTENCING EVALUATION
NAME: Marcus Alexander
DATE OF BIRTH: January 1, 1991
DATE OF REPORT: February 29, 2010
AGE: 19
Judge: _____
Commonwealth's Attorney: _____, Esq.
Defense Attorneys: _____, Esq.
_____, Esq.
Case No: ####-###

Referral

Mr. Alexander was referred for an evaluation in the context of capital sentencing. Section 19.2-264.3:1 of the Code of Virginia requires that evaluators appointed to conduct capital sentencing evaluations must prepare a report regarding the history and character of the defendant and the defendant's mental condition at the time of the offense. Specifically, the report is to include opinions as to *(1)* whether the defendant acted under extreme mental or emotional disturbance at the time of the offense, *(2)* whether the defendant was significantly impaired with respect to his or her appreciation of the criminality of his or her conduct or his or her capacity to conform his or her conduct to the requirements of the law, and *(3)* whether there are other factors in mitigation relating to the history or character of the defendant or the defendant's mental condition at the time of the offense.

Qualifications of the Forensic Expert

Dr. Eileen Ryan is a board-certified general/adult, child and adolescent, and forensic psychiatrist licensed to practice medicine in the Commonwealth of Virginia. Dr. Ryan is an Associate Professor of Psychiatry and Neurobehavioral Sciences at the University of Virginia Health System.

Dr. Ryan is Section Chief of Community Services and Public Policy, and she is the Medical Director of the Institute of Law, Psychiatry and Public Policy at the University of Virginia, as well as the director of the Institute's juvenile forensic clinic. Dr. Ryan is the director of pediatric consultation, Division of Child and Family Psychiatry, Department of Psychiatry and Neurobehavioral Sciences, at the University of Virginia. She supervises and trains medical students at the University of Virginia, as well as residents in general psychiatry and fellows in child and adolescent psychiatry and forensic psychiatry and postdoctoral fellows in forensic psychology. She has presented continuing education programs and lectures to other mental health professionals, as well as to attorneys, judges, law enforcement personnel, and probation officers. She has been appointed to serve as an expert witness in Circuit and Juvenile courts in Virginia, and her credentials have been accepted in every court or proceeding in which she has been offered as an expert.

Sources of Information

As typical of capital evaluations, this report is based on a broad range of information and evaluation procedures because the Code of Virginia requires evaluators to develop a comprehensive understanding of the defendant's character and mental condition. Specifically, my evaluation considered information from the following sources:

1. Forensic psychiatric interviews with the defendant by Drs. Eileen Ryan and Jeffrey D. Raynor; approximately 10 hours on December 18, 2009 and February 19, 2010
2. Neuropsychological testing conducted by Dr. Scott Bender on February 19, 2010
3. Telephone interview with Brenda Davison, relative of the defendant, conducted March 1, 2010 by Dr. Eileen Ryan
4. Telephone interview with Jane Smith, defendant's aunt, conducted by Dr. Eileen Ryan on February 14, 2010
5. Telephone interview with Lashonna Alexander, defendant's mother, conducted by Dr. Eileen Ryan on February 26, 2010 and March 2, 2010
6. Telephone interview with Jessica Gordon, former girlfriend of defendant, conducted by Dr. Eileen Ryan on February 26, 2010
7. Telephone interview with Paul Alexander, Jr. ("P.J."), the defendant's brother, conducted by Dr. Eileen Ryan on March 5, 2010
8. Telephone interview with Jackson Evans, cousin of the defendant, conducted by Dr. Eileen Ryan on March 6, 2010

9. Telephone interview with Paul Alexander, defendant's father, conducted March 21, 2010 by Dr. Jeff Raynor
10. Telephone interview with Paul Alexander, conducted by Dr. Eileen Ryan on April 24, 2010
11. Copy of Grand Jury Indictment of Marcus Alexander dated August 1, 2009
12. Copy of Commonwealth's Response to Defendant's Motion for Discovery dated October 24, 2009
13. Copy of autopsy report on Dalton Smith dated March 17, 2006 and amended April 6, 2009
14. Copy of autopsy report on Melba Smith dated March 17, 2006 and amended April 6, 2009
15. Transcript of police interview with Marcus Alexander on March 18, 2006 and March 19, 2009
16. Diagram of crime scene, unsigned and undated
17. Copy of Defendant's criminal record dated October 24, 2009
18. Defendant's employment records from Shell Motor, Hardee's, Kentucky Fried Chicken, Taco Bell, and Kmart
19. Copies of defendant's medical records from Children's Hospital, Anytown, Virginia, dated September 27, 2008 through September 29, 2008
20. Copies of defendant's medical records from Sentara Leigh Hospital, Anytown, Virginia, dated December 29, 2002, February 2, 20May 05, 14, 2007 and September 27, 2008
21. Copies of defendant's school records from Anytown Public Schools
22. Copies of defendant's school records from Virginia Beach City Schools
23. Copy of court records relating to prior offenses
    a. Intake complaint form dated June 23, 2008
    b. Verdicts and sentences in Virginia Beach Juvenile and Domestic Relations District Court dated February 9, 2007, February 19, 2008, and July 13, 2008
    c. Criminal Complaints and Petitions dated March 6, 2005, March 3, 2006, and October 11, 2008
    d. Detention Assessment dated October 11, 2008
    e. Commonwealth's intent to transfer case to Cityville Circuit Court dated November 30, 2008
    f. Verdict and sentence in Cityville Juvenile and Domestic Relations District Court dated December 8, 2008
24. Copy of defendant's records from Cityville Juvenile Services
25. Copy of defendant's probation file from 99th Judicial District Court Service Unit in City, Virginia
    a. Risk Assessment dated December 20, 2008
    b. Workload Running Report, Contact period December 29, 2008

through March 2, 2009
c. Social History dated January 24, 2009
d. Letter from Probation Officer Karen L. Alexander to Probation Officer Kevin Curling, dated February 21, 2009
e. Cover letter dated September 10, 2009
26. Records from Cityville Correctional Center

Disclosures

At the beginning of the interview, the nature, scope, and purpose of this capital sentencing evaluation, as well as the limits of evaluator confidentiality, were fully explained to Mr. Alexander. In discussing the nature of the present evaluation, Mr. Alexander displayed a clear understanding of the nature, scope, and purpose of this evaluation and provided informed consent for proceeding with the evaluation. Mr. Alexander signed consent forms, allowing us to gather further information from varied sources. He also readily gave permission for family, friends, neighbors, and others to be interviewed for the purpose of this evaluation.

Identifying Information

Marcus Alexander is a 19-year-old African American male being held at the Cityville Correctional Center in Cityville, Virginia. He was transported by deputies for interviews at the Institute of Law, Psychiatry, and Public Policy at the University of Virginia.

Circumstances Surrounding the Offenses

Commonwealth's version: According to the grand jury indictment dated August 1, 2009, the Commonwealth alleges that the defendant willfully, deliberately, and with premeditation, murdered Dalton Smith, his uncle, and Melba Smith, his aunt, on March 16, 2009. He is also charged with using a firearm during the commission of these alleged offenses.

Defendant's version: The defendant's statements about the alleged offense are protected against disclosure until such disclosure is compelled, or until the defendant waives his privilege.

Mental State Since Arrest

According to Mr. Alexander and jail records, he was arrested on March 18, 2009, and has been housed at the Cityville Jail since that time. He said he was voluntarily placed in segregation several times due to his concern about other inmates retaliating against him for his alleged offenses. He said there were several inmates who had threatened to "jump" him. He said he generally has kept to himself and tried to avoid conflicts. He endorsed feeling depressed. He endorsed feeling hopeless, having low energy, no interest in activities, frequent crying spells, and thoughts of suicide. He said he once tied a sheet around his neck to "see how it worked" and also contemplated obtaining a blade to cut himself. He said he decided not to pursue suicide after thinking about the effect his death would have on his parents.

Mr. Alexander stated that a mental health provider evaluated him on one occasion since his arrest. He remembered the staff telling him he would begin treatment with an antidepressant, but he reported this never occurred. Review of jail medical records confirm he reported feeling depressed on March 18, 2009, at which time he also mentioned thoughts of suicide. According to the records, he reported the aforementioned symptoms to a social worker on January 10, 2010, including his reasoning for not acting on his suicidal thoughts. The social worker's plan was to refer Mr. Alexander to the psychiatrist for possible treatment with medication. According to Mr. Alexander, his symptoms began to resolve spontaneously prior to this appointment.

Mr. Alexander presented to both interviews in jail-issued clothing and appeared to have normal attention to personal grooming. He was calm and cooperative throughout the evaluations. No abnormal movements were noted. He maintained appropriate eye contact. His facial expressions were full range and congruent with topics of discussion. His speech was fluent with normal rate, tone, and volume. His vocabulary was average. He appeared to put forth good effort in responding to the interviewers' questions. Based on his statements, his thought process was linear and logical. He described his mood as depressed, but he noted that his mood had improved significantly in recent months. He admitted that he occasionally thinks of suicide, but he has no plans to act on this. He did not voice any delusional thoughts during either interview. He did not report or exhibit behavioral evidence of hallucinations or any other perceptual alterations.

Test Results

Neuropsychologist Scott Bender, Ph.D., performed neuropsychological testing and reported the following:

> When age and education are taken into account, Mr. Alexander shows generally intact neurocognitive functioning at this time. While verbal learning and memory are below average, they do not appear to be significantly below his baseline level. Measures sensitive to executive dysfunction are generally commensurate with his estimated intellectual level and low educational achievement. He appears to have a somewhat haphazard and inefficient approach to planning.

Opinions

i) *Whether the defendant acted under extreme mental or emotional disturbance at the time of the offenses.*

Mr. Alexander had been using a variety of intoxicating substances in the days leading up the offenses. This included use of cocaine, alcohol, and marijuana. His use of drugs and alcohol had accelerated in the 3 months leading up to the offense. He was intoxicated on a variety of substances at the time of the offense, including alcohol and cocaine. These drugs significantly altered his perceptions of reality and his impulse control.

ii) *Whether the capacity of the defendant to appreciate the criminality of his conduct or to conform his conduct to the requirements of the law were significantly impaired.*

As described earlier, Mr. Alexander had been using drugs and alcohol prior to the offense. Intoxicating effects of cocaine and alcohol can include impulsivity and impaired perceptions and impaired judgment.

iii) *Whether there are other factors in mitigation relating to the history and character of the defendant or the defendant's mental condition at the time of the offense.*

There are several mitigating factors related to the defendant's mental condition at the time of the offense as well as to his history and character:

1. Mr. Alexander's age at the time of the offense:

    Adolescents are inherently more impulsive and have greater difficulty considering long-term consequences of their actions. Emotional and psychosocial maturity is not achieved abruptly at a particular age, but rather develops slowly over time. Mr. Alexander's decision making prior to the offense was shortsighted and immature.

2. Mr. Alexander's intoxication at the time of the offense:

    The level of intoxication was so severe as to interfere with perception, thinking, and emotional regulation.

3. Abuse that precipitated Mr. Alexander seeking a "family" outside of the home:

    The disciplinary style of Mr. Alexander's parents, combined with a rigid and uncompromising view regarding childrearing, was a factor in Mr. Alexander seeking acceptance outside of the home and family. Unfortunately, his cognitive and psychosocial immaturity rendered him more susceptible to the lure of gang life, which initially appeared to offer him the acceptance and nurturance that he craved.

4. Early recruitment into an organized street gang by adults:

Mr. Alexander became involved in a gang, and subsequently drug use and violence at an early age. He described being recruited by older gang leaders when he was approximately 13 years old, in large part because of his home life. He developed a highly idealized and immature image of gang life. He viewed the gang leaders as powerful role models and more supportive and nurturing than his own parents. Mr. Alexander clearly chose to join and participate in a gang, but his emotional and mental immaturity prevented him from appreciating the long-term consequences of this choice.

In the months leading up the offense, Mr. Alexander had become disillusioned with the gang, and he decided to leave the gang, despite threats to his life that would likely result from this choice. While his decision to leave the gang was appropriate, his lack of planning and forethought regarding his own safety in the wake of such a decision was characteristic of his immature and impulsive thought processes. The fear of retaliation from his former gang and the loss of an overidealized surrogate family contributed to an escalation in his drug use in the weeks prior to the offense.

5. Early exposure to drugs and alcohol:

Facilitated by his gang involvement, Mr. Alexander began using drugs at an early age. The effect of drug use on the developing brain is not fully understood, but research has shown that it can be harmful. Mr. Alexander's pattern of drug and alcohol use continued unabated throughout his adolescence and until the night of the offense.

The findings and opinions presented in this report are based upon information available at the time this report was prepared. These findings and opinions will be subject to reconsideration and possible modification in the event new information is forthcoming from any source.

Eileen P. Ryan, D.O.
Associate Professor of Psychiatry and
Neurobehavioral Sciences
University of Virginia Health System
Medical Director
Institute of Law, Psychiatry, and Public Policy
University of Virginia

Report 6: Competence for Execution

Contributor Introduction (Patricia Zapf, Ph.D.): The evaluation of competency for execution (CFE) generally occurs at a time when all other avenues have been exhausted and a convicted offender has spent a good deal of time in prison on death row. Thus, there is typically a good amount of file information that has accumulated about the offender and his or her behavior while on death row as well as correctional officers who can be interviewed about their observations of the offender while incarcerated. Recall that competency refers to current mental state and so the importance of these collateral information sources cannot be minimized. These and other third-party or collateral information sources should be strongly considered in this type of evaluation, especially in light of the severity of the consequences of being found competent and the strong incentive to malinger.

Incompetence for execution is a relatively low base-rate phenomenon. As such, the courts have, relatively speaking (as compared to competence to stand trial, for example), had limited opportunity to define what is meant by and to delineate a standard for CFE. A constitutionally minimal standard was set out by the U.S. Supreme Court in *Ford v. Wainwright* (1986), which includes only that the offender be able to understand the nature of the punishment and the reasons for it. Recently, the Supreme Court in *Panetti v. Quarterman* (2007) expanded the minimally constitutionally adequate test for competency for execution to include both rational as well as factual understanding. Although considered a constitutional minimum, states are free to expand this standard. Currently in the United States, 35 states allow capital punishment and, of these, 30 have outlined a standard for CFE. Over half of these states ($n = 18$) have delineated a one-prong standard for CFE, requiring that the offender understand the nature of the punishment and the reasons for it, with no requirement that the offender be capable of assisting counsel (commonly referred to as a two-prong standard and used in every state for competence to stand trial). The two-prong standard has been adopted by the American Bar Association and appears to have been advocated for in Justice Marshall's plurality opinion in *Ford*.

Since the courts continue to grapple with the notion of CFE, it is, arguably, important to evaluate *all* potential aspects of CFE and to set this information out for the legal decision maker. Thus, in any CFE evaluation, regardless of jurisdiction, important elements to consider include the ability to *(a)* factually understand the nature of the death penalty, *(b)* factually understand the reasons for the impending execution, *(c)* rationally understand the reasons for the impending execution, and *(d)* consult with counsel in making final appeals. For an extended commentary on CFE and the *Ford* and *Panetti* cases and their implications for the assessment of CFE, see Zapf (2009).

Name: J. Smith
Date of Birth: 01-01-1952
SSN: xxx-xx-xxxx
Case No(s): CAxxxx-xxx
Date of Evaluation: 02-02-10
FORENSIC EVALUATION REPORT
Date of Report: 02-05-10

Referral Information

Mr. J. Smith, a 58-year-old African American male, was ordered to undergo an evaluation of his competency to be executed by the Honorable J. H., U.S. Court of Appeals for the 11th Circuit, on November 30, 2009. Mr. Smith was evaluated with respect to his competency to be executed on February 2, 2010. Mr. Smith was convicted of Murder in the First Degree in 2004 and was sentenced to death. He has resided on death row in Florida since his conviction.

Notification

Prior to beginning the evaluation, Mr. Smith was informed of the nature and purpose of the evaluation and the limited confidentiality of the information to be obtained. He was told that the results would be submitted to the court in the form of a written report and that copies of this report would be made available to his attorney (legal counsel for the petitioner), legal counsel for the respondent, and the Clerk for the 11th Circuit Court of Appeals. He was also informed that these results might be used in appeals proceedings, in the form of either the written report or testimony by the examiner. He was further informed that the information obtained might be used to help the court reach a decision regarding his competency to be executed. Mr. Smith indicated that he understood the information provided in the notification but refused to sign the notification of rights form, indicating his belief that "God is my witness" and that, therefore, this somehow eliminated the need for him to sign a form indicating his awareness of the limited confidentiality and/or his willingness to participate in the evaluation. Although I have some doubt as to whether this defendant truly understands the implications of this evaluation, given the nature of this evaluation and the fact that it has been ordered by the court and agreed to by all parties, I did not press the issue or ask for further indication of his ability to understand or provide consent.

Summary of Offense and Sentence

Mr. Smith was convicted of the murder of a convenience store clerk during an attempted robbery and was sentenced to death for this crime 6 years ago. Court records indicate that Mr. Smith was under the influence of crystal methamphetamine at the time of the offense and that he has an extensive, documented history of severe mental illness and substance dependence dating back to when he was a teenager.

Since being sentenced, Mr. Smith has been housed on death row with regular stints in administrative segregation for disorderly conduct and possession of contraband (in the form of illegal drugs). At Mr. Smith's sentencing 6 years ago the issue of his mental health was raised as a mitigating factor to the crime because he has a lengthy history of paranoid schizophrenia and depression with bouts of suicidality and substance dependence dating back almost 40 years. The issue of Mr. Smith's competency, however, was not an issue at the time of his trial or at the time of sentencing. Similarly, the issue of mental state at the time of the offense was only raised as a mitigating factor at sentencing, not as a defense to the crime.

Data Sources

Data sources that were reviewed for the purposes of this evaluation include the following:

- Court records and trial transcripts for index offense and sentencing
- Treatment records from RMC Emergency Room for 9-22-81
- Lab report from health care authority dated 9-22-81
- Treatment records for hospitalization at RMC from 9-23-81 to 10-11-81
- Report from the Disability Determination Service dated 12-6-1983
- Treatment records from XX Mental Health Center dated 10-11-1981 through 8-27-2001 (with a note that further records date back to 1970)
- Treatment records from XX Psychiatric Hospital dated 7-5-1992 through 6-4-1994
- Treatment records for an admission to XX Hospital Secure Unit from 3-1-1995 through 3-22-1995
- Treatment records from XX Mental Health Center dated 4-2-1996 through 3-5-2000
- Treatment records for hospitalization at RMC from 4-17-97 through 4-26-97
- Treatment records for care by Dr. M. C. from 4-17-97 through 6-30-97 and 5-31-99 through 6-14-99
- Forensic Evaluation Report dated 4-3-2002
- Florida State Prison Detainment Logs dated from 2004 to present
- Florida State Prison Solitary Confinement Incident and Progress Reports dated from 2004 to present
- Interview with Mr. Smith on 2-2-2010, 2-3-2010, and 2-4-2010
- Interview with Mr. X, Mr. Smith's brother, on 2-3-2010
- Interview with Officer Y, Mr. Smith's Classification Officer at Florida State Prison Death Row

Data sources that were requested but not forthcoming at the time of this evaluation include the following:

- Treatment records for hospitalization at PMHS in December 2000

Background Information

It was difficult to obtain much self-reported background information from Mr. Smith. His speech was confused, tangential, and disorganized at times. The following is a summary of the background information that I was able to piece together from the interviews with Mr. Smith, his brother, and his primary correctional officer as well as from the historical file information and multiple treatment records that I had obtained on Mr. Smith.

Mr. Smith reported that he was the third child of four and that his mother and father separated when he was very young. He reported that he was born in XXX and raised by his mother. He has apparently lived in XXX all his life. Mr. Smith indicated that he lived with his brother from approximately 22 years of age for approximately 25 years but that he was in and out of various treatment facilities and jails during this time. Mr. X (Mr. Smith's brother) indicated that Mr. Smith was living on the street at the time of the Index Offense because Mrs. X (Mr. X's wife) had asked Mr. Smith to leave their house, as she was increasingly afraid of Mr. Smith because he "was acting weird and has violent tendencies." Mr. Smith's brother reported that their mother (now deceased) also acknowledged that Mr. Smith has violent tendencies and she asked Mr. Smith to leave her house when he was 20 years old.

Mr. Smith reported that he dropped out of school after the eighth grade (however, file information indicates that he attended school until the 10th grade). Mr. Smith reported that he attended the "future program," which, as far as I understand, is a program for individuals with behavioral problems. File information indicates that Mr. Smith showed multiple behavioral problems in school and did not get along well with his peers or his teachers. Mr. Smith was vague with respect to how he did in school but did report that he got into trouble for possession of marijuana and was sent to "boot camp." Mr. Smith indicated that he dropped out of school "to start buying cars."

Mr. Smith reported that he has never been married but acknowledged that he has a daughter who is approximately 25 years old and with whom he has no contact because she lives out of town.

Mr. Smith reported that he has only held one job—at a fast food place "for a good 4 weeks." He indicated that he was fired from this job because of some difficulties he was having with a female coworker. His brother indicated that he was fired because the manager saw him hanging around when he was not scheduled to work and perceived him as "about to rob the place." This was apparently the only job that Mr. Smith has held and his brother had him evaluated for disability income shortly after he was fired. Apparently, Mr. Smith collected a disability income until he was sentenced to death for the index offense but was not considered competent to manage his own financial affairs and so his brother was appointed as his financial guardian.

Mr. Smith was evasive with respect to his drug and alcohol use. He reported that he smoked marijuana heavily when he was "a juvenile" but was unable to indicate how long this lasted or how old he was at the time. He also indicated that he "snorted some powder" (cocaine) but again was unable or unwilling to indicate how much or how often. He acknowledged that he was under the influence of crystal meth at the time of the index offense and that he has since used illegal drugs while on death row "to pass the time." His brother indicated that Mr. Smith has a lengthy history of drug use and had been addicted to crystal meth for "approximately 3 years" before the index offense. With respect to his alcohol use, Mr. Smith indicated that he used to "drink a bottle of Tanqueray [Gin] straight every now and then" but would not elaborate. He stated that he has never gotten "carried away" with alcohol. File records indicate that Mr. Smith has been convicted of driving while under the influence and has a number of drug-related charges. Mental health records from XXX Mental Health Center indicate that Mr. Smith has had serious drug and alcohol problems from the time he was in his early 20s.

Treatment records, dating back to 1970 when Mr. Smith was 18 years old, indicate that Mr. Smith has a lengthy history of drug and alcohol dependence. In addition, Mr. Smith has been diagnosed with Major Depressive Disorder; Major Depressive Disorder, Severe with Psychotic Features; Schizophreniform Disorder; and Schizophrenia, Paranoid Type since 1970. An extensive review of the available treatment records appears to indicate that Mr. Smith was treated for depression and substance dependence from 1970 through 1981. In September 1981, Mr. Smith was admitted to RMC Hospital after being brought to the emergency room by police after he was found wandering the streets and yelling obscenities at no one in particular. Lab records from that admission indicated that Mr. Smith tested negative for illegal or prescription drugs. Mr. Smith was given a diagnosis of Schizophreniform Disorder, as the psychotic symptoms had been present for less than 6 months at that time. At the time of admission, records indicated that he was cognitively disorganized, paranoid, hallucinating, and guarded. In addition, he had significant attention problems. Treatment records also noted that Mr. Smith had religious delusions about the devil. He was put on psychotropic medication while hospitalized but was noncompliant with medication after discharge. As far as I can tell, this was Mr. Smith's first psychotic break, at the age of 29 years. Since that time, Mr. Smith has had numerous hospitalizations, mainly for psychotic symptomatology related to diagnoses of Major Depressive Disorder, Severe with Psychotic Features and/or Schizophrenia, Paranoid Type. In addition, Polysubstance Dependence has been a comorbid diagnosis throughout all of Mr. Smith's treatment records.

Mr. Smith reported that he was hospitalized "a couple of times" at XX Psychiatric Hospital but was unable to indicate why or when this was. His brother reported that he had Mr. Smith hospitalized three times—in July 1992, May 1994, and April 1997 (for just under 3 weeks each time)—while he was living with Mr. X and his wife because Mr. Smith would "act strangely and would do bizarre things." Mr. X reported that Mr. Smith would often act paranoid and look over his shoulders all the time. Mr. Smith's brother reported that Mr. Smith has acted "strangely" since the early 1980s. He indicated that there was a history of mental illness on the paternal side of their family. Mr. X reported that he and his wife asked Mr. Smith to leave their home in late 1997 because he was becoming increasingly difficult to manage and refused to stay on his prescribed medications. After Mr. Smith served a brief stint in jail, Mr. X found his brother living on the street, unkempt and not taking care of himself. Mr. Smith refused to go to a shelter or to take his prescribed medications, telling his brother that he was "living the life the Devil intended." After this, Mr. X lost contact with his brother until he read about the index offense in the newspaper. He has been a loyal visitor since Mr. Smith's conviction.

Clinical Assessment

Mr. Smith, a 58-year-old single African American man, was interviewed on February 2, 3, and 4, 2002, in the attorney conference room at Florida State Prison, in Starke, FL. Mr. Smith is tall and has a slight build. He was dressed in the appropriate Florida Department of Corrections uniform—blue pants and an orange t-shirt. He smelled strongly of smoke. He had short, dark hair that was graying at the temples and a full beard, which was also graying. He was missing several of his front teeth and had the habit of sucking his lip through the hole left by his missing teeth.

Mr. Smith appeared to be cooperative with the evaluation; however, he was extremely difficult to communicate with, as he was tangential (often veered off topic and randomly from topic to topic), paranoid (holding beliefs not based in reality), and religiously preoccupied. His cognitive functioning appeared to be generally intact as he was able to perform a number of operations in different areas; however, he had to be directed to stay on task. He demonstrated appropriate immediate, recent, and remote memory skills and appeared to be able to concentrate well enough to recall short strings of numbers (five or fewer).

Mr. Smith appeared to have an adequately developed fund of information, as evidenced by his ability to answer elementary general knowledge questions. He was able to demonstrate some abstract reasoning ability, although he then became perseverative (visiting the same theme over and over again) and religiously preoccupied in his responses. For example, he was able to indicate the similarities between an apple and an orange (stating that both were fruit), but then replied "they're Lords, Christ" to queries regarding the similarities between a bird and a tree, a table and a chair, and a poem and a statue. Mr. Smith was able to correctly answer social judgment questions and was oriented to person, place, time, and situation.

Mr. Smith presented with expansive affect (irritable, easily annoyed, and provoked to anger) throughout the interview and continuously spoke even when cut off. He evidenced flight of ideas (moving from one topic to the next at a quick rate) and loose associations between topics (having little logical connection between topics). His speech was somewhat pressured and his affect was labile (abnormal with sudden, rapid shifts in mood). He would raise his voice to shouting level when speaking about the "so-called police."

He denied any homicidal ideation or intent but was vague and would veer off topic when asked about suicidal ideation or intent. He acknowledged auditory and visual hallucinations (hearing and seeing things that are not present), but I was unable to make sense of the form or content of these hallucinations. He appears to hold a delusional belief system surrounding the other inmates in his cellblock and the narcotics police. He reported that his "cell block has been flooded with whores, whoremongers, bitches, and bastards by the Narcs" and that he has been "set up to take the fall for the sins of others." His thought style and speech productivity appeared to be excessive and tangential. He maintained appropriate eye contact with the interviewer but exhibited an excessive level of motor activity. Mr. Smith appears to believe that he has been sent to death row as part of a conspiracy against him by the "narcotics police" since he was using crystal meth at the time of his crime and God intends to punish him for his drug use. Furthermore, Mr. Smith appears to believe that his being caught with illegal drugs and being sent to administrative segregation for this was the result of a "drug lord, Christ the Lord" set up and that he is "taking the fall" for "all their sins" (he was unable to meaningfully elaborate on who "they" were, but kept repeating, "They are all part of it, all of them"). Mr. Smith was extremely religiously preoccupied and treatment records dating back to the early 1980s indicate that religiously preoccupied delusional beliefs have been a consistent theme of Mr. Smith's when he is actively psychotic.

Treatment records from XXX Mental Health Center indicate that Mr. Smith has a lengthy history of treatment dating back to 1970. He has been diagnosed with paranoid schizophrenia and his behavior at the time of interview appeared to be consistent with this diagnosis. He has been prescribed numerous psychotropic medications in the past, but treatment records indicate that he has not seen the psychiatrist for medication since October 2004. He indicated that he has not renewed his prescriptions, because he likes the way he is now. He admitted to using illegal drugs whenever he can and stated that these "black market medications" (which include methamphetamine, Ecstasy, and Ritalin) work best for him. Mr. Smith does not appear to have any insight into his mental disorder. Denial and minimization of his psychiatric symptoms as well as the aforementioned lack of insight have been documented through over 30 years of treatment records from various psychiatric hospitals, correctional institutions, and mental health facilities.

I attempted to administer the *Structured Interview of Reported Symptoms* (SIRS; Rogers, Bagby, & Dickens, 1992); however, Mr. Smith was unable to concentrate well enough to answer the questions meaningfully. He was perseverative and kept coming back to religiously preoccupied themes. His behavior appeared to be consistent with someone who was responding to internal stimuli. Given that his current presentation appears consistent with treatment and admission records for periods when he has been in a psychotic state over the last 30 years, and that interviews with both Mr. Smith's brother and his classification officer corroborate his current presentation, I do not believe that Mr. Smith is malingering or exaggerating his current presentation.

Treatment records indicate that when Mr. Smith is compliant with his medication regime his psychotic symptoms are held in check and he is able to communicate in a meaningful way. This indicates to me that if he were to be treated and placed on a regime of psychotropic medications, with which he is compliant, there is a good chance that his symptoms will again be held in check. Whether this treatment regime is appropriate, feasible, or desirable under Mr. Smith's current circumstances is an issue for the court and for Mr. Smith's medical treatment team.

Forensic Assessment

Mr. Smith was evaluated with respect to his competency to be executed. The Interview Checklist for Evaluations of Competency for Execution (Zapf, Boccaccini, & Brodsky, 2003) was used to structure the evaluation of competency for execution.

Competency for Execution

Section 922.07(3) of the Florida Statutes states that an inmate is considered incompetent to be executed if he "does not have the mental capacity to understand the nature of the death penalty and why it was imposed on him" (Fla. Stat. Ann. § 922.07(3), 2009). In addition, under the Florida Rules of Criminal Procedure "a person under sentence of death is insane for purposes of execution if the person lacks the mental capacity to understand the fact of the impending execution and the reason for it" (Fla. R. Crim. Pro. 3.811(b), 2010). Furthermore, the U.S. Supreme Court in *Panetti v. Quarterman* (2007) expanded the minimally constitutionally adequate test for competency for execution that was set out in Justice Powell's concurring opinion in *Ford v. Wainwright* (1986) to include both rational as well as factual understanding. Therefore, Mr. Smith was evaluated with respect to his ability to *(a)* factually understand the nature of the death penalty, *(b)* factually understand the reasons for his impending execution, and *(c)* rationally understand the reasons for his impending execution. In addition, although a strict interpretation of the Florida Statutes and Florida Rules of Criminal Procedure might suggest a one-prong standard for competence for execution in this jurisdiction (the ability to understand; as opposed to a two-pronged standard, which would include the ability to understand as well as the ability to assist counsel), Mr. Smith was also evaluated with respect to his ability to consult with counsel in making his final appeals given that nearly half of the jurisdictions that articulate a standard for competence for execution use a two-prong standard and a two-prong standard has been adopted by the American Bar Association and other organizations with germane expertise (in addition, Justice Marshall's plurality opinion in *Ford* appears to have advocated a two-prong test).

Mr. Smith was able to give a brief but jumbled account of his time on death row; however, his version was punctuated by paranoid beliefs about the inmates in his cellblock and the "Narcotics Task Force." He was extremely difficult to communicate with and my lengthy interviews with him were marked by religiously preoccupied delusional beliefs and perseveration on religiously preoccupied themes.

Mr. Smith was able to indicate that he was on death row and that the reason why people come to death row is because they are going to be "killed like vermin for their sins." He was able to report that he was found guilty of murder but then went on to elaborate that he was sent to death row because he was being "punished by God for using drugs" and that "they only say murder to make it legal." When asked whether he was also sent to death row because he had committed the crime of murder, he indicated that he was "found guilty of sinning, not of murder." When he was asked whether someone could be sent to death row only for their sins if they did not commit murder, he stated, "they can do whatever he [*sic*] wants." When asked to elaborate he replied, "I am just here to live in purgatory, punishment for sins but not murder, she isn't even dead." When Mr. Smith was questioned further about the index offense, it appears to be the case that he is under the impression that the convenience store clerk was a woman who did not die but "pretended" to in order to set him up (there is no mention of a woman in the police reports or court documents for the index offense; all accounts indicate that the clerk was a male; no female was implicated in any of the reports). Mr. Smith indicated his belief that he was "set up" to come to death row as a "purgatory" for his sinning and drug use.

Mr. Smith appeared unwilling or unable to believe that individuals on death row are put to death. He reported his belief that death row was a "purgatory," where people lived out their existence and moved to "different levels of hell." It is unclear whether Mr. Smith believes that anyone actually dies; he appears to believe that there are different levels of hell and that he will not die because he has been set up to live forever in purgatory for using drugs. When pressed, Mr. Smith conceded, "Some of them around here must die" but then went on to say that "maybe they just move to the next level."

Mr. Smith is extremely difficult to communicate with, because his speech is confused, tangential, paranoid, and religiously preoccupied. He was unable to rationally discuss any of the important aspects of his current situation or his appeals. Mr. Smith appears to hold numerous paranoid and irrational beliefs about the inmates on his cellblock and his attorney being a part of the "Narcotics Task Force," which compromises Mr. Smith's ability to trust and relate to his attorney. In addition, Mr. Smith's understanding of his appeals and the legal appeal process appears to be religiously preoccupied, which compromises Mr. Smith's ability to rationally understand the nature of his impending execution.

Interviews with Mr. X (Mr. Smith's brother) and Officer Y (Mr. Smith's Classification Officer) confirm that Mr. Smith's current presentation, religious occupation, and delusional belief system have been in place for at least the past 5 months. Mr. X noted that his brother was "more in touch" about 6 months ago but that, even then, he still "had some weird beliefs." Officer Y reported that Mr. Smith "acts crazy all the time and really seems to be nuts." He elaborated that Mr. Smith will often present as "talking to himself or yelling at someone we can't see" and that he makes the other inmates uncomfortable with his "weird beliefs and behavior." Officer Y noted that Mr. Smith has spoken of his beliefs regarding being "set up" and "forced to live in purgatory" for at least 2 years but that he has gotten "much worse over the last 5 months." Mr. X noted that Mr. Smith has spoken of "purgatory" and of religiously occupied themes for "most of his entire adult life."

Summary and Recommendations

In summary, Mr. Smith is a 58-year-old African American male who currently appears to meet criteria for diagnoses of *(1)* Schizophrenia, Paranoid Type; and *(2)* Polysubstance Dependence, currently in remission.

Mr. Smith is not currently taking any psychotropic medications and displays limited insight into his mental illness. He currently appears to be experiencing a number of symptoms of formal thought disorder and, as a result, is unable to communicate in a meaningful way. Although it seems likely that he is able to understand factually the nature of the death penalty and the reasons for it, he does not appear to appreciate the personal importance of the proceedings against him and, in fact, denies that he will be put to death. He does not appear to have a rational understanding of the reasons for his impending execution. In addition, he appears unable to communicate effectively with his counsel, whom he also believes to be part of a conspiracy against him.

As a forensic psychologist, I recognize that the determination of a defendant's competency for execution is ultimately a matter for the court to decide; therefore, the opinions rendered here are of an advisory nature only. I will be happy to provide the court with any further information, records, or testimony that it may require.

Respectfully submitted,
Patricia A. Zapf, PhD
Licensed Psychologist
Certified Forensic Examiner

Report 7: Competence for Execution

Contributor Introduction (Mary Alice Conroy, Ph.D.): The following evaluation was conducted in the State of Texas, and, as with any forensic evaluation, should assess the standard prescribed in the particular jurisdiction. In Texas, the standard for competence for execution (CFE) is two pronged (Tex. Code Crim. Proc. art. 46.05(h)):

A defendant is incompetent to be executed if the defendant does not understand the following:

1. That he or she is to be executed and that the execution is imminent
2. The reason he or she is being executed

Texas law *does not* include the third prong, specified in some states, that the defendant is incompetent if he or she cannot assist his or her attorney in the appeals process. In *Panetti v. Quarterman* (2007), the U.S. Supreme Court further made it clear that "understanding" was to include rational, as well as factual, understanding in all jurisdictions.

In conducting CFE evaluations, I take the position that the evaluation should focus on the elements prescribed by statute and not stray into other areas such as revisiting the issue of mitigation, while others have argued evaluators should provide all information that could possibly be relevant (Zapf, Boccaccini, & Brodsky, 2003). Although others have differed with this approach (Ebert, 2001), I would include psychological testing and extensive collateral interviews only in so far as they would aid my judgment relative to this focus.

An additional issue to consider is whether it is essential to interview the individual on more than one occasion. I would agree with the majority of CFE evaluators interviewed for a recent study (Young, Boccaccini, Lawson, & Conroy, 2008) that "it depends." Often a plethora of collateral records will provide greater insight into a defendant's general functioning and presentation than would a second visit. Texas statute *requires* that for a CFE evaluation to be conducted "the defendant waives any claim of privilege with respect to, and consents to the release of, all mental health and medical records relevant to whether the defendant is incompetent to be executed" (Tex. Code Crim. Proc. art. 46.05(j)). Additionally in Texas, if a court orders a CFE evaluation, the court is required to appoint "at least two mental health experts" to examine the defendant (Tex. Code Crim. Proc. art. 46.05(f)), allowing for not only at least two separate observations but observations by at least two different people. And then, of course, there is the issue of time. In Texas, as is true in some other jurisdictions, CFE evaluations are not generally ordered until the issue is "ripe"—meaning the execution is very close at hand. Of course, should some elements of a particular case make it impossible to complete the necessary evaluation in the allotted time, appropriate motions could be filed.

Name: J. B.
Cause No.
Date of Evaluation: _____, 2002

Identification and Reason for Referral: J. B. is a 42-year-old Caucasian male currently housed on Texas Death Row subsequent to a conviction for capital murder. The _____ Court of _____ County ordered he be evaluated for competence to be executed as defined in Article 46.05 of the Texas Code of Criminal Procedure. At the time of this evaluation his execution was scheduled to be carried out on _____, 2002.

Evaluation Procedures: As part of the evaluation Mr. B. was interviewed on the TDCJ Death Row Unit for a little over 2 hours. In addition, the following documents were reviewed:

Confession of J. B., undated.

Psychological Evaluation of J. B. by _____, Ph.D., dated _____ 1995.

Forensic Psychiatric Assessment of J. B. by _____, M. D., dated _____, 1997.

B. v. Texas, _____.

Response to J. B.'s Appellate Lawyer and Psychiatrist by ____, Ph.D., dated ____, 1998.

Affidavit of _____, M. D., dated _____, 1998.

Affidavit of _____, dated _____, 1998.

TDCJ disciplinary and medical records relative to J. B.

Prior to beginning the interview, the purpose and scope of the evaluation were explained to Mr. B. He was also advised of the limits of confidentiality, that a report would be provided to the court to be shared with both attorneys, and that the evaluator could be called to testify at a hearing to decide the issue of his competency. He was given an opportunity to ask questions and was provided with a written Statement of Disclosure regarding the evaluation. He evidenced an understanding of the information given.

Background Information: Detailed social histories were outlined in previous reports and relevant information will be summarized here. Mr. B. was born on _____, 1960, in _____, Texas. His parents separated when he was very young, and he was raised primarily by his maternal grandparents.

Mr. B. said he has difficulty remembering his early childhood, but he said he was having problems in school by the time he reached junior high school. These included fighting and truancy. He recounted being sexually molested by more than one person by age 12. At about the same time, he began abusing alcohol and drugs. He admitted this became a lifelong problem and included almost all of the widely used illegal drugs, with the exception of heroin.

At age 15, Mr. B. reportedly returned to live with his mother, stepfather, and three younger siblings. He now believes his mother and one brother may have had mental health problems, but he cannot provide specific information. He said he continued to have behavioral problems in school and his drug abuse steadily increased. He reported being raped at 16. That same year he was arrested for the first of multiple juvenile offenses. At 17 he dropped out of school prior to completing the 10th grade.

Mr. B. received his first mental health evaluation of record at age 17. He said his mother sought the evaluation due to escalating substance abuse and odd behavior, such as creeping about the house naked. In 1978, he was treated briefly at the _____ Hospital and then hospitalized for 9 months at another facility in _____. Although original records were not available, a record review summary by Dr. _____ indicated Mr. B. was thought to be experiencing the early onset of Schizophrenia. He discharged from the hospital against medical advice (AMA).

At age 19, Mr. B. was committed to _____ State Hospital for 3 months subsequent to charges of DWI and motor vehicle theft. He was diagnosed with Paranoid Schizophrenia, exacerbated by severe substance abuse, and treated with psychotropic medications (per the record summary provided by Dr. _____).

At age 20, Mr. B. said he was committed to TDCJ for the first time on a charge of Aggravated Robbery. After spending much of the ensuing decade in prison, the defendant was paroled in 1987 or 1988. He said he had previously been involved in a common law marriage, but he had never lived with his "wife." He entered into what he considered to be his second common law marriage in 1988 and a third in 1989. No children resulted from any of the marriages.

In 1990, Mr. B. was once again incarcerated due to an arson conviction in state court and a federal conviction on firearms violations. After completing his state time he was transferred to federal custody. While housed at a general federal correctional institution, he attempted suicide by drinking window cleaner and was transferred to a federal medical center. There he was diagnosed with Major Depression, Recurrent, with Psychotic Features and treated with psychotropic medications.

Once released from federal custody, Mr. B. returned to Texas. He was treated on an outpatient basis by Dr. _____ of MHMRA from 1993 to 1994. He was prescribed numerous medications, including Prolixin-D (a long-acting antipsychotic that is administered by injection). Simultaneously, the defendant admitted he was again abusing drugs and alcohol.

In June of 1994, Mr. B. was charged with murder, later convicted, and sentenced to death. He has resided on Texas Death Row since his conviction, because his case has been appealed. During that time, he has been under continuous psychiatric care. There have been a number of suicide attempts and other instances of self-mutilation. He has been transferred to a psychiatric inpatient unit on a number of occasions, most recently 2 months ago. At that time he was found to be eating and drinking excrement. Since his return to the Death Row last month, he has been maintained on a regimen of Thorazine and Nortriptyline. During his most recent tenure with TDCJ he has been variously diagnosed with Paranoid Schizophrenia, Schizoaffective Disorder, and Major Depression with Psychotic Features.

Mental Status: When Mr. B. appeared for interview he was somewhat disheveled and displayed nervous mannerisms. Nonetheless, he was polite and cooperative throughout the interchange. His speech was spontaneous and normal in rate and tone. He made adequate eye contact and evidenced occasional fleeting humor.

Mr. B. was correctly oriented to time, place, person, and situation. If allowed to ramble, he could become somewhat tangential and disorganized. However, he responded well to the examiner's efforts to redirect and focus the interview. His concentration was adequate for the entire 2 hours. Although there were no obvious indications of hallucinations during the examination, the defendant described in detail a long history of both auditory and visual hallucinations.

He also referred to his "delusions." However, none of the ideas described during the interview would qualify as delusional thinking.

The defendant's affect was generally flat, regardless of the topic of discussion. He described no symptoms, either past or current, that would be characteristic of mania. He said at the present time his sleep and appetite were generally adequate, although he does have occasional crying spells. Despite a history of intermittent depression and suicidal ideation, he denied current symptoms of this nature.

Case Formulation: J. B. has a lengthy history of mental health problems. Over many years he has evidenced symptoms, primarily hallucinations, of Schizophrenia. Although the visual phenomena he described were more characteristic of the sequelae of drug abuse or nighttime dreaming, the auditory hallucinations were congruent with those commonly experienced by those with Schizophrenia. He noted that some of these "voices" often took the form of commands but said he had developed strategies to resist them. Although he did not appear to have a fixed delusional system, he harbored some bizarre ideas (e.g., drinking urine can allow you to come back as a ghost after you die). Although not prominent, the defendant displayed evidence of tangential thinking and flat affect. Despite the lengthy history, Mr. B.'s psychosis appears to be in adequate remission at this time. Although still bothered by auditory hallucinations, he can identify them as symptomatic of his illness and resist complying with commands. He is also capable of focusing on reality without interruption from bizarre ideas. He expressed considerable insight into his treatment needs and said he wanted to continue his medications.

History also establishes a diagnosis of Polysubstance Dependence for this individual. He has, by his own admission, abused a plethora of illegal drugs, as well as alcohol, from his early teenage years. Whether in an institution or in the community, he has rarely resisted an opportunity in this regard. Although this may well have exacerbated his psychotic condition, current evidence would indicate the psychosis continued to exist even when the substances were removed.

Mr. B. also has the features characteristic of Antisocial Personality Disorder. Much of his very lengthy criminal history appears unrelated to a psychotic condition. Even in his current treatment-compliant state he admitted to many of the attitudes and motivations common to this character structure. However, this in no way mitigates the severity of his psychotic condition.

Diagnostic Impressions

Axis I: 295.30 Schizophrenia, paranoid type, in partial remission
  304.80 Polysubstance Dependence
Axis II: 301.7 Antisocial Personality Disorder

Opinion Regarding Competence for Execution: Throughout the interview, Mr. B. was focused on reality. He was able to discuss his defense attorney's current strategy in regard to issues of treatment. Personally, he said he believes the court does not really understand his mental condition and that the crime he committed was not premeditated. He said he believed the sentence was somewhat unfair because he thought the 12th juror was pressured to conform by the others. He also said that the system is unfair because some people who commit more heinous crimes than he only get life—noting that he only killed one adult, whereas some people are serial killers and some murder children. Regardless of whether one agrees with him, none of his contentions appeared irrational or based in any delusional thinking. Regardless of whether he agrees with it, he could clearly articulate the reason the state is planning to execute him.

Some time was spent discussing the defendant's understanding of death. He expressed the traditional Christian teaching about heaven and hell. He also said he thought he might be able to come back as a ghost and haunt people. However, he then appeared somber and said he did not know for certain what happened after death. He was very aware that, absent some action from the court, he is scheduled to be executed in a little over 2 weeks. He volunteered that this meant he would not be alive for Thanksgiving or Christmas this year. He said he thought the state was rushing things and wished it could at least be delayed until after the holidays. He then discussed several people, including members of his family and his spiritual advisor, with whom he was planning a final meeting.

In my professional opinion, J. B. currently meets the standard of competence for execution outlined in Texas statute. That is, although he does suffer from a serious mental illness, he does understand that he is to be executed and that the execution is imminent. He also understands the specific reason that sentence has been imposed.

It should be noted that at the time of the evaluation Mr. B. was receiving a regimen of antipsychotic and antidepressant medication. He was adamant that he needed this medication, despite an understanding that it may keep his mental faculties sufficiently intact to face execution. However, should the medication be discontinued, it is entirely possible that his mental status and level of competence could change, thus necessitating additional evaluation.

Mary Alice Conroy, Ph.D. Date
Diplomate in Forensic Psychology
American Board of Professional Psychology

References

42 Pa. Cons. Stat. Ann. § 9711(e)(8), 2010 42 Pa. Cons. Stat. Ann. § 9711(e)(8) (2010).
Abramson, J. (2004). Death-is-different jurisprudence and the role of the capital jury. *Ohio State Journal of Criminal Law*, *2*, 117–164.
Acker, J. R. (2009). Actual innocence: Is death different? *Behavioral Sciences and the Law*, *27*, 297–311.
Ackerman, M., & Kane, A. (1998). *Psychological experts in divorce actions* (3rd ed.). New York, NY: Aspen Law & Business.
Ackerson, K. S., Brodsky, S. L., & Zapf, P. A. (2005). Judges' and psychologists' assessments of legal and clinical factors in competence for execution. *Psychology, Public Policy, and Law*, *11*, 164–193.
Ake v. Oklahoma, 470 U.S. 68 (1985).
Ala. Code § 13A-5-52 (2010).
Alexander, J., & Austin, J. (1992). *Handbook for evaluating objective prison classification systems*. Washington, DC: NIC.
American Academy of Psychiatry and the Law. (2005). *Ethics guidelines for the practice of forensic psychiatry*. Bloomfield, CT: Author.
American Association of Intellectual and Developmental Disabilities. (2010). Definition of intellectual disability. Retrieved from http://www.aamr.org/content_100.cfm?navID=21.
American Association of Mental Retardation. (2002). *The AAMR definition of mental retardation*. Retrieved from http://www.aamr.org/content_100.cfm?navID=21.
American Bar Association. (1989). *American Bar Association criminal justice mental health standards*. Washington, DC: Author.
American Bar Association. (2003). *American Bar Association guidelines for the appointment and performance of counsel in death penalty cases*. Retrieved from http://www.abanet.org/legalservices/downloads/sclaid/deathpenaltyguidelines2003.pdf.

American Educational Research Association, American Psychological Association, & National Council on Measurement in Education. (1999). *Standards for education and psychological testing*. Washington, DC: American Educational Research Association.

American Law Institute, Restatement (Second) of Torts § 282 (1965).

American Medical Association. (2001). *Code of medical ethics*. Retrieved from http://www.ama-assn.org/ama/pub/physician-resources/medical-ethics/code-medical-ethics.shtml.

American Medical Association. (2008). *Code of medical ethics of the American Medical Association* (2008-2009 ed.). Chicago: Author.

American Psychiatric Association. (2000). *Diagnostic and statistical manual of mental disorders* (4th ed., text rev.). Washington, DC: Author.

American Psychiatric Association. (2008). *Capital punishment: Position statement*. Retrieved from http://www.psych.org/Departments/EDU/Library/APAOfficialDocumentsandRelated/PositionStatements/200801.aspx.

American Psychiatric Association. (2009). *The principles of medical ethics with annotations especially applicable to psychiatry*. Arlington, VA: Author.

American Psychological Association. (2002). Ethical principles of psychologists and code of conduct. *American Psychologist, 57*, 1060–1073.

Apodaca v. Oregon, 406 U.S. 404 (1972).

Appelbaum, P. (1986). Competence to be executed: Another conundrum for mental health professionals. *Hospital and Community Psychiatry, 37*, 682–684.

Appelbaum, P. (2007). Death row delusions: When is a prisoner competent to be executed? *Psychiatric Services, 58*, 1258–1260.

Archer, R. P. (Ed.). (2006). *Forensic uses of clinical assessment instruments*. Mahwah, NJ: Lawrence Erlbaum.

Atkins v. Virginia, 536 U.S. 304 (2002).

Banner, S. (2002). *The death penalty: An American history*. Cambridge, MA: Harvard University Press.

Barefoot v. Estelle, 463 U.S. 880 (1983).

Barnard v. Collins, 13 F.3d 871 (5th Cir. 1994).

Baroff, G. S. (2003). Establishing mental retardation in capital cases: An update. *Mental Retardation, 41*, 198–202.

Bartol, C., & Bartol, A. (2006). History of forensic psychology. In I. B. Weiner & A. K. Hess (Eds.), *The handbook of forensic psychology* (3rd ed., pp. 3–27). Hoboken, NJ: Wiley.

Batson v. Kentucky, 476 U.S. 79 (1986).

Beecher-Monas, E. (2003). The epistemology of prediction: Future dangerousness testimony and intellectual due process. *Washington and Lee Law Review, 60*, 353–416.

Bersoff, D. N. (2002). Some contrarian concerns about law, psychology, and public policy. *Law and Human Behavior, 26*, 565–574.

Bersoff, D. N. (2004). The differing conceptions of culpability in law and psychology. *Widener Law Review, 11*, 83–94.

Bersoff, D. N. (Ed.). (2008). *Ethical conflicts in psychology* (4th ed.). Washington, DC: American Psychological Association.

Blackstone, W. (1978). *Commentaries on the laws of England* (9th ed.). New York, NY: Garland.

Blanks, R., & Pinals, D. A. (2007). Competence to be executed: Eighth Amendment and mere "awareness" rather than "rational understanding" of reason for execution. *Journal of the American Academy of Psychiatry and the Law, 35*, 381–384.

Bloche, M. G. (1993). Psychiatry, capital punishment, and the purposes of medicine. *International Journal of Law and Psychiatry, 16*, 301–357.

Blume, J. H., Garvey, S. P., & Johnson, S. L. (2001). Future dangerousness in capital cases: Always "at issue." *Cornell Law Review, 86*, 397–410.

Blume, J. H., Johnson, S. L., & Seeds, C. (2009). *Of* Atkins *and men: Deviations from clinical definitions of mental retardation in death penalty cases.* Cornell Law School Research Paper No. 09-001, Cornell Law School, Ithaca, NY. Retrieved from http://ssrn.com/abstract=1327303.

Blystone v. Pennsylvania, 494 U.S. 299 (1990).

Bobby v. Bies, 129 S. Ct. 2145 (2009).

Bonnie, R. J. (1990). Dilemmas in administering the death penalty: Conscientious abstention, professional ethics, and the needs of the legal system. *Law and Human Behavior, 14*, 67–90.

Bonnie, R. J., & Gustafson, K. (2007). The challenge of implementing Atkins v. Virginia: How legislatures and courts can promote accurate assessments and adjudication of mental retardation in death penalty cases. *University of Richmond Law Review, 41*, 811–860.

Bonta, J., Law, M., & Hanson, R. K. (1998). The prediction of criminal and violent recidivism among mentally disordered offenders: A meta-analysis. *Psychological Bulletin, 123*, 123–142.

Borum, R. (1996). Improving the clinical practice of violence risk assessment: Technology, guidelines and training. *American Psychologist, 51*, 945–956.

Borum, R., Otto, R., & Golding, S. (1993). Improving clinical judgment and decision making in forensic evaluation. *Journal of Psychiatry and Law, 21*, 35–76.

Borum, R., & Verhaagen. (2006). *Assessing and managing violence risk in juveniles.* New York, NY: Guilford.

Bowers, W. J., & Steiner, B. D. (1999). Death by default: An empirical demonstration of false and forced choices in capital sentencing. *Texas Law Review, 77*, 605–717.

Boykin v. Alabama, 395 U.S. 238 (1969).

Branch v. Texas, 408 U.S. 238 (1972).

Brief for Amicus Curiae of the American Bar Association in Support of Petitioner, Panetti v. Quarterman, 2007 U.S. S. Ct. Briefs LEXIS 151 (Feb. 22, 2007) (No. 06-6407).

Brief for Amicus Curiae of the American Psychiatric Association, Barefoot v. Estelle, 1983 U.S. S. Ct. Briefs LEXIS 1529 (March 4, 1983) (No. 82-6080).

Brief for Amicus Curiae of the American Psychological Association in Support of Defendant-Appellant, *United States v. Fields* (April 4, 2005) (No. 04-50393), Retrieved from http://www.apa.org/about/offices/ogc/amicus/fields.pdf.

Brief for Amicus Curiae of the Criminal Justice Legal Foundation in Support of Respondent, Panetti v. Quarterman, 2007 U.S. S. Ct. Briefs LEXIS 313 (March 29, 2007) (No. 06-6407).

Brief for Amici Curiae American Psychological Association, American Psychiatric Association, and National Alliance on Mental Illness in Support of Petitioner, Panetti v. Quarterman, 2007 U.S. S. Ct. Briefs LEXIS 152 (Feb. 27, 2007) (No. 06-6407).

Broderick, D. (1979). Insanity of the condemned. *Yale Law Journal, 88*, 533–564.

Brodsky, S. (1990). Professional ethics and professional morality in the assessment of competence for execution: A response to Bonnie. *Law and Human Behavior, 14*, 91–97.

Brodsky, S. (1991). *Testifying in court: Guidelines and maxims for the expert witness.* Washington, DC: American Psychological Association.

Brodsky, S. (1999). *The expert expert witness: More maxims and guidelines for testifying in court.* Washington, DC: American Psychological Association.

Brodsky, S. (2004). *Coping with cross-examination and other pathways to effective testimony.* Washington, DC: American Psychological Association.

Brodsky, S., & Galloway, V. (2003). Ethical and professional demands for forensic mental health professionals in the post-*Atkins* era. *Ethics and Behavior, 13,* 3–8.

Brodsky, S. L., Zapf, P. A., & Boccaccini, M. T. (2001). The last competency: An examination of legal, ethical, and professional ambiguities regarding evaluations of competence for execution. *Journal of Forensic Psychology Practice, 1,* 1–25.

Brodsky, S. L., Zapf, P. A., & Boccaccini, M. T. (2005). Competency for execution assessments: Ethical continuities and professional tasks. *Journal of Forensic Psychology Practice, 5,* 65–74.

Broeders, T. (2003). The role of a forensic expert in an inquisitorial system. In P. J. van Koppen & S. D. Penrod (Eds.), *Adversarial versus inquisitorial justice: Psychological perspectives on criminal justice systems* (pp. 245–253). New York, NY: Kluwer/Plenum.

Bruininks, R. H., Woodcock, R. W., Weatherman, R. F., & Hill, B. K. (1996). *Scales of Independent Behavior Revised: Comprehensive manual.* Rolling Meadows, IL: Riverside.

Buffington-Vollum, J., Edens, J. F., & Keilen, A. (2008). Predicting institutional violence among death row inmates: The utility of the Sorensen and Pilgrim Model. *Journal of Police and Criminal Psychology, 23,* 16–22.

Butcher, J., Dahlstrom, W., Graham, J., Tellegen, A., & Kaemmer, B. (1989). *MMPI-2: Manual for administration and scoring.* Minneapolis, MN: University of Minnesota Press.

Burch v. Louisiana, 441 U.S. 130 (1979).

Butler, B., & Moran, G. (2002). The role of death qualification in venirepersons' evaluations of aggravating and mitigating circumstances in capital trials. *Law and Human Behavior, 26,* 175–184.

Butler, B., & Moran, G. (2007). The impact of death qualification, belief in a just world, legal authoritarianism, and locus of control on venirepersons' evaluations of aggravating and mitigating circumstances in capital trials. *Behavioral Sciences and the Law, 25,* 57–68.

Cal. Penal Code § 190.3(k) (2010).

Caldwell, C., & Seamone, E. (2007). Excusable neglect in malpractice suits against radiologists: A proposed jury instruction to recognize the human condition. *Annals of Health Law, 16,* 43–77.

Canivez, G. L., & Watkins, M. W. (1998). Long-term stability of the Wechsler Intelligence Scale for Children-Third Edition. *Psychological Assessment, 10,* 285–291.

Caritativo v. California, 357 U.S. 549 (1958).

Ceci, S., Scullin, M., & Kanaya, T. (2003). The difficulty of basing death penalty eligibility on IQ cutoff scores for mental retardation. *Ethics and Behavior, 13,* 11–12.

Cherry v. Florida, 959 So.2d 702 (Fla. 2007).

Christy, A., Douglas, K., Otto, R., & Petrila, J. (2004). Juveniles evaluated incompetent to proceed: Characteristics and quality of mental health professionals' evaluations. *Professional Psychology: Research and Practice, 35,* 380–388.

Cicchetti, D. (2006). Development and psychopathology. In D. Cicchetti & D. J. Cohen (Eds.), *Developmental psychopathology* (2nd ed., pp. 1–23). Hoboken, NJ: John Wiley & Sons.

Cicchetti, D., & Aber, J. L. (Eds.). (1998). Contextualism and developmental psychopathology [special issue]. *Development and Psychopathology, 10*, 137–426.
Cicchetti, D., & Cohen, D. J. (1995). Perspectives on developmental psychopathology. In D. Cicchetti & D. J. Cohen (Eds.), *Developmental psychopathology* (Vol. 1, pp. 3–16). New York, NY: Wiley.
Cicchetti, D., & Rogosch, F. A. (1996). Equifinality and multifinality in developmental psychopathology. *Development and Psychopathology, 8*, 597–600.
Clark v. Quarterman, 457 F.3d 441 (5th Cir. 2006).
Clemons v. Alabama, 2005 Ala. Crim. App. LEXIS 128.
Coe v. Bell, 209 F. 3d 815 (6th Cir. 2000).
Cohen, B. J. (2010). Conducting capital sentencing evaluations. In *Conducting mental health evaluations for capital sentencing*. Training sponsored by Commonwealth of Virginia and Institute for Law, Psychiatry, and Public Policy, Charlottesville, VA.
Coker v. Georgia, 433 U.S. 584 (1977).
Colbach, E. M. (1981). Integrity checks on the witness stand. *Bulletin of the American Academy of Psychiatry and the Law, 9*, 285–288.
Collins, P. A. (2009). The effects of cognitive disability evidence on death penalty dispositions: An analysis post *Atkins v. Virginia*. *Criminal Justice Studies, 22*, 17–38.
Committee on Ethical Guidelines for Forensic Psychologists. (1991). Specialty guidelines for forensic psychologists. *Law and Human Behavior, 15*, 655–665.
Committee on the Revision of the Ethical Guidelines for Forensic Psychologists. (2006). Specialty guidelines for forensic psychology: Second official draft. Retrieved from http://www.ap-ls.org/links/SGFP January 2006.pdf.
Connell, M. A. (2003). A psychobiographical approach to the evaluation for sentence mitigation. *Journal of Psychiatry and Law, 31*, 319–354.
Connell, M. A. (2008). Ethical issues in forensic psychology. In R. Jackson (Ed.), *Learning forensic assessment* (pp. 55–72). New York, NY: Routledge/Taylor & Francis Group.
Conroy, M. E., & Murrie, D. C. (2007). *Forensic assessment of violence risk: A guide for risk assessment and risk management*. Hoboken, NJ: John Wiley & Sons.
Coons, P. (1989). Iatrogenic factors in the misdiagnosis of multiple personality disorder. *Dissociation: Progress in the Dissociative Disorders, 2*, 70–76.
Costanzo, S., & Costanzo, M. (1994). Life or death decisions: An analysis of capital jury decision making under the special issues sentencing framework. *Law and Human Behavior, 18*, 151–170.
Council on Ethical and Judicial Affairs. (1993). Physician participation in capital punishment. *Journal of the American Medical Association, 270*, 365–368.
Cunningham, M. D. (2006a). Informed consent in capital sentencing evaluations: Targets and content. *Professional Psychology: Research and Practice, 37*, 452–459.
Cunningham, M. D. (2006b). Special issues in capital sentencing. In M. A. Conroy, P. M. Lyons, & P. P. Kwartner (Eds.), *Forensic mental health services in Texas* [special issue]. *Applied Psychology in Criminal Justice, 2*, 205–236.
Cunningham, M. D. (2006c). Dangerousness and death: A nexus in search of science and reason. *American Psychologist, 61*, 827–839.
Cunningham, M. D. (2008). Forensic psychology evaluations at capital sentencing. In R. Jackson (Ed.), *Learning forensic assessment* (pp. 211–238). New York, NY: Routledge/Taylor & Francis Group.
Cunningham, M. D. (2010). *Evaluation for capital sentencing*. New York, NY: Oxford University Press.

Cunningham, M. D., & Goldstein, A. M. (2003). Sentencing determinations in death penalty cases. In A. M. Goldstein & I. B. Weiner (Eds.), *Handbook of psychology, Vol. 11. Forensic psychology* (pp. 407–436). Hoboken, NJ: John Wiley & Sons.
Cunningham, M. D., & Reidy, T. J. (1998). Antisocial personality disorder and psychopathy: Diagnostic dilemmas in classifying patterns of antisocial behavior in sentencing evaluations. *Behavioral Sciences and the Law, 16,* 331–351.
Cunningham, M. D., & Reidy, T. J. (1999). Don't confuse me with the facts: Common errors in violence risk assessment at capital sentencing. *Criminal Justice and Behavior, 26,* 20–43.
Cunningham, M. D., & Reidy, T. J. (2001). A matter of life or death: Special considerations and heightened practice standards in capital sentencing evaluations. *Behavioral Sciences and the Law, 19,* 473–490.
Cunningham, M. D., Reidy, T. J., & Sorensen, J. R. (2005). Is death row obsolete? A decade of mainstreaming death-sentenced inmates in Missouri. *Behavioral Sciences and the Law, 23,* 307–320.
Cunningham, M. D., Reidy, T. J., & Sorensen, J. R. (2008). Assertions of "future dangerousness" at federal capital sentencing: Rates and correlates of subsequent prison misconduct and violence. *Law and Human Behavior, 32,* 46–63.
Cunningham, M. D., & Sorensen, J. R. (2006). Actuarial models for assessment of prison violence risk: Revisions and extensions of the Risk Assessment Scale for Prison (RASP). *Assessment, 13,* 253–265.
Cunningham, M. D., & Sorensen, J. R. (2007). Predictive factors for violent misconduct in close custody. *Prison Journal, 87,* 241–253.
Cunningham, M. D., & Sorensen, J. R. (2010). Improbable predictions at capital sentencing: Contrasting prison violence outcomes. *Journal of the American Academy of Psychiatry and the Law, 38,* 61–72.
Cunningham, M. D., Sorensen, J. R., & Reidy, T. J. (2005). An actuarial model for assessment of prison violence risk among maximum security inmates. *Assessment, 12,* 40–49.
Cunningham, M. D., Sorensen, J. R., & Reidy, T. J. (2009). Capital jury decision making: The limitations of predictions of future violence. *Psychology, Public Policy, and Law, 15,* 223–256.
Cunningham, M. D., & Tasse, M. J. (2010). Looking to science rather than convention in adjusting IQ scores when death is at issue. *Professional Psychology: Research and Practice, 41,* 413–419.
Cunningham, M. D., & Vigen, M. P. (1999). Without appointed counsel in capital postconviction proceedings: The self-representation competency of Mississippi death row offenders. *Criminal Justice and Behavior, 26,* 293–321.
Cunningham, M. D., & Vigen, M. P. (2002). Death row inmate characteristics, adjustment, and confinement: A critical review of the literature. *Behavioral Sciences and the Law, 20,* 191–210.
Daubert v. Merrell Dow Pharmaceuticals, Inc., 509 U.S. 579 (1993).
Deitchman, M. A., Kennedy, W. A., & Beckham, J. C. (1991). Self-selection factors in the participation of mental health professionals in competency for execution evaluations. *Law and Human Behavior, 15,* 287–303.
Dekleva, K. B. (2001). Psychiatric expertise in the sentencing phase of capital murder cases. *Journal of the American Academy of Psychiatry and the Law, 29,* 58–67.
DeMatteo, D., & Edens, J. F. (2006). The role and relevance of the Psychopathy Checklist-Revised in court: A case law survey of U.S. courts (1991-2004). *Psychology, Public Policy, and Law, 12,* 214–241.

DeMatteo, D., Edens, J. F., & Hart, A. (2010). The use of measures of psychopathy in violence risk assessment. In R. K. Otto & K. S. Douglas (Eds.), *Handbook of violence risk assessment* (pp. 19–40). New York, NY: Routledge/Taylor & Francis Group.

DeMatteo, D., Marczyk, G., Krauss, D. A., & Burl, J. (2009). Educational and training models in forensic psychology. *Training and Education in Professional Psychology, 3,* 184–191.

DeMatteo, D., Marczyk, G., & Pich, M. (2007). A national survey of state legislation defining mental retardation: Implications for policy and practice after *Atkins. Behavioral Sciences and the Law, 25,* 781–802.

Diamond, B. L. (1992). The forensic psychiatrist: Consultant vs. activity in legal doctrine. *Bulletin of the American Academy of Psychiatry and the Law, 20,* 119–132.

Doane, B. M., & Salekin, K. L. (2009). Susceptibility of current adaptive behavior measures to feigned deficits. *Law and Human Behavior, 33,* 329–343.

Dorland, M., & Krauss, D. (2005). The danger of dangerousness in capital sentencing: Exacerbating the problem of arbitrary and capricious decision-making. *Law and Psychology Review, 29,* 63–104.

Dowling, A. K. (2003). Post-*Atkins* problems with enforcing the Supreme Court's ban on executing the mentally retarded. *Seton Hall Law Review, 33,* 773–810.

Drope v. Missouri, 420 U.S. 162 (1975).

Dusky v. United States, 362 U.S. 402 (1960).

Duvall, J. C., & Morris, R. J. (2006). Assessing mental retardation in death penalty cases: Critical issues for psychology and psychological practice. *Professional Psychology: Research and Practice, 37,* 658–665.

Dvoskin J. A. (2006, June). *Psychological evidence in juvenile and family court.* Presentation given to the North Carolina Association of District Court Judges, Wrightsville Beach, NC.

Dvoskin, J. A., & Guy, S. L. (2008). On being an expert witness: It's not about you. *Psychiatry, Psychology, and Law, 15,* 202–212.

Ebert, B. (2001). Competency to be executed: A proposed instrument to evaluate an inmate's level of competency in light of the Eighth Amendment prohibition against the execution of the presently insane. *Law and Psychology Review, 25,* 29–57.

Eddings v. Oklahoma, 455 U.S. 104 (1982).

Edens, J. F., Buffington-Vollum, J. K., Keilen, A., Roskamp, P., & Anthony, C. (2005). Predictions of future dangerousness in capital murder trials: Is it time to "disinvent the wheel"? *Law and Human Behavior, 29,* 55–86.

Edens, J. F., Colwell, L. H., Desforges, D. M., & Fernandez, K. (2005). The impact of mental health evidence on support for capital punishment: Are defendants labeled psychopathic considered more deserving of death? *Behavioral Sciences and the Law, 23,* 603–625.

Edens, J. F., & Cox, J. (2010, March). *Examining the prevalence, role and impact of evidence regarding antisocial personality, sociopathy and psychopathy in capital cases: A survey of defense team members.* Paper presented at the 2010 Annual Conference of the American Psychology-Law Society (AP-LS), Division 41 of the American Psychological Association (APA), Vancouver, British Columbia, Canada.

Edens, J. F., Desforges, D. M., Fernandez, K., & Palac, C. A. (2004). Effects of psychopathy and violence risk testimony on mock-juror perceptions of dangerousness in a capital murder trial. *Psychology, Crime, and Law, 10,* 393–412.

Edens, J. F., Petrila, J., & Buffington-Vollum, J. K. (2001). Psychopathy and the death penalty: Can the Psychopathy Checklist-Revised identify offenders who represent "a continuing threat to society"? *Journal of Psychiatry and Law*, *29*, 433–481.

Eisenberg, J. R. (2004). *Law, psychology, and death penalty litigation*. Sarasota, FL: Professional Resource Press.

Eisenberg, T., & Wells, M. T. (1993). Deadly confusion: Juror instructions in capital cases. *Cornell Law Review*, *79*, 1–17.

Ellis, J. W. (2002). *Mental retardation and the death penalty: A guide to state legislative issues*. Albuquerque, NM: University of New Mexico School of Law.

Estelle v. Smith, 451 U.S. 454 (1981).

Everington, C. E., & Keyes, D. W. (1999, July-August). Diagnosing mental retardation in criminal proceedings: The critical importance of documenting adaptive behavior. *The Forensic Examiner*, *8*, 31–34.

Everington, C., & Olley, J. G. (2008). Implications of *Atkins v. Virginia*: Issues in defining and diagnosing mental retardation. *Journal of Forensic Psychology Practice*, *8*, 1–23.

Ewing, C. P. (1987). Diagnosing and treating "insanity" on death row: Legal and ethical perspectives. *Behavioral Sciences and the Law*, *5*, 175–185.

Ex parte Jose Garcia Briseno, 135 S.W.3d 1 (Tex. Crim. App. 2004).

Ex parte Clarence Curtis Jordan, 758 S.W.2d 250 (Tx. Ct. App. 1988).

Ex parte Jerry Jerome Smith, 2003 Ala. LEXIS 79.

Fabian, J. M. (2005). Life, death, and IQ: It's much more than just a score: The dilemma of the mentally retarded on death row. *Journal of Forensic Psychology Practice*, *5*, 1–36.

Fabian, J. M. (2006). State supreme court responses to *Atkins v. Virginia*: Adaptive functioning assessment in light of purposeful planning, premeditation and the behavioral context of homicide. *Journal of Forensic Psychology Practice*, *6*, 1–25.

Fabian, J. M. (2009). Mitigating murder at capital sentencing: An empirical and practical psycho-legal strategy. *Journal of Forensic Psychology Practice*, *9*, 1–34.

Faigman, D. L., Kaye, D. K., Saks M. J., & Sanders, J. (2009). *Modern scientific evidence: The law and science of expert testimony*. St. Paul, MN: West/Thomson Publishing Co.

Farringer, J. L. (2001). The competency conundrum: Problems courts have faced in applying different standards for competency to be executed. *Vanderbilt Law Review*, *54*, 2441–2493.

Fearance v. Scott, 56 F. 3d 633 (5th Cir. 1995).

Federal Death Penalty Act, 18 U.S.C.A. §§ 3591–3598 (1994).

Federal Rules of Evidence (2010).

Ferris, R. (1997). Psychiatry and the death penalty. *Psychiatric Bulletin*, *21*, 746–748.

Fla. Stat. § 921.141(6)(h) (2010).

Flanagan, T. J. (1980). Time served and institutional misconduct: Patterns of involvement in disciplinary infractions among long-term and short-term inmates. *Journal of Criminal Justice*, *8*, 357–367.

Flynn, J. R. (1984). The mean IQ of Americans: Massive gains 1932 to 1978. *Psychological Bulletin*, *95*, 29–51.

Flynn, J. R. (1985). Wechsler intelligence tests: Do we really have a criterion of mental retardation? *American Journal of Mental Deficiency*, *90*, 236–244.

Flynn, J. R. (1998). WAIS-III and WISC-III gains in the United States from 1972 to 1995: How to compensate for obsolete norms. *Perceptual and Motor Skills*, *86*, 1231–1239.

Flynn, J. R. (1999). Searching for justice: The discovery of IQ gains over time. *American Psychologist, 54,* 5–20.

Flynn, J. R. (2006). Tethering the elephant: Capital cases, IQ, and the Flynn Effect. *Psychology, Public Policy, and Law, 12,* 170–189.

Flynn, J. R. (2007). *What is intelligence? Beyond the Flynn effect.* New York, NY: Cambridge University Press.

Flynn, J. R. (2009). Requiem for nutrition as the cause of IQ gains: Raven's gains in Britain 1938-2008. *Economics and Human Biology, 7,* 18–27.

Foot, P. (1990). Ethics and the death penalty: Participation by forensic psychiatrists in capital cases. In R. Rosner & R. Weinstock (Eds.), *Ethical practice in psychiatry and the law* (pp. 207–218). New York, NY: Springer.

Ford v. Wainwright, 477 U.S. 399 (1986).

Frederick, R. (1997). *Validity Indictor Profile manual.* Minnetonka, MN: NSC Assessments.

Freedman, A. M., & Halpern, A. L. (1998). A crisis in the ethical and moral behavior of psychiatrists. *Current Opinion in Psychiatry, 11,* 1–15.

Freedman, A. M., & Halpern, A. L. (1999). The psychiatrist's dilemma: A conflict of roles in legal executions. *Australian and New Zealand Journal of Psychiatry, 33,* 629–635.

Frye v. United States, 392 F. 1013 (D.C. Cir. 1923).

Furman v. Georgia, 408 U.S. 238 (1972).

Gagliardi, G. J., & Miller, A. K. (2008). Writing forensic psychological reports. In R. Jackson (Ed.), *Learning forensic assessment* (pp. 539–563). New York, NY: Routledge/Taylor & Francis Group.

Gendreau, P., Goggin, C., & Law, M. A. (1997). Predicting prison misconduct. *Criminal Justice and Behavior, 24,* 414–431.

Gendreau, P., Little, T., & Goggin, C. (1996). A meta-analysis of the predictors of adult recidivism: What works! *Criminology, 34,* 575–607.

Goldstein, A. M. (2001). Expert opinion. *American Psychology-Law Society News, 21,* 8–14.

Goldstein, A. M., Goldstein, N. E., & Kalbeitzer, R. (2006). Assessing childhood trauma and developmental factors as mitigation in capital cases. In G. Koocher & S. Sparta (Eds.), *Forensic mental health assessment of children and adolescents: Issues and applications* (pp. 365–380). New York, NY: Oxford University Press.

Goldstein, A. M., Morse, S. J., & Shapiro, D. L. (2003). Evaluation of criminal responsibility. In A. M. Goldstein (Ed.), *Handbook of psychology, Vol. 11. Forensic psychology* (pp. 381–406). Hoboken, NJ: John Wiley & Sons.

Goodman-Delahunty, J., & Foote, W. (1995). Compensation for pain, suffering, and other psychological injuries: The impact of *Daubert* on employment discrimination claims. *Behavioral Sciences and the Law, 13,* 183–206.

Gould, J. W., & Martindale, D. A. (2007). *The art and science of child custody evaluations.* New York, NY: Guilford.

Grassian, S., & Friedman, N. (1986). Effects of sensory deprivation in psychiatric seclusion and solitary confinement. *International Journal of Law and Psychiatry, 8,* 49–65.

Greene, R. L. (1997). Assessment of malingering and defensiveness by multiscale inventories. In R. Rogers (Ed.), *Clinical assessment of malingering and deception* (2nd ed., pp. 169–207). New York, NY: Guilford Press.

Green v. Johnson, 515 F.3d 290 (4th Cir. 2008).

Green v. United States, 365 U.S. 301 (1961).
Greenberg, S. A., & Shuman, D. W. (1997). Irreconcilable conflict between therapeutic and forensic roles. *Professional Psychology: Research and Practice, 28*, 50–57.
Greenberg, S. A., & Shuman, D. W. (2007). When worlds collide: Therapeutic and forensic roles. *Professional Psychology: Research and Practice, 38*, 129–132.
Greenspan, S. (2006). Issues in the use of the "Flynn effect" to adjust IQ scores when diagnosing MR. *Psychology in Mental Retardation and Developmental Disabilities Newsletter, 31*, 3–7.
Greenspan, S., & Switzky, H. N. (2003). Execution exemption should be based on actual vulnerability, not disability label. *Ethics and Behavior, 13*, 19–26.
Gregg v. Georgia, 428 U.S. 153 (1976).
Griffin, M. L., & Hepburn, J. (2006). The effect of gang affiliation on violent misconduct among inmates during early years of confinement. *Criminal Justice and Behavior, 33*, 419–448.
Grisso, T. (1986). *Evaluating competencies: Forensic assessments and instruments.* New York, NY: Plenum Press.
Grisso, T. (1988). *Competency to stand trial evaluations: A manual for practice.* Sarasota, FL: Professional Resource Exchange.
Grisso, T. (1998). *Forensic evaluation of juveniles.* Sarasota, FL: Professional Resource Press.
Grisso, T. (2003). Advances in assessments for legal competencies. In T. Grisso (Ed.), *Evaluating competencies: Forensic assessments and instruments* (2nd ed., pp. 1–20). New York, NY: Kluwer.
Grisso, T. (2010). Guidance for improving forensic reports: A review of common errors. *Open Access Journal of Forensic Psychology, 2*, 102–115.
Grisso, T., & Appelbaum, P. S. (1998). *Assessing competence to consent to treatment: A guide for physicians and other health professionals.* London, England: Oxford University Press.
Grisso, T., & Tomkins, A. J. (1996). Communicating violence risk assessments. *American Psychologist, 51*, 928–930.
Guy, L. S., Edens, J. F., Anthony, C., & Douglas, K. S. (2005). Does psychopathy predict institutional misconduct among adults? A meta-analytic investigation. *Journal of Consulting and Clinical Psychology, 73*, 1056–1064.
Haas, L. J. (1993). Competence and quality in the performance of forensic psychologists. *Ethics and Behavior, 3*, 251–256.
Hagen, M. A. (1997). *Whores of the court: The fraud of psychiatric testimony and the rape of American justice.* New York, NY: Harper-Collins.
Hagan, L. D., Drogin, E. Y., & Guilmette, T. J. (2008). Adjusting IQ scores for the Flynn effect: Consistent with the standard of practice? *Professional Psychology: Research and Practice, 39*, 619–625.
Hall, T. A., Cook, N. E., & Berman, G. L. (2010). Navigating the expanding field of law and psychology: A comprehensive guide to graduate education. *Journal of Forensic Psychology Practice, 10*, 69–90.
Haney, C. (1995). The social context of capital murder: Social histories and the logic of mitigation. *Santa Clara Law Review, 35*, 547–610.
Haney, C. (2003). Mental health issues in long-term solitary and "supermax" confinement. *Crime and Delinquency, 49*, 124–156.
Hans, V. P. (1986). An analysis of public attitudes toward the insanity defense. *Criminology, 24*, 393–414.

Hanson, R. K., & Morton-Bourgon, K. (2005). The characteristics of persistent sexual offenders: A meta-analysis of recidivism studies. *Journal of Consulting and Clinical Psychology, 73*, 1154–1163.

Hare, R. D. (2003). *Hare Psychopathy Checklist-Revised (PCL-R), 2nd ed.: Technical manual.* Toronto, ON: Multi-Health Systems, Inc.

Harris, G. T., Rice, M. E., & Quinsey, V. L. (1993). Violent recidivism of mentally disordered offenders: The development of a statistical prediction instrument. *Criminal Justice and Behavior, 20*, 315–335.

Harrison, P. L., & Raineri, G. (2008). Best practices in the assessment of adaptive behavior. In A. Thomas & J. Grimes (Eds.), *Best practices in school psychology* (5th ed., pp. 605–616). Bethesda, MD: NASP Press.

Heilbrun, K. S. (1987). The assessment of competency for execution: An overview. *Behavioral Sciences and the Law, 5*, 383–396.

Heilbrun, K. (1992). The role of psychological testing in forensic assessment. *Law and Human Behavior, 16*, 257–272.

Heilbrun, K. (2001). *Principles of forensic mental health assessment.* New York, NY: Kluwer Academic/Plenum Press.

Heilbrun, K. (2003). Principles of forensic mental health assessment: Implications for the forensic assessment of sexual offenders. *Annals of the New York Academy of Sciences, 89*, 1–18.

Heilbrun, K., & Brooks, S. (2010). Forensic psychology and forensic science: A proposed agenda for the next decade. *Psychology, Public Policy, and Law, 16*, 219–253.

Heilbrun, K., & Collins, S. (1995). Evaluations of trial competency and mental state at the time of the offense: Report characteristics. *Professional Psychology: Research and Practice, 26*, 61–67.

Heilbrun, K., DeMatteo, D., & Marczyk, G. (2004). Pragmatic psychology and forensic mental health assessment: Applying principles to promote quality. *Psychology, Public Policy, and Law, 10*, 31–70.

Heilbrun, K., DeMatteo, D., Marczyk, G., Finello, C., Smith, R., & Mack-Allen, J. (2005). Applying principles of forensic mental health assessment to capital sentencing. *Widener Law Review, 11*, 93–118.

Heilbrun, K., DeMatteo, D., Marczyk, G., & Goldstein, A. M. (2008). Standards of practice and care in forensic mental health assessment: Legal, professional, and principles-based considerations. *Psychology, Public Policy, and Law, 14*, 1–26.

Heilbrun, K., Grisso, T., & Goldstein, A. M. (2009). *Foundations of forensic mental health assessment.* New York, NY: Oxford University Press.

Heilbrun, K., Marczyk, G. R., & DeMatteo, D. (2002). *Forensic mental health assessment: A casebook.* New York, NY: Oxford University Press.

Heilbrun, K., Marczyk, G., DeMatteo, D., & Mack-Allen, J. (2007). A principles-based approach to forensic mental health assessment: Utility and update. In A. M. Goldstein (Ed.), *Forensic psychology: Emerging topics and expanding roles* (pp. 45–72). Hoboken, NJ: John Wiley & Sons.

Heilbrun, K., Marczyk, G. R., DeMatteo, D., Zillmer, E., Harris, J., & Jennings, T. (2003). Principles of forensic mental health assessment: Implications for neuropsychological assessment in forensic contexts. *Assessment, 10*, 329–343.

Heilbrun, K. S., & McClaren, H. A. (1988). Assessment of competency for execution: A guide for mental health professionals. *Bulletin of the American Academy of Psychiatry and the Law, 16*, 205–216.

Heilbrun, K., Radelet, M. L., & Dvoskin, J. (1992). The debate on treating individuals incompetent for execution. *The American Journal of Psychiatry, 149,* 596–605.

Heilbrun, K., Rogers, R., & Otto, R. (2002). Forensic assessment: Current status and future directions. In J. Ogloff (Ed.), *Psychology and the law: Reviewing the discipline* (pp. 120–147). New York, NY: Kluwer Academic/Plenum Publishing.

Heilbrun, K., Warren, J., & Picarello, K. (2003). Third party information in forensic assessment. In A. M. Goldstein (Ed.), *Handbook of psychology, Vol. 11. Forensic psychology* (pp. 69–86). Hoboken, NJ: John Wiley & Sons.

Hensl, K. B. (2005). Restoring competency for execution: The paradoxical debate continues with the case of *Singleton v. Norris. Journal of Forensic Psychology Practice, 5,* 55–68.

Hirschi, T., & Gottfredson, M. (1983). Age and the explanation of crime. *American Journal of Sociology, 89,* 552–584.

Hitchcock v. Dugger, 481 U.S. 393 (1987).

Hoffman, L. W. (1991). The influence of the family environment on personality: Accounting for sibling differences. *Psychological Bulletin, 110,* 187–203.

Howell, J. C. (1995). *Guide for implementing the comprehensive strategy for serious, violent, and chronic juvenile offenders.* Washington, DC: Office of Juvenile Justice and Delinquency Prevention.

Huebner, B. M. (2003). Administrative determinates of inmate violence. *Journal of Criminal Justice, 31,* 107–117.

Idaho Code Ann. § 19-2515 (2010).

In re Grandy, 623 P.2d 666 (Or. Ct. App. 1981).

Ind. Code Ann. § 35-50-2-9(c)(8) (West 2010).

Jackson v. Georgia, 408 U.S. 238 (1972).

Jacobson, J. W., & Mulick, J. A. (Eds.). (1996). *Manual on diagnosis and professional practice in mental retardation.* Washington, DC: American Psychological Association.

J. E. B. v. Alabama ex rel T. B., 511 U.S. 127 (1994).

Jenkins v. United States, 307 F.2d 637 (D.C. Cir. 1962).

Johnson v. Louisiana, 406 U.S. 356 (1972).

Johnson v. Zerbst, 304 U.S. 458 (1938).

Jurek v. Texas, 428 U.S. 262 (1976).

Kanaya, T., Scullin, M. H., & Ceci, S. J. (2003). The Flynn effect and U.S. policies: The impact of rising IQ scores on American society via mental retardation diagnoses. *American Psychologist, 58,* 778–790.

Kane, H. (2003). Straight talk about IQ and the death penalty. *Ethics and Behavior, 13,* 29.

Kaufman, A. S. (1990). *Assessing adolescent and adult intelligence.* Columbus, OH: Allyn & Bacon.

Kaufman, A. S. (1994). *Intelligent testing with the WISC-III.* New York, NY: Wiley.

Kaufman, A. S., & Lichtenberger, E. O. (2002). *Assessing adolescent and adult intelligence* (2nd ed.). Columbus, OH: Allyn & Bacon.

Keesler, M. E., DeMatteo, D., Murrie, D. C., & Anumba, N. (2010, March). *The evolution of future dangerousness as an aggravating factor in capital litigation: Once endangered, soon to be extinct?* Poster session presented at the 2010 Annual Conference of the American Psychology-Law Society (AP-LS), Division 41 of the American Psychological Association (APA), Vancouver, British Columbia, Canada.

Kennedy v. Louisiana, 128 S. Ct. 2641 (2008).

Kermani, E. J., & Drob, S. L. (1988). Psychiatry and the death penalty: Dilemma for mental health professionals. *Psychiatric Quarterly, 59,* 193–212.

Keyes, D. W., Edwards, J. D., & Derning, T. J. (1998). Mitigating mental retardation in capital cases: Finding the "invisible" defendant. *Mental and Physical Disability Law Reporter, 22*, 529–539.

Knauss, L., & Kutinsky, J. (2004). Into the briar patch: Ethical dilemmas facing psychologists following *Atkins v. Virginia. Widener Law Review, 11*, 121–135.

Knight v. Florida, 746 So.2d 423 (Fla. 1998).

Koocher, G. (2003). IQ testing: A matter of life and death. *Ethics and Behavior, 13*, 1–2.

Kraemer, H. C., Kazdin, A. E., Offord, D. R., Kesler, R. C., Jensen, P. S., & Kupfer, D. J. (1997). Coming to terms with the terms of risk. *Archives of General Psychiatry, 54*, 337–343.

Krauss, D. A., & Lee, D. (2003). Deliberating on dangerousness and death: Jurors' ability to differentiate between expert actuarial and clinical predictions of dangerousness. *International Journal of Law and Psychiatry, 26*, 113–137.

Krauss, D., Lieberman, J. D., & Olson, J. (2004). The effects of rational and experiential information processing of expert testimony in death penalty cases. *Behavioral Sciences and the Law, 22*, 801–822.

Krauss, D., & Sales, B. D. (2001). The effects of clinical and scientific expert testimony on juror decision-making in capital sentencing. *Psychology, Public Policy, and Law, 7*, 267–310.

Krauss, D. A., & Sales, B. D. (2006). Training in forensic psychology: Training for what goal? In I. B. Weiner & A. K. Hess (Eds.), *The handbook of forensic psychology* (3rd ed., pp. 851–871). New York, NY: Wiley.

Kuanliang, A., Sorensen, J. R., & Cunningham, M. D. (2008). Juvenile inmates in an adult prison system: Rates of disciplinary misconduct and violence. *Criminal Justice and Behavior, 35*, 1186–1201.

Kumho Tire Co. v. Carmichael, 526 U.S. 137 (1999).

Kuhn, M. (1974). House Bill 200: The legislative attempt to reinstate capital punishment in Texas. *Houston Law Review, 11*, 410–420.

Kwartner, P., & Boccaccini, M. T. (2008). Testifying in court. Evidence-based recommendations for expert-witness testimony. In R. Jackson (Ed.), *Learning forensic assessment* (pp. 565–588). Mahwah, NJ: Lawrence Erlbaum Associates.

Lacritz, L. H., & Cullum, C. M. (2003). The WAIS-III and WMS-III: Practical issues and frequently asked questions. In D. S. Tulsky, D. H. Saklofske, G. J. Chelune, R. K. Heaton, R. J. Ivnik, R. Bornstein, … M. F. Ledbetter (Eds.), *Clinical interpretation of the WAIS-III and WMS-III* (pp. 491–532). Boston, MA: Elsevier.

Lahm, K. F. (2008). Inmate-on-inmate assault: A multilevel examination of prison violence. *Criminal Justice and Behavior, 35*, 120–137.

Lally, S. (2003). What tests are acceptable for use in forensic evaluations? A survey of experts. *Professional Psychology: Research and Practice, 34*, 491–498.

Lander, T., & Heilbrun, K. (2009). The content and quality of forensic mental health assessment: Validation of a principles-based approach. *International Journal of Forensic Mental Health, 8*, 115–121.

Latzer, B. (1998). *Death penalty cases: Leading U.S. Supreme Court cases on capital punishment*. Boston, MA: Butterworth-Heinemann.

Ledford v. Head, 2008 U.S. Dist. LEXIS 21635 (N.D. Ga.).

Leistico, A. R., Salekin, R. T., deCoster, J., & Rogers, R. (2008). A large-scale meta-analysis relating the Hare measures of psychopathy to antisocial conduct. *Law and Human Behavior, 32*, 28–45.

Leonard, P. B. (2003). A new profession for an old need: Why a mitigation specialist must be included on the capital defense team. *Hofstra Law Review, 31*, 1143–1155.

Leong, G. B., Silva, J. A., Weinstock, R., & Ganzini, L. (2000). Survey of forensic psychiatrists on evaluation and treatment of prisoners on death row. *Journal of the American Academy of Psychiatry and the Law, 28*, 427–432.

Leong, G. B., Weinstock, R., Silva, J. A., & Eth, S. (1993). Psychiatry and the death penalty: The past decade. *Psychiatric Annals, 23*, 41–47.

Lidz, C. W., Mulvey, E. P., & Gardner, W. (1993). The accuracy of predictions of violence to others. *Journal of the American Medical Association, 269*, 1007–1011.

Lieberman, J. D., & Sales, B. D. (2006). *Scientific jury selection*. Washington, DC: American Psychological Association.

Lockett v. Ohio, 438 U.S. 586 (1978).

Lockhart v. McCree, 476 U.S. 162 (1986).

Loeber, R., Pardini, D., Homish, D. L., Wei, E., Crawford, A., Farrington, D. P., ...Rosenfeld, R. (2005). The prediction of violence and homicide in young men. *Journal of Consulting and Clinical Psychology, 73*, 1074–1088.

Luckasson, R., Schalock, R. L., Spitalnik, D. M., Spreat, S., Tasse, M., & Snell, M. E., ... Tasse, M. J. (2002). *Mental retardation: Definition, classification, and systems of supports* (10th ed.). Washington, DC: American Association of Mental Retardation.

Luthar, S. S., Cicchetti, D., & Becker, B. (2000). The construct of resilience: A critical evaluation and guidelines for future work. *Child Development, 71*, 543–562.

Mabli, J., Holley, C. Patrick, J., & Walls, J. (1979). Age and prison violence. *Criminal Justice and Behavior, 61*, 175–186.

Macvaugh, G., & Cunningham, M. D. (2009). Atkins v Virginia: Implications and recommendations for forensic practice. *Journal of Psychiatry and Law, 37*, 131–187.

Marczyk, G., Heilbrun, K., DeMatteo, D., & Bell, B. (2003). Using a model to guide data gathering, interpretation, and communication in capital mitigation evaluations. *Journal of Forensic Psychology Practice, 3*, 89–103.

Marczyk, G., Knauss, L., Kutinsky, J., DeMatteo, D., & Heilbrun, K. (2008). The legal, ethical, and applied aspects of capital mitigation evaluations: Practice guidance from a principles-based approach. In H. V. Hall (Ed.), *Forensic psychology and neuropsychology for criminal and civil cases* (pp. 41–91, 779–791). Boca Raton, FL: CRC Press (Taylor & Francis Group).

Marquart, J. W., Ekland-Olson, S., & Sorensen, J. (1989). Gazing into the crystal ball: Can jurors accurately predict future dangerousness in capital cases? *Law and Society Review, 23*, 449–468.

Marquart, J. W., Ekland-Olson, S., & Sorensen, J. R. (1994). *The rope, the chair, and the needle: Capital punishment in Texas, 1923–1990*. Austin, TX: University of Texas Press.

Marquart, J. W., & Sorensen, J. (1988). Institutional and postrelease behavior of Furman-commuted inmates in Texas. *Criminology, 26*, 677–693.

Marquart, J. W., & Sorensen, J. (1989). A national study of the Furman-commuted inmates: Assessing the threat to society from capital offenders. *Loyola of Los Angeles Law Review, 23*, 5–28.

Martin v. Florida, 515 So. 2d 189 (Fla. 1987).

Martindale, D. A., & Gould, J. W. (2007). Custody evaluation reports: The case for empirically-derived information. *Journal of Forensic Psychology Practice, 7*, 87–99.

Masten, A. S. (2001). Ordinary magic: Resilience processes in development. *American Psychologist, 56*, 227–238.

Mathias, R. E. (1988). Assessment of competency for execution: Assessment and dissonance on death row: The dilemma of consultation. *Forensic Reports, 1*, 125–132.

McCann, J. (1998). *Malingering and deception in adolescents.* Washington, DC: American Psychological Association.
McCleskey v. Kemp, 481 U.S. 279 (1987).
McCoy v. North Carolina, 494 U.S. 433 (1990).
McGautha v. California, 402 U.S. 183 (1971).
Meany, K. A. (2004). *Atkins v. Virginia*: The false finding of a national consensus and the problems with determining who is mentally retarded. *Widener Law Review, 11,* 137–170.
Melton, G. B., Petrila, J., Poythress, N., & Slobogin, C. (2007). *Psychological evaluations for the courts: A handbook for mental health professionals and lawyers* (3rd ed.). New York, NY: Guilford.
Messick, S. (1980). Test validity and the ethics of assessment. *American Psychologist, 35,* 1012–1027.
Messick, S. (1995). Validity of psychological assessment: Validation of inferences from persons' responses and performances as scientific inquiry into score meaning. *American Psychologist, 50,* 741–749.
Miller, H. (2001). *Miller-Forensic Assessment of Symptoms Test (M-FAST): Professional manual.* Odessa, FL: Psychological Assessment Resources.
Miller, R. D. (1988). Evaluation of and treatment for competency to be executed: A national survey and an analysis. *Journal of Psychiatry and Law, 16,* 67–90.
Miller v. State, 373 So.2d 882 (Fla. 1979).
Millon, T. (1994). *Millon Clinical Multiaxial Inventory-III manual.* Minneapolis, MN: Interpretive Scoring Systems.
Mills v. Maryland, 486 U.S. 367 (1988).
Miranda v. Arizona, 348 U.S. 436 (1966).
Monahan, J. (1981). *Predicting violent behavior: An assessment of clinical techniques.* Beverly Hills, CA: Sage.
Monahan, J. (1996). Violence prediction: The past twenty and next twenty years. *Criminal Justice and Behavior, 23,* 107–120.
Monahan, J. (2003). Violence risk assessment. In A. M. Goldstein (Ed.), *Handbook of psychology, Vol. 11. Forensic psychology* (pp. 527–540). Hoboken, NJ: John Wiley & Sons.
Monahan, J., Steadman, H. J., Silver, E., Appelbaum, P. S., Robbins, P. C., Mulvey, E. P., Roth, L. H., Grisso, T., & Banks, S. (2001). *Rethinking risk assessment: The MacArthur study of mental disorder and violence.* New York, NY: Oxford University Press.
Moore, R. B. (2006). Modification of individual's IQ scores is not accepted professional practice. *Psychology in Mental Retardation and Developmental Disabilities Newsletter, 31,* 11–12.
Morey, L. (1991). *Personality Assessment Inventory professional manual.* Odessa, FL: Psychological Assessment Resources.
Morris v. Dretke, 379 F.3d 199 (5th Cir. 2004).
Morris, R. G., Longmire, D. R., Buffington-Vollum, J., & Vollum, S. (2010). Managing career inmates: Differential parole eligibility and institutional misconduct among capital inmates. *Criminal Justice and Behavior, 37,* 417–438.
Morse, S. J. (1978a). Crazy behavior, morals, and science: An analysis of mental health law. *Southern California Law Review, 51,* 527–654.
Morse, S. J. (1978b). Law and mental health professionals: The limits of expertise. *Professional Psychology, 9,* 389–399.
Mossman, D. (1987). Assessing and restoring competency to be executed: Should psychiatrists participate? *Behavioral Sciences and the Law, 5,* 397–409.

Mossman, D. (1994). Assessing predictions of violence: Being accurate about accuracy. *Journal of Consulting and Clinical Psychology, 62*, 783–792.
Mossman, D. (1995). Denouement of an execution competency case: Is *Perry* pyrrhic? *Bulletin of the American Academy of Psychiatry and the Law, 23*, 269–284.
Mossman, D. (2003). Atkins v. Virginia: A psychiatric can of worms. *New Mexico Law Review, 33*, 255–291.
Mumola, C. J. (2005). *Bureau of Justice Statistics special report: Suicide and homicide in state prisons and local jails*. Washington, DC: U.S. Department of Justice.
Munsterberg, H. (1908). *On the witness stand: Essays on psychology and crime*. New York, NY: Doubleday.
Murrie, D. C., & Warren, J. I. (2005). Clinician variation in rates of legal sanity opinions: Implications for self-monitoring. *Professional Psychology: Research and Practice, 36*, 519–524.
National Institute on Drug Abuse. (1993). Numerous factors implicated in drug-related violence. *NIDA Notes, 8*(5), 1–4.
National Institute of Justice. (2000). *1999 annual report on drug use among adult and juvenile arrestees*. Washington, DC: U.S. Department of Justice.
Neal v. Texas, 256 S.W.3d 264 (Tex. Crim. App. 2008).
Nicholson, R. A., & Norwood, S. (2000). The quality of forensic psychological assessments, reports, and testimony: Acknowledging the gap between promise and practice. *Law and Human Behavior, 24*, 9–44.
Nobles v. Georgia, 168 U.S. 398 (1897).
North Carolina v. Lippard, 568 S.E. 2d 657 (N.C. Ct. App. 2002).
Ohio v. Stallings, 2004 Ohio App. LEXIS 4167.
Okla. Stat. Ann. Tit. 21, § 701.12 (2010).
Ore. Rev. Stat. § 163.150 (2010).
Orpen, C. A. (2003). Following in the footsteps of *Ford*: Mental retardation and capital punishment post-*Atkins*. *University of Pittsburgh Law Review, 65*, 83–102.
Otto, R. K. (2009). Meaningful consideration of competence to be executed. In R. F. Schopp, R. L. Wierner, B. H. Bornstein, & S. L. Willborn (Eds.), *Mental disorder and criminal law: Responsibility, punishment, and competence* (pp. 191–204). New York, NY: Springer.
Otto, R. K., & Douglas, K. (Eds.). (2010). *Handbook of violence risk assessment*. New York, NY: Taylor/Francis.
Otto, R. K., & Heilbrun, K. (2002). The practice of forensic psychology: A look toward the future in light of the past. *American Psychologist, 57*, 5–18.
Otto, R. K., Slobogin, C., & Greenberg, S. A. (2007). Legal and ethical issues in accessing and utilizing third party information. In A. M. Goldstein (Ed.), *Forensic psychology: Emerging topics and expanding roles* (pp. 190–208). Hoboken, NJ: John Wiley & Sons.
Packer, E. (2007). Associations concur on mental disability and death penalty policy. *Monitor on Psychology, 38*, 14.
Panetti v. Dretke, 401 F. Supp. 2d 702 (W.D. Tex. 2004), aff'd, 448 F.3d 815 (5th Cir. 2006).
Panetti v. Quarterman, 551 U.S. 930 (2007), remanded, 2008 U.S. Dist. LEXIS 107438 (W.D. Tex. 2008).
Pastroff, S. M. (1986). Eighth Amendment–The constitutional rights of the insane on death row. *Journal of Criminal Law and Criminology, 77*, 844–866.
Pearson v. Yewdall, 95 U.S. 294 (1877).

Penry v. Lynaugh, 492 U.S. 302 (1989).
People v. Superior Court, 129 Cal. App. 4th 434 (Cal. Ct. App. 2005).
People v. Taylor, 9 N.Y.3d 129 (2007).
Phyle v. Duffy, 334 U.S. 431 (1948).
Pirelli, G., & Zapf, P. A. (2008). An investigation of psychologists' practices and attitudes toward participation in capital evaluations. *Journal of Forensic Psychology Practice, 8*, 39–66.
Porter v. Virginia, 661 S.E.2d 415 (Va. 2008).
Proffitt v. Florida, 428 U.S. 242 (1976).
Radelet, M. L., & Barnard, G. W. (1986). Ethics and the psychiatric determination of competency to be executed. *Bulletin of the American Academy of Psychiatry and the Law, 14*, 37–53.
Randa, L. E. (Ed.). (1997). *Society's final solution: A history and discussion of the death penalty*. Lanham, MD: University Press of America.
Regnier, T. (2004). *Barefoot* in quicksand: The future of "future dangerousness" predictions in death penalty sentencing in the world of *Daubert* and *Kuhmo*. *Akron Law Review, 37*, 469–508.
Reid, W. H. (2001). Psychiatry and the death penalty. *Journal of Psychiatric Practice, 7*, 216–219.
Reidy, T. J., Cunningham, M. D., & Sorensen, J. R. (2001). From death to life: Prison behavior of former death row inmates. *Criminal Justice and Behavior, 28*, 67–82.
Reisner, R., Slobogin, C., & Rai, A. (2004). *Law and the mental health system: Civil and criminal aspects* (4th ed.). St. Paul, MN: Thomson/West.
Ring v. Arizona, 536 U.S. 584 (2002).
Rivera v. Quarterman, 505 F.3d 349 (5th Cir. 2007).
Roberts v. Louisiana, 428 U.S. 325 (1976).
Rodriguez v. Florida, 919 So.2d 1252 (Fla. 2005).
Roesch, R., & Golding, S. L. (1980). *Competency to stand trial*. Urbana, IL: University of Illinois Press.
Rogers, R. (1984). Towards an empirical model of malingering and deception. *Behavioral Science and the Law, 2*, 93–112.
Rogers, R. (1986). *Conducting insanity evaluations*. New York, NY: Van Nostrand-Reinhold.
Rogers, R. (1997). (Ed.). *Clinical assessment of malingering and deception* (2nd ed.). New York, NY: Guilford.
Rogers, R. (2008). (Ed.). *Clinical assessment of malingering and deception* (3rd ed.). New York, NY: Guilford.
Rogers, R., Bagby, R. M., & Dickens, S. E. (1992). *Structured interview of reported symptoms*. Odessa, FL: Psychological Assessment Resources.
Rogers, R., & Ewing, C. P. (1989). Ultimate opinion proscriptions: A cosmetic fix and a plea for empiricism. *Law and Human Behavior, 13*, 357–374.
Rogers, R., Sewell, K. W., & Gillard, N. D. (2010). *Structured interview of reported symptoms* (2nd ed.). Odessa, FL: Psychological Assessment Resources.
Rogers, R., & Shuman, D. (2000). *Conducting insanity evaluations* (2nd ed.). New York, NY: Guilford Press.
Roid, G. H. (2003). *Stanford-Binet fifth edition: Technical manual*. Rolling Meadows, IL: Riverside.
Roper v. Simmons, 542 U.S. 551 (2005).
Rosales v. Quarterman, 2008 U.S. App. LEXIS 17964 (5th Cir. 2008).

Salekin, K. L. (2004, March). *Forensic evaluation, mental retardation, and methodology: Is there a consensus?* Paper presented at the 2004 Annual Conference of the American Psychology-Law Society, Scottsdale, AZ.

Salekin, K. L. (2007). Capital mitigation from a developmental perspective: The importance of risk factors, protective factors, and the construct of resilience. In M. Costanzo, D. Krauss, & K. Pezdek (Eds.), *Expert psychological testimony for the courts* (pp. 149–176). Mahwah, NJ: Lawrence Erlbaum Associates.

Salekin, K. L., & Doane, B. M. (2009). Malingering intellectual disability: The value of available measures and methods. *Applied Neuropsychology, 16*, 105–113.

Sameroff, A. J. (2000). Developmental systems and psychopathology. *Development and Psychopathology, 12*, 297–312.

Satterwhite v. Texas, 486 U.S. 249 (1988).

Scarr, S., & McCartney, K. (1983). How people make their own environments: A theory of genotype environmental effects. *Child Development, 54*, 424–435.

Schalock, R. L., Buntinax, W. H. E., Borthwick-Duffy, S., Bradley, V., Craig, E. M., Coulter, D. L., et al. (2010). *Mental retardation: Definition, classification, and system of supports*. Washington, DC: American Association on Intellectual and Developmental Disabilities.

Schiro v. Summerlin, 542 U.S. 348 (2004).

Schopp, R. F. (2009a). Psychological expertise and amicus briefs in the context of competence to face execution. In R. F. Schopp, R. L. Wierner, B. H. Bornstein, & S. L. Willborn (Eds.), *Mental disorder and criminal law: Responsibility, punishment, and competence* (pp. 205–230). New York, NY: Springer.

Schopp, R. F. (2009b). Treating criminal offenders in correctional contexts: Identifying interests and distributing responsibilities. *Behavioral Sciences and the Law, 27*, 833–855.

Scullin, M. H. (2006). Large state-level fluctuations in mental retardation classifications related to introduction of renormed intelligence test. *American Journal on Mental Retardation, 111*, 322–335.

Scullin, M. H. (2008, March). *The Flynn effect helped establish the IQ criterion of mental retardation in an Atkins hearing.* Poster session presented at the 2008 Annual Conference of the American Psychology-Law Society (AP-LS), Division 41 of the American Psychological Association (APA), Jacksonville, FL.

Shah, S. (1978). Dangerousness: A paradigm for exploring some issues in law and psychology. *American Psychologist, 33*, 224–238.

Shandera, A. L., Berry, D. T. R., Clark, J. A., Schipper, L. J., Graue, L. O., & Harp, J. P. (2010). Detection of malingered mental retardation. *Psychological Assessment, 22*, 50–56.

Shapiro, D. (1991). *Forensic psychological assessment: An integrated approach*. Boston, MA: Allyn & Bacon.

Shapiro, D. L. (1999). *Criminal responsibility evaluations: A manual for practice*. Sarasota, FL: Professional Resource Press.

Shapiro, M. (2009). An overdose of dangerousness: How "future dangerousness" catches the least culpable capital defendants and undermines the rationale for the executions it supports. *American Journal of Criminal Law, 35*, 145–200.

Shayer, M., Ginsburg, D., & Coe, R. (2007). Thirty years on–A large anti-Flynn effect? The Piagetian test volume and heaviness norms: 1975-2003. *British Journal of Educational Psychology, 75*, 25–41.

Shuman, D. W., & Greenberg, S. A. (2003). The expert witness, the adversary system, and the voice of reason: Reconciling impartiality and advocacy. *Professional Psychology: Research and Practice, 34*, 219–224.

Simmons v. South Carolina, 512 U.S. 154 (1994).
Simon, R. J. (1970). "Beyond a reasonable doubt": An experimental attempt at quantification. *The Journal of Applied Behavioral Science, 6*, 203–209.
Simon, R., & Gold, L. (Eds.). (2004). *Textbook of forensic psychiatry*. Washington, DC: American Psychiatric Publishing.
Skeem, J., & Golding, S. (1998). Community examiners' evaluations of competence to stand trial: Common problems and suggestions for improvement. *Professional Psychology: Research and Practice, 29*, 357–367.
Skeem, J., & Monahan, J. (in press). Current directions in violence risk assessment. *Current Directions in Psychological Science*.
Skipper v. South Carolina, 476 U.S. 1 (1986).
Slobogin, C. (2000). Mental illness and the death penalty. *Mental and Physical Disability Law Reporter, 24*, 667–677.
Slobogin, C. (2003). What *Atkins* could mean for people with mental illness. *New Mexico Law Review, 33*, 293–314.
Slobogin, C. (2006). *Proving the unprovable*. New York, NY: Oxford University Press.
Slobogin, C. (2007). The Supreme Court's recent criminal mental health cases: Rulings of questionable competence. *Criminal Justice, 22*(3), 1–8.
Slobogin, C., Rai, A., & Reisner, R. (2009). *Law and the mental health system: Civil and criminal aspects* (fifth ed.). St. Paul, MN: Thomson/West.
Small, M. A., & Otto, R. K. (1991). Evaluations of competency to be executed: Legal contours and implications for assessment. *Criminal Justice and Behavior, 18*, 146–158.
Smith v. Texas, 543 U.S. 37 (2004).
Snell, T. L. (2009). *Capital punishment, 2008–Statistical tables*. Washington, DC: U.S. Department of Justice, Office of Justice Programs, Bureau of Justice Statistics.
Solesbee v. Balkcom, 339 U.S. 9 (1950).
Sorensen, J. R., & Cunningham, M. D. (2009). Once a killer always a killer? Prison misconduct of former death-sentenced inmates in Arizona. *Journal of Psychiatry and Law, 37*, 237–267.
Sorensen, J. R., & Cunningham, M. D. (2010). Conviction offense and prison violence: A comparative study of murderers and other offenders. *Crime and Delinquency, 56*, 103–125.
Sorensen, J. R., & Pilgrim, R. L. (2000). An actuarial risk assessment of violence posed by capital murder defendants. *Journal of Criminal Law and Criminology, 90*, 1251–1270.
Sorensen, J. R., & Wrinkle, R. D. (1996). No hope for parole: Disciplinary infractions among death-sentenced and life-without-parole inmates. *Criminal Justice and Behavior, 23*, 542–552.
Spaziano v. Florida, 468 U.S. 447 (1984).
Sroufe, L. A., & Rutter, M. (1984). The domain of developmental psychopathology. *Child Development, 55*, 17–29.
Stallings v. Bagley, 561 F. Supp. 2d 821 (N.D. Ohio 2008).
Stanford v. Kentucky, 492 U.S. 361 (1989).
State v. Mata, 745 N.W. 2d 229 (Neb. 2008).
Sterling v. Texas, 830 S.W.2d 114 (Tex. Crim. App. 1992).
Stevens, K. B., & Price, J. R. (2006). Adaptive behavior, mental retardation, and the death penalty. *Journal of Forensic Psychology Practice, 6*, 1–29.
Stone, A. A. (2002). Forensic ethics and capital punishment: Is there a special problem? *Journal of Forensic Psychiatry, 13*, 487–493.
Strickland v. Washington, 466 U.S. 668 (1984).

Summerlin v. Stewart, 341 F.3d 1082 (9th Cir. 2003).
Sundby, S. E. (1997). The jury as critic: An empirical look at how capital juries perceive expert and lay testimony. *Virginia Law Review, 83*, 1109–1188.
Swanson, J. W. (1994). Mental disorder, substance abuse, and community violence: An epidemiological approach. In J. Monahan & H. J. Steadman (Eds.), *Violence and mental disorder: Developments in risk assessment* (pp. 101–136). Chicago, IL: University of Chicago Press.
Sweet, J. J., & Moulthrop, M. A. (1999). Self-examination questions as a means of identifying bias in adversarial assessments. *Journal of Forensic Neuropsychology, 1*, 73–88.
Tarasoff v. Regents of the University of California, 551 P.2d 334 (Cal. 1976).
Task Force on Mental Disability and the Death Penalty. (2006). *Report of the Task Force on Mental Disability and the Death Penalty.* Retrieved from: http://www.apa.org/pubs/info/reports/mental-disability-and-death-penalty.pdf.
Tasse, M. J. (2009). Adaptive behavior assessment and the diagnosis of mental retardation in capital cases. *Applied Neuropsychology, 16*, 114–123.
Taylor, R. L. (1997). *Assessment of individuals with mental retardation.* San Diego, CA: Singular Publishing.
Teasdale, T. W., & Owen, D. R. (2005). A long-term rise and decline in intelligence test performance: The Flynn effect in reverse. *Personality and Individual Differences, 39*, 837–843.
Teasdale, T. W., & Owen, D. R. (2008). Secular declines in cognitive test scores: A reversal of the Flynn effect. *Intelligence, 36*, 121–126.
Tennard v. Dretke, 542 U.S. 272 (2004).
Tex. Code Crim. Proc. art. 37.071 (2010).
Tex. Code Crim. Proc. art. 37.0711 (2010).
Thompson, D. C., & Wachtell, M. F. (2009). An empirical analysis of Supreme Court certiorari petition procedures: The call for response and the call for the view of the solicitor general. *George Mason Law Review, 16*, 237–302.
Thompson v. Oklahoma, 487 U.S. 815 (1988).
Tillbrook, C., Mumley, D., & Grisso, T. (2003). Avoiding expert opinions on the ultimate legal question: The case for integrity. *Journal of Forensic Psychology Practice, 3*, 77–87.
Tobolowsky, P. M. (2003). *Atkins* aftermath: Identifying mentally retarded offenders and excluding them from execution. *University of Notre Dame Journal of Legislation, 30*, 77–141.
Toch, H. (1975). *Men in crisis: Human breakdowns in prison.* Chicago, IL: Aldine Publishing Co.
Toch, H., & Adams, K. (1986). Pathology and disruptiveness among prison inmates. *Journal of Research in Crime and Delinquency, 23*, 7–21.
Tolman, A. O., & Mullendore, K. B. (2003). Risk evaluations for the courts: Is service quality a function of specialization? *Professional Psychology: Research and Practice, 34*, 225–232.
Tombaugh, T. N. (1997). *TOMM: Test of Memory Malingering manual.* Toronto, ON: Multi-Health Systems.
Trop v. Dulles, 356 US 86 (1958).
United States v. Fields, No. 04-50393 (5th Cir. 2007).
United States v. Green, 407 F.3d 434 (1st Cir. 2005).
United States v. Horowitz, 360 F. Supp. 772 (E.D. Pa. 1973).

United States v. Lee, 89 F. Supp.2d 1017 (E.D. Ark. 2000).
United States v. Lee, 274 F.3d 485 (8th Cir. 2001).
United States v. Sablan, 555 F. Supp. 2d 1177 (D. Colo, 2006).
United States v. Sampson, 335 F. Supp. 2d 166 (D. Mass. 2004).
United States v. Satan and His Staff, 54 F.R.D. 282 (W.D. Pa. 1971).
United States v. Taylor, 320 F. Supp.2d 790 (N.D. Ind. 2004).
United States v. Williams, 400 F.3d 277 (5th Cir. 2005).
United States v. Young, 424 F.3d 499 (6th Cir. 2005).
Va. Code Ann. § 19.2-264.2 (2010).
Va. Code Ann. § 19.2-264.3:1(A) (2010).
Wainwright v. Witt, 469 U.S. 412 (1985).
Walker v. Sauvinet, 92 U.S. 90 (1876).
Walker v. True, 399 F.3d 315 (4th Cir. 2005).
Walsh, T., & Walsh, Z. (2006). The evidentiary introduction of Psychopathy Checklist-Revised assessed psychopathy in U.S. courts: Extent and appropriateness. *Law and Human Behavior, 30*, 493–507.
Walter v. Angelone, 321 F.3d 422 (4th Cir. 2003).
Walters, G. D. (2003). Predicting institutional adjustment and recidivism with the Psychopathy Checklist factor scores: A meta-analysis. *Law and Human Behavior, 27*, 541–558.
Walton v. Johnson, 407 F.3d 285 (4th Cir. 2005).
Ward, B. A. (1986). Competency for execution: Problems in law and psychiatry. *Florida State University Law Review, 14*, 35–101.
Washington v. Harris, 789 P.2d 60 (Wash. 1990).
Washington v. Rice, 757 P.2d 889 (Wash. 1988).
Water Energizers, Ltd. v. Water Energizers, Inc., 788 F. Supp. 208 (S.D.N.Y. 1992).
Wechsler, D. (1997). *Wechsler Adult Intelligence Scale, 3rd ed. Administration and scoring manual*. San Antonio, TX: Psychological Corporation.
Wechsler, D. (2003). *Wechsler Intelligence Scale for Children, 4th ed. Administration and scoring manual*. San Antonio, TX: Psychological Corporation.
Wechsler, D. (2008). *Wechsler Adult Intelligence Scale, 4th ed. Technical and interpretive manual*. San Antonio, TX: Psychological Corporation.
Weiner, I. B. (2006). Writing forensic reports. In I. B. Weiner & A. K. Hess (Eds.), *The handbook of forensic psychology* (3rd ed., pp. 631–651). Hoboken, NJ: Wiley.
Weiner, I. B., & Hess, A. K. (2006). *The handbook of forensic psychology* (3rd ed.). Hoboken, NJ: John Wiley & Sons.
Weinstock, R., Leong, G. B., & Silva, J. A. (1992). The death penalty and Bernard Diamond's approach to forensic psychiatry. *Bulletin of the American Academy of Psychiatry and the Law, 20*, 197–210.
Weinstock, R., Leong, G. B., & Silva, J. A. (2010). Competence to be executed: An ethical analysis post *Panetti*. *Behavioral Sciences and the Law*, DOI: 10.1002/bsl.951.
Weithorn, L. A. (2008). Conceptual hurdles to the application of *Atkins v. Virginia*. *Hastings Law Journal, 59*, 1203–1234.
Weiss, L. (no date). *Technical Report: Response to Flynn*. Harcourt Assessment. Retrieved from: http://www.pearsonassessments.com/hai/Images/Products/WAIS-III/WAIS-III_TR_lr.pdf.
Werner, E. E., & Smith, R. S. (1982). *Vulnerable but invincible: A study of resilient children*. New York, NY: McGraw-Hill.
Werner, E. E., & Smith, R. S. (1992). *Overcoming the odds: High risk children from birth to adulthood*. Ithaca, NY: Cornell University Press.

Wexler, D. B., & Winick, B. J. (Eds.). (1996). *Law in a therapeutic key: Developments in therapeutic jurisprudence*. Durham, NC: Carolina Academic Press.

White, C. G. (1982). Ethical guidelines for psychologist participation in death penalty proceedings: A survey. *Professional Psychology, 13*, 327–329.

Widroff, J., & Watson, C. (2008). Mental retardation and the death penalty: Addressing various questions regarding an *Atkins* claim. *Journal of the American Academy of Psychiatry and the Law, 36*, 413–415.

Wiggins v. Smith, 539 U.S. 510 (2003).

Williams v. Florida, 399 U.S. 78 (1970).

Williams v. Quarterman, 2008 U.S. App. LEXIS 20148 (5th Cir. 2008).

Winick, B. J. (1992). Competence to be executed: A therapeutic jurisprudence perspective. *Behavioral Sciences and the Law, 10*, 317–337.

Witt, P. H. (2010). Forensic report checklist. *Open Access Journal of Forensic Psychology, 2*, 233–240.

Woodson v. North Carolina, 428 U.S. 280 (1976).

Wyo. Stat. Ann. § 6-2-101 (2010).

Young, B., Boccaccini, M. T., Conroy, M. A., & Lawson, K. (2007). Four practical and conceptual assessment issues that evaluators should address in capital case mental retardation evaluations. *Professional Psychology: Research and Practice, 38*, 169–178.

Young, B. A., Boccaccini, M. T., Lawson, K., & Conroy, M. A. (2008). Competence-for-execution evaluation practices in Texas: Findings from a semi-structured interview with experienced evaluators. *Journal of Forensic Psychology Practice, 8*, 280–292.

Zant v. Stephens, 462 U.S. 862 (1983).

Zapf, P. A. (2008). Competency for execution. In R. Jackson (Ed.), *Learning forensic assessment* (pp. 239–261). New York, NY: Routledge/Taylor & Francis Group.

Zapf, P. A. (2009). Elucidating the contours of competency for execution: The implications of *Ford* and *Panetti* for the assessment of CFE. *Journal of Psychiatry and Law, 37*, 269–307.

Zapf, P. A., Boccaccini, M. T., & Brodsky, S. L. (2003). Assessment of competency for execution: Professional guidelines and an evaluation checklist. *Behavioral Sciences and the Law, 21*, 103–120.

Zhang, Z. (2004). *Drug and alcohol use and related matters among arrestees, 2003*. Washington, DC: U.S. Department of Justice, National Institute of Justice.

Index

AAIDD. See American Association on Intellectual and Developmental Disabilities
AAMR. See American Association of Mental Retardation
Accreditation of forensic psychology (APA), 4
Adaptive Behavior Assessment System, 195, 196
Adaptive Behavior Scales (AAMR), 196
Adaptive functioning, 192–196
  AAIDD definition involving, 169
  ambiguities in state defined deficits, 177
  assessment recommendations, 196, 308
  best practice assessment strategy, 192–193
  Clark v. Quarterman example, 195
  Clemons v. Alabama example, 195
  correctional context use of, 194
  defined, 168–169, 192
  difficulties in assessing, 182
  evaluator assessment procedures, 193–194
  evaluator inability in choosing measures, 301
  Ex parte Briseno example, 195
  Ex parte Smith example, 195
  IQ scores and, 178–180
  measurement developmental limitations, 309
  mental retardation diagnosis and, 168
  Rodriguez v. Florida example, 195–196
  in sample report, 323–324, 330, 344–345, 349, 351
  Williams v. Quarterman example, 193
Ake v. Oklahoma (1985), 214, 297
Alito, Samuel, 144n8
American Association of Mental Retardation (AAMR), 133, 162, 168
  adaptive functioning measures, 192, 196
  mental retardation definition, 133, 168, 192
American Association on Intellectual and Developmental Disabilities (AAIDD)
  adaptive behavior assessment, 195
  intellectual disability criteria, 351
  IQ scoring guidelines, 187
  mental retardation definition, 168–169, 178, 192, 196, 302, 329

435

American Bar Association (ABA)
  amicus brief, Panetti case, 142
  competence to stand trial standard, 138, 397, 404–405
  Guidelines for the Appointment and Performance of Counsel in Death Penalty Cases, 231
  Individual Rights and Responsibilities Section, 197
  staying of execution recommendations, 138
American Board of Forensic Psychology, 290
American Medical Association (AMA)
  Code of Medical Ethics, 149, 207*n*6
  Principles of Medical Ethics, 147
  stance in capital cases, 149
American Psychiatric Association, 133, 142
  amicus brief filing, 142, 153, 263
  Annotated Principles, 148
  antisocial personality disorder criteria, 162
  Barefoot v. Estelle amicus curiae brief, 263
  mental retardation definition, 133, 162, 168–169, 329
  Task Force formation, participation, 143, 197
American Psychological Association (APA)
  competence defined/described, 213
  forensic psychology accreditation, 4
  mental retardation definition, 169
  Panetti amicus brief filing, 142
  Task Force formation, 197
Annotated Principles. See *The Principles of Medical Ethics with Annotations Especially Applicable to Psychiatry*
Anthony, C., 273
Antisocial personality disorder (APD), 131, 160, 162, 280, 342, 411
Appeals process role (of mental health professionals), 22
Atkins type evaluations, 134
  characteristics of defendants referred for, 289
  components included in, 313–314
  ethical challenges of, 144
  evaluator qualifications for, 290–291
  Flynn effect, 184–190
  front end/posttrial conduction, 19, 20
  IQ measurement error, 182–184
  mental retardation focus of, 305
  Morse/Grisso model application to, 299–300
  procedural issues relevant to, 180–182
  Report 1 (sample), 318–324
  Report 2 (sample), 325–351
  state minimum qualifications for conducting, 295
  testing conditions influence, 303–304
  test-retest effects, 190–191
Atkins v. Virginia (2002), 17, 19*n*9, 20, 25, 159, 231
  described, 20, 131–134, 165–166
  Eighth Amendment protections of, 197
  FMHAs of (2002, 2004, 2005), 191
  implications of, 166–169, 177–180
  IQ testing and, 159
  on mental retardation, 166, 180–181, 199, 203, 205, 231, 253
  need created by, 295
  Penry v. Lynaugh as prelude to, 129–132, 165
Automatic appeals/review, in capital cases, 47
Autonomy issues, 9–10

Back-end evaluations (in capital contexts), 20–23, 165. *See also* Front-end (pre-trial) evaluations in capital contexts
  defined, 19
  Eddings v. Oklahoma, 21
  Lockett v. Ohio, 21
Barefoot v. Estelle (1983), 153, 263–266
Barnard, G. W., 207
Barnard v. Collins (1994), 139
Bersoff, D. N., 179–180
Bifurcation of capital trials, 20, 43–44
Blackmun, Harry, 264
Blume, J. H., 198
Blystone v. Pennsylvania (1990), 229, 232
Bonnie, R. J., 184, 198, 207
Borum, R., 294

Boundaries of competence (of mental health professionals), 152–154
Brodsky, S., 207, 293, 315
Buffington-Vollum, J. K., 273
Burch v. Louisiana (1979), 39
Burger, Warren E., 226*n*4

Capital mitigation evaluation, 19
  application of Heilbrun's principles, 288
  areas for exploration, 253–256
  caution regarding, 258
  cognitive/neuropsychological testing, 252–253
  collateral interviews component, 250–251
  collateral records component, 249–250, 251*t*
  conducting evaluations, 247–253
  defined, 223, 234–235
  developmental psychopathology report, 240–241
  equifinality, 242
  evaluation expert role, 246–247
  evaluator requirements for, 153–154
  evaluator's task in, 235
  focus required for, 223
  interview component, 247–249
  issues relevant to, 157
  mitigation, defined by case law, 224–232
  "mitigation specialist" consulting role, 244
  moral culpability considerations, 235–240
  multifinality, 242
  presentation of findings, 256–259
  protective factors, 241–242
  resilience, 242–243
  risk factors, 241
  roles for mental health professionals, 243–247
  in state statutes, 233–234
  "teaching expert" consulting role, 245–246
  testing component, 252
Capital offenses
  aggravating factors by state, 54–102
  childhood abuse connection to, 21
  death penalty decision, 42–43
  defined, 40
  eligible capital offenses, 40–42
  Federal list, 50–51
  mitigating factors by state, 102–121
  by state, 51–53
  state clemency procedure differences, 121–122
Certiorari, writ of, 31, 33
Cherry v. Florida (2007), 183
Child abuse, 7*t*, 330
Civil law context evaluations, 5
Clark v. Quarterman (2006), 195
Clemency option, 48
  state procedure differences, 121–122
Clemons v. Alabama (2005), 195
Clinical assessment-FMHA comparison, 7*t*–8*t*
  client, 10
  consent, 9
  data sources, 11–12
  examinee's perspective, 11–12
  pace and setting, 12–13
  purpose, 6–9
  relationship, 12
  report, 13–14
  response style/threat to validity, 11
  testimony, 14
  voluntariness/autonomy, 9–10
Code of Hammurabi (Babylon), 125
Code of Medical Ethics (AMA, 2001), 149, 207*n*6
Coker v. Georgia (1977), 23, 25, 40
Colbach, E. M., 293
Committee on Ethical Guidelines for Forensic Psychologists, 147
Competence
  to waive counsel, 19
  to waive Miranda rights, 5, 19
Competence for execution evaluations, 18, 19, 22–23, 200–222. *See also* Competence for execution evaluations; *Ford v. Wainright; Panetti v. Quarterman;* Sample FMHA reports and components
  absence of substantive legal standard, 203
  ambiguity of standards for, 137, 203–205, 207

Competence for execution evaluations (*cont'd*)
  application of Morse/Grisso models, 299–300
  cases relevant to, 203–205
  clinical considerations, 210–212
  clinical interview of offender, 214–216
  competence-specific instruments, 217–219
  conducting competence for, 212–221
  ethical considerations relevant to, 151, 205–209
  evaluator competence standards, 202, 213–214, 312
  impaired thought process of offenders, 215–216
  informed consent/notification of purpose, 214
  Justice Kennedy's opinion, 204
  Justice Powell's opinion, 137
  length of evaluation, 215
  Panetti v. Quarterman and, 140
  present focus of, 301, 305
  privately conducted evaluations, 297
  rarity of, 202, 290
  report writing for, 220
  response style of defendants/civil litigants, 219–220
  scope limitations, 301
  Supreme Court rulings, 18, 128, 202–203
  traditional psychological measures used, 216–217
Competency for Execution Research Rating Scales (CERRS), 218
Comprehensive Test of Adaptive Behavior-Revised, 196
Consent. *See also* Informed consent
  clinical vs. forensic, 9
  formal/explicit, 7*t*, 9
  given by parties to the court, 33
Constitution (U.S.). *See also* Eighth Amendment
  Article III, 30n10, 33n15
  capital punishment violations of, 289
  Equal Protection Clause, 37, 197
  Fifth Amendment, 26, 34, 247
  Fourteenth Amendment, 26, 125, 224
  Fourth Amendment, 33
  primacy of, 32
  Sixth Amendment, 22, 26–27, 34–39
  as source of Federal law, 26
  Supreme Court's interpretive role, 30
  Tenth Amendment, 27
Court system, structure of (U.S.), 28–33. *See also* Supreme Court
  binding vs. pervasive legal authority, 31–32, 32n12
  hierarchies/tiers, 29–31
  jurisdictional differences, 28
  state-level court system, 28–31
  writ of certiorari, 31, 33
  writ of habeas corpus, 19, 22, 33
Criminal Justice Legal Foundation (CJLF), 142
Cruel and unusual punishment. *See* Eighth Amendment
Cultural fairness and biases
  of assessment instruments, 161
  Ethics Code guidelines, 161
  native vs. nonnative English speakers, 162
  principles of, 160–161
Cunningham, M. D., 17, 22, 157–158, 187, 189, 269–270, 272–273

Data sources
  Dept. of Justice/correctional facility homicide data, 270
  examinee's perspective of, 11–12
  Grisso/Morse data gathering model, 299–300
  violence risk evaluations/prison violence data, 270–271
Daubert v. Merrell Dow Pharmaceuticals, Inc. (1993), 32, 191, 264–265
Death penalty, historical background, 124–127
  Ancient Greece, Rome, Babylon, 125
  assessment instrument development, 4
  England, 1800s, 3
  law enforcement/psychological fitness testing, 3–4
  modern U.S. jurisprudence, 125–127
  1972 abolishment, 125
Death penalty cases, U.S. proceedings
  automatic appeals, review, 47

bifurcated trials, 20, 43–44
clemency, 48
decision for seeking, 42–43
eligible capital offenses, 40–42
execution, 48
felony murder rule, 41
guilt/innocence phase, 44
nonmurder capital offenses, 41
sentencing phase, 44–47
standards for seeking, 43
states ruling on, 40–41
Death penalty jurisprudence. *See also Gregg v. Georgia*
Ancient World, 124–125
historical background, 124–127
modern U.S., 125–127
Death penalty litigation
key players
defendants, 34
defense attorneys, 35
judges, 36
jury, 37–40
prosecutors, 35–36
sources of law, 26–27
structure, U.S. court system, 28–33
Death Penalty Protocol (U.S. Dept. of Justice), 42–43
Death sentence. *See also* Execution
Arizona judge decision, 39
biasing jury towards, 38
defense strategy for averting, 46
ethical practice in assessment, 148–152
IQ/eligibility for, 17
judicial scrutiny regarding, 123–124
for nonmurder offense, 41
possible inappropriateness, 21
waiving right to appeal, 22
Defendants
constitutional protections for, 13, 34–36
described, 34
felony murder rule application, 41
initial presumption of innocence, 38
post-sentencing *Atkins*-type evaluations, 20
waiving of rights by, 36–37
Defense attorneys
appointment of/rights to, 35

Atkins argument, 193
cross examination of defendant, 40n20
evaluations requested by, 214
goal at trial, 46
minimal acceptable standards for, 227
moral culpability and, 237
Panetti argument, 142
Penry argument, 129
reasonable effort standard of, 234
retention of private evaluator, 297
Supreme Court standards for, 231
DeMatteo, D., 169, 177–178, 286
Diagnostic and Statistical Manual of Mental Disorders, 4th edition (DSM-IV)
antisocial personality disorder inclusion, 162
intellectual disability criteria, 351
mental retardation criteria, 168, 169, 178, 192, 196, 302
"Do no harm" principle, 154–155, 205, 206
Draconian Code of Athens, 125
Droskin, Joel, 314
Due Process Clause (Fourteenth Amendment), 26, 125, 224
Dusky v. United States (1960), 16, 18, 19
"Duty to protect" against third parties, 10n4
Duvall, J. C., 181

Ebert, B., 217
Eddings v. Oklahoma (1982), 21, 25, 127, 226–228
Edens, J. F., 273
Education of defendants
age of onset determination, 198
Individualized Education Plan, 13
risk assessment factor, 278–279
special education, 185
use in mitigation evaluation, 251*t*, 254*t*
use in response style assessment, 219
Education of professionals
Ethical Standards and, 146
of psychiatrist, 148
of psychologists, 146, 148, 152–153, 213
training opportunities, 4

Eighth Amendment (Constitution), 32.
  See also Atkins v. Virginia (2002)
  evolving standards and, 27
  Ford v. Wainwright case, 22, 133,
    135–138
  four-Justice plurality opinion, 136
  historical background, 125
  interpretation considerations, 41
  Justice Powell on, 137
  Justice Warren on, 27
  Panetti v. Quarterman case, 22, 135,
    139–144, 203, 204, 207
  Penry v. Lynaugh case, 129–131,
    129–132, 165
  rights of, 20, 26, 32
  Trop v. Dulles case, 130, 136
England
  death penalty history, 125
  medical expert testimony, 3
Equal Protection Clause (Constitution),
    37, 197
Estelle v. Smith (1981), 262–263
Ethical practice in death penalty
    assessments, 148–152, 205–209
  mental health vs. law dilemmas,
    148–151
  physicians barred from execution
    participation, 149
  psychiatrist guidelines, 149
  psychologist lack of guidelines,
    149–150
  standards of adherence, 152
*Ethical Principles of Psychologists and
    Code of Conduct*
    (APA, 2002), 213
Ethical Standards of Psychologists
    (APA), 146
Ethics Code (*Ethical Principles of
    Psychologists and Code of
    Conduct*, APA)
  competence acceptability
    standard, 213
  components, 146–147
  cultural fairness principle, 160–162
  "do no harm" principle, 154–155,
    205, 206
  malingering assessment, 162–163
  psychologist scope of practice
    limitations, 152–153
  psychometric tools standards, 159

Ethics codes
  for psychiatrists, 147–148
  for psychologists, 146–147
*Ethics Guidelines for the Practice of
    Forensic Psychiatry* (American
    Academy of Psychiatry and the
    Law), 148
Everington, C., 178, 193
Execution. *See also* Competence for
    execution evaluations
  ABA competence standard, 138
  Eighth Amendment and, 129, 131
  forms of and constitutionality, 32
  historical background, 125
  state death penalty statutes, 48, 49t
  waiving right to appeal and, 22
Ex parte Briseno (2004), 195
Ex parte Smith (2003), 195

Family law evaluations, 5–6, 11, 286
Federal court system (description),
    28–31
Federal Death Penalty Act (1994),
    42, 44
Federal Rules of Evidence, 32, 264n2,
    311n5
Felony murder rule, 41
Fifth Amendment (Constitution), 26,
    34, 247
Florida statutory law, 135, 183
Flynn, J. R., 186
Flynn effect
  AAIDD guidelines, 187
  cases involving, 186
  court statutory guidance and, 186
  defined, 160, 184
  forensic evaluator considerations,
    188–189
  IQ scores and, 160, 184–190
  measurement errors, 189
  mental retardation determination
    and, 185
  test-retest effects, 190–191
Ford v. Wainright (1986), 22, 133,
    135–138, 166–167, 203
Forensic mental health assessment
    (FMHA). *See also* Forensic
    mental health assessment,
    violence risk assessment; Mental
    retardation; Principles of forensic

mental health assessment; Sample
FMHA reports and components
of *Atkins v. Virginia* (2002, 2004,
2005), 191
authorization for conducting, 156–157
clinical assessment comparison, 7t–8t
client, 10
consent, 9
data sources, 11–12
examinee's perspective, 11–12
pace and setting, 12–13
purpose, 6–9
relationship, 12
report, 13–14
response style/threat to validity, 11
testimony, 14
voluntariness/autonomy, 9–10
defined/described, 5–6
ethical practice in, 148–152
malingering assessment, 162–163
psychometric considerations, 158–160
quality of, 14–23
relevant Supreme Court cases, 127–144
violence risk assessment, 265–284
Forensic mental health assessment,
violence risk assessment, 265–284
age of defendant, 277–278
background information, 266–267
base rates of violence relevancy,
270–276
context determination, 267–270
educational background, 278–279
evaluator choice of considerations,
282–284
factors unrelated to prison violence,
280–282
offense characteristics, 279
poor prison terms, 278
prior prison violence, 278
prison gang membership, 279
risk communication, 282–284
Forensic psychology
conventions/standards, 8t
criticism of, 295
Specialty Guidelines for, 147
"ultimate legal question" debate, 220,
239, 310
Fourteenth Amendment
Due Process Clause, 26, 125, 224
violations of, 289

Fourth Amendment, 33
Freedman, A. M., 207
Front-end (pre-trial) evaluations in capital
contexts
Atkins v. Virginia, 17, 20
defined, 19
Dusky v. United States, 16, 18, 19
Miranda rights and, 19
types of, 19–20
Frye v. United States (1923), 32,
191, 301
Full Scale IQ score, 129, 182, 183, 190,
195–196
Furman v. Georgia (1972), 25, 125,
224–225, 261–262, 271–272, 289
"Future dangerousness" decision,
263–264, 273
Future violence, risks of
assessment of, 21–22
court receptivity to, 264
jury consideration of, 260–262, 272
prior prison act consideration, 278
recommendation for rejection of, 264
unpredictability of, 150

General Principle A ("do no harm," Ethics
Code), 154–155, 205
Golding, S., 294
Goldstein, A. M., 5–6, 16, 17, 22
Great Britain, death penalty history, 125
Greenspan, S., 186
Gregg v. Georgia (1976), 25, 40, 43, 123,
224–225, 229
Grisso, T., 5–6, 15, 16, 302–303
Grisso data gathering model, 299–300
Guidelines for the Appointment and
Performance of Counsel in Death
Penalty Cases (ABA), 231
Guilt/innocence phase, capital trials, 44
Gustafson, K., 184, 198

Habeas corpus (writ of habeas corpus)
evaluations, 19
Ohio v. Stallings (2004), 198–199
Panetti v. Quarterman (2007),
140–141
Penry v. Lynaugh (1989), 129
translation (meaning), 33
Hagan, L. D., 187
Halpern, A. L., 207

Heilbrun, K., 5–6, 16, 137–138, 211–212, 286, 288, 289, 303, 307, 310–311
Hippocratic Oath, 154
Hitchcock v. Dugger (1987), 228

Impaired thought process or form of offenders, 215–216
Individualized considerations of defendants, 261–262, 276, 309
Individualized Education Plan (IEP), 13
Individual Rights and Responsibilities Section (ABA), 197
Informed consent, 155–158
  for competence for execution evaluation, 214
  consequences of absence of, 306–307
  discussions with defense counsel, 158
  FMHA vs. clinical assessment, 6, 7*t*
  obtaining, 9, 214, 298
  reason for not needing, 304
  sample report (example), 319
  variance of requirements, 156–157
Insanity defense, 5, 10*n*3, 15, 20, 129–130, 140, 167
Interview Checklist for Evaluations of Competency for Execution (Zapf), 217
IQ (intelligence quotient) scores. *See also* Mental retardation
  Cherry v. Florida case, 183
  death penalty eligibility and, 17
  Flynn effect on, 160, 184–190
  Full Scale IQ score, 129, 183, 190, 195–196
  measurement errors, 182–184
  mental retardation and, 159, 168, 169, 178–180, 232
  native/non-native English and, 161–162
  recommendations for evaluators, 191–192
  score cut-offs, 179
  Stanford-Binet measures, 182
  state acceptability standards, 172*t*, 175*t*, 177
  state requirements, 159
  Supreme Court on, 134
  testing concerns, 180
  test-retest effects, 190–191
  variability factors, 185
  Wechsler Adult Intelligence Test, 182–183
Irreversibility of death sentence, 123

Jenkins v. United States (1962), 4
Judiciary Act (1789), 30–31*n*10
Jurek v. Texas (1976), 262
Juries
  deliberation process, 39–40
  described, 36–40
  responsibilities of, 39
  selection process, 37–38
    death penalty cases, 38
    size, 38–39
Justices of the Supreme Court. *See* Alito, Samuel; Blackmun, Harry; Burger, Warren E.; Kennedy, Anthony; Marshall, Thurgood; O'Connor, Sandra Day; Powell, Lewis F.; Roberts, John; Scalia, Antonin; Stevens, John Paul; Thomas, Clarence

Kanaya, T., 186
Keilen, A., 273
Kendall, George, 125
Kennedy, Anthony, 144, 204
Kennedy v. Louisiana (2008), 25, 41–42
Keyes, D. W., 193

Law, sources of, 26–27
Ledford v. Head (2008), 186
Life without possibility of parole (LWOP), 268, 273–275, 279
Lockett v. Ohio (1978), 21, 25, 225
Lockhart v. McCree (1986), 38

Malingering assessment, 162–163
Marczyk, G., 286
Marquart, J. W., 271–272
Marshall, Thurgood, 136, 397, 405
McClaren, H. A., 211–212
McCoy v. North Carolina (1990), 229
Mental health professionals
  boundaries of competence guidelines, 152–154
  do no harm principle adherence, 154–155, 205, 206
  ethical challenges of, 148–152

informed consent delivery, 155–158
role of in capital cases, 18–23
   appeals process, 22
   back-end evaluations, 19, 20–23
   front-end evaluations, 17–20
   habeas corpus evaluations, 19
   mitigation evaluations, 19
   sentencing decisions, 19
   teaching witness/"teaching testimony," 18
   waiving rights appeals, 22
Mental retardation. *See also* Antisocial personality disorder; IQ (intelligence quotient) scores
   AAIDD/AAMR definitions, 133, 168, 169, 192, 196
   APA definition, 169, 192, 196
   Atkins decision on, 180–181, 199, 203, 205, 231, 253
   diagnosis, 152, 154, 163, 178, 180, 193
   dismissing claim of, 195
   DSM-IV-TR definition, 162, 168, 169, 178, 179, 192, 196
   Equal Protection Clause and, 197
   feigning by offender, 198
   Flynn effect influence on, 185
   pretrial noneligibility determination, 201
   significance of diagnosis, 166
   state statutory definitions, 170*t*–177*t*, 180, 182, 194
   Supreme Court clinical definition, 182
   term shift to "intellectual disability," 165*n*2
   traditional diagnostic measures, 169, 182–183, 185, 187, 190, 191, 196, 321, 328, 346–349, 348*t*
Mental retardation and the death penalty. *See also Atkins* type evaluations; *Atkins v. Virginia*
   age of onset determination, 196–199
   Barnard v. Collins, 139
   competence to face execution, 134–135
   competence to stand trial, 15, 16, 18, 19–20
   determination of retardation, 19, 133
   feigning mental illness, 11
   Ford v. Wainright, 22, 133, 135–138, 166–167, 203

Panetti v. Quarterman, 22, 135, 139–144, 203, 204, 207
Penry v. Lynaugh, 129–131, 129–132, 165
Tennard v. Dretke, 134, 231–232
Trop v. Dulles, 130, 136
Walton v. Johnston, 139
Miller Forensic Assessment of Symptoms, 308
Mills v. Maryland (1988), 228
Minnesota Multiphasic Personality Inventory (MMPI), `63, 216, 220
Minnesota Multiphasic Personality Inventory-II (MMPI-II), 163
Miranda rights, 5, 19
Missouri court system, 273
Mitigation, as defined by case law, 224–232. *See also* Capital mitigation evaluation
   Atkins v. Virginia, 231
   Blystone v. Pennsylvania, 229, 232
   Eddings v. Oklahoma, 226–228
   Furman v. Georgia, 224–225
   Gregg v. Georgia, 224–225, 229
   Hitchcock v. Dugger, 228
   Lockett v. Ohio, 225–228
   McCoy v. North Carolina, 229
   Mills v. Maryland, 228
   Ring v. Arizona, 230–231
   Schiro v. Summerlin, 230
   Skipper v. South Carolina, 228
   Strickland v. Washington, 227
   Summerlin v. Stewart, 230
   Tennard v. Dretke, 231–232
   Wiggins v. Smith, 231
Moral culpability consideration, in capital sentencing, 21, 235–240
   in *Atkins v. Virginia,* 237
   factors for consideration, 237–238
   forensic clinician's lack of knowledge about, 239–240
   medical/psychiatric condition influence, 245
   nonpartisan nature of, 238
   in *Roper v. Simmons,* 237
   value of, 235
   variances among offenders, 236
Morris, R. J., 181

Morse data gathering model, 299–300
Moulthrop, M. A., 294
Munsterberg, Hugo, 3

National Alliance on Mental Illness (NAMI), 142, 197
Neal v. Texas (2008), 186
Nelson, Evan, 131–132
Nonmurder capital offenses, 41
North Carolina v. Lippard (2002), 41

O'Connor, Sandra Day, 130
Ohio v. Stallings (2004), 198
Olley, J. G., 178
On the Witness Stand (Munsterberg), 3
Otto, R., 212, 221, 294

Panetti v. Quarterman (2007), 22, 135, 139–144, 203, 204, 207
Penry v. Lynaugh (1989), 129–132, 165
People v. Superior Court (2005), 186
Personality Assessment Inventory, 163, 220
Pervasive and binding authority, 31–32
Pilgrim, R. L., 277–278
Powell, Lewis F., 137, 139, 141, 203–204, 215, 404
Pretrial evaluations. *See* Front-end (pre-trial) evaluations
Principles of forensic mental health assessment (FMHA), 287*t*–288*t*
  1: differences between clinical-forensic domains, 289–290
  2: education, training, experience in specialization area, 290
  3: legal, ethical, scientific, practice literatures familiarity, 291–292
  4: recognition/limiting evaluator bias, disclosure of inconsistent data, 292
  5: control of evaluator bias, 292–294
  6: focus on substantive/procedural legal knowledge, 294
  7: avoidance of conflict during expert testimony, 294–295
  8: identification of relevant forensic issues, 295
  9: acceptance of referrals only within area of expertise, 295–296
  10: impartiality of evaluator, 296–297
  11: evaluator's role with attorney, clarification of, 297
  12: clarification of financial arrangements, 297–298
  13: obtaining proper authorization, 298
  14: avoidance of dual therapist/evaluator roles, 298
  15: determination of assessment role, 298–299
  16: choice of data gathering, interpretation, reasoning model, 299–300
  17: use of multiple sources of information, review of background information, seeking missing elements, 300–301
  18: use of relevance/reliability as guides, 301
  19: obtaining relevant historical information, 301–302
  20: reliability of psychological measurements, 302
  21: assessment of legally relevant behavior, 302–303
  22: quiet, private, distraction-free evaluation conditions, 303–304
  23: providing notification of purpose/obtaining appropriate authorization, 304–306
  24: determination of defendant's understanding of evaluation, 306–307
  25: use of third party information in assessing response style, 307–308
  26: using testing when indicated in assessing response style, 308
  27: using idiographic evidence in assessing clinical condition, functional abilities, causal connection, 308–309
  28: use of nomoethic evidence in assessing clinical condition, functional abilities, causal connection, 309–310
  29: use of scientific evidence in assessing causal connection

between clinical condition and functional abilities, 310
30: considerations for answering the "ultimate legal question," 310–312
31: describing findings/limits to avoid cross-examination changes, 312
32: attribute information to sources, 312–313
33: use of plain language/avoidance of technical jargon, 313
34: write reports in sections using models, procedures, 313–314
35: testimony based on properly performed FMHA, 314
36: effective communication, 315
36: preparation, 314–315
37: control of message/meaning, impact of presentation in testimony, 315
identification of, 286, 287*t*–288*t*
The Principles of Medical Ethics (AMA, 2001), 147
The Principles of Medical Ethics with Annotations Especially Applicable to Psychiatry (APA, 2001), 147–148
Prosecutors
cross-examination of defendant, 40*n*20
Death Penalty Protocol and, 42–43
described, 35–36
seeking death penalty decision, 42
Psychological testing
benefits of, 216
capital mitigation de-emphasis of, 252
cultural fairness of measures, 160–162
forensic evaluation reliance on, 300
formal/explicit consent for, 9
offender's functional abilities vs., 212
reason for using, 407
use of, in death penalty contexts, 159–160
Psychometric considerations in FMHA, 158–160
benefits of, 158–159
instrument requirements, 159
psychological assessment, 159–160

validity/generalization limitations of, 160
Psychopathy Checklist-Revised (Hare), 281

Racial considerations
psychological evaluation and, 160–161
questioning of jurors, 37
Radelet, M. L., 207
Reidy, T. J., 157
Reports. *See also* Sample FMHA reports and components
admittance to public record, 10
for competence for execution evaluations, 220
forensic (samples), 24
post-evaluation, 13
self-reports, 8*t*, 11
written, clinical vs. forensic, 8*t*, 13–14
Ring v. Arizona (2002), 25, 39, 47, 230–231
Roberts, John, 144*n*8
Rodriguez v. Florida (2005), 195
Roman Law of the Twelve Tables, 125
Roosevelt, Franklin, 31*n*10
Roper v. Simmons (2005), 25, 164, 166
Roskamp, P., 273

Salekin, K. L., 194
Samenow, Stanton, 131–132
Sample FMHA reports and components, 317–355
Atkins-type evaluation (Report 1), 318–324
Atkins-type evaluation (Report 2), 325–351
cognitive functioning assessment, 343–345
employment history, 336*t*
legal history of adults, delinquency, 335, 337–342
observations/mental status evaluation, 345–347
psychological evaluation history, 342
Scales of Independent Behavior-Revised, 349–351
Stanford-Binet (SB5) Intelligence Scale results, 347, 348*t*

Sample FMHA reports and components (*cont'd*)
    Woodcock-Johnson III Tests of Achievement, 348–349
Scales of Independent Behavior (Woodcock-Johnson), 196, 328, 349, 352t
Scalia, Antonin, 132n3
Schiro v. Summerlin (2004), 230
Sentencing phase, capital trials, 44–47
Sixth Amendment (Constitution)
    defined, 22, 26–27, 34, 157
    guarantees of, 35–37
    on jury vs. judge responsibility, 38–39
Skipper v. South Carolina (1986), 45–46, 228
Small, M. A., 212, 221
Sorenson, J. R., 271–273, 277–278
Sources of law, 26–27
Spaziano v. Florida (1984), 25
Specialty Guidelines *(Specialty Guidelines for Forensic Psychologists)*
    capital evaluator's use of, 292
    cultural fairness principle, 160–162
    forensic psychologist information obligation, 156
    practitioner competence vigilance, 153
    psychometric tools standards, 159
    purpose of, 147
    third-party information source importance, 162–163
Stallings, Michael, 198
Standard errors of measurement (SEM) of the WAIS reports, 182–184
Stanford-Binet intelligence measures, 182, 185, 191, 321, 328, 346, 347, 348t
Stare decisis system (defined), 31
State-level court system (description), 28–31
Stevens, John Paul, 132
Street Survival Skills Questionnaire (SSSQ), 323
Strickland v. Washington (1984), 227
Structure Interview of Reported Symptoms (SIRS; Rogers, Bagby, Dickens, 1992), 163, 219, 308, 403
Summerlin v. Stewart (2003), 230

Supreme Court. *See also* Constitution (U.S.); individual cases throughout the index
    on bifurcation of capital trials, 43–44
    binding authority of, 32
    certiorari petitions, 33, 129, 132, 141
    competence of offender standards, 16, 18, 22
    death penalty exceptions, 15n8
    death penalty moratorium, 25, 125
    death penalty reinstatement, 21, 25, 262
    death sentence irreversibility, 123
    Eighth Amendment, four-Justice plurality opinion, 136–137
    expert testimony admissibility rulings, 264–265
    framework for imposing death penalty, 262
    "future dangerousness" decision, 263–264
    judicial composition, 30–31
    jurisdiction of, 31
    on juror decisions, 37
    on mentally retarded offenders, 20, 24
    petitioning procedure, 31
    psychiatric violence assessment rulings, 262–263
    reduction of arbitrariness, 25–26
    Roosevelt's expansion attempt, 31n10
    shaping of FMHAs by, 23
    violence risk assessment decision, 263
Sweet, J. J., 294

Tarasoff v. Regents of the University of California (1976), 10n4
Task Force on Mental Disability and the Death Penalty, 143, 197
Tasse, M. J., 187
Teaching witness role (of mental health professional), 18
Tennard v. Dretke (2004), 134, 231–232
Tenth Amendment (Constitution), 27
Testimony, clinical vs. forensic, 14
Test of Memory Malingering, 220, 308
Test-retest (IQ) effects, 190–191
Texas Court of Criminal Appeals, 129
Texas Death Row, 273

Thomas, Clarence, 144*n*8
Treatment frequency, open-ended vs. deadline-driven, 13

Ultimate legal question
 answering, by mental health professionals, 16
 avoidance of answering recommendation, 212
 capacities/abilities underlying, 295
 debates about answering, 220–221, 288*t*, 310–312
United States v. Green (2005), 43
University of Virginia Institute of Law, Psychiatry and Public Policy, 290
U.S. Dept. of Justice
 correctional facility homicide data, 270
 Death Penalty Protocol, 42–43
U.S. Government, eligible capital offense crimes, 41–42

Validity Indicator Profile, 219–220, 308
Vineland Adaptive Behavior Scales, 196
Violence risk evaluations (factors), 260–284
 age of defendant, 277–278
 base rates of violence relevancy, 270–276
 case law and statute related to, 261–265
 context determination, 267–270
 crucial assessment elements, 266–267
 educational background, 278–279
 evaluator choice of considerations, 282–284
 expert testimony admissibility rulings, 264–265
 factors unrelated to prison violence, 280–282
 "future dangerousness" consideration, 263–264
 future release considerations, 268–269
 individualized considerations of defendants, 261–262, 276, 309
 offense characteristics, 279
 poor prison terms, 278
 post-*Barefoot* changes in, 265
 postconviction prison violence
  by death-sentenced capital offenders, 271–273
  by other capital offenders, 273–274
 prior prison violence, 278
 prison context for, 268
 prison gang membership, 279
 prison violence data, 270–271
 psychiatric assessment rulings, 262–263
 risk communication, 282–284
Virginia Supreme Court, 131–132
Voir dire process, 37
Voluntariness and autonomy issues, 9–10

Waiving rights appeals, 22
Walker v. True (2005), 186
Warren, Earl, 130
Wechsler Adult Intelligence Test (WAIS), 169, 182–183, 187, 190, 323
White, Byron, 262
Wiggins v. Smith (2003), 231
Williams v. Florida (1970), 39
Williams v. Quarterman (2008), 193
Woodcock-Johnson Test of Achievement, 196, 328, 346–349
Wrinkle, R. D., 273
Writ of certiorari, 31, 33
Writ of habeas corpus, 19, 22, 33
Writs of certiorari, 33
Wundt, William, 3

Young, B. A., 193

Zapf, P. A., 212, 217

DISCARD

EAST BATON ROUGE PARISH LIBRARY
BATON ROUGE, LOUISIANA

ZACHARY

I want to hear the prayers that were offered up to God-beyond-the-ceiling-and-roof.

I want to hear the voices of sometimes-joy.

I want to know what caused the joy.

I want to know how the giving way took place.

It would be a story worth writing.

1998

[*"Giving Way"*]

even worse—Colored Only water fountains, sitting in the balcony of The Royce Theater, buying from the side door at Wray's, getting the throw-away meat at hog killings.

In college, I would read clinically cold studies from those sociologists who were examining the nature of decentralization—studies where every sort of human behavior and condition could be explained to some degree of satisfaction by the clever use of theory and conclusion—and it occurred to me that, again and again, the sociologists were pointing their scholarly fingers at the word *economics* and fixing the blame. The economics of the South created sharecropping, they declared, just as it had created slavery.

They were right, of course—those sociologists, with their theories and conclusions. It was a matter of economics. There were those who had and those who didn't have, which seems to me to be the bottom line of human history. Haves and have nots. The only thing left out of the conclusions of the sociologists was a sense of the drudgery of life suffered by the have-nots. Yet, it is not a deliberate omission. Only those who lived it could understand what it meant to be not much better off than anyone else.

That is why I would like to hear the stories of the house.

I am not interested in the economics of the people who lived there.

I would like to know about the trembling moments—the uncertainties, the fears, the anger, the rage, the bullying, the begging.

"Don't know what we're going to do."
"Look for a second job somewhere."
"Doing what?"
"Whatever's out there."
"God help us."
"If He's planning on it, He's taking his own sweet time getting around to it."
"Don't talk about God like that."
"Next time He plows a round for me, I'll tell Him I'm sorry."

I know there was talk. Had to be.

Sometimes the words did slip out.

I remember a conversation between two sharecroppers at the Vanna Cotton Gin, two men old before their time, smoking finger-rolled cigarettes from Prince Albert tins, two men lamenting the boll weevil and the dry weather and the short staple of the cotton packed in their wagons and the bill at the store.

One of them said, "We ain't much better off than niggers."

The other wagged his head in agreement.

Today, much would be made of the comment. It would he called racist and mean-spirited. Critics would put a spin on it by talking indignantly about the "N-word."

And they would be so wrong, so very wrong.

It wasn't a racist comment, not even meanspirited. It was merely a point of reference, a hard and despairing truth. Class-to-class reality. The white sharecropper's family lived, in many ways, exactly like the black sharecropper's family. Being not *much better off* simply acknowledged that blacks were treated

[*"Giving Way"*]

limbed kind of songs. We had electricity and an indoor toilet, a wringer washing machine on the back porch, vegetables in the garden, meat on the hoof, a Sears and Roebuck catalog to order from, if we couldn't find what we wanted at Gallant Belk, or Thornton's, or Blumenthal's, or one of the other enterprises located in Royston.

We were giving way, all right. Yessiree. Giving way to good times after bad.

Zip-a-dee-doo-dah, zip-a-dee-a. Me, oh my, what a wonderful day . . .

That is how we lived.

But we were not sharecroppers.

We owned our farm and our home.

The Careys did not. They were tenants, sharecroppers.

Every bale of cotton we picked was ours. Every bale of cotton the Careys picked was only partly theirs. The rest they surrendered to the landlord. The same with corn and wheat and oats.

I do not remember ever hearing the Careys singing in the fields. Maybe they did. I simply don't remember it.

I think the Careys, like all tenant farmers, were balanced between giving way and giving up.

If the house could talk, I would ask it to tell me stories of the night-whispering that must have taken place among the Careys and the Cromers and the Harts and the Carters and the Humans and the Crafts.

But the house has lost its words, and in its silence, I can only invent.

Yet, safe within our boundaries, little of it mattered, more than talk. Some of it even seemed senseless—a doctor named Benjamin Spock writing about raising children. My mother had given birth to eleven children at home, one in the hospital. What could this Dr. Spock teach her?

In Vanna, the community of my childhood, we crept along cautiously, following the philosophy my father once recited as advice: "Be not the first by which the new is tried, nor yet the last to lay the old aside."

In summer, the canning plant operated on the grounds of Vanna Junior High School, where crowds of women and children gathered to shell peas, snap beans, peel peaches, and to talk of how things were among the people they knew.

Dennis Harris, who sold Watkins products, still drove the backroads with his goods stuffed in his vehicle, bringing the aroma of vanilla and spices to linger invitingly in the heavy, hot air.

We still fished Beaverdam Creek for catfish, still raided watermelon patches, still played pasture baseball and football, still had our petty, temper-triggered fights, still smoked rabbit tobacco, still took our walks to Royston, still wondered about the carryings-on of people in such faraway places as Elberton and Hartwell and Athens.

And then, in 1947, electricity came to the farm families of Vanna, and nothing was the same.

In the fields, my brothers and sisters and I were singing "Zip-a-dee-doo-dah," "Shoo-Fly Pie and Apple Pan Dowdy," and "Doin' What Comes Nacherly." Dancing kind of songs. Loose-

[*"Giving Way"*]

but things were rolling down where the fish lived. Odd things. Funny things. Frightening things.

In Roswell, New Mexico, a flying saucer supposedly malfunctioned and crashed to Earth, leaving little human-like creatures scattered over the ground.

Jackie Robinson, born in a Georgia sharecropper's house, showed up in a Brooklyn Dodgers uniform, the first black man to play baseball in the white man's major leagues, and in Royston, hometown of the great Ty Cobb, tongues clucked in disbelief.

In Walton County, four black people were assassinated, but the details were pretty much hushed up.

The Dead Sea Scrolls were discovered in Wadi Qumran, and revivalists bellowed "Amen!" over more hard proof of what they had been preaching.

Henry Ford, who gave us the automobile from the assembly line, died in 1947. So did Al Capone, who gave us crime to remember.

Joe Louis, the great Brown Bomber, was still heavyweight cham-peen of the world.

An electronic brain was put together at the University of Pennsylvania and people grinned at such nonsense and muttered, "Wonder what they're going to do with that?"

A United States airplane flew at supersonic speeds, as if getting some place was more important than the pleasure of the trip.

Everything was moving so fast that it made your head spin if you tried to take it all in at one sitting.

gish with them, a penny pack of Kits could last through a cowboy movie and a serial (*The Phantom,* or *Batman and Robin,* or *The Green Arrow,* or someone else equally remarkable). After the movie, maybe an ice cream cone from Wray's Drug Store, with a nickel or dime left for the collection plate on Sunday.

A Saturday afternoon in Royston was familiar adventure. Going to Elberton, or Hartwell, or Athens, was almost unimaginable. You might as well set your sights on Atlanta, or Miami, Florida, or New York City, New York. Elberton and Hartwell and Athens were miles away, and if you ever got there you never really felt good about it. All those strangers looking at you, funny-like, wondering who you were and why you were in their town, and if you had ever listened to rumor, you knew there were plenty of reasons to beware of such places. You couldn't expect a bargain in Elberton or Hartwell, even if they were advertising one with a carnival barker and a clown, and in Athens there was the University of Georgia, which turned normal people arrogant and sometimes rowdy. In Athens—the older boys vowed with wide-mouthed grins—there was a famous brothel. Everyone knew someone who had been there, or bragged that they had. If you had a lick of sense, you stayed in Royston. Royston was good enough. Everything a person could want could he found in Royston.

I think of those years fondly, as the best years, years of my Age of Innocence, before innocence gave way to experience, before I began my own exodus.

We bobbed along with the times, like fishing corks on a two-acre fish pond. On the surface, all seemed peaceful and serene,

[*"Giving Way"*]

great distances, and once having passed, whizzing in their automobiles, they were not likely to return that way again. The Highway 17 Gang watched those passing people and believed directions—north and south, east and west—were gray concrete roads drawn in heavy lines on service station maps.

The Highway 17 Gang did not have boundaries. They had yards. Somehow, they believed they were blessed.

When I wrote those words, in the early '70s, I had recently experienced the death of my mother, and a yearning for my youth—for the joy of those sparkling discoveries of the child-who-once-was—had become an unshakable obsession. I wanted to be the child again. From my fingertips, striking the words, the child returned. Magically, he returned. North and south, east and west, the child again roamed the boundaries of his boyhood, protected from the flood of change that would erode everything except memory.

But the writing of books is often as much an illusion as the magician's trick.

I think now that the Highway 17 Gang was better prepared for change than Our Side. They understood the meaning of *people moving, going great distances.*

A great distance for us—Our Side, the dirt-road farm youngsters—was a Saturday afternoon trip to Royston, a hard-earned quarter allowance in our pocket, and a system for spending it: nine cents for admission to The Royce Theater, a penny left for a penny pack of Kits. Best buy for the money anywhere. If you weren't pig-

value, we learned of imperatives; and, in imperatives, we realized perspective.

To the members of Our Side, perspective was conditioned by boundaries. Boundaries gave us reach, held us, dared us; boundaries tutored us in the deeper significance of belonging.

Wesley and I lived by the boundaries of Black Pool Swamp, circling us in a horseshoe from the south and east and west. To the north we were somehow contained by Banner's Crossing and Rakestraw Bridge Road.

There was a sense of being centrifugally leashed to the center of our north and south, east and west boundaries; the center was Home and Home would spin us out, but only to the invisible, protective edges of where we wandered, and then Home would draw us back again.

We could not mark those boundaries by stake and flag. They were not taught by a line drawn in shoe-edge, or plotted on some map from the Official Office of Official Boundaries. Our boundaries were established by instinct. We knew. We simply knew. We could chase after laughter and echoes of laughter until we were exhausted with exhilaration, and we could wander farther and farther away, safe, protected, until that one step—that one step too far, too threatening—and then we would retreat. No one told us to return. We knew. We simply knew. We knew when we had ventured too far, as though our sense of equilibrium had been savagely attacked.

But the Highway 17 Gang did not understand about boundaries. Highway 17 was alive with people moving, going

[*"Giving Way"*]

to do with belonging to the units of a place and a family, of having boundaries.

In my first novel, *The Year the Lights Came On*, I wrote about it, and offer here an excerpt to describe it as I first realized it:

The Great Depression and World War Number Two had been our only experience with the Larger World, and we had inherited—through some curious process of osmosis—a possessed sense of belonging. Belonging was our constant defense, our way of warding off the suspected Great End. The Larger World had issued messages that we lived in a temporary time, that we, ourselves, were temporary. (The atomic bomb was one thing; now, in 1947, there was rumor about a bomb of such unpredictable destruction that certain international scientists were afraid it would create a molecular reaction and Earth would disintegrate in a series of explosions, like a string of Chinese firecrackers.)

Because of the Larger World, and what it said to us in the voices of the Radio Evening News Network and eight-point type of the Anderson Independent, *we had been mightily influenced and had adopted the habit of clustering, as though clustering was an affirmation of our existence: if we saw one another, spoke with one another, then it must be true—we had survived.*

In clustering, we became isolationists; in isolation, we assumed identities; in identity, we were assigned value; in

the war ended, a blurred-memory age. I have a dreamy sense of celebration, like spying on an adult party where glad-faced people preened with glad-faced smiles and behaved in a way that a child could not understand, but felt good about anyway.

The soldiers and sailors and war workers had stories and memories and ideas. They knew a thing or two about bravery. And tyranny. They knew a lot about tyranny. They weren't so easily bought by old promises of charge accounts at the fertilizer and feed store. No sir. They'd played that game. Or their parents had. And if they were old enough to fight, they had suffered the Great Depression first-hand, knew too well how long that belly-gnawing bad time had lingered. Enough was enough. They had the G.I. Bill and maybe some trade they'd picked up in the war— mechanics, welding, cooking. It didn't take them long to assess their options. Going back to the ass-end of a mule on someone else's place gradually gave way to getting on with their lives.

It was the true beginning of the thing called decentralization, especially for the sharecropper. Poetically, I think of it as an exodus of slow-moving people—farm to town, town to city, one state to another, generation following generation, leaving behind gravestones that carry the codes of a personal, yet dim, history.

I have always been intrigued with that period of time—the post-war years. Two of my novels are set in that period. I was at the right age, in the right place, for developing memories that are still clear and certain, and the clearest, most certain sensation from that period is the opposite of decentralization. It has

[*"Giving Way"*]

knew it. The steel plow beam of a middle-buster from a Georgia field might be the very thing that turned the tide in a close fight with the Nazis somewhere in France, or with the Nips on a tiny Pacific island.

The day that Franklin Delano Roosevelt died, I heard it from Cousin Allie Skelton, who came rushing from her home, wailing, "The President's dead, the President's dead!" We were playing in the yard, joyfully whirling in circles on a spinning jenny, and the shriek of that surprising news terrified us. The only picture more prominent than Franklin Delano Roosevelt in rural homes of the South was the picture of Jesus praying in Gethsemane. Ironically, the President had died while sitting for a portrait at the Little White House in Warm Springs. *The Unfinished Portrait*, it would be named. And in the gloom after his death, on the slow train crawl through Georgia, up to Washington, D.C., America also seemed unfinished. Like Moses, Roosevelt had led his people out of the wilderness of despair and, like Moses, he would die too soon, too soon.

But the war that seemed to scorch the globe was ending even as a nation mourned.

On April 30, 1945, eighteen days after the President's death, the madman, Adolf Hitler, killed himself in a place called the Führerbunker in Berlin.

In August, A-bombs fell on Hiroshima and Nagasaki.

And then the war was over and the soldiers and sailors and war workers came home, and a kind of jubilation (or maybe it was a sigh, singing relief) hummed across the land. I was seven the year

had to do was take a look at what had happened since the start of World War II.

The war, the professors declared, had given change a boot in the pants. All that new technology. The atomic bomb. People playing with rockets with thoughts of the moon in their mind. Everything. If the Great Depression had numbed people, the war had put a jolt into them.

And I think they were right. Giving it a backward look, at an age when backward looks have perfect vision or perfect illusion, I think they knew what they were talking about.

During the war, we watched gliders being pulled across American skies by four-motored airplanes, and we wondered what would happen if one of the gliders snapped free of its tether and began to ride the wind above us. Would it circle peacefully like a buzzard and skim to a landing on the white runway of cotton rows? Or would it drop like a rock and splinter into a million pieces of balsa wood?

At play, we fought the Japs and Germans with tree-limb guns and dirt-clod hand grenades, made rifle-firing, pinging-off-rock ricochet sounds in our mouth, held the enemy at bay from foxholes of gullies, and rushed machine gun nests through scrub pine and mountain laurel. Took hits ourselves, of course. Never fatal, of course. Just hits. Nicks. Barely enough to draw blood. Something a saw briar would make.

We collected scrap iron—plow points, railroad spikes, tin cans—to be made into tanks and submarines and anti-aircraft shells the size of our legs. It was kill or be killed, and everyone

["Giving Way"]

clutter. Leaf drifts against porch steps. Hand-dug wells covered with cement slabs. Kudzu gone mad.

One of my professors had called change a giving-way thing, and that is what I saw while looking carefully at deserted sharecropper houses:

The mule giving way to the tractor.

The grain thrasher giving way to the combine.

The cotton-mop giving way to the airplane duster.

The field hand giving way to the cotton picker.

The kerosene lamp giving way to the electric light.

The radio giving way to the television.

The row crop giving way to chicken houses.

And the sharecroppers giving way to town houses, giving way to age, giving way to jobs in textile mills, or on the pipeline, or in repair shops, giving way to migrations that would carry them away from memories of long, sun-sapping days in worked-out fields. Sharecroppers giving way to the paycheck, knowing the paycheck—no matter how small—was not as risky as the summing-up of shares.

In college, the professors gave it a word: *Decentralization*. It was one of the things of change, and it meant the breakdown of the unit system—family, community, region, state. (I always thought of it as being *deboned*, taking out the skeleton that held everything together.)

Because of this decentralization, there were remarkable and possibly grave things ahead, the professors predicted. All you

Someone told me years ago that Marie and her husband had gone to Alaska in search of gold. I hope so. I hope they found a wheelbarrow load of nuggets the size of bricks. It would have been a great adventure for a pretty girl who was reared in a sharecropper's house on a sharecropper's farm.

If the house could talk, I would ask it to tell me if Marie, as a child, had dreamed of finding gold buried under the red clay of cotton fields.

I do not know when the Careys moved from the house, or if they were the last to occupy it. I am certain the family still lived there when I went away to college in the mid-'50s. I know only that on some visit home, I realized the house was empty.

In college, professors of sociology were telling us that things were popping. Change was everywhere, merrily evolving. It was like being in the middle of a county fair with the snappy blaring of calliope music beating against you. So much going on, it was impossible to see everything, and everything was tempting.

You had to look carefully to see change, the professors said. Best to pick one thing and watch it. Then you'd see.

I began to look carefully at deserted sharecropper houses on drives over country roads, houses like the one where the Careys once lived.

There was a sameness about them. Unpainted clapboard, bleached gray by rain and sun. Some wrapped in tarpaper. All with a tin roof water-stained the color of tobacco juice. Yard

[*"Giving Way"*]

he would amble out across the field, crooning his Blueberry Hill love song.

Or so goes the story.

I do not remember the Harts or the Carters or the Humans or the Crafts. Barely remember the Cromers.

The Careys I remember.

Most of them, at least.

Wallace, Martin, Marie. And there were others. Twins, I think. A boy named Laron. An older daughter, who, like Marie, was remarkably beautiful. Gladys. I believe her name was Gladys. She lived away somewhere, and would come for visits that made for gladness among the Careys. Maybe that was her name: Gladness.

Wallace was older than I. Four years older. The first person I ever idolized. More man than boy, he seemed. Fiercely proud. So much pride it radiated from him in a bright aura that could have been the polished armor of a knight. When we had chinaberry war-games, I would put myself near him, behind his back, and watch in awe. Green-berry bullets, hard as creek pebbles, zipped away with the rubber-snap of his flip. Yelp of someone across the yard, taking the berry in the chest—or back. Wallace would have driven off the Huns with his flip and a fistful of chinaberries. I have written of him in bits and pieces. The bits and pieces are all heroic.

I knocked Martin's tooth out one afternoon in an anger-fit. He had called my dog, Red, a son of a bitch, which was right, technically speaking, but sounded bad enough for a fight.

fallen away and it has a cracked backbone on the roof line and it is waiting for the vines of poison ivy and fox grape to pull it down. Can't see it from the roadbed for so many vines and the trash trees and saw briars and privet bushes growing wild and lush.

Snakes live there. You know it without seeing or hearing them. Snakes hiding in dust and grass in perfect-O curls of cold-blooded muscle. Rats, too. Or maybe not. Maybe the snakes have feasted on the rats.

I wish the house could talk, but it cannot. Time has taken the talk out of it, all the words spilled from broken-out windows and doors. Some floated up the rock chimney, I would guess. Some seeped through floor cracks. Some wiggled out where tongue-and-groove walls used to be, wiggled around heart-pine studs, through rough-planed clapboards.

If the house could talk, I would make a sitting-down place near it—away from the snakes—and ask questions I've always wanted to ask.

The Careys lived there. And before them, the Cromers. Before them, the Harts. Before them, the Carters. Before them, the Humans. Before them, the Crafts.

It was one of the Carter boys who used to sing about finding his thrill on Blueberry Hill to my sister, Nell.

Or so goes the story.

Spied on her from the house, the gossip has it, and when she would go from our home to check the mailbox at the cemetery turnaround—expecting letters from her gone-away boyfriend—

"Giving Way"

The house sits on a knoll off Viola Winn Road leading to Beaverdam Creek, a half-mile or so from the home of my childhood. Viola Winn Road is named for my mother. Winn was her maiden name.

Once, drooping boughs of large oaks shaded the house. A few shrubs were tucked neatly against it. The dirt yard was always swept clean by hand-made twig brooms. Chinaberry trees grew in the side yard. Peach trees, too, I think. Peach trees that bore nubby peaches. A well for drawing water was between the house and the barn. Chickens promenaded over the grounds, clucking, claw-scratching for bugs, pecking aimlessly. Dogs slumbered in the shade, blowing dust with their breathing. In spring, the air was scented with sassafras and pine and fruit blossoms. In summer, perfume from honeysuckle seeped up from the pasture. In winter, a cold wood musk—a water musk—floated in from the creek and the swamp.

The house is important to me, personally and professionally.

It is the model for every tenant-sharecropper house, every rural setting, I have ever written about.

It is deserted now. Has been for many years. The front porch has

Some of them believe what they are saying; some are charlatans out to line the silk of their pockets with the widow's mite. The charlatans sell sacred oil from the Holy Land, prayer scarves, inspired scribblings dictated by the voice of God himself—the same voice that spoke to Moses from the burning bush.

The best of the radio sermons are remarkably poetic, the same as the best of the sermons from the revivals of old. The messages are leashed to a single verse of scripture—often chosen at random, which, in itself, is considered an act of divine intervention—and the repetitive saying of that verse, in a singsong rhythm almost hypnotic in its power is amazingly persuasive.

Whenever I hear the summer whisper of the revival, I think of James Weldon Johnson's wonderful story about the famous preacher who decided to deliver a prepared sermon because there were a number of distinguished visitors present, but discovered quickly that he had lost the attention of his audience. According to Johnson, the preacher stepped from behind the pulpit and, abandoning his notes, began to "intone" in the voice of a musical instrument—a trombone—the story from Genesis about the creation of the world. Johnson began then to make notes for the poem that would become "The Creation," which is included in one of the remarkable achievements of American literature—*God's Trombones*.

And I think of the man of The Calling, who chose the streets of Royston to conduct his curbside revivals. I loved him and I'm proud that I was his backslider for a few weeks of my youth.

1990

[*"Give Me that Old-Time Religion"*]

kept them alive as much as the meager sustenance of their tables because it gave them the will to work for improvement.

For others, it was an illusion that carried them to ruin as they waited, hopefully and dumbly, for the multiple riches purchased by their pennies. Carl Sandburg's poem "To a Contemporary Bunkshooter" was a scathing denunciation of such hollow promises. Karl Marx took aim at the same condition in his comment about religion being the opium of the people.

In a period of relative economic comfort, today's revival often addresses the emotional well-being of the here and now more than the promised spiritual tranquility beyond St. Peter's cloudy gates. Messages once springing from the red-lettered words of the King James' Jesus are now tempered by psychological insights of human behavior ("I'm OK, You're OK"); and hot-button language (ownership, choices, consequences, etc.) influenced by the corporate world make many pulpit sermons sound curiously like an executive report at an Annual Meeting. (Could it be that our people of The Calling are breaking too many paradigms?)

Yet the appeal of the old revival, the revival of the oppressed, worked. And still it works. For those with nothing, there must be something and that something is the right, the need, to wish for a grander experience, even if in the afterlife.

You can hear men and women who profess The Calling preaching from radio stations and their message is almost always one of fundamental interpretation: leave all your troubles to Jesus and Jesus will reward you with riches on earth and in heaven.

He, or she, would be the evening's confessor, something of a DB—a designated backslider. He, or she, would kneel at the altar and the man of The Calling, beaming with gladness, would declare victory over the legions of The Fallen Angel.

The revival of that time was one of the special, high dramas in small, isolated communities, with the visiting preacher treated as a celebrity compensated by love offerings dropped into collection plates.

And then the drama began to weaken. Television changed it as much as anything. Television had celebrities who did not require love offerings or backsliders, celebrities who made you laugh instead of tremble. Television had faces in grainy black and white, beamed mysteriously from New York or some other faraway place—technology very much like a miracle. Television told easy-to-take stories not found in the Old Testament. Television was watched at home from the comfort of a padded chair or sofa. (And we wonder about the power of the televangelist. It is simply a matter of joining them if you can't beat them; a natural drama finding a natural medium and even such poor players as Jim Bakker will not end its run.)

Economics also influenced the revival. In the lingering of the Depression, in regions of sharecropping poverty, the man of The Calling promised a better life, golden streets, no more hunger, no more pain. Relief—blessed, blessed relief—was an act of surrender and faith. Ask and you will receive. Give and you will get. And the more you give, the more you will get.

For millions of people it was the best offer they had, and it

[*"Give Me that Old-Time Religion"*]

less, of the opinion that revivals, like everything, have changed over the years and air conditioning is only partly responsible. With exceptions, of course, the modern revival is a matter of spiritual enrichment rather than a safari hunt for those unwashed in the Blood of the Lamb or for those guilty of the human frailty called backsliding.

Once, the unwashed and the backsliders were essential for a successful revival. "Revive Us Again" was more than a hymn for lusty voices; it was a battle cry, an anthem of renewal, of getting straight, of resurrected life in a failing spirit. On a hot summer night, with the urgency of salvation reaching its crescendo in a mix of choir voices and prayerful commands from a man of The Calling, "Revive Us Again" was an absolute guarantee to exorcise Satan from the most worthless of sinners.

The backslider was particularly important. In many small Baptist, Methodist (before the United was attached), Church of God, Holiness and churches of other denominations, there would be few in the congregation who were not baptized. Thus saving became resaving, and any determined man of The Calling would refuse to pronounce a benediction without at least one backslider coming forward.

I have watched it. Man of The Calling in front of the altar, choir softly singing "Just as I Am," verse after verse after repeated verse (there are six verses, for the record, and they sound as appealing the second time through as they did the first), until someone in the congregation surrenders (for the right to go home as much as the need for redemption).

red-faced glory with belief. He had enough belief to fling the Appalachian mountain range into the middle of the Pacific ocean, and there were moments—grand, high-pitched frenzies—when I thought he was about to accomplish the feat.

In the years since, I have heard Billy Graham in Madison Square Garden, Oral Roberts in a tent, and once attended a double-portion-of-the-spirit night in a rented movie theater. The double portion required a double donation and, lo, the looser the purse strings got, the more splendid the sermonizing became.

It would be easy to present those experiences as histrionic moments played by talented con artists cut from the clerical cloth of Elmer Gantry, but for many of us reared in the fundamental Protestant traditions of the South's rural Bible Belt, there is a faint summer urge—like a genetic whisper—to take to the pew for the sort of annual soul-purging that only revivals offer.

Why summer? Summer was once the season of the revivals, between the lay-by and harvesting of crops. Late July and August. Also, summer was the right climate for the revival in those pre-air conditioner days. Sweltering weather has a touch of hell about it. ("You think it's bad hot today, brothers and sisters? It ain't nothin' compared to hell. It's as cold as ice water where you're sittin' right now, if you put it up against Satan's fire.")

Even funeral parlor fans with pictures of Jesus praying in Gethsemane failed to stir the July and August air when hellfire and brimstone spewed from the tongue of a man with The Calling.

Not to engage in ecclesiastical debate with those blessed by verse-proof insight into the ways of the Almighty, I am, neverthe-

"GIVE ME THAT OLD-TIME RELIGION"

There was, in my youth, a man who made Saturday appearances on the streets of Royston to conduct curbside revivals for those squandering time and money on such gratifications as ice cream cones and ten-cent movie tickets. He was a man of The Calling and he believed passionately that God's word was worth delivering to anyone at any time. He believed also that God's voice was large, and to emulate that voice, he had to shout. He was a great shouter, this man of The Calling, and he noisily performed salvation on me more than once near the Royce Theater, with my ice cream melting and my dime to see Hopalong Cassidy clenched protectively between my thumb and index finger.

People are amused when they hear this story. They conjure an image of a maniacal evangelist, hopscotching on hot pavement, jabbering in tongues, delirious with the joy of having wrestled another soul from the greedy grasp of Satan—a Jack Davis caricature out of a William Price Fox short story.

And there was a touch of humor about it, I suppose, but I came to love that man of The Calling. He believed. He blazed in

peared. Off. On. Off. On. Light and shadow danced in the room.

And then Gary, my younger brother (twelfth of the twelve), moved to my sister, Patsy, who was his selected second mother. He tugged at her and said, "Peggy better quit doing that. She's gone burn out all the batteries."

I have never forgotten that day, that scene, those words from Gary. Many years later I would make a book of it. And I would try, in that book, to say that the REA mattered, that the REA equalized the rural classes of haves and have-nots. I wanted it to be a story of children swept into change by the absolute act of a technology more powerful than their environments of isolation. I wanted the readers—those who remembered—to nod and say, "Yes, that is the way it was."

But books are feeble voices—more echo than voice. Books make much of fragments. More than necessary. Sometimes it takes only a picture in an aging woman's house to tell the story.

A lot of us would be blind without the REA.

1985

[*"As the Room Is Lit, So Is the Future"*]

The REA was for her, as it has been for millions, an expression of status, a password into some unimaginable and unbridled future. The REA was the lighting of homes.

The agency was created by President Roosevelt on May 11, 1935, by an executive order signed at the Little White House in Warm Springs, Georgia. Congress passed the Rural Electrification Act a year later.

But that is the history of the fact, the footnoting of a government agency. The REA—the REA of lights—arrived in the backwoods of the Vanna community in northeast Georgia in 1947. And that is where the Kays lived, on the road that crossed Beaverdam Creek at the upper end of Blackgum Swamp and ended on the Goldmine ridge, near Moss's gin.

And, yes, that frail ancient woman with the pictures of Jesus and Roosevelt on her wall was correct: the best thing that ever happened to us was the REA.

There were six of the twelve children still living at home on that day in 1947 when the REA lights were turned on. We gathered with our mother and father at the announced hour in the middle room of our house, stood there, staring silently at a naked ceiling bulb. And then the bulb popped with light—light flooding the room, spilling over it like a nova erupting with its sudden, blinding power.

We did not move, or speak. My sister, Peggy, who was standing near the wall switch, pulled the switch down, to Off, and the light snapped away. She pushed it to On, and the light reap-

"As the Room Is Lit, So Is the Future"

Once, in my failed few weeks as an insurance salesman, I made a call on an aging woman who lived alone in a house with a broken-rib tin roof and a front porch that sagged forward. She occupied only one room, did hand-stitching for neighbors and listened to religious programs on her radio. She also kept a pistol on a small table beside her rocker. She told me it had belonged to her late husband and she had it near because she had heard too much from her radio about robbers preying on old people in old houses.

There were only two pictures on the wall of her live-in room. One was of Jesus praying in Gethsemane. The other was a yellowed, curling newspaper clipping of Franklin D. Roosevelt. She saw me looking at the pictures and she talked about each, about Jesus, who had not betrayed her, and about Roosevelt, who had put her husband to work on the WPA and who had given them electricity.

"I'd be blind if I had to sew by lamplight," she said. "Best thing ever happened to us was the REA."

[*"Jesus in Jasper"*]

the same compassion, the same pleading. One was Joel's former wife, Mary. "She's very religious," he says. "She has high moral standards, a strong faith. She was there, praying for Ray."

I have shown pictures of the face in the door to friends. They are intrigued. They tell their own stories of their own images. They see features I have not seen—the face of a fox in the eyes, a wooden teardrop, a gargoylish mask, profiles that turn in as well as out. (One, a Jewish friend, laments, "Why is it always the face of Jesus? Why not Moses? Or Abraham?")

Listening to Joel Naramore, it is easy to believe that he does not want to profit from any claim of having discovered the image in the door. He is uncomfortable with the celebrity of it all. He simply saw the face. It gave him comfort.

1981

It is a significant statement in Christian acceptance, this believing without seeing, and it is one of the early stories taught in church school studies. "Don't be a doubting Thomas," teachers warn in hushed voices. And, when you are small, the fear of being a doubting Thomas is hard to shake. Believe. Just that. Believe. Nothing else matters.

There are people everywhere willing to help you believe: hawkers, like carnival barkers, with promises as powerful as hope, itself; mail-order bargains for a dwindling supply of holy cloths; special, precious vials of water or oil—as pure as the tears of God, himself,—going for less than it would cost to buy a pack of cigarettes or a gallon of gasoline; packaged grains of sand from the roads that Jesus walked.

All of it is supposed to change us, like some unmistakable cosmic magic.

But does it? Has Joel Naramore changed because he saw a face in a door's grain and his son escaped death?

Yes. And no.

"It's made me take things more seriously," he admits. "It's made me more aware of the Christian life. Though I've been a church member [Baptist], I wasn't active. I was having a high old time. I still haven't been going to church, since my job interferes, but I've been re-evaluating myself."

Part of Joel Naramore's re-evaluation is the knowledge that he was not alone in the aching prayer ("I was talking to my son, telling him to pull through . . . .") for help when his son was dangerously ill. There were others, others with the same yearning,

[*"Jesus in Jasper"*]

is all right to look, that if we have seen Him, we have seen God, telling us to love and care and forgive and believe. The two persuasions are supposed to integrate, to lock into place, but they do not always. Our understanding is too feeble. Here is this God of the signs, of metaphor, manifesting Himself in anger and vengeance and absolute power. Then there is this Jesus, son of God, this Jesus who was so remarkably unblemished, who told parables as innocent as lullabies, who took abuse, was passive and good. And in this Jesus, followers are to find peace.

But we want to see Him. To know for certain.

And we do see Him. We see Him in clouds over war-killing places like Korea and Vietnam. We see Him in the licking flames of a house fire. We see Him in the flickering static of a television screen. We see Him behind night-dark windows, like a face peering through to the quick of our lives.

We see Him in the Shroud of Turin, in the stains of His ancient death sheet.

And now we see Him in Jasper, Alabama, in a door.

We see Him because proof is important. Yet, in Christian doctrine, the need for proof, for manifestation, is often considered a troublesome matter. In the twentieth chapter of the Gospel according to John, the disciple Thomas touches the nail punctures and spear wound of Jesus as proof of the resurrected Christ. And Jesus says, "Thomas, because thou hast seen me, thou hast believed: blessed are they that have not seen, and yet have believed."

are 70,000 people in Walker County, 14,000 in Jasper. The economy is not robust, nor anemic. There are the poor, the wealthy, the in-between. Service stations, fast-food restaurants, car lots, mini-markets—the businesses of a town—line the highways and streets. There are many churches—small, large, old, new. The voice of the people is a feathered drawl, with few *g*-endings of words pronounced.

Jasper is a town of the rural South. And maybe that is why the door is in Jasper.

In the rural South—as in other rural areas of the world—we are born to this: the God image.

We begin early with it, balancing on the hips of our mothers outside Protestant church schoolrooms where (when our mothers leave us) we learn to sing "Jesus Loves the Little Children" and where we hear awesome stories about the visitations of God—God flying through the pages of the Old Testament with extraterrestrial might, the visions of Him burned into our inner seeing. God of the flood. God of the plagues. God of the burning bush. God of the great fish. God of the lion's den. God of David and the giant, of blind Samson and the pillars.

God of the metaphor.

We learn much in our early years from the Old Testament, setting the images quite firm. ("You can't stare down God, eye-to-eye," a boyhood friend once told me. "You can't even look at Him without being struck down if He's mad.") In contrast, we sing songs of the New Testament Jesus, look at His picture thumbtacked to walls. Gentle, tolerant, suffering Jesus, telling us that it

[*"Jesus in Jasper"*]

would have faced it into the room. But we didn't hang it that way. We don't know what happened. Something."

Jesus?

Those who come to see for themselves, who make pilgrimages to the third-floor corridor of the hospital (reportedly there have been more than 70,000), are strangely affected.

Some kneel and genuflect.

Some touch.

Some declare it has healing powers.

Some take pictures, the reflection of their flashbulbs spitting off the corridor walls like white heat.

Some say, "I don't see nothing."

Some say, "It's there. Plain as day."

And, yes, Armour confesses, the promoters have appeared. A T-shirt company made an offer. A minister wanted to buy the door to build a church around. There was a rumor that Billy Graham had offered $100,000 for it. *That's Incredible* has visited as has the *National Enquirer*. And surely there is someone waiting in the wings of a carnival tent, readying an offer to tour it to county fairs and shopping centers, like Bonnie and Clyde's death car. Fifty cents for a look at Jesus in the Jasper door.

And that, too, is a question: why Jasper?

Jasper, Alabama, is located in Walker County, approximately forty miles northwest of Birmingham, off Highway 78. It is coal country—strip-mining and tunneling. ("As coal goes, so goes Walker County," the people proclaim.) In round numbers, there

Officials of Walker County Medical Center—an impressive, three-year-old private hospital—produced a paper about the door that is distributed to visitors. The paper states that ". . . a phenomenon has occurred."

Phenomenon is a carefully chosen word. James Armour, administrator of the 227-room, not-for-profit facility, says, "We think miracles are in healing, in seeing someone who had been ill walk out of the front door, healthy. When we see that happen, it confirms there are miracles in medicine.

"In the young Naramore boy's case, I'm grateful that we have doctors on staff who acted quickly and properly and were able to stabilize him. As for the door, the image is there. We don't have an opinion of the meaning of it. We let people draw their own conclusions."

To the people of the hospital, the image on the door is only one distinctive feature. The discoloration is, perhaps, even more astonishing.

The door, which was finished and hung by the hospital's plant engineering staff, is two-tone. At the top, where the image can be seen, the door is a lighter color. It is as though a kind of bleaching has occurred along a straight line approximately a third of the way down, between the top and middle hinges. The rest of the door is coated in a mahogany darkness.

"I've been through that door hundreds of times," asserts Margaret Reed, day supervisor of nurses, "and I know the color changed."

Armour agrees. "We wouldn't have hung a two-tone door," he says. "If we had, we wouldn't have had it facing the corridor; we

[*"Jesus in Jasper"*]

Jesus?

On April 10, the day following his near-fatal reaction to anesthesia, Ray Naramore was transferred to University Hospital in Birmingham. He was released on April 21. A few days later, gradually regaining his strength, he went fishing at his grandfather's cabin.

Jesus?

"On the morning that Ray was transferred to Birmingham, I was showing one of my sisters and her husband [Janet and Danny Olive] the face on the door," Joel explains. "A nurse who was getting off duty came over to tell us she hoped Ray would be all right and I pointed out the image to her. She said, 'It looks like the face of Jesus. He's been with you.' That was the first person outside my family I'd said anything to about it. If I'd seen her anywhere else in the hospital, I wouldn't've mentioned it.

"Then we went to Birmingham with Ray, who was still in a coma. It was during the time we were there that the excitement about the door was being generated. We didn't even know it was happening."

Joel learned that the story of the door had become news when a television reporter in Birmingham asked for an interview. He thought she wanted to talk about Ray's reaction to the anesthesia.

"She asked, 'What about the image in the door?'" Joel says. "And I asked her how she knew about that. She told me that people were filing through there by the hundreds to see it."

Jesus?

the first to see the face and that seeing came at a time when he desperately needed something for reassurance. His sixteen-year-old son, Ray, was in the operating room, in critical condition.

Ray had been riding a Kawasaki trail bike alone near a place called Cedar Lake. As he was crossing a bridge, he apparently hit a hump in the road and was thrown from the motorcycle. He was not seriously hurt, but doctors at Walker County Medical Center decided he needed plastic surgery to faintline the scars that would be left from healing lacerations. Ray was taken to the One-Day Surgery Room. Anesthesia was administered and Ray suffered an allergic reaction. His temperature soared to above 107 degrees—a state that can cause brain coagulation. His condition immediately deteriorated and the doctors began trying to stabilize him. One of the doctors told Joel they were packing his son in ice and preparing to move him to an ice tank.

"I could tell by his voice—because it was nervous—that things were bad," Joel remembers. "He ran back into the room. We knew it was life or death."

Tim Williams, a reporter with the *Daily Mountain Eagle* in Jasper, later questioned Joel about the experience of fear and yearning and seeing the face in the door. From that interview:

"I was leaning against the wall in an almost daze and I noticed the image which looked so real," he [Naramore] said. "The first thing I noticed were the eyes and then I could see the other features of the face such as a nose and mouth. I thought to myself then that somebody was looking over us."

[*"Jesus in Jasper"*]

ment of pinholes in the wood-shingled roof.

"You're just imagining things," they told us.

And there are those who think that is what has happened this year in Jasper, Alabama, in the Walker County Medical Center. There are those who think a face-image in the door leading into the One-Day Surgery Room is nothing but imagination, a freak of nature, a kind of wood-veneer Rorschach inkblot that had been there all the time, but never attracted attention until April 9, 1983, when it was first noticed. Since then, thousands have seen it. Few deny they have seen a face.

Most of them say it is Jesus. Yes, Jesus.

But the doubters ask how anyone could possibly know what Jesus looked like since he never posed for a portrait in oils or had a Polaroid snapshot taken of him by curious tourists.

None of that matters, the believers argue. Look in the picture books of the Bible. Bloch and Van Dyck and Dore and Raadsig and Bellini and Storch and Jouvenet and all the other master artists know how Jesus looked: long hair, beard, gentle face, soft, hurting eyes. And that is the face in the door in Jasper. Just like the picture books of the Bible show it. Besides, why should it matter? Wouldn't God have the power to transmit the picture of Jesus looking the way people expect him to look?

It is. It isn't. It is. It isn't.

To Joel Naramore, a divorced thirty-nine-year-old father of three and an employee of Alabama Power Company, the argument can rage forever. Let people think as they will. Joel Naramore was

"Jesus in Jasper"

I slept, as a child, in a large bedroom with a wallpapered ceiling. Leaks in the roof had left water stains, like a horizon of clouds, on the wallpaper and, in the light of early morning, those stains would become images. John, my brother, and Peggy, my sister, and I could see them: there was Dick Tracy (old sharp chin), the Joker from Batman and Robin, the Durango Kid, in mask, and Cochise, proud-faced and silent under a feathered headdress. Whatever we had seen or read about, we could find in those rain stains.

God was one of the images. He was there, floating on an air current, his long hair upswept, his great body flung out along the same lines that, on some mornings, were shorelines of continents. God was there, his muscular arm thrust forward, his hazy finger pointing across the room to a brown star burst just over the chifforobe. He had the majestic look of power. Small, delicate angels fluttered like butterflies about his face.

It was a grand ceiling. God and Cochise in the same blot of stain, depending on how we squinted our eyes and force-fed our imaginations. And I think only we could see those faces. Everyone else saw rain-puddled wallpaper and sighed over the embarrass-

[*"I Was a Teenage Quarterback"*]

Actually, we had a decent season in 1954. We won five games, lost six, and even made Charlie Roberts' Top Ten in the *Atlanta Constitution's* Class C listing one week.

I have not written this to make fun of my former teammates. Truthfully, I've never been around a better group of fellows, and I still enjoy seeing them on occasion.

All this jumped forward in my memory not long ago when my ten-year-old son went out to play one morning and returned a couple of hours later wearing a football uniform. His smile was as wide as the face bar on his helmet. "I think I'll play football, Dad," he said, making an effort to flex every muscle in his body at the same time.

I had this strange feeling, as though twenty years ago happened yesterday. I looked at him, proud and speechless. God, he was handsome!

"That O.K. with you, Dad?"

"Yea, son, Sure. But you need to know a few things about playing football, and we'll have to talk about it."

"Like what, Dad?"

"Well, like listening to what the quarterback has to say, and paying attention to the game."

"That all?"

"Naw. There are other things. When you get older, I'll tell you about them."

He gave his shoulder pads a little hitch. "Why not now?"

"O.K." I said. "Let's begin with a guy named Eddie LaBaron..."

1973

The moment came in the fourth quarter. It could not have been computerized by IBM to come at a worse time. We were actually leading, and Irby and Mason and Johnson were having their best night running the ball.

A sub came into the huddle. "Coach said to run the Hoo Doo Voo Doo," he said.

"Now?"

"He said to tell you he'd kick your ass all over downtown Royston if you didn't."

"It's first down. Who the hell's gonna believe we're punting?"

"Coach said now."

We ran the Hoo Doo Voo Doo.

We ran the Hoo Doo Voo Doo three straight times.

We lost exactly forty-five yards.

On fourth down, Coach sent in the Hoo Doo Voo Doo. We punted instead. He never knew the difference.

"I told you it'd work," he said proudly.

There are other stories I could tell. About hitchhiking to one game when the bus gave out. About the water boy suiting up and kicking off the second half, and booting the ball into the end zone. About playing in a rain so heavy no one showed up to watch and the ball kept floating away. About the year only eleven boys showed up for practice.

I do not mean to suggest we were terrible football players, even if we did look pitiful enough to come from Boys' Town. It's just that we were small; our line averaged 165, or less, and the backfield weighed in at 135, or less.

["I Was a Teenage Quarterback"]

The Hoo Doo Voo Doo made the Statue of Liberty look sandlot. It required five pages in our playbook. But Coach loved that play. He had used it once to beat another team, and he was determined to use it again.

I will try to explain the Hoo Doo Voo Doo.

We lined up in punt formation. On this particular play, I was the punter, which was a dead giveaway in its own right. I never punted. Nevertheless, to my right, slightly staggered, were two running backs; to my left, in a blocking position, was the third running back. The line was in tight, end to end.

On the snap, I took the ball, did a little fake like a punter and then handed the ball off to the nearest running back on my right, who would be in motion to his left. He would take the ball and hand it off to the running back lined up on my left, who would be in motion to his right. This second running back would then hand the ball off to the other running back on my right, who would, by this time, be in motion to his left. The second running back on my right, who was the fourth person in the backfield and third running back to handle the ball, would then lateral the ball back to me. At this point I had the option to (a) punt, (b) run, or (c) pass.

The night that Coach planned to use the Hoo Doo Voo Doo finally arrived. He was restless as a thief. He giggled. Did little dance steps on the sideline. But, most important, he waited. Coach wanted the timing to be right. He wanted to spring his surprise of surprises at the precise time, the moment of truth.

a thing of beauty. The University of Georgia would have looked like amateurs in comparison.

But adversity has a way of turning the tables. No one knew it, but history would be made that night: My passing record.

We had the normal three options against Stephens County. We could run, pass or punt. It took one play to eliminate running. And a runner. Punting was also out of the question. Stephens County had the punt rush down to a science. If one of their guys couldn't get back fast enough to block the ball, he picked up one of our guys and threw him into the punter. It was a very discouraging technique. Down to one option. Ol' Eddie LaBaron's good right wing.

That night I threw the J5V a total of twelve times. The first pass was complete, but was called back. Our flanker had lined up in the wrong backfield. The second pass was dropped by the same flanker. The next ten were intercepted, a record that causes my heart to ache whenever I see a picture of Eddie LaBaron.

We lost to Waynesboro but won the next three games, a feat so startling it seemed the mood at R.H.S. bordered on canonizing the entire First Team. Pep rallies that had previously attracted one pyromaniac to light the bonfire, now drew dozens of students willing to fling their bodies before us in sacrificial homage. We had assemblies to cheer us on. The *Royston Record* carried the stories of our exploits, written with generous exaggeration by one of our own players. We even got a new J5V and another towel.

Then we added the Hoo Doo Voo Doo to our playbook.

["I Was a Teenage Quarterback"]

"What play was that?" Coach asked. "We make a first down?"

"Jameson pooted on my hand again."

"Well, punt the damn ball."

That fall we played the first football game in Georgia—Royston vs. Lavonia. We lost, 19-0. I threw one incomplete pass and one interception. I also got knocked senseless by my own fullback and a defensive end from Lavonia caved in my back. Lavonia had a thing about disabling Royston quarterbacks and he was the elected hatchet man; he had the contract. Also, it didn't help a hell of a lot that he believed I was making a play for a Royston girl he had been dating.

Our second game was against Stephens County, which came as a mild surprise when we first got the schedule. We had booked a game against Eastanollee, a school with a reputation for losing football games with remarkable consistency. We were interested because it would have given us at least one even match. Little did we know they would pick that year to consolidate four or five small mountain high schools into one that would be called Stephens County.

Thus, Stephens County arrived to a freshly watered Royston football field. To the screams of enthusiasm for a new school, the team trotted out between the goal posts on the west end of the field. It was unbelievable. There must have been seventy-five guys wearing new McGregor uniforms and Riddel helmets, none weighing less than 170. Stephens County had more football players than we had students. When they went through their warmups, we all sat down and watched. Their unison was

be thinking pass. Indeed, I had learned to be tricky watching Ol' Eddie.

I walked behind Jameson. *"Ready."* I yelled. I slapped my right hand under Jameson's rump. *"Set..."*

And then it happened.

Jameson broke wind.

Not with sophistication. Not small and tooty.

Jameson broke wind like a hurricane hitting Florida. Like the naval attack on Iwo Jima. It was a rolling clap of thunder. It jumped up into the still, soundless night and echoed off the corn stalks. Cows began to moo in the pasture. It paraded up and down the field like a John Phillip Sousa march. It killed gnats and mosquitoes on the fly. It jarred people awake in the stands and brought the cheerleaders to their feet in a single bound.

"Hit 'em again! Hit 'em again! Harder! Harder!"

I jumped back like I'd been hit point blank with a twelve-gauge shotgun. I yelled, "arrrrrrgh!" I couldn't believe it. Jameson had actually pooted on Eddie LaBaron's throwing hand. It would be forever ruined.

A halfback started it. *"Jameson pooted!"* he said, coughing with laughter. *"Jameson pooted!"*

Then everyone broke up. Rolled in the dust. Cried great tears. Even the officials.

Everyone but me. I held my right hand up with my left, as though it had been broken, and I ran to the sidelines.

"Water bucket! Water bucket!" I screamed. And I stuck my hand down in the water, up to the elbow.

[*"I Was a Teenage Quarterback"*]

"Yea. Yea. Kay. Kay. If Kay can't do it, nobody can."

It was the voice of a lone cheerleader who had my name in the "If (blank) Can't" cheer. She didn't even get up from the hogwire fence or miss a stroke with her emery board.

No matter. They'll all be up in a minute, I said to myself.

I rushed out to the field. The team was sitting down.

"Is this a timeout?" I asked, authoritatively.

"Naw."

"Time out!" I yelled. "Time out, Mr. Ref!"

He blew the whistle. I did my best Eddie LaBaron kneel. "All right, men. Let's get this thing going. We've still got a quarter, men."

"Crap." It was Jameson, the center and team captain.

I will ignore that, I thought.

"Now I've been studying their left defensive end," I said. "He's crashing too much inside. We can wipe him out. I want to try something we haven't tried all night—28 Option, but I'll likely lateral and take out the end myself."

The timeout was over. I jumped up in the huddle position. No one else moved. "28 Option on Two. Got it, men? All right, let's get 'em!"

We went to the line of scrimmage. I gave the left defensive end a long, sinister look. I will chew him a new one and lay on the ol' Reverse Body Block, I thought. *Ha! Fool!*

I looked left and then right. I checked my backs. I pushed up on my shoulder pads, and gave the fingers on my right hand a slobbery swipe across my tongue. That'll fool them, I thought. They'll

place I had ever been, and I was reared in the horseshoe of Blackgum Swamp.

Anyway, late in the third quarter, having been thoroughly and convincingly thrashed, the enthusiasm of the Panthers had begun to ebb. More to the point, the Panthers didn't give a damn. The line wouldn't even get on point. The backfield lolled around like it was waiting for the next Greyhound to Atlanta. The cheerleaders were resting against a hog-wire fence, emery-boarding their nails and not even talking to one another. People were actually asleep in the stands. Coach was whispering to the water boy about "... the quiet ones." It was so hushed, you could hear the flag drop when an official called a penalty.

On the sideline, watching, listening, wondering which play would work in such-and-such a situation, I had begun to lose interest in the game. I knew this because Coach's lecture to the water boy had caught my attention. Suddenly, a figure was standing before me. It was the first-string quarterback. He was gasping.

"What's the matter?" I asked.

He looked around and picked up the water bucket and drank from the side. "God, I'm thirsty." He swallowed again. "And tired. Hey. Hey, Kay, you wantta take it a minute? God, it's quiet."

I bounced up. Desire burned in my heart. I paused to test the ache in my throwing arm. I could hear the P.A. in the hollow cave of my imagination: *"Ladies and gentlemen, off the injured list and now playing quarterback—Eddie LaBaron."* The roar of the crowd was deafening.

[*"I Was a Teenage Quarterback"*]

room and hear him coming. *"Ho, Rinny!"* he would yell. And we would answer, *"Ho, Rinny!"* On Friday nights, he suited up and took his position.

Thinking about it, everything seems terribly insane and funny now. It didn't when I wore Number 1 across my back and chest and had visions of leading my men against the Pittsburgh Steelers. If you are a Teenage Quarterback, you take life serious.

I should explain the reason I became a Teenage Quarterback. There were three reasons, actually: (1) I was the only person who knew what everybody was supposed to do on every play; (2) I was the fastest man on the team, which meant running for your life more often than not, and (3) I could do an Eddie LaBaron that would have made Ol' Eddie weep with pride. I mean, I had him down to a split-T. His posture. The sassy strut he had coming out of a huddle. The way he surveyed his own line, checked his backs and read the enemy's defense. His little shoulder pad hitch. The commanding way he slapped his hands under the butt of his center. Oh, I knew LaBaron. I used to want to change my name to Eddie.

The most embarrassing thing that ever happened to me occurred in my Eddie LaBaron days. It was my junior year and I was playing second-string quarterback on offense and wayback on defense. (Wayback is a position in the defensive secondary played by 130-pound safeties.)

We were in south Georgia on a still, soundless, Indian summer Friday night. The football field was next to a corn patch and a pasture. I never did see the high school. It was the most remote

the sub would be squashed in the ground and Coach would say. "That's the way you gotta treat the bourgeoisie." And he would laugh.

Ha. Ha.

I am not suggesting Coach was a character who warped our minds or misguided our values. Not at all. He helped a lot of us build a personal pride we would not have otherwise experienced. And pride was important to those of us who grew up as the last generation of forty-acre, plow-and-mule dirt farming. We were the agents, and victims, of an uncertain economy and a baffling social awareness that had already begun to stir and rumble with its thunder of inevitable change. We had seen the rag-tag coattail of The Great Depression, had felt its bitterness and sadness and knew the business of keeping in our place.

Football was a relief from that sense of anonymity. It made us Somebody. And we played the role with style. We wore our Levi's with the tell-tale pair of white athletic socks dangling out of a back pocket. We had slicked-back ducktails and measured G.I.'s. We attended classes together, walked down halls together and stayed together at recess.

But as similar as we were collectively, we were also learning the adventure of being distinctively individual.

There was one boy, for example, who played first string guard. He was individual because he never reported to practice. He went home and watched "Rin-Tin-Tin" on television. After practice, he would drop by and tell us about Ol' Rin-Tin-Tin and who had been bitten on the tail. We could sit in the dressing

[*"I Was a Teenage Quarterback"*]

Coach got confused a lot. One time, he sent in a substitute for me. When I arrived at the sideline, he grabbed me by the shoulder pads and began to shake me like a malted milk.

"Dammit!" he screamed. *"When I send in for you to punt the damn ball, you damn well better punt!"*

"Co-o-o-o-ch," I stuttered like a chorus from "K-K-K-Katy."

"Punt, damn you!"

"Co-o-o-o-ch, we ca-ca-n't pun-punt. We ai-ain't got the ball. We-we-we're on de-de-de-defense."

Coach stopped shaking me. He blinked wildly.

"Oh . . . Well, when you get it, punt."

Coach had a great coaching technique. He had plays written in his Blue Horse tablet, but he kept things simplified. If you played on the line, you hit anybody in front of you, any direction he would move. If you played backfield, you ran wherever you could without stepping on your own men.

That was offense.

On defense, you looked for the J5V and did anything required to stop the other team in its act of moving the J5V forward. Absolutely anything. We did not practice defense. Ever. But we played it with the glee of a New York gang rumble out of the real "West Side Story."

I have two distinct memories of Coach teaching refinements. He taught me to pass without snapping my wrist to one side, and he taught all of us the Reverse Body Block. Occasionally, to prove he was our superior, Coach would administer the Reverse Body Block on an unsuspecting substitute. One swift lick and

tric light poles, each with four or five 500-watt bulbs aimed in the general direction of the playing action. You could have been mugged in the middle of the fifty-yard line and no one would have been able to identify the culprit. It pains me to think about the passing records I might have established if Poss Johnson could have seen the ball. The same is true of those quarterbacks I followed—Billy Ford, Ben Dickson, George Adams and the rest. In the blindness of our football field, there might have been an All-American.

We had one uniform each. Almost. Some of the lower subs wore tennis shoes. Thigh pads were hard to come by. Our helmets were of assorted style and color and came from the Punic Wars. No one knew what a face mask, or bar, looked like. Our water bucket came without a dipper. We had one roll of tape per game for the entire team. You should have seen the towel. We used Ben Gay for everything from broken bones to athlete's foot to jock itch. And we had one J5V official game ball that Coach kept wrapped in a White Lily flour sack. Coach regarded that J5V as a virgin needing his full attention and protection. At the closing whistle of every game, Coach would start screaming to the water boy: "Goddammit! Where's the J5V? You find that J5V or I'll skin you."

We didn't have much to be proud of, but we did have one thing that was unusual: We had the damnedest coming together of coach and young men in the history of sport.

Coach. I liked Coach, but always thought he needed more rest than he got. A year after I was graduated he entered an institution just for that purpose, and I understand he is still there.

[*"I Was a Teenage Quarterback"*]

A guy named Travis Reed carried the ball a half dozen times. Travis was six feet tall and weighed around 180 pounds, and everytime he got the ball the line opened like the Red Sea obeying Charlton Heston. It was brutal. The first time I hit Travis, he knocked me ten yards—in all directions. By the sixth time, the only thing left to make a grease spot was my Wildroot Creme Oil. I think the reason I survived was because Travis had never before killed anyone and a sense of humanity seized him.

When it was over, Coach stood looking down on my remains. He found the place where my nose had been and knowing the eyes were in close proximity, he gave me a man-to-man stare.

"Now, you gonna run track or play football?"

"But . . . but, we ain't got a track team."

Coach blinked wildly.

Well, this is to say I did play football. I made it, old sport. I mean First Team. I became a Teenage Quarterback and established a national single game passing record that, to my knowledge, has never been challenged. But I will explain that in detail a few paragraphs from now.

Our football field was weed-less and grass-less. It was a naked piece of ground with all the comforts of crushed granite. (As God is my witness, the city would send out a couple of trucks of water to settle the dust when the Purple Panthers played at home. Practice was another thing. They wouldn't send out spit for practice. But, then, we really never stirred up much dust practicing.)

Our weed-less, grass-less, dust-and-granite football field was illuminated by six or eight used Georgia Power Company elec-

In those days, I could run for hours in my PF Flyers. Everyday I ran laps. For two weeks I ran laps. One day I said to Coach, "Coach, I am tired of running laps; I want to play football."

"You ain't going to play football," he said flatly. "You're going to be on the track team."

"Coach, we ain't got a track team."

Coach blinked wildly. He always blinked wildly when reality broke in to flood his brain.

"Well, dammit, we may have one someday."

"Coach, I'd like to play football."

"You little poot, you ain't big enough."

"Coach, I'd like to try."

It was a day I will always remember. Coach told me I would play linebacker.

"What's a linebacker?" I was not versed in sophisticated sports terminology in those days.

"He lines up on the defensive tackle and he kicks hell out of anybody that runs by him with the ball."

"Sure, Coach."

Coach took the rest of the team down to one side of the field and they kneeled and talked in whispers. I thought they were saying The Lord's Prayer and I wouldn't be invited until I'd been formally introduced around. Occasionally a head would bob up from the huddle and someone would giggle aloud.

That's no way to treat The Lord's Prayer, I thought.

The huddle broke. "All right, men," Coach yelled, "let's scrimmage." He looked at me and smiled. "Kay, play linebacker, son."

"I WAS A TEENAGE QUARTERBACK"

(Author's note: Part of what you are about to read is true; part of it is the natural liar of the writer. But it could have happened as reported . . . if you knew how it was. Oh yes, it could have happened. That is why some of the names have been changed, to protect the guilty.)

The first day I reported to football practice, I weighed 118 pounds. Coach looked at me and "ummm-m-m-med." He rubbed his chin with the one philosophic gesture he had. He backed off and sized me up. "Ummm-m-m-m." He walked around me, reached down suddenly and caught me by the calf of my left leg. "Ummm-m-m. Good legs." I thought of Hansel being goosed by the witch. Coach continued around me, stalking, looking, rubbing his chin and going "Ummmmm-m." I felt a great compulsion to open my mouth and show him my teeth. He stopped and was very still. Then he noticed my PF Flyers.

"Go run some laps, boy."

"Yessir."

The South & Tradition

[*"What If Nancy Reagan Was Right?"*]

She sees what she sees, and she tells it as she sees it. Why else would she be called Madam?

But what I really want to believe comes from none of them. It comes from a fortune cookie randomly passed to me after a meal in a charming, but run-of-the-mill Chinese restaurant.

In the broken-apart fortune cookie was the message: YOU ARE THE MASTER OF EVERY SITUATION.

I'll accept that, thank you.

1992

"I told you, didn't I?" the young palmist said.

"Yes, yes you did. You told me," the young model enthused.

"Good. Now, I want you to come back tomorrow. We have things we must talk about."

The young model's face clouded for a moment. "I can't," she said. "I have to work."

"Then call me," she was told. "It's important we talk."

I saw in that exchange a mood of hope and belief and desperation, and I began to ask friends if they had ever been to a psychic, or a palmist, or a numerologist, or if they had had an astrological reading performed. I was stunned at how many admitted to consulting at least one such medium.

I learned that a lot of well-to-do people—from the retired and settled to the yuppies—get some kind of emotional fix by having regular counsel with an agent of the metaphysical arts. It's what might be called the Nancy Reagan mentality, I suppose, but there are a lot of believers, and a lot of people conduct their personal and business lives by what they are told.

That's the danger, of course. If someone tells me that I am going to end a friendship, or a business relationship, in anger and I believe it, I think I could easily make it happen. And then I could say, "I knew it. It was inevitable."

The psychic told me she was eighty-five percent accurate. (I think I will lower her average.)

The astrologer told me he was speaking only of influences, that how I responded to those influences was the key.

The palmist did not worry about percentages, or influences.

[*"What If Nancy Reagan Was Right?"*]

All gave me comments on events and moods that were amazingly accurate. All said that a tiresome period was ending, but they disagreed on the outcome. One saw tragedy. One saw hope learned from hard lessons. One saw adjustments, a leveling of the ups and downs.

The palmist and the astrologer informed me that I had been born under a special spirit and, therefore, had something special awaiting me in the future. The palmist suggested it was something I had never considered, something unrelated to the other experiences in my life. When I left her, I had an image of working the senior citizens' shift at McDonald's.

I went into these sessions as an interested observer and came out of them with the same attitude—though the palmist did make me tremble with one or two comments that were so dead-center I could feel the blood drain from my face. "But you know these things, don't you?" she said. "No matter what you are being told, you know the truth of these things. You have a great psychic power yourself." I do not know about the psychic power, but I do know she was right about what she told me.

What now intrigues me about these practices that some consider the devil's doings and others consider a gift from God is how many people turn to them for answers.

While waiting to see the palmist, I watched a lovely young woman anxiously talking to another young woman—I think she was the daughter of the palmist and is also a reader—about her future as a fashion model. The world seemed to be spinning golden dreams for her.

All informed me that I was in a troubled period, but all said I was beginning a new-life phase, one that would find direction in 1993. The astrologer—a fascinating, intense, intelligent fellow—told me that my time in the sun, so to speak, would begin about 1997, or thereabouts. It has to do with the "primal triad"—the sun, the moon and the ascendant. At the hour of my birth, a few light years ago, the sun was in Aquarius, the moon in Gemini, and Sagittarius was ascending. Not a bad mix, he told me, and he was very certain there was sufficient planetary evidence among other heavenly bodies to keep me striding in eager step for whatever it is I am supposed to be striding for.

All suggested that I would never own a yacht, or a Rolls Royce, or live in a penthouse suite, or travel the world on first-class tickets. All also agreed that if I *had* money, I would manage it badly. Only the astrologer gave me credit for having good business judgment. "However," he correctly noted, "you don't use it very often." The psychic was almost too blunt regarding the matter: "You dislike legal entanglements," she said, "such as contracts. They always annoy you." I wondered if she knew my agent.

My writing, they determined, would become focused in late spring or early summer of 1993. The psychic used the description "rocket," a word any writer enjoys hearing. The astrologer predicted good works beginning in 1993, but held to the 1997 date for the icing on the career. The palmist said the novel I was writing and would finish in 1993 would be popular and have great impact. She said a second novel would begin slowly, then blossom. (I wonder if she wants to *be* my agent.)

[*"What If Nancy Reagan Was Right?"*]

This interest in the metaphysical—using metaphysical in its most elastic meaning—began when I was twelve.

It was at a Halloween carnival at Vanna Junior High School. As part of the merriment, the local mystic/palm reader, who was renowned for telling a woman where her lost diamond ring would be found, was employed to read palms. It was a silly sort of experience—standing there, giggling, moving up in line, wiping our palms clean, waiting to have our future declared.

I remember it distinctly. The reader took my hand, held it, palm-up, and scanned it with her small, narrow eyes. She then looked up to me. She said, "You will be a writer." She dropped my hand and motioned to the person behind me.

When you are twelve, you want more out of a palmist, especially if you despise writing.

I lied when asked what the palmist said. I told my classmates she predicted that I would be a great athlete, that I would have more money than I could count, that I would be surrounded by beautiful females.

None of them believed me.

And that made it even: I did not believe the palmist.

Then.

When I was twelve.

But becoming what she said I would become has caused me to pause, and wonder.

I do not think any of the recent experiences were as profound as the one at Vanna Junior High School, but they were interesting, especially in a few common perceptions, or findings.

"WHAT IF NANCY REAGAN WAS RIGHT?"

I have always been leery of those who have the "sixth sense," those who seem to have found a peephole in the steel curtains that we wrap around ourselves, covering our past, masking our future.

The person who can look into your palm and tell you things that you have done, or will do, after all, is not your normal, walking about representative of the human species.

Better still, the person who can pluck images out of the air while merely holding an object that belongs to you is, indeed, a marvel.

But none of that holds a candle to an astrological reading, which informs you of planetary influences that begin the moment you get your butt-slap jump into life.

I am like a lot of people I know.

I don't *believe* any of it.

Yet, I don't doubt it, either.

But, I've had a go at it lately (partly as your envoy, and partly, frankly, to satisfy an abiding personal curiosity). Not only a psychic reading, but a palm reading, and an astrological chart reading.

trust on their faces. Dreams of my family avoiding me out of shame. Dreams of my friends laughing hysterically.

Now I know something important: Most of those friends in my dreams have admitted to me that they, too, have been in counseling.

"Best thing I've ever done," they say.

Maybe we have become a society that needs adjustments we can get only in professional counseling. Talking to a friend has always been a good, soul-lifting experience for me, but I want my friends to think of me as someone who can handle the disturbances that occur.

Some disturbances are too powerful to handle alone, however.

Some moments—a thought, a remembered scene, an old comment—can break the shell.

And all of this is to say that the skeptic has put aside his skepticism.

After twenty years of Never, I did it.

And I feel better because I did.

1992

I know people who have been in counseling for years and still have not shared their most searing experiences with their counselor. They talk around those experiences, reference them lightly or lie outrageously. They disguise them well. It is as though the experiences were too horrific, or too grand, to release.

They sometimes tell me what the counselor has said to them, and I want to argue, "But that's what you wanted him [or her] to say, isn't it?"

And there are others who go in with tongues wagging, spilling their guts, and they seem to come out relieved or, in some cases, frightened.

I did go to another counselor several years ago. A onetime visit. She was a very nice lady. She invited me to talk and I began. Fifty minutes later, I stopped. Then she made a mistake—for me. She said, "You very badly need counseling.

I stood, thanked her for her time, and started for the door. She said, "You're coming back, aren't you?"

I said, "I don't think so."

I made a mistake.

I was one of those who wagged his tongue and walked out frightened.

It was a throwback to an old conditioning: How will I feel if I see her again? Embarrassed? Guilty? Will I imagine that she is telling the person with her, "Do you see that man? That's Terry Kay. He's certifiably crazy. Let me tell you what he said to me."

I had dreams about it. Dreams of walking down the street in my hometown and people retreating, with looks of fear and dis-

[*"The Shell Game"*]

get up and walk out and go handle this thing that bothers me? I've always done it. Why not now?

I think that is a fear that many people have about counseling—not being able to handle what they believe they should handle alone. A sign of weakness, they have convinced themselves.

Dr. Tom Gable, a psychiatrist and a friend, explains that people fear counseling because they think they may ". . . find out that they're crazy, or have something sinister bottled up inside them. If they 'unlock' it, it will consume them. In a specific sense, they fear there will be some emotional uproar.

"The issue isn't so much a matter of telling what people believe is the truth," Dr. Gable contends. "The issue is being able to tell things in a complete and undisguised manner, but with many people the thought is, 'If I let these horrors come forward, I will be viewed as a vulgar, bad person.'"

I can give him an endorsement on that view. It is exactly what I felt as I revealed myself to my counselor. When the session was over, I wanted to apologize.

Yet, what I learned is this: It's a little like losing weight. You get rid of something excessive and it feels better. And if the person who is hearing you is able to say things that you think he or she has read from the inside of your heart, you no longer feel so alone with whatever demon—mild or fierce—resides with you.

The requisite, I suspect, is in doing the one thing that is, perhaps, most difficult—putting your cards on the table, as the cliché goes.

thing. After my son left, I thought that I had recovered, that it was merely a passing moment. I called a friend, and as I was talking to her, the shell broke again.

The next several hours were the most despairing of my life. The friends who called, who were concerned, asked the same question: What caused this?

And I lied. "Nothing," I said. "Nothing. It just happened."

I lied because I did not know I was lying. Not until the next day did I understand what had caused it.

It was my third visit to the counselor. She asked, "How are you?"

"I had a very bad day yesterday," I confessed.

"Tell me about it," she said.

And I think that in the hour I spent with her, I came closer to sharing some moments of absolute truth than I ever have—with anyone.

This stranger, this woman who sat properly and quietly in a rather dull office, this person I had seen only twice before, heard what I could not tell those who are closest to me. And there is nothing really terrible about it. I have not molested children. I am not on drugs. I have not mugged anyone. I do not have anxieties over my sexual orientation. I simply have not been in sync with life, and that has confused me.

Even while talking to her—or babbling, as I felt I was doing—I was amazed. I kept thinking, Why am I doing this? Why am I telling her these things that I won't tell anyone else? Why don't I

[*"The Shell Game"*]

On the day the shell broke, I was at my machine, my word processor, working on a story that was only mildly interesting. Then, like a ministroke, a thought, a remembered scene, an old comment, flashed in my mind and I could not move my hands.

I am told that similar things happen to everyone, in one degree or another, but it had never happened to me.

I sat for a moment, frightened. And I forced my fingers to close, then open, close again, open.

I pushed away from the machine and went upstairs and walked out onto the deck. My son was at home with a friend. He came out to tell me they were leaving. When he saw me, he knew something was wrong.

"What's the matter?" he said in a worried voice.

And that is when the shell—the fragile thing that I think of as control—broke. I began to weep. Just that. Weep. He came to me and took my hands and knelt before me, and he said, "Dad, what is it?"

I wanted to tell him that I was all right, that it was just a momentary thing, a lapse, the final drag-down of fatigue, but I could not speak.

He led me inside the house and helped me stretch out on the sofa and he sat and talked to me until I became calm. I apologized for my behavior, told him I was tired, urged him to go with his friend. Reluctantly, he did. I think he knew I needed time to be alone.

I am not a psychiatrist, or a psychologist, but I believe that when the shell breaks, it tries to repair itself, and that is a tricky

advantage of counseling, and since it seemed to have worked for John Smoltz during his bad days with the Braves in 1991, I thought, Why not? This has been a year of bad days. Friends who know me well said, "Do it. God knows, you need it. Besides, what harm is it going to do?"

Also, I was beginning to feel lonely. Almost everyone I know either is, or has been, in counseling. When idle chatter is about the wisdom of one's therapist, and you have nothing to contribute, you begin to feel deprived.

And, so, I jotted down the name and the number of the counselor the insurance company recommended, and I called and made an appointment.

I was asked, "Is this drug-related?"

"No," I said.

"Stress?"

"I'll accept that," I answered.

On my first visit, I talked in circles, saying nothing of significance. (At least, that is the way I remember it; her notes may be more telling.) I had writer's block, I said. I couldn't concentrate. I was restless, worried about money. I was annoyed because my grown children won't keep their rooms clean. That sort of thing.

I think I bored the lady.

On the second visit, I began to peel away some layers of insecurity—cautiously, of course.

On the third visit, I think she may have saved my life, which is a melodramatic way of saying she helped and I knew it.

"The Shell Game"

Many years ago, there was a clinical psychologist in Atlanta who counseled a number of my writer friends. She was, to them, something of a miracle worker, a mind-cleanser, someone who took the stagger out of their step and put them back on stride. When they spoke of her, they beamed happily and they marveled at her insights to their problems.

I thought it was hogwash.

Why in the name of God would anyone pay someone else—especially at an appointed hour—to hear their stories of burden?

We were at a party one night and I was introduced to her. She said, smiling, "You're next."

"Never," I said. "Not me."

I was, you see, a skeptic. Sew up my cuts, reset my bones, slice out ailing and unnecessary organs, but leave my mind alone.

"I wouldn't say that," she said sweetly.

"Never," I repeated.

Never lasted almost twenty years.

And then, a few months ago, there was an opportunity through the benevolence of my insurance company to take

gets the idea that the Postseason is a money-maker, be forewarned that this is a copyrighted article, but I'll be happy to discuss a sellout.

That way, I could be in the Bahamas, and I could be slapping expensive cologne on my face in hopes of running into Michelle Pfeiffer.

Who knows? The two of us could be having dinner in a poetic Italian restaurant, and she could be slipping me grapes from her lips as we kissed to sweet string music. I might even be wearing my old PF flyers.

As my daddy used to say, if the shoe fits, wear it.

1992

[*"Keds Say the Darndest Things"*]

Does the name matter? You can bet your last dollar it does. In fact, with some of these brands, you can pay your last dollar. They don't come cheap.

Case in point. My grandson, Brooks, is a shoe fanatic. He would rather go to a shoe store than the zoo. And he is a determined little rascal. He enters a store with one thing in mind: a name brand. Not long ago it was British Knights. For whatever reason—some ad, I am sure—he had to have British Knights. And, yes, he got them. And, yes, they were more expensive than another brand that I deemed equally good.

Because the competition to fit your feet is keen among shoemakers, they often sign celebrities like Michael Jordan or Dominique Wilkins or Spike Lee to hawk their goods. The hawking is effective. What kid wouldn't want to be Michael Jordan in the solitary play of his imagination?

And the beat goes on. Even among sport shoes, there's always a new angle.

Reebok is now promoting the Preseason, something of a cross-trainer, but the concept behind the name is to convince people that they need a shoe for wearing before putting on the real shoe for the game. It's a little like a warm-up jersey, I suppose. And if we have the Preseason, can the Postseason be far behind? Naturally, it would be a lightweight thing, comforting to sore, aching soles. It would also have an optional medicated insert—color of green, I think—that would time-release the chemical equivalent of Ben-Gay to relieve irritation.

Oh, in case any shoemaker—or ad agency—reads this and

SPECIAL KAY *the wisdom of terry kay*

First, it is no longer a shoe. It is a species of shoe. There are shoes for walking, running, aerobics, racquetball, basketball, baseball, soccer, football, cross-training (a little bit of everything), wrestling, etc. There are even shoes for tennis.

And these are not canvas/rubber/glue/string shoes that have tops and bottoms. Oh, no. These are engineered footwear, and I'm not speaking only of the air-pump gizmo that swept the nation a couple of seasons ago. I'm speaking of shoes that have sock liners, trampolines, midsoles, midsole chambers, outsole windows, outsoles, and motion-control devices. How do I know? An ad from Turntec tells me. There are also shoes with air bubbles, shoes with gel, shoes with—well, whatever. And if you really want to get technical, Adidas has this thing called a FootScan for individualized perfection. The FootScan, I have read from the *Adidas Running News,* not only determines foot morphology (you look it up), but also "... measures the pressure under the foot in standing and in running using a pressure-sensitive sensor mat."

If you want a pair of sport shoes, you have enough choices to boggle the imagination—Adidas, Nike, Reebok, Tretorn, British Knights, Wilson, K-Swiss, Avia, Asics, Fila, Diadora, Saucony, Turntec, Brooks, Etonic, New Balance, Mizuno, etc. Old timers can even get the Converse All Star, with the round rubber patch that hits the ankle bone. Today, they are multicolored. (And, by the by, most of these shoes are made in Taiwan, Japan, Korea, or the Republic of China, which is one way of keeping us on our toes, I suppose.)

[*"Keds Say the Darndest Things"*]

Good advertising is a novel, a play, a movie, in miniature. It is quintessential storytelling, making us all believe that what we have seen, heard, or read, is—or could be—our story.

We could be partying in the Bahamas, or we could be rubbing our faces with cologne that would make Michelle Pfeiffer do a double take in a crowded restaurant. For that matter, we could be dining selectively in one of those eateries with a poetic Italian name, instead of sitting impatiently in the drive-through lane of a hamburger palace.

Even the more delicate matters of our daily lives look dreamy in ads. Tell me that Preparation H didn't score one with that fellow riding a bicycle after a couple of treatments, or that women aren't impressed with the soft, confidential chatter between mother and daughter about Summer's Eve. We could be one of those people, upbeat and happy with the way life treats us.

The point is, advertising makes us dream, makes us strive to get what we don't have, and that, in turn, makes the economy healthy. Or so they say.

But we are suckers.

We fall for what the advertising folk say. These people know their business. Always have. And from the moment they decided to turn their attention to our feet, we never had a chance.

I don't really believe that putting on a pair of Air Jordans will get me into the NBA, but I—and a lot of other shoe buyers, apparently—am willing to suspend that disbelief for a brief dream-moment of kinship with Michael Jordan.

Thus, the sport shoe has been, and is, a hot commodity.

A lot of boys believed the same thing. A young man I knew in elementary school once vowed that he could run sixty miles an hour in his PF Flyers. He said he had done it. Said that his father had tested him by driving the family car an even sixty on a straightaway, and he had kept up.

Ah, magic. Long-ago magic. It is still wonderful.

Basically, the old PF Flyer was canvas, rubber, glue and string. The shoe, itself, was fine. It simply was not as good, or as fast, as its advertising.

Advertising. Telling us what we want. Telling us to go get it. In the matter of shoes and practically everything else, advertising greases the wheels of America. Without it, the capitalistic system we promote in the name of free enterprise would be generic boredom. Say it right, with style, with celebrity spokespersons and, by heavens, Americans can sell anything.

I would also say, with deep regret, that advertising clearly represents the instability of our ever-changing culture, because advertising folk are quick to pick up on, or invent, the latest fad. The latest fad sells, of course, and I don't care if we're talking about double-knit suits or some kid pumping the air with his fist and shouting "Yo!" What is our culture if it is not the newest thing out of the mold?

Yet good advertising is remarkable.

It's the bad stuff (advertisements for new or previously owned cars at local dealerships come immediately to mind) that is horrendous.

"Keds Say the Darndest Things"

Years ago, when I was into heroic fantasies, I wore PF Flyers. I wore them because there were ads in the newspapers and magazines that told of heroic acts by those with PF Flyers laced to their feet. They could turn on the speed and, in that nick-of-time suspense that still makes us hold our breath, these guys (it was guys in those days) could pluck a lovely, sensuous, but distressed lady from helplessness in such spectacular fashion, I would have dreams of them. Dreams of being them.

I wore my PF Flyers with pride, waiting for some lovely, sensuous, distressed woman to find herself in a helpless situation. It never happened. Most of the women I knew in those days were perfectly capable of handling their own problems with frying pans or uppercuts.

Still, I believed what I read. And, to my own way of thinking, I was faster in my PF Flyers than in any other shoe. They were magical. I could have raced Jesse Owens and Carl Lewis at the same time, and left them gasping. I could have climbed Mt. Everest, or danced the ballet with my feet tucked inside a pair of Flyers. Magic has no limits on the imagination.

But all of this is the business of toys, which doesn't necessarily have anything to do with the spirit of toys. The spirit touches the heart, not the wallet.

In his book, *Without Reservations*, Fred Alias presents a story about a hotel clerk who was shopping one day in a thrift store and overheard a small girl begging her mother for a doll's house that was in need of repair. The mother tried to explain that there was no money for dollhouses, that a winter coat was more important.

The hotel clerk followed the mother and child when they left the store, noting their address. He then went back to the thrift shop, purchased the dollhouse and spent his spare time repairing it. On Christmas Eve, he tied a bow around the dollhouse and delivered it in the middle of the night to the front steps of the home where the girl lived.

Forgive me for being sentimental, but I like that story. It reminds that there are things that can't be purchased in Toys "R" Us, or any other shop.

And I think it confirms something that's important at Christmas: A doll's house given out of caring is more valuable than diamonds—if your heart is the heart of a child. If it isn't, you will never understand what giving, or receiving, really means, anyway.

1992

[*"Gift Rap"*]

getic gather. She is even featured in a wedding dress, which makes me wonder if she's managed to trap Ken at the altar. Oh, yes, Ken's still around. Still smiling, the little devil that he is. Personally, I think he's got his eye on Midge, Barbie's best friend.

And the Cabbage Patch Kids are plentiful. My favorite is the one called Newborn (but it's not Lucy). It is advertised with a "magical monitor," and it "cries, giggles, and calls 'Ma Ma.'" Cute, real cute.

But there always seems to be a head-liner Christmas gift, and, if the pleading of my oldest grandson—son of Lucy's mother— is an indicator, that gift would have to be from Nintendo.

The Nintendo games are advertised as the World of Nintendo. There's no brag in the claim. It is a world. Strange. Baffling. And every year, something new.

That, of course, is the key to toy manufacturing: Keep it coming with upgraded and improved product. The new look, the new appeal. It's a little like adults who collect Christmas plates from Hummel. If it's another year, there's another edition.

According to Matt Dodge, the assistant inventory control manager for the Southeast region of Toys "R" Us, the key to the business of toys is ". . . always to keep fresh."

Dodge admits that even Nintendo has leveled off over the years, but, ". . . they keep bringing out new generations of software, offering new and more exciting games."

Dodge must be right. My grandson tells me the same thing, insisting that he will be considered the neighborhood oddball if he can't have his fingers flying over the latest Nintendo challenge.

He thinks I am a sucker for his woeful expression. He is right.

around search to find them at a slashed-price deal. (And I am referring only to children's toys, not that gaudy nonsense annually advertised for over-rich adults. A Mercedes golf cart? May it dogleg left and find the fairway to hell.)

An investigative tour of one of the Toys "R" Us stores is a trip into a latter-day land of fantasy. Little wonder the corporate powers that be are building twenty-five to thirty of these toy-stacked emporiums each year in America. They know that cash flow is bound to follow the squeal of childish joy.

We used to be happy with a simple game of checkers. Now they have a board that can be used for checkers, chess, backgammon, Parcheesi, Chinese checkers and something called Chutes & Ladders.

The standards are still available, but they're often hard to recognize.

The toy truck we once pushed around in the back yard has now been upgraded by Tonka to the size of a riding lawn mower.

The roller skate is now an in-line skate, or something called a Rollerblade.

You can now buy a kite that looks like a fighter plane and has electronic battling sounds.

And I swear there are bicycles with more gears than spokes in the wheels.

Barbie, the doll's doll, is still as youthful and fetching as Brenda Starr, and still on the shelves, but she's a modern woman of action. She can be found in a Patio Party box, or a Backyard Cookout box, or a Sunshine Holiday box, and a few other places where the ener-

[*"Gift Rap"*]

- Educational—With boxes, children must use their imagination. Does a greater instrument of education exist than the imagination?

- Durable—Boxes are like good dogs around children. They can take the punishment and still be there.

- Relatively inexpensive—How much can a box cost in comparison to the gift it holds?

- Child Delight Meter—Refer to "popular" and "educational" items above, or better yet, refer to experience.

In addition, a box does not require batteries, which are never included when they should be included. It does not need late-night home assembly with directions that not even the CIA could follow. It can be drawn on with Magic Marker and become magical. And when it is finally crushed from the weight of imagination—from being submarines and spaceships, dollhouses and dark caves—it may be recycled for such mundane purposes as holding items for sale. It is even biodegradable for those too casual to recycle.

Yet, to my knowledge, no one makes cardboard shipping boxes for the express purpose of functioning as a toy, and in that decision or oversight is a statement about our values that is worth pondering: If we get a wrapped box, we expect something other than possibility to be inside it.

Still, like most shoppers, I enjoy the annual dilemma of the what and how many of Christmas toys, and then the rushing-

Point is, shopping for Christmas toys is not an easy task, especially today.

The choices are too many, too appealing.

Used to be—or so memory tells me—it was as simple as a walk-through in a five-and-dime store.

Boys got something from the sports table, or toy pistols, or toy cars. Maybe some Tinker-toys, or pick-up sticks. Maybe even a Red Ryder BB rifle.

Girls got dolls, and other stuff. I don't know what, make-believe makeup kits, maybe. Imitation jewelry. I didn't pay very much attention.

No one fretted that what was being given would be sneered at, or refused, or ignored. A gift was something, and something was considerably better than nothing.

Not so today.

Today, everyone seems to want a toy that is popular, safe, educational, durable, relatively inexpensive, and one that ranks high on the Child Delight Meter.

The only thing I know that comes close to meeting the above requisites is a large cardboard shipping box:

- Popular—How many of us have watched children tear open a gift, turn it over a couple of times, toss it away, and pick up the box it came in?

- Safe—Sure, youngsters can get hurt playing with, or in, boxes, but chances are the toy inside the box is far more dangerous.

"Gift Rap"

The best memory I have of Christmas, as a parent, was the evening that my oldest daughter—then a one-year-old—pulled a wrapped package beneath the tree two days earlier than Santa Claus would have liked, and proceeded to rip it open.

Inside the package was a doll, a squint-eyed thing that I considered on-purpose, new-born-baby ugly. I had protested to my wife that it would cause nightmares or even more severe traumas. My complaints were ignored with a stare that said, "This is a mother-daughter thing."

Of course, she was right. My daughter's face was radiant when she tore open the box.

"Baby," she whispered in awe. "Baby." She held it to her face, like a mother being tender with her child.

That doll became Lucy, and from that Christmas until she was lost on a trip many years later, Lucy was always within reach of my daughter. The tears of woe over that sad mishap were so great, I have spent almost thirty years trying to duplicate Lucy in flea markets and doll shops.

My daughter had cried, "There's only one Lucy."

After all these years, I believe her.

published in 1969 and remains popular. In it, Kübler-Ross identifies five stages of response to death—Denial and Isolation, Anger, Bargaining, Depression and Acceptance. The final stage is followed by Hope.

I submit that her five stages are equally applicable to other stressful events—loss of job, divorce, betrayal, any number of painful experiences. I can't speak for others, but I've picked my way through those five moods more than once. That's the sort of dysfunctional fellow I am.

Thank God for Hope—whatever its source.

1992

[*"If the Dysfunction Fits, Read It"*]

author is an M.D. or a New Age spiritualist. If the teacher provides an answer, or an understanding, the credentials hardly matter.

I have a friend—one from that inquisitive and sometimes annoying younger generation—who can quote chapter and verse from any number of self-help books. She believes the reason for their success is the failure of traditional sources—the church, the schools, the family, the community—to address serious contemporary issues of a dysfunctional nature. They dodge the bullet, so to speak. Avoid unpleasant realities.

A quick scan of titles suggests she may be right: Marianne Williamson's *A Return to Love* (Reflections on the Principles of *A Course in Miracles*); Chris Griscom's *The Healing of Emotion* (Awakening the Fearless Self); Stormie Omartian's *A Step in the Right Direction* (Your Guide to Inner Happiness); Lynne Finney's *Reach for the Rainbow* (Advanced Healing for Victims of Sexual Abuse); Jacquelyn Small's *Awakening in Time* (The Journey From Co-Dependence to Co-Creation); Jean Shinoda Bolen's *Gods in Everyman* (The New Psychology of Men's Lives and Loves); Lois Frankel's *Women, Anger and Depression* (Strategies for Self-Empowerment).

There is even a cookbook—Gina Ogden's *Food for Body and Soul* (Recipes for Recovery).

I cannot recommend any of these titles. I've scanned some, but I haven't read them. I have copied their titles merely as evidence of the variety of topics that seem to plague us as a society.

But I have read passages from one that does interest me—Elisabeth Kübler-Ross's *On Death and Dying*, which was first

be so debilitating that we become slaves to the memories of them. It is possible to have closure. We do have the right to make choices from an expansive list of possibilities.

From what I know of them, the self-help books feast on dysfunctional situations. Some, I am certain, offer good advice; others may cause harm. But they all promote one thing: the self matters. Who, with good sense, would want to believe otherwise?

Self-help books also sell, which is why most bookstores keep a good supply of them prominently displayed.

Chris Wooster, the publicity coordinator for Borders Book Shop, calls the self-help section "one of the strongest in the store, one that is constantly trafficked." He observes that interest is particularly keen among the younger crowd, those in their twenties and thirties and even into their early forties. The older buyer, he adds, is more likely to seek publications that are strictly inspirational.

Gigi Weinrich, head buyer for Oxford Book Stores, confirms that the self-help market, embracing such peripheral areas as spirituality and psychology, is a large part of their business, ". . . perhaps ten to fifteen percent." She is not surprised by the response she sees from customers. She thinks of them as students seeking answers. "When you're ready, the teacher will appear," she suggests philosophically.

Those of my acquaintance who have benefited from the self-help racks were all reluctant seekers, until it became necessary to stand up and be counted because enough was enough. Perhaps that explains why no one is too concerned about whether an

[*"If the Dysfunction Fits, Read It"*]

A friend from my corporate days is, in part, responsible. When I worked with him, he was a rounder of sorts. Not bad, mind you, but always ready for a beer and a laugh. Still, he could not disguise that he was also burdened. It was in the moods that would fall on him like a stroke, sending him reeling into remorse and apology. When I saw him recently, he was serene and confident. The smile was different, the aura no longer troubled. I asked him about it, and he told me that he had been involved with an encounter group inspired by Robert Bly's *Iron John* (A Book About Men).

"I finally began to realize some things about myself," he said. "Some things I didn't want to face."

The word he used was *dysfunctional*, and it is a powerful word, one that society seems only now willing to accept freely and, in fact, to embrace. Check your literature, or your television programming, or your movie offerings to see how hot the topic is. Anything that fails to have a few moments of dysfunctional angst lacks fire. Or, in commercial terms, it won't sell.

What may have been guarded as too horrible to admit in one's life is now open for discussion and revelation. The father who neglected his children because he was neck-deep in work, or because he really didn't give a damn, is no longer dismissed with a pitying, "Well, that was just the way he was." The young girl who was raped no longer has to be controlled by it. There are exorcisms that work.

What we are learning is that such dysfunctional experiences—and there seems to be no end to them—do not need to

Recovery for Women Involved With Sex-Addicted Men), if there's a problem in one's life, it is—I promise—addressed by someone in some manner.

There's no reason for confusion, either. The titles of self-help books can be as appealing as a Tom Clancy novel, and they all seem to have subtitles cleverly calculated to tell the reader what his, or her, problem really is, in case of doubt. When puzzled, a person needs, and appreciates, such certainty.

There is, in fact, an impressive order-by-mail catalog from Health Communications Inc., out of Deerfield Beach, Florida, called Personal Caring. It, too, has a subtitle: A Recovery Catalog. In it, one can find books, audiotapes, videotapes, pamphlets, booklets—you name it—covering the troubles of sexual abuse, divorce, co-dependency, addictions, etc.

I used to be skeptical of these publications. I cringed if friends whipped out the latest work of M. Scott (*The Road Less Traveled*) Peck from pocketbooks or briefcases and began to read in reverence from some highlighted section. It was, I thought, another success from the slick marketing of psychobabble. More swill in the trough for the gullible. I am from that era that says a person takes a licking and keeps on ticking. You lift rocks, you are bound to find worms. Leave well enough alone. Men don't cry.

You may know the philosophy.

Well, I've changed somewhat. Not because I've suddenly found my Inner Child, or a John 3:16 equivalent, in a self-help book, but because it doesn't make a great deal of sense to live by such hardnosed codes, or clichés.

"IF THE DYSFUNCTION FITS, READ IT"

You have seen them, I am sure.

They stand there, an intensely involved lot, their heads bowed over the opened pages of a book like supplicants seeking wisdom in twenty-five, or fewer, words. They appear oblivious to the people around them. Their auras—if one believes in such—are often dark and troubled.

And there are a lot of them out there.

In their local bookstore. Lolling before the self-help rack.

Sometimes they stand and scan. Sometimes they buy and leave. What they want—and maybe what we all want—are instant answers for ancient problems, healings from words that are somehow blessed with magic.

And all of it leads me to believe that self-help books have become the scriptures of our age.

From John Bradshaw's best-selling *Homecoming* (Reclaiming and Championing Your Inner Child) to Joy Browne's *Nobody's Perfect* (How to Stop Blaming and Start Living) to Jennifer P. Schneider's *Back From Betrayal* (A Ground-Breaking Guide to

card. I know people who have cars that tell them such imperative information as the need to fasten their seal belts. But what is the old saw? If you can't fight them, join them.

And I, like millions, have joined them. I have an answering machine, one that I can access by pressing in a coded set of numbers. The first I'm-sorry-but-we're-not-at-home message I put on it sounded like Gomer Pyle trying to imitate Richard Burton, and my friends gave me hell. I wrote a script, rehearsed, and recorded it four or five times before I was satisfied that it sounded casual.

It doesn't. Not really. It sounds like my insurance agent urging me to leave my name and number.

1992

[*"For Frustration, Press 1"*]

functionary with limited skills, who does nothing more than dial an extension. They—the executives—are fools.

Yet, there are advantages to some of this electronic voice business. If you are tolerant, you can get to a voice mailbox and leave a message, and that's better than being put on hold until hell freezes over, and it's better than the endless ringing of a telephone that is never answered.

Also, in most cases, you can understand what is being said, especially if the voice is electronically produced, and I offer a case in point—the train system at Hartsfield vs. MARTA. At Hartsfield, I do not have to wonder if I am on Concourse A or Concourse B, or if the color-coded signs match the gate, or if I am keeping the train door open. In clear, understandable monotone, I am told. On MARTA, I hear mumbling, with one or two recognizable words, like order-takers at drive-through hamburger emporiums.

The fact is, it is senseless to argue the issue. The electronic voice, with its Voice Information Processing, is with us, and it is not a fad. I am sure that everyone has answered the telephone at night to hear a recording hawking goods and services, and because some of us are still throwbacks to a polite society, we feel uncomfortable hanging up. At least I do. I always say, "Excuse me," before I slam the receiver into its cradle. But it's not just a telephone thing. The voice is everywhere. I think it started with talking dolls. I had one of those instant cash bank machines speak to me not long ago. It told me to remove my

shop, I assume. The woman who answered yawned the name of the firm. I said. "Good morning. I've got a couple of questions I'd like to ask someone."

There was a pause. She said, in a hiss, "Cut out that bull'_ _ _ _."

"Excuse me?" I replied.

"Knock it off. Get your lazy butt out of bed."

"Uh, I don't understand," I said.

There was a pause.

"Who is this?" she asked.

I gave her my name and explained again that I wanted to ask someone a couple of questions.

"Oh, my God," she moaned. "I'm sorry. You sound exactly like my husband. I thought he wanted me to come home to make him some breakfast."

We had a great talk, one I could not have had with a Voice Information Processing system. A Voice Information Processing system would have invited me to press 1, 2 or 3. She promised to have her husband—and partner—call when he pulled his lazy butt out of bed.

Later, he did, and she was right about the sound-alike. I thought I was talking to myself.

I've always believed if I owned a company, I would have those who answered the telephone among my highest-paid employees. With patience, they solve more problems of irritation than the CEO and his elite staff. But, alas, too many executives think of the switchboard operator as little more than a funnel, a mere

[*"For Frustration, Press 1"*]

whoever was calling. He urged me to leave a detailed message.

The woman spoke again: "At the tone, please record your message. When you have finished recording, you may hang up, or press 1 for more options."

I left a message and hung up. My brain would have fried with more options. I had already listened to four voices, and besides, I couldn't afford the time; my policy was in danger of being canceled.

It is a long exposition into a complaint, but I know I am not alone in the above experience. I've shared grumbling with too many others over this hellish change in our society. One friend calls it the sperm of Big Brother. "It ain't voice mail," he explains. "It's the mating call of all them damn computers. One of these days, we won't have to say nothing to nobody. We'll carry along a little hand-held thingamajig and it'll do the talking for us. We ain't got a chance. Not anymore, They've got our number."

But, as with every good argument, there are pros and cons. It is, to me, a shock that businesses—especially those offering services—have elected to do away with the switchboard operated by a real person, one who greets you with, "Good morning. May I help you?" If you are a caller, you have an immediate sense of contact. You are speaking to someone, not something. You do not have to punch keys on a telephone pad. You do not have to worry about options. You say, "I'd like to speak to John Doe, please," and you get a reply. It may be pleasant, or it may be a snarl, but you know, by God, that it's real.

Not long ago, I had reason to call an agency, a two-person

Well, good morning to you, too. I pressed 1. Another voice—this one a bit breezy and excited—answered. She said: "Welcome to [Brand Name] Voice Information Processing. To be transferred to an extension, please spell the name of the person you are calling. Spell the last name first, using the keys on your touchtone phone. To enter the letter q, press for 7; for z, press 9."

Two letters into my touchtone touching, the lady spoke again: "You have spelled—"

My agent answered, pronouncing his name like a man delivering his own eulogy.

The lady said: "If this is the name of the person you are calling, press 1. To spell a different name, press 2. To hear the name again, press 3."

I pressed 1. The woman said: "Please hold." I listened to recorded music and a message about insurance. The messenger was a man, most likely a radio talk-show host moonlighting for a few extra dollars. After a moment, the woman's voice returned to inform me: "That extension does not answer. To enter another number, press 1. To disconnect, press 2. To leave a voice message for"—my agent again interrupted to give his name in his grave, machine voice. The woman continued: "—press 3, or simply stay on the line."

I decided to stay on the line. Then my agent spoke from the Voice Information Processing system. He sounded like the son of HAL, out of *2001: A Space Odyssey,* or the voice that advises you which concourse is up next at Hartsfield International Airport. He gave a spiel about being unavailable, but eager to speak to

"For Frustration, Press 1"

I have realized recently that America is in trouble with progress, that in our romancing of things new, we are becoming mutants of a sort.

Bluntly put, in the Age of Communication, we are losing our voice (and perhaps our soul) to electronics.

A letter from an insurance company warned me.

Certainly, it was my fault. In oversight, I had allowed an insurance policy to lapse and the aforementioned letter followed, informing me that I was living in peril, that I must call ASAP if I wanted to be reinstated with forgiveness and without penalty.

I called. ASAP. A voice—a lady's voice, very pleasant—answered. It said something on the order of: "You have reached the Blank-Blank Insurance and Financial Services Office. Our office hours are from 8 o'clock A.M. to 4 o'clock P.M., Monday through Friday. If you know the extension number of the person you are calling, enter it now. If you know the name of the person you are calling, press 1. If you are calling concerning homeowners or automobile insurance, press 2. All other calls, to leave a message, press 3. Thank you."

In cow baseball, however, people have enough sense to realize that what they have engaged in is a lively afternoon of sport. Games end with a win, a loss or a call because of darkness.

In politics, things are not quite so definite. Sides keep compiling points, but the game never ends. It simply changes leads.

I agree with the fellow who was interviewed after hearing a debate among the candidates. He trusted none of them, he said to the reporter. "They keep smiling," he complained. "They're talking about the most serious stuff in the world, and they keep smiling. I wonder what they're smiling about."

I can't tell him. They're in the Big Game, and the cameras are on, and they know it.

All they've got to do is watch where they step in the cow pasture.

1992

[*"That's Entertainment"*]

the losers. It has not been good television, however, and I suspect if we didn't have Bill (someone called him "Breezy" on a radio program, and it seems to fit) and the warts beneath his handsome face, we'd be bored silly.

Maybe it's discourteous to suggest, but such people as Paul Tsongas, who strikes me as a truly decent and capable man, never stood a chance. On television, he comes across as wholesome and as bland as natural peanut butter. Once we could elect such men, because the string-pullers wanted them, but not anymore. Now, we want someone who is as likely to show up on the front cover of a supermarket tabloid as at a peace conference in Geneva.

Our problem may be in the way we select our candidates. Perhaps we should leave it up to some central casting office, or to an executive head-hunting firm.

And maybe it's just me, getting more disenchanted by the day with politics.

I vote, but I really don't care for politics or politicians—with a few, special exceptions. The problem is, I've known too many of them, the real, party-affiliated, type. Most of them are egocentric and potentially dangerous, the sort who, for personal gain or temporary pleasure afflict abuse with such sweet guile, it seems almost provocative.

The whole razzmatazz of political goings-on has always struck me as a kind of confused choose-up game of cow pasture baseball, where the overbearing and the strong make up the rules, the weak get left out or are used only for stand-around purposes, and the umpiring goes to the person with the loudest voice.

take a bloodhound to find it, the role of the candidate's spouses.

Now such matters are as compelling as the issues.

What did Hillary really mean by her cookies-and-tea comment? Was Bill's affair alleged? Is Hillary a suffering woman standing by her man, or is she manipulative egotist with designs on the queenly role of a first lady?

Why does Bill smile so much?

Does George need to have a skeleton ripped from the closet to get equal attention? Should someone ask whose lips his lips have touched before we read them?

In the old days, it was entertainment for the sake of entertainment, an acceptable circus of wheeling and dealing as slick as Wildroot Cream Oil. Today, with television, it's competitive entertainment. If we're going to watch a political debate, it damn well better be as engaging as Geraldo dropping his pants to have some fatty tissue extracted.

I don't know about others, but to me, the great issue of the current campaign seems a bit tiring and predictable. Yes, the economy is in shambles. Everyone knows it, and everyone knows none of the candidates has the power to magically make things better. Fortunately, our government remains a democracy with enough checks and balances to stop a Mack truck on the downhill side of a mountain.

Thus, it has been a campaign of shadowboxing, of dogging the trail from state to state, tallying the results, listening to the roar of the winners and the remarkably optimistic reasoning of

[*"That's Entertainment"*]

the buck board, the men in the Ford, to the sky, the swamp and down the drain ditch the length of Calhoun County.

"And you got Eugene Herman Talmadge of Sugar Hill, Georgia, and I want you to know it."

It is fiction, and, as a purist, I must report that Price was wrong in naming his character Eugene Herman (he was actually Eugene Thomas Talmadge, but he dropped the Thomas). Yet the spirit of the story is as real as the occasion might have been.

The television folk would have been astonished. They would have packed the gear and hightailed it back to whatever big city they were dispatched from.

No one snaps suspenders on television. Not George Bush. Not Bill Clinton. Not Pat Buchanan. Not Jerry Brown.

They stand before the cameras in the tailor-cuts, looking like models in a magazine advertisement. They are politically correct to those who support them, raving fools to those who do not. And even in the most outrageous moments—Bill telling Jerry he is not fit to stand on the same platform as Hillary—they are so civilized they could star in daytime soap operas.

It's something of a given that all of this started with John Kennedy's matinee charm in his televised debates with Richard Nixon, who, in comparison, was a bumbler on trial for heinous crimes.

But it was tame in those early days, election-by-looks.

No one really got into the juicy stuff—the stories of dallying by JFK, the slew of money going in so many directions it would

No one has ever written of the old days of politics as colorfully as the Southern humorist William Price Fox. In his *Southern Fried Plus Six,* there is a marvelously funny story called "Eugene Talmadge and Sears Roebuck Co." It tells of the late Georgia governor's campaign tactics.

Quoting from the last few paragraphs:

Gene stood in the very center of the gallery and rared up as tall as he could and snapped his suspenders. He addressed the men and women in the back row.

"You got three friends in this here world and I want you to know it."

"Tell us, Gene."

He raised one finger, pointed it at the sun and spoke to the back row and the two men leaning on the buckboard.

"You got Sears Roebuck Company—and I want you to know it."

"That's right, Gene."

A second finger . . . a louder voice to the back row . . . the two leaning on the buckboard and the two seated in the Ford by the drain ditch drinking corn whiskey out of a mayonnaise jar.

"You got God Almighty—and I want you to know it."

"That's right, Gene."

And then he crashed his steel heels into the gallery boards, snapped his suspenders, raced back like he was going to lift a whole bale of cotton single-handed and roared to the men by

"That's Entertainment"

The culprit, of course, is television. Television has ruined politics.

And it is sad. Sad because our children will never know what it used to be like when a political rally in a small Georgia town was as celebrated as the county fair or a good hellfire tent revival that had the legends of sin on their knees, confessing to transgressions that fanned gossip for a year.

Lord, those were good days, even if they did give us some corrupt politicians and tightened the screws on progress. The show was almost worth the sacrifice.

In some places they still try to pull it off. The barbecues and the speeches and the hand-shaking and the baby-kissing and the awed whispers, "That sucker knows everyone here by his given name."

But it's only a sham. Not like the old days where a political gathering was a to-do reported with serious analysis in the local newspaper, and disagreed with by almost everyone who read it. (Think of a rerun of an *Andy Griffith* television show, with a gubernatorial candidate at a town rally in Mayberry—Otis in high spirits, Barney on the loose and the mayor being official—and you get a general idea of what it was like.)

one of a row planted by my brother in-law, Harry, before he went away to die in France. It tells me that he was here, and that his dying should be remembered.

Someday, I hope to get to Arlington National to show him (or me) that I do.

1991

[*"From the Ashes of Infamy"*]

startling than the stories in books. They received letters from friends in Brooklyn, Dallas, and Miami and other odd, out-of-the way places. Occasionally, other people would stop by in their car as they drove to Florida—people with unpronounceable names, speaking too fast to be heard, and there would be merriment that would be talked about for months. Those who had gone away to, or for, war, seemed more tolerant, more sensitive. I don't think any of them knew they had experienced a mild form of what we now call culture shock.

War is the tragedy, even the contradiction, of civilization, yet it is historically true that war jolts nations out of all sorts of dilemmas, from economic depression to political tyranny. That is what happened to America, and especially the American South, during and after World War II. The bombs on Pearl Harbor fifty years ago were a jolt that changed us.

Sometimes when I return to visit the rural community where I lived during World War II, I drive over the hard-clay roads and try to find the turnoffs to those sharecropper houses where the last generation of tenant farmers lived. Those turnoffs are mostly overgrown with scrub bushes and briars, and the houses—those still standing—are covered in kudzu. Occasionally I will see one with the spine of the roof bowed and twisted, and I think of it as a symbol of that dreary past of the bowed backs of the people—white and black—who lived in the lock of unmoving time, before the changes began.

There is one other thing I see when I return home. On a ridge that divided our land from the Brown place, there is a pine tree,

of that sounded too good to pass up. They'd had a war under their belt, as Andrews observed; they deserved being inside.

But almost everything had changed, or was in the process of changing in those war years. The stubborn mule, plowed by stubborn farmers, was being replaced by the tractor, and the mechanical cotton picker was making its appearance in the fields of the forty-acre farms where sharecropper homes now stood empty.

It was a new South, with vigorous young veterans building the groundswell for what would be called the Sunbelt Movement. And as they moved from the fields to the factories, they began to realize they were just beginning. There was one other lesson to be learned, and that was the lesson of learning itself. Education, never a serious consideration for many Southerners, became an imperative.

The G.I. Bill made education possible, and there are those who believe (I am one of them) that the G.I. Bill turned America inside out. Thousands of veterans enrolled in schools to learn trades or to get advanced degrees, and by those bold acts, made the first giant step away from a past that had encumbered their families for generations.

And there was something else the soldier and the war worker picked up while they were away for World War II: awareness of other people in other places. I have heard talk of it since childhood, about the change in those who returned home. They spoke a few words of German, or French, or Italian, or Japanese. They had souvenirs and the souvenirs had histories more

[*"From the Ashes of Infamy"*]

What I now know about World War II is that it changed things in the South—perhaps more than any event of the twentieth century, including all the other wars (and, God knows, they never stop, do they?).

World War II changed the soldier who came home from the war of foreign lands, and it changed those who were working in war-effort factories in American cities. Soldier and worker alike returned as different people, people who somehow knew they were more special than they had been.

In his novel, *Jessie and Jesus and Cousin Claire*, writer Raymond Andrews introduces a magnificent character—the Private—in the following manner:

> *"When he came home to Appalachee, Georgia, from World War II on Thanksgiving Day Eve, 1945, he swore he wasn't going back to his old job at Nickerson's sawmill where he had worked before being drafted. With a war under his belt he felt he deserved better. He wanted an "inside" job like the one he had had in the war as an orderly room file clerk filing Army regulations and other important papers and where just before getting discharged he had been learning to type on the typewriter . . ."*

There were a lot of Southern men, and women, like the Private. They returned home and stopped at the service stations and the drugstores in town to have a soft drink, and someone said something about a new textile mill hiring workers, and all

We are now fifty years beyond that day called Infamy. By our habit of marking time, it is a highlighted anniversary year, but such anniversaries in a nation's history are, at best, somber celebrations. (What is there to celebrate, other than victory and the benefits of victory? Can any war be grand enough for great, lasting gaiety?)

You've read the stories and heard the talk about this anniversary, of course. The camps have called their followers to order— the forgivers on one side, the Jap-bashers on the other, spitting across a dare-me line that someone drew in the dirt to aggravate the situation.

Among many, there is a *Forget, hell!* mentality that is intense enough to make them want to attack Hondas with pitchforks, if there weren't so damn many of the cars. Humanitarians, who believe that men of arms should take their fingers off the triggers when war has ended, are astounded by such behavior. Out of war there should be some progress. Otherwise, what have we gained?

To me, it's a curious argument. I don't know that Japan is buying America, piece by piece, but it seems to me that if the electronic gizmos the Japanese produce are spurring our own industry on to improvement, we should take it in stride.

But the memory of war is a powerful image, and I guess you had to be there to know what it was like and how it can linger, and I wasn't. I was at home, a small boy, not exactly understanding who was fighting whom, or why. I knew that Harry had been killed, and that Lula, my sister, was sad. Small boys are often confused.

"From the Ashes of Infamy"

I have never been to my brother-in-law's grave at Arlington National Cemetery in Washington, D.C., and I am ashamed. I have wanted to go there, to that orderly field of the dead, many times, on many trips, but there was always something that ate away the hours—some place to be on a typed-out agenda, someone else to meet with for whatever business purpose seemed urgent at the time.

His name was Harry Patat. He was a first lieutenant with the Eighth Army, and he was killed on Jan. 6, 1945, in a forest in the Alsace-Lorraine region of France. He was a month shy of his twenty-eighth birthday. I was too young then to remember him clearly, though there is an image that swims in my imagination like a slightly familiar face smiling from a last-night dream, but I do remember his photographs and I see the resemblance to that swimming image and to those photographs in his children, my nephew and niece (he never saw her, never held her).

Harry was one of more than four-hundred thousand Americans who perished in the hellish years of killing that began, for the United States, on Dec. 7, 1941, when the Japanese showered bombs on Pearl Harbor.

that's a healthy (pardon the pun) group. Speaking for all of them, we would be most grateful.

You see, I think all of us would like to believe the purpose of life is more important than trying to pay the price to stay well enough to enjoy it.

As it is, I'm having a tough time of it—and there must be others in the same boat.

I did one last calculation. I subtracted everything—insurance, taxes, monthly bills, etc.—from the projected income and there was just enough left for a bottle of aspirin.

I need them.

I have one God-awful headache.

But if I called my doctor, I couldn't meet the deductible.

1991

["High-Rate Robbery"]

Unless my little calculator has slipped a silicone, that adds up to $24,000 a year. For health insurance—only health insurance. I didn't see any reference to a dental plan or to deductibles. For all I know, the $24,000 per year could be only a catastrophic policy.

Surely someone of influence is incensed enough about this to be rattling a few cages, but if not, I've got a health-coverage plan that Gov. Miller and the state's lawmakers should consider: Every bona fide citizen of the state of Georgia would be eligible for a state-operated group insurance policy, with some reasonable cap on the monthly rate—say, twenty bucks or so per person. For my family of four, it would cost $80 a month, or $960 a year. Put a deductible on it of a couple of hundred. Hold the maximum coverage to $1 million per person.

Don't scoff. If such a plan pulled in five million citizens (the others would be considered noncitizens and a noncitizen's tax would be levied against them), it would bring in $1.2 billion a year. And if that's not enough, heck, I'd be pleased to throw in another $10 or $15 a month.

Oh, one other thing: We can't link this plan with socialized medicine. That's a fight that Schwarzkopf couldn't win. Promote it as a way to attract new industry, or as an act of startling benevolence for a deserving citizenry. It seems to me that a state-operated family health plan for those who can't afford what the private industry is leveling would be as progressive as a lottery.

It would also relieve anxiety, especially for those of us who are out of the group-size business world. And what with the layoffs we've experienced lately—Eastern, Sears and a few others—

ing of security in knowing that a check-writing machine in some distant city, like Minneapolis, will click out a payment that would have left you in total ruin.

I remember the year that my father took the first health plan for his family. It was in the early 1950s and he was president of the Hart County Farm Bureau, which had initiated a group policy for its membership. To demonstrate leadership, he signed up, though he had never been ill a day of his life. A few months after the policy became effective, he was hospitalized for the better part of a summer. Without the coverage, we might well have lost everything the family owned.

Some people live in such jeopardy. One of my children told me recently of a young woman who had heart surgery following a stroke. She was not insured. Her bill, according to rumor, was in the $85,000 range. She has no idea how it will be paid.

A horror story?

If it is, it is more common than we think. And it is exactly the sort of everyday drama that makes us fearful of being caught with a notice of expiration because we let the grace period for renewal slip away.

Still, if trends continue, the question will not be a matter of having insurance, but of paying for insurance. One agent who discussed my plight with me whipped out a paper that had a sweeping bar chart keyed to increased rates. One well-known company had estimated that monthly health-care rates by the turn of the century (that's barely eight years from now) will exceed $2,000.

[*"High-Rate Robbery"*]

year, or an average of $641.65 per month, including some policies that we carry for our children. If we had elected to keep our old health policy, the one that took the leap to $587.00 per month, we would have been paying $14,743.76 a year, or an average of $1,228.65 per month.

We did not elect to keep the old policy. After casting about, comparing policies (try that exercise for a joyful use of discretionary time), we settled on a plan that was far less comprehensive than our old policy (no dental, higher deductible), but with a cost of slightly more than $400 per month.

I wanted to celebrate. I told my wife, "It's only costing us about $5,000 a year."

She scoffed.

We added up everything once again. Not bad. I am now paying only $12,544.76 a year for all my insurance policies, an average of $1,045.40 a month.

By comparison, my mortgage payments are slightly over $800 per month.

Yet, by further comparison, my first house cost only $12,500, and I had thirty years to pay off the debt.

I do not want this lamentation to be misread. I believe in insurance. Without it I would have been terrified to raise a family, and I have benefited on more than one occasion because a policy did what it said it would do—such as replacing the roof when the wind blew the shingles across the neighborhood, or paying for my son's emergency appendectomy (the one that cost as much as my entire college education). There is a strange feel-

But a leap from $2,808 a year to $7,044—especially when I seldom exceeded the deductible? Something is wrong here, out of whack, bordering on insanity.

I called my wife and told her about the letter. She shrieked over the telephone and demanded to know how I had let things get so far out of control.

I told her I had little, or nothing, to do with it.

"How can it cost that much?" she cried.

"How do I know?" I snapped. "All I do is write the check." I promised I would inquire, and I did. It was the expected response. Rising health costs, re-evaluation of the existing policy (supposedly the first such analysis in a couple of years), etc. I have learned that there is a kind of litany that insurance people use to explain problems. It is delivered with a sad clucking of the tongue, with empathy, and with apology for the necessity of such high rates. They always tell you about an incident personal to them that agrees with your complaint. You always thank them for understanding.

"What are we going to do?" my wife asked.

"Look for something cheaper," I said.

"I still don't know how you let it get out of control," she replied.

The fact is, in my family, the matter of insurance is out of control. We sat one Sunday and put on a sheet of paper all that we are paying to be insured for something that may or may not happen (except for the life policy, of course; that's a certainty). Discounting the health policy, we were shelling out $7,699.76 a

"HIGH-RATE ROBBERY"

We can stop looking for the purpose of life. I have found it.

It is not service to mankind.

It is not spiritual peace.

It is not the gaining of great knowledge.

It is not discovering new solar systems or exploring marine life on the bottom of the world's oceans.

It is not safeguarding the world from dictatorships. It is not waiting for the Atlanta Braves, Falcons and/or Hawks to hang a championship banner.

It is not an annual pilgrimage to Graceland.

The purpose of life is to make enough money to pay for health insurance.

I say this because of a letter that arrived recently. The letter informed me that my family health policy was being increased from $234 to $587 a month.

And that is one hell of an increase.

Don't get me wrong. It was a good policy. One of those with a small deductible, a dental plan, reasonably clear and understandable forms to fill out, and not much hassle from the home office.

she said. "If you loathe it, we're the first people in line." I told her I was pleased to learn they had begun reading.)

Movie advertising can be more deceptive than meets the eye. I remember engaging in an argument with the managing editor of the *Journal* over the review of a film that he felt particularly offensive. "We're not going to promote that sort of filth in this newspaper," he said. I told him that if he was concerned about obscenity, he should read the ads, specifically one celebrating a particular dance scene in a XXXX-rated adult film. "So?" he said. "That's dance." I explained it to him. He paled. The ad was dropped in the next edition.

Certainly, I realize there are more important subjects to consider than the come-ons in movie advertising, but it does represent an understudied, and persuasive, field of communication—the blurb. From movies to books to rented videotapes to you-name-it, the blurb is with us, declaring in frenetic-word voices that So-and-So is available for our having, and suggesting that we would be fools to be without it.

What the blurb ultimately communicates, then, is promise—a teasing quality that, sadly, is too seldom delivered.

Yet, we read and watch and wonder. And we respond.

If we didn't, the blurb wouldn't exist.

Which would be a pity.

We would then never know just how rip-roaring, spine-tingling, nail-biting, heart-rending, and spellbinding the world really is.

1991

[*"Revenge of the Blurbs"*]

beautiful, rip-roaring adventure for all ages." There we go. Another rip-roaring.

Ah, here's an old standard. Ralph Novak of *People* magazine promotes *Kindergarten Cop* as "One of the year's 10 best." All movie producers like that catchy little tagline, though it has always puzzled me how any reviewer can make such judgement so early in the year. And, someday, in the name of trivia, I would like to tally how many movies make the "Top 10" lists.

Still, Peter Rainer of the *Los Angeles Times* goes Ralph one better in his assessment of *The Grifters*. It is, declares Peter in bold letters, locked in quotes and stabbed with an explanation point, "The Best Film of the Year!" Peter has been captivated.

One must be careful in falling victim to such excessive enthusiasm, of course. Not long ago, I saw *Home Alone,* a movie that had been trumpeted as the funniest of the season, and one that was making zillions of dollars. It was, for the time spent, a pleasant diversion, but its Two Stooges vs. Little Boy plot was also a bit inane and tiresome. Another case of the parts—the promotions—being grander than the whole.

When I became a movie reviewer, I realized immediately that a quarter-page ad, with select, doctored excerpts in dark ink, could steamroll any writer in America. The reason was simple: More people read ads than read reviews, and those who do read reviews often do so only to improve their cocktail culture. Others simply like to be disagreeable. (Once an acquaintance, angry with me at the time, confessed that she and her husband faithfully read my reviews. "If you recommend it, we avoid it,"

ing all at a single sitting. It makes me wonder if some clever editor didn't cut and paste. Did Patrick really write those words? And if he did, is such an outpouring of emotion the behavior of a thinking man?

As for Zeffirelli's *Hamlet,* Larry Frascelia of *US* magazine has decorated it with four stars and declared it ". . . rip-roaring. The most musing, robust, and briskly entertaining *Hamlet* ever." A few thousand theater companies may take exception, and Shakespeare's spirit may be wondering what a rip-roaring is, but it does come across as a shout of approval, and it is, after all, the sort of thing that will cause a man in search of a Clint Eastwood Western to pause and wonder what the racket is about. (Well, face it, they could have used "To See or Not to See.")

My favorite guideline is the Siskel and Ebert system of thumbing down and thumbing up, as Roger Ebert does for *Alice.* An S&E up-thumbs is cause for jubilation among producers. Two down and you might as well put it on ice. One down, one up, and you still have a chance. Personally, I've seen some up-thumb movies on S&E's recommendation, and it is my opinion that they used the wrong digit to express their judgment on one or two of them.

Continuing with the Sunday paper.

Janet Maslin of *The New York Times* finds *The Godfather, Part III* to be ". . . irresistible," which carries me back to the first *Godfather,* and the deal that couldn't be refused. Richard Freeman of Newhouse Newspapers announces that *White Fang* is "more gripping than *Dances With Wolves*" and, further, is "a

[*"Revenge of the Blurbs"*]

manager of the Rialto, a friend, knew the film was risky, but he knew also that the power of promotion could wipe out a bad review like a Patriot locked on a Scud.

A couple of days later, he called and urged me to visit with him at the theater. "Got something to show you," he said. And he snickered over the telephone.

When I arrived, I saw in the window, in block letters that appeared to be several feet high, this: ". . . BRILLIANT. . . ." My name, and my association with the newspaper, was beneath the quote.

"I didn't say that," I protested.

"Sure you did," my friend retorted. He pulled out the review. Well, yes, the word was there. It had been plucked from a sentence that said something like. "At a time when movie makers are capable of brilliant work, it is tragic that such trash is allowed to be released."

I remembered this story when I decided I wanted to see a movie recently, and I opened the Sunday newspaper and turned to the arts and entertainment section, and began reading the advertisements.

Nothing has changed. No industry in the world can get your attention as quickly, or as dramatically.

"Spellbinding, nail-biting, heart-rending tension. . . the thinking person's thriller." All of this from one Patrick Stoner, of PBS. The movie in praise is *Not Without My Daughter*.

I haven't seen the movie, but I am somewhat suspicious about anything that causes one to suffer binding and biting and rend-

irresistible deal at Blah-Blah's place, where the after-sales service is the best on God's planet.

These are blurbs of a sort. They put the commoners—us—in something of the same class as Bo Jackson doing his thing(s) for Nike and the guy next door buying a car. A laudatory word or two about anything from someone else, especially if that someone is one of us, may be all that we need to be swayed.

Blurbism is everywhere. "Pre-Inventory Sale" is, to me, a blurbish statement. Ditto on "We Will Not Be Undersold" and "0% Interest Rate" and "Double Coupons Specials" and "Buy One, Get One Free." Though not taken from personal endorsements, the effect is the same. Such statements are attention-getters.

Sometimes a blurb works wonders. There was a story (and it may have been just that; a story) about the first of the *Walking Tall* movies. When first released, it fizzled, bringing panic upon the producers. Then someone—a reviewer, or a patron—attended a showing where the audience stood up and applauded when it was over. From that occasion came the line, "When was the last time you applauded a movie?" That line was enough. People flooded to theaters to see what caused such spontaneous adoration.

We've all been caught by a blurb. Or blurbed. Well, victimized.

Once upon a time, it was my misfortune, as the reviewer for the *Atlanta Journal,* to sit through a disgracefully bad movie at the Rialto Theatre.

I ripped it. I ripped it with vigor and enthusiasm and with every vile description then allowed in family newspapers. The

"Revenge of the Blurbs"

Of the refinements that America has given the world, few have had the impact of the blurb.

As the blurb goes, so goes the cash register.

My dictionary tells me that a blurb—a word allegedly coined by F. G. Burgess—is "a brief advertisement or announcement, especially a laudatory one. . . ." *Laudatory* is the essential word. It is the reason we read only praise from book-jacket blurbs and why we've never read an ad for a movie that called it a dog.

Commonly, the blurb takes the form of a comment from a person about a product.

Some are obviously paid-for testimonials—Bo Jackson for shoes, Jim Palmer for underwear—purchased for advertising purposes. Others are plucked selectively from reviews and used for advertising.

Sometimes it's hard to tell which is which. I have noticed a tendency for advertisers to use the man-on-the-street approach to promotion. Television grocery spots introduce us to a lady, cart filled with items, enthusing over the amount of money she is saving by shopping store X. Automobile dealerships feature a pleased new-vehicle owner vowing he/she has been afforded an

I have a theory about this—about why we are so tolerant, so forgiving, with our heroes: It is because we all think of ourselves as being heroic in some odd, secretive way, and we all know that we could not pass the test of perfection.

Still, we want it clearly defined in the absolutes of black and white that used to mark the villains and heroes of Western movies. And that is difficult in a world shaded with grays, a world that celebrates the rough edges of the antihero.

But having the absolutes turn gray does not change our basic instinct: We want movies and television shows and novels and, yes, an everyday-real world, where right ultimately triumphs over wrong.

And that is why we want Hulk Hogan to rise up from the canvas in a trembling of determination, to the begging applause of the crowd. We want Hulk to kick butt. For us.

And that is why I watch professional wrestling. I know who the enemy is. And I know the heroes.

I can't say that about anything else.

1991

[*"Lords of the Ring"*]

Even down to the role-switching.

Our dilemma, of course, is that nothing in everyday life is as easily defined as it is in the WWF or the WCW. We may know right from wrong, good from evil, but we no longer know who the heroes are, because deep in our souls we have learned to be suspicious of heroes. Too many of them are crumbling before our glued-to-the-television-tube eyes—clergy, politicians, businessmen, athletes. They are caught with their hands in the cookie jars, or elsewhere, and we are left to deal with shock and with the horror that they, like us, must be human.

And this is what we do: We rationalize.

Why, yes, it is a pity what happened to Pete Rose. But Pete's all right. You've got to remember what he did on a baseball field.

Or Oliver North. Wasn't Ollie merely following orders?

Or Marion Barry. Hey, was it fair that they trapped the mayor that way?

In everyday life we agonize and argue over Rose and North and Barry. We accuse and defend, and we wonder what in heaven's name has happened to us.

In wrestling, Rose and North and Barry would have a few weeks of sneering arrogantly at the crowd and of beating up on anemic-looking opponents (guys who appear as though they were selected from the audience in a lottery), and then they would suddenly see the light and join the Steiner Brothers in pounding The Nasty Boys to a pulp. And we would stand as one, cheering the return of our heroes—knowing that what they had suffered was merely temporary insanity.

Give them the old blockade. Cut off their food and water. Blow Little Hitler to hell and gone.

The wind was in the flag, the strut in the soldier's step.

It was advertised as Operation Desert Shield.

The WWF (that's World Wrestling Federation) or the WCW (that's World Championship Wrestling) would have called it the Saudi Showdown or the Persian Pitfight. Steel-cage matches in a sandstorm.

Of course, it did not last—that great early hurrah against Insane Hussein. We found another enemy.

Our own government. The budget mess, you remember.

Throw the bums out. Bring our boys home.

And then Desert Shield became Desert Storm and the Eerie War—the great television special, the for-real Nintendo zapping—began, and our niggling quarrels over such matters as the latest savings and loan failure suddenly paled.

We had a greater argument, a classic argument: Were we right or wrong? Good or evil? Do we praise or protest?

In wrestling, with its vaudevillian showmanship and its silly carnival pitch-people—Boni (Where's the Camera?) Blackstone, Mean Gene Okerland, Sir Samuel F. Kent, Bobby (The Brain) Heenan, et al.—there are no doubts. Evil is evil and good is good, right is right and wrong is wrong, and to keep the juices flowing, the roles are switched with such regularity that you have to keep watching to sort through the dramas.

It is a bit like another experience we all have—everyday life.

[*"Lords of the Ring"*]

flinging themselves into the ring, scattering Nasty Boys like bowling pins.

Another nick-of-time rescue. God love the Steiners.

Absurd? Okay, a little. Unless you understand it. The rescue by the Steiner Brothers was not made to save two sacrificial beginners from The Nasty Boys. And it was not made only to hype an upcoming match. It was made to save the audience from madness, to give the audience something to wish for, to believe in, to hold on to.

In other words, it was not unlike the frenzy that flooded America with its tidal wave of emotion last year when President George Bush first decided to rescue Kuwait from Iraq. America was ripe for something, or someone, to hate, having lost the threat of its ancient enemy, communism, to declarations of freedom in Iron Curtain countries. Even more confusing was Mikhail Gorbachev's democratic reforms in Mother Russia herself.

Such sudden and surprising change from the Evil Empire(s) took us aback, to say the least. It was like, well, like Ric Flair turning on Sid Vicious, a Bad becoming a Good. We need our enemies. How in heaven's name can we feel good about being good if we don't have someone bad being bad?

And then along comes Saddam Hussein and the snarl was back. The president dispatched troops to the Persian Gulf in a show of might-and-right that had Americans standing on interstate overpasses cheering convoys headed for port cities. It was a loud, ringing hurrah, the most dizzying demonstration of national pride for the military since World War II.

SPECIAL KAY *the wisdom of terry kay*

Certainly, it's the point. I watch professional wrestling not because it is the King of Sport, but because it is one of the few activities in America that does not beat around the bush on Good vs. Evil.

We are dealing here with something far more important than Wildfire Tommy Rich's amazing powers of recovery from a pounding that would total a Buick. We are dealing with metaphor, with a stand-in for everything good from Mother Teresa to motherhood vs. everything bad from cancer to cocaine.

And, God knows, we need a hero or two to balance the insanity that has infected us with epidemic killspeed.

Professional wrestling puts it in focus.

My son and I were watching a recent tag-team bout on TBS between The Nasty Boys (hailing, appropriately from New York City) and a couple of beginners who approached the ring wreathed in an aura of decency and innocence. This was a sure thing; you could bet the house against a doughnut and never furrow a brow in concern. Nasty could have phoned in an armlock and won the thing. And it was bad. Body slams. Elbow drops. Clawing, punching, jabbing, jeering. The sort of predicament that makes one yearn for Superman to stop the punishment.

Of course, that is what happened. Just when human life seemed to be at stake, when the body of one of the fallen innocents had begun to quiver in the onset of rigor mortis, there was a mighty roar from the crowd, a startling squeal from the announcer, and, lo, from a corner of the auditorium/theater, the Steiner Brothers—Rick and Scott—sprinted across the distance,

"LORDS OF THE RING"

I am going to fling the closet doors wide open on this one. Sometimes I watch professional wrestling (or 'rassling) as it is enacted (or acted) on television.

Thank you, Ted Turner.

Being so afflicted does not please anyone in my family—except for my son, Scott, who is my chief researcher in this—but I simply don't care. I am a Hulkamaniac. One of Sting's Stingers. A Kerry Von Erich fanatic.

I howl with the Junkyard Dog. I get down and boogie with the Rock 'n' Roll Express.

And I am a booer and a hisser over the despicable and evil-intended behavior of such unsportsmanlike fellows as The Four Horsemen, Doom, The Fabulous Freebirds, Steve (The Brawler) Lawler, Dirty Dick Murdoch, Stan (The Lariat) Hansen, the turncoat Sergeant Slaughter, the Black Scorpion and the madman from the Sudan, Abdullah the Butcher.

The emotional strain is tremendous. It makes me ache to know that Andre the Giant has gone bad, or that Jake (The Snake) Roberts has gone good.

Or maybe that's vice versa.

And there is one last, bothersome fact: The lottery is easy to play. You don't have to know if the 2, 3, 4, 5 and 6 of hearts can beat three of a kind, or what it means to have jacks or better to open. All you have to do is make a mark on a piece of paper, and if that's too taxing, you can trust the computer to pick the numbers for you. A child could do it. And children will, no matter what the rules say about minors being ineligible.

What was Professor Harold Hill's warning in *The Music Man*? Something about trouble. "Trouble, trouble, trouble, right here in River City..."

Take it from Stoopid.

Gambling can be a seductive thing.

1991

[*"Sucker Hunch"*]

about "new" money, contending that the figures usually promoted do not consider the impact of that money going out of circulation. Also in question are the ultimate benefits the state would gain.

And there is, always, the moral issue. Do the poor suffer because there is a compulsion to wish, to want, to believe? Do their dollars go to the one-in-millions odds, to the quick-rich dreams of places and cars and trinkets?

The cons argue *yes*. The cons say the five dollar lottery bet is milk out of the refrigerator. The pros say such reasoning is a tired overstatement, a sentimental, unfounded argument.

As with all issues of emotion and personal conviction—such as quarrels over abortion—there is not an answer to satisfy, absolutely and permanently, the lottery debate. It would appear that Georgia will have a state-operated lottery because Georgians, on the whole, want it, and because, with today's technology, armchair wagering seems as inevitable as a fax in every home.

For me, however, a lottery is not an entirely good alternative to taxes—and not because of illusions about money or arguments about empty refrigerators. I believe it is risky business because it comes across as a panacea, a cure-all to changing times and fiscal irresponsibility. It's a bit like the old Medicine Man with his bottled elixirs and his spiel about youth and vitality, when, in fact, he was selling high-proof intoxication. People are easily duped, and one can become as drunk on dreams as on alcohol.

are being written in exchange for money is evidence. Had I won the lottery, there would be a line in this space, parenthetically wrapped, announcing that Terry Kay is on a prolonged vacation. Not only did my whispering tickets lie like Eve's snake, they did not contain a single correct number.

A couple of weeks later, six people split more than $100 million dollars in Florida's biggest Lotto drawing, and it did get a trifle wild in those last few hours. People were plucking down $100 million to increase their chances. Otherwise dependable wage-earners in Georgia were taking off from work to drive to Florida for what Kipling described in his poem, "If," as "one turn of pitch and toss."

What kind of experience was it, this five dollar investment in fate? Nothing personally harmful, I think, but I am not one who believes next time will be *the* time. I am a quitter when it comes to losing money. In the few visits I've made to Las Vegas, I've fed the little metal mouths of slot machines to a ten dollar limit, and that was enough. Even then, it felt as though I was paying tribute to a graven image against my better instincts.

The real question is whether or not a lottery—in Florida, Georgia, or anywhere—is all that it's cracked up to be, a kind of volunteer contribution to the state's welfare (education system, primarily), or is it, in fact, a dangerous, addictive excuse for obsessive gambling?

The pros have it that a lottery is little more than an amusement-park game that provides untold dividends for an already-stretched economy. The cons speak passionately of illusions

[*"Sucker Hunch"*]

with others: I began to wish, to want, to believe. The lottery tickets in my billfold seemed to have a personality of their own. They whispered sweetly to me, "I'm the one, I'm the one, I'm the one."

What *would* I do with the money, I wondered secretly. I'd have to call my friend, Grady, one of the few lawyers on earth I trust. I would call him at three o'clock in the morning and tell him to meet me in disguise at a Waffle House, and then I'd get him to do some lawyer magic to make sure everything was in order. When all of that was done, I'd find some land in the mountains and build a cabin the size of a convention center, and maybe I'd get a place on the ocean for those few days of the year when I long to hear waves lapping over sandbars. Oh, yes, I'd get a new car—a big one, for long-distance comfort. I would travel the world in style, staying only in Americanized hotels with private toilets and large towels. And I suppose the family would want a few dollars, which I would distribute with genuine gladness. So the kids want some trinkets. Sure. Nothing wrong with trinkets, if you've got the money.

"I'm the one, I'm the one, I'm the one," the tickets whispered.

On Saturday following, when the numbers were to be selected, I was verging on the blasphemous act of greedy prayer ("Oh, please, God. Ten percent goes to you. I promise"). I stayed up to watch the late news, holding my still-purring tickets, believing there would be a national announcement of the numbers following the latest report from the Persian Gulf.

I did not win the lottery, of course. The fact that these words

ing a pecan log. There are some things too powerful, too alluring to ignore. Like that of millions of first-time lottery ticket buyers, mine was an impulse purchase, one of those "Sure, why not?" decisions, a vacation frivolity. And I went for the big one, the Lotto. It was up to $24 million at the time.

The young lady who explained the procedure asked if I wanted to select my own numbers or have the computer select for me. "I'll do it," I told her. What can a computer know about my personal destiny, a destiny mystically locked into an alignment of numbers that is surely more blessed than mere chance? The computer be damned.

I chose the numbers most significant in my life—birthdate, Social Security, street address, telephone, zip code, that sort of thing—and paid the young lady. She said, "Good luck."

I shrugged a thank you. "It's just a lark," I said blithely.

"Of course," she replied, smiling.

She knew. She'd heard it all before.

Anyone who has ever purchased a lottery ticket understands there is a required behavior for players: cool.

Cool says, "What are you going to do with all those millions?"

Cool answers, "Be rich. Buy me some things. Pay off the bills."

A yuk follows. None of this is to be taken seriously. What are the odds anyway? One in several million? You're more likely to get hit by lightning, the risk-makers say.

But still . . .

This is what happened to me, and I suspect that it is the same

"Sucker Hunch"

I am not a gambler.

My knowledge of the games of wagering and the rules supposedly governing those games is woeful. Many years ago I was dismissed with not-too-gentlemanly derision from the only poker game I have played which involved real money (high ante, ten cents), simply because I did not know that the 2, 3, 4, 5 and 6 of hearts would beat three of a kind, or most anything else. The only words uttered to me the rest of the evening were, "Hey, Stoopid, bring me a Blue Ribbon."

This is to announce that Stoopid is back.

Last summer I bought lottery tickets in Florida.

I couldn't help it.

If you're in Florida, you have to buy lottery tickets.

Well, you don't *have to* have to. It's not a law, or anything quite so absolute. There are no Lottery Police Officers shaking you down. No one holds the muzzle of a gun to your temple. In fact, you are far more likely to be hustled by a time-share boondoggler than by someone behind the counter of the local lottery outlet.

It's just that it's—well, it's hard to resist. To not buy a lottery ticket in Florida would be like being in a Stuckey's and not buy-

The fence around Fernbank Forest says a lot about us. It brings to mind lines from *The Night Thoreau Spent in Jail,* a play by Jerome Lawrence and Robert E. Lee. In the closing of Act One, Ralph Waldo Emerson cries out to Henry David Thoreau, "Henry! Henry! What are you doing in jail?" And Thoreau answers (defiantly, according to stage directions), "Waldo! What are you doing *out* of jail?"

If we must surround our environment with chain-link to preserve it, a lot of us are on the wrong side of the fence.

1990

[*"Recycling the Rah-Rah"*]

effect—and resolve gets lost in the swell of Us vs. Them emotion.

Also, there is the matter of post-excitement apathy, inspired by the comfort of taking an obligatory stand. It's easy to say, "I tried, but I am only one person." Apathy is the sin of sins.

And, not least among the downsides, public declarations issued by environmentalists will be used by industry and politicians much in the same manner as the discovery process is used in litigation—to refine and reposition and maintain. No one could say it is a practice of determining which way the wind blows or of testing the waters, but without great concern over how thick the wind is with pollution or how contaminated the water is with waste. A good, lawyer-approved position paper is as passionate as scripture in certain circles.

Still, it is inarguable that, as a civilization, we are not good stewards of the resources of Earth. Greed is greater than reason, ignorance more gratifying than understanding, waste more fashionable than conservation. We cannot drain off our wetlands, or chain saw away our trees, or thicken our air with the soup of chemicals and expect Earth to heal itself and still tolerate our destruction. We cannot. It doesn't work that way.

Among the many stories about Earth Day, *Life* magazine's issue on trees was particularly interesting. One of the feature stories was on Fernbank Forest in DeKalb County, a beautifully wooded holdout against the restless forces of progress. Yet there was one sad note about the story: Fernbank Forest must be fenced to protect the integrity of nature.

these actions had not occurred. Others contend such claims are overstated, that legislation on behalf of nature was inevitable.

What was, and is, inevitable, is the argument.

Thus, there are pros and cons to an Earth Day.

The first positive is national attention. Ballyhooing the issue. Putting it in the headlines of media specials. Getting people to read and listen and talk, so perhaps, out of knowledge they will commit to individual acts of rebellion against old and careless habits.

Second, an event like Earth Day does apply discomforting pressure on industry and politicians. (Frankly, there is considerable benefit to nationalistic public crusading. Pressure exerted on public officials is often more effective when the topic is broad-based, and the environment is about as broad-based as one can get. Challenge existing regulations on specific issues—industrial waste, for example—and the system can bureaucratize the argument into oblivion.)

Third, because there are rare individuals among the power elite who respond to voices crying in what little wilderness is left, positive change does occur. And even if some of those decisions are subject to charges of public relations posturing—Maynard Jackson's call for recycling in Atlanta comes to mind—the results are still encouraging.

But the downsides, the cons, of an Earth Day campaign are equally certain.

For one thing, the rah-rah tone of its call to action invites lively debate over alleged generalities—i.e., the green house

[*"Recycling the Rah-Rah"*]

we're after, or is it excess?) But it is not only the plazas that account for the heaps of red dirt blighting the roadsides. Subdivisions jam against subdivisions, with quick-built houses on narrow slabs of land. Apartment complexes sprout from the ground like brick weeds. And with these developments come the necessity to accommodate—accommodate traffic and garbage and all the other signatures of mankind's lofty notion of living.

It is called progress. With progress, we are informed, there must be sacrifice as well as gain, which makes one wonder if the word shouldn't really be semi-progress, or quasi-progress, or, perhaps, compro-progress.

The positions at cross-purpose in this obsession for progress are economics and environment. An example is the clean air dispute. Unquestionably, we are polluting the air with our cars and industrial plants, but we linger, linger, linger over the question of what to do about it. The environmentalist wants action. Industry wants more study, more proof. Industry is rich. Rich matters. Rich can hire consultants to argue ably that the so-called greenhouse effect on Earth is as much myth as fact. The political body responsible for making responsible decisions listens attentively and furrows its collective brow and intones grave-sounding warnings about the costly error of hasty judgments. Few of them rail against the expense of foot-dragging.

The original Earth Day, in 1970, is credited with the creation of the Environmental Protection Agency and other conscientious reform and we are assured by celebrants of that occasion that, as bad as things are, they would be alarmingly worse if

mostly in the holy name of progress. And for all the skepticism generally, and smugly, leveled at such sensible purposes—usually by those profiting from progress—Earth Day was a spirited event.

Credit the media for getting out the message, or messages, for there are many stories to be told, many horrors to be witnessed, many facts to astound us. And credit the schools. The schools realize a good lesson is a good lesson is a good lesson, and that an inquisitive, imaginative child experiencing the first pure rush of social consciousness is a persuasive force in the home. There have been many aluminum cans and discarded newspapers recycled because students have been badgering, insistent little soldiers for the environment.

The question is, Will any good come of the effort? Or was Earth Day little more than a group of latter-day beatniks humming, perhaps off-key, a national mantra? And, if so, was it a prayer to a god, or one in search of a god? Was it, in short, aimless blathering?

A look around makes one hope for the best.

Once a person could drive into Atlanta, catching the city's skyline in peekaboo glimpses through trees lush with vegetation, and there was a clean, sweet aura that cupped the clustering of buildings. It is no longer an aura. It is a haze. There are not so many trees to see through or around or over.

And it is almost impossible to drive the fringe of Atlanta without seeing land stripped and leveled for yet another shopping plaza on yet another crossroads corner. (What is the ratio, anyway? One plaza for every twenty people? Is it convenience

"Recycling the Rah-Rah"

Alex the cat—so named because a suspected *he* later became a pregnant *she*—merely wanted to please.

For a day, she deposited baby rabbits at my feet. Five of them. She had found them nested in the narrow strip of overgrowth separating my back yard from my neighbor's back yard.

"What are they doing there?" my wife anguished.

"They are there," I told her, "because the woods are gone."

And that is true. The woods that used to be at the back of our property and the woods across the street have been bulldozed away over the past few years. Subdivisions now occupy the space. The few trees left standing are more for ornament and shade than for baby rabbits.

Alex the cat, with her offerings, prompts these thoughts.

In late April, Planet Earth, like fathers and mothers and groundhogs, had its own day—a day devised and promoted by the one animal species hell-bent on putting wobble in its spin. That would be mankind. *Homo sapiens.* Upright creatures with advanced reasoning and splendidly usable thumbs.

The purpose of Earth Day was to call attention to a cancerous spread of pollution and other injurious acts infecting the globe,

vate themselves above their gifts and their once-humble expectations of admiration have become their demands. And they wonder why fans get disgruntled. The Tee-League center fielder slays dragons with pebbles; the professional athlete slays himself with his tongue.

The Braves and the Falcons and the Hawks and other professional teams make a grave mistake when they ask the question, "Why aren't they supporting us?"

They should be asking, "Why should they support us?"

When they get the answer to that one and do something about it, there won't be any empty blues, because the seesaw will be in another position.

Until then, the discretionary dollar is up for grabs and a lot of grabbing is going on. The Tee-League bake sale intrigues me at the moment.

1990

[*"The Days of Whine and Ruses"*]

ond desperation by the team's most awkward substitute. Such are the moments that *oohs* and *aahs* and glad laughter and bellowing cheers are made of. That is why parents and siblings and grandparents and assorted other relatives skip Atlanta-Fulton County Stadium in favor of lawn chairs along chain-link fences.

There is something else about watching the youngsters play: It's good, relaxing fun—discounting a few parents and coaches who are obnoxious fanatics, full of more *hiss* and *boo* than *attaboys* or *attagirls*. In sour moods, I go often to watch the Tee-Leaguers and leave always with a feeling of joy. Few things refocus perspective as surely as a Lilliputian center fielder building sand castles for imaginary kings or throwing pebbles at invisible dragons while the game rages around him and the score ends in numbers too high to count.

Over the next few months reasonably rational adults will write letters to the sports pages berating fair-weather fans for their failure to support the Braves, and distressed callers to radio sports programs will announce, as though it is a revelation, that the city doesn't deserve to have professional baseball. It is the same for football and, in past years, has been the same for basketball. Fan-fickleness is the charge. It is a weak argument. The fans, to me, are less fickle than many of the athletes, who leave their talents with the scribbled signatures of their obscenely lucrative contracts. It is not fan-fickleness; it is fan-exasperation over muscular, arrogant demigods behaving boorishly, snarling about empty seats as though the seats are pews for worshipers. Somewhere along the way too many of these gifted men have chosen to ele-

cretionary dollar Rankin Smith wants in order to calm the hair-trigger disposition of the foolish child-man, Neon Deion.

And before the first story appears in print or the first radio/television voice utters shame over the Braves leading the league in no-shows, I hereby declare there are thousands of people who believe, with good reason, that the baseball/softball/soccer game at the local park is far more entertaining, far more exciting, and far more involving than watching Dale Murphy—a truly good human—strike out on a 3-2 count with a man at third. (It is also far less expensive.)

Some of my most enjoyable days have been spent on playgrounds and in gymnasiums watching one of the offspring suffer and/or triumph in those same games that our professionals play. In fact, the most thrilling basketball game I have ever seen was not between the Hawks and the Bulls—Dominique vs. Michael—but between two teams of eighth-grade-age players, when excessive fouling left one team with only two players against five for the other team. You got it: The two beat the five. In that same year I saw my own son score forty-seven points in a game, a memory that is almost chilling in its splendor.

Of course, the act of splendor is what all parents seek for their children, and that includes those who declare, "Oh, I just want them to have a good time." The beauty of the playground game is that splendor can come out of accident and error as well as skill—the surprise catch by a startled third baseman trying to avoid a baseball streaking across the infield like a comet, the basketball that miraculously arcs into the basket, flung in last-sec-

[*"The Days of Whine and Ruses"*]

small countries and then selectively spend their time strutting and posing for scrapbook material. (I pray I am not alone in dislike of athletes who describe games in terms of their own glory— i.e., "I knew they were depending on me, you know, so I just went out, you know, and done it, because, you know, I was the only one who could of done it." Once upon a time, compliments were earned, and praise was offered sensibly by others, not proclaimed stupidly by the athlete.)

If I am going to peel off $30, $40, $50, $60 to pay for transportation, parking, tickets, food, programs and other incidentals, I want to make certain that I see a Joe DiMaggio, not somebody whose best performance is spitting expertly while kneeling in the on-deck circle. You may recall it was DiMaggio who explained the reason he always played full-speed was because there might be people in the stands seeing him for the first time. An ancient philosophy by today's standards, but a good one.

Our professional teams need to understand their game is not the only one around. Distractions abound.

It is an interesting fact that downtown Atlanta is surrounded on all four sides by exurbs that have become suburbs, which are inhabited by people eagerly willing to be entertained and whose choices are many. For example, in the distance separating my settlement (Lilburn) from the epicenter of Atlanta, there are ten zillion (or so it seems) movie theaters, shopping centers at every crossroads, eateries offering gluttony-of-choice dishes, health clubs, recreational centers, etc.—all after the same devalued dis-

they be mentally prepared, remembering the tragic sight of empty blues in Atlanta-Fulton County Stadium [now Turner Field]? Will Jerry Glanville leave tickets to entire sections for departed, quasi-departed and/or mythical guests?

And what of the Atlanta Braves, now limbering their muscles for yet another season of rebuilding? How disconcerting will it be if fans never get past Underground Atlanta on the way to the stadium? Will the failure of a crowd to cheer (or even to insult lustily) affect the hit-and-run, the double play, the costly balk, the RBI when the RBI is something other than a feeble attempt at catch-up?

In-person support is an issue that seems to infest our teams of professional sport with the same predictability as—well, the performance of said teams. It works on the seesaw principle: Up performances get up support; down performances get down support. Sadly, in Atlanta we are far more familiar with down than with up.

Still, the question lingers: If our fellows are out there in their play-as-work vocations, why aren't we crowding appreciatively around them?

Other than the effect of the seesaw principle, I suggest two reasons inextricably related: money and distraction.

I don't know about others, but it's my experience that the discretionary dollar—which our teams of sport continue to require for attendance—has lost as much of its actual value as the nondiscretionary dollar. I am thus less disposed to share it with ballplayers who annually accumulate more wealth than

"THE DAYS OF WHINE AND RUSES"

When the Atlanta Falcons last in the barnyard faded—in December [1989], against Detroit; their Sanders (Barry) flying, our Sanders (Deion) sitting—there appeared the following day in the sports pages a story of complaint about fan support or, more accurately, lack of it.

Some of the Falcons were suffering greatly from injured feelings as well as postgame embarrassment and occupational bruises.

One reported that he had tried to give away tickets to the game but could not find any takers.

Upon reading the story, my reaction was: What?

Did this really happen? Did some poor, unappreciative, workingman slob, a week before Christmas, on a miserably cold day, actually resist free tickets to watch the 3-and-12 Falcons become the 3-and-13 Falcons?

I mean, dear God, have we lost all sense of propriety and responsibility? Do we not care about the fragile emotions of our athletes, those finely outfitted warriors who go forth as our alter egos in search of heroism? Are we to expect them to heal overnight from such disregard? What about next season? Will

high of the opium of power, most politicians are bright, often gifted and, on the whole, are dedicated stewards of their office. But that office is not easily obtained. It requires more than platform or personality or catchy advertising slogans; it also requires money. A lot of money.

As a consequence, politicians seem always to be squirming on a hot seat of controversy. Why, for example, is it necessary for a congressman from Georgia to accept political contributions from someone residing in Colorado or New Mexico or Nevada or some other out-of-Georgia location? Are the home-folk so bad off they can't elect their own representatives without outside help?

The fact is, covering the cost of an election every couple of years is a monumental task, one that would be impossible if left to the generosity of the individual voter. And that is why special interest groups—from Georgia and elsewhere—attend receptions and barbecues and other forms of fund-raising activities.

Several years ago, a Georgia politician of some renown was defeated in his bid for high office. A number of his cohorts and supporters organized an event—a big bash, as they say—to retire his campaign debt.

The best letter to the editor I have ever read followed in the daily newspaper. Paraphrasing, it said, "I just wonder: How would he [the politician] have paid off his debt if he had been elected?"

It's our system. Love it or lump it.

Sadly, it demands that we play games to keep it going.

And, yes, it has all the intrigue of a good novel.

1990

[*"The Fall Guys"*]

records are clean and orderly. Not Top Brass; he is insulated by organizational distance and corporate policies. The vulnerable are those responsible for the nitty-gritty. In the case of Jake Horton, it is alleged that vendors were enlisted to make contributions and then charge back the cost through goods and services.

In the pecking order of larger companies there is usually yet another player, a Person-in-Charge—a Jake Horton—lodged between Top Brass and the lobbyist. Holding such a position is a little like playing bunt-depth at third base when Wade Boggs is swinging away. You may be pleased to be in the lineup, but you never see the shot that strikes you between the eyes; and when you regain consciousness you find that the same manager who signaled you to play in is benching you for not being back.

Yet that may be only the beginning of your woes. Your corporate teammates—a very serious concept in contemporary business—suddenly avoid you and you are likely to discover that you are portrayed as (a) a sexual deviate, (b) a liar, (c) a communist, (d) a thief, (e) an incompetent or (f) all of the above. And if there is a corporate trial, you can bet the mortgage it will be conducted without your testimony.

Frankly, the politician is as much a victim of the system as the corporate body or the individual contributor. Following the letter of the law is relatively simple: Keep good, accurate records and avoid accepting unlawful contributions. However, living with the spirit of the practice—knowing how it really works—must be discomforting, for these are not naive, unaware people. Just the opposite. Discounting a few egomaniacs who live off the

SPECIAL KAY *the wisdom of terry kay*

But there are many who will think of Jake Horton as someone victimized by a political system so layered in Catch-22s that it has become a parody of itself.

The law says utilities cannot make political contributions, per se. If the contribution can't be made through a Political Action Committee (a PAC), it must be as a personal donation. It is, on the surface, good law. It keeps down the braying of favoritism by public officials over the always-sensitive question of public utilities.

It is also false, a cosmetic swipe across the aging face of democracy.

The same lawmakers who support the law governing political contributions are not at all ashamed to inquire if a lobbyist plans to attend such-and-such reception, at $250 or $500 (or more) a pop, and if he will be bringing others along. The lobbyist is not a fool. If there is any chance that said lawmaker will have influence over an important piece of legislation affecting the lobbyist's interests, why, yes, he'll be at the reception, and, yes, there will be others with him. (For those who have never attended these receptions, it is more a matter of being seen—acknowledging that a contribution has been made—than having a rare opportunity to negotiate the fine points of an issue.)

The result is obvious and inevitable: Even with PAC money, there is a limit to how many receptions can be attended and how many lawmakers can be supported before someone is taking from Peter to pay Paul.

Who, then, is at great peril in the delicate manipulation of satisfying both the law and political pressure? Not the politician; his

[*"The Fall Guys"*]

then picked up the telephone and called his office to inquire about a pending case.)

Issues are seldom resolved, or even clearly defined, in this expository exercise. It simply provides everyone with a memorandum to file confirming that, indeed, a meeting did occur and that, somewhere, someone is attending to the matter.

That someone most often is the lobbyist working diligently with the note-scribbling aide, who in turn helps develop strategy for the politician's ultimate decision. In the meantime, if anything goes awry, Politician and Top Brass can say, legitimately, that it's all a mystery to them; beyond an initial meeting, they haven't been involved. Exposition becomes confrontation seeking resolution, which, ironically, is the critical track of every good tale, from the comedian's joke to classic literature.

A few months ago Jake Horton, a senior vice president for Gulf Power Co. with the responsibility for governmental affairs, died tragically in an airplane accident en route to Atlanta, reportedly after learning that he would be dismissed over political contributions that failed to meet the standard of law and ethics. His death and the subsequent admission of guilt by Gulf Power officials turned the hot beam of the spotlight on the relationship between business and politics.

This is not to accuse or defend Jake Horton, but to suggest that his name will now become a metaphor for conduct, and it won't mean the same as in "everything's jake," that quaint, turn-of-the-century slang for satisfactory.

places the word *lobbyist* between *lobbygow* (an errand boy) and *lobe* (as in earlobe) and defines the word as "a person who tries to influence legislation on behalf of a special interest; a member of a lobby."

Special interests abound, from tobacco farmers to pharmaceutical distributors, from automobile manufacturers to foreign importers, from utilities to unions. If a thing or an issue can't be lobbied, there should be serious doubt of its existence. And, of course, there are degrees of intensity in the lobbying effort, as demonstrated of late by the uncivil war over abortion, with politicians caught in the crossfire of deadly word bullets.

It may be inappropriate to call all of this a game, but it is, and well-played, it is as complex and invigorating as a good page-turning mystery.

The first rule to understand is that posturing matters. Here is an example:

Politician meets with Top Brass representatives of XYZ Co. or Cause to discuss Serious Impending Issue. There is much furrowing of collective brows as Politician's aides furiously scribble notes, or depending on the circumstance, Politician avoids the issue by name-dropping, or he resorts to bullying, as in "Do it this way, or I'll have a bill in the hopper before you get to the door." (Once I heard a distinguished state legislator laughingly tell a group making a courtesy call that he didn't mind what they did; as an attorney litigating against them in private practice, he expected to make a great deal of money. He

"THE FALL GUYS"

Memory is dim on the details, but I believe the invitation that my parents received and proudly displayed was for Carl Sanders' inauguration as governor of Georgia. They did not attend, but the invitation was a cherished family document, a confirmation that a politician could, as Kipling phrased it, keep "the common touch."

To my parents, a politician had an important obligation: To keep democracy untainted and vigorous was a lofty calling, up there with that of the preacher and the teacher. Politicians were to be treated with respect, honoring protocols of behavior inherently bestowed with the taking of office—a practice, I suspect, that is primeval in its origins but refined by the British.

My parents did not know many politicians.

More important, they did not know a single lobbyist. Ergo, they did not understand a lot about politics, because anyone who knows a constituent from a kumquat realizes that government does not operate solely at the direction of elected officials, but also at the persuasion of the hired lobbyist.

The *Random House Dictionary of the English Language* (second edition, unabridged), properly, and perhaps significantly,

what he/she is doing than the mother "mixing" the same batter.

These are splendid little people, with imaginations that blaze from the heat of language. Limitation to them is an afternoon nap, and even then they have the joy of dreams.

And then we commit the necessary crime of education against them. We take them from homes and kindergartens and place them in schools, and our teachers say to them, in various demonstrations and in precise, listen-to-me tones, "Look, Jane, look. See the dog. See the cat. Run, Spot, run." The startled child (it is not the face of intrigue, teacher; it is the face of confusion) subconsciously thinks. "Oh, no, I've been doing it wrong." Give them six weeks. Their sentences are punctuated on a three-breath count. They say, "Hello, Daddy. How are you? I am fine. Where is Spot?"

"Beatering" becomes mixing.

Without realizing it, our acts of education temper the process of discovery and unintentionally take away the imagination of the child who beaters cake batter. The great teacher, the adult Johnny(ie) with daring and passion and love and excitement for the smell of the chalk dust and the energy of the mind at learning—at discovering—does one thing: He/she intentionally gives back to the child the freedom of the imagination. The imagination, once gained, is more powerful than a great hall of framed degrees.

The adult Johnny(ie) can't teach because we, the public, are afraid of that power and we don't want him/her to fire the fuse.

We haven't learned that a "beatered" cake is the food of life.

1989

[*"Why Johnny(ie) Can't Teach"*]

and happy surprise it leaves the viewer envious of both teacher and student. And it poses the question, Why can't it be like that?

The answer is painfully obvious: Movies are magic; reality is not. Students must learn basic skills, and most often that is a matter of drill—do, repeat, do, repeat. And different subjects beg different teaching philosophies. It may be exciting to fling the spirit to its outer limits with Milton or Whitman or Thoreau, but pouring unlabeled chemicals at random into a blender to see what happens is silly.

Still, the teacher of chemistry should have zeal for his/her task. Too few do. Maneuvering around land mines buried in the maze of the formula seems more compelling than the wonder of possibilities offered by the formula.

Because the adult Johnny(ie) can't teach, or is prevented from teaching, the student becomes a victim of the locked-in, locked-down process of education. Preschool children quickly discover that the ability to use words is a remarkable experience. Words will get you attention. A lot of words will get you a lot of attention. Wonderfully clever words will get you a performance contract.

There's freedom to be gained in words. Four-year-olds speak in unrelenting, periodless sentences, sentences that flutter majestically in the atmosphere, like a kite unreeling in a brisk March wind. They invent words far more poetic and descriptive than those in any alphabetized, unabridged inventory from the editors of *Webster's* or *Funk & Wagnalls*. The child assisting his/her mother by "beatering" cake batter has a much clearer idea of

steel-lined shell of obstinacy many students develop in their conditioning to the classroom.

The brave are few. One teacher in a private school in Atlanta once locked a student in a closet until that student began to shove pages of an assigned writing project under the door. In public schools the teacher would have been lynched, lawyers for the student would have salivated over such cruel and unusual punishment, and Ted Koppel would have consulted Harvard educators and government experts to examine the merits of outrageous behavior. Today, that student is a graduate of Yale and an Oxford scholar.

That same teacher begins each school session by having his students stand before the class and remain until he/she reveals something of him/herself, even if foolish or funny (especially if foolish or funny), thereby proving that everyone is capable of absurdity and everyone is capable of achievement.

That same teacher has fourteen-year-olds who are far more accomplished as writers than many college seniors.

A summer movie that nudged itself into respectable popularity amid the shameless roar of a shamelessly poor *Batman* was *Dead Poets Society*, featuring Robin Williams in the role of an unconventional and inspiring teacher on the campus of a very proper and very private preparatory school. Though overwrought in many of its dramatic points (subtlety is a casualty of modern theatrics), this latter-day reminder of Pat Conroy's *Conrack* celebrates the passion for teaching with such tenderness

[*"Why Johnny(ie) Can't Teach"*]

water. They'll make it to safety even if it's by dog-paddling. (And we wonder why there are peer groups. Students will identify *themselves* if they must, and to avoid being perceived as common, routine, everyday at-home people who suddenly seem as useless as dandruff, they can be incredibly creative, as many stunned parents will attest.)

The adult Johnny(ie)s can't teach because the system has more muscle than the individual. The system orders from its master plan: Teach here, teach this, teach in this manner. Johnny(ie) can't teach because conformity is easier than resistance, and for the dollar paid, it makes one hell of a lot more sense to join the uniformed, smart-stepping troops than to wage battle as a guerrilla.

The adult Johnny(ie)s can't teach because their students are addicted to the great mind-killer, situation-comedy commercial television, and because the parents of their students are also addicted, transformed by ratings wars into apathetic, carping custodians who would rather watch the inane babbling of *Perfect Strangers* or *Roseanne* or (fill in the blank) than engage their child in a review of the school day. Johnny(ie)s can't teach because their students suffer from neglect, abuse, poverty, selfishness—those sorry, sad conditions that ravage the soul and seem forever perpetuated by genetic handcuffs linking generations with markings as telling as the color of eyes.

The adult Johnny(ie) can't teach because he/she lacks the confidence for the job. It is easy enough to give monotone renderings of basal-skill directions, or to ramble incoherently about totally unrelated subjects, but it requires bravery to break through the

Plan, smilingly approved by the Elders of Administration, who themselves have consulted the Oracles of Academese for guidance. (Curious about those Oracle folk—they're always bickering among themselves about salvation's path to wisdom.)

We do not want unconventional, inspired and inspiring teachers, those with a maverick spirit and a passion for the act of discovery (which is the act of learning). We want readin', writin' and 'rithmetic, which, by God, were good enough for me and my daddy and mama and ought to be good enough for anybody. Let the teachers teach what's in the book. If they can't do that, then get somebody who can. We want marionettes, with enough string attached to their appendages and their tongues that we can dance them at will or hang them on a whim.

It is bad enough that good (and poor) teachers must work in the shopping-mall atmosphere of too-crowded schools—consolidation being the accomplishment of Satan with a Ph.D.— where a child's fragile identity is in danger of being shattered and then trampled into oblivion on the first day. Ah, yes, proclaim the Oracles, but that is part of the learning experience, this elbow-rubbing with the large and crowded world, and if the student doesn't understand it at twelve, thirteen, or fourteen, he/she will forever muddle about meekly as a catch-up. Never mind that the student has been conditioned to think of him/herself as belonging, even if it's with the kids on the cul-de-sac or in a vacant lot; before he/she can become a Somebody, he/she must understand what it's like to be a Nobody. Throw them in the deep end of the pool. Let them thrash about and churn up the

"Why Johnny(ie) Can't Teach"

There are wonderful teachers in America and there are teachers—far too many—who simply should not be in the presence of students. They should be organizing terrorist groups in Lebanon, inflicting fear and pain on captors with sharp-pointed red pencils, or they should be lecturing roadside rocks, which have the material composition to withstand ceaseless boredom. Enough of deliberating why the child Johnny(ie) can't read or write or speak or count to three on his/her fingers. Why can't the adult Johnny(ie)s—even those who belong in a classroom—teach?

Maybe it's because we don't want them to.

We want them to understand our children, but not to offend them. We want them to accept mysterious, yet earnest, explanations of temporary, yet recurring, failures. We want them to chaperone and supervise and protect and favor and coddle and attend the needs of our sons and daughters. At the same time, we want them to be as accountable as junior executives with a claw-grip on the crowded rungs of the corporate ladder. We want them to live by the commandments of the Great God Lesson

Social Commentary

My youngest son called me in February. He wanted to borrow my tiller to break up some ground in his backyard in preparation for planting grass where his dogs had eroded the land. I had this image of my son behind the tiller. Comic, I thought. My son and a tiller. I volunteered to take a look at his task, volunteered to transport the tiller in my truck, understanding that I would be the one to demonstrate it.

Yet, I am sixty-two, a defining age for me.

I said to my son, "Come get the tiller."

And then I added, "Do the best you can."

I have decided that being a father is a matter of faith as much as anything.

Yet, I do wonder if it will be a hot summer, if grass will grow for him.

2000

[*"Lay-By Time"*]

Yet, that year, the year of sixteen, my father gave me a task—his work.

Now, at my father's age of illness, I realize how profoundly influenced I was by that summer, and by him. A bond developed between us that seemed somehow different from the bond that I saw between other fathers and other sons. I do not think he ever worried about me being on my own, and over the years, through other illnesses, he privately shared with me a few of those trembling moments that we all try to disguise. It was that sense of knowing him that made the writing of *To Dance with the White Dog* a simple task. I did not have to tell of his life; I merely had to translate it.

I know this: from that year, from the summer of 1954, my parents never again considered me a child.

And I wish to God I could do the same with my own children. I cannot.

I have confidence in them, believe in them, yet I think of myself as their safety net, as someone who secretly knows incantations of magic that will soothe them, the same kind of trickery I used on them when they were very small and very impressionable.

Of course, those who deal professionally in such matters have long advised that we must snip the cord of dependency. Push them out of the nest and let them fly on their own. That sort of thing.

And I am not a fool. I know they are right.

The trick, perhaps, is picking the right time, the right situation.

the row and back on the other side. Run-around. It was called run-around.

We each plowed one row and were sweat-soaked. The mules were in white lather.

I said to John, "I declare this field of corn laid-by." We unhitched the mules from the plows, put the plows back into the wagon and went home. I was terrified of my father's reaction. Lay-by was an ancient practice, a ritual almost as sacred as communion. Only a lazy man would skip the lay-by.

My father merely nodded when I told him what I had done.

Curiously, it was the only crop that gave back anything for the labor that year. A meager harvest, but a harvest all the same. Later, my father would judge that we had not torn up the feeder roots with plowing. He said he had learned something from it. In future years, he would skip the lay-by plowing.

I am old enough now to see metaphor in all of this. Then, I was sixteen, restless as a young animal, the slippery jelly of manhood intoxicating me with its promises. The wagging finger of a beckoning dream could easily have led me to imitate the laziness of other young men I knew—town boys who spent their summer afternoons at swimming pools or leaning across the fountains of drug stores sipping from cherry-flavored Cokes, always in the company of a smiling, bright-eyed young woman.

Mule-plowing does not compete well with cherry-flavored Cokes.

[*"Lay-By Time"*]

He spent much of that summer in the hospital. Kidney stones. A slipped disc. Sciatica. Another ailment I do not remember.

With John helping when he could in the afternoons of his pre-college summer job as a surveyor for cotton allotments, I would plow the land and plant the crops and cultivate them and harvest them, and it would teach me lessons no other experience has ever provided.

Lessons that were literally burned into me.

The summer of 1954, in Hart County, Georgia, was a summer of drought. Cloudless days following cloudless days. Sun-baking heat that blistered the crust of the earth until it turned to powder.

Cotton does not grow in powder. Neither does corn, nor wheat, nor oats.

From the hospital, my father would advise, "Do the best you can, son."

I learned that, when you are young, doing the best you can requires a lot of guesswork and guesswork is not always as fifty-fifty as a coin toss.

Still, you do remember when you are right.

There was an airless day in July when John and I went to a rented field to lay-by a few acres of wilting corn that grew on a slope not far from Beaverdam Creek. Lay-by was the last plowing, done with plow points called gophers and with sweeps that would roll the dirt in a mound against the plants. Up one side of

leaving me and our younger brother, Gary, with our father. Gary was ten years old at the time; I was sixteen.

I assisted my father to the tub and instructed Gary to keep watch over him, then went to the barn to milk the cows.

A few minutes later, Gary came racing to the barn, fearfully calling that our father was screaming in pain. I found him writhing in the tub. He said, "I need a doctor, son."

It is not easy at age sixteen to become a man in a few minutes.

The first call I made was to my sister, Jean, who lived in Royston, four miles away. Jean had been a nurse. At the time, she did not have a car. "I'll come for you," I told her.

I got my father back into his bed and took Gary with me in the car, stopping at a neighbor's home—our cousins, the Ginns— dispatching him to alert them about our father's condition. The drive to Royston took only minutes. The car was a Ford. A 1950, I think. Or a '51. I do not have an obsession for the makes and models of cars, remember them vaguely even if I've driven them to junk-yard ruin. Oddly, though, I do remember that a mechanic had said the radiator on the Ford was clogged and needed a change-out, and I was supposed to take it soon to his garage. The drive—fast, dangerous, foolish—blew out the trash and the radiator was never repaired.

On the trip back to the farm with my sister, we met our cousin, Emiel Ginn, transporting our father to the hospital in Elberton.

Jean remembers the terrible pain in our father's face. He did not want to waste time talking with us. He wanted a doctor. This powerful man—ox-strong, never sick—wanted a doctor.

"Lay-By Time"

I have done the math and the math does not lie.

At age sixty-two—my age—my father suffered his first serious illness.

It happened on an early-spring morning in 1954, the day we were to take the mules and the turning plows and begin to plow the fields for planting. Tedious work; yet, in my memory, good work. The slicing of the ground, rolled over to the right of the plowblade, leaving ripples. At day's end it was pleasing to lean against the crossbar of the plow handles and to see the evenness of the ripples, and to breathe in the winter dampness of the dirt —a scent like rain closing in over distant pine stands.

We did not make it to the fields that morning.

My father awoke with a searing pain in his lower back. Told me to run hot water in the bathtub for him, and to go about the morning chores with the livestock.

My mother was not at home. She had been staying in Elberton attending my Aunt Lula Peek, who was suffering from cancer. My mother had wanted to be a nurse. Being with Aunt Lula was like a calling for her. John, my older brother by eighteen months, was in Washington, D.C. on his senior class trip,

What I am really saying to those who are about to send their child(ren) off to Wherever, is this: If you close the door behind them, don't lock it. Because that's what a home is for, isn't it? A place to be from, and a place to return to.

1991

[*"The Full Nest Syndrome"*]

But before this sounds too one-sided, it should be acknowledged that stay-at-home children (mine and yours) are not always shiftless moochers who are willing to trade a few hours of excited parental lecture for a place to sleep. A lot of them are home because it's too expensive to be anywhere else, and I don't care if they've got a pretty decent job and their own credit cards. It's not as easy to get started now, without some seed money, as it used to be.

And there are a lot of children living with parents because of divorce, or illness, or because they have been given the dreaded pink slip, or because of other matters a bit out of their control.

Parents may find themselves moaning over these circumstances, but the experience doesn't have to be total frustration. In fact, there are moments when those stay-at-homes make it right—as they did when they were babies and they gave you that curious, warming look of gladness.

My youngest son, Jon, will sometimes take his guitar and play for me a ballad he has written, and I marvel at the way he can hold music on his fingers.

My oldest son, Scott, reads me perhaps better than anyone. I can spend ten minutes with him in quiet talk and feel magically well.

Sometimes Heather will lean over and kiss me and I want to lock the doors to make sure she can never again leave me.

And then there's my older daughter—Terri—who sent me into mourning when she left home. She returns, too. For visits. And when she does, she brings the grandsons. I would keep them if she would let me. The house is big enough.

And the younger, home-from-college daughter—well, what can I say? She is home, and she has her dormitory stuff with her. It baffles me how she could make all of that fit into her half of a teensy dormitory room, and yet could not fit it into three larger rooms of a full-size house. We do not answer the telephone any longer with the customary "Hello." We say, "Heather's Answering Service."

In stories from books and magazines, and in some of the more heartwarming television ads of the seasons, family holidays involving adult children seem always to depict life with sweet violin music in the background. You know the setting: Christmas Eve, getting on toward nightfall, new-fallen snow on the boxwoods and Mama and Daddy peering longingly out of the curtained window to see if Junior will make it home from Pittsburgh, where he is climbing the executive ladder for a steel company. And just when all hope seems lost and the logs are turning to ash in the fireplace, when Mama is standing in front of the Christmas stockings, her eyes moist with memories, the door flings open and Junior explodes into the living room, trailed by radiant wife and squealing children.

I love those kinds of things. My throat always lumps up when I see them, even if they're only hawking cheap champagne. That is what I want to experience—that sort of passionate bonding.

We do not need such suspense in my family, however. Gathering the clan is relatively simple: Wake them up. (Well, actually, that's not at all simple, especially since they believe that one of the privileges of being an adult is sleeping late enough to have the energy to stay up all night.)

[*"The Full Nest Syndrome"*]

ownership right to both countries. She wears joy like a splendid aura, and when she is out of the house for even the shortest time, the place takes on a silence that is absolutely eerie.

There: That's the word. Silence. That's what makes the Empty-Nest Syndrome so damnably painful. Silence.

I first experienced that silence when my older daughter left home. I wept for days, wept great, aching tears, wept in such mourning I became ill. She was too young, too little, too much in need of her daddy. She, of course, believed she was ready to leave. Her daddy, of course, was right, but that is another matter.

But that first leaving did make me understand that our children would, in their time, pack up one day, smile that I'm-out-of-here smile, and roar away. And I knew that, with each leaving, I would somehow be diminished, reduced to a kind of nothingness.

I believe now that my children want to spare me the pain of loneliness.

They are home.

Yes, they are.

My youngest son has transformed the basement—where, once, I had an office—into a rehearsal studio for his band. His band does not play elevator music. His band can crack concrete, which, perhaps, is the reason his music is called rock music.

My oldest son, who is in the landscaping business, also inhabits the basement. Sometimes he brings his work home with, and on, him. Potting soil. Regular dirt. Fertilizer. I believe I could throw marigold seeds into his room and they would spring up and bloom overnight.

SPECIAL KAY *the wisdom of terry kay*

We do not live like other people. I have friends whose children have been so long gone from home, rooms have been sealed off, and when I visit, I am astonished at how orderly their lives appear to be. There are no tracks across their up-nap carpets, no breakfast dishes on the coffee table in front of the television set, no trails of clothing from the front door to a bedroom. The telephone does not ring every ten seconds.

In my home, I need commercial carpet suitable for forklift traffic and at least three sets of dishes. The way my children scatter their clothes suggests to me that they were frightened by the story of Hansel and Gretel and are determined never to be lost. As for telephones, I need an in-house operator.

I began to realize the seriousness of this subject in June, when I packed an eighteen-wheeler's worth of dormitory stuff into my older daughter's Chevrolet van and fetched my younger daughter home from her first year of college.

My younger daughter, you must understand, is not the product of careful family planning. Twenty years ago, my wife and I had decided to borrow some money for a trip to England and Ireland and, amazed that we had been so devil-may-care about our finances, we celebrated too exuberantly. The trip we eventually made was to the maternity ward of Emory Hospital, which is nice, but it is not England, or Ireland. We did, however, name our new daughter Heather, in part to commemorate the put-aside dream.

Please accept that this is not to complain about a pregnancy foiling a vacation. I would not trade my daughter for the sole

"The Full Nest Syndrome"

These words are applied to this space as a service for those thousands of parents who have had a child—or children—recently leave home for college (or some other experience of the Great Unknown).

You are probably suffering from the shock of Empty-Nest Syndrome, an emotional malady that can cripple the spirit.

This is my advice: Do not worry. They are likely to return—not as your children, of course, but as privileged lodgers. I know about this. I am an expert, and being an expert I can tell you the first question you will have about the Empty-Nest Syndrome is: How can I possibly bear it?

The second question—the one that follows their return—is exactly the same, but from a different perspective.

The reason I am an expert in this matter is that three of my four children currently reside with my wife and me. Their combined ages are seventy, which puts them five years past retirement. And as they say in those grade-B westerns, this town ain't big enough for all of us—which is why, for this writing, I have accepted Tom Bodett's invitation and have taken a twenty-four-hour refuge in the place where they forget the pillow mints, but leave the light on for you.

Not everyone was of the Break-Away Generation, of course. Most of us were simply a little dysfunctional—but enough so to make us feel isolated and bewildered. When we began to find little shops that had warm, good reminders of our past, we began to experience little moments of healing. The old chair that used to be shoved in the corner at the homeplace suddenly became what it was always meant to be—an heirloom.

I have such heirlooms from the home of my parents. I hope, someday, that my children will be pleased to have those heirlooms in their own homes.

And I hope one of them will take care of the typewriters, even if they have no idea at all what they meant to their father as he toiled before an impersonal machine, trying to dodge radiation from a blinking cursor.

1991

[*"Collected Wisdom"*]

It is more than coincidental that today's collecting craze began in the 1960s, during the same period that we were being torn, by the centrifugal force of society's spinning madness, from a still-familiar heritage. It was as though the more we quarreled among ourselves and with ourselves, and the further we traveled from our touchstones of comfort, the more we needed a tangible identity. A brass bed may not have been a grandfather, but it was a reminder of a grandfather's age and wisdom. We could say, "Look at this, it's from Pennsylvania." But what we meant was. "I'm still connected."

I do not remember my parents, or any neighbors, going on "junking" missions for collectibles. They had items—heirlooms—that were handed down from meager or grand estates, and they knew who had possessed them, knew their family histories. It was right-of-ownership with price. Except for rare, certified antiques (the Louis Roman Numeral stuff from France, for example), no one associated these heirlooms with great monetary value. It was more a matter of sentiment.

What happened had a lot to do with the economy, and with a change in lifestyles, I suppose. There was a prevailing opinion in the 1960s that the young belonged to a Break-Away Generation, that they were adopting new philosophies and new desires, and in that evolutionary process they were rejecting anything older than twenty minutes. What could a seventy-year-old rolltop desk possibly mean to them? And a lot of those desks, and other items, were sold to men driving the territory in pickup trucks, looking for good buys.

- There are people who will collect anything associated with Elvis Presley.

- Some of the most interesting storytellers in America work in roadside antique/junk shops.

- If a national magazine with a circulation of six declares that whatever you are collecting has value, it is going to skyrocket in cost.

- Nothing can make you feel quite as triumphant as finding a good deal on a collectible.

- Furniture buyers must beware of clever reproductions, lately assembled in the basement of the dealer. (The smell of fresh wood is a clue.)

- Some antique/junk centers are as wonderful as museums, and the dealers are as grand as curators if they know their stuff.

- "Junking," the practice of traveling about in search of collectibles, is as therapeutic as a hot tub after a stressful day.

- I will buy anything that is five-for-a-dollar.

[*"Collected Wisdom"*]

Her latest preoccupation is with belt buckles and buttons, which I consider relatively sensible; there was a time when she had a more-than-passing interest in used chicken coops.

I have a neighbor who collects bottles—blue bottles. I have no idea why a green bottle won't do, or a plain, clear one, but she wants only blue bottles. There are people who collect pins from political campaigns, and are proud of the fact. Other people collect unicorns, salt and pepper shakers, coffee mugs, rolling pins, paper dolls, book markers, books, cuff links, tie clips.

Baseball cards are collected. Old tobacco tins, tidbits of paper with *Gone With the Wind* references, thimbles, Brownie cameras, comic books, turn-of-the-century eyeglasses. If it has existed, someone will collect it.

I have concluded these things about collecting:

- Only old things are true collectibles. The older, the better. People who collect new things—like posters of rock bands—are not so much collecting as they are gathering. Some do this because they are foolish. A few do it because they are gambling on the stuff being valuable when it gets old enough to be a collectible rather than a gatherable.

- Of devices, no one collects anything electronic; it is all mechanical. Having to plug a collectible into a wall socket somehow cheapens the experience.

stuff—some wonderful, some useless. I could feel a rush, a tingling in my arms and fingers. Someone had left a piece of paper in the machine. There were names typed on the paper from passersby who wanted to know what it felt like to type in the old days. I could not leave it there, on the floor. I had a feeling that it was looking at me with sad Underwood eyes, begging for a home. I told the man in the booth I would give him ten dollars—not be cause I needed a typewriter, but because I had learned to type on an Underwood at Royston High School, and, well, I was a sentimental sort of fellow.

It was the beginning of a madness, an obsession. I now have twenty-five or thirty old typewriters. They surround me when I am I writing in my basement office. I turn my head and see the Underwood and a Royal and two Remington portables and a Woodstock and a Corona and a Corona hyphenated with a Smith. They comfort me. They are objects of my heritage. The only person who does not love them is my wife. She has threatened to have them melted into a typewriter glob.

I am not alone in this obsession. Almost everyone I know stays on the watch for something special. A doctor friend collects old tools. He is especially fond of saws. (I must ask my proctologist if he has such a hobby. If he shows me a brace-and-bit, I'm out of there.)

My wife (the typewriter hater) collects Santa Clauses. She has dozens of them. At Christmas, they occupy the house like bearded little ghosts. Once she collected inkwells. After that it was baskets, then weighing scales, then fountain pens for the inkwells.

[*"Collected Wisdom"*]

I began collecting these typewriters one spring day a few years ago, not long after I had been introduced to the computer, with all its word-processing gimmickry. I am, in fact, using such a machine now. The words are popping up from beneath the cover of a blinking doo-dah that the computer people call the cursor.

It is not of my heritage. It is not a typewriter. It has no personality. I cannot hit it with my fist in a fit of artistic emotion. There is no sound of metal letter facings striking against paper wound around a hard-rubber roller. When a thunderstorm blows in, I must turn off the machine for fear of losing whatever it is that I have typed from beneath the cover of a blinking cursor.

When I first began using the computer at the office where I worked, it was necessary to have a typewriter nearby for reasons of personal security—a kind of Linus' blanket assurance. The typewriter looked wise and dependable, if a bit forlorn and sad. Occasionally, I would twirl a piece of paper into it and type *The quick brown fox jumped over the lazy dogs.* There is music in that line when it is typed on a real typewriter. It has symphonic beauty, the way it engages every key. On a computer, *The quick brown fox jumped over the lazy dogs* sounds like every other line. Soft clicking. Monotonous soft clicking. The blinking cursor blinks the same. It never stops blinking. I am certain the blinking cursor is spitting out radiation.

On the spring day that I saw the old Underwood, it was on the floor of a booth at Elco, which was, then, a giant junkyard of

"Collected Wisdom"

I t is lamentable that we have achieved—in our state of celebrated progress—such distancing from our heritage as to become orphans.

Even sadder are the arguments that we are better off leasing all that old baggage from the past in the train station if we are to ride space shuttles into the future. It's a persuasive message set to alluring music, and it may be sweet to the senses, but it doesn't work. Not totally.

There is something in us that won't let go, some homing device that picks up the whistle of an ancestor's call. There are instincts that prevail. We do not want to be totally new creatures; we want to have (and thus to leave) evidence that we were from someone, or something, on the way to being ourselves.

It is why we collect old things—because we have a need to connect with the past, with our heritage, as we are hurled blindly into the unknown.

I, for example, collect old typewriters. They're called manuals, meaning they are worked by the hand, or hands, rather than by electronic devices.

[*"The Strange Dance of White Dog"*]

I do not know about such things. But I like the thought, and I like the memory of my father's gentleness with White Dog, as though he wanted to embrace a caring he had lost.

And then White Dog left. On February 4, 1980. On February 5, my father wrote in his journal: "The weatherman says we will have snow before sunup tomorrow. Have just had a phone call from my granddaughter Ann in Knoxville. It is snowing up there. Whitey, my dog, has not been here since yesterday. I hope no harm has come to him."

On February 6, he wrote: "A beautiful four-inch snow this morning. No school today. Fred and Jimmy did not go to work. Snow is practically gone tonight. Gary has just phoned me. The snow over there is not melting. He has talked with Pat. Debbie's baby has not arrived. Whitey is still missing. I guess he is gone for no return. He was my best friend. I will miss him."

My sisters say that my father would stand in the yard, leaning on his walker, and call for White Dog and look in the skies for buzzards circling.

"Maybe somebody killed him," we said among ourselves.

"Maybe he just left, like he came."

My father died of cancer on August 16, 1980.

I like to think that White Dog left because he knew my father was being tended by his children.

Or my mother believed that it was time, at last, to leave him in our care.

1985

father's fingers scrubbing at his neck and later he learned to stand on his hind legs and put his front paws up on my father's walker across the front bar—and he'd walk that way with my father, like a man-dog dance in a carnival act.

That is the way the two of them lived for years. Special. Attentive. White Dog eating from my father's leftovers (he overcooked on purpose, though he never admitted to it—table scraps, he said). White Dog always in seeing or calling distance. White Dog playing walking games in the yard, paws up, face bobbing with the steps, my father talking to him, "You know what I'm saying, don't you, boy? You know, don't you?" (We'd watch from the windows, amused, wondering.)

White Dog did not take to anyone else. I am told my sister Lula once touched him, but no one else ever did that I know of. Whenever any of us went to the home place, to the farm, we could expect to see White Dog skirting the hedges by the tractor barn, body close to the ground, almost invisible in the ground light, or we could hear him slipping through the shrubbery at the base of the house, scrubbing against the clapboard. But we could not call him to us, could not coax him with promises of food, and we could not touch him. He was there and we knew it. Even when we could not see him, we could sense White Dog.

"Funny how that dog is," I said to Betty, one of my sisters. "Taking to Daddy like that."

"Daddy thinks it's Mama," Betty said. "He told me that. He said he thought it was Mama watching over him."

[*"The Strange Dance of White Dog"*]

again. (I think that is the way it was with White Dog, too—why he had to call on Fred to get his gun to do the killing.)

Maybe my father got to thinking about all of that. Maybe he got to thinking that he'd killed out of need and, as it sometimes happens, out of habit. But he'd no need to kill White Dog, except mercy, and, besides, he had enough to eat and to share with a dog, now that nobody was left at home but him and he didn't eat much, not working like he'd always done.

And there was the other thing (as he later told me): It played on his mind that White Dog appeared only a short time after my mother had died, about the same time the grievers had begun to leave him alone. Strange, it happening that way. Him being alone. Nothing to do but watch the television and sit in his rocker beside his rolltop desk and, at night, laboriously write in his journal of fragments of memories. And then White Dog. White as an apparition. Eyes that looked into him. A beggar dog that would not leave. Strange. All of it.

"Well, we'll just let him live, I guess," my father said to Fred when Fred came out one day with his gun. "He's trying hard enough." Fred didn't argue. He'd never wanted to kill the dog. "I don't know why; I just didn't," Fred said. "Not that dog."

And White Dog seemed to know the talk of killing was over. He crawled out from the bellied-in place he'd made in the sand under the house (directly under my father's bed) and he crept day by day closer to my father's offerings of food. One day, he took the food from my father's hand and then he took my

ness in the way he wanted to do things for himself. When he could not chase White Dog away by shouting from the door, he pushed his way outside and got his weight under his good leg and took his walker and jabbed it at White Dog like some ancient animal trainer, and White Dog jumped and whimpered and ducked his head and crawled away under the house only to show up later, begging with dull eyes at some safe distance from my father.

This went on for days, the shouting and jabbing and whimpering, but White Dog would not leave, and my father said to Fred, my brother-in-law, "Somebody ought to take a gun and put that starving dog out of his misery." And Fred, who knew my father well (knew he was asking, not discussing), said he'd do it first chance he got.

"Somebody ought to," my father repeated philosophically. "I'd do it myself, but I can't hold a gun leaning on this thing. Anyhow, my eye's gone for shooting."

So was his heart. He couldn't kill animals then, at his age. He'd had to kill too many in his years. Stall and lot and pasture animals. Cows and pigs he'd grown from newborns trembling unsteadily in the womb-steam of their mothers, their wet faces slapping instinctively at swollen teats—animals he'd have named (likely from magazine stories or radio shows) and petted until they followed after him like puppies. And then he'd have to put a gun to their heads and kill them for food at killing time. And over the years he'd had enough of it. He couldn't do it

"The Strange Dance of White Dog"

White dog came starving. Just showed up one day, as dogs will.

My father saw him from the middle-room window. He was at the back-door steps, where there'd been grease dripped from frying pans my mother'd taken across the yard to pour out at the edge of the pasture. There was not much left of the grease—my mother having died weeks earlier—but White Dog licked hungrily at the spots, licked the blood out of his tongue on the cement steps, he was so starved.

A stray, my father thought. A beggar dog wandering backyards for scraps left by pets too well-fed to fight. Skittish, from the looks of him. Maybe locked up too long by somebody mean enough to do such things. Best to run him off. Not let him get used to food for the taking.

My father was on his walker then, balancing on one fairly good leg and four stems of aluminum, pulling along like a slow metal spider. He was no match for White Dog, but he had pride (and remembered muscles) and there was a beautiful stubborn-

mourn among ourselves as the family portrait becomes less crowded. And that is what my father learned as he studied the geneology of his people: the worth of family is now.

The reunion was over too quickly. We put the leftovers in our cars and drove away, past the homeplace with its pecan shade yards. I slowed to look at the portion of the land that is now mine, drawn from a lottery of numbers that marked the slicing of the inherited property. I had been fortunate. It was the acreage that I had always wanted, the highest part of the farm, near the small overgrown cemetery that predates the Civil War.

I will not live there again and I know it. But it is a place to return to and care about. To my mother and father it was the extent of their lives. It was where their children worked and played and I think they never wanted us to be so far away that it would not call us back. They wanted it to be in us like a delicate homing device that would play a lovely, haunting music, like the whisper of a flute. It was there that we were together. There, we were family.

1982

["Reunion"]

"Precious Lord, take my hand . . ." And we would pick it up, one by one, shyly, in our childish, nasal voices.

It was very Southern, very Bible Belt, very good those Sundays. And that was part of the silence we left with our father when we ended our holiday visits with him.

After the last of his brothers had died, my father became the patriarch of a scattered tribe. That was when the Kay-Peek get-togethers began, when the call went out and strangers with the same genetic imprints, like the presence of a ghost, began gathering each year in the old Sardis Junior High School auditorium. My father sat in the middle of all this and read tags and remembered histories that none of us knew, and he was very proud.

Not all of my brothers and sisters made all the reunions. It was never easy. So many of us, so far-flung. It always distressed my father. "You ought to plan it," he would say. "How else will you know who everybody is?"

And then he died, my father, and we were again together and we talked about the need to keep close, to see one another.

That is how the Toombs and Viola Winn Kay Reunion was started.

There will be another next year, a barbecue at the home of my niece and her husband. "There'll be more people next year," some of my sisters predicted. They sounded excited about it. And though no one said it, next year is more important. There are so many of us. As years pass, there will be fewer. We will

Old people left alone suffer silence. You can read it in them. Sometimes it is the look of fear. Silence does not pass as swiftly as the babel of voices.

Life changed for my father and mother with the one-by-one leaving of their children and the emptying of the house. Once there had been Sundays of crowded dinner tables, with Aunt Lula Peek driving up from Elberton in her black Pontiac, terrifying us with her austere bearing. Sisters returned with their husbands and children and it was all pleasant chaos, the playful fury of running through rooms and slamming doors and yard games and too much talk for any room to hold.

In the afternoon, the adults would retire to the pecan shade off the back porch and sit in chairs taken from the kitchen. Sometimes there would be a freezer of ice cream, slow-cranked in shifts, packed with block ice. Block ice from the icehouse, pick-chipped as needed or hammered in a fertilizer sack. And rock salt. The ice and rock salt mixed and spewed out the overflow in the side of the wooden freezer, leaving a stain like an elongated tear.

If he was there, my brother-in-law, Jim McBath, would go to his car and raise the trunk and bring out his accordian or guitar and sit in a straight-backed chair and begin to find music with his fingers. It was always done casually: Jim, sitting, leaning over his guitar, head cocked, his ear close to the guitar well, listening for the right tension of the strings. Pleased, he would lean back and begin strumming and we would leave our games and creep to him, close, waiting. And then he would begin, softly:

[*"Reunion"*]

orderliness—he became certain that his own family should be more than footnotes of research. Family should be together. Family should know the good and bad of each other, suffer the failures, celebrate the triumphs. Family should laugh, cry, touch. Family should have collectibles of good memories, like albums of smiling faces. Family should be glad.

He liked for us to be home on holidays (before it was a reunion). Liked the busy sound of things. Liked the heaps of food. Liked the way the men gathered, out of sight but within calling. Liked the giggly, chattering voices of his daughters and daughters-in-law. He liked driving his grandchildren and great-grandchildren around the farm in his truck, a wonderful rusting relic that could never have passed inspection and therefore had charm. (There were such piles of squealing children bouncing in the truck bed as he sputtered across fields, it seemed as though he had harvested them like produce.)

My father began each of those days the same: an early bath and shave and the ritual of selecting his suit and shirt and tie. (He liked colors but was not aware that some did not match; most often he was vividly attired.) He would piddle about in the kitchen until one of his daughters chased him out—gently. And then he would sit in his chair and watch and be pleased.

He also ended each of those days the same: sitting alone in his chair, by his desk, quietly staring into his hands. He often wore his felt hat when the good-byes were said. It was not easy to see his face and the sadness that grew on him as car after car pulled away from the front yard.

that made the absence of Thomas bearable; hurt and joy balancing precariously across the nerves of emotion.

The next time we were together was in 1973 at the funeral of my mother, and it was that sad reality that began the obsession of the family.

Before my mother's death, my father had seldom spoken of his history. I knew my uncles, but I did not know there was an aunt who had died in an epidemic in South Carolina and was buried there. I did not know of another aunt who had died in infancy. I did not know the names of my grandparents. (Once we were looking at some old photographs, and I found a picture of a woman of incredible beauty. I asked my father, "Who's this?" He looked at the picture, turned it once in his hand and gave it back to me. "That was my mother," he said simply.)

During the years that he spent alone in the house he had shared with his wife and their twelve children—children noisy as a parade—my father became intrigued with genealogy, the who-were-we bloodlines that had become obscured, if not diluted, by time and wanderings. He wanted desperately to thread those names into a single, spectacular object, like an artistic work of jewelry. He discovered, to his joy, that the novelist Pat Conroy was a relative from the Peek (his mother's) line. He learned, to his concern, that Jimmy Carter was part of it. He was never quite sure he agreed with President Carter's politics.

As he worked alone at his rolltop desk in the middle room, reading through the type-face of names on paper—cold in their

[*"Reunion"*]

has turned it into a scam. "Betty calls me every few days to send money for flowers," he said at the reunion. "Then I come home and meet the people who are supposed to be dead, walking down the street." Gary knows the need to keep things light.

We took pictures, the brothers and sisters standing by age, Lula to Gary. It is the same pose we have always taken. Only now we are older. There is more gray in the hair. We need more space per person. We talk more about out grandchildren than our children. (I confess that it pleased me to pass around the wallet-size Olan Mills picture of my own grandson, Brooks, though I am too young for the experience.)

We sat under the trees in folding lawn chairs and loosened our belts and watched the children scampering over the old truck that my father had had. They begged for rides across the fields. Someone tried to take pictures at the truck, separating the grandchildren from the great-grandchildren. No one knew exactly where the generations were divided. ("Aw, heck. Just get them all." "Can't. Not in one picture.")

"It's good, this reunion," one of my brothers-in-law said. "Keeps the family together. Lets the cousins know one another."

Someone asked: "When was the first time we were all together?"

It was the fiftieth wedding anniversary of my mother and father, in 1966. Even then, not all of their children were there. Thomas, my brother, had been killed in 1941, before Gary was born. And though my mother never treated it as a son-for-son experience, it was. In a way, Gary was the assuaging presence

SPECIAL KAY *the wisdom of terry kay*

The reunion was on an August Saturday, on a clean, blue-brilliant day of summer with enough green and bloom to hurt the eye. We met at Betty's house, which is a few hundred yards from the homeplace, in a field where we used to find flint arrowheads in corn furrows. There were fifty-eight of us. Children, grandchildren, great-grandchildren. I did not know all the names of my grandnieces and nephews. Some I had never seen. ("Whose child is that?" "That's Peggy's grandbaby." "Naw, that's not Peggy's. That one came in with Nell?" "Oh, then where's Peggy's?" "That one with red hair." "No, that's Patsy's son's baby. I've seen it before.")

The sisters took the food that had arrived in boxes and baskets and arranged it by categories—meats, vegetables, salads, desserts—on outside tables near the edge of the woods, and stationed people to fan away the flies and bugs, and Fred, Betty's husband, said grace and we ate until we ached.

We had a private family meeting, and Toombs (Junior) presided as the patriarch. (It is part of our lives that the oldest son present assumes the patriarchal role. It is not a sexist act, only a lovely heritage.) We talked about the community. Who was ill. Who had died. Cousin Allie Skelton, who lived across the branch and was like a mother to us, had not long been buried, I was playing at her house the day Franklin Roosevelt died, and I remember her sobbing, telling us about it. Betty said she had sent flowers for Cousin Allie's funeral from the Toombs Kay family, and she assessed us for our share. It is the way we want it, we have agreed. Flowers from the family. Family. All of us one. Betty had assumed much of the responsibility for that dreaded communication. Gary asserts she

"Reunion"

I do not know who decided there would be a reunion. One of the sisters, perhaps. There are a lot of sisters and they are often together, at least in twos and threes, and they do talk excessively about matters of the family.

Or maybe it was Gary who suggested the idea.

Gary is the youngest and the most earnest about keeping us together, especially in the physical way of embraces and voices and seeing. Gary rightfully believes that progeny is more than the product of mating; it is also a cry of allegiance, like a high-frequency whistle out of some European-lunged ancestor.

I know that I was surprised when Betty—one of the sisters—told me about it. Reunion was a strange word for the family. It sounded as though something had happened to rip us apart and now there would be this occasion to mend the tear. We had never had a reunion. We had simply gotten together, as families do.

"What are we going to do?" I asked Betty.

"Just have lunch. Nothing special," she said.

"Oh. Like we've always done?"

"That's right. It's just a reunion?"

bewilderment in me. She stood before me and I could see the brush strokes of makeup around her eyes and I breathed the air of her perfume samples. Then, as if on cue, she threw her arms around me and hugged me. She told me about her adventures with Lana and asked if I liked the way she looked.

I think she was trying to tell me that she understood. And she was beautiful.

1982

[*"Reflections on a Mother and Child"*]

tic tubes and through a needle almost as large as her veins. Sometimes the veins would break when she moved and the needle would be replaced in another part of her body—in her arms, in her feet, even in her head. She lay very still in our arms when we fed her, as though pulling milk from the bottle was a mighty effort. We talked to her constantly, trying to say all that we knew to say, all that might be said in years to come, because we were never certain of the next hour or the next day. It did not matter that she could not understand us; we had to talk to her.

We stayed at Egleston for days, my wife and I swapping shifts, and I learned to trust the doctors and nurses who were caretakers of our child. They were gentle and concerned and understood the panic that would not leave us until we could see Heather begin to stretch back into health.

Heather is ten years old now. She has blue eyes and dimples and soon she will need braces on her teeth. She is becoming a young woman and those same intuitive senses possessed by her mother are beginning to swim in her. She senses the perplexity I feel in losing the baby she has been. She senses it and yet she cannot resist the lure of womanhood that is pulling on her like a magnetic field. Sometimes she holds me desperately, as though telling me she is sorry all this is happening. She understands, as her mother understands, there is a privacy I cannot share, and that I am confused.

Last Christmas she went shopping with our new neighbor, Lana, and they played girlish games at cosmetic counters in department stores. When they returned home, Heather saw the

poised above his son on the sacrifice stone, taking God's test to heart without a question, drawing back only at the last dangerous second. God had cut it short with Abraham, we were told, but Abraham never whimpered about it. He was willing to give up his child because God had commanded it. Abraham was a man we could learn from, they said. But I was not Abraham and I knew I could not give up my child. Not that way. Not that willingly.

I did not sleep that night. I stayed awake and wondered and could not stop the trembling. I do not think I have ever felt so alone.

I have never asked my wife when her own fear, the fear that she had handled so magnificently, began to spill out. I know that she tried to bring me into her grief, but could not. (I am not strong when my children are hurting; she knows that and always braces for the failures of my self-pity.) During all the days of Heather's illness, I saw her put aside her privacy only once. It was with the visit of a minister. He came into the room and in his soft minister's voice, told her he was sorry and sad about Heather. I saw her drink comfort from his eyes as though her lips were pressed on the cold silver of a Communion cup. Though I understood it then (and do now), it was painful, because I could not give her the assurance she most needed. One person alone can never fill the droughts of emotion in another.

The antibiotics—the remarkable antibiotics—were fed into Heather intravenously from upside-down bottles, through plas-

[*"Reflections on a Mother and Child"*]

He spoke of remarkable antibiotics, of the telltale signs of improvement or failure, of having confidence, of patience, of parental care. "Not long ago, we wouldn't have given this much of a chance," he confessed. "Now we do."

It was well after midnight. I asked my wife to go home and rest. An awful anger snapped into her eyes and she told me, no, she would not leave. "My baby's sick," she said. "I can't leave." I had never seen her so determined. "You go," she told me, almost as an order. I knew she meant it. She wanted to be alone.

On the drive home I thought of Heather, so tiny a pillow could have been her entire bed. I thought of the needle that had been slipped into her and how it must have hurt, being with strangers. I think I cried. And maybe I prayed. Or cursed. (Sometimes there is little difference between the two.)

I thought of my wife, aching in the privacy that she has always called about her when bothered. I thought about the silence that had somehow fallen between us during the night. There had been no sorrowful embraces—like those in photographs of the great holocausts with people hanging to one another in heaps, slowly dressing each other in shrouds of expectation. We had been matter-of-fact—what to do at home, the schedule of when I would return—and quiet and awkward.

I also thought of something else on that drive home (the mind skitters wildly when it is frightened). It was from earlier years, a poster picture of Abraham and Isaac that had been thumbtacked to the wall of a Sunday school room at Vanna Methodist Church. Abraham, old, old Abraham, with his knife

always of baby talc. I loved holding her when she was stripped and swimming into sleep across the skin of my bare chest, warm and soft and purring.

My wife and I had laughed about her pregnancy with Heather. Such timing, such poor timing. We had planned a trip to Europe that summer, had planned to borrow the money as we would have borrowed it to purchase a car, and it was supposed to make us realize how grand the world outside Decatur, Georgia, really was. Then the pregnancy. "Oh, well," we said, "we don't know any languages, anyway. Maybe we should name her for some European country."

Her. Yes, her. My wife was very sure the child would be a girl, just as she had been sure that Jon, before Heather, would be a boy. Jon was supposed to be the last of our children, and before Jon, Scott. Terri and Scott. Girl and boy. That was the order of families in the 1960's. Neat. Clean. Two children. Two cars. Two bathrooms. It was the era of the great "one each" dream. Four children was considered excessive.

"Doesn't matter. I like large families," I said, philosophically.

The doctor who led me into the hallway outside the waiting room was young and athletic. I remember thinking that he would be a weekend athlete—touch football, softball, soccer. (The mind wanders even when all senses beg it to be still; the mind has jitters that cannot easily be checked.)

The young, athletic doctor told me bluntly that Heather might have been dead by morning. "Be grateful for your wife's instincts," he said. "Be grateful for Dr. White. He's a great doctor, a great one."

[*"Reflections on a Mother and Child"*]

believe because there is a weight of too much fear and the long minutes of silence become as sluggish as sleep.

I heard her cry through the walls. I knew it was Heather. My wife's eyes (they are large, like pools) filled and she looked toward the crying like an animal mother locked away from her young. I swallowed hard. My throat ached.

I cannot remember who told us—Dr. White, perhaps—but the tests were conclusive: Heather had meningitis.

It is an acid word, meningitis; a hissing, awful word. It is a word that speaks of squirming parasites with wide mouths and gutless bodies, bloating like balloons on the liquids that feed life. It is a word of death, mysterious and as frightening as the assault of wars.

It is strange how you feel when you know death is close. It is a feeling of bravery, of horror, of calm, of screams that do not rise. It is a numb, hypnotic feeling, like a slumber crowded with too many dreams.

My wife and I stood, not touching, as though we were separately responsible for the message we had received, and we listened to explanations we could not understand, from voices that were distant and sounded like fragments of static.

"She . . . tonight . . . feed her intra . . . know more tomorrow . . . you . . ."

Heather was only six weeks old. She had not been a large child at birth. I could cup her in both my hands and her legs would dangle about my wrists and tickle them when she kicked. She was light, almost weightless in her doll clothes that smelled

"He doesn't mind," she said to me, defiantly. "You should know him better than that."

Yes. She was right. He is beautiful with babies, this Dr. Penn White, this large man with large hands. He handles babies as though he is holding delicate material and is awed by its silk or velvet feel. Babies smile a lot around him, even those who are sick. Babies seem to know him.

As he held Heather and looked and listened, his face became heavy with the same fear that my wife wore like makeup. My wife saw it. "What is it?" she asked.

He shook his head. "I want to take her to Egleston," he said. "I don't know. I can't find anything wrong, why there would be a fever. There should be something, but I can't find it."

God, I thought. Dear God. My wife held Heather and blew into her face and talked quietly to her.

I do not remember going to Henrietta Egleston Hospital, or how we got into the examination room, or the faces of the nurses who took our baby from us. They were antiseptic people, coolly white. They did not talk to us. Heather did not cry.

"They're going to do a spinal tap." Dr. White explained. "They're good." he said. "They're good." He wandered nervously, pacing, thinking. It was as though his mind was whirling through microfilms of textbooks, reading for the one sentence that would tell him something new and certain.

Waiting is most terrible when someone else—some stranger— controls the time. Waiting is most terrible when you are not certain, when you want to believe and you do not know what to

[*"Reflections on a Mother and Child"*]

I have lied because *it*—what ever *it* is—belongs not to me, but to my wife. And knowing that, I am isolated from those secrets that pass from mother to child, child to mother, in their radar beeps of understanding.

Once, in late May, or early June, 1972, 1 saw proof of *it*.

It happened on a night when my wife was visiting Mildred, our neighbor, and returned home late. When she came into the house there was an aura of tension about her, like a primordial alert.

She asked, "Where's Heather?"

"In bed with Terri," I said. "Terri wanted to hold her."

"Is she all right?"

"She's fine. Why?"

"I think I'll check on her."

There was a fever. My wife knew it by touch. She leaned to Heather and put her face on Heather's forehead. She gathered Heather into her arms and pulled her close to her breast and began to sway in the dance of mothers and whisper in a soft repetition of chanting, "It's all right, it's all right. . . ." Her face burned with fear.

"I'm going to call Dr. White," she said.

"It's late," I protested. "She's not very hot. He'll be asleep."

"I don't care. I'm calling him."

She called and talked and answered questions and Dr. White told her to bring Heather to his office. It did not matter that it was late.

ately after childbirth and touched the faces of a million babies and picked hers from the lot.

When the children were tiny, she could hear their soft whimpers, over a thunder of surrounding noise. She could awake from sleep two heartbeats before they cried, could tell by touch where they hurt and why and how badly. *(You have seen it: mothers in playgrounds, reading from paperback books as their children scurry about them like squirrels, and then the sudden yelp and the one uplifted face, jerked out of its book, knowing the yelp above all others.)*

She knew also the exact balance of prejudice, holding the one who most needed it, keeping the others aware that soon, very soon, she would also hold them.

All of this has always awed me, partly because it is her nature (and, I am guessing, the nature of most mothers) and partly because I have never truly belonged to it. It is something beyond my reach and touch, as though I am intruding.

I have lied about it to myself, of course. I have said I know my children well, that I can sense them and transport myself by astral projection into their minds and into their emotions. It is my pride that makes me lie, or my jealousy of my wife's gifts. (I am fascinated by the mysticism of those types of precognitions. Such as the one of my own mother when Thomas, my brother, was killed. My mother knew before she was told, as though Thomas had been to her in an electric pass-by.)

"Reflections on a Mother and Child"

There is something—rich as primeval blood—that exists between my wife and our children. Something shared before birth when the child, floating inside its web of umbilical membranes, drew freely from its mother. It is a private and holy sensation, like an unnamed religion.

Because of this something, this exquisite, undefinable something, my wife knew instantly each time she became pregnant, as though the dewdrop of fetus had its own sudden personality, and, always, she would wrap herself in a blanket at night and curl into a nest of fabric and wait until there was movement (or imagined movement). Then she would uncurl from her nest and prepare herself in a celebration of gladness.

Intuitively, she knew much about each child. She knew which would be girl, which would be boy. She knew, almost precisely, if the child would deliver itself early, or on time, or late. She knew their weights and lengths, the color of their eyes, that each would be born bald. She could have been blindfolded immedi-

my mother. I read the bare facts of their years cut into the granite of their headstone and think how closed they are from us, how deep in the ground. I think about the loneliness that my father endured after Mother died (he did not hear well and sometimes you could slip up on him, unnoticed, and watch him staring off numbly, resigned, knowing the only thing left was the quick hugs of grandchildren and the fuss of children).

He is dead and I look for him in my own face and in the faces of my own children. Sometimes I see him. And that is enough.

1981

[*"T. H. Kay, Proprietor"*]

did not have a wanderlust (the fartherest he ever traveled was New York City for the national Farm Bureau convention; he returned with a flannel shirt for me and tales of walking for blocks in the basement of Macy's). He fished occasionally, but never hunted. He did not play games with us or lie about being a grand athlete. He did not curse, except to mutter an occasional mild expletive. I doubt if he ever drank a quart of whiskey in his life, though he enjoyed his wine and sometimes a cold beer, and during one illness, he sipped a good quantity of sherry that I would buy for him as medicine. He did not do idle things because he was never idle. Even when he could not walk, when he ached inside with the cancer that was there before he knew it, when he became dizzy in the sun, he would drag himself along with his walker and try to hoe weeds from around his trees.

He was also a man who knew hurt and in his last years his great pride obsessed him and he would cry with the wailing moan of an injury that he could not, or would not, understand. It was, to him, the obsession of betrayal and it turned into a kind of internal evil that blinded his reasoning. I ached for him. I ached for him because I, too, knew that despair. I, too, had felt the evil of betrayal. I would say, "Look, Daddy, you can't dwell on those things. There's too much that's better. There's too much for you to teach us, to leave us." And he would look at me and his small eyes would be red from crying and he would simply shake his head. And I knew what he felt.

He is dead and we have buried him. When I return to Royston I go by Rose Hill Cemetery and visit his grave and the grave of

SPECIAL KAY *the wisdom of terry kay*

The last time I visited my father before he died, I sat beside his bed and listened as he wept and begged for me, for anyone, to tell him why he had been condemned to live in such great pain. He was coherent that day. I know it. He was thin and his eyes were filmed and his mouth, without his teeth, was drawn into a wrinkled O, and his head was buried into the indention of his pillow. But he was coherent, and as I dabbed water over his lips with a cloth he began to whisper about his animals.

"I wouldn't do this to them," he said. "I wouldn't let them suffer. They're keeping me alive and I want to die, son."

He knew the word euthanasia: death by mercy. He knew he would die and be folded into the ground and become part of its fertilizer, and he could not understand why someone had not loaded the slender barrel of a hypodermic with some sweet, colorless liquid that would seize the cancer at its heart and kill it and him with the pleasantness of a long sleep.

When I left that day, I kissed him on the forehead and his face sighed in pain from the touch of my lips. I told him I loved him. I'm glad I did. He had already died when they called me a week later. Gary said he died at midnight. They had given his body tiny sips of morphine that day and the pain had eased its ravaging—quietly he surrendered to the history that had so fascinated him.

My father? He was not a character. There was not an ounce of Jeeter Lester or Snuffy Smith in him. He did not wear bib overalls and stand around the cotton gin chewing tobacco and clucking his tongue over hard times, though he did love those men. He

[*"T. H. Kay, Proprietor"*]

our visits home. During his hard, working years, he had been a silent man who seldom laughed. We knew little of his history, or how he felt about things. He had principle, little codes of conduct, and when he delivered those messages to us it was like a brief litany that we should hear and remember. When he began to tell his stories he laughed often and his eyes watered with merriment or with a sudden, striking vision that snatched him out of his age and landed him in another time. I think he loved our amazement. I think he loved teasing us. (Once he told my wife about making a churn of beer from skimmings of cane syrup. He said he put it away in the smoke house and covered the top with a milkcloth. When he went back, a few days later, he found that a rat had plopped on the top of the milkcloth and died. "You know," he said, "I almost didn't drink that beer.")

He told stories of crimson clover festivals, with red fields waving like dance. Stories of the freshmen boys at the University of Georgia and how some of them (he was one, but never admitted it) became agitated with a certain train engineer and found a way to urinate on his head when he stuck it out of the cab of the train as it rounded a curve. Stories of selling Bibles in Kentucky. Stories of men he had known, men so rich in character they could have slept wrapped in the linen sheets of literature. He had a remarkable memory. "In '25 . . . ," he would recount. Or, "In 1933, I sold . . ." He told all of us that he could remember back to 1893, or "maybe it was 1894." It was his earliest memory, of a fly crawling over the fly net on his crib, finding a hole, and diving into the crib with him.

My father thought most of it was unnecessary. He had little need for it. Set yourself steady. Don't compromise. He was that kind of man.

He did not change after my mother died, but he was different. He became interested in genealogy and spent much of his time researching and tidying up the mysteries of his history. He started with the cemeteries of his family and my mother's family. New headstones. New granite borders. We often walked those cemeteries and I listened as he told the stories of those who were buried, as though the coffins were private libraries that had been locked shut and forgotten. Once we were at the Vanna cemetery and I asked him about a miniature grave. "That's a baby," he said. "I remember that child. Used to be that children were tied in chairs when their parents went outside to work. The mother of that child went out to milk one morning and tied her baby in the rocking chair and put it in front of the fireplace The child rocked itself over into the fire." I whispered, "My God." My father kicked at a rock on top of the sunken grave and then walked away.

On Easter Sunday Gary gave me two cassette tapes of an interview he had had with our father in 1975. On the tapes, in his voice (which is strange to hear again), were stories of his grandparents and parents, his brothers and sisters, his uncles and aunts, stories of my mother, of my brothers and sisters, of the mule, Kate, who could jump fences like a trained horse.

My father was a marvelous storyteller but none of us knew it until Mother died and he was forced to say something to us on

[*"T. H. Kay, Proprietor"*]

told, we are different). Those bred to it cannot bleed it from them. It is as incurable as leprosy, as unmistakable as a mutation, as noble as the collective rush of mankind to leap evolution and reside among the gods. It is both poetic and demonic. My father was a bearer of that history. He carried it in the pods of his organs, and he and my mother endowed each of us, their children, with tracings of ancient cultures, like microscopic germs. They endowed us with the heat of work, with stubbornness, with pride, with failings.

My father was born in the bridge years of the nineteenth and twentieth centuries and when he was stretching into boyhood and manhood, his arms spread in both directions of time. He had the powder burns of the Civil War on the hand that reached into the past and the searing heat of rocket ships scorching the hand that groped for the future. He would live in a world that changed with epidemic speed, like an unstoppable madness. It would be a world of wars and depressions, of prophets bellowing about doom, of peace-peddlers and hate-baiters. It would be a world smogged by the thick, gray cloud of internal combustion motors, a world that would gut its own earth like a starving predator feeding on itself, slurping up its own blood. It would be a world drunk on moods—jazz to rock, Prohibition bootleg to frozen daiquiris, the sex of falling and rising hemlines and necklines, zoot suits, and Nehru jackets. It would be a world talking gibberish to itself on the analyst's couch, a world of split atoms and soy beans turned into steak. It would be a world impossible to comprehend; the pace was too furious.

journal in his lap and I wondered if he had written anything about my mother's death. He had not. Not in that journal, not at that time. I think he could not force himself to finalize her dying.

And there, that night as we talked about family and old stories, and I watched his fingers drumming against the *Planters Register,* I knew suddenly that the inheritance I would receive from my father was at his fingertips. I knew that I was bound inextricably to him and to his history and that the writings at his fingertips and the journals he would later fill in his day-by-day habit of diary-keeping were his testaments. I knew that he was a patriarch who had long ago made his covenants with living. That night, with the flash of Suddenly Knowing, I began to write a word play of my father, and the setting was the middle room, at his rolltop desk, where he lived. The first words of that play were: "I know this room. I can walk it with my fingers in the blackest of nights and tell you the whispers of every scar in its walls and on its floors. My father lives here, in this room. He told me these stories...."

I wanted it to be a play of a Southern father and his family, of the privacy and pride of their growing and of the one-by-one leaving of the children. I wanted it to carry the heavy space of the left-alone parents in a silent house. I wanted it to say this is a history that was noisy, that burned intensely, then died away.

It was a romantic thought, soggy with sentiment, but not entirely wrong. Perhaps history is the essence—the elusive, indulgent, invisible essence—of the Southerner (if, as we are

[*"T. H. Kay, Proprietor"*]

"Lindbergh flying the Atlantic."

Yes, I thought. Yes, that would be it. Lindbergh, alone, daring to be first because he believed. Lindbergh fighting what he could not know, forcing his tiny craft to skim air currents above the shimmering glass of an ocean, his eyes straining to find France or England. My father would have liked being Lindbergh. Perhaps he even pretended that he was, as he guided his plow in the monotonous silence of work.

It was on one of the visits with my father that I had an experience of Suddenly Knowing. It was, again, late at night. We were in the middle room, in the chest cavity of the house, and my father was sitting in his padded armchair, pulled next to his rolltop desk. He had his feet propped against the aluminum bar of his walker and his right arm and hand rested across the shelf of his desk and his fingers drummed rhythmically on a book. The title of the book was the *Planters Register,* published in 1895. It was a journal, my father's journal. In it was a history of our lives—of diseases, the births and names of cattle, the layout of crops, the sad, short notes of disaster. And for a moment I was back to the day of my mother's death, back to the exact time that I had stepped into the middle room and into the arms of a neighbor I had not seen in years. It was an eerie day, an eerie experience. My mother was dead. Dead. She was not in her kitchen. Other women were there, searching the cabinets for spices and dishes, quietly preparing their mourners' meals. My father was sitting in his chair when I entered. I knelt and embraced him and said, "I'm sorry, Dad. I'm sorry." He had his

God, he was a worker. When it rained us out of the fields, we went to the corn crib. When the rain stopped, we pulled bitterweeds from the pasture until it became dry enough to go back to the fields (My father had two stories about work and his children. He said once that he had twelve children because he needed them to work the farm; he said another time that he ran the farm, as well as his nursery, because he had to have something for his children to do.)

I know this: he loved work. He loved to he in the fields, his hand on the stock of a plow or around the handle of a hoe or shovel. He loved the evenness of rows, the muscular sweep of terracing, the delicate green of finger-long plants breaking through the soil-crust in spring. He loved the smell of the earth. He loved the song of a steel plow slicing through dirt and clay, a song that ran up the plow's heel and beam and along the handles and leaped into the hands and tickled the biceps and shoulders. He believed, for years, that tractors ruined the earth in their straight-line gutting of rows. (I am sorry he never read Steinbeck's *Grapes of Wrath.*)

After my mother died in 1973 (in a clean, sudden stroke, like an ambush), I would visit my father, often without my family, and he and I would sit together until late at night and he would drink his homemade grape wine mixed with Pepsi Cola, and we would talk about things that were grand and unique. One summer night, with the windows open and the woods below us filled with singing, I asked him about the most amazing incident that had happened during his lifetime. He said without pause,

[*"T. H. Kay, Proprietor"*]

proprietor. It was a word that had dignity and integrity. It meant that he was responsible. It also meant that he would do damn well what he pleased with the plants and trees that he grew. He gave away much of it. Down-on-luck farmers counting out change from their bib purse for a single tree could drive away with the car's trunk stuffed with grape, pear, apple, any kind of plant they mumbled a desire for—except pecan. T. H. Kay, Proprietor, was not timid about scolding a man for failing to follow his planting instructions.

He was an expert with trees and it was with trees that he found peace. (I think that is what I wanted my sons to see on Easter Sunday, but they would not have seen it for I must admit I have not found my trees, my peace.) On Sundays, when other men carted their children to churches to sing and pray to God, or themselves, my father would dress in his suit and tie (always a mistake of colors) and he would walk among his trees and plants and care for them. He did not hear sermons, he performed them with the surgery of his budding knife.

In those years, in Vanna, at the home place, my father became a hard, stubborn man who earned respect because he lived respect. I never heard more than five men call him anything but Mr. Kay. He taught carpentry, ran the canning plant, was chairman of the board of education of Vanna Junior High School for more than thirty years (it took that long to get his children through), was president of the Farm Bureau, and an arbiter of disputes that baffled other men. And he was a worker. Oh, my

He stayed a year, went home for a year, then returned to Madison in 1912 and remained until he was graduated in 1915 with a high school education. He attended the University of Georgia briefly, then accepted a position as superintendent of farms at Madison A & M. There he met my mother, Mamie Viola Winn, who had ambitions of being a nurse.

"First time I saw her I thought she had a pretty big nose," he would later say, "but she was pretty nice otherwise." He said this with humor and tenderness. From his first sighting of Mamie Viola Winn, my father was taken. They were married a few months later, in 1916, in Madison, before a Judge Winter, a man who had vowed during the Civil War never to shave until the South had defeated the North. He was very old in 1916 and his beard, my mother would tell me, was waist-length. The wedding and Judge Winter must have been memorable. As the eleventh child, I would bear the judge's name: Terry Winter.

Over the next dozen years, my parents lived in a number of places, trailing after the carpentry trade that my father had mastered. Every two years, there was another child. In 1928, they settled at the home place. The home place was a forty-odd-acre farm willed to my mother and her heirs by my grandfather Winn. It became the location of Kay Nurseries, successors to the Hartwell Nurseries, which had been established in 1881. My father's stationery carried that banner, which included the notation: T. H. Kay, Proprietor.

Proprietor. I thought of that word on Easter Sunday. It was a good word for my father. He was not just a farmer. He was a

[*"T. H. Kay, Proprietor"*]

and I tell it the same way: we have never been hit as hard by anyone else.

My father was born in 1892, in Hart County, the city of Hartwell, on Benson Street. He was born before the use of automobiles and airplanes and radio and television. His uncle, Zachariah Peek, had fought in the Civil War and my father loved him because Uncle Zack was a little crazy from the shelling and had renamed himself Zachariah, Beauregarde, General Bee, Stonewall Jackson, Robert E. Lee, Peek. Sometimes I think Uncle Zack was the greatest pleasure of my father's youth.

My father's parents were dead before he was a teenager and he was shuffled about in the foster families of relatives like a migrant. It was a displacement and hurt that he seldom spoke about but would never forget.

He was, he remembered, around eighteen when a friend named Harry McGill told him about a school called Madison A & M, where a boy could work for his education. "Go with me," urged Harry. "Why?" my father asked. "Even if they teach you how to farm, you've got to have a farm to do it." Harry assured him that land was no problem; after all, Harry's brother-in-law was Asa Candler Jr., who owned the first automobile to roll through Hart County, and Asa Junior would buy each of them a farm.

My father had the equivalence of a seventh-grade education when he arrived by train (without Harry McGill) in 1910 to begin study and work at Madison A & M. "I ain't got a penny," he announced, "but I'll work."

months in the hospital with kidney stones and a slipped disc, or something, and it began a life of pain and illness. We became close during that summer because I worked the fields for him. It was 1954—the same year that Aunt Lula Peek died of cancer—and it was a baking, hot summer, a summer of withered crops and oppressiveness. My brother John and I tried to farm in that killing heat; tried, but failed. I would visit my father in the hospital and tell him of the sad news of the weather and the spindly, dying corn and burned cotton, and he would say, "Do what you can, son. Keep working."

We became close, but that closeness did not break him. We were father and son, not friends or partners. Each had his place and place was imperative to my father. That fall, when he was recuperating, I returned late from a football game in south Georgia, bruised and tired and aching. At seven o'clock on Saturday morning I was out working. At ten I came into the house for water and my mother told me to remove the trash from the back porch. "Aw, I'll get around to it," I said sardonically. My father was leaning against the kitchen cabinets. He reached me in one step, caught me by my shirt with his left hand, lifted me from the chair, and struck me flush across the face with his right fist. I hit the wall "Son, don't ever talk to your mother that way," he said quietly. "Yessir," I replied.

He did not hit me because I was disobedient (that would have been cause for assassination), but because I had violated, by the tone of my voice, respect for my mother. Years later he would do the same thing to my brother Gary, for the same reason. Gary

[*"T. H. Kay, Proprietor"*]

"Everytime I say gee the damn mule goes to the right; everytime I say haw, it goes to the left" (My father looked at me incredulously. He said, "Son, if you had a lick of sense you'd know gee means right and haw means left. It wasn't the damn, crazy mule, it was the damn, crazy boy.")

My father had reason to be concerned about me.

I remembered those things on my Easter Sunday walk across the fields. Remembered the awesome strength of my father's body as he lifted two-hundred-pound sacks of fertilizer on the brace of his shoulder. Remembered the day he told me that I could plow a furrow as straight as my brother Thomas, who was killed when I was three. Remembered the rumble of his voice as he cleared his throat and warned us of his presence. Remembered the steel in his stare.

We did not always understand one another, my father and I. I performed for his approval, but he gave it sparingly, inched it out, qualified it, made me stretch for it. He saw me play one game of football. Against Stephens County, who could have beaten the University of Georgia that year. Our entire team was less than heroic, but I did score a touchdown against the third-team reserves and I thought he would be proud. "Son," he told me after the game, "it seems like a senseless way to get beat up."

He was sick that year. He had never before been sick, had never had a cold. Smallpox shots would not take on him. He could rub poison oak over his body and never break out. Kerosene cured his cuts and scratches overnight. But he awoke screaming one morning in the spring and he spent the next few

He would not have treated his other children so cruelly. He would have listened and then advised them to write, not to waste money on telephone calls from pay booths. He hung up on me. He did not say, "I'm glad," or "I'll tell your mother," or anything. He slammed down the receiver with his long-distance vigor and left the violence of that act ringing in my ear. It was a long time before I understood what he had done and why: it was for me, not for his other children. My father knew me well. He knew that I was lonely, that I wanted to be home. He knew I had to be angered to stay. And he knew I had to stay.

For men of my father's age and environment (Southern, rural), it was not easy to turn out sons and send them away to jobs or schools or wars. Sons were never quite finished with being boys. Sons were too impressionable, too easily lured by the charm of carnival promises.

I was no different, except, perhaps, my father felt I was more of a risk than his other sons. I was impatient, quick to temper. I was a dreamer. I was the one who hurried the family to the fields, then found a way to avoid the task. I was the con, the one who once sold three cotton stalks for a dollar apiece, telling the New York visitor that he had just purchased one of the rare, delicate plants of the South, warning him that it might not survive the harsh climate of the North, but not to worry if it began to wilt before be got out to the highway. I was the one who had the nerve (the stupidity) to curse in front of my father, telling him that his damn, crazy mule did not know gee from haw.

[*"T. H. Kay, Proprietor"*]

and let it slide through the funnel of my hand into a pyramid of sand. I wanted them to see me pulling weeds and trimming sprouts from fruit trees with my pocket knife. I do not know if they would have understood any of it, as I never fully understood it with my father, but I wanted them to be with me.

Alone that day, where I could not be seen, I cried over my father. I think it was the first time I had wept painfully since his death. The home, the home place, was empty without him. The only thing left was the music of the land, and the memories.

I called him once from the Catskill Mountains. It was 1955. I was seventeen and working as a busboy in one of those tiny villages that rest beautifully in the forests of lovely white birches. I had earned exactly one hundred dollars for a week's work and I wanted to celebrate.

"What do you want?" my father asked sternly.

"Nothing," I said. "I just wanted to call and see how things are and to tell you and Mother that I earned exactly one hundred dollars this week."

There was a pause of long-distance static and then my father, said, "Are you paying for this call, or am I?"

"I am, Daddy. I'm at a pay station with a fistful of quarters."

"You're paying for it?" he asked again.

"That's right."

"Well, son, you don't have a hundred dollars anymore, do you?" And then he hung up.

Then, when I was seventeen, I cried over his blunt disregard for my loneliness. Dammit, it was my money, my time, my need.

SPECIAL KAY *the wisdom of terry kay*

Last Easter Sunday I returned home, to the home place, and attended services at Vanna United Methodist Church to hear my brother John preach. Some of us gathered for lunch in the house where my father and mother had lived and reared their twelve children. The house is now owned by my nephew and his wife. They have painted and remodeled and stippled the ceilings and there is a fresh, open, just-married feeling about the rooms. On Easter Sunday they tried mightily to make it our home again, to give it over to us, to say, "It will always be here for you." I know they are earnest. I know they want us to feel at ease. But it is a strange house, just vaguely familiar. And it is not because of the cosmetic surgery of a carpenter's tools; it is the absence of what had been there. The home of my parents, of my brothers and sisters, no longer exists.

In the afternoon of Easter Sunday I walked the farm, as I had walked it with my father. Around the horseshoe road that circled the house, past the Cedrus deodara we had planted together when it was waist-high (now tall as a tree), up to the old cemetery bordering our farm with the Ginns, down along the gully of the property line to where the pine stand had been (now cut and brown with clutter). I walked the fields where we had planted cotton and corn and grain and peach trees, where we had worked and turned brown in the heat of still, summer days. I wanted my sons to walk with me, but they were satisfied with play or television or something. I wanted to tell them, in my father's voice, about the growing of things. I wanted them to watch me dig a handful of dirt and crush it soft with my fingers

"T. H. Kay, Proprietor"

My father had a fear of cancer. His Aunt Lula Peek had died of the disease in 1954, slowly, in torture, and the ugliness of that suffering—the ugliness of the two-syllable sound of the word—had remained with him. He often said that he wanted to die quickly, wanted death to surprise him with a clean, sudden stroke, like an ambush. When they found cancer in his prostate in 1969 and cored it out and removed his testicles, he believed that it was controlled. (They told him it was controlled; they did not believe he would be alive when it began to grow again.) Then, in autumn of 1979, he was watching a television program that gave symptoms of cancer and he knew. From that day, he began his dying. From that day be began to understand the unending feast that was occurring inside him, like a worm crawling through the hard earth of his body, leaving it weak and sunken.

He had said he would live to be one hundred.

He did not. He died on August 16, 1980, in his eighty-eighth year.

And I have missed him.

Family & Heritage

[*Foreword*]

Strange Dance of White Dog," quickly done. I did not think anyone would find it very interesting.

One man did, however: Joe Beck.

Joe, an attorney and writer, sent a letter of compliment. In it he said he thought I had made a mistake, though he enjoyed the story. He thought I should write a book about this strange dog. I knew immediately he was right. I began *To Dance with the White Dog* that day.

(Writers can be—often are—astonishingly dumb, which may be why many of them are successful. They start with a smidgen of knowledge and experience and set about tracking a story through the hot-scented ground of their imagination. It is an intoxicating process of discovery.)

When Judy Long, editor-in-chief of Hill Street Press, proposed this collection of essays (as she called them), she produced a list of titles. I remembered four or five of them. Then I began to scan-read them, to call back the what and why of them, and the memories were special.

I hope the reader finds in them some enjoyment.

They were written by a man accidentally, but gladly, engaged in an interesting profession.

Terry Kay
Athens, Georgia

write what would become *The Year the Lights Came On.*

I was thirty-five years old, terrified by the prospects of writing a hundred thousand words, I had no idea it was only a beginning.

As I have suggested in the dedication page of this work, it would be my long-time friend, Lee Walburn, who would force the magazine stories from me.

He would call with an idea, tell me the subject suited me perfectly, give me a pep talk that Knute Rockne would have applauded, and I would feel my fingertips beginning to itch. "I hate magazine writing," I would tell him, "but I'll do it."

The greatest con artists in the world are friends.

Yet from such stories, miracles can happen.

When my father died, Lee gently urged me to write about him. It took seven months to complete the story. Afterward, Lee and I were having lunch, talking about it, and I said to him, "Maybe I should have mentioned the white dog."

"What white dog?" he asked.

And I told him about the white dog that appeared at my father's home immediately after the death of my mother.

Lee became agitated. "You fool," he growled, "that *was* the story. Now write it."

It would be years before I obeyed his instruction. When I did write it—on orders from Jim Townsend, who was then working as an advisor for Lee—it was a short magazine piece, "The

[*Foreword*]

pilot ("The Great Santini") and knows how to laser-lock on a target when he becomes passionate about his mission.

One afternoon, Pat called Anne Barrett, his editor at Houghton Mifflin in Boston. He told her he had just finished reading 150 pages of a manuscript being written by his friend, Terry Kay. He added that he thought it was wonderful. A few days later I received a letter from Anne, begging me for the manuscript Pat Conroy had raved about.

I did not know about his conversation with her, and other than the "Teenage Quarterback" story, I had never written a word of fiction (though some people I had interviewed over the years thought otherwise).

Pat suggested that I had two options. One, I could tell Anne the truth—that he had lied. Two, I could write 150 pages.

I think he knew what I would do.

In one month, on a manual typewriter, I wrote exactly 150 pages consisting of four short stories with the setting alternating between plowing a mule on a northeast Georgia farm and what I thought of as my Hollywood years. The transition line, thin as a spider's rope, was the incongruity of those experiences. I did not correct the spelling, or the punctuation. I submitted it with an honest cover letter saying I was not impressed with any of it, though I believed a novel might be fashioned out of the vignette about getting electricity on the farm where I was reared.

I knew Anne Barrett would write a soothing, gracious rejection, and that would be that.

To my surprise, she offered me a contract and an advance to

"What do you want?" I asked. "A monthly film column?"

"Well, yeah," he told me. "That, and some stories."

"What kind of stories?"

"I don't know," Jim said. "Stories. You're a writer and I'm going to prove it to you."

Each month I would deliver my essay on movies to Jim. Each month he would ask me to begin work on a story, failing always to tell me what he meant.

One day, weary of the badgering, I said to him, "I'll write a story if you'll let me do a mixture of truth and fiction."

"Fine," he said. In fact, I think it delighted him. Jim loved to mix fiction with fact. It made better reading. He also understood that writers needed to be jump-started, that it was important for writers to learn through encouragement as well as mistakes. To Jim, rejecting someone was a sad business, not a triumph, and he did as little of it as possible, especially if he had chosen a writer as his *find*. It was his genius as an editor. Give writers an opportunity to be published and they would learn by doing, and they would become better writers.

And that, I believe, was what he was telling me by his insistence that I create a story—definition unnecessary—for him. One afternoon I wrote "I was a Teenage Quarterback," which is included in this collection and is a perfect example of error-burdened first fiction. Yet, it was popular and it prompted my friend Pat Conroy to encourage me to write a novel.

I did not want to write a novel. Told Pat I had no interest in it. It was the wrong thing to say to him. Pat is the son of a Marine

[*Foreword*]

Bill Robinson—and, of course, Bisher—I learned discipline and the richness of language. (During those years, I began a writing exercise of occasionally copying Bisher's columns. I wanted to *feel* the words, wanted to pretend they had fallen from my fingers, not his. It is an exercise I still practice when brain-locked over a story, and I remain in awe over the power that is transferred from the likes of John Steinbeck, Thomas Wolfe, William Faulkner, Flannery O'Connor, Jesse Stuart, Pat Conroy, Gabriel Garcia Marquez. I have never understood why such an exercise is not used in classrooms.)

In 1965, I was awarded the position of Entertainment Editor of the *Journal* and for eight years covered film and theater (and sometimes nightclubs and concerts). I did the hobnobbing thing with such celebrities as Alfred Hitchcock, Vincent Price, Jimmy Stewart, Ann-Margret, Kim Novak, Burt Reynolds, Vanessa Redgrave, Gregory Peck, Michael Caine, Hal Holbrook, Paul Newman, Pearl Bailey. It was a great job, yet, in those days, journalism was a low-paying, tiring profession, and in 1973 I resigned from the *Journal* to accept a position as creative director for a film and television production company specializing in commercials and industrials. The pay was an astronomical $350 per week.

I believed my writing career was essentially over.

Jim Townsend called. The founding editor of *Atlanta Magazine* and one of the most persuasive men I have known, Jim was then editing a magazine called *Georgia*. He announced to me over the telephone that he wanted me to become a regular contributor.

educated man. The position available was for a strong-bodied high school dropout. I think I won him over when he asked, "Where did you study journalism? The University of Georgia?"

I thought my answer would give me the boot, but I had to be truthful. "I've never had a course in journalism," I confessed.

A smile cracked on his face. "Good," he said. "We won't have to knock all that nonsense out of you."

And, so, in 1959—October, I believe it was—I resigned my position with the Reserve Life Insurance Company of Dallas, Texas, and became a multipurpose journalism flunky.

A few months into the job, I asked Linton Broome, who was the executive editor, if I might submit an occasional story. Linton welcomed the offer. It is not easy to fill the columns of a weekly newspaper with two or three contributors.

At the *Decatur-DeKalb News* I covered sports events and city hall meetings, fashioned want ads, and wrote a front-page column called "DeKalb After Dark" under several pseudonyms. Coincidentally, I became acquainted with a young man at Decatur High School who was the sports writer for the *DeKalb New Era*, another weekly. His name was Roy Blount Jr.

In late February, 1962, I was hired as a sportswriter by Furman Bisher at the *Atlanta Journal*, joining a staff which may well have been the finest ever assembled in one department at a Southern newspaper. It was to be my apprenticeship as a writer. In the company of Jim Minter, Greg Favre, John Logue, Lee Walburn, Ed Miles, Gerry Chatham, Tom Willow, Gene Asher,

Foreword

In 1959, I read an advertisement in the classified section of the *Decatur-DeKalb News* which, today, I would find suspicious, the times being what they are. The ad stated:

Wanted: Young man to learn interesting profession.

A telephone number was given.

Out of curiosity, I called.

I was, then, a young man, and any profession other than selling life insurance (which, at the time, I was attempting to do) seemed interesting.

It was a blind ad for the newspaper, a giveaway weekly publication fashioned from Linotypes and Ludlows and printed on a flatbed press that seemed to bleed ink. The owners were in need of someone to run errands, sweep up the place, glue address labels on subscription copies.

The pay was forty dollars per week.

And I almost didn't get the job.

Bud Crane, who, with his wife Mary, owned the *Decatur-DeKalb News,* was noticeably displeased that I was a college-

125 "For Frustration, Press 1"
131 "If the Dysfunction Fits, Read It"
137 "Gift Rap"
143 "Keds Say the Darndest Things"
149 "The Shell Game"
156 "What If Nancy Reagan Was Right?"

The South & Tradition

165 "I Was a Teenage Quarterback"
180 "Jesus in Jasper"
190 "As the Room Is Lit, So Is the Future"
193 "Give Me that Old-Time Religion"
199 "Giving Way"

Contents

xi   *Foreword by Terry Kay*

Family & Heritage

3   "T. H. Kay, Proprietor"
21   "Reflections on a Mother and Child"
31   "Reunion"
39   "The Strange Dance of White Dog"
44   "Collected Wisdom"
51   "The Full Nest Syndrome"
57   "Lay-By Time"

Social Commentary

65   "Why Johnny(ie) Can't Teach"
71   "The Fall Guys"
77   "The Days of Whine and Ruses"
83   "Recycling the Rah-Rah"
89   "Sucker Hunch"
95   "Lords of the Ring"
101   "Revenge of the Blurbs"
107   "High-Rate Robbery"
113   "From the Ashes of Infamy"
119   "That's Entertainment"

blood thickens, the bond becomes steel, and friendship becomes brotherhood.

And, so, this book is Lee's book, my brother's book. His touch is on it, his presence is in it. I merely supplied the words.

Dedication

Almost everything in this collection of works was inspired, or assigned, by Lee Walburn during his reign as editor for *Atlanta Weekly* and *Atlanta Magazine*. Thus, it is fitting that this book should be dedicated to Lee.

Yet there is more to it than that.

I met Lee (then known as Mose) as a freshman at West Georgia College in 1955. He had, somehow, managed to become editor of the college newspaper and he persuaded me to do some columns—my first published writing. The camaraderie we established continued at LaGrange College, where we both earned degrees in 1959. Later, Lee would recommend me for a position in the *Atlanta Journal* sports department. Still later, we would work together at Walburn & Associates, his public relations firm, and at Oglethorpe Power Corporation.

During the years—the adventures of those years—we have laughed together, wept together, bellowed at one another, and, thank God, we have also shared many of those warm-coated, melancholy moments that make humbling oneself an art worthy of the gods. In such unguarded moments of sharing, the

A HILL STREET PRESS BOOK
Published in the United States of America by
Hill Street Press LLC
191 East Broad Street, Suite 209   Athens, Georgia 30601-2848 USA
706-613-7200
info@hillstreetpress.com   www.hillstreetpress.com

Hill Street Press is committed to preserving the written word. Every effort is made to print books on acid-free paper with a significant amount of post-consumer recycled content. No material in this book may be reproduced, scanned, stored, or transmitted in any form, including all electronic and print media, or otherwise used without the prior written consent of the publisher. However, an excerpt not to exceed 500 words may be used one time only by newspaper and magazine editors solely in conjunction with a review of or feature article about this book, the author, or Hill Street Press, LLC. Attribution must be provided including the publisher's name, author's name, and title of the book.

Copyright ©1973, 1981, 1982, 1985, 1989, 1990, 1991, 1992, 1998, 2000
by Terry Kay Corporation. All rights reserved.

The author wishes to acknowledge the Georgia Museum of Art for permission
to reprint "Giving Way" which originally appeared in *Before 1948*
and which includes a passage from *The Year the Lights Came On*
(University of Georgia Press).

Text and cover design by Anne Richmond Boston.
Printed in the United States of America.

Library of Congress Cataloging-in-Publication Data

Kay, Terry
Special Kay: the wisdom of Terry Kay / by Terry Kay.
p.   cm.
ISBN 1-892514-69-9 (alk. paper)
I. Title
PS3561.A885 S64 2000
814'.54—dc21   99-088324

ISBN 1-892514-69-9

10   9   8   7   6   5   4   3   2   1

First printing

TERRY KAY

HILL STREET PRESS ATHENS, GEORGIA

SPECIAL KAY

the wisdom of terry kay

ALSO BY TERRY KAY

The Years the Lights Came On
After Eli
Dark Thirty
To Dance with the White Dog
To Whom the Angel Spoke
Shadow Song
The Runaway
The Kidnapping of Aaron Greene
Taking Lottie Home